# The Rocky Road
# to Reform

# The Rocky Road to Reform

Adjustment, Income Distribution, and Growth in the Developing World

edited by Lance Taylor

The MIT Press
Cambridge, Massachusetts
London, England

United Nations University/World Institute for
Development Economics Research (UNU/WIDER)
Helsinki, Finland

The United Nations University Press has exclusive rights to distribute in Japan.

The United Nations University Press / The MIT Press have open rights to distribute in Southeast Asia.

The MIT Press has exclusive rights to distribute throughout the rest of the world.

This book was set in Palatino by Asco Trade Typesetting Ltd., Hong Kong, and printed and bound in the United States of America.

Library of Congress Cataloging-in-Publication Data

The Rocky road to reform : adjustment, income distribution, and growth in the developing world / edited by Lance Taylor.
    p.  cm.
Includes bibliographical references and index.
ISBN 0-262-20093-7
   1. Economic development—Case studies. 2. Developing countries-Economic conditions—Case studies. I. Taylor, Lance.
HD82.R648   1993
338.9′009172′4—dc20                          92-39611
                                                     CIP

# Contents

# Contributors

| | |
|---|---|
| Korkut Boratav | University of Ankara, Ankara |
| François Boye | University of Dakar, Dakar |
| Dionisio D. Carneiro | Pontifical Catholic University, Rio de Janeiro |
| Rob Davies | University of Zimbabwe, Harare |
| José María Fanelli | CEDES, Buenos Aires |
| Carlo Fonseka | North Colombo Medical College, Colombo |
| Roberto Frenkel | CEDES, Buenos Aires |
| Bill Gibson | University of Vermont, Burlington, VT |
| Lal Jayawardena | WIDER, Helsinki |
| Somchai Jitsuchon | Thailand Development Research Institute, Bangkok |
| Jomo K. S. | University of Malaya, Kuala Lumpur |
| S. A. Karunaratne | Ministry for Finance and Planning, Colombo |
| Joseph Y. Lim | University of the Philippines, Quezon City |
| Nora Lustig | Brookings Institution, Washington, DC |
| Thandika Mkandawire | CODESRIA, Dakar |
| Manuel F. Montes | East-West Center, Honolulu |
| Benno J. Ndulu | African Economic Research Consortium, Nairobi |
| José Antonio Ocampo | FEDESARROLLO, Bogota |
| T. Ademola Oyejide | University of Ibadan, Ibadan |

| | |
|---|---|
| Agnes R. Quisumbing | World Bank, Washington, DC |
| Mufutau I. Raheem | University of Ibadan, Ibadan |
| Jørn Rattsø | University of Trondheim, Trondheim |
| Jaime Ros | University of Notre Dame, Notre Dame, IN |
| Ardeshir Sepehri | University of Manitoba, Winnipeg |
| Andres Solimano | World Bank, Washington, DC |
| Chalangphob Sussangkarn | Thailand Development Research Institute, Bangkok |
| Lance Taylor | Massachusetts Institute of Technology, Cambridge, MA |
| Oktar Türel | Middle East Technical University, Ankara |
| Rogerio L. F. Werneck | Pontifical Catholic University, Rio de Janeiro |

# Foreword

Previously, WIDER research had focused on stabilization policies essentially designed to tackle short-term problems arising out of external and internal shocks. Among the findings of that research, which were reported in a book by Lance Taylor, *Varieties of Stabilization Experience* (Oxford: Clarendon Press, 1988), was the need to address adjustment questions in developing countries from a longer-term perspective. A logical follow-up is therefore to explore the implications of returning to a long-run growth path supported by a degree of external self-reliance and a socially acceptable internal income distribution. These concerns, which formed the core of traditional development economics, had been relegated to the background during the 1980s mainly due to the pressing preoccupations of coping with internal and external shocks in much of the developing world. The comparative neglect of these concerns at present in mainstream North Atlantic economics is also in part due to a commitment to essentially neoclassical approaches. This book, which brings together the findings of research on medium-term development issues, takes stock of different approaches to questions of adjustment and examines the application of the existing body of knowledge to practical problems faced in developing countries in the Third World.

The country studies in this volume follow the premise that each economy can be sensibly analyzed only in terms of its own history and institutions. Consistent with this perspective, the medium-term prospects have been explored in terms of an interacting set of saving and foreign and fiscal constraints. However, there are no standard prescriptions or solutions emerging out of the country studies. What these studies highlight are the implications of specific given circumstances for each of the country economies. For example, the sensitivity of the growth rate to foreign exchange availability differs significantly from country to country depending on the size of their economies. The analysis focuses on the likely trade-offs possible in macroeconomic decision making under given situations, and seeks to address the central issue of whether reform packages to cope with changes in internal and external circumstances are feasible in the context of a country's historical and institutional background.

The sample set of country exercises provide a basis for extrapolating the net additional resource requirements for achieving socially necessary growth in the Third World as a whole during the 1990s. Professor Lance Taylor has estimated that if the developing countries are to maintain growth rates permitting the achievement of minimum socially necessary development goals, additional external resource inflows rising from U.S. $40 billion in 1990 to U.S. $60 billion by the turn of the century would be required. Of the initial amount of U.S. $40 billion, broadly speaking, sub-Saharan Africa is estimated to require U.S. $7 billion, Asia (except the Middle East) U.S. $18 billion, Europe, the Middle East, and North Africa (EMENA) U.S. $7 billion, and Latin America U.S. $8 billion. This amount can be obtained, for example, from the budgets of OECD countries by doubling the present level of its Overseas Development Assistance from 0.35 % of OECD GNP to reach the internationally agreed target of 0.7 %. This conclusion is consistent with the Six Point Global Programme of Immediate Action of the South Commission, in particular, the objective of "doubling the volume of concessional transfers of resources to developing countries by 1995."

The studies provide a representative cross-section of development experiences and prospects in the Third World. These include countries where growth and reform seem to be under way; some countries in delicate transition of one form or another; and a third set of countries where the prospects for reform appear to be blocked for the present due to political or distributional reasons. In terms of bringing about an understanding of the complex nature of these economies and the possible set of macroeconomic corrections and policies in each case, the present volume marks a significant advance on the earlier WIDER studies on stabilization experiences.

Lal Jayawardena
Helsinki

# 1     The Rocky Road to Reform

## Lance Taylor

This book is about the difficulties of sustaining equitable economic growth in the Third World, as illustrated by country case studies founded on structuralist policy analysis. The work is based on the collective insights of the authors as they have interacted since 1985 in conferences and correspondence under the auspices of the World Institute for Development Economics Research (WIDER). This entire volume is very much a joint effort.

The basic message, set out synthetically in chapters 2 and 3 and elaborated in the country study papers, is that attempts at economic reform must fit the situation at hand. Orthodox packages may well be appropriate in some situations; for practical purposes, policies must substantially vary in others. Much of the discussion is devoted to sketching plausible initial and boundary conditions on feasible policy choices.

At least seven common features unite the synthesis chapters and country studies:

1. They follow structuralist macroeconomic methodology in starting from aggregate accounting relationships featuring categories such as saving, investment, and foreign capital flows, and examining growth and distributional performance in terms of causal mechanisms connecting these categories. Sectoral and microeconomic linkages are analyzed in institutional terms as opposed to the stylized optimization theater of neoclassical models.

2. In particular, at the macro level a recently developed "three-gap" model emphasizing problems with government finance in addition to the traditional saving and external gaps is used to analyze growth prospects and implications for policy design.

3. This model, and structuralism more generally, allow an integrated discussion of both stabilization problems in the short run and medium-term

limitations on growth. An awkward division of labor, at times demonstrated in policy conflicts between the International Monetary Fund (IMF) and the World Bank, is thus avoided in the analysis.

4. There is an explicit emphasis on issues of income distribution and poverty.

5. The authors are conscious of political economy questions concerning the nature of the state and its relationship to other significant actors in the political arena.

6. They are also aware of the fact that economic development and policies aimed to support it are historically and institutionally contingent, depending on the situation of the economy at hand. Successful economic reforms are sui generis; contrary to mainstream doctrine, they cannot be devised on the basis of economic theory (especially the neoclassical variety) alone.

7. Finally, most contributors generally approve of state intervention in economic activity, and are critical of typical IMF austerity-based stabilization packages and the World Bank's emphasis over the past decade on the virtues of completely liberalized external trade and fully deregulated national markets. However, they do not go to the opposite extreme of rejecting all such policies, especially the need to maintain fiscal balance. They generally support activist but restrained state intervention in the economic system.

## 1.1   Plan of the Book

Chapters 2 and 3 are a general introduction to the models and modes of analysis in the country papers. The former sets out the three-gap model, which is based on the fact that macroeconomic discussion in developing countries takes place "essentially in terms of four sets of accounts—the balance of payments accounts, the fiscal accounts, the consolidated accounts of the banking system, and the national income and product accounts which usually offer only a pale reflection of what is going on in the real economy, out there. Now fairly simple models can be constructed using the type of accounting identities represented by the four sets of accounts just mentioned" (Sobhan 1990).

In fact, two fairly simple formulations based on some or all of the accounts almost always frame the debate. One feeds the fiscal, monetary, and balance of payments numbers into the IMF's financial programming exercises, which have scarcely changed since they were designed by Polak (1957).[1] The other fits all the accounts into various gap models that have been set up over the years. As chapter 2 describes in detail, three-gap formulations emphasize how linkages between foreign and fiscal constraints placed new limitations on macroeconomic policy formation during the 1980s.

This discussion is extended in chapter 3 to take up other factors influencing short-term macroeconomic stabilization and medium-term adjustment, which are supposed to add up to economic "reform." The chapter amounts to a detailed map of the many rocks that developing economies encounter on the road to reform. It begins by summarizing mainstream or orthodox views of development policy, as codified in a recently christened "Washington consensus" (or WC). One striking aspect of the consensus is its neoliberal obsession with removing price distortions to enhance static, allocative efficiency. Regrettably, policy movements in this direction often do little to boost efficiency in production, an essential condition for raising the level of income per capita in the medium run.

Besides the distinction between allocative and productive efficiency, the structuralist approach stresses other factors that affect prospects for economic growth and equitable distribution: overriding saving, fiscal, and foreign exchange constraints on macroeconomic performance of the sort emphasized in the three-gap model; an inescapable link between changes in the distributions of income and wealth and processes of accumulation and growth; the role of an activist state in managing the dynamic forces that affect productive efficiency and avoiding the dangers of financial fragility; and the importance of market structures and institutions in affecting possibilities for change.

The first of these issues addressed in chapter 3 is how ideas about the state and economic development have evolved since World War II. The conclusion is that, contrary to recent orthodox theorizing, public intervention continues to play an essential developmental role. The discussion then turns to macroeconomics, complementing the three-gap model's emphasis on quantity adjustment by asking how movements in relative prices and the distributions of income and wealth affect aggregate behavior. Next, non-WC perspectives on stabilization and adjustment are set out in terms of boundary conditions that limit freedom of maneuver to reform in any economy's specific historical and institutional circumstances. These considerations lead in the chapter's conclusion to a "non-Washington synthesis" shared by the authors of this volume.

## 1.2   The Country Studies

Quite a bit is said in passing in chapters 2 and 3 about the past performances and future prospects of the economies in the WIDER sample, and much more detail appears in the country chapters. They are presented in three groups: countries where growth and reform seem to be under way, subject to some risks; those in delicate transitions of one form or another; and a final set in which reform is politically or distributionally blocked.

There have been relatively good growth performances recently in Sri Lanka, Thailand, Malaysia, Colombia, and Chile—they have both "stabilized" and "adjusted." However, a series of caveats applies:

1. All benefited from foreign assistance during key periods: Sri Lanka from official donors since 1977, Chile from the same sources during the 1980s (when foreign assistance as well as government access to copper mine revenues helped make meeting its debt obligations less burdensome than in other Latin American economies), and Thailand and Malaysia from direct foreign investment (or DFI) from Japan, South Korea, and Taiwan after the middle of the decade. In Sri Lanka as well as other small, primary-exporting economies discussed below, capital inflows in the range of 10 %– 20 + % of GDP have been involved, supporting potential output growth rates of about 5 % per year. How long such transfers (with such relatively low payoffs in terms of growth) will be politically feasible remains to be seen. Similar doubts apply to Asian DFI, a traditionally unstable source of funds.

2. Distributional conflicts have not been absent, for example, between ethnic groups differentially favored by policy changes in Sri Lanka and Malaysia, popular classes and the bourgeoisie in Chile, and rural and urban groups in the primary-product-exporting countries. All these tensions led to violence (suppressed at substantial cost), which paradoxically also increased in Colombia, where for Kuznets-type reasons of the sort discussed in chapter 3, the income distribution has become more equal. Income concentration in Thailand has recently risen markedly, both regionally and between rural and urban areas, as average productivity levels have diverged, without major political consequences as yet. Malaysia's rapid growth has softened interethnic rivalries, which could resurge if world trade in the 1990s is less kind to the economy than it has been in decades past.

3. Thai and Malaysian exports jumped in the mid-1980s. Their currency devaluations at that time (induced by pegging to the dollar while the yen strengthened) ratified a swing of comparative advantage in their favor in assembly industries for which production in the first wave of Asian newly industrializing countries or NICs (South Korea, Taiwan, Singapore, and Hong Kong) had become too high-cost. But Thailand now has a large trade deficit, while Malaysia's export potential in timber and oil may be running out.

4. Because their public investment reduces or crowds out private capital formation (contrary to the general rule, as we will see in chapter 2) and tax receipts are unresponsive to output, Colombia and Chile are likely to be fiscally constrained if they try to accelerate growth via state intervention. Chile must also raise revenues with the economy already at full capacity to pay for its progressive, post-Pinochet redistributional agenda; with escalating unemployment and unresolved ethnic conflicts, Sri Lanka faces similar problems.

5. Colombia has not had a leading sector since tacitly abandoning import-substituting industrialization (or ISI) in the mid-1970s; in the interindustry sense, Malaysia has a disarticulated production structure. To a lesser extent, the other countries in this group have similar difficulties, suggesting a need for rethinking industrial strategies in the medium run.

Zimbabwe, Uganda, Turkey, Tanzania, the Philippines, Nigeria, and Mexico find themselves in delicate transitions toward reform. Both distributional and political obstacles may frustrate these attempts. Turkey had significant export growth in the 1980s, relying on price incentives, domestic demand contraction, growth of external demand from culturally compatible countries in the region (due to the second oil shock and the Iran-Iraq war), and the fact that decades of highly distorted ISI had created a viable industrial base. However, there has been little capacity expansion and price incentives now are eroding as the exchange rate has been appreciated to slow inflation and assuage distributional strife. The current government never truly eliminated rent-seeking[2] as it had promised and is now veering toward "bastard populism." Without political restructuring and a new economic model, full reform may prove beyond its grasp.

Similar doubts arise in the Philippines, where an elite-dominated but weak government grapples with land reform while hoping to receive enough Asian DFI to keep a fiscally driven demand expansion going. Whether the government can settle into a serious attempt to restructure its industry to compete with its Asian rivals at a moderate but sustainable growth rate remains to be seen. Rather large concessional inflows would be required; otherwise foreign debt would grow twice as fast as output (as in Thailand recently). A fiscal adjustment of 2%–3% of GDP would also be necessary. As in Mexico, these problems are not eased by the threat of capital flight, which requires high interest rates to gratify the wealthy and finance profits in the oligopolistic banking system.

In wake of the 1982 debt crisis, Mexico practiced stop-and-go austerity for almost a decade, with zero average GDP growth rates for 1982–90. On the other hand, it achieved a degree of real devaluation (after the exchange rate appreciated sharply for "Dutch disease"[3] reasons during the oil boom of the 1970s) while oil revenues helped solidify a fiscal reform. Together with incomes policies, these changes fed into a successful "economic solidarity pact," which stabilized inflation late in the decade.

The relatively strong Mexican state has been pushing the economy toward privatization and market liberalization. As of the early 1990s, one key question is whether DFI and a reversal of capital flight will raise internal saving flows enough to support a return to historical rates of per capita income growth in a liberalized system. A second query is whether investment will pick up; if not, a speculative financial boom as in Chile in the 1970s is a distinct possibility. As noted in chapter 3, the WC package that the economic authorities religiously applied for 10 years provides no automatic transition to growth. For Mexico, that is what the wager in the proposed free trade agreement with the United State is all about.

Nigeria has a far weaker state, and in an adverse scenario for the 1990s would continue drifting from Dutch disease and the debt-led boom of the 1970s via slow growth toward stagnation with rent-seeking rampant throughout the economy. Reform efforts began in the mid-1980s with heavy austerity and devaluation aimed at cutting the trade deficit and inflation along with redressing overvaluation (the latter with some success). In the 1990s the emphasis will have to be on resuscitating moribund food and export agriculture while grappling with fiscal and external deficits. Addressing the distributional implications and orchestrating renewed economic growth in an ideological ambience of privatization are likely to be tricky.

Zimbabwe had a tightly controlled import regime in the 1980s, while the government ran a deficit of about 15 % of GDP. It was financed in nonmonetary fashion by borrowing from financial intermediaries (insurance companies, pension funds), which received savings inflows of over 20 % of GDP from the private sector. If import compression is relaxed, the private saving rate may well fall as more consumer goods become available. But then fiscal reform will be necessary to avoid massive monetary emission. Whether the current house of cards can be rearranged into a viable structure remains to be seen; foreign transfers of 5 %–10 % of GDP (not unusual for Africa) from external donors would certainly ease the transition.

Uganda and Tanzania have received such massive capital inflows; their output growth rates are correspondingly positive, but not outstandingly strong. Both economies will be constrained by structural factors for a long time. Beyond potentially binding foreign and fiscal constraints, these include the needs to restructure the government apparatus to make it minimally effective (WC emphasis on cutting public expenditure to the bone is not helpful in this regard), and to distribute the fruits of modest output expansion more rapidly than via simple trickle-down.

For both three-gap and distributional reasons, reform has been effectively blocked in Zambia, Senegal, Nicaragua, Brazil, and Argentina. Although they are not there yet, Argentina and Brazil are marching more rapidly than other countries in the sample toward rent-seeking stagnation of the sort discussed in chapter 3. Both are fiscally constrained due to external debt service obligations, with powerful coalitions blocking any attempts to reduce the public deficit from either the tax or current spending side. Numerous attempts at eliminating inflations fed by both cost-based inertial forces and money creation (exacerbated by foreign exchange limitations on aggregate supply) have failed in both countries, and both have relatively distorted price systems due to past programs for ISI.

As the country papers demonstrate, there are complex historical reasons why Brazil and Argentina arrived at their current political and distributional deadlocks. Although the macroeconomic corrections these countries have to make are reasonably clear, they are not trivial—making fiscal adjustments on the order of 5 % of GDP, figuring out how to stop built-in inflations, and so on. How appropriate steps can be taken in the face of political impasse is obscure. Beyond stabilization, the problem of finding dynamic leading sectors to replace those created under ISI also looms. In both countries, agroindustries may prove to be a solution, but only if the public sector regains its capacity to finance the required transportation and processing infrastructure.

Nicaragua, Senegal, and Zambia are small, primary-exporting economies, with their activity levels highly dependent on volumes of external sales. Bad luck externally or expansionary policy inside push them rapidly against import restrictions, which can only by met by economic contraction induced by policy or the joint actions of forced saving and the inflation tax. Although simple, their economic structures allow policy makers few degrees of freedom.

Nicaragua was severely destabilized by the Contra invasion of the 1980s as well as by overly ambitious investment projects and extreme overvaluation. The invasion forced government spending to rise to 50 %–60 % of GDP while tax receipts could only be pushed to a bit over 30 % (a strong performance in a poor economy): The resulting money emission provoked a hyperinflation. A new government in the early 1990s was struggling to restore stable economic policy with external assistance, but as the country study here argues, it may face major problems rooted in the class contradictions that permitted the Sandinista revolutionary victory in the first place.

Zambia was once a rich country by African standards, with a strong labor movement based in the copper mines and ambitious past programs in social welfare, import substitution, and investments in large-scale farming. Although each generated a productive base, neither ISI nor the agricultural initiative was highly successful. The country went through stop-go growth cycles in the 1980s, breaking and then making up with the IMF. Through these maneuvers, Zambia also became highly indebted. If, like Uganda and Tanzania, it gets access to large capital inflows, then growth may be possible. But that would require internal agreement to accept World Bank and IMF medicine enthusiastically; as of the early 1990s, such a social compact had not been attained.

Finally, Senegal, as a member of the West African monetary union, has no control over its exchange rate. It is also under chronic fiscal duress, but ultimately can borrow as much as it wants from the French Treasury. Local political factions are in a mutually blocking position, and it is not clear whether they would accept short-term losses in exchange for policy changes that might permit the economy to stop transforming capital inflows from France into zero growth. Nor, given the strictures of the monetary union, would such policies be easy to design.

### Notes

1. How financial programming works in practice is discussed in chapter 3.

2. In the 1980s rent-seeking became an important mainstream economic category, which structuralists also use. See chapter 3.

3. "Dutch disease" is professional jargon for the difficulties economies confront in adjusting to bonanza inflows of foreign exchange. For further discussion, again see chapter 3.

### References

Polak, J. J. (1957). "Monetary Analysis of Income Formation and Payments Problems." *International Monetary Fund Staff Papers*, 6: 1–50.

Sobhan, Rehman (1990). "Introduction" in R. Sobhan et al., *Structural Adjustment in Third World Countries*. Dhaka: Bangladesh Institute of Development Studies.

# 2

# A Three-Gap Analysis of Foreign Resource Flows and Developing Country Growth

## Lance Taylor

This chapter has two goals: to set out the three-gap framework used in most country papers in this volume, and to apply it to calculations of global resource requirements for renewed output growth in the developing world. Much of the discussion focuses on the specific version of the model used for the latter task, but a final section sketches extensions devised by the country authors.

The 1980s were difficult years for developing economies: Most suffered low or negative per capita income growth rates and adverse trends in trade and capital flows. With some exceptions (mainly in Asia), poor countries' prospects for the 1990s are not much brighter, despite the fact that they have taken big steps toward economic reform. There is a chance that continued structural change plus additional foreign exchange inflows (or reductions of some countries' outflows from several percent of GDP to something closer to zero) can support a return to adequate growth rates as the decade unfolds, but the foreign resource requirements will be high. A model incorporating the interactions of saving, foreign, and fiscal limits to growth is a natural tool for evaluating possibilities for economic recovery based on plausible structural adjustments plus enhanced capital inflows in countries from the WIDER sample; the results easily lead to extrapolations to the rest of the developing world.

The discussion begins in section 2.1 with a review of ideas about the contribution of foreign resource flows to output and capacity growth. Models have evolved since development became a matter of international policy concern after World War II, but present growth rates are still constrained by factors perceived in the past. There is an excess capacity overhang in many economies, and they face linked internal (or fiscal) and external (or balance of payments) problems as well. These constraints are illustrated numerically for countries in the WIDER sample in section 2.2.

Section 2.3 gives a verbal description of how a simple flow-of-funds model involving three resource limitations or "gaps" can be used to analyze growth prospects, and a formal description appears in section 2.4. Quantitative assessments of how growth rates of productive capacity and output in the countries in the WIDER sample might respond to structural changes and greater capital inflows are the topic of section 2.5, using model simulations. In section 2.6, these results are extended to provide an estimate of global resource "needs" for modestly renewed growth in the Third World. As already mentioned, section 2.7 outlines variations of the basic model employed by specific country authors.

## 2.1  Complications of Foreign Resource Flows

An economy's trade deficits and surpluses (with offsetting capital movements or flows of external aid or finance) affect its style and rate of growth. Economists began to map the linkages for developing countries about 40 years ago. Because their analysis has become more sophisticated by steps, it is instructive to review the mechanisms that different authors proposed.

The first studies—epitomized by Rosenstein-Rodan (1961)—presumed that output was strictly determined by local productive capacity, specifically the physical capital stock. "Foreign saving" in the form of a financial capital inflow covering an external current account deficit could supplement domestic accumulation, permitting physical (and perhaps human) capital to grow faster. Output would respond according to the magnitudes of the incremental output-capital ratio, the national saving rate, and the volume (relative to output or the capital stock) of foreign resources obtained. The algebra came from the Harrod-Domar growth model popular at the time.

One problem with Rosenstein-Rodan's and similar calculations is that they failed to take into account specific foreign exchange requirements for both current production and capital formation in developing economies. The initial steps toward industrialization involve substitution of imports of final goods by domestic products. The difficulty is that this mode of manufacture always depends on imported intermediate inputs (textiles to make garments, pharmaceuticals in bulk for local packaging, and so on). Similarly, agricultural modernization creates demands for fuels, fertilizers, and pesticides that often are not produced at home. Neither sector can function without hard currency to pay for intermediate imports to keep production moving. On the investment side, few poor economies extend import substitution to machinery and equipment, that is, foreign-made investment goods. Thus, hard currency is an essential input into capital formation as well.

These multiple requirements for external capital—to provide additional saving and also to finance required intermediate and investment imports—were highlighted in the two-gap model proposed by Chenery and collaborators, for example, the foreign aid computations in Chenery and Strout (1966). The gaps were, respectively, the saving-investment balance emphasized by Rosenstein-Rodan (1961) and the trade account with the forms of external dependence just described. The Chenery-Strout model also included an absorptive capacity constraint, stating the peak capital inflow that a poor country could effectively utilize. Given the dearth of transfers toward the Third World in the 1980s, such a restriction is not brought in formally here. We do, however, consider possible absorptive capacity limitations in specific country cases.

In early two-gap calculations, output was set equal to productive capacity in the manner proposed by Rosenstein-Rodan, and one constraint was treated as being more "binding" than the other in the sense of putting a lower limit on growth for available capital inflow. In macro equilibrium, this "gap between the gaps" must disappear, that is, the trade deficit must equal investment minus saving. Bacha (1984) was among the first to point out that the two gaps are equivalent to the familiar internal and external balances of open economy macroeconomics, with developing country twists. He described adjustment mechanisms that can drive the gap between the gaps to zero; as discussed later in this chapter and in chapter 3, output changes induced by forced saving and the inflation tax were conspicuous in the 1980s. They effectively make the output-capital ratio an endogenous macroeconomic variable instead of a "technically determined" parameter as it was for Rosenstein-Rodan, and Chenery and Strout. Bacha's insights were a key step toward the model developed in sections 2.3 and 2.4.

The interest in income distribution that bloomed in the 1960s added a more humane dimension to all this macroeconomics, as economists asked how big a capital inflow might be required to build up capacity to deliver "basic needs," say to half the population by the year 2000 or something similar. Cline (1979) reviewed calculations of this sort, along with gap models. In a similar vein, one can also compute "socially necessary" growth rates on employment or distributional grounds and ask what resource inflows would be needed to support them.

With the oil, debt, interest rate, and terms-of-trade shocks of the 1970s and 1980s, distributional concerns along with gap computations faded from view and discussion shifted to how poor countries were involuntarily adjusting to repeated blows from abroad. Typical studies concentrated on changes in comparative export and import performance of different economies as well as the extent of economic contraction and investment cutbacks that they undertook. For example, Helleiner (1986) used an approach to "differentiating the balance of payments" proposed by Bacha to quantify investment reductions and also show that the economic contraction that poor countries suffered in the 1980s drove their levels of output well below available capacity. Utilizing excess capacity to raise output was a possibility not considered in the early two-gap models; it is brought explicitly into the analysis here.

## 2.2   Initial Economic Conditions

For many developing economies, fiscal, foreign exchange, and financial constraints tightened sharply during the 1980s due to successive oil, interest rate, debt, and terms-of-trade shocks. In 1990, real GDP growth for typical economies in three of the four regions of the World Bank's global classification continued the disappointing trends of a decade. The average country growth rate for Latin America and the Caribbean (LAC) was 0.0 %; Europe, Middle East, and North Africa (EMENA), $-1.0$ %; Sub-Saharan Africa (SSA), 1.5 %; and Asia, 5.5 %.

The countries in the WIDER sample were subject to these shocks. Their specific initial conditions are summarized numerically in tables 2.1 and 2.2, with most column headings being symbols from the model set out in section 2.4. The one labeled $Q$ in table 2.1 gives potential or full capacity output (defined below), expressed in billions of dollars for each economy in its model's base year. The column headed $g$ gives growth rates of potential output as calculated in the country growth exercises, and $u$ stands for the fraction of capacity being utilized.

Several points stand out in these three columns. First, developing economies are small by world standards. Total capacity in the 18 countries is only $1,380 billion or roughly one-third of GDP in the United States. This figure reflects the low incomes of even relatively large and prosperous nations like South Korea and Brazil.

Second, there is wide variation in both rates of growth and capacity utilization. Eight countries have capacity growth rates of 4 % or more, giving margin for sustained output increases in excess of the population growth rates (for 1980−87, at annual rates) appearing in the last column. Seven economies, on the other hand, show negative capacity growth per

**Table 2.1**
Country production, fiscal and external data

| | $Q$ | $g$ | $u$ | $\pi$ | $i_g$ | $\phi + t$ | Population growth |
|---|---|---|---|---|---|---|---|
| Argentina (1988) | 76.9 | 0.0046 | 0.978 | 0.0644 | 0.0705 | 0.0362 | 0.014 |
| Brazil (1987) | 315.6 | 0.033 | 0.8 | 0.0 | 0.048 | −0.01 | 0.022 |
| Chile (1988) | 23.0 | 0.074 | 1.0 | 0.019 | 0.069 | 0.056 | 0.017 |
| Colombia (1988) | 46.3 | 0.0434 | 0.877 | 0.03 | 0.059 | −0.0074 | 0.019 |
| India (1987−88) | 262.7 | 0.05 | 0.866 | 0.098 | 0.105 | 0.016 | 0.021 |
| South Korea (1987) | 146.0 | 0.091 | 1.01 | −0.04 | 0.05 | −0.062 | 0.014 |
| Malaysia (1988) | 47.8 | 0.068 | 0.8 | 0.028 | 0.0606 | −0.042 | 0.027 |
| Mexico (1988) | 170.3 | 0.011 | 0.879 | 0.021 | 0.052 | 0.014 | 0.022 |
| Nicaragua (1989) | 2.8 | 0.028 | 0.9 | 0.0344 | 0.016 | 0.128 | 0.034 |
| Nigeria (1986) | 91.1 | 0.013 | 0.7 | 0.0444 | 0.052 | 0.004 | 0.034 |
| Philippines (1988) | 46.4 | 0.04 | 0.87 | 0.0269 | 0.0233 | 0.036 | 0.025 |
| Sri Lanka (1987) | 8.0 | 0.052 | 0.93 | 0.094 | 0.124 | 0.057 | 0.015 |
| Tanzania (1986) | 5.4 | 0.03 | 0.7 | 0.026 | 0.055 | 0.088 | 0.035 |
| Thailand (1987) | 55.8 | 0.078 | 0.949 | 0.0121 | 0.0579 | 0.0065 | 0.02 |
| Turkey (1987) | 66.2 | 0.04 | 0.995 | 0.0448 | 0.117 | 0.012 | 0.023 |
| Uganda (1987) | 4.7 | 0.0317 | 0.75 | 0.09 | 0.028 | 0.051 | 0.031 |
| Zambia (1987) | 3.8 | 0.03 | 0.82 | 0.187 | 0.048 | 0.067 | 0.036 |
| Zimbabwe (1986) | 6.7 | 0.035 | 0.88 | 0.1538 | 0.0943 | −0.001 | 0.037 |

Note: Potential output ($Q$) in billions of dollars. Other variables are defined in the text and are measured relative to $Q$ except $\pi$, which is relative to output.

capita. Capacity utilization ranges from 101 % in Korea to figures in the 70 % range in several African economies.

The column headed $\pi$ gives the internal public sector borrowing requirement (or PSBR), measured as a fraction of output rather than $Q$ because that is how the concept is usually expressed. The PSBR is the amount that the government must raise in national financial markets to pay for its expenditures net of tax and other revenues. Roughly speaking,

PSBR = Government current spending − local revenues

+ public investment + foreign interest payments

− net transfers to government from abroad.　　　(2.1)

**Table 2.2**
Country external accounts data

|            | $m_{int}$ | $m_{cap}$ | $m_{oth}$ | $e$    | $D$      | $\phi + t$ | $j^*$  | $\xi$ |
|------------|-----------|-----------|-----------|--------|----------|------------|--------|-------|
| Argentina  | 0.056     | 0.017     | 0.024     | 0.115  | −0.018   | 0.036      | 0.054  | 0.88  |
| Brazil     | 0.03      | 0.016     | 0.002     | 0.083  | −0.035   | −0.01      | 0.025  | 0.75  |
| Chile      | 0.13      | 0.059     | 0.096     | 0.31   | −0.025   | 0.056      | 0.081  | 0.67  |
| Colombia   | 0.045     | 0.029     | 0.009     | 0.105  | −0.022   | −0.001     | 0.021  | 0.83  |
| India      | 0.037     | 0.02      | 0.001     | 0.042  | 0.016    | 0.018      | 0.002  | 0.9   |
| South Korea| 0.2       | 0.127     | 0.04      | 0.448  | −0.081   | −0.062     | 0.019  | 0.48  |
| Malaysia   | 0.145     | 0.075     | 0.176     | 0.463  | −0.067   | −0.042     | 0.025  | 0.88  |
| Mexico     | 0.064     | 0.02      | 0.001     | 0.115  | −0.03    | 0.014      | 0.044  | 0.89  |
| Nicaragua  | 0.134     | 0.093     | 0.049     | 0.148  | 0.128    | 0.128      | 0.0    | 0.0   |
| Nigeria    | 0.012     | 0.026     | 0.013     | 0.052  | −0.001   | 0.004      | 0.006  | 1.0   |
| Philippines| 0.089     | 0.034     | 0.082     | 0.213  | −0.008   | 0.036      | 0.044  | 0.3   |
| Sri Lanka  | 0.096     | 0.054     | 0.103     | 0.22   | 0.033    | 0.057      | 0.022  | 0.45  |
| Tanzania   | 0.038     | 0.079     | 0.007     | 0.061  | 0.063    | 0.088      | 0.021  | 1.0   |
| Thailand   | 0.084     | 0.074     | 0.114     | 0.285  | −0.013   | 0.007      | 0.02   | 0.82  |
| Turkey     | 0.118     | 0.009     | −0.016    | 0.131  | −0.02    | 0.012      | 0.032  | 0.84  |
| Uganda     | 0.04      | 0.061     | 0.014     | 0.068  | 0.047    | 0.051      | 0.004  | 1.0   |
| Zambia     | 0.193     | 0.05      | 0.021     | 0.296  | −0.032   | 0.067      | 0.099  | 0.8   |
| Zimbabwe   | 0.088     | 0.056     | 0.058     | 0.228  | −0.026   | −0.001     | 0.025  | 0.66  |

How the government obtains resources to cover the PSBR is a key policy question, highly conditioned by the nature of local financial institutions. Options may range from monetary emission through placement of government securities with non-bank financial intermediaries to running up arrears on foreign debt. Table 2.1 shows that for many countries the PSBR is a large share of output, running to over 15 percent in Zambia and Zimbabwe, for example.

The column headed $i_g$ illustrates one reason why developing country PSBRs are high: their governments pursue large public investment programs (measured relative to $Q$ in table 2.1). As described later in this chapter, state capital formation is an important factor driving growth in poor countries, and the relatively high $i_g$ shares reflect this fact. But investment by governments also strains their finances.

The next-to-last column in table 2.1 shows the sum of financial transfers from abroad—the $\phi$ and $t$ components flow respectively to the private and public sectors. In other terminology, $\phi + t$ is the current account deficit on the balance of payments. This deficit is a standard indicator of resources coming into the economy, and it takes a reassuringly positive sign in 13 of the 18 countries.

Unfortunately, Table 2.2 reveals that these resource transfers are much more apparent than real. Omitting minor items, it is true that

Current account deficit − total foreign interest payments = trade deficit.

(2.2)

This accounting shows that the trade deficit is a more reliable signal of resource flows, basically because interest payments must be covered by foreign exchange revenues from trade plus net transfers from abroad. The column headed $D$ in table 2.2 shows the trade deficit relative to potential output. Its entries are negative (i.e., there is a trade surplus) for 13 of the 18 countries, not a reassuring sign.

These surpluses exist for historically diverse reasons. In South Korea, three decades of export expansion unprecedented in economic history accompanied by trade deficits of several percent of GDP culminated in a switch to surpluses in the mid-1980s. Although it now has a deficit, if Thailand's current export growth rates continue, it may be poised for a structural surplus late in this decade. On the other hand, as its timber and petroleum resources deplete, Malaysia probably is not. Other countries have had less autonomy and far less time to move to a surplus position.

One important reason why exports exceed imports in the late 1980s is because many countries' foreign interest obligations relative to potential output are large, as shown in the column headed $j^*$. Especially for the nations that ran up major external debts with commercial banks in the 1970s, $j^*$ values run to several percent. Moreover, they are a burden on the state. The column headed $\xi$ gives the fraction of total foreign interest owed by the government. For two types of economies—those in which private foreign obligations were taken over by the government in the wake of the debt crisis, and poorer countries depending on overseas development assistance (ODA) in the form of more-or-less soft loans—$\xi$ takes values close to one. In turn, public interest burdens $\xi j^*$ adding up to 2 % or 3 % of potential output reappear as part of the PSBR ratio $\pi$ in Table 2.1.

These numbers illustrate a "double transfer" problem that plagues many developing countries in the 1990s. They have to send hard currency abroad to meet interest obligations; hence they need a trade surplus since net transfers toward the economy ($\phi + t$ in table 2.1) are less than the flow of money out. Second, the state is responsible for a large share of these payments; it either has to run a fiscal surplus (apart from interest obligations) or find local finance for a large PSBR. To increase cash flow, the government may cut back on its investment, with adverse consequences for long-term growth.

These considerations suggest that debt-ridden developing countries confront a financial as opposed to the real external constraint emphasized by traditional two-gap models. Like Korea, they shifted from trade deficits of a few percent of GDP to surpluses of the same order, a transformation that would have been viewed as little short of miraculous two decades ago. But unlike Korea, they accomplished these miracles with low capacity utilization, price inflation, declining public investment, and slow growth. Moreover, the old problems of external strangulation remain, as illustrated by the left-hand entries in table 2.2.

The first three columns give shares of intermediate, capital goods, and other imports in potential output (the last category includes food, competitive imports, and items not elsewhere accounted for). For several reasons, there is substantial variation in these ratios across the sample:

1. Populous countries tend to have lower trade shares because of their relatively expansive domestic markets, for example, Brazil, India, Mexico, and Turkey, with South Korea as a notable exception.

2. Policy-induced trade "orientation" does matter. Import and export ratios can change over time in response to the policy climate; for example, Chile's shares were much lower in 1970 than they are today. In a medium run of about five years, however, import coefficients stay relatively stable.

3. All the countries in the sample are dependent on intermediate imports (with ratios to potential output running as high as 15 %), and most are also large purchasers of foreign capital goods. In smaller and more openly oriented economies, other imports are high.

4. Because most countries in the sample have trade surpluses, exports (in the column headed $e$) are correspondingly large.

As noted previously, the 1980s were difficult years for non-Asian (plus a few other) developing economies. Figures 2.1 through 2.4 illustrate the typical adjustment pattern as it showed up in four countries from the WIDER sample: Mexico, the Philippines, Tanzania, and Turkey.

The lines labeled $S$, $E$, and $F$ crossing through the observed utilization and growth rate points represent saving, external, and fiscal trade-offs between $u$ and $g$ in the short to medium run; the details are explained in the following sections. These restrictions determine local options for policy change, valid for shifts of a percentage point or so in the growth rate and perhaps a bit more for capacity utilization. All four figures show that the countries in question were subject to nonlocal economic shocks.

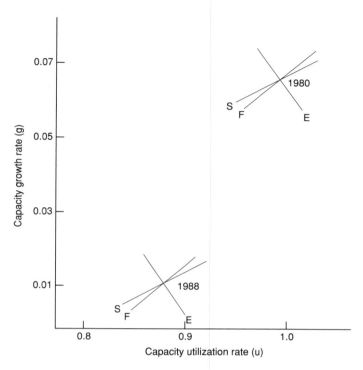

**Figure 2.1**
Capacity growth and utilization rates in Mexico, 1980 and 1988

Their magnitudes were on the order of 5 % of GDP (say a change from a trade deficit of 2.5 % to an equivalent surplus). More telling is that fact that they amounted to 20 % or 30 % of the volatile items in the national accounts: import, export, saving, and investment flows. The effects were large. The capacity growth rate fell by 5.5 % and capacity utilization by 11 % in Mexico between 1980 and 1988, corresponding decreases in the Philippines were about 4.4 % and 25 % between 1978 and 1985, and so on. At the same time, in many countries the wealth and income distributions adjusted in regressive fashion (typically accompanied by inflation) to reduce aggregate demand to foreign resource constrained supply. The violent policy maneuvers and structural shifts that countries went through to deal with 5 % shocks are discussed in the country papers here as well as in a set of previous WIDER studies on economic stabilization summarized by Taylor (1988). Often, drastic stabilization did not lay a foundation for future economic growth.

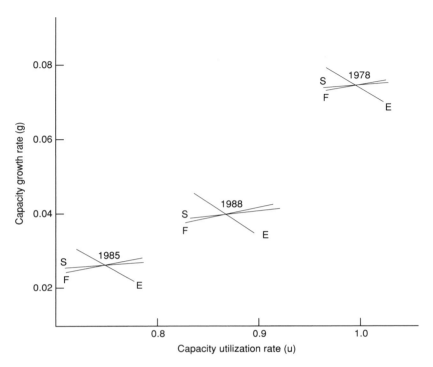

**Figure 2.2**
Capacity growth and utilization rates in the Philippines, 1978, 1985, and 1988

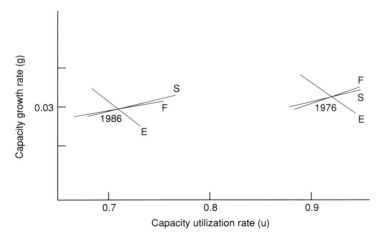

**Figure 2.3**
Capacity growth and utilization rates in Tanzania, 1976 and 1986

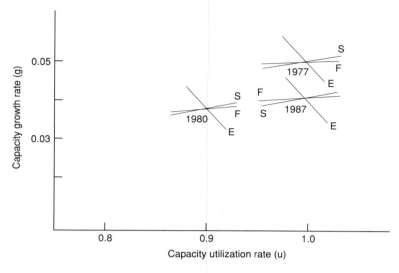

**Figure 2.4**
Capacity growth and utilization rates in Turkey, 1977, 1980, and 1987

## 2.3   A Three-Gap Model

The foregoing discussion suggests that at least a third gap should be added to the traditional foreign exchange and saving constraints, to take into account the linked fiscal and foreign transfer limitations on policy choice that have become crucial in many countries. In principle, further effects of fiscal deficits on inflation or the public debt-output ratio should be explored: They are of central policy (and political) importance. However, these linkages depend strongly on national financial institutions and diverse forms of social resistance to financing increased government claims via higher taxes, spiraling prices that transfer resources toward the state through the inflation tax and forced saving, or increases in real volume of nationally held fiscal debt. To ease cross-country comparisons, we concentrate on the PSBR. Inflation gaps and potential debt traps are taken up in the following chapter, the country studies, and recent research at the foundation of this section's model, for example, Fanelli, et al. (1987), Carneiro and Werneck (1987), Bacha (1990), and Taylor (1991b).

The models used in most of the country papers in this volume have six major features:

1. The data just presented demonstrate that output and capacity growth rates are not closely linked. Figures 2.1 to 2.4 dramatically portray how

output can fall below its potential when the economy is subject to strong enough shocks. To permit production to fall below capacity, the model incorporates a traditional incremental output-capital ratio (or IOCR) equation to determine the growth of potential output or capacity as a function of new investment along Harrod-Domar lines, but it also allows the utilization rate u to be less than 100%. In most papers, output is defined in somewhat non-standard fashion as the sum of real GDP and intermediate imports, reflecting the importance of these inputs as summarized in the first column of table 2.2.

2. An important feature of the model is its treatment of capital formation. A burgeoning literature in the late 1980s emphasized that public and private investment are often complementary; for references and discussion, see Shapiro and Taylor (1990). One practical implication is that the government's infrastructure, public utility, and even manufacturing projects are likely to "crowd in" investment by the private sector by making it more profitable, instead of crowding it out through the mechanism of higher government borrowing putting pressure on financial markets.

This possible linkage was tested by the country paper authors using a private sector investment function with a term $\alpha i_g$ for crowding-in or -out as well as a contemporaneous accelerator effect $\beta u$ on capital formation. As shown in table 2.3, the $\alpha$ coefficients take values ranging from $-0.4$ and $-0.23$ in Colombia and Chile (where there is crowding-out) to 1.6 in South Korea and Malaysia. Because investment is the sum of public and private components, additional public capital formation increases the rate of growth of potential output even in the two South American countries. Both the $\alpha$ and $\beta$ coefficients influence how effectively public investment stimulates capacity expansion: Low values mean that larger foreign exchange transfers to the state, a more vigorous tax effort, or a bigger PSBR is required to underwrite public investment in support of a given increase in the rate of capacity growth.

3. The model contains explicit accounting for the public sector. The key operating assumption is that national public revenue net of current expenditure (say Z) is an increasing function of the rate of capacity use—taxes and other receipts rise more rapidly than real spending when economic activity goes up. The strength of this response is measured by $z_1$ coefficients, which take nonnegative values except in Zambia. There, taxes fall and output rises in response to the copper cycle, giving a negative estimated response of Z to $u$.

Public investment enters the fiscal accounts as shown in equation 2.1. For given values of the PSBR ratio $\pi$ and the net revenue coefficient $z_1$,

its volume (relative to potential output) $i_g$ will be tied to capacity utilization, foreign transfers to the government, and interest payments to abroad. By crowding in private investment, a higher $i_g$ raises the rate of capacity growth $g$. We arrive at the upward-sloping "F" lines in Figures 2.1 to 2.4, which show how a higher $u$ can push up $g$ by generating more net fiscal revenue that is channeled to capital formation. A lower interest burden or more foreign transfers to the government will shift the F-schedule upward, while increases in $\pi$ or $z_1$ make it more steep.

4. Available saving puts a limit on investment and potential output growth. Three sources are considered: net government saving or the PSBR minus public investment from (1), net foreign transfers from abroad ($\phi + t$ in table 2.1), and national saving by the private sector. We assume that private saving increases with the rate of capacity utilization according to a coefficient named $\sigma_1$. Together with the positive effect of $u$ on $Z$, this hypothesis underlies the upward-sloping $S$ curves in Figures 2.1 to 2.4. Depending on parameter values, the saving limit on growth may rise more or less steeply than the fiscal constraint $F$ as a function of $u$. A steeper $S$-schedule means that an raising public investment to stimulate overall capital formation will land the government in fiscal difficulties, even though saving is in principle available to finance the additional aggregate demand.

Two other aspects of private saving are important in specific countries. First, its level may decline as more foreign transfers $\phi$ flow toward the private sector. This potential displacement of national by foreign saving was emphasized by early critics of the two-gap model such as Griffin (1970) and Weisskopf (1972), and was visible econometrically in Thailand and Zambia among the countries in the sample.

Second, in a related point not all private saving may be directed toward investment at home; it can filter out of the country via capital flight. Typical vehicles are overinvoicing of imports and underinvoicing of exports. Their outcomes in terms of national accounting conventions are lower national and higher foreign savings. According to chapter 16, on Argentina, in the 1970s "government savings averaged 1.9 percent of GDP, those of the private sector ... 19.2 percent, and the external sector ... about 0.6 percent. After the debt crisis, during the eighties, the saving/GDP ratios for the government, the private sector, and the external sector were − 3.4 percent, 13.2 percent, and 4.3 percent respectively." Similar shifts are notable in other economies prone to capital flight, for example Mexico.

5. The last important linkage in the model is the foreign exchange constraint. As noted previously, production and capital formation depend cru-

cially on imports of intermediate and investment goods. Especially for the small, open economies in the sample, these requirements at the margin can be large.

The story for exports is more complicated. In most countries, producers appear to cut back on foreign sales as domestic demand rises so that exports decline as a function of $u$. In a few export-led economies, however, higher domestic production flows naturally abroad; when $u$ goes up then so does export volume. The country models suggest that domestic demand crowds out foreign sales except in Zambia, Thailand, and South Korea.

Putting all these responses together gives a scenario as follows: Rising output pulls in intermediate imports and (more often than not) reduces export sales, a higher $u$ requires more foreign exchange. Because faster capacity growth $g$ also depends upon imports, an increase in one variable forces the other down: We get the downward-sloping external restriction or $E$ schedules in figures 2.1 to 2.4.

The sensitivity of the growth rate to foreign exchange availability varies markedly across the countries in the sample. Calculations show that a 1 % increase in capital inflows (relative to potential output) may permit $g$ to rise by 0.5 % in small economies and by as much as 2 % in large economies that have pursued import substitution of capital goods. A 1 % increase in capacity utilization $u$ may reduce $g$ by 0.1 % in closed economies and up to 1 % in those that are highly open.

Such trade-offs are central to macroeconomic decision making in the medium run. In Africa, for example, policymakers targeted measures such as import quotas and credit restrictions explicitly toward sustaining either capital formation or current production when external strangulation became acute. At the same time, aid donors imposed pressures to keep ongoing investment projects underway. As figure 2.3 illustrates, the outcome in Tanzania was continued investment, while capacity utilization fell by 20 % between 1976 and 1986. Other countries subject to import compression such as Zimbabwe, which had fewer donor obligations, reacted the other way.

6. The last issue to be discussed is how the model hangs together. Which variables drive the others in practice? How should they be deployed in simulations to illuminate problems of policy choice? Answers to both questions rely on understanding of the institutions and adjustment mechanisms of the economy at hand; some of the possibilities are discussed in section 2.7 and in greater depth in chapter 3.

## 2.4 Formal Statement of the Model

We begin by setting up accounts. Let $X$ stand for real output, or the sum of GDP (or real value-added) *and* real intermediate imports in base year prices. This slightly nonstandard definition underlines the importance of intermediates to the production process in most of the developing world.

The model is based on a simple set of relationships around $X$. The "material balance" equation can be written as

$$X = C + \theta I + G + E - M,$$

where the symbols have their usual meanings except that $\theta$ is the share of investment demand satisfied by goods produced domestically and $M$ stands for competitive imports only.

If $W$ represents tax revenues less transfers plus public enterprise profits, etc. (that is, $W$ is the net revenue that the government receives from the private sector), private consumption $C$ can be expressed as

$$C = X - aX - \lambda S_p - (1 - \lambda)S_p - W,$$

where $aX$ stands for real intermediate imports ($a$ is the import/output ratio), $S_p$ is private saving, and $\lambda$ and $1 - \lambda$ are respectively the shares of $S_p$ directed to asset accumulation within and outside the country. In other words, $(1 - \lambda)S_p$ is capital flight, usually reflected in the trade account through over-invoicing (under-invoicing) of imports (exports). In addition to this external transfer, the model carries along three others. One is foreign interest payments $J^*$, of which the government pays a share $\xi$ and the private sector $1 - \xi$. The others are incoming net capital flows or foreign transfers $T$ and $\Phi$, respectively to the government and private sector. The balance of payments thus becomes

$$M + (1 - \theta)I + aX + (1 - \lambda)S_p + J^* - E = \Phi + T.$$

Putting the consumption function together with the material balance and balance of payments gives the investment-saving balance:

$$I = [W - G - \xi J^*] + [\lambda S_p - (1 - \xi)J^*] + [T + \Phi].$$

The terms in brackets on the right-hand side are savings flows that can finance national investment from government, recorded private, and foreign sources respectively. They underlie the three gaps of a model built around flows of funds of the state, the private sector, and the rest of the world.

To analyze growth, it is convenient to normalize the model around potential real output $Q$, defined as the highest level of $X$ that can reasonably be produced with existing capacity. In the base year, the level of $Q$ was estimated by the country authors using various methods. Extrapolating lines through previous peak outputs was adopted by some, but that approach does not make sense in economies that simply have not been growing. In such circumstances, the best guess at $Q$ was based on a judgment about how far output could rise without running into bottlenecks if foreign exchange (or some other critical input) were freely available.

Let $g$ stand for the rate of growth of potential output, and assume that

$$g = \frac{Q(t+1) - Q(t)}{Q(t)} = g_0 + \kappa \frac{I(t)}{Q(t)} = g_0 + \kappa i. \tag{2.3}$$

Here $I(t)$ is gross capital formation in year $t$, $\kappa$ is the incremental potential output/capital ratio, and $g_0$ is a base level of growth (which could be negative to account for depreciation, or positive because of technological change). Let $i = I/Q$, or investment normalized by potential output. As noted, this sort of normalization is used extensively in what follows.

We define $i_g$ and $i_p$ respectively as public investment (undertaken by the government along with parastatals and public enterprises) and private investment normalized by $Q$. Using a linear behavioral equation for simplicity, we can assume a private investment function of the form

$$i_p = i_0 + \alpha i_g + \beta u. \tag{2.4}$$

Coefficient $\alpha$ captures crowding-in effects of public investment on private capital formation, while $\beta$ is the simplest version of an accelerator. As discussed previously, a negative $\alpha$ represents conventional financial crowding-out: increased fiscal deficits drive up interest rates and reduce private investment demand.

Because $i = i_p + i_g$, equation (2.4) implies that overall investment demand is

$$i = i_0 + (1 + \alpha)i_g + \beta u. \tag{2.5}$$

The next step is to set out savings functions preparatory to writing equations for gaps. Real public saving can be written as

$$S_g = (W - G) - \xi J^* + T = Z - \xi J^* + T,$$

where we implicitly assume that $W$ and $G$ are unaffected by changes in foreign transfers $T$ (a similar hypothesis is discarded for private saving later in this chapter).

The new variable $Z$ is net revenue less current government spending. Let $Z = z_0 Q + z_1 X$, so that normalized government saving is

$$s_g = S_g/Q = z_0 + z_1 u - \xi j^* + t, \tag{2.6}$$

in which $j^* = J^*/Q$ and $t = T/Q$. Typically $z_1 > 0$, as tax takes and public enterprise profits rise with the level of economic activity.

In addition to government saving, it is of interest to consider the public borrowing requirement. If $\pi$ is the share of the PSBR in total output $X$, we have PSBR/$Q$ = (PSBR/$X$)($X/Q$) = $\pi u$, and

$$\pi u = i_g - (z_0 + z_1 u) + \xi j^* - t. \tag{2.7}$$

The reason to use a parameter such as $\pi$ is that PSBR targets are usually set relative to actual instead of potential output. In interpreting numerical values of $\pi$, bear in mind that $X$ exceeds GDP.

Relative to capacity, private saving can be expressed in linear form as

$$s_p = \sigma_0 + \sigma_1 u - \sigma_2 \phi, \tag{2.8}$$

where $\phi = \Phi/Q$. The parameter $\sigma_0$ implicitly includes private foreign interest payments $-(1 - \xi)j^*$; this is one reason why it is in practice negative. As described later, the observed value of $\sigma_0$ may also shift over time in response to capital flight. The marginal saving rate $\sigma_1$ implicitly includes the effects of transfers and taxes. A positive value of $\sigma_2$ means that capital inflows partially substitute for domestic saving along the lines suggested by critics of the two-gap model such as Griffin (1970) and Weisskopf (1972).

Uses less sources of foreign exchange for the economy can be written as

$$S_f = M + (a_0 Q + a_1 X) + (1 - \theta)I + J^* + (1 - \lambda)s_p u Q - (\varepsilon_0 Q - \varepsilon_1 X)$$

$$= T + \Phi.$$

As in the material balance expression, $M$ stands for competitive imports or other inflow items in the current account. Intermediate imports are $aX = a_0 Q + a_1 X$, or $au = a_0 + a_1 u$ in normalized form. Demand for intermediates may be more than unit elastic with respect to capacity utilization, in which case $a_0 < 0$ and $a_1$ is just the product of the average intermediate share $(a)$ and the import elasticity.

Similar tricks can be applied to other items of the trade balance. In most countries export sales seem to be cut back as producers turn to local sales when domestic activity rises according to the parameter $\varepsilon_1$. However, a few authors found complementarity between exports and production, making $\varepsilon_1 < 0$. Export and intermediate import expansion at the same rate as potential output is built into the equations, because $\varepsilon_0(a_0)$ stands for the share of exports (intermediate imports) in $Q$, which is presumably growing. These shares change as exports (imports) grow faster or slower than $Q$.

The parameter $\theta$ is the share of nationally produced goods in total investment. The import share $1 - \theta$ in some circumstances may be elastic to investment itself: $(1 - \theta)i = v_0 + v_1 i$ is a specification adopted in several papers. We have already noted that falsified trade accounting may reflect the term $(1 - \lambda)s_p u Q$, or capital flight.

In normalized form, foreign saving is

$$s_f = m + (a_0 + a_1 u) + (1 - \theta)i + j^* + (1 - \lambda)s_p u - (\varepsilon_0 + \varepsilon_1 u)$$

$$= t + \phi. \tag{2.9}$$

We can now set up three gap equations, treating the capacity growth rate $g$ (or public investment $i_g$) and capacity utilization $u$ as the variables that trade off to give macro equilibrium.

Setting investment from (2.5) equal to the sum of savings flows gives a saving gap:

$$(1 + \alpha)i_g - (\lambda\sigma_1 + z_1 - \beta)u = z_0 - \xi j^* + (1 - \lambda\sigma_2)\phi + \lambda\sigma_0 - i_0 + t, \tag{2.10}$$

in which the standard macro stability condition is $\lambda\sigma_1 + z_1 > \beta$. Higher capacity utilization in this equation generates more (private plus public) saving, permitting $i_g$ and the growth rate $g$ to rise.

Using (2.3) and (2.5), the saving gap can be written in growth rate form as

$$g = \kappa(\lambda\sigma_1 + z_1)u + \kappa[z_0 - \xi j^* + (1 - \lambda\sigma_2)\phi + \lambda\sigma_0 + t] + g_0, \tag{2.10'}$$

which is used for the calculations in section 2.5. Growth is limited by capacity utilization according to the coefficient $\kappa(\lambda\sigma_1 + z_1)$, in Harrod-Domar form.

Rewriting (2.9) gives a *foreign exchange gap*:

$$(1 - \theta)(1 + \alpha)i_g + [a_1 + (1 - \theta)\beta + \varepsilon_1 + (1 - \lambda)\sigma_1]u$$

$$= [1 + (1 - \lambda)\sigma_2]\phi - m - j^* - (1 - \theta)i_0 - a_0 + \varepsilon_0 + t - (1 - \lambda)\sigma_0. \tag{2.11}$$

The positive terms in $i_g$ and $u$ on the left-hand side reflect the inverse trade-off between imports of capital goods for investment and of intermediates to support current output (and exports) that African and other authors stress. For example, Figure 2.3 shows that Tanzania reacted to its external shocks by reducing intermediate imports and capacity utilization while keeping up investment and potential output growth. Other countries such as Zimbabwe responded in the opposite way.

The growth rate version of this equation is

$$g = -\frac{\kappa[a_1 + \varepsilon_1 + (1 - \lambda)\sigma_1]}{1 - \theta}u + \frac{\kappa}{1 - \theta}\{[1 + (1 - \lambda)\sigma_2]\phi - m - j^*$$

$$- a_0 + \varepsilon_0 + t - (1 - \lambda)\sigma_0\} + g_0, \tag{2.11'}$$

with $g$ responding negatively to $u$.

Finally, rewriting (2.7) gives a *fiscal gap*:

$$i_g - (\pi + z_1)u = z_0 - \xi j^* + t. \tag{2.12}$$

Here, with the PSBR target $\pi$ set in terms of output, greater capacity utilization permits an increase in government capital formation and growth. Higher foreign transfers $t$ permit greater public investment, while increased interest obligations $\xi j^*$ cut $i_g$ back.

In growth rate form, the fiscal gap becomes

$$g = \kappa[(1 + \alpha)(\pi + z_1) + \beta]u + \kappa(1 + \alpha)(z_0 - \xi j^* + t) + g_0 + \kappa i_0. \tag{2.12'}$$

Note that the investment function parameters $\alpha$ and $\beta$ appear only in (2.12'), but not in (2.10') and (2.11'). In effect, we adopt a closure for the three-gap model similar to the one used by Johansen (1960) in his pioneering computable general equilibrium model: Public borrowing is used to accommodate an independent investment function. As discussed later, several country authors selected other closures as being more appropriate to their particular cases; the Johansen approach is followed here to ease cross-country comparisons.

In full equilibrium, the three gaps cross each other as shown in Figures 2.1 through 2.4. The negatively sloped external gap will be steep when $a_1$ and/or $\varepsilon_1$ is large, or $1 - \theta$ small, while either the saving or fiscal constraint may have a bigger positive slope. A steeper saving than fiscal schedule means that an attempt to speed up growth will land the government in fiscal difficulties, even though overall saving is, in principle, available to finance additional investment demand. Many developing countries find themselves in this predicament in the 1990s.

**Table 2.3**
Key country parameters

| | $\kappa$ | $\alpha$ | $\beta$ | $\sigma_1$ | $z_1$ | $a_1$ | $\varepsilon_1$ | $1 - \theta$ |
|---|---|---|---|---|---|---|---|---|
| Argentina | 0.26 | 0.5 | 0.0 | 0.364 | 0.234 | 0.1 | 0.0 | 0.13 |
| Brazil | 0.286 | 1.0 | 0.2 | 0.2 | 0.285 | 0.01 | 0.05 | 0.15 |
| Chile | 0.333 | −0.23 | 0.059 | 0.16 | 0.10 | 0.487 | 0.0 | 0.645 |
| Colombia | 0.32 | −0.4 | 0.13 | 0.36 | 0.02 | 0.128 | 0.0 | 0.21 |
| India | 0.4 | 0.232 | 0.091 | 0.3 | 0.36 | 0.1 | 0.15 | 0.092 |
| Malaysia | 0.3 | 1.6 | 0.024 | 0.3 | 0.2 | 0.62 | 0.01 | 0.48 |
| Mexico | 0.47 | 0.9 | 0.054 | 0.096 | 0.199 | 0.16 | 0.16 | 0.387 |
| Nicaragua | 0.25 | 0.5 | 0.0 | 0.15 | 0.2 | 0.182 | 0.05 | 0.46 |
| Nigeria | 0.29 | 0.853 | 0.185 | 0.25 | 0.012 | 0.045 | 0.094 | 0.318 |
| Philippines | 0.286 | 0.5 | 0.05 | 0.069 | 0.012 | 0.153 | 0.0 | 0.237 |
| Sri Lanka | 0.236 | 0.458 | 0.0 | 0.473 | 0.141 | 1.362 | 0.161 | 0.31 |
| Tanzania | 0.25 | 0.148 | 0.089 | 0.2 | 0.083 | 0.076 | 0.179 | 0.33 |
| Thailand[a] | 0.317 | 0.546 | 0.25 | 0.527 | 0.07 | 0.33 | −0.169 | 0.363 |
| Turkey | 0.181 | 0.185 | 0.05 | 0.245 | 0.0 | 0.2 | 0.144 | 0.22 |
| Uganda | 0.27 | 1.0 | 0.086 | 0.127 | 0.034 | 0.195 | 0.0 | 0.5 |
| Zambia[b] | 0.255 | 0.249 | 0.756 | 0.775 | −0.0136 | 0.292 | −0.12 | 0.749 |
| Zimbabwe | 0.197 | 0.5 | 0.05 | 0.2 | 0.1 | 0.15 | 0.1 | 0.313 |

a. Private saving in Thailand responds negatively to capital inflow ($\phi$) with a coefficient of 0.63.
b. Private saving in Zambia responds negatively to $\phi$ with a coefficient of 0.69.

The parameters defining the curves for each economy are summarized in table 2.3. Country authors used a combination of econometrics and informed judgment in arriving at these numbers. Both methods require substantial expertise and experience regarding the economy at hand. In other words, the table presents as good a statistical representation of each economy's fiscal and growth trade-offs as one is likely to find.

The following observations about the parameters apply:

1. There is a wide range of values for $\alpha$, the public investment crowding-in coefficient, but in most cases it is positive. Countries with high accelerator coefficients $\beta$ also have high marginal public and private saving shares $z_1$ and $\sigma_1$, so that overall macroeconomic stability is attained.

2. As is to be expected, marginal import coefficients $a_1$ and $1 - \theta$ are bigger in smaller economies.

3. The papers for Thailand and Zambia came up with a positive response of exports to output changes, that is, $\varepsilon_1 < 0$. Elsewhere, an increase in the domestic activity level crowds out exports, as hypothesized previously.

4. Zambia also demonstrates a negative effect $z_1$ of output on net public revenue. The econometrics captures the fact that output rises and the tax effort declines in response to the copper cycle.

5. Capital flight was not estimated directly, so all models implicitly set $\lambda$ to one. Flight does, however, show up clearly as a declining trend in recorded savings flows in Argentina, Mexico, and elsewhere.

## 2.5  Three-Gap Simulations

In this section, we deploy equations (2.10′) to (2.12′) to illustrate interactions between foreign transfers and developing country policy choice. In line with the Johansen model closure, we first ask how capacity utilization $u$, public investment $i_g$, foreign transfers to the government $t$, and the PSBR ratio $\pi$ would have to adjust to meet one percent faster growth in capacity $g$.

Specifically, we solve the saving and external gaps for changes in capacity utilization and foreign transfers $\Delta u$ and $\Delta t$, given $\Delta g = 0.01$, and then use the fiscal gap to find the change in the PSBR ratio $\Delta \pi$ that supports 1 % faster capacity growth. If the economy is at or near full capacity, then the change in the base level of government net revenue $\Delta z_0$ is taken as the adjusting variable in place of $\Delta u$. In a planning context, this exercise estimates the volume of foreign resources required to support modestly more rapid medium term expansion in the countries in the WIDER sample.

A second exercise computes foreign capital requirements $\Delta \phi$ and capacity utilization and PSBR shifts $\Delta u$ and $\Delta \pi$ needed for 1 % faster capacity growth under plausible changes in policy and external conditions, as specified for each economy. Using the variable $\Delta \phi$ implies that capital inflows go to the private sector. The goals are to check how resource "needs" may vary if the countries are affected by plausible structural changes and luck, and to see if fiscal limitations tighten due to actions of the private sector and its financiers.

Lines (1) and (2) for each economy in table 2.4 summarize these calculations. We take up policy implications after discussing the general outcomes of the first set of simulations. The resulting $\Delta t$ values are given relative to potential output and (in parentheses) in billions of dollars.

There is a fairly wide range of net transfers required to support the 1 % increment in potential output growth. With their relatively large, diversified economies, Argentina, Brazil, India, and the Philippines have $\Delta t$ values less than 1 % (although their corresponding dollar resource flow increments are

**Table 2.4**
Simulations for increasing the capacity growth rate by 1%

| | $\Delta t$ or $\Delta\phi$ | $\Delta i_g$ | $\Delta u$ | $\Delta\pi$ | Other changes | |
|---|---|---|---|---|---|---|
| Argentina (1) | 0.0072 (0.554) | 0.0256 | 0.022* | −0.0064 | $\Delta z_0 =$ | 0.0181 |
| (2) | 0.02    (1.538) | 0.0123 | 0.022* | 0.0005 | $\Delta i_0 =$ | 0.02 |
| | | | | | $\Delta z_0 =$ | 0.0053 |
| | | | | | $\Delta\varepsilon_0 =$ | −0.0128 |
| Brazil (1) | 0.0085 (2.68) | 0.012 | 0.0546 | −0.015 | | |
| (2) | 0.0063 (2.0) | 0.0158 | 0.0175 | −0.0118 | $\Delta z_0 =$ | 0.0202 |
| Chile (1) | 0.0194 (0.446) | 0.039 | 0.0* | 0.009 | $\Delta z_0 =$ | 0.0106 |
| (2) | 0.0194 (0.446) | 0.039 | 0.0* | 0.009 | $\Delta z_0 =$ | −0.02 |
| | | | | | $\Delta z_1 =$ | 0.05 |
| Colombia (1) | 0.0129 (0.597) | 0.0417 | 0.0488 | 0.0301 | | |
| (2) | −0.0158 (−0.732) | 0.0394 | 0.0584 | 0.0131 | $\Delta\varepsilon_0 =$ | 0.03 |
| | | | | | $\Delta z_0 =$ | 0.025 |
| India (1) | 0.0085 (2.243) | 0.0184 | 0.025 | −0.0018 | | |
| (2) | 0.0031 (0.807) | 0.0201 | 0.0031 | −0.0016 | $\Delta z_0 =$ | 0.02 |
| Malaysia (1) | 0.0256 (1.224) | 0.0127 | 0.0154 | −0.0205 | | |
| (2) | 0.0245 (1.172) | 0.0128 | −0.0024 | 0.0042 | $\Delta\varepsilon_0 =$ | −0.01 |
| | | | | | $\Delta z_0 =$ | 0.01 |
| Mexico (1) | 0.015   (2.555) | 0.0106 | 0.0212 | −0.0103 | | |
| (2) | 0.0047 (0.8) | 0.0089 | −0.0112 | 0.0128 | $\Delta z_0 =$ | 0.02 |
| | | | | | $\Delta i_0 =$ | 0.005 |
| Nicaragua (1) | 0.027   (0.076) | 0.0267 | 0.037 | −0.01 | | |
| (2) | 0.015   (0.042) | 0.0267 | 0.0716 | 0.011 | $\Delta\varepsilon_0 =$ | 0.02 |
| Nigeria (1) | 0.0191 (1.741) | 0.0127 | 0.0587 | −0.0138 | | |
| (2) | 0.0157 (1.429) | 0.0152 | 0.0339 | 0.0048 | $\Delta z_0 =$ | 0.01 |
| Philippines (1) | 0.0063 (0.292) | 0.0224 | 0.0277 | 0.0173 | | |
| (2) | 0.0031 (0.144) | 0.0238 | −0.0138 | 0.005 | $\Delta z_0 =$ | 0.02 |
| Sri Lanka (1) | 0.0353 (0.282) | 0.029 | 0.0145 | −0.0104 | | |
| (2) | 0.0303 (0.242) | 0.029 | 0.0244 | 0.0251 | $\Delta\varepsilon_0 =$ | 0.02 |
| Tanzania (1) | 0.028   (0.151) | 0.031 | 0.06 | −0.005 | | |
| (2) | 0.006   (0.032) | 0.031 | 0.05 | 0.0079 | $\Delta\varepsilon_0 =$ | 0.02 |
| | | | | | $\Delta z_0 =$ | 0.02 |
| Thailand (1) | 0.0157 (0.876) | 0.0162 | 0.0265 | −0.0147 | | |
| (2) | 0.0156 (0.866) | 0.0162 | 0.0261 | 0.0043 | $\Delta z_0 =$ | 0.01 |
| Turkey (1) | 0.0122 (0.808) | 0.0468 | 0.0* | −0.0087 | $\Delta z_0 =$ | 0.0432 |
| (2) | 0.0072 (0.477) | 0.0468 | 0.0* | −0.0115 | $\Delta z_0 =$ | 0.0582 |
| | | | | | $\Delta a_0 =$ | −0.005 |
| | | | | | $\Delta\sigma_1 =$ | −0.01 |
| Uganda (1) | 0.0287 (0.135) | 0.0163 | 0.0521 | −0.0252 | | |
| (2) | 0.0186 (0.087) | 0.0166 | 0.052 | −0.0002 | $\Delta z_0 =$ | 0.01 |
| | | | | | $\Delta a_0 =$ | −0.01 |
| Zambia (1) | 0.0315 (0.112) | 0.0241 | 0.0121 | −0.0098 | | |
| (2) | 0.0214 (0.081) | 0.0287 | 0.0044 | 0.0226 | $\Delta z_0 =$ | 0.01 |
| | | | | | $\Delta\varepsilon_0 =$ | 0.01 |
| Zimbabwe (1) | 0.0318 (0.213) | 0.0318 | 0.0636 | −0.0183 | | |
| (2) | 0.0159 (0.107) | 0.0339 | 0.0 | −0.0016 | $\Delta z_0 =$ | 0.035 |

Notes: Capacity use changes ($\Delta u$) marked with an asterisk are determined by the full capacity use condition $u = 1$. Public saving ($\Delta z_0$) is assumed to adjust to balance the saving gap in this case. The adjusting capital flow variables in simulations (1) and (2) are $\Delta t$ and $\Delta\phi$ respectively, measured as fractions of potential output and in billions of dollars (in parentheses).

not trival sums). At the other end of the spectrum, the small, import-dependent economies of Nicaragua, Sri Lanka, Tanzania, Uganda, and Zimbabwe require transfers of around 3 % of capacity for 1 % faster growth.

It is easy to show analytically that the effect of capital inflows on capacity use ($\Delta u/\Delta t$) exceeds the effect on capacity growth ($\Delta g/\Delta t$) when the saving and foreign gaps are solved together. The implication for the line (l) simulations is that, except when capacity limits bind, increases in $u$ exceed 1 %. In some country cases, the extra foreign exchange required for 1 % capacity growth is adequate to support the output expansion "necessary" for social ends such as employment and income redistribution.

In part because foreign inflows $\Delta t$ are assumed to go directly into the fiscal accounts, 14 of the 17 countries have reduced PSBR ratios ($\Delta \pi < 0$) in the first simulation, even though public investment has to go up to make overall capital formation rise. Other contributory factors to the fiscal improvement are increased capacity use which generates more net government revenue and the postulated increase $\Delta z_0$ in public saving when capacity limits bind; offsetting factors are a weak public investment effect on private capital formation ($\alpha$ is negative in Chile and Colombia, which have positive $\Delta \pi$s) and low tax responsiveness $z_1$ as in the Philippines.

Adding up the foreign transfers needed for 1 % faster capacity growth gives a total of $15 billion ($12.1 billion for the second set of simulations). This flow is 1.2 % of the total potential output of the 17 economies ($1,234 billion), and would be associated with output growth of $43.8 billion, or 3.5 % of capacity (perhaps 4.5 % of base year GDP). These growth versus inflow relationships look favorable, but an additional resource transfer of $15 billion is large compared to net ODA flows to all developing economies, which are about $40 billion. This requirements estimate is extended to the rest of the developing world in the following section.

Uniform application of the simulation model should not divert attention from the fact that each economy evolved in its own institutionally and historically unique fashion during the 1980s. Specific country results are discussed in Taylor (1991a) and the following chapters, but in general the second set of simulations underscores the following points:

First, enhanced fiscal and/or export and import substitution efforts (i.e., $\Delta z_0 > 0$, $\Delta \varepsilon_0 > 0$ and/or $\Delta a_0 < 0$) can reduce external requirements and hold down the PSBR, e.g., Colombia, India, the Philippines, Tanzania, Turkey, Uganda, and Zimbabwe. Nevertheless, the PSBR ratio $\pi$ goes up in 12 of the 17 economies when private agents instead of the government benefit from bigger capital flows. As we have noted, effectively recycling funds from the private to the public sector as $\pi$ rises can be a tricky financial question.

Second, if there is repatriation of flight capital (modeled as $\Delta\phi > 0$) which goes into private investment ($\Delta i_0 > 0$) in Argentina and Mexico, faster capacity growth with a reduced export effort may be possible but there still may be problems with the PSBR.

Third, in economies at or near full capacity (Argentina, Chile, and Turkey) an increased public revenue effort ($\Delta z_0 > 0$) is required to maintain macro balance when there is faster potential output growth supported by higher public capital formation. Chile will have to raise taxes substantially ($\Delta z_1 = 0.05$) to offset the new, nondictatorial government's increased social expenditures ($\Delta z_0 = -0.02$) under full capacity. Elsewhere, increased capacity use $u$ helps generate both fiscal revenue and saving to finance increased public and private capital formation.

Fourth, likely trends in export growth may help some countries and harm others, for example, Colombia and Malaysia respectively.

Finally, these simulations with $\Delta g$ at 1 % leave countries such as Mexico and Brazil well below their three or 4 % historical rates of per capita output growth. These shortfalls should be borne in mind as we extrapolate our 17-country projections to the rest of the Third World in the following section.

## 2.6   Extrapolations to the Rest of the Developing World

The most direct way to extend the results to other countries is by simple regression analysis based on the first set of projections just described. Based on 1987 data taken from the World Bank's 1989 *World Development Report*, the following equation was estimated for the capital inflow (FLOW) required for 1 % faster capacity growth in the 17 countries according to the first simulation in table 2.2:

$$\ln\left(\frac{\text{FLOW}}{\text{GDP}}\right)$$

$$= -7.15 + 2.067\left(\frac{\text{Exports}}{\text{GDP}}\right) - 0.478\ln\left(\frac{\text{GDP}}{\text{Pop}}\right) - 0.238\ln(\text{Pop}),$$

$$(-7.25)\quad(1.68)\qquad\qquad(-3.19)\qquad\qquad(-2.35),\ \bar{R}^2 = 0.56,$$

$$(2.13)$$

where *Pop* stands for population, and *t*-ratios are in parentheses.

The goodness of fit is adequate for an empirical regression on a small cross section, and the coefficients have signs that agree with considerations already raised. Populous countries have lower import coefficients and thus require smaller foreign transfers (relative to GDP) for a given increment in growth. But given population, a higher export ratio signals more openness, leading to a greater FLOW. As might be expected, reliance on capital inflows to support faster growth declines with GDP per head.

Taylor (1991a) presents detailed results from applying equation (2.13) to compute capital inflow "needs" for 1% faster capacity growth in 76 countries with populations exceeding one million for which data from the 1989 *World Development Report* were available. The total flow estimate is $35.309 billion, which can be disaggregated in several ways.

First, there are 25 "large" countries with populations exceeding 20 million, and 51 "small" economies. The estimated flows to the former group are $24.793 billion, and $10.516 billion to the latter. Even if they absorb less in relation to output, big countries still take in the bulk of foreign transfers.

Second, total flows to the countries grouped by per capita output are: 34 low income countries (per capita GNP less than $450), $14.319 billion; 31 low middle income (per capita GNP between $450 and $2000), $13.598 billion; 11 high middle income, $7.392 billion. In the low income group, China and India account for $6.921 billion, or almost half the total. Aside from a few other large absorbers, many small, poor economies (concentrated in sub-Saharan Africa) require inflows in the 100 million dollar range.

By region, flows to the World Bank's four major groupings are: Asia (except Middle East), $13.349 billion; Latin America and the Caribbean (LAC), $8.246 billion; Europe, Middle East, and North Africa (EMENA) $7.252 billion; and sub-Saharan Africa (SSA), $6.462 billion. Again, big countries dominate these regional flows. The SSA total is heavily influenced by Nigeria and South Africa (a total of $2.201 billion) and the LAC total by Mexico and Brazil ($3.5 billion). India and China would take more than half the Asian total. In EMENA, three "post Socialist" economies (Poland, Hungary, and Yugoslavia) take $2.364 billion, and Egypt and Turkey together require $1.645 billion.

These estimates can be compared to other computations of foreign exchange needs or supplies, especially for sub-Saharan Africa and Latin America and the Caribbean, the two most visibly troubled zones.

For SSA, a recent World Bank (1989) report estimates that a regional increase of 1.5% in the output growth rate in the late 1980s would require additional capital inflows of $4 billion. In the year 2000, 5% output growth would require flow support of $19 billion (compared to $8 billion in 1986–87). These numbers are similar to those just derived and contrast sharply with the region's external financial losses averaging $7.6 billion per year between 1979–81 and 1985–87 (United Nations, 1988). Three major negative shifts were adverse movements in the terms of trade, $2.9 billion; increased interest payments, $2.1 billion; and reduced net credit flow, $2.4 billion.

The importance of worsened terms of trade for African economies stands out in the fact that total exports from SSA countries (excluding Nigeria and South Africa) are about $22 billion. A 19.4 % increase in export prices would be equivalent to the $4.26 billion in additional aid flows required for 1 % faster capacity growth in these economies. The United Nations (1988) and World Bank (1989) both estimate that the deterioration in SSA terms of trade has been in the 40 to 50 percent range since the late 1970s. Similar losses afflicted other small, primary exporting economies, for example, Nicaragua and Sri Lanka in the WIDER sample.

Finally, potential absorptive capacity constraints merit consideration in the African context. The data on current account deficits ($\phi + t$) in table 2.1 of chapter 1 show that African countries in the WIDER sample are now absorbing gross transfers amounting to 5 % to 10 % of potential output. GDP in 1987 for the entire region was $134 billion. Our postulated additional transfers of $6.5 billion for one percent faster capacity growth are almost 5 % of GDP, and socially acceptable growth rates would require two or three times as much money. But with such inflows, many economies would be running current account deficits of 20 % to 25 % of GDP. Whether they could absorb such a volume of resources effectively is an open question.

For countries in the LAC region, interest obligations not offset by "fresh money" are the main external burden. According to the Economic Commission for Latin America and the Caribbean (ECLAC, 1990), the regional net transfer on credit transactions peaked at over $20 billion in 1982, fell steadily to − $27 billion in 1985, and was around − $20 billion per year at the end of the decade. The estimate here of $8.25 billion required for 1 % faster capacity growth is dwarfed by these numbers; they are closer to the $25 billion (approximately) that would be needed to support historical growth rates of per capita GDP.

As discussed in more detail in Taylor (1991a), programs to offset the debt burden have been ineffective. The latest initiative is the Brady Plan, begun in 1989. ECLAC (1990) estimates that for countries in its region,

Brady will provide well less than $5 billion per year in net relief of interest burdens, a bagatelle in comparison to the requirements estimates here.

Returning to global figures, we can round up our grand estimate of $35.309 billion to account for omitted countries (inter alia, Iraq, Iran, Afghanistan, and Vietnam) to get a total of at least $40 billion in additional flows in the late 1980s, needed for 1 % faster capacity growth in all the developing world. For some Asian economies, this increment would more than suffice for reasonable social goals, but such a judgment clearly does not apply to sub-Saharan Africa and Latin America. In those regions, double or triple the regional estimates presented would be needed to underwrite per capita growth rates of 2 % or 3 % per-head. Also, if a target annual growth rate of capacity (or $Q$) in the developing world as a whole is 4 %, $40 billion around 1990 would have to rise to $60 billion in constant prices by the year 2000 to hold the FLOW/$Q$ ratio stable. These numbers should be compared to an ODA flow of about $40 billion in the late 1980s and a net transfer from developing to developed economies in the $20 to $40 billion range at the decade's end (down from $50 billion in 1985).

The conclusion is that a substantial realignment in international payments flows would be required to accelerate growth for developing nations overall. The repercussions of such an effort on global macroeconomic equilibrium—in particular on interest rates and macroeconomic performance in the "North"—remain to be explored.

## 2.7 Variant Specifications

The model sketched in sections 2.3 and 2.4 can be modified in many ways to fit particular country circumstances. The extensions in the country papers include the following:

1. As already noted, several papers used marginal import, export, and saving coefficients (with capacity utilization as the explanatory variable).

2. In some cases, the real exchange rate $eP^*/P$ (where $e$ is the nominal exchange rate, and $P^*$ and $P$ are foreign and domestic price indexes respectively) also was used as an explanatory variable for trade performance and/or inflation (see the studies for Colombia and Chile).

3. The model can be extended dynamically, with ratios of foreign and domestic fiscal debt to potential output as state variables with considerable policy interest. Under unchanged conditions in Argentina, for example,

these ratios may well explode as the country falls into external or internal debt traps.

4. The three gaps also can be treated as a disequilibrium system as in the original two-gap approach. Consideration of possible scenarios via which disequilibria can be eliminated can prove illuminating, as in the Brazil and Mexico papers herein, or Fanelli et al. (1987).

## References

Bacha, Edmar L. (1984). "Growth with Limited Supplies of Foreign Exchange: A Reappraisal of the Two-Gap Model" in Moshe Syrquin, Lance Taylor, and Larry Westphal (eds.), *Economic Structure and Performance: Essays in Honor of Hollis B. Chenery*. New York: Academic Press.

Bacha, Edmar L. (1990). "A Three-Gap Model of Foreign Transfers and the GDP Growth Rate in Developing Countries." *Journal of Development Economics*, 32: 279–296.

Carneiro, Dionisio, and Rogerio Werneck (1987). "External Debt, Economic Growth, and Fiscal Adjustment." Rio de Janeiro: Departamento de Economia, Pontificia Universidade Catolica.

Chenery, Hollis B., and Alan M. Strout (1966). "Foreign Assistance and Economic Development." *American Economic Review*, 56: 149–179.

Cline, William R. (1979). "Resource Transfers to Developing Countries: Issues and Trends" in W. R. Cline (ed.), *Policy Alternatives for a New International Economic Order*. New York: Praeger.

Economic Commission for Latin America and the Caribbean (ECLAC) (1990). *Latin America and the Caribbean: Options to Reduce the Debt Burden*. Santiago.

Fanelli, Jose Maria, Roberto Frenkel, and Carlos Winograd (1987). "Argentina" *Stabilization and Adjustment Policies and Programmes Country Study* No. 12. Helsinki: WIDER.

Griffin, Keith B. (1970). "Foreign Capital, Domestic Savings, and Economic Development." *Bulletin of the Oxford University Institute of Statistics*, 32: 99–112.

Helleiner, G. K. (1986). "Balance of Payments Experiences and Growth Prospects in Developing Countries: A Synthesis." *World Development*, 14: 877–908.

Johansen, Leif (1960). *A Multi-Sectoral Study of Economic Growth*. Amsterdam: North-Holland.

Rosenstein-Rodan, Paul N. (1961). "International Aid for Underdeveloped Countries." *Review of Economics and Statistics*, 43: 107–138.

Shapiro, Helen, and Lance Taylor (1990). "The State and Industrial Strategy." *World Development*, 18: 861–878.

Taylor, Lance (1988). *Varieties of Stabilization Experience*. Oxford: Clarendon Press.

Taylor, Lance (1991a). *Foreign Resource Flows and Developing Country Growth*. Helsinki: WIDER.

Taylor, Lance (1991b). *Income Distribution, Inflation, and Growth*. Cambridge, MA: MIT Press.

United Nations (1988). *Financing Africa's Recovery* (Report and Recommendations of the Advisory Group on Financial Flows for Africa). New York.

Weisskopf, Thomas E. (1972). "The Impact of Foreign Capital Inflow on Domestic Savings in Underdeveloped Countries." *Journal of International Economics*, 2: 25–38.

World Bank (1989). *Sub-Saharan Africa: From Crisis to Sustainable Growth*. Washington, DC.

# 3 Stabilization, Adjustment, and Reform

## Lance Taylor

In this chapter, we take up questions of short-term macroeconomic stabilization and medium-term adjustment, which are supposed to add up to economic "reform." As the title of this book implies, the road to reform is often hard to traverse. Some of the worst obstacles are pointed out in the following discussion.

We begin in section 3.1 by considering the mainstream or orthodox view of development policy, as codified in a recently christened "Washington consensus" (or WC). Thinking about alternatives to the WC package is important, because it has been widely applied with modest results and high social costs. The WC's major intellectual drawback is that its underlying assumptions and empirical generalizations do not fit the facts. In particular, a neoliberal obsession with removing price distortions to enhance static, allocative efficiency does little to raise efficiency in production, the essence of what economic development is supposed to be about.

As observed in chapter 1, an alternative view also emphasizes other factors: overriding saving, fiscal, and foreign exchange constraints on macroeconomic performance of the sort emphasized in last chapter's three-gap model; an inescapable link between changes in the distributions of income and wealth and processes of accumulation and growth, the role of an activist state in managing the dynamic forces that affect productive efficiency and avoiding the dangers of financial fragility, and the importance of market structures and institutions in affecting possibilities for change.

We begin to address these issues in section 3.2, describing how theories about the state and economic development have evolved since World War II. The conclusion is that, contrary to recent orthodox theorizing, public intervention continues to play an essential developmental role. Section 3.3 takes up macroeconomics, complementing the three-gap model's emphasis on quantity adjustment by asking how movements in relative prices and the distributions of income and wealth affect aggregate behavior. Sections

3.4 and 3.5 set out non-WC perspectives on stabilization and adjustment in terms of "boundary conditions" that limit freedom of maneuver to reform in any economy's specific historical and institutional circumstances. These considerations lead in section 3.6 to a "non-Washington synthesis" largely shared by the authors of this volume.

## 3.1    The Washington Consensus

On the whole, economics does not provide guidance about how to design macro and sectoral policies to support the incomes of all groups in the population, control inflation and internal, external, and fiscal balances, and guarantee output growth, especially in less developed countries. If the policy means were readily at hand, presumably the industrial nations' comparatively stable and egalitarian prosperity would have been extending itself toward the rest of humanity over the past 10 to 15 years; as we saw in chapter 2, just the opposite has frequently been taking place.

One implication of their failure as architects of change is that in given circumstances, certified economists from the neoliberal to radical extremes typically agree on one-half or three-quarters of their policy recommendations. There are only a few instruments available, and the arguments center around their unfavorable effects on one or another of the targets just mentioned. Moreover, there has been a convergence of views over the past 10 to 15 years about initiatives that are likely to self-destruct, as bold programs of both orthodox and heterodox intellectual persuasion have failed spectacularly.

Nonetheless, differences between mainstream and structuralist thought about development persist, as the WC exemplifies. For the record as well as comparison with the counterpoints set out in section 3.6, a widely accepted version of the consensus due to Williamson (1990) embodies:

W1. balancing the fiscal budget, with a deficit of at most a few percent of GDP, tight spending controls, and broadly based taxation programs with low marginal rates;

W2. price reform, aiming at positive (presumably moderate) real interest rates and a weak, stable exchange rate;

W3. trade liberalization and a cordial attitude toward direct foreign investment (DFI);

W4. privatization of state enterprises; and

W5. deregulation of markets, especially for labor.

To these principles, Fischer (1990) and the World Bank's 1991 *World Development Report* (or *WDR*) would add

W6. a need for "sound" macroeconomic policy and at least a rudimentary social safety net,

with the World Bank also stressing

W7. the positive effects on growth and distribution of accumulation of human capital.

Finally, there is agreement on policy sequencing:

W8. "Stabilization" or removal of macroeconomically disabling balance of payments and fiscal gaps as well as inflation has to come before "adjustment" or creation of conditions for sustainable growth. As noted at the outset of this chapter, together with institutional changes, stabilization and adjustment are supposed to produce viable "reform."

These recommendations are transmitted toward developing economies principally by the International Monetary Fund (IMF) and World Bank, the twin Bretton Woods Institutions (BWIs). Especially for low income countries—usually with few professional economists in government to argue back to visiting BWI missions and negligible international clout—both stabilization and adjustment measures in recent years have been tied together in a "policy framework paper" or PFP. This document is supposed to be written in collaboration by BWI and local government staffs, but it is usually clear who sets the tone. Because even in relatively advanced economies like Mexico or the Philippines PFP-style policies are regularly applied, we can take them as a generic description of the options available throughout the Third World.

To expand a bit on Williamson's list, stabilization attempts typically encompass most or all of the following policy moves:

1. Fiscal austerity, that is, reductions in public investment, consumption, and subsidy programs; increased taxes; and the privatization of state enterprises.

2. Monetary austerity beyond simple reduction of the public sector borrowing requirement or PSBR, for example, interest rate increases and credit restraint.

3. Devaluation of the local currency, unification of multiple exchange rates, and so on.

4. Trade liberalization, which is supposed to improve the economy's "efficiency" in the medium run. Both BWIs stress that policymakers should steer toward a liberal, market system, even though social costs in terms of output losses, regressive redistribution, and rapidly rising deregulated prices may be high.

5. Redistributions of income and wealth are implicit in all the policies just mentioned, as discussed in section 3.3. At times explicit interventions are also pursued, for example, manipulating key prices at both the producer and consumer levels (farmgate prices, food subsidy rates, interest rates, etc.) or regulating bargaining processes such as the imposition of less than 100 % indexation of wages to ongoing price inflation.

One portion of a PFP will set out performance criteria incorporating such stabilization measures, for example, ceilings on PSBR levels for several periods (quarters or years), the recommended pace of devaluation, and perhaps targets for wage restraint and moves toward liberalization. Although they are not included in the document, the IMF will also prepare tables projecting the balance of payments (BOP) situation, monetary balances, and government financial operations (in a table called the TOFE, a French acronym for Tableau des Opérations Financières de l'Etat). Figure 3.1 illustrates the IMF's financing programming computations, with the arrows indicating how the logic runs from objective or target variables

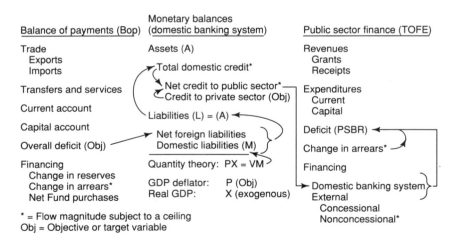

**Figure 3.1**
Illustration of the Fund model

(most notably, the external deficit and the inflation rate) to operational ceilings on the PSBR and public sector borrowing from the banks.[1]

The PFP will also include a "policy matrix," mainly the handiwork of the World Bank. It specifies both macroeconomic and sectoral measures the country is supposed to undertake to be eligible for World Bank credits. Conditionality is involved in that if certain policies are not undertaken, then adjustment credits will not be released. Typical examples include the following.

1. Again, liberalized trade policies (including exchange rate management) are emphasized, with an eye toward helping exporters get access to intermediate inports and credit. There is growing tension in both the Bank's rhetoric and actions between trying to "level the playing field" between import substituting and exporting sectors, and illiberal policies that benefit exporters outright. Indeed, the institution is under growing pressure from a major stockholder to advocate interventionist industrial/trade policies of the sort discussed in section 3.5, with some internal staff support.[2]

2. Fiscal restructuring may be suggested, for example, the establishment of a core public investment program, and better targeting of social expenditures when overall transfers and subsidies are being cut (somewhat ostentatious creation of a "safety net" has been a feature of Bretton Woods programs in a few countries, for example, Chile and Ghana). Although perhaps desirable, BWI sponsorship of fundamental tax reforms or more thoroughgoing asset redistributions such as land reform has been rare.

3. Increasing public sector efficiency is a frequently stated goal, although the Bank continues to experiment with the mechanics. It may fall back on measures such as employment freezes, and ceilings on budgetary transfers or preferential credit lines to public sector firms.

4. Financial sector reform can take the form of restructuring of intermediaries, their recapitalization, and creation of a new (usually liberalized) regulatory climate. Transparency in credit transactions is the long-term goal, supported by real interest rates that are moderately positive for savers and not excessively high on the lending side.

5. Specific sectoral programs, for example in agriculture, industry, energy, or transport, combine external support for investment projects with reform packages that typically emphasize pricing policy.

The country studies in this volume suggest that the simple PFP/WC dichotomy between stabilization and adjustment is too strict; development takes place in a broader context. The real question is whether economic reform, or reconfiguration of the system to meet challenges posed by changes in both internal and external circumstances, is feasible in a given country's historical and institutional context. As we will see in the following discussion, policies that have worked in practice are definitely a mixed bag.

## 3.2  The State and Economic Development

The state has to be a major actor in putting reform policies into place. Indeed, its role in directing economic development is an old concern, and central to the papers here. Before delving into the details of why a government should or should not choose certain policies, it makes sense to explore the limits to what it can achieve. Although Josef Schumpeter (1934) had stated its basic ideas in the German-language version of his *Theory of Economic Development* as early as 1910, for practical purposes development economics emerged as a separate discipline just after World War II; both the problems and possibilities for public intervention that its practitioners perceived and the ones they failed to comprehend remain relevant today.

As observed by Shapiro and Taylor (1990), mainstream views about economic governance have clearly shifted. The discussion no longer centers on remedies for market failure and whether or not a liberal environment can capture dynamic efficiencies. The claim of the "new neoclassical political economy" that emerged in the 1980s is much more radical: Although markets may be imperfect, any state intervention just amplifies distortions and inhibits growth to such an extent that it makes a bad situation worse.[3]

The mainstream consensus came to this turn in three stages. The first was shared by the development economists who dominated the field until the 1960s, and the second and third respectively by "old" and "new" neoclassical critics. The points stressed by early scholars included the following:

1. Development is a disequilibrium process involving successive transitions from one configuration of steady growth or "circular flow" to another. A transition may be induced by technical innovation, and its implementation via new investment requires endogenous credit creation and inflationary forced saving as described in section 3 (Schumpeter, 1934).[4]

2. One can postulate conditions under which development will be increasingly rapid, capital-intensive, and reliant upon a greater role of the state. In nineteenth-century Europe, for example, greater relative "backwardness" called forth more dramatic transitions (Gerschenkron, 1962).

3. Economies of scale are important. Coordinated investment across many sectors in a "Big Push" is required to give balanced output and demand expansion to take advantage of decreasing average costs economy-wide (Rosenstein-Rodan, 1943; Nurkse, 1953).

4. The investment must be planned, because pervasive market failures such as decreasing costs and imperfect tradeability mean that price-driven, decentralized investment decisions will not be socially optimal (Scitovsky, 1954).

5. Modern analytical tools such as input-output models and social cost-benefit analysis make public investment planning possible (Chenery, 1961).

6. On the other hand, planning tools are at best approximations, so one should be on the lookout for inflationary, balance of payments, and other bottlenecks, and figure out how to break them in a process of perpetually unbalanced expansion (Hirschman, 1958).

7. Given the breakdown of the world trading system in the 1930s, export-led growth was a strategy option not worth detailed exploration (implicit consensus). An emphasis on growth through import-substituting industrialization or ISI was an obvious corollary.

This 40-year-old literature was highly suggestive, but it had at least two major drawbacks. One was that although it was rich with diagnoses of development problems, it provided little concrete policy advice. Circular flow, relative backwardness, balanced and unbalanced growth, and so on were intriguing metaphors but did not help much with practical decisions. Planning models and cost-benefit analysis also proved to be more of academic than managerial interest.

The second problem is that the early development economists placed limitless faith in the capacity of the state to intervene in the economic system. Its inability to carry out its assigned development role(s) became apparent, almost equally fast. The contrast with liberal teachings could not be more striking. Realistically or not, neoclassical economics at most requires that the state should be a "night watchman." The development economists needed the state to be proactive and effective, but provided no reasons why it could or should fulfill its tasks.

Around 1970, the first wave of critics concentrated on the "inefficiency" of state intervention as it had evolved, particularly in its emphasis on ISI. Using new analytical tools from trade theory, such as effective rates of protection and domestic resource costs, economists Little et al., 1970; Balassa, 1971; and Krueger, 1984 showed that the incentive structures created by import substitution were highly unequal for different economic actors. They further sought to correlate "distorted" policy regimes with poor economic performance; their modest success in this endeavor is described later.

One of their empirical problems is worth describing. When they applied computable general equilibrium models—their highest tech analytical tools—to estimate "welfare losses" from distortions, the outcomes were meager: 100 % distortions might reduce GDP by 0.5 %. Implicitly, then, the first neoclassical critique reduced to an assertion that eliminating distortions will lead the economy to jump to a noticeably more rapidly growing configuration of circular flow. The question of just how such a transition is supposed to happen instantly arises; as we will see, the dynamics of miracles by the invisible hand are not easy to describe.

Regardless of this difficulty, when the critics showed that many industries in developing countries had "negative value-added" at world prices, they took the profession by storm. But they also transmitted a more powerful message. Read between the lines, these economists advocated laissez-faire as the only viable alternative to an incentive mare's nest. The rapid growth rates of Taiwan and South Korea—at the time unrealistically postulated to have noninterventionist governments—were cited in support of the free market. Although they are not easy to substantiate, the notions that observed distortions inhibit growth and that rapid growers are noninterventionist now permeate the rhetoric and advice of mainstream development scholars and lending institutions; as already observed, such ideas are built solidly into the WC.

In the 1980s, the debate took its second turn. Echoing P. T. Bauer (1972, 1984), who had questioned the efficacy of state intervention early on, recent authors postulate that "bureaucratic failure" is worse than "market failure." Figure 3.2 is a schematic representation of the latest neoclassical critiques. The point that it tries to depict is that the critics are not fully relevant because their models push them into extreme positions with regard to the nature of both the market (highly distorted or fully competitive) and the state (pluralistic and reacting passively to pressures or monolithic and proactive). On the other hand, the obstacles to intervention that they emphasize do help understanding of blocked attempts at economic reform.

For example, Olson (1982) argues that because of bargaining costs and the presence of free riders (both major themes of the new institutionalists), coalitions within the society form to protect their own interests. They seek to redistribute income toward themselves, instead of increasing efficiency

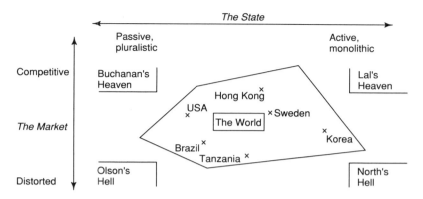

**Figure 3.2**
The new neoclassical political economic vision

in the national interest. A weak state cannot intervene, so the system tends toward a highly distorted market structure with the coalitions distributing the spoils: "Olson's Hell" in the diagram. Developing countries that have helped coalitions form around ISI or other strategic interventions may drift toward infernal situations as the subsidized groups take over decision making: Argentina comes to mind for this pathology (along with numerous others).

The public choice school led by Buchanan (1980) elevates rent-seeking induced by government interventions—lobbying for state favors, paying a bribe to get an import quota or Pentagon contract, fixing a ticket for a traffic violation—to a deadly social ill. If real resources are devoted to pursuing rents or directly unproductive profit-seeking (DUP) activities in the jargon, the outcome can be a form of suboptimality resembling Olson's for the society as a whole. Inventing DUP was a technical advance because deep wells of postulated corruption allowed numerical models to give satisfyingly large estimates of welfare losses from distortion. Moreover, the saving social grace became a thoroughly night-watchmanly state supervising a competitive market—the latter condition to be guaranteed by international free trade. Under these conditions, DUP activity supposedly becomes unrewarding, and the invisible hand will guide society toward "Buchanan's Heaven." Unpleasant externalities, such as transnational corporations (TNCs) taking advantage of a country's fully unregulated trade and external capital markets, are banished from the scene.

A second form of bliss takes a more authoritarian cast. For Buchanan (1980), the ideal state mimics the Cheshire cat by vanishing to avoid being taken over by the interests. Alternatively, the state can force the interests to vanish, or in Lal's (1983) words, "A courageous, ruthless, and perhaps undemocratic government is required to ride roughshod over these newly created special interest groups": The current Mexican leadership may share such dreams. In the diagram, we ascend to another heaven, although it is not clear why Lal's ruthless generals and bureaucrats will abstain from taking over the market. The record of Third World authoritarian states in avoiding corruption and distortions is not encouraging in this regard.

Indeed a market distorted by the state for its own ends is a final, extreme possibility in the diagram, which can be associated with North's (1981) theories of economic history, not to mention Kennedy's (1987) good read about how their military-industrial complexes force great powers into economic decline. In a typical North example, a state may choose to raise revenue by creating monopolies and then marshall political arguments in their support. The fate of Leninist centrally planned systems suggests that economic damnation may well lie at the end of such a path.

The message of the diagram is that, in principle, the state and market can arrive at extreme configurations that are easy to characterize. However, the Buchanan combination of a purely night watchman state and a completely undistorted market has never been observed in practice (certainly not in eighteenth-century Britain and contemporary Hong Kong, the two most widely cited putative examples). If it were ever created, a Lal equilibrium would probably not be stable; recent events suggest that even North's Hell is not forever (the same is true for Olson's form of anarchy).

Indeed, as the central section of the picture illustrates, existing societies combine mixtures of state activism with market distortions. The national placements are arbitrary but are meant to illustrate stylized facts. (Readers are encouraged to think about where their own favorite countries may lie!) Moreover, if it were possible to attach numerical coordinates to nations' points in the diagram, statistical analysis would almost certainly detect scant association between their positions or movements and indicators of economic performance such as GDP growth rates, except for the likelihood of poor growth in countries with hellishly distorted markets.

Beyond this hypothetical regression, a much more fundamental point is that the new neoclassical theory of the state is ahistorical and timeless; although it may shed light on tendencies, it elides the messy dynamics of transitions. A typical new institutional economics (NIE) story would please Dr. Pangloss: Its "agents" successfully optimize over all possible choices so that the system inevitably arrives at the best (and only, presuming uniqueness) possible world. In such models there is not much hope for "development" in Schumpeter's sense of jumping from one pattern of circular flow to another.

Abba Lerner caught the flavor when he remarked that "economics has gained the title of queen of the social sciences by choosing solved political problems as its domain." He was certainly correct with regard to the theorists at the corners of our diagram. The last topics that they can address are the complex, real time interactions between state and market that have characterized economic development since it began three centuries ago. The essays in this volume go far more deeply into these historical issues than any simple analytical formulation ever can.

### 3.3   Distribution and Model Closure

We now turn to policy analysis in detail. To trace how the state's economic interventions work out in practice, a natural way to start is by considering how macroeconomic balance is attained. To a first approximation, shifts in schedules like those in figures 2.1 through 2.4 in chapter 2 can be used to explore adjustment to macroeconomic shocks. For example, with the parameters of its three-gap model, Mexico's output growth rate increase of about 2 % per year in 1990–91 is consistent with the increment of 1.5 % of GDP in capital inflows that it received. Contrary to a WC interpretation, no great improvement in the efficiency of resource use due to Mexico's drastic liberalization moves during the 1980s appears to have occurred.

In addition to output changes, additional adjustment channels are opened by changes in the national distributions of income and wealth induced by price and quantity fluctuations. For its own ends, the state may seek to alter distribution, for example, an attempt to raise real wages on the part of a government with strong working class support such as Salvador Allende's in Chile in the early 1970s. Later that decade, the successor Pinochet regime undertook massive redistribution of wealth-favoring its own bourgeois "Chicago Boy" clients by selling them the enterprises nationalized under Allende at knock-down prices. As described later in this chapter, their subsequent financial speculation cost the country dearly in the medium run.

Alternatively, distributional changes may result from other policies. An ISI program typically switches relative prices against agriculture by a variety of methods (import tariffs or quotas, an "overvalued" exchange rate,[5] and soon); pro-farmer strategies move sectoral prices and incomes the other way. As noted in chapter 2, after the debt crisis many governments nationalized private external obligations—a wealth transfer deemed essential to save local financial systems.

Distributional shifts—both endogenous and policy-induced—thus emerge as the keys to changes in capacity utilization, capital inflows, the public sector borrowing requirement or PSBR, and capital formation. Along lines set out in Taylor (1991), at least eight sets of linkages recur in developing economies, and are summarized here:

1. If output is not limited by available capacity or other constraints, it may well be stimulated from the side of aggregate demand by progressive income redistribution in general and higher real wages in particular: "wage-led growth" appears to be the rule in much of the developing world. Demand expansion due to real wage increases may crowd out exports and pull in intermediate imports as described in the previous chapter, creating stabilization problems. A positive wage-output linkage also complicates adjustments to rising labor productivity. If surplus labor is present, a productivity gain (or a fall in the labor/output ratio) is not likely to be accompanied by a higher real wage. At the initial level of output, total wage payments will decline, reducing consumption demand and ultimately investment and potential output growth via the accelerator. On the other hand, if exports are sensitive to local production costs which are reduced by the productivity increase, they may jump up enough to raise total output. The price elasticity of "our" exports becomes a crucial parameter, via which productivity and wage changes can feed into dynamic growth processes as described in the section 3.5.

2. In the short run, currency devaluation drives up prices from the side of costs (recall the large intermediate import component in developing country cost structures—an artifact of ISI—from table 2.2 in chapter 2). If money wages are not fully indexed to rising prices, real wages will fall and output contract. This effect is reinforced if there is an initial trade deficit, for then devaluation raises exporters' incomes less than importers' costs, again reducing local spending power.

An offsetting possibility is that devaluation along with other moves to "get prices right" may boost exports enough to create net aggregate demand. This happened in the mid-1980s in Malaysia and Thailand where devaluation in effect ratified a shift in comparative advantage in low-wage manufactures in their direction from countries like South Korea and Taiwan and encouraged their transformations into export platforms.

A third contingency is that depreciation may be accompanied by large incoming transfers from foreign donors, making it look expansionary and anti-inflationary as the foreign exchange constraint is lifted. Ghana early and Tanzania late in the 1980s are examples.

A reverse scenario applies when, with a binding external constraint, lower capital inflows provoke inflation (for reasons to be discussed shortly), leading to exchange appreciation and further deterioration in the balance of payments. This instability applied in Ghana in the 1960s and 1970s and Tanzania in the 1970s and 1980s before they got Fund-Bank religion and reaped the foreign exchange rewards. Any Nicaraguan recovery in the 1990s will require-similar foreign support to offset the Sandinistas' external strangulation.

3. This last possibility illustrates how getting the exchange rate badly "wrong" can be self-destructive, a point on which WC and nonmainstream economists agree in the wake of Latin and African policy disasters of the last decades. They stemmed from the common temptation to let the local currency/dollar rate increase less rapidly than inflation, because real appreciation may well hold down price increases and stimulate local demand.

The resulting overvaluation or income redistribution from foreignors toward nationals is a step down a primrose path. As in the classic Argentine and Chilean cases of the late 1970s (Taylor, 1988), it leads ultimately to an unsustainable trade deficit and capital flight in anticipation of a maxi-devaluation that will surely follow. This is a clear example of how distributional changes constrain macroeconomic policy choice and how financial adjustments can have strong effects on the real side of the macro system.

4. Another problem can show up when there is a foreign exchange bonanza, from oil discoveries, ample foreign aid, or other sources. Some extra foreign exchange will flow toward imports or a reduced export effort, but the balance may spill over into demand for nontraded goods. As their prices rise, the real exchange rate appreciates, leading to a further loss in output diversification in an example of Dutch disease. Mexico and Nigeria had severe cases after their oil discoveries, as did the Philippines under Marcos when the country received big inflows of foreign aid.

It is also difficult to prevent reserve gains from the extra foreign exchange from being monetized (open market operations not being available in most developing country financial structures). Fiscal-monetary policy complications can arise as in Colombia with its recurrent coffee bonanzas. A possible offset is for either the state or the private sector to save the inflows abroad. As noted in chapter 2, capital flight was a frequent final voyage for the resources flowing toward developing countries in the 1970s when they accumulated huge stocks of foreign debt.

5. Output may suddenly be bounded from above, often by foreign exchange shortfalls like those of the 1980s. Another contingency is that progressive redistribution in the manner of Allende may drive production up against capacity limits. How can aggregate demand then be limited to available supply? One mechanism is through prices that rise more rapidly than nominal wages, thereby cutting real wages and demand. This is the simplest example of inflation-induced "forced saving," which may also occur via shifts in prices favoring or harming groups with differential saving propensities from current incomes, for example, workers, capitalists, farmers, foreignors, or the state. As a result, real wage reductions during the 1980s were surprisingly large, ranging up to 50 % and more in some Latin American and African economies.

6. Changes in the distribution of wealth may also influence aggregate demand. The most widely cited example is the "inflation tax" on money balances, a transfer from firms or people with cash (or unindexed deposits) to the state or other borrowers through the banking system that printed the paper in the first place. The value of money erodes with rising prices, usually leading to reductions in real producer and consumer purchases.

7. When inflation settles in, different social groups learn to protect themselves against its adverse distributional effects by continually bidding up the prices over which they have control, for example, firms via mark-ups, labor via money wage increases, or wealth-holders via higher nominal interest rates. As such informal or formal contract indexation spreads, eliminating inflation becomes correspondingly more difficult. Shortening the waiting periods between indexation steps makes the problem worse. These inertial responses to ongoing price increases immensely complicated attempts to reduce inflation in places such as Argentina and Brazil. By deindexing wages, Chile effectively braked inflation in the 1980s with wage-earners bearing the social cost.[6]

In the mid-1980s, so-called heterodox shock stabilizations were tried in Argentina and Brazil to attack inertial inflation where the orthodox approaches just described had failed. They involved price freezes and deindexing contracts, and stopped inflation in the short run. But when the inflation tax and forced saving disappeared, the real wage and aggregate demand rose. Internally, pressures for additional wage increases appeared, feeding in turn back into more demand. Externally, as imports rose the foreign resource constraint began to bind, reintroducing forced saving, the inflation tax, and indexation. A few years later, Israel and Mexico made heterodox stabilizations stick through social compacts to hold wages in line and the use of foreign resources (from capital inflows and international reserves, respectively) to relax the foreign constraint.

8. Especially when low capacity utilization and slow potential output growth are accompanied by regressive redistribution and high interest rates, *ex ante* saving by the wealthy tends to exceed investment demand. Often in such circumstances, speculation in real estate, local financial paper, and foreign currency (especially if the exchange rate is overvalued) increases, because higher savings flows have no natural outlet into capital formation. The stage is then set for a speculative boom and crash, which can be worsened by the fetish of financial market deregulation.

Chile in the late 1970s is a classic example: Financial conglomerates based on captive banks organized themselves around denationalized industrial firms. In a stock market boom, each one started borrowing from its bank to bid up its own share prices, until the banks became so extended that the scam fell apart. Interest on the public sector bonds used to restructure the financial system during the 1980s will cost Chilean taxpayers a couple of percent of GDP for the foreseeable future. The foreign debt assumed (and recreated within the economy) during this operation amounted to over one-third of one year's GDP.

All of the foregoing points suggest that questions about the causal structure of an appropriate macro model inevitably arise. Structuralist economists emphasize that causality often runs from demand injections such as exports and investment to savings and output (at times with strong financial interactions), the importance of distributional processes of the sort just discussed, and frequently binding foreign exchange and fiscal restrictions on capacity utilization and growth.

More orthodox analysts, including many from the BWIs, often postulate supply-side determination of output with ample price responsiveness. The implication is that monetary and fiscal austerity will reduce inflation but not the level of economic activity, and that the primary impact of relative price changes will be on the compositions of the nation's production and demand baskets but not its functional and sectoral distributions of income and wealth.

The unreality of these notions is beginning to be recognized (Dornbusch, 1990), but has yet to be corrected in standard practice. The BWIs remain impervious to the fact that the invisible hand plus a minimal government (especially in its fiscal, regulatory, and investment roles) do not necessarily act together to support sustained economic growth. How public intervention can help the transition is the topic of the following sections.

## 3.4   Stabilization Policy

Despite recent rhetorical flourishes, IMF programs have not fundamentally changed since the 1950s: They still aim at cutting the inflation rate and trade deficit by restraining aggregate demand through fiscal and monetary austerity. There is always a risk that IMF-inspired adjustment policies will drive their recipients toward prolonged "stabilized stagnation," because they ignore crucial macroeconomic factors such as linked foreign exchange and fiscal constraints, financial fragility, and the dynamics of the inflation process. Here we discuss the issues of fiscal austerity, monetary control, anti-inflation policy, and exchange rate complications.

### 3.4.1   Austerity and the Linkages between the Fiscal and Foreign Constraints

According to the 1991 *World Development Report* (World Bank, p. 8), "experience shows that when government spending has expanded too far, the result has often been large deficits, excessive borrowing or monetary expansion which has been quickly followed by inflation, chronic overvaluation of the currency, and loss of export competitiveness. Excessive borrowing can also lead to domestic and external debt problems and to crowding out of private investment." In other words, developing economies destabilize themselves through fiscal or foreign exchange bonanzas.

This view of the causes and effects of fiscal duress follows WC logic in presupposing that macroeconomic disequilibrium uniquely results from an imbalance between domestic income and absorption; it implies that adjusting the fiscal deficit is sufficient to restore stability. It is wrong because it ignores structural features linking the saving, external, and fiscal gaps and thereby understates the complexity of stabilization, especially if stagnation is to be avoided.

Orthodox stabilization theory is particularly inappropriate for highly indebted economies. As argued in chapter 2 and several country papers in this volume, policy there is constrained by two new stylized facts that emerged during the past decade. The first is that the nature of the external constraint has changed. Before the debt crisis, periodic external imbalances caused short-run instability but did not impede growth in the long run. From time to time, scarce foreign exchange did induce misalignment between income and absorption; IMF-style policies helped restore foreign balance without completely stopping accumulation over time.

Since the debt crisis, however, external disequilibrium has become structural. It is not being generated by differences between flows of income and spending but from a stock-flow disequilibrium between foreign obligations and current income as reflected by a high debt/GDP ratio. Although previously scarce foreign exchange used to create liquidity squeezes in the short run, during the 1980s chronic trade surpluses reflected a solvency as opposed to a liquidity problem. The result was negative long run growth rather than a recession for a limited period of time.

The second stylized fact is that the external crisis assumed a fiscal form. In most highly indebted economies, governments hold nearly all the external obligations; therefore, solvency problems fall into the hands of the public sector. The impact effect of the crisis was to raise ratios of the stock of public debt to current revenue to unsustainable levels.

In order to reduce their exposure, governments reacted by slashing expenditures, including public investment. This fall in capital formation still crowded in private investment, but in reverse. Through the third gap, the government budget constraint became an independent restriction on growth. An essential question for the 1990s will be how to restore public investment in physical and human capital with associated externalities, while at the same time maintaining fiscal responsibility.

Because of the strong linkage between fiscal weakness and external solvency, the two problems have to be addressed simultaneously—both in debtor nations with an external double transfer problem and in primary product exporting nations where incoming donor transfers simultaneously finance the trade deficit and PSBR. Using three-gap models simulated over time, it is easy to see that if fiscal and solvency difficulties are not jointly resolved, then the economy is almost certain to stagnate due to inadequate capital formation at the same time as ratios of external and internal debt to potential GDP shoot up toward infinity (see the chapter 16, on Argentina, in this volume). Bolivia, Uruguay, and numerous other small, primary exporting economies are observable examples.

Countries that had severe external shocks but succeeded in restoring growth all utilized foreign exchange up front—for example, Colombia, Chile, Turkey, Ghana, Tanzania, Israel, Sri Lanka, and Mexico—and benefitted from other favorable circumstances. These included the ability of the state to tap natural resource rents (Colombia, Chile, Mexico), a fortuitous increase in demand for its manufactured exports (Turkey), and truly massive external support (the rest).

Countries that avoided major disruptions (mostly in Asia) were relatively balanced in fiscal terms and in some cases lucky: As observed in section 3.3, exchange rates in ASEAN countries apart from the Philippines weakened against the yen after the mid-1980s since they pegged to the dollar. They also received ample DFI from Japan and the diversifying newly industrialized economies. This foreign investment financed capital goods and intermediate imports, which fed into export growth.

Continuing inflows even permitted repeated botched stabilizations while adjustment proceeded apace: Chile between 1973 and 1985 and Turkey in the early 1980s are cases in point. The stabilize-then-adjust sequence recommended by the WC may be common but is not essential; such a smooth progression is certainly unlikely if a country is expected to attempt reform entirely by itself.

### 3.4.2   Monetary Policy and Financial Relationships

Depth, amplitude, and persistence have been the salient features of macroeconomic instability in developing countries over the past 15 to 20 years. Unsustainable current account positions, government and private financial crashes, capital flight, and abruptly accelerating inflations (becoming hyperinflations in Latin America and economies making the transition from socialism) became the rule.

The long-lasting consequences of these coincident maladies for the fragility of the financial system, the dynamics of inflation, and relative price movements scarcely figure in the orthodox approach to stabilization, though they are grudgingly recognized by commentaries such as those in the 1991 *World Development Report* (World Bank, p. 115): "reform of the financial sector often calls for distressed financial institutions to be restructured; in the short run this may raise public spending and make it harder to cut the budget deficit."

As we have already observed, the implication is that causality does not always run from fiscal imbalance to financial disequilibrium. This interesting "trade-off among policies" is not followed up in orthodox discourse, even though its practical relevance is far from nil. In Chile, monetary restructuring through the fiscal and foreign balances cost more than one-third of GDP and Chile was not the only country in which such an episode occurred. The savings and loan-junk bond misadventures in the United States naturally spring to mind, not to mention developing country cases discussed in this volume.

Another problem for national economies is the disarticulation of finance. Debt and terms of trade shocks led to demonetization as inflation accelerated and capital flight sped up. The natural consequence was "dollarization" of financial relationships, which in turn created an inconsistency between the demand for and supply of financial assets (i.e., it created excess demand for external assets and excess supply of domestic ones). Movements of the relevant rates of return were unable to restore equilibrium without driving the public and parts of the private sector toward insolvency.

Because the main source of supply of domestic assets is the government, these portfolio adjustments made it extremely difficult to finance the public deficit; for a given national propensity to save, dollarization and the denationalization of savings put a tighter financial limit on the public sector than otherwise would have occurred. Solving this problem will take more than mere remonetization if and when inflation is contained; there has to be renewed access to foreign finance. Official lenders can play a fundamental role in providing credits to restore growth before (and to assist) the restoration of creditworthiness and the reversal of capital flight. That is, they can decisively support government investment and restructuring of the public finances. In most countries (largely for political reasons on the part of the donors), the BWIs have not demonstrated much enthusiasm for this task.

### 3.4.3 Anti-inflation Policy

Analysis of inflation as a disequilibrium process that plays a crucial role in closing (ex post) the gaps in a highly imbalanced macroeconomic setting is complex. But the issue is essential precisely because in one developing country after another, price spirals accelerated as the economy sought some sort of macro balance after suffering an adverse foreign shock.

As discussed in section 3.3, steady price increases amount to a crude but effective means for cutting aggregate demand to an externally constrained level of supply, via the inflation tax on money balances (which ultimately proves self-defeating as people and firms reduce cash holdings to a few percent of GDP) and forced saving resulting from inflation-induced income redistribution against low savers (real wages have fallen by more than 50 % in economies all over Africa and Latin America). In Argentina and elsewhere, unexpected accelerations in inflation helped stave off massive bankruptcy by reducing the real liabilities of heavily indebted economic actors in both the public and private sectors.

In Israel and several Latin American countries, the "equilibrating" role of faster inflation had major institutional implications, including destabilization of the dynamics of prices. Because of the spread of implicit or explicit contract indexation, a "high inflation regime" came to be established, making anti-inflation policy a central social question.

There are basically only five ways to break a cumulative inflationary process:

1. Relative prices can be manipulated, for example, the exchange rate can be allowed to appreciate in real terms or the real wage to fall (by allowing the nominal exchange rate or wage to rise less rapidly than a general index of prices). Ultimately, the nominal wage or exchange rate has to be held fairly stable as an anchor against further price increases.

2. Imports can be increased to ease local supply bottlenecks, at least for internationally traded goods. Often, purchases abroad (and capital flight) must be financed by the central bank as it spends reserves to support an exchange rate pegged as a price anchor.

3. Incomes policies and other forms of market intervention can be deployed to muffle the most acutely conflicting social claims. A common example is a "social pact" to reduce wage inflation while holding profit claims in line.

4. In a more extreme case, a price freeze plus contract deindexation—a heterodox shock in the jargon—can be attempted as a policy surprise.

5. Austerity can be applied, that is, a cut in the public sector borrowing requirement coupled with monetary restriction based on increased interest rates and credit restraint.

As noted earlier, the WC approach leans toward austerity, but successful anti-inflation packages, which are relatively few and far between, always combine several of the listed measures. Each economy's inflation process is unique, making it difficult to generalize about which policies will be effective in any case at hand. A few observations are worth making.

Austerity is likely to work better when "most" market transactions occur in a regime of flexible prices, that is, mark-up pricing and contract indexation are not widely spread. In practice, the IMF often combines austerity with real wage cuts, reductions in income support programs and subsidies, and so on. All these measures reduce demand, so that the outcomes include output contraction and a lower trade deficit (via import cuts) along with slower inflation. The exact mix of outcomes is obviously a politically relevant question.

Blending austerity with incomes policies and foreign exchange outlays has been a recipe for success in other circumstances. Mexico and Israel, for example, combined a modicum of demand restriction with heterodox shocks in successful packages; Nicaragua relied on a nominally pegged exchange rate after a maxi-devaluation in 1991. The first two efforts included social pacts more or less democratically ratified while Nicaragua just let real wages erode along Bolivian lines. Dollars to spend came from external sources in Israel and Nicaragua and reserves built up over several years of austerity in Mexico. These conditions are all somewhat unusual, to say the least, and underline the difficulties of coordinating several policies simultaneously in the anti-inflation fight.

### 3.4.4   The External Gap and Exchange Rate Policy

The WC posits that maintaining a competitive exchange rate is one of the most important guarantees for achieving a sound closure of the external gap. The problem is that the prestabilization situation often includes an "overly strong" exchange rate, making it necessary to devalue early on.

As observed in section 3.3, devaluation has complicated, economy-wide effects. By increasing import costs, it may be price inflationary and output contractionary. If, however, foreign exchange is severely constraining the system, the outcomes may go the other way: *Any* net export response to depreciation generates scarce dollars. They can be used to reduce excess demand by allowing intermediate imports and production to rise, with a corresponding reduction in inflation.

Problems also arise in coordinating devaluation with other policies, in both stabilization and adjustment contexts. For anti-inflation purposes, the exchange rate may be frozen as a nominal anchor. But then if inflation continues, there will be real currency appreciation. Imports will rise and export growth will decline, upsetting the real side of the economy as in numerous failed stabilization attempts in Latin America over the past two decades.

With regard to fiscal policy, if depreciation is expansionary, then it can usefully be combined with austerity. The exchange rate change improves the trade balance, while fiscal policy helps avoid an inflationary, excess demand situation. If devaluation is contractionary, on the other hand, combining it with austerity can lead to the sort of policy "overkill" for which the IMF is (un?)justly renowned.

Indeed, especially in an African context with many parastatals and marketing boards present, the exchange rate must not only be coordinated with tax and spending initiatives but is a tool of fiscal policy in and of itself. Exchange rate changes affect parastatal cash-flow positions that ultimately feed into either fiscal revenues or outflows or net credit creation by the banking system. Tracing through these linkages can be very tricky.

A further question is whether devaluation will by itself markedly improve trade performance. A considered answer might well be in the negative. As discussed in section 3.5, getting rid of extreme price distortions appears to be a necessary condition for (or at least is correlated with) greater "tradeability" of domestic activities. However, price incentives are never sufficient. A real exchange rate with a reasonable, stable value is an invaluable stimulant to net exports. But it must be supplemented with directed trade-promotion policies such as tax drawbacks, export subsidies, and cheap credits, as well as state interventions to improve infrastructure and the economic environment more generally.

Finally, how should the real exchange rate be held stable? Crawling peg policies involving frequent nominal mini-devaluations to keep the exchange rate in line with the domestic price level have a fairly respectable track record in all corners of the developing world. The outcomes of exchange auctions have been spotty, because they lead at times to speculative surges of consumer imports.

In addition to the exchange rate, one also has to consider the implications for stabilization of commercial and capital market policy. Import quotas can be deployed intelligently to offset external shocks; as discussed later, they can also play a pivotal role in industrial policy. Changes in trade regimes can bring substantial benefits, for example, permitting "own-exchange" imports (no questions asked!) creates some problems with big imports of luxury goods but can also effectively widen forex bottlenecks and perhaps reduce incentives for smuggling. Removing exchange controls in general, however, can prove an open invitation to capital flight. All such possibilities have to be weighed in terms of the nature of the economy at hand.

## 3.5   Boundary Conditions on Reform

In conjunction with reform, what more can be said about the possibilities for reconfiguring the economy to support sustained and equitable growth? This section with 14 subdivisions is devoted to delimiting the economic space in which policymakers have room to maneuver, at a "meso" level somewhere between macroeconomic and strictly firm- and household-level interventions. The discussion is set up in terms of reasonable boundary conditions on policy, which can be inferred from cross-country and historical comparisons. The country papers in this volume draw in diverse fashion on all the approaches sketched here.

### 3.5.1 Patterns of Growth

Several papers invoke the lore developed in cross-country "patterns" studies of structural change of the type made famous by Kuznets and Chenery, and reviewed by Syrquin (1988). Here we take up shifts in sectoral output shares, trends in productivity, and other matters.

The most familiar patterns are declining shares of the agricultural sector in both total employment and GDP as per capita income rises; the other side of the coin is that the GDP share of manufacturing increases from less than 10 % in poor countries to around 30 % (with a standard deviation of 10 points or so) in rich ones.

Across countries and over time, one also sees a sequence of manufacturing subsectors appearing, as the economy advances (in old-fashioned development economics parlance) from "easy" to "hard" ISI. Syrquin and Chenery (1989) use cross-country regressions to split 11 branches into "early," "middle," and "late" groups, "according to the stage at which they make their main contribution to the rise of industry." Their classification is as follows:

Early: Food, beverages, and tobacco; textiles and clothing; other manufacturing. Peak share of GDP = 8.3 % at a per capita GNP of $1000 (1980 prices).

Middle: Wood and products; chemicals and rubber; nonmetallic minerals. Peak share = 6.5 % at $4000.

Late: Printing; basic metals; metal products and machinery. Peak share = 13.2 % at $5000.

This sequence provides useful background for industrial planning and historical analysis. But, of course, the cross-country average patterns say nothing about when specific products or even broad commodity groups may enter into production in a specific country context. There is also an old question as to whether growth curves from international regressions in some sense provide a "center of gravity" for any given economy's structural change. The answer is likely to be in the negative, although extreme deviations may be a source of satisfaction as in Korea or a source of worry as in the lagging output and productivity levels in African agriculture since about 1975. Industrial "catch-up" to typical sectoral shares may describe some country experiences, for example, the recent decades in Colombia.

With regard to labor productivity, Kuznets (1966) postulated a narrowing of intersectoral differences as development proceeds. Observed patterns are more complex. Syrquin and Chenery (1989) find that productivity in agriculture declines relative to the rest of the economy up to a per capita GNP of about $3000, while Rothschild (1985) shows a widening gap between productivity in services and other sectors in OECD countries. Over time, labor productivity trends can importantly affect the income distribution, as discussed in the country studies for Colombia and Thailand (chapters 4 and 6).

A great deal of effort has also been put into more (neoclassically) fashionable studies of the residual or total factor productivity (TFP) growth. Pack (1988) gives a review, although he ignores causal questions about what the "residual" means in a context of varying capacity use. In particular, is a high rate of TFP growth or a rising output-capital ratio simply an artifact of rapid supply expansion (resulting, say, from relaxation of the foreign exchange constraint and/or fiscal activism) or does it reflect autonomous productivity increases under full employment of resources? This question is rarely considered in macro or sectoral level productivity studies, leaving them subject to diverse interpretations.

Based on the usual full employment hypothesis, the conventional wisdom is that in developing as opposed to developed economies, the growth of inputs (specifically, capital and labor) is more important than TFP increases as an "explanation" of output expansion. The TFP contribution is about one-half the total growth rate in advanced economies, and one-third in the developing world. From this angle, the three-gap model computations in chapter 2 and the country studies (which presume varying capacity utilization and often treat productivity growth as a function of changes in output) are relevant from even a neoclassical perspective.

### 3.5.2   Country Size

As noted in chapter 2, the size of a country, best measured by population, influences its trade and industrial prospects. Typical Chenery-style analysis distinguishes "large" and "small" nations, with the boundary at a population of (say) 20 million. The equations fit better for large countries: They seem to follow a more uniform pattern of industrial change. This observation is consistent with the importance of specialized, niche-oriented trade strategies for small, open economies.

The econometric results for a big country can be summarized as follows: It typically enters earlier into import substitution and has a higher manufacturing share of GDP than does a small country at the same per capita income level; and it pursues import substitution further into intermediate and capital goods and producers' services. The statistically "typical" large country's import and export shares of GDP are likely to be around 10% (with a standard deviation of about the same size, e.g., South Korea with import and export shares in the 30% range is far more open than the norm) although a small country's shares may be more than one-half.

Both the regressions and (more importantly) country histories suggest that big countries exploit import-substitute-then-export (ISTE) strategies in manufacturing. The basic premise is that big, protected markets permit economies of scale and scope. At the same time, they allow the luxury of allocative inefficiency for extended periods of time; high-cost production creates economic loss, but need not represent a binding restriction on inward-oriented growth. In a favorable context, a statically inefficient industrial sector can become the base for breaking into world trade with import-substituted products, as suggested by Turkey's example.

With due care to avoid facile country comparisons, South Korea and Brazil make an interesting contrast. Korea, with its unusually high trade shares, successfully designed policies to direct the transformation of domestic production for a protected local market into export capability. A highly skilled labor force and rapid growth of a capital stock embodying world-class technology have played a central role. Brazil historically directed more of its output toward the domestic market and has lower trade shares; for example, Brazilian commodity exports were about 8% of GDP in the early 1980s, as opposed to South Korea's 38%.

Brazil's industrial strategy relied on rapid demand growth in the domestic market to generate scale economies and technical change. One disadvantage is that sales prospects at home are more limited than for the world as a whole, and a concentrated income distribution may be required to support purchases of modern goods. Indeed, there is always a risk that the domestic market will become saturated. Without access to external credit, domestic demand in an ISI strategy cannot grow much faster than exports in the medium to long run, that is, there *are* lower bounds on the ratio of imports to GDP. If foreign resource flows decline, then, as we have seen, the state may be forced toward austerity as the fiscal gap begins to bind. Foreign obligations may be especially vexing if (as in Brazil's case) much technology was imported via TNCs.

Because small countries are far more open to foreign trade, they are likely to find the ISTE approach less fruitful. Sector level inefficiencies can easily degenerate into a binding foreign resource constraint. With benefit of hindsight, one can see that now prosperous small economies earned foreign exchange by exploiting niches in which they could be efficient producers for export trade, for example, downstream expansion of forest products plus high skill-high tech manufacturing in Canada, Sweden, and Finland, shipping in Norway (before oil), industry and financial services in Switzerland, and so on.

Within the WIDER sample, Chile has been a successful small country in the recent period. Its trade shares have risen rapidly, buoyed by favorable copper prices and expansion of fishery, fruit, and forestry exports from $191 million to $2,134 million between 1972 and 1988. This case is of interest because Chile's success rests on collaboration between the public and private sectors. The laissez-faire rhetoric of the Pinochet government obscured this fact, but also aided the mental reorientation of the business class from being a "bourgeoisie of the aperitif" (in Paul Rosenstein-Rodan's conversational phrase) to profit-seeking.

The Chilean production development corporation, or CORFO, created the base for the noncopper export push by afforestation programs and promotion of pulp and paper production; solving problems of transport, cold storage, quality control, and marketing for fruits; and setting up a mixed public-private fishmeal industry, rationalizing production from several pre-existing plants. There were also subsidies for pine plantations, soft credits for fruit growers, significant devaluation (real wage reduction in other language), elimination of export red tape, relaxation of labor legislation, ownership guarantees, and so on. With all these initiatives designed to support private sector activity, Chile's "miracle" was very much a state-bourgeoisie joint affair (ECLAC, 1990). How labor can be brought in remains to be seen.

As noted previously, downstream expansion from an initial export niche can be crucial to sustained export growth. Following the Canadian "staple school" of economic historians, Hirschman (1977) raised a practically important question about the growth potential of the resource base. Timber and oil may favor downstream industrial and marketing activities more than, say, sugar and bauxite (although not much seems to be happening with either wood or petroleum in Malaysia). Local production of such raw materials can lead to capacity to manufacture the relevant capital goods, for example, paper machines and components for oil refineries or petrochemical plants with associated engineering skills. The policy issues center around manipulating effective protection for downstream activities so that they can develop in efficient fashion.[7]

Building upon a "staple" service is also an option to be explored. Entrepôt trade can be an extremely productive base, as exemplified recently by Hong Kong, a small economy that skipped much import substitution (in part because the Shanghai textile industry, a child of earlier ISI, migrated there in wake of the Chinese revolution) and rapidly attained export capability in many lines. Its experience is hard to replicate, however, because Hong Kong follows a prosperous city-state model of great antiquity, which is not open to the overwhelming majority of poor countries in the world.[8]

A special political economy may underlie small country successes, as Katzenstein (1985) points out for the prosperous European economies. Historically, the private sector took the lead and absorbed the failures in opening niches, but bankruptcies were cushioned by "oligarchic" politics (close linkages among large industrial firms, labor unions organized from the top down, and a stable state) plus publicly supported safety nets.

Small, prosperous countries practiced protection at times in the past, but now maintain undistorted trade regimes. The Scandanavians explicitly sought to create large-scale enterprises to utilize best-practice technology and reap economies of scale, while letting relatively free trade hold domestic prices in line (Hjalmarsson, 1991). They adjust to rapid technical change through close cooperation among public, corporate, and labor leadership, with strong emphasis on job retraining. Examples of this model have yet to become fully visible in the developing world.

### 3.5.3    Internal vs. External Orientation

The degree of "openness" of an economy has at least two interpretations: the levels of its trade shares (obviously affected by the nation's size), and the comparative absence of interventionist commercial policies. On both definitions, openness has implications for development strategy. But, as we have already seen, just how it influences industrialization and growth is a topic of intense debate.

The mainstream view is that high foreign trade shares in GDP—especially exports—are associated with faster growth. This conclusion is typically based on the "average" experience reflected in cross-country regression equations. The methodology is compact, but like all naive data comparisons, it is easily misled by diverse country histories.

Syrquin and Chenery (1989) provide one example. They split a sample of 108 countries according to size and whether they are more specialized in primary or manufactured exports. Within each resulting group, they then ask whether economies with higher export shares of GDP grew faster. In all four cases, average growth rates were higher for the subgroup with more exports, especially for small countries. But these arithmetic means hide skewed within-group distributions of growth that suggest specific explanations for the results:

1. By far the biggest difference in growth rates for the 1950–83 period was in small, primary exporting countries (1.4% for averages of GDP growth by high- and low-export subgroups, and 1.1% for subgroup median rates per capita). This outcome reflects poor endowments or bad management more than the benefits of openness per se. It is precisely a poor, small exporter such as Chad, Ghana, or Madagascar (the three slowest growers) that will both contract and have low observed export shares when it is hit by adverse supply shocks, downswings in export volume and the terms-of-trade, or smuggling as national macroeconomic policy unravels. The policy implications are that somehow overcoming internal disruption and finding profitable export lines are prior conditions for economic viability, not that liberalizing an economy will miraculously "open" it to growth through trade.

2. Small economies with high shares of manufactured exports grew 1.0% faster on average than the primary exporters in the Syrquin-Chenery sample, in part because the former group includes 10 European economies as well as Taiwan, Singapore, and Hong Kong. Among the manufactured export specialists, the more export-oriented economies had a 1% faster mean growth rate, but the difference in subgroup medians was only 0.2%. The three small Asian tigers badly skew the mean.

3. A similar conclusion applies to large countries more specialized in manufactured exports. The outliers are Japan and South Korea, and they substantially raise the mean but not the median of the more open subgroup.

An agnostic conclusion about the benefits of openness follows from other studies. For example, McCarthy et al. (1987) find in another sample that fast-growing countries did not on average have either high or increasing shares of exports in GDP between 1962 and 1984. Examples are easy to cite: Among middle income countries, Jamaica (12%), Uruguay (5%), and Portugal (16%) have high industrial export shares of GDP and grow slowly; Colombia and Brazil have shares of 2% or 3% and their growth historically has been fast. Poorer countries' growth rates are more subject to the vagaries of capital inflows and primary product trade, but similar observations hold: Cameroon and Egypt have grown fairly rapidly with industrial export shares of about 1% while traditionally slow-growing India and Honduras both have shares of 3% or more.

Despite these inconclusive results, the empirical literature does present six boundary conditions that appear to apply fairly widely:

1. Least controversial, the ratios of manufactured to primary products both produced and exported tend to rise as per capita GDP goes up. In a broad sense, industrialization is concomitant to economic growth.

2. Trade and output data suggest that at the two-digit level of industrial classification, import substitution usually precedes production for exports, as we have already observed. The lag may be very short, as in the case of South Korea (except for automobiles, where the transition took 20 years), but normally one must think in terms of lustra or decades. Needless to say, this sector-average generalization does not rule out the possibility of a country's exporting a particular product the day it begins to be produced.

3. Both production and trade shares vary within narrower ranges in large countries than in small ones, emphasizing the importance of niche-seeking strategies for the great majority of economies in the world. The relatively few large economies that exist shape their industrial structures more in line with domestic demand.

4. Countries poor (rich) in natural resources tend to have high (low) shares of industry in both exports and GDP. Japan and Korea on the one hand, and the United States and Brazil on the other are obvious examples.

5. Fishlow (1985) raises a useful distinction between "export-led" and "export-adequate" growth. In terms of broad regional distinctions, the labels describe Asian (externally oriented) and Latin (internally oriented) strategies. The current problem for countries pursuing the latter line is how to regain a viable growth process under fiscal duress.

6. Recent experience has shown big increases in exports and reductions in imports in many countries as they have adjusted to external shocks (recall tables 2.1 and 2.2). Whether these adjustments over the past decade will cumulate into renewed growth is, as we have emphasized, very much an open question.

The bottom line is that empirical regularities linking country size, observed trade shares, and economic performance help set limits on how policy can affect openness and growth. Boundary conditions suggest that the trade and production patterns of Costa Rica will never resemble Brazil's, for a variety of reasons. The implication is that policy should not be formed in one economy taking a vastly different one as a model. If, however, some intervention is effective in (say) Jamaica, it might pay off in Costa Rica as well, as both small, open countries share many of the same limits to growth.

### 3.5.4   Liberalization and Growth

Is there any reason to expect that openness defined as a low degree of trade intervention is associated with faster growth? What about internally oriented moves such as deregulation and privatization? Theoretical models in diverse contexts suggest that such questions have no clear answer (Buffie, 1991; Taylor, 1991). Nor is empirical evidence conclusive. Among the countries discussed in this volume, for example, trade liberalization perhaps aided Chile's growth spurt since the mid-1980s (at least psychologically), but after its mid-decade devaluation, faster-growing Thailand raised tariffs for revenue purposes. Turkey's export boom was accompanied by real depreciation and export subsidies of up to one-third of sales value, combined with replacement of a baroque system of import quotas with arbitrarily manipulated levies. Meanwhile, Mexico liberalized conscientiously and grew slowly. Among the relatively poor performers, Argentina and Zambia dabbled with liberalization while until very recently Brazil, Nicaragua, and Senegal did not.

Turkish experience with trade-industrial strategy is illuminating in this regard. The economy entered early into ISI, with an explicitly etatist thrust under Atatürk in 1931. Waves of industrialization followed on 10-year cycles, through the Syrquin-Chenery sequence already discussed. Between 1950 and the late 1970s, GDP growth fluctuated around 6% per year, but there was less than full employment and each cycle ended in an inflationary contraction as the saving, foreign, and fiscal gaps began to bind. Inefficiency as measured by the standard methods ran rampant; indeed, Turkey was the launching pad for Krueger's (1974) early generalizations about rent-seeking and DUP.

Then in 1980, following a relatively mild but regressive IMF-style stabilization with ample capital inflows, Turkey broke from ISI and launched into state-sponsored export growth in illiberal fashion. Boratav's (1988) WIDER study shows that the export miracle rested upon the preexisting industrial base created by ISI, the regressive redistribution and other policies leading to contraction of domestic demand for manufactures, the export subsidies and import quota and levy manipulations mentioned earlier, and rapid growth in demand for products such as cement and steel on the part of culturally compatible buyers in the region (the Gulf and the Iran-Iraq War). Had any of these factors been missing, the boom could well not have happened. but it was clearly capitalist-led (although scholars disagree about whether or not Turkey has a "mature" bourgeoisie). Perhaps in Aesopian language, providing the groundwork for a profitable private sector excursion is what liberalization rhetoric is all about.

### 3.5.5   Allocative vs. Productive Efficiency

As observed in section 3.1, the distinction between allocative and productive efficiency offers a clue about how rapid growth may be stimulated by liberalization or other moves in practice (Hjalmarsson, 1991; UNCTAD, 1991). Experience suggests that efficiency in production is by no means assured by removing price distortions to put allocative gains into place. Many factors—market and capital stock structures, forms of financial intermediation, resource "endowments" and their creation or destruction by changes in technology and tastes, the size of the economy, historical fetters from colonialism, access to geopolitically determined capital inflows and penetrable markets, and so on—affect productive efficiency in ways the neoliberal worldview cannot comprehend.

If productive efficiency is not assured by liberalization, then how can it be enhanced? There are no foolproof stimulants, but intriguing possibilities can be read from historical experiences. One example is the model of accumulation followed by the Nordic economies after 1930 and South Korea two decades later. It emphasized the advantages of workers' productivity growth when they were employed by firms big enough to benefit from best practice technology and economies of scale. Such enterprises were consciously sanctioned by Nordic and Korean authorities as monopolies or oligopolistic participants in export trade. After relatively short learning periods, governments sought allocative efficiency by supporting their local champions in competition with counterparts abroad (the Nordics, though not the Koreans, also opened national markets to foreign import competition). They learned to meet world prices of commodities and services with elastic export demands, so that labor productivity increases could be absorbed into foreign sales.

Pressures toward productive efficiency came not from capital markets, but from Scandinavian trade unions and the South Korean state. The Nordic workers promoted higher productivity on the understanding that it would be translated rapidly into real wages; without underwriting wage growth, the South Korean economic bureaucracy followed their Japanese mentors in adopting a pro-productivity line. Given the tightly held nature of (say) the Swedish Wallenberg bank-centered "group" of companies and the *chaebol*, stock market discipline did not figure in production or investment decisions. Industrial subsidies and targeted, cheap credit in restricted national capital markets certainly did (Kosonen, 1991; Amsden, 1989).

### 3.5.6   Boundary Conditions on Liberalization: Trade

These experiences raise an obvious question as to whether market liberalization in general and removing trade restrictions in particular play much of a role in stimulating growth in output per worker or installed capital stock. Neoclassical and structuralist economists clash over this issue, especially with regard to trade (see, for example, the 1991 *World Development Report* for an impassioned defense of external liberalization). Their opposing arguments are worth spelling out in detail.

Neoliberal advocacy of trade liberalization rests on textbook theorems about how interventions should be designed. If an economy is initially very distorted (say from an extended period of ISI with a high and complicated tariff structure and/or strict import quotas), most economists agree that steps should be taken to rectify the situation. There is professional consensus in this regard; the problem is that different authors' policy remedies diverge. Evans (1991) suggests that the neoliberal pharmacopeia goes as follows:

1. The mainstream does recognize arguments for intervention, for example, nurturing infant industries, attempting to repel foreign dumping (however defined), and implementing optimal export taxes. In terms of complexity, red tape, and inflexibility, however, quotas and tariffs aimed at correcting these problems may well proliferate beyond reason under ISI.

2. When there is a market imperfection, the corrective policy should be applied as "closely" to it as possible, for example, a subsidy for an infant industry makes more sense than a tariff, because the latter will induce a by-product consumption distortion.

3. Under competition in the standard Heckscher-Ohlin model, an import quota has an "equivalent" tariff, which will let the same quantity of foreign goods come in. Because the government gets the tariff's proceeds while producers benefit from quota rents, the tariff may be preferable.

4. If producers have market power, they can squeeze extra rents from a quota. If they go in for rent-seeking or DUP by devoting productive resources to lobby for more quotas, this form of protection looks even less desirable.

5. All this leads to a standard WC sequence of recommended policies. First there should be macroeconomic stabilization; thereafter, quotas should

be "tariffized," and then the tariff schedule should be simplified to two or three rates in the 10 % to 50 % range, sufficient for some protection and revenue generation.

6. As part of the exercise, the real exchange rate will probably have to depreciate to hold the trade deficit constant as quota and tariff protection is cut back. For this reason, capital market liberalization that may lead to appreciation should be postponed.

All these arguments are irrefutable on their own terms. As often with neoclassical formulations, they contain practical reason and at times are policy-relevant. But they still are deficient because of incompatibilities between their underlying assumptions and the world as it really functions. For example, all DUP activity is assumed to focus on state interventions, although the private sector readily generates its own distortions and rents. The nation-state has to deal with external agents with significant market power such as TNCs, local monopolies, and the divide-and-rule tactics of indigenous capitalists when confronting labor, in just a few important cases.

The WC model treats its "distortions" as small perturbations to an economy assumed to be at full employment with investment determined by available saving (perhaps mediated by a variable interest rate) and all actors satisfying the familiar "marginal this equals marginal that" behavioral conditions. When these hypotheses are relaxed in investment-driven growth models, protection to a given sector can easily lead to faster overall expansion if it leads to a spurt in investment demand or to endogenous technical advance (Buffie, 1991; Taylor, 1991).

Finally, the WC model does not incorporate the LDC trade patterns pointed out in chapter 2 and sections 3.51 and 3.52. Yet programming the level and composition of noncompetitive intermediate and capital goods imports has been key to the success of developmentalist states. In South Korea, for example, authors as diverse as Amsden (1989) and Pack and Westphal (1986) agree that instruments such as quotas, directed credits, and targeting were used to promote import substitution that led to export growth. Brazil used protection and licensing to build an automobile sector that flourished until growth was detailed by macroeconomic forces in the 1980s (Shapiro, 1993). In India's large market, small-scale producers of bicycles and machine parts were helped by local authorities and cross-firm cooperation/competition in Ludiana in the Punjab. They now sell throughout India and are expanding abroad (Tewari, 1991) .

Pack and Westphal (1986) emphasize interlinked factors underlying these examples. Technology is imperfectly tradeable, because local producers and workers have to gain know-how to operate physical capital goods which are not produced at home. There are economies of scale in both production and technology acquisition, and externalities among output levels, prices, and technical choice. Evans (1991) underlines the following implications:

1. Protection is justified, and may be programmed more effectively if it is based on quotas. Quota rents on strategic, technology-bearing imports can help subsidize export activity. Quotas on competitive imports (which persist in Japan and South Korea to this day) turn the national market into a place for profitable learning. Costs can be held down if firms are exposed to foreign competition on the export side; real wage increases force the cost reductions to come from productivity advance.

2. Rent-seeking may characterize the process of allocating quotas, but ultimately they can be tied to export and output performance. Ideology and public pressure can help keep DUP within "reasonable" bounds.

3. Two-way information flows are essential, whether top-down as with Korean bureaucrats dealing with the vertically integrated, conglomerate *chaebol*, or from the bottom up, as among small producers and local authorities as in the Punjab.

If a reformed quota allocation system under this second line of policy action leads firms to use strategic inputs to acquire technology and expand nontraditional exports, it may well expand potential output faster than WC trade reform (especially if investment responds). Moreover, it does not suffer from coordination problems such as guessing tariff equivalents of quotas, phasing the liberalization to avoid bankrupting viable domestic producers by taking away effective protection, and getting the exchange rate "right." In other words, policymakers are not forced to solve a realistically dynamic computable general equilibrium model to reprogram the price system for the economy at hand—a Herculean labor if there ever was one.

The implication is that interventionist policies have been and can be effectively utilized, which is more than can be said of orthodox reforms such as Argentina's program in the late 1970s. Its effective protection and other incentive signals were all wrong, and this neoliberal "mistake" aborted economic growth for at least a decade.

By contrast, on the other side of the Andes, we have seen how a rhetorically laissez faire government's public investments in copper mines and quiet promotion policies for fruits, forestry products, and fisheries laid the base for Chile's export boom after 1985. These interventionist steps were taken while the economy reeled through a 12-year sequence of disastrous stabilization experiments amply supported by the BWIs. The WC's recommended stabilize-then-adjust sequence was exactly reversed (Meller, 1991).

Of course, there have been interventionist failures as well; the 1991 *World Development Report* presents an ample collection of horror stories. The implication for both structuralist and neoliberal economists is that there is room for debate about such questions: the study of how states have acted effectively in given circumstances is likely to provide far more policy guidance than any number of theorems about the gains from international trade

### 3.5.7 Financial Reform

Financial restructuring is another broad plank in the WC program, but neither Williamson's (1990) version of the consensus nor the 1991 *World Development Report* goes into much detail about the means by which savings flows are intermediated into capital formation through financial markets. Their basic policy suggestions are to increase interest rates and deregulate the system. As observed by UNCTAD (1991), the goal again is to enhance allocative efficiency, in the sense that returns on saving instruments and investment projects should tend toward equality, perhaps with "the" marginal product of physical capital.

Just as price liberalization does not ensure that firms will efficiently produce commodities, there is no particular reason to expect that removing wedges separating rates of return will guarantee a low-cost supply of financial services. As we have already observed, WC-style reform packages in practice have *reduced* productive efficiency in finance, leading to increased credit costs. The outcomes also included stagflation (lower capacity utilization coupled with faster inflation), a fall in investment demand, and a speculative flurry ending in a financial crash as in the widely discussed case of Chile.

The WC model of finance has the same basic shortcoming as its counterpart for trade and industrial policy: It ignores existing market structures. In most developing economies, the "formal" financial sector comprises public institutions, large private enterprises, and banks. Financial claims typically have short maturities, and the ratio of the outstanding value of either assets or liabilities to GDP is a fraction (well less than ratios in the 1.0 to 1.5

range observed in industrialized economies). Although their size is difficult to judge, informal markets may account for as much as one-half of total credit outstanding.

The typical initial conditions for a high interest rate-deregulation package include ceilings on nominal interest rates, and directed formal sector credit allocations by sector and form of use. Immediately imposing a reform gives the following sorts of results:

1. Getting rid of ceilings on bank deposit rates removes a nominal anchor on the pricing system. Particularly if the external capital account has been deregulated, the alternative to a bank deposit in a citizen's portfolio is a foreign holding, with a domestic return equal to the foreign interest rate plus the expected rate of exchange depreciation plus a premium for lower risk. Such an alternative puts a floor under the local deposit rate that is usually strongly positive in real terms. Deposit institutions have to pass along their higher costs into interest rates on their loans.

2. Eliminating credit targets in the absence of effective prudential regulation leads banks toward high risk-high return loans (a moral hazard made more acute if the government implicitly promises that failing banks will be rescued). The proportion of nonperforming loans in bank portfolios rises; this hidden cost has to carried by debtors still meeting their obligations.

3. Higher interest rates on loans for working capital tend to be passed along by firms into higher prices (especially if they have market power, common enough under ISI). Because production costs rise, supply may also be reduced, giving stagflation. Higher lending rates and lower output will constrict investment demand.

4. More attractive deposit rates can also pull funds from the informal market, reducing its credit flows and raising curb or bazaar borrowing costs with unfavorable effects on output and prices.

5. Although banks can (up to a point) protect themselves from these developments by raising the spread between borrowing and lending rates, the same is not true of their borrowers. The financial position of the private productive sector becomes more precarious, while a higher proportion of the government's fiscal receipts must be dedicated to interest payments on its internal liabilities outstanding. Refinancing these flows can reach manic dimensions as in the "overnight" market in Brazil during the 1980s. Profits on turning over the federal debt made bankers partisans of inflation in that country, a peculiar and risky situation.

6. The Brazil example suggests that with high rates and low investment, speculative holdings become attractive. Turkey had Ponzi schemes around

bank CDs, Chile its stock market boom for shares of prematurely privatized public firms, and Argentina destabilizing flows of foreign exchange. In all cases, speculation went together with deteriorating enterprise balance sheets to pave the way for a crash. The taxpayers ended up with bills totaling tens of percent of GDP to put the financial system back together.

These scenarios amount to a substantial list of neoliberal "mistakes" to be added to those involving trade policy. A more gradual reform in newly industrialized South Korea avoided a debacle, while after presiding over its stock market boom and crash around 1980, the Chilean government later took advantage of ample support from the BWIs to reprivatize, restructure its internal debt, and set up a pension fund program permitting the state (at fairly high interest costs) to capture savings flows. From these experiences and those of now developed economies, can anything sensible be said about productively efficient directions for LDC financial evolution?

UNCTAD (1991) points out that two broad forms of financial organization present themselves. In one, since the last century, banks in Germany and Scandanavia have been closely associated with productive firms, owning stock and holding seats on boards of directors. With insider knowledge and their own incomes in mind, bankers can impose discipline on managers while at the same time providing cheap credit (often rolling over short-term loans). Similar market structures have also emerged in Japan. Insider speculation along 1970s Chilean lines is a risk with this form of market organization, but it can be avoided with adequate regulation and a financial ideology of prudence.

In an alternative Anglo-American model, firms pay for investment by borrowing from banks (or, more recently, by entering the money market), and then refinance short-term debt from internal saving and by issuing long-term liabilities in the capital market. One implication is that the final cost of funds tends to be higher in the United States, because German and Japanese shareholder banks can internalize information flows and exploit scale economies in credit provision. The U.S. cost disadvantage widened in the 1980s as financial deregulation removed nominal anchors on interest rates. A broad, liberalized capital market may help equalize returns to different sorts of holdings, but it can also be productively inefficient, creating high costs of finance and shortening economic horizons.

The implication is that developing countries might consider German bank-type institutions to provide long-term finance, instead of trying to underwrite capital markets (which in many cases have proven to be heavily subsidized playgrounds for ruling oligarchs and generals). Indeed, credit provision by the state—either directly or through development banks—has functioned successfully on all three poor continents.

Modernizing the development bank institution with due care to avoid rent-seeking and inflationary finance for the benefit of chronically derelict parastatals is at least as appealing an option as the high interest rates, stagflation, deregulation, and financial crashes that orthodox financial reforms have provided. Because (especially after fiscal restructuring) development banks can tap public savings flows, they fit naturally with the public-private patterns of saving and capital formation set out in chapter 2.

### 3.5.8   Privatization

The practical implications of the privatization component of the WC package are difficult to judge. Nor are they fully addressed by the studies in this volume, which were largely completed before a worldwide surge of privatization (at least on the rhetorical level) got underway in the early 1990s. Nonetheless, accounting considerations in regard to gap models and the general approach followed by the country authors can shed some light on the question.

It is clear that across nations, different historical divisions among public, local private, and foreign ownership of productive enterprises have emerged. There is no solid evidence that firms of one stripe are consistently more efficient in static terms than those of another. Dynamically, scholars such as Amsden (1989) argue that Korea's home-owned but publicly subsidized private conglomerates are more adept at indigenizing technology than TNC affiliates, while in Brazil before the debt crisis public enterprises were effective motors for capital accumulation and technical change (Shapiro, 1993).

In economic terms, the effects of privatization on savings and investment flows will be the only means of evaluation available for years. Even these calculations are tricky when discounting is taken into account. Marcel (1989) argues, for example, that in Chile's 1985–88 second go at privatization, firms were sold below present value and half the receipts were allocated to uses such as tax reduction. In other words, there were probably no positive impacts on capital formation, along with a flow portfolio shift from public liabilities toward enterprise equity on the part of the private and external sectors.

More generally, Fanelli, Frenkel, and Rosenwurcel (1990) observe that local private sectors can finance acquisitions of public firms in four ways: 1. an increase in private saving, 2. a fall in private investment, 3. a decrease in private sector flow demand for financial assets, and 4. an increase in private sector flow demand for credit.

Alternative (1) could be helpful for growth if accompanied by a jump in investment. The public sector would probably have to be the motor, taking into account the crowding-in effects discussed in chapter 2. In other words, privatizing governments should reinvest the proceeds instead of following Chile's example of cutting the current fiscal deficit. This observation becomes doubly relevant if the private sector cuts its own capital formation to take over public firms in alternative (2).

Alternative (3) is more likely than (4), especially in countries where financial markets have contracted in the wake of adverse shocks. But then the government will find it increasingly difficult to place its own liabilities, provoking it to emit money or bear higher interest burdens or both. As in the Chilean paradigm case, there will be strong pressures to use the proceeds of privatization just to cover the PSBR with no spill-over to capital formation.

Finally, if public firms are sold to foreigners, is their DFI "additional" to what would have arrived, in any case? What about remittance obligations in the future? It *is* true that TNCs that are doing more than simple sourcing do not readily leave a country once they have entered and built up sunk capital, and that they can serve as vehicles for technology acquisition. But can the same be said of debt-swapping banks? Even in terms of current financial flows, privatization need not produce great benefits.

### 3.5.9 Deregulation and Real Wages

Quite a bit has already been said about deregulation in the context of trade reform. Here, we can just add a few observations regarding wages and labor markets. The WC perception is that protective labor legislation is at best an impediment to adequate market functioning and that lower real wages can go a long way toward improving a country's export competitiveness.

As usual, the WC fails to see crucial elements of market structure. For example, in his classic study of the industrial revolution, Polanyi (1944) observed that economic modernization necessarily involves a "double movement" toward creation of markets for commodities and production inputs (such as labor), together with their regulation by the state for social and productive ends. Such changes are as necessary for long-run socioeconomic development as for human capital accumulation of the sort that the 1991 WDR singles out.

Labor market decontrol is also likely to lead to regressive income redistribution, which can stifle aggregate demand. Compositional shifts may occur, although country level evidence suggests that the new commodity demand basket may be either more or less labor-intensive (i.e. wealthier segments of the population who gain in the redistribution may bias their consumption toward either labor-intensive services or capital-intensive commodities, depending on context). There is also likely to be an increase in the import-intensity of demand.

These compositional shifts are all relatively weak, so that the short run effect of real wage changes on the sectoral breakdown of output can probably be ignored. But beyond the conjuncture, dynamic feedbacks become important. Real wages are central to the distributional process, and their secular growth appears essential for industrialization in the long run. Now-popular efficiency wage arguments emphasize how worker motivation and efficiency depend on good pay. The bulk of demand for advanced products must come from exports or wage income. These linkages mean that which classes gain from productivity increases is an important question.

On the one hand, worker motivation and internal demand require real wage increases; on the other, if real wages rise more slowly than productivity, unit labor costs fall, which can help trade. But it is clear that aiming for low wages alone is *not* a viable or sustainable strategy. South Korea would never have shifted its exports from human hair and cheap garments to automobiles and electronics had its wages stayed at the levels of 1955. It has combined steady real wage increases with even more rapid productivity growth to underwrite industrial expansion. Small European economies did the same thing while creating the welfare state. The WC's comparative static exercises ignore these dynamic processes.[9]

## 3.5.10   Labor Skills and Education

There is no question that high skills are required of workers in industrial modes of production; substantial literacy and numeracy are required to produce commodities ranging from Green Revolution wheat to computer code for microprocessors. Successful industrializers since World War II exemplify the pattern; Korea has virtually complete literacy and world-class ratios of engineers and technically trained persons to the overall population. Across countries, there is a positive correlation between education levels (especially of technical personnel) and output growth.

Despite this evidence, an obvious question is whether human capital acquisition is a more-or-less necessary or a sufficient condition for sustained development and growth. As usual, cross-country averages blur historical distinctions, with counterexamples running both ways: Sri Lanka has a healthy, well-educated population but prior to the late 1970s when its foreign aid inflows took a quantum jump it had a slow rate of growth; Brazil's level of literacy is dismal but its growth prior to the 1980s was extremely fast. Sri Lanka suggests that one can overemphasize the direct economic benefits of education, at least in some contexts. Nor is Brazil to be congratulated for having an undereducated population; its low average labor productivity underscores the point. As always, single-factor explanations of growth performance cannot be supported.

The same observation applies to the distribution of income: Education is just one of a number of influential factors. Within the WIDER sample, Thailand's recent increase in inequality can in part be associated with growing educational disparities among groups of the population, while Colombia's decrease in the 1960s and 1970s was helped by the spread of public schooling. Sri Lanka's well-educated, egalitarian citizenry has been unable to avoid ethnic strife, in part because of rising unemployment. Both improved distribution and more widely spread education (especially for women) tend to slow the rate of population growth. These linkages may be essential for the economic salvation of some nations, for example, Nicaragua in the WIDER sample.

In the 1990s, policy questions about education in many countries may have to be defined in narrow fiscal terms. For example, how can formal education and on-the-job training be geared toward higher productivity in a period of tightened budget constraints? Quoting UNESCO data, Schultz (1988) observes that public expenditure on education per child more than doubled during the 1970–80 period in all developing regions, and then decreased in 1982. A fair guess (confirmed by the 1991 *World Development Report*) is that this tendency toward stagnation or decline continued through the 1980s.

Even if industrial jobs are successfully created, these trends suggest that skill constraints may increasingly bind. Policies to encourage the private sector to shoulder a greater share of the national educational effort may be required. Regulatory action supporting on-the-job training and similar activities may partially replace the state's inability to tax the private sector in this regard. In African countries such as Tanzania and Uganda, private schools for those who can afford them have proliferated, despite a longstanding political commitment to public education. How the two systems can be integrated and regulated is a pressing policy concern.

### 3.5.11   Access to Technology

International competitiveness depends on steadily growing productivity and access to best practice technology. Despite isolated exceptions (e.g., Korean and Brazilian design of new models of cars and armored personnel carriers), little technical innovation occurs in the developing world. New technology must be obtained through deals with international suppliers, involving licensing and royalty costs, or via direct foreign investment on the part of transnational firms (Helleiner, 1989). Either route involves extensive bargaining between local public and private sector firms and external suppliers, under the aegis of the state.

The conditions of these bargains vary with a country's own industrial history and time. Dealing in the 1980s with Suzuki about setting up an automobile industry, India was in a weaker position than was Brazil when it dealt with Ford and Volkswagen 30 years before: The corporations were groping almost as blindly as their potential host at that stage. The main similarity is that a process beginning with assembly and leading toward rising domestic content is one policy goal. The time frame for such a change may be fairly short, because NIC industrial sophistication has by now reached the point at which international unit labor cost levels in greenfield plants can be rapidly attained, as in production of car engines during the past decade in Mexico.

Even this comfortable generalization breaks down, however, when new technologies like those based on microprocessors are at issue. Stimulating local applications rather than production of hardware has emerged as the relevant policy objective. Sweden, the most computerized economy in the world, does minimal local manufacture. In developing countries, pursuing computer literacy and familiarity emerges as the relevant policy goal. Traditional ISI strategies do not apply, but state and privately supported educational initiatives may.

### 3.5.12   Managerial Capability of the State

As noted in chapter 2, recent evidence suggests that in many countries public investment stimulates private capital formation via complementarities. Despite the importance of crowding-in, many governments found public investment impossible in the 1980s because (even with improved tax performance and current spending cuts) they were fiscally constrained.

Besides fiscal problems, an important empirical question is whether the state can in fact handle all the obligations we have discussed. Theories of how it functions aside, it is not an easy task to find an existing government capable of making use of the local resource base, utilizing the advantages and avoiding the problems inherent in the country's size, maintaining an intelligent stance between import substitution and export promotion, seeking export niches, hastening skill creation, and dealing effectively with new technologies such as microprocessers. Optimal performance in all areas is impossible. The question is whether the state can effectively cope. Its managerial capacity—even to supervise a regime of laissez-faire—is perhaps the most important boundary condition of all.

Here, we can only flag the issue; Evans (1989) takes up some of the problems it creates. But one observation (especially relevant for Africa) follows naturally from the discussion earlier in this chapter: Arguments for liberal policies may be based on desperation about the capacity of the state. Because the public sector does so badly, the reasoning goes, an unfettered private sector could not possibly do worse. This view ignores the objective difficulties—unfavorable ecological conditions, plummeting export volumes and prices, political turmoil—that African and other poor countries have confronted, as well as the historical fact that development does not happen in a fully free market regime.

However, the fact that the private sector is unlikely to create sustained expansion on its own does not answer the question about how state capacity can be improved. Even under favorable macroeconomic conditions, a painful learning process is likely to be involved. It is clear, however, that the last thing a poor African country like Uganda needs is further reduction in the government payroll. As the country study in this volume argues, this is a BWI policy recommendation that any sensible person would reject.

### 3.5.13   Development Transitions

Development is a historical process: Each economy must be seen as traversing a particular dynamic path. For a poor country, initial conditions obviously matter. South Korea in the 1950s had a low per capita income and little capital stock. There had been a recent, successful land reform, however, and the population was well educated and had been exposed to industrial culture during the colonial period under the Japanese. Ample human capital, generous foreign aid, privileged access to U.S. and Japanese markets, and other intangible factors set the stage for the Korean industrial miracle. The contrast with African countries, which still struggle with relics of a much more exploitative form of colonialism, could not be sharper.

Their lack of physical and educational infrastructure and even rudimentary industrial experience stands out.

As an economy develops, transitions continue to occur. Toward the end, rich nations enter more or less competitively into world markets with levels of export subsidies, import barriers, and activities such as dumping restrained to "normal" levels (with normality being a flexible concept—consider Japanese import restrictions and the increasing interest of the United States in "strategic trade"). In the developing world, the import-substitute-then-export strategy means that large economies may hold themselves (or at least many of their products) away from international competition for periods measured in decades. Small countries are necessarily more open to trade, and arguably have fewer opportunities for dynamic gains from distorting prices in the short run. Conceivably, their size deficiencies could be offset by regional production-trading groups, although their record of success so far is bleak. Flexible manufacturing processes as discussed by Piore and Sabel (1984) may also provide opportunities for surmounting problems posed by economies of scale, but the evidence about them so far is mostly confined to industrialized economies.

Neither import substitution nor the return toward international competitivness is typically led by the invisible hand. Internally, as the small prosperous European economies exemplify, an interlocking institutional network allows negotiation among well-organized groups—unionized labor, transnational companies, and big government. *Chaebol* and *zaibatsu*—competing among themselves while confronted by labor and activist state—demonstrate the same tendencies in Korea and Japan.[10]

Externally, an export push may be required to compensate (so to speak) for a period of import substitution. As we have observed, successful newly industrializing countries (or NICs) followed this pattern, although there are historical exceptions; the United States remained quite closed throughout its industrialization and India is now. But would both these economies improve their performance by pushing sales abroad?

The benefits of more exports are easy to enumerate. They can support the current account as imports are liberalized (except when there are negative domestic resource costs), and by simple arithmetic, raising a modest export share of GDP toward unity is likely to be a less painful process than further reducing an already low import coefficient toward zero. Also, when world trade is expanding faster than world GDP, exports tap into a rising source of demand. The unknown for countries making the transition over the next decades is whether or not international trade will continue to grow as rapidly in the future as it has in the recent past. As Hobson (1902) observed long ago, progressive income redistribution and creation of a welfare state can also underwrite growth in demand.

Rapid export expansion aside, the "return" involves a transition from noncompetitive to competitive trade, as Chenery (1975) pointed out. On the export side, the emphasis shifts from primary products with a small internal market to manufactures and services sold both abroad and at home. Goods initially produced to substitute imports (often creating a further dependence on imported intermediates and capital goods) must ultimately find external markets if world class costs and variety are to be provided to domestic consumers.

There is no reason why production for appropriate niches should not initially be supported by import barriers and export subsidies; indeed "opportunity costs" of distorting trade have to be ignored until learning and scale effects take hold. The point is that growth can stagnate if infant firms do not grow up to compete more or less effectively on international terms. The issues raised by DUP theorists are important in this context: Why should a firm try to compete with foreigners instead of seeking national rents?

Directed public interventions, social consensus, and profit opportunities in world-market competition necessarily must play a role in the difficult transition from noncompetitive to more competitive trade.

A final question has to do with "leading sectors," which are mentioned in several of the country papers. The concept is well-established, but analytically ill-defined: Basically, it refers to an interlinked, rapidly growing set of economic activities that stimulate growth in the rest of the system via interindustry and investment demands, or other spillovers. Stimulating formation of a leading sector is the implicit goal of much public intervention.

Historically, supporting ISI as in Turkey's successive waves of early, middle, and late industrialization and directing incentives toward manufactured exports as in Korea can help the relevant sectors play a leading role. The country studies for Chile and Malaysia suggest that agroexports under certain circumstances can have strong spillover effects; the same observation applies to import substitution of rice in Sri Lanka. Whether agroexports and capital goods import substitution combined with a free trade agreement under negotiation will reenergize the Argentine and Brazilian economies in the 1990s remains to be seen.

### 3.5.14 The Agrarian Question

Far more strongly than exports—the WC's favorite explanatory variable for growth—a good agricultural performance is correlated with sustained output expansion. Although the sector's product rarely expands more rapidly than the population growth rate plus two or three percent per year, falling short of this pace can hold down development overall. Moreover, land and labor productivity rates in many developing countries are low (and indeed have been declining in sub-Saharan Africa since the mid-1970s). They are at levels one-half or less of those in the industrialized nations when they had similar per capita incomes. Because in many places agriculture's share of total investment is considerably less than a "reasonable" 20 %, there is room for expansion. As posed by Timmer (1988) and Rao and Caballero (1990), the question is how it is to be organized.

Unsurprisingly, the WC-BWI view is that agriculture has been handicapped by policy-induced distortions such as currency overvaluation, negative effective protection, and so on, which are supposedly caused by "urban bias," excessive pursuit of ISI, and populist pressures to subsidize urban consumers. Offsetting factors such as low or nonexistent agricultural taxes and input subsidies are ignored from this perspective, as well as the fact that total crop and livestock supplies are price-inelastic in the short to medium run.[11]

As usual, simply eliminating distortions provides no royal road to productivity improvements in agriculture. Many factors can force the sector's output to grow slowly or income distribution to be unequal; they also condition its influence on growth of the macroeconomic system.

1. Market structures and institutions can adversely affect adoption of new technologies, employment, and income distribution. Dominant rural classes may block or inappropriately bias directions of technical change.

2. Rural poverty is not just due to low level technology (Schultz, 1964); there is also exploitation in both the neoclassical (monopoly positions) and Marxist (extraction of surplus labor value) senses of the word.

3. Especially with tight fiscal constraints, higher public investment in agriculture (with likely crowding-in effects) is going to have to be financed by higher taxes. For example, raising taxes on agricultural exports or tariffs on nonagricultural imports could worsen allocative distortions of the sort that WC partisans emphasize. In growth rate terms, a capital formation push may outweigh mere allocative losses, but a trade-off is involved that merits investigation in specific cases.

4. Hunger in rural and urban contexts is not just due to lagging agricultural supply; effective demand limitations have to be overcome as well. One key question is whether shifts in the terms of trade toward agriculture will inhibit or stimulate aggregate demand. Farmers would presumably

spend more because their real incomes go up, but nonfarmers (or farmers who produce less than they consume) whose real spending power is reduced by the price shift would have to cut back on real consumption in a form of forced saving. Feedbacks from income changes into investment can influence growth overall, as argued shortly.

5. The WIDER country studies for Malaysia and Chile suggest that agroexports can, in some circumstances, support a growth spurt, but rapid expansion of primary product sales abroad is always at risk of running afoul of low income and price elasticities of demand. The international terms of trade were not favorable in the 1980s on average, and show no clear signs of improving.

6. Similar dangers arise, of course, for "agriculture first" strategies aimed at expanding food and other farm outputs for national consumption, of the sort proposed by Chakravarty (1987). A supply increase is not helpful to farmers if the price falls more than in proportion to permit the extra output to be sold. The outcome will depend on demand compositional effects of the form just discussed: If falling prices strongly stimulate food consumption by nonfarmers while higher output benefits the rural poor, agricultural real income losses may be avoided.

The possibility of adverse price shifts can be characterized in terms of a simple growth model permitting two potential equilibria for agriculture in the macroeconomic system (Rao and Caballero, 1990; Taylor, 1991). In the "low" position a shift in resources toward the sector reduces its terms of trade enough to cut its real income; slow growth follows from induced low investment demand. In the "high" equilibrium, the terms of trade are stable enough to raise agricultural incomes after the resource reallocation; they spill over into higher demand and investment in nonagriculture, and the economy overall. How can the system be shifted from one equilibrium to the other?

1. Demand for agricultural products can be enhanced (and strong adverse shifts in the terms of trade forestalled) by progressive redistribution within the sector; such an income shift is also likely to reduce population pressure by accelerating the demographic transition. Both labor absorption and rural distribution can be improved by directed policies, for example, land reforms in Chile just prior to Pinochet and perhaps the Philippines or South Africa in the future. Where a peasantry persists, its rapid transformation to a capitalist mode of production can be socially catastrophic as well as cutting back on rural incomes. Will this be the case for Mexico's maize-producing *ejidos* as a consequence of that country's drive toward liberalized trade?

2. Macro policies also have to be designed with present institutional features in mind. Turkey's peasantry, for example, is not likely to continue self-exploitation to raise yields in the face of publicly orchestrated farmgate price reductions, as in the 1980s. Chances are that further shifts in the terms of trade toward agriculture (for food, exports, or both?) will be needed in Africa, while Indian landlords are socially (but not politically) ripe to be taxed. They would also resist redistribution within rural India, to the detriment of agricultural demand.

3. Fiscal and foreign exchange limitations continue to apply. But it is fair to recognize that public investment in agriculture may well have stronger crowding-in effects than in other sectors. Infrastructural improvements may be essential for both producing and marketing higher outputs, for example, in Africa, or else for upward jumps in productivity as in Sri Lanka's Mahaveli project, Turkey's Central Anatolia scheme, and perhaps in Argentina and Brazil during the 1990s. Agriculture's input structure may also be less foreign exchange-intensive than the economy's on average, and import substitution of inputs (not to mention some capital goods for the sector) may be "easy." Pursuing such possibilities is one way to make higher rural incomes feed back into demand for products of other sectors.

4. Bringing new lands into cultivation may be feasible in a few places, for example, Nicaragua and Brazil, but elsewhere new technologies are required, for example, dryland crop improvements, livestock disease control, and small-scale irrigation projects.

5. Incentives in addition to prices may be crucial, for example, access to incentive consumer goods (a key issue in import-compressed Africa) and needed inputs, as well as a satisfactory lifestyle in rural towns and on the farm. These can provide important possibilities for intersectoral complementarity.

6. Transition toward a high-level agriculture-nonagriculture equilibrium is likely to be a lengthy process, requiring extensive investment and technical innovation and diffusion. The road is not likely to be easy, and the journey will require public action much more extensive than endless exhortations from Washington to get farmers' prices right.

## 3.6   A Non-Washington Synthesis

Consensus is too strong a word for any set of policy recommendations; few economists have new ideas, but all are willing to argue long and hard in support of proactive or inactive positions cherished from their personal pasts. Neither a Washington nor a non-Washington consensus about development policy exists, but there still would be fair agreement among progressive economists both within and without the Beltway about the following counterpoints to the summary of the WC in section 3.1.[12]

1. Fiscal equilibrium is desirable, but can be devilishly difficult to attain. The fiscal, foreign, and savings gaps are closely linked. Improvement in the first is not likely without gains for the other two as well. External support may well be required on all three fronts; it was certainly available in the (provisionally) successful reform cases of the 1980s. Reducing a fiscal deficit is always tricky in political terms; in some corners of the world, distributional conflicts make it well nigh inconceivable.

2. Changing real "macro" prices such as the wage, exchange rate, and interest rate is not easy. Movements in their nominal counterparts have complicated, economy-wide effects and overall inflation is difficult to control. Numerous orthodox programs postulating big changes in exchange and interest rates have resoundingly failed. Gains in allocative efficiency when real macro prices are revised can be misleading, if improvements in productive efficiency are trivial at best.

3. External liberalization programs have fared no better than packages based on intelligent use of quotas and controls. The advantages of the latter include the possibility of using the threat of withdrawing protection to extract efficient production from the private sector without having to estimate and impose a whole set of allocatively "correct" prices. Direct foreign investment bolsters the balance of payments and may help with acquisition of technology, but home-based firms may be able to do the latter better still.

4. Privatization brings no obvious productivity gains, and if done in slapdash fashion it can adversely perturb saving, investment, and financial flows. The same observation applies to attempts to restructure a "repressed" financial system by raising interest rates and abdicating prudential control.

5. Labor market deregulation may slash wage costs in the short run, presumably to some export advantage. But it may prove inimical to long-run socioeconomic development, and can slow accumulation of productive human assets.

6. Sound macroeconomic policy is always desirable, like stable family relationships and apple pie. Whether it is feasible under LDC political and distributional conditions is another question. If "soundness" means austerity, it runs a grave risk of inducing secular stagnation.

7. An increasingly educated, healthy, and well-paid population is necessary for long-run productivity growth. However, speeding up human capi-

tal accumulation is not a sufficient condition for raising actual or even potential output in the short run.

8. Stabilization before (or concurrent with) adjustment sounds sensible but does not always work out. Maybe basic improvements in fiscal or balance of payments positions are required before macroeconomic difficulties can be overcome. There are recent examples both ways.

9. Indeed, there are examples of successes and failures of both orthodox and heterodox policy initiatives worldwide. The problem is how to invent and sequence policy changes effectively in each economy's historical and institutional context. We know a little bit about how such factors as the structure of the existing capital stock, the size of the population, and natural resource endowments put somewhat flexible boundary conditions on policies aimed at raising productive efficiency, but a general solution is nowhere at hand. The Washington consensus and the BWIs do not make groping for it any easier by turning themselves into latter day reincarnations of Polonius and preaching neoliberal common sense for the benefit of deafened ears. They are even less helpful when they use financial clout to impose their ideas on poor economies where neoliberalism does not comfortably fit.

## Notes

1. For a more analytical presentation of IMF logic, see Taylor (1988), which also summarizes a previous round of WIDER country papers focusing on stabilization. As Figure 3.1 shows, the IMF's macroeconomic causal scheme is as follows: (1) The country at hand basically called in the IMF because it got into external imbalance; its goal is an improved trade balance, which means that foreign reserves will grow. (2) On the other hand, "excessive" money creation will be inflationary. (3) To avoid this peril, with rising reserves as a source of new money supply, domestic credit creation must be restricted. (4) If the economy recovers, so will private sector credit needs. (5) Therefore, the government's demand for credit should be reduced, that is, in polyglot acronyms, the PSBR must fall in the TOFE.

2. For details of a Japanese proposal urging the World Bank to take a more interventionist role, see Overseas Economic Cooperation Fund (1991) as well as a discussion in terms of received development theory by Jayawardena (1992).

3. Related ideas are developed by practitioners of the "new institutional economics" or NIE who "attempt to modify or broaden the mainstream toolkit and then to use its broadened analytical framework to explain phenomena that previously seemed inpenetrabie" (Nabli and Nugent, 1989). Adepts of NIE often stress the "path dependence" of economic events with emphasis on technological change (Arthur, 1989). For professional economists, such open-mindedness is refreshing but the insight that historical events are irreversible and interrelated can scarcely surprise anyone with an adequate secondary education.

4. The saving counterpart of extra investment could also come from capital inflows or higher output, but Schumpeter ignored these possibilities because he implicitly worked with a closed economy model and abhorred the notion that the economy could be at less than full capacity, in the mode of Keynes, Kalecki, and the papers in this volume.

5. Exchange rate "overvaluation" has at least two partially overlapping meanings: (1) Nominal peso/dollar rate increases can lag inflation for a time, increasing costs of national exports to the rest of the world and cheapening imports at home. Overvaluation in this sense ranged from a few to a few thousand percent in the countries studied herein. (2) The current rate—interpreted as a relative price between traded and nontraded goods—can be compared to a "shadow" rate that would lead to trade balance (or the current level of the trade deficit) if all import protection were removed. Calculations of shadow rates usually suggest that the actual rate is overvalued in the double digit percentage range. The text reference invokes the latter definition; the former is taken up in the observations about distributional adjustment channels.

6. Outside the WIDER sample, the widely publicized Bolivian stabilization of 1985 also was built around massive wage cuts and unemployment for government functionaries and erstwhile tin miners, as well as overvaluation and export stagnation when the exchange rate was frozen as a "nominal anchor" (Pastor, 1991). The latter outcomes recall the Chilean and Argentine stabilizations of the late 1970s, which had unfavorable and long-lasting real and financial repercussions. The course of real wages in the wake of Nicaragua's exchange rate-anchored stabilization of 1991 (amply supported by foreign donors) remains to be observed.

7. "Effective" protection refers to the implicit tax or subsidy to some economic activity when the taxes and subsidies on local production of its intermediate inputs are taken into account. As the text implies, how to structure degrees of effective protection across different industries is a vexing policy issue.

8. For a large nation, a Hong Kong-type city selling largely to the internal market is a mixed blessing (because of regional disparities, migration flows, etc.) but it is also an omen for general growth—inward-looking industrialization seems to need an "engine." Hong Kong's metropolitan economic numbers are not more striking than São Paulo's or Bombay's, even though the hinterlands of Brazil and India grow far more slowly than their national city-states.

9. In a practically important case, primary product exporters that face inelastic demand structures can find productivity growth feeding into lower terms of trade, to the benefit of consumers in rich countries but not at home. Part of Chile's and Malaysia's recent success with primary exports is tied to the fact that they chose (or stumbled into) commodities with rapidly rising world demand. Past ISI may pay off in this regard, because it at least teaches local industries how to produce products with high income elasticities. Among the WIDER countries, the industrial exports of Brazil, Colombia, Thailand, and Turkey exemplify this observation. The point that productivity growth does not benefit a producer confronting inelastic demand is an old one, recognized by economists as diverse as Prebisch (1959) and Houthakker (1976).

10. Chang (1990) observes that the conglomerate nature of the *chaebols* led to a "bundling of issues" that eased bargaining among themselves and the state. Their size and ability to move into almost any line of business generated competitive pressures and held down start-up costs. The social benefits of their rapid productivity growth outweighed the ample subsidies that they received. Similarly, Shapiro (1993) observes that tax receipts from the subsidized, protected Brazilian automobile industry in the 1960s outweighed costs as stringent domestic content requirements began to be satisfied and per unit production costs fell.

11. Supply elasticities in the 0.1 to 0.3 range are statistically typical; econometricians usually find that agricultural investment is a more robust explanatory variable than price for yield or output. These results are, of course, consistent with the observation that substitution elasticities among different crops (especially in multi-crop, irrigated agriculture) can be bigger than one.

12. Similar ideas are set out by Fanelli, Frenkel, and Rosenwurcel (1990) and the United Nations (1991).

## References

Amsden, Alice (1989). *Asia's Next Giant: South Korea and Late Industrialization*. New York: Oxford University Press.

Arthur, W. Brian (1989). "Competing Technologies, Increasing Returns, and Lock-in by Historical Events." *Economic Journal*, 99: 116–31.

Balassa, Bela (1971). "Trade Policies in Developing Countries." *American Economic Review (Papers and Proceedings)*, 61: 178–87.

Bauer, P. T. (1972). *Dissent on Development*. London: Weidenfeld and Nicolson.

Bauer, P.T. (1984). *Reality and Rhetoric: Studies in the Economics of Development*. London: Weidenfeld and Nicolson.

Boratav, Korkut (1988). "Turkey." *WIDER Stabilization and Adjustment Policies and Programmes Country Study* No. 5. Helsinki: WIDER.

Buchanan, James (1980). "Rent Seeking and Profit Seeking," in J. M. Buchanan, R. D. Tollison, and G. Tullock (eds.), *Toward a Theory of Rent-Seeking Society*. College Station: Texas A&M University Press.

Buffie, Edward F. (1991). "Commercial Policy, Growth, and the Distribution of Income in a Dynamic Trade Model." *Journal of Development Economics*, 37: 1–30.

Chakravarty, Sukhamoy (1987). *Development Planning: The Indian Experience*. Oxford: Clarendon Press.

Chang, Ha-Joon (1990). "Interpreting the Korean Experience—Heaven or Hell?" *Faculty of Economics and Politics Research Paper* No. 42. Cambridge: Faculty of Economics and Politics.

Chenery, Hollis B. (1961). "Comparative Advantage and Development Policy," *American Economic Review*. 61: 18–51.

Chenery, Hollis B. (1975). "The Structuralist Approach to Development Policy." *American Economic Review (Papers and Proceedings)*, 65: 310–316.

Dornbusch, Rudiger (1990). "Policies to Move from Stabilization to Growth," in *Proceedings of the World Bank Annual Conference on Development Economics*, Washington, DC: The World Bank.

Economic Commission for Latin America and the Caribbean, (ECLAC, 1990). *Changing Production Patterns with Social Equity*. Santiago: United Nations.

Evans, David (1991). "Institutions, Sequencing, and Trade Policy Reform." University of Sussex: Institute of Development Studies.

Evans, Peter (1989). "Predatory, Developmental, and Other Apparatuses: A Comparative Analysis of the Third World State." *Sociological Forum*, 4: 561–587.

Fanelli, José María, Roberto Frenkel, and Guillermo Rozenwurcel (1990). "Growth and Structural Reform in Latin America: Where We Stand." Buenos Aires: CEDES.

Fischer, Stanley (1990). "Comment" on Williamson, in John Williamson (ed.), *Latin American Adjustment: How Much Has Happened?*. Washington, DC: Institute for International Economics.

Fishlow, Albert (1985). "The State of Latin American Economics," in *Economic and Social Progress in Latin America*. Washington, DC: Interamerican Development Bank.

Gerschenkron, Alexander (1962). *Economic Backwardness in Historical Persgective*. Cambridge, MA: Harvard University Press.

Helleiner, G. K. (1989). "Transnational Corporations and Direct Foreign Investment," in Hollis Chenery and T. N. Srinivasan (eds.), *Handbook of Development Economics*, Vol. 2. Amsterdam: North-Holland.

Hirschman, Albert O. (1958). *The Strategy of Economic Development*, New Haven, CT: Yale University Press.

Hirschman, Albert O. (1977). "A Generalized Linkage Approach to Development, with Special Reference to Staples." *Economic Development and Cultural Change (Supplement)*, 25: 67–98.

Hjalmarsson, Lennart (1991). "The Scandanavian Model of Industrial Policy," in Magnus Blomstrom and Patricio Meller (eds.), *Diverging Paths: Comparing a Century of Scandinavian and Latin American Economic Development*. Washington, DC: Johns Hopkins University Press.

Hobson, John (1902). *Imperialism: A Study*. London: J. Nisbet.

Houthakker, Hendrik S. (1976). "Disproportional Growth and the Intersectoral Distribution of Income," in J. S. Cramer, A. Heertje, and P. Venekamp (eds.), *Relevance and Precision: Essays in Honor of Pieter de Wolff*. Amsterdam: North-Holland.

Jayawardena, Lal (1992). "Comments" on a paper by Paul Krugman. World Bank Annual Conference on Development Economics, Washington, DC: The World Bank.

Katzenstein, Peter (1985). *Small States in World Markets: Industrial Policy in Europe.* Ithaca, NY: Cornell University Press.

Kennedy, Paul (1987). *The Rise and Fall of the Great Powers.* New York: Random House.

Kosonen, Katri (1991). "Saving and Economic Growth in a Nordic Perspective," in Jukka Pekkarinen, Matti Pohjola, and Bob Rowthorn (eds.), *Social Corporatism—A Superior Economic System?.* Helsinki: WIDER.

Krueger, Anne 0. (1974). "The Political Economy of the Rent-Seeking Society." *American Economic Review,* 64: 291–303.

Krueger Anne O. (1984). "Comparative Advantage and Development Policy 20 Years Later," in Moshe Syrquin, Lance Taylor, and Larry Westphal (eds.), *Economic Structure and Performance: Essays in Honor of Hollis B. Chenery.* New York: Academic Press.

Kuznets, Simon S. (1966). *Modern Economic Growth: Rate, Structure, and Spread.* New Haven, CT: Yale University Press.

Lal, Deepak (1983). *The Poverty of "Development Economics."* Hobart Paperback No. 16. London: Institute of Economic Affairs.

Little, Ian M. D., Tibor Scitovsky, and Maurice Scott (1970). *Industry and Trade in Some Developing Countries: A Comparative Study.* London: Oxford University Press.

McCarthy, F. Desmond, Lance Taylor, and Cyrus Talati (1987). "Trade Patterns in Developing Countries, 1964–82." *Journal of Development Economics,* 27: 5–39.

Marcel, Mario (1989). "Privatizacion y Finanzas Publicas: El Caso de Chile." *Colecion Estudios CIEPLAN,* No. 26: 5–60.

Meller, Patricio (1991). "Review of the Chilean Liberalization and Export Expansion Process (1974–90)." Santiago: CIEPLAN.

Nabli, Mustapha K., and Jeffrey B. Nugent (1989). *The New Institutional Economics and Development.* Amsterdam: North-Holland.

North, Douglass C. (1981). *Structure and Change in Economic History.* New York: W. W. Norton.

Nurkse, Ragnar (1953). *Problems of Capital Formation in Underdeveloped Countries.* Oxford: Basil Blackwell.

Olson, Mancur (1982). *The Rise and Decline of Nations.* New Haven, CT: Yale University Press.

Overseas Economic Cooperation Fund (Government of Japan, 1991). "Issues Related to the World Bank's Approach to Structural Adjustment—Proposal from a Partner." Mimeo, Tokyo.

Pack, Howard (1988). "Industrialization and Trade," in Hollis B. Chenery and T. N. Srinivasan (eds.), *Handbook of Development Economics,* Vol. 1. Amsterdam: North-Holland.

Pack, Howard, and Larry E. Westphal (1986). "Industrial Strategy and Technological Change: Theory vs. Reality." *Journal of Development Economics*, 22: 87–128.

Pastor, Manuel, Jr. (1991). "Bolivia: Hyperinflation, Stabilization, and Beyond." *Journal of Development Studies*, 27: 211–37.

Piore, Michael J., and Charles F. Sabel (1984). *The Second Industrial Divide: Possibilities for Prosperity*. New York: Basic Books.

Polanyi, Karl (1944). *The Great Transformation: The Political and Economic Origins of Our Time*. New York: Rinehart.

Prebisch, Raul (1959). "Commercial Policy in the Underdeveloped Countries." *American Economic Review*, 49: 257–69.

Rao, J. Mohan, and José María Caballero (1990). "Agricultural Performance and Development Strategy: Retrospect and Prospect." *World Development*, 19: 899–913.

Rosenstein-Rodan, Paul N. (1943). "Problems of Industrialization of Eastern and South-Eastern Europe." *Economic Journal*, 63: 202–211.

Rothschild, Emma (1985). "A Divergence Hypothesis." *Journal of Development Economics*, 23: 205–226.

Schultz, T. Paul (1988). "Education Investment and Returns," in Hollis B. Chenery and T. N. Srinivasan (eds.), *Handbook of Development Economics*, Vol. 1. Amsterdam: North-Holland.

Schultz, T. W. (1964). *Transforming Traditional Agriculture*. New Haven, CT: Yale University Press.

Schumpeter, Josef A. (1934). *The Theory of Economic Development*. Cambridge, MA: Harvard University Press.

Scitovsky, Tibor (1954). "Two Concepts of External Economies." *Journal of Political Economy*, 62: 143–51.

Shapiro, Helen (1993). *Engines of Growth: The State and Transnational Automobile Companies in Brazil*. Cambridge: Cambridge University Press.

Shapiro, Helen, and Lance Taylor (1990). "The State and Industrial Strategy." *World Development*, 18: 861–78.

Syrquin, Moshe (1988). "Patterns of Structural Change," in Hollis Chenery and T. N. Srinivasan (eds.), *Handbook of Development Economics*, Vol. 1. Amsterdam: North-Holland.

Syrquin, Moshe, and Hollis B. Chenery (1989). "Patterns of Development, 1950 to 1983." Discussion Paper No. 41. Washington, DC: World Bank.

Taylor, Lance (1988). *Varieties of Stabilization Experience*. Oxford: Clarendon Press.

Taylor, Lance (1991). *Income Distribution, Inflation, and Growth*. Cambridge, MA: MIT Press.

Tewari, Meenu (1991). "The State, Intersectoral Linkages, and the Historical Conditions of Accumulation in Ludiana's Industrial Regime," Massachusetts Institute of
Technology: Department of Urban Studies and Planning.

Timmer, C. Peter (1988). "The Agricultural Transformation" in Hollis Chenery
and T. N. Srinivasan (eds.), *Handbook of Development Economics*, Vol. 1. Amsterdam:
North-Holland.

United Nations (1991). "Economic Stabilization Programmes in Developing Countries: Report of the Secretary-General." New York, Document No. A/46/385.

United Nations Conference on Trade and Development, (UNCTAD, 1991). *Trade
and Development Report 1991*. New York: United Nations.

Williamson, John (1990). "What Washington Means by Policy Reform," in John
Williamson (ed.), *Latin American Adjustment: How Much Has Happened?*. Washington, DC: Institute for International Economics.

World Bank (1991). *The Challenge of Development: World Development Report 1991*,
New York: Oxford University Press.

# 4         Colombia

## José Antonio Ocampo

This paper explores growth in Colombia in historical perspective, claiming that the economy's post-war expansion can be best understood as the result of the interplay between foreign exchange shortages and the dynamics of structural change, with factor productivity playing an accommodating role. On the other hand, neither the balance of payments nor factor growth will be binding constraints in the next few years, but accumulation will be subject to a severe domestic financing constraint. The latter is largely the result of the aggressive devaluation policy implemented in recent years to facilitate adjustment to the trade liberalization program, and may be interpreted as a sign of contradictions between the long-term goals of exchange rate management and its short-run effects. Economic dynamics in the next few years will depend on how this financing constraint is managed and how the structural paralysis which the economy has faced since the mid-1970s is overcome. Finally, the paper argues that the remarkable resilience of the Colombian economy to violence indicates that this factor is likely to play a secondary role in the near future.

## 4.1   Post-War Economic Growth

The literature on economic development has emphasized three aspects of the growth process in less developed countries (LDCs). The first is the relation between factor accumulation, productivity, and growth. The second is the constraint which particular sectors may pose on economic growth. Although agriculture has been repeatedly mentioned in this regard, the usual focus of the literature is on foreign exchange availability. The third is the role of structural transformation in economic development.

The first relation is shown in table 4.1 for the period 1945 to 1987. The upper part displays the traditional Harrod-Domar linkages between capital accumulation and growth. Following the neoclassical tradition, the lower

**Table 4.1**
Colombia: Economic growth and factor accumulation, 1945−1987

|  | 1945−56 | 1956−67 | 1967−74 | 1974−80 | 1980−87 |
|---|---|---|---|---|---|
| **A. Growth and fixed capital accumulation** | | | | | |
| GDP Growth | 5.1% | 4.5% | 6.5% | 4.8% | 3.1% |
| Marginal capital-output ratio | 2.9 | 2.2 | 1.5 | 1.9 | 3.2 |
| Net investment rate | 14.8 | 9.8 | 9.7 | 9.3 | 9.9 |
| Depreciation funds | 6.6 | 7.6 | 6.9 | 6.4 | 6.9 |
| Gross investment rate | 21.4 | 17.4 | 16.6 | 15.7 | 16.8 |
| Relative price of capital goods (1975 = 100) | 74.2 | 100.0 | 107.8 | 98.6 | 100.7 |
| Gross investment rate at current prices | 15.9 | 17.4 | 17.9 | 15.5 | 16.9 |
| Memo item: Marginal capital-output ratio with capital stock lagged two years | 2.1 | 2.4 | 1.3 | 1.7 | 3.1 |
| **B. Growth and total factor accumulation** | | | | | |
| GDP growth | 5.1 | 4.5 | 6.5 | 4.8 | 3.1 |
| Growth of capital stock | 7.0 | 4.2 | 4.5 | 4.7 | 4.8 |
| Growth of employment | 1.9 | 2.4 | 2.8 | 4.2 | 3.0 |
| Contribution to aggregate growth (capital stock lagged two years) | | | | | |
| Capital accumulation | 2.9 | 2.4 | 2.1 | 2.3 | 2.0 |
| Employment | 0.9 | 1.3 | 1.5 | 2.1 | 1.8 |
| Education | 0.1 | 0.5 | 0.7 | 0.6 | 0.9 |
| Total factor productivity | 1.2 | 0.3 | 2.2 | −0.2 | −1.6 |

Source: Ocampo and Crane (1988), chapter 5. Estimates of Part B are those using variable labor shares.

part shows the growth contributions of capital accumulation, employment, education, and factor productivity. The post-war period has been divided into five stylized phases: the post-war boom (1945−1956), the years of foreign exchange strangulation which followed it (1956−1967), the "golden age" of post-war development (1967−1974), the coffee boom of the 1970s (1974−1980), and the recession and recovery of the 1980s (1980−1987). The capital stock series is the intermediate estimate of Ocampo and Crane (1988) and refers only to fixed capital.[1]

According to the first of these exercises, the net investment rate has been fairly constant since the years of foreign exchange strangulation of the 1950s and 1960s. This feature reflects the stability of the nation's development in the post-war period as well as its mild crisis in the 1980s as compared to her Latin American neighbors. The high investment rate of the post-war boom was associated with war-time repression of demand for industrial and transport equipment and the low relative price of capital goods. However, because the demand for capital goods is price-inelastic in Colombia (Ocampo 1989d), the high real investment rate of this period was the lowest, if measured at current prices.

Given the relative constancy of the investment rate, the *ex-post* marginal capital-output ratio has adjusted to variable growth in different periods (particularly when estimated by lagging the capital stock two years). This indicates that, in a broad sense, capacity utilization has been the accommodating variable. This result casts doubts on the interpretation of changes in the capital-output ratio as reflecting varying *ex-ante* efficiency of investment. For example, faster growth in the 1967 to 1974 period can hardly be attributed to better investment decisions, as reflected in a lower *ex-ante* capital-output ratio. Rather, the very low *ex-post* ratio typical of this period was the *result* of more intensive use of the existing stock. Similarly, the relatively poor growth of the 1980s can hardly be attributed to the capital-intensive character of investment projects underway—a central feature of the period, nonetheless. On the contrary, the high marginal capital-output ratio was a reflection of growing excess capacities induced by a sharp slowdown.

Following a pattern typical of developing countries (see Chenery et al., 1986), factor accumulation rather than productivity growth has been the central feature of post-war development. Part B of table 4.1 shows that factor accumulation was dominated by fixed capital investment in the early post-war period. Since the mid-1970s, employment cum human capital has ruled the process. Except for 1967–74, total factor productivity growth has been very slow and, if adjusted by human capital, negative since the mid-1970s.[2] On the other hand, factor accumulation does not explain variable performance across the different post-war periods. Mirroring the cross-country pattern typical of developing and Latin American countries (Chenery et al., 1986; de Gregorio, 1991), variable growth performance has been closely associated with factor productivity.[3]

This result may be interpreted in two different ways. If we assume that the growth rate is the independent variable in this relation, it is consistent with Verdoorn's or Kaldor's low; that is, policies which promote growth will be ratified by more intensive and efficient use of existing factors (higher capacity utilization, falling informality, and so on; see, for example, Ocampo, 1989c). The causality can also be interpreted in the opposite way:

growth would be accelerated by promoting productivity, *if* factors displaced find alternative employment in a rapidly growing economy. An open economy partly satisfies this condition, to the extent that faster productivity growth increases the relative supply of tradable goods facing elastic world demands.

The causality test can hardly be settled at a macroeconomic level. Existing studies of the determinants of productivity in the manufacturing sector provide additional clues. Sandoval (1982), Echavarría (1990a), and Ocampo (1992) support the first of these interpretations, that is, a strong Verdoorn effect characterizes productivity performance. On the other hand, capacity utilization has been found to be a major mechanism of adjustment in Colombian manufacturing (Ocampo, 1990a), whereas research on labor market adjustment indicates that the relative growth of both formal employment and more productive "informal" activities is largely determined by economic growth (Misión de Empleo, 1986; López et al., 1987); and Londoño (1987). Import competition and domestic concentration also have been found to influence productivity performance in the manufacturing sector, but the effects of these variables have uncertain signs and are weak relative to the traditional Verdoon effects (Roberts, 1988; Echavarría, 1990a; Ocampo, 1992).[4]

All these results leave the major phases of post-war development largely unexplained. What role, if any, do other factors emphasized by the development literature play? Changes in exchange rate and trade policies help shed light on the foreign gap. From the late 1940s to the late 1960s, there was a chronic foreign exchange shortage, if a few years of high coffee prices in the early 1950s are excluded (Ocampo, 1989c). The adjustment policies of the mid-1980s also reflect balance of payments considerations.

Table 4.2 presents the crudest test of the link between the balance of payments and growth in the post-war period: a simple correlation between the deviation of GDP from trend and a similar deviation of import capacity (purchasing power of exports). The results are striking: For 1945 to 1989, the correlation is weak (and nil for 1970 to 1989), but the purchasing power of exports explains, by itself, 66 % of the variance of GDP performance in 1950 to 1969. This method cannot be used to test the relevance of the foreign exchange gap in the recent past, although contrary to the gap hypothesis, the correlation between these two variables is less weak for the 1970 to 1985 period than if the most recent years are included in the sample.

Two decades ago, Landau (1971) suggested an alternative test, based on the hypothesis that, when the foreign exchange gap is binding, there will

**Table 4.2**
Relation between GDP and import capacity ($t$ statistics in parentheses)

| Period | Constant | Effect of import capacity | $R^2$ |
|---|---|---|---|
| 1945–1989 | −0.055<br>(−0.10) | 0.068<br>(2.59) | 0.135 |
| 1945–1969 | −0.976<br>(−3.46) | 0.059<br>(4.41) | 0.459 |
| 1950–1969 | −1.418<br>(−6.55) | 0.057<br>(5.88) | 0.658 |
| 1970–1985 | 2.706<br>(2.91) | 0.104<br>(2.22) | 0.260 |
| 1970–1989 | 1.111<br>(0.98) | 0.063<br>(1.06) | 0.059 |

Note: Both variables expressed as deviations from trend.

be strong substitution between external and (*ex-post*) domestic savings. According to this test, such gaps played a crucial role in the 1950 to 1969 period, when substitution was very high (−0.74 according to Ocampo, 1988). On the contrary, in the 1970 to 1980 period, substitution was weak (−0.31). Unless other factors affected the relation between domestic and external savings in that period, these results support the evidence presented above.

The role of structural change in post-war economic growth is illustrated in tables 4.3 and 4.4. Up to the mid-1970s, transformation was rapid. It was led by manufacturing along with public utilities, communications, transportation, and financial services. Within manufacturing, the intermediate sectors that had dominated industrial growth in the 1930s continued to expand in relative terms in the post-war boom, but the leading role was taken over by "late" industries. Agricultural production was also transformed: coffee, cattle raising, and traditional food crops grew at slow rates, as noncoffee commercial crops boomed after the 1950s (Kalmanovitz, 1978). This process was accompanied by a relative expansion of public sector expenditure, particularly in the late 1960s and early 1970s. It was also "inward-looking," as reflected in the downward trend of the export coefficient. The import coefficient did not show any clear trend but rather cyclical behavior, associated with the evolution of the terms of trade.

Tariff and nontariff protection played a crucial role in these changes, but other factors were also present. Until the early 1960s, manufacturing underperformed relative to Kuznets-Chenery patterns: "Catching-up" may have played a role. Relative prices were significantly affected by the 1957

**Table 4.3**
Colombia: Structural change, 1945–1989

| | GDP structure (1975 prices) | | | Manufacturing value added (1975 prices) | | Net public sector expenditure[d] as % of GDP (current prices) |
|---|---|---|---|---|---|---|
| | Share of manufacturing | Share of dynamic services[a] | Share of mining | Intermediate sectors[b] | Late sectors[c] | |
| 1945–49 | 14.9% | 8.0% | 2.9% | 37.9% | 10.6% | 9.1%[e] |
| 1950–54 | 17.6 | 10.5 | 3.4 | 38.4 | 13.2 | 11.0 |
| 1955–59 | 19.5 | 11.5 | 3.3 | 36.9 | 20.1 | 11.7 |
| 1960–64 | 20.7 | 12.7 | 3.2 | 37.0 | 23.1 | 13.5 |
| 1965–69 | 21.2 | 13.7 | 3.0 | 35.5 | 24.1 | 15.4 |
| 1970–74 | 22.5 | 15.4 | 2.3 | 36.2 | 29.7 | 18.1 |
| 1975–79 | 22.9 | 16.6 | 1.4 | 35.7 | 31.6 | 17.9 |
| 1980–84 | 21.3 | 18.3 | 1.4 | 34.2 | 31.8 | 21.6 |
| 1985–89 | 21.2 | 17.2 | 3.8 | 34.4 | 32.4 | 21.7[f] |

devaluation induced by the collapse of the coffee terms of trade in the mid-1950s. This factor supported import substitution and export diversification during the 1960s and the first half of the 1970s (see table 4.3). The latter process was encouraged by active export policy, for example, a preferential exchange rate since 1948, a drawback mechanism since 1957, tax incentives for nontraditional exporters since 1960, and subsidized credit since 1963. This "mixed" strategy, combining protectionism with export promotion and active exchange rate management, helps explain why the structural transformation was more akin to that of a "small primary-producing country" than to that of a large economy, and why "late" manufacturing activities remained small relative to the normal cross-country pattern (Chenery et al., 1986; Londoño, 1989a and 1990; Ocampo, 1991b; Syrquin, 1987).

The "golden age" of post-war development was abruptly interrupted in the mid-1970s. The repercussions included a dramatic fall in the elasticity of manufacturing production to total GDP and retrogression of the industrial and export structures (tables 4.3 and 4.4). Slow manufacturing growth is particularly worrisome, because disequilibrium analysis indicates that rather than export growth, it was the major determinant of total factor productivity growth in the 1925 to 1980 period (Echavarría, 1989).

Structural trends over the past 15 years have been linked to the Dutch-disease effects of the coffee boom of the second half of the 1970s and easy access to external financing in the late 1970s and early 1980s (Ed-

**Table 4.3** (continued)

| Public sector investment as % of total fixed capital investment (current prices) | | Foreign trade as % of GDP (1975 prices) | | Export structure (current $) | | |
|---|---|---|---|---|---|---|
| Public construction | Total public sector investment | Exports | Imports | Coffee | Mining | Other (Non-traditional) |
| | | 21.0% | 14.4% | 72.1% | 20.2% | 7.7% |
| 16.9 | | 18.4 | 18.4 | 78.7 | 16.3 | 5.0 |
| 20.6 | | 17.2 | 15.9 | 76.2 | 16.8 | 7.0 |
| 18.9 | | 16.0 | 14.1 | 68.9 | 18.9 | 12.2 |
| 18.9 | | 15.6 | 14.1 | 61.0 | 15.2 | 23.7 |
| 29.5 | 32.1 | 14.9 | 16.9 | 50.5 | 8.7 | 40.8 |
| | 36.0 | 15.1 | 16.0 | 57.9 | 6.6 | 35.4 |
| | 44.7 | 14.1 | 19.3 | 48.7 | 13.0 | 38.3 |
| | 51.1[f] | 17.7 | 15.6 | 35.6 | 31.0 | 33.5 |

a. Public utilities, communications, transportation and financial services.
b. Beverages, textiles and apparel, and nonmetallic minerals.
c. Paper and printing, chemicals, basic metals, metallic products, machinery and equipment.
d. Estimated on the basis of tax receipts and the consolidated public sector deficit.
e. 1946–1949.
f. 1985–1987.

wards, 1984; Ocampo, 1989a); no doubt the drug boom played a reinforcing role. Exchange-rate revaluation and trade liberalization adversely influenced nontraditional exports and import-competing activities, due both to legal and illegal trade. Nonetheless, this interpretation does not explain why the structural paralysis continued long after the Dutch disease was over. As argued later in this chapter, the structural crisis can be traced to the lack of a consistent industrial policy since the early 1970s. This vacuum became a fertile ground for the severe short-term shocks which the industrial sector experienced after the mid-1970s including the Dutch disease.

Some important transformations nonetheless took place: Coffee production experienced a technological revolution, mining (oil, coal, gold, and nickel) activities boomed, and public expenditures continued to expand in relative terms up to the mid-1980s. The latter process reflects the rising share of public sector in total investment, associated with infrastructure and mining. Overall, however, structural transformation has become erratic, as the high standard errors of most sectoral elasticities in table 4.4 indicate.

**Table 4.4**
GDP trend and structure, 1945−1990

| | Trend growth and sectoral GDP elasticity | | | Standard error of estimated coefficient | | |
|---|---|---|---|---|---|---|
| | 1945−74 | 1975−90[a] | 1985−90[b] | 1945−74 | 1975−89[a] | 1985−90[b] |
| Trend GDP growth | 0.0477 | 0.0370 | 0.0427 | 0.0006 | 0.0014 | 0.0025 |
| Sectoral elasticities with respect to total GDP | | | | | | |
| Agriculture | 0.636[c] | 0.830[c] | 1.110 | 0.017 | 0.029 | 0.134 |
| Mining | 0.816[c] | 3.471[c] | 4.069[c] | 0.059 | 0.490 | 0.635 |
| Manufacturing | 1.352[c] | 0.812[c] | 0.954 | 0.023 | 0.038 | 0.051 |
| Construction | 0.985 | 1.317[c] | 0.176[c] | 0.059 | 0.133 | 0.288 |
| Transportation | 1.320[c] | 0.803[c] | 0.635[c] | 0.047 | 0.066 | 0.069 |
| Public utilities and communications | 2.004[c] | 1.896* | 1.084 | 0.027 | 0.110 | 0.225 |
| Government services | 1.086[c] | 1.426* | 1.314[c] | 0.017 | 0.032 | 0.043 |
| Commerce | 1.173[c] | 0.725* | 0.855[c] | 0.032 | 0.017 | 0.053 |
| Financial services | 1.750[c] | 1.193* | 1.651[c] | 0.033 | 0.089 | 0.230 |
| Other services | 0.960[c] | 0.893* | 0.722 | 0.015 | 0.024 | 0.026 |

a. 1975−89 for public utilities, financial and other services.
b. 1985−89 for public utilities, financial and other services.
c. Significantly different from one at 95 % confidence level.
Source: National accounts.

Deficient macroeconomic management and contamination by the Latin American debt crisis go far to explain the relatively slow economic growth of Colombia since the mid-1970s and, particularly, the recession of the early 1980s. The "leading sectors" of the past 15 years have been imperfect substitutes for manufacturing production and the complementary sectors that played that role up to the mid-1970s.[5] Given stagnant world demand and Colombia's high share in the market, the growth of modernized coffee production was soon exhausted. Investment in large-scale capital-intensive mining and infrastructure lacks the linkages necessary to induce, by itself, a dynamic growth process. Indeed, the parameter estimates for the three-gap model suggest that it may have the crowded out investment in the rest of the economy.

In sum, the interplay between the foreign exchange constraint and the dynamics of structural change dominated post-war economic growth in Colombia, with factor productivity playing an accommodating role. When the economy was not constrained by the external gap and structural change was at full swing, growth rates peaked. Equally, when balance of payments limitations mattered or structural change slackened, growth rates fell. The implication is that renewed growth in Colombia will require a healthy balance of payments and dynamic structural change.

## 4.2  The Recent Recovery

Contrary to her international stereotype, Colombia was not free from the macroeconomic disequilibria common to Latin America in the 1980s. Following (with a lag) the regional pattern, the early 1980s were characterized by fiscal and balance of payments deficits. These were the joint product of external shocks—the collapse of coffee prices and world recession—and the 1978 to 1982 Turbay administration's combination of expansionary fiscal policy with exchange rate appreciation and trade liberalization. Worsening economic conditions were reflected in rapid erosion of the strong net debt position of the country. Moreover, the aggregate demand effects of external shocks and macroeconomic policy were strongly contractionary. As fiscal and external balances deteriorated, the economy experienced the worst recession of the post-war period (Lora and Ocampo, 1987; Ocampo, 1989b).

Two distinct stabilization attempts were made by the Betancur administration (1982–86). During 1983 and the first half of 1984, a "heterodox" package included mild fiscal adjustments, strong import and exchange controls, higher tariffs and export subsidies, and a faster exchange rate crawl. The foreign exchange drain typical of this period forced a policy shift in mid-1984. The "orthodox" program that followed combined contractionary fiscal policy with rapid devaluation and mild trade liberalization (Junguito, 1986; Garay and Carrasquilla, 1987; Lora and Ocampo, 1987; Ocampo, 1989b).

Despite adverse aggregate demand effects of the adjustment programs, particularly the "orthodox" package adopted in mid-1984, the correction of external and fiscal imbalances was accompanied by growth. From 1983 to 1985, the rate reached 3.2 % a year, a significant improvement over the dismal record of 1980 to 1983 (1.6 %). By late 1985, basic macroeconomic balance had been restored. The country was able to use the temporary boost of coffee prices generated by draughts in Brazil in 1985 to raise economic growth (table 4.5).

Macroeconomic management during the Barco administration (1986–90) had four major features: (1) continued fiscal restraint—the consolidated public sector deficit was reduced to 1 % to 2 % of GDP after 1987; (2) a remarkable stabilization of real domestic coffee prices at fairly high levels,

**Table 4.5**
Economic performance, 1984–1990

| | 1984 | 1985 | 1986 | 1987 | 1988 | 1989 | 1990 |
|---|---|---|---|---|---|---|---|
| GDP growth | 3.4 | 3.1 | 5.8 | 5.4 | 4.1 | 3.2 | 4.3 |
| (manufacturing)[a] | 5.5 | 3.6 | 4.8 | 8.3 | 4.0 | 2.2 | 6.6 |
| Inflation (CPI, Dec.–Dec.) | 18.3 | 22.5 | 20.9 | 24.0 | 28.1 | 26.1 | 32.4 |
| Consolidated public sector deficit (cash-flow basis; % of GDP)[b] | 6.7 | 5.9 | 3.3 | 0.8 | 2.2 | 2.0 | 0.9 |
| Real exchange rate (1975 = 100) | 78.2 | 89.4 | 106.1 | 108.8 | 108.9 | 111.1 | 124.6 |
| Real coffee price (1975 = 100) | | | | | | | |
| External | 156.9 | 160.4 | 208.0 | 103.4 | 109.2 | 90.7 | 83.7 |
| Domestic | 85.1 | 86.3 | 139.9 | 126.3 | 116.0 | 116.3 | 110.8 |
| Exports (Million $) | | | | | | | |
| Coffee | 1734 | 1702 | 2742 | 1633 | 1621 | 1477 | 1482 |
| Mining | 790 | 955 | 1227 | 2065 | 1866 | 2410 | 2942 |
| Nontraditional | 1099 | 1125 | 1363 | 1556 | 1856 | 2145 | 2595 |
| Total | 3623 | 3782 | 5331 | 5254 | 5343 | 6032 | 7019 |
| Exports and imports of goods and services as % of GDP (1975 prices) | | | | | | | |
| Exports | 14.1 | 15.6 | 17.8 | 18.2 | 17.5 | 18.5 | 19.7 |
| Imports | 17.6 | 15.9 | 15.6 | 15.6 | 16.0 | 14.7 | 15.1 |
| Other external indicators (Million $) | | | | | | | |
| Trade balance | −404 | 109 | 1922 | 1461 | 827 | 1474 | 1917 |
| Current account balance | −2088 | −1586 | 463 | −21 | −216 | −194 | 480 |
| Net financial transfer[c] | −687 | 2 | −666 | −1467 | −390 | −1503 | −1279 |
| Net external debt | 10555 | 11996 | 11509 | 12213 | 12624 | 12382 | 12388 |

a. Excludes coffee hulking.
b. Excluding the National Coffee Fund.
c. Debt disbursements net of amortizations and interest payments.
Source: DANE—National accounts and Banco de la República—Balance of payments statistics. Consolidated public sector deficit and estimates for 1990 according to the National Planning Office. Real exchange rates according to Banco de la República. The real domestic coffee price has been deflated by the CPI, whereas the external price has been deflated by the IMF export unit value of industrial countries.

despite the dramatic fall in international prices generated by the normalization of world supplies in 1987 and the collapse of the International Coffee Agreement (ICO) in 1989—the basis was the surplus generated by the National Coffee Fund during the 1986 boom (3.5% of GDP) and the aggressive commercialization policy followed by the country after the collapse of ICO; (3) a gradual liberalization of non-tariff barriers and a simultaneous reduction of tariff levels, particularly since February 1990, when a more aggressive program was adopted;[6] and (4) a "high" (peso/dollar) real exchange rate policy, due to the already devalued real rate achieved during the years of macroeconomic adjustment and acceleration of the crawl since mid-1989 to facilitate adjustment to trade liberalization.

In many regards, economic performance since 1986 has been remarkable, despite the short duration of the coffee boom that propelled the initial recovery, the collapse of ICO, and a substantial negative financial transfer. Even with trade liberalization, devaluation has kept the import coefficient at moderate levels. This fact, together with growing mining exports (associated with past investment decisions) and a rapid recovery of non-traditional exports, has been reflected in strong trade and current account balances and the stabilization, since 1987, of the external debt, net of international reserves. The export coefficient increased rapidly, reaching levels unknown to the country since the early 1950s (see tables 4.3 and 4.5).

Nonetheless, growth has been far from satisfactory. After two years at rates higher than the post-war average but lower than those of the 1967 to 1974 boom, growth slowed down. The inability to sustain a rapid expansion of manufacturing production was particularly worrisome. If any leading sector can be singled out, it would be mining, with its high GDP elasticity and contribution to export growth (tables 4.4 and 4.5). However, as emphasized by FEDESARROLLO (1990), economic expansion in recent years may be characterized as a succession of short-lived sectoral booms without a clearly discernible structural pattern.

It should also be emphasized that, contrary to the experience of the early 1980s, when recession was reflected in falling inflation rates, the recent slowdown has been accompanied by rising inflation. Given the nature of macroeconomic management, this process cannot be attributed to fiscal pressure. Rather, it may be interpreted as the result of a series of supply shocks—domestic agricultural prices in 1987, external prices of traded goods in 1988–89, and devaluation in 1990—accompanied by spreading domestic indexation (Correa and Escobar, 1990; Ministerio de Desarrollo, 1990). Also, the aggressive devaluation policy adopted to complement trade liberalization may have generated a "domestic financing constraint," of a kind that the country only experienced in the past when international coffee prices boomed.

## 4.3   Medium-Term Prospects

The medium-term prospects of the Colombian economy can be analyzed with the help of a revised version of the three-gap model developed by Villar (1991). It follows the literature, but introduces explicitly the effects of exchange rate adjustments and trade policy on external and internal balances.

The basic parameters were estimated with data for the 1970 to 1990 period and calibrated for 1990. The model uses a marginal capital-output ratio (*gross* of depreciation) of 3.1, which is an intermediate level, according to post-war evidence summarized in table 4.1.[7]

Coffee and mining exports, fuel imports, transfers from the rest of the world, and debt service are exogenous. Nontraditional exports depend on the real effective exchange rate (which includes direct subsidies) and world economic activity. Demand for imports depends on relative prices, direct controls, and an activity variable—capacity utilization or the investment rate, according to the goods involved. Net exports of nonfinancial services are determined by the real exchange rate and global commercial activity.

Private investment depends directly on capacity utilization, and inversely on public investment, relative prices, and import controls. The influence of public investment is captured by a strong but debatable "crowding out" effect (−0.36), which may be conceived of as being transmitted through the traditional financial mechanisms or congestion in the import licensing process.[8] Given the high import content of machinery and equipment, relative prices of capital goods are strongly affected by the real exchange rate.

Private savings depend on capacity utilization and the real exchange rate; the latter effect captures the redistribution of income from wages to profits generated by devaluation and the higher savings propensity of profit recipients. In turn, public savings depend on capacity utilization and strongly on coffee and oil exports, which are heavily taxed on the margin. Finally, the net domestic interest payments of the consolidated public sector are assumed to be negligible.[9]

The economy can be visualized as facing three different constraints. The first is available capacity. Because capacity utilization was low in 1990 (table 4.6) and investment levels guarantee a rate of growth of potential

**Table 4.6**
Historical evolution and 1990 levels of basic variables used in the model

|  | 1971–75 | 1976–80 | 1981–85 | 1986–90 | 1971–90 | 1990 |
|---|---|---|---|---|---|---|
| e = Real exchange rate (1975 = 100) | 95.3 | 84.5 | 78.7 | 111.9 | 96.2 | 124.6 |
| g* = Potential GDP growth rate | 5.2 | 4.9 | 5.2 | 4.5 | 4.9 | 4.4 |
| g = Actual GDP growth rate | 5.7 | 5.4 | 2.2 | 4.4 | 4.4 | 3.7 |
| u = Capacity utilization | 98.0 | 98.5 | 90.2 | 86.9 | 93.4 | 85.7 |
| ig = Public sector investment (% of potential GDP at 1975 prices) | 5.2 | 5.9 | 7.2 | 5.9 | 6.0 | 5.5 |
| ip = Private-sector investment (% of potential GDP at 1975 prices) | 10.5 | 9.7 | 8.5 | 7.9 | 9.2 | 7.7 |
| xnt = Nontraditional exports (% of potential GDP at parity exchange rate) | 5.2 | 5.7 | 3.9 | 3.8 | 4.6 | 4.4 |
| m = Imports of goods (% of potential GDP at parity exchange rate) | 11.1 | 13.0 | 13.8 | 8.6 | 11.6 | 8.6 |
| def = Consolidated public-sector deficit (% of GDP at current prices) | 1.8 | 0.7 | 6.1 | 0.8 | 2.3 | 0.9 |
| ca = Current account balance (% of GDP at current prices) | −2.6 | 1.4 | −5.9 | 0.3 | −1.7 | 1.2 |

Source: Estimated from DANE—National Accounts and Banco de la República—Balance of Payments statistics, 1990, according to the National Planning Office. Real Exchange Rate: 1970–76, FEDESARROLLO; 1976–90: Banco de la República.

GDP of 4 % or more, this constraint is never binding in the projections. In other words, as in the past, factor accumulation will play a passive role. The second constraint is on foreign exchange, specified as a maximum level of the current account deficit (foreign savings) that the economy can sustain. Given the experience since the debt crisis and existing projections, this level can be set as roughly 2 % of current GDP (slightly over US $800 million).

Finally, there may be a "domestic financing constraint," which is more relevant than the usual fiscal constraint for Colombia. It may be defined as the maximum level of high-powered money creation the economy can sustain, given a "normal" inflation rate. Money creation depends on: (1) the public sector deficit, which is financed with either external or central bank credits, (2) the current account of the balance of payments, and (3) private capital inflows from the rest of the world or central bank credits to the private sector. This constraint is approximated in the model by forcing the sum of the public sector deficit and the current account surplus to be less than some 1.0 % to 1.5 % of current GDP, consistent with a ratio of high powered money to GDP of about 6 % and an inflation rate of 20 % to 25 %.

If monetary policy is prudent and the constraint is binding, the government must finance part of the budget deficit by selling domestic debt instruments, undertake massive open-market operations, control private capital inflows, or reduce domestic credit to the private sector. In all of these cases, private financing would be crowded out. Over the past two decades, net average money creation from the public sector deficit and the current account balance was positive by some 0.6 % of GDP. When it rose to 2 %, during the coffee boom of the 1970s and, more recently, in 1990, monetary policy became quite complex and strongly contractionary (table 4.6).

The model can be used to simulate the effects of fiscal policy (specified in terms of either deficit or public-sector investment targets), the real exchange rate, and trade policy on potential and current GDP growth, capacity utilization, the current account of the balance of payments and domestic financing requirements, as defined earlier. Table 4.6 summarizes the historical evolution of the basic variables and the initial conditions faced by the economy in 1990: low capacity utilization, sluggish public and private investment, and slow actual and potential GDP growth *with* a binding domestic financing constraint. This peculiar mix was mainly determined by an external surplus due to a high real exchange rate. The most recent official projections of exogenous balance of payments variables are summarized in table 4.7; this table also shows the rate of growth of the rest of the

**Table 4.7**
Projection of exogenous balance of payments and external variables (million dollars and rates)

|  | 1990 | 1991 | 1992 | 1993 | 1994 |
|---|---|---|---|---|---|
| National Planning Office (Mar. 1991) |  |  |  |  |  |
| Coffee exports | 1482 | 1486 | 1561 | 1643 | 1725 |
| Fuel exports | 1907 | 1630 | 1628 | 2036 | 2214 |
| Other mining exports | 1035 | 1096 | 1191 | 1358 | 1585 |
| Total exogenous exports | 4424 | 4212 | 4380 | 5037 | 5524 |
| Fuel imports | −310 | −191 | −247 | −257 | −332 |
| Transfers | 1037 | 1063 | 1100 | 1100 | 1100 |
| Net interest payments | −1105 | −1005 | −1078 | −1095 | −1100 |
| Net profit remittances | −820 | −762 | −787 | −1028 | −1194 |
| Net exogenous balance of payments |  |  |  |  |  |
| Variables | 3226 | 3317 | 3368 | 3757 | 3998 |
| External variables Rest of the world growth rate | 1.8 | 1.0 | 1.5 | 2.0 | 2.5 |
| World inflation rate |  | 5.0 | 4.5 | 4.5 | 4.5 |

world used in the simulations. The economy will face weakly adverse external conditions in 1991–92, which will improve in 1993 and 1994. A world economic recession in 1991 is incorporated in the model, followed by a weak recovery thereafter.

The base scenario presented in table 4.8 assumes that the real exchange rate and the public sector deficit remain at their 1990 levels and that the trade reform adopted by the Gaviria administration in late 1990 does not take place. Real GDP growth results at 4.4% a year, with potential GDP lagging slightly behind. To guarantee the fiscal target, public sector investment must fall with respect to 1990, and remain significantly below historical levels. Even then, the economy will be subject to a domestic financing constraint throughout the period. Thus, major policy corrections are necessary. As the second scenario in the table indicates, a deterioration of exogenous balance of payments variables (by 5% of the projected values in 1991, rising annually by an equivalent proportion to 20% in 1994) will reduce economic growth, with additional adverse effects on public sector investment. The domestic financing constraint would be eliminated by 1992, but the economy would still not be under a foreign exchange gap.

**Table 4.8**
Prospects for growth in the 1991 to 1994 period

| | | Yearly levels | | | | Average change 1991–94 | | | |
|---|---|---|---|---|---|---|---|---|---|
| | | 1991 | 1992 | 1993 | 1994 | | | | |
| 1. Base scenario | g | 3.2 | 3.5 | 5.5 | 5.3 | g | 4.4 | u | 0.9 |
| (unchanged external | ca | 0.5 | 0.2 | 0.7 | 1.0 | g* | 4.1 | xnt | 0.6 |
| and fiscal policies) | def | 0.9 | 0.9 | 0.9 | 0.9 | ig | 4.5 | m | −0.2 |
| | | | | | | ip | 8.0 | | |
| 2. Base scenario with | g | 1.8 | 2.1 | 3.8 | 3.6 | g | 2.8 | u | −3.7 |
| adverse exogenous | ca | 0.0 | −0.8 | −0.9 | −1.1 | g* | 3.9 | xnt | 0.6 |
| balance of payments | def | 0.9 | 0.9 | 0.9 | 0.9 | ig | 3.8 | m | −0.9 |
| conditions | | | | | | ip | 8.0 | | |
| 3. Elimination of QRs | g | 2.9 | 3.6 | 5.6 | 5.4 | g | 4.4 | u | 0.6 |
| in late 1990 | ca | 0.0 | −0.3 | 0.2 | 0.5 | g* | 4.2 | xnt | 0.6 |
| | def | 0.9 | 0.9 | 0.9 | 0.9 | ig | 4.7 | m | 0.3 |
| | | | | | | ip | 8.2 | | |
| 4. Global trade reform | g | 2.2 | 2.7 | 4.7 | 4.9 | g | 3.6 | u | −1.5 |
| | ca | −0.3 | −0.9 | −0.8 | −0.7 | g* | 4.1 | xnt | 0.5 |
| | def | 0.9 | 0.9 | 0.9 | 0.9 | ig | 4.0 | m | 1.2 |
| | | | | | | ip | 8.3 | | |
| 5. Global trade reform | g | 3.4 | 3.0 | 5.0 | 5.3 | g | 4.1 | u | 0.1 |
| and 3% real | ca | 0.2 | −0.4 | −0.2 | 0.0 | g* | 4.1 | xnt | 0.7 |
| devaluation | def | 0.9 | 0.9 | 0.9 | 0.9 | ig | 4.2 | m | 1.2 |
| | | | | | | ip | 8.3 | | |
| 6. Scenario 5 with | g | 2.3 | 2.8 | 4.9 | 5.1 | g | 3.8 | u | −0.7 |
| elimination of fiscal | ca | 0.5 | −0.1 | 0.1 | 0.3 | g* | 4.0 | xnt | 0.7 |
| deficit in 1991 | def | 0.0 | 0.0 | 0.0 | 0.0 | ig | 3.5 | m | 1.0 |
| | | | | | | ip | 8.5 | | |
| 7. Scenario 5 with | g | 4.8 | 3.9 | 5.5 | 5.9 | g | 5.0 | u | 2.2 |
| public sector | ca | −0.2 | −0.9 | −0.8 | −0.7 | g* | 4.4 | xnt | 0.7 |
| investment at | def | 2.2 | 2.8 | 3.0 | 3.2 | ig | 5.8 | m | 1.8 |
| 1987–88 levels | | | | | | ip | 8.0 | | |
| 8. Global trade reform, | g | 2.0 | 3.2 | 4.7 | 4.9 | g | 3.7 | u | −2.0 |
| public sector | ca | −1.9 | −2.9 | −3.1 | −3.3 | g* | 4.3 | xnt | −0.2 |
| investment at 1987– | def | 2.9 | 3.6 | 3.9 | 4.2 | ig | 5.8 | m | 2.0 |
| 88 and 10 % real | | | | | | ip | 7.7 | | |
| appreciation | | | | | | | | | |
| 9. Scenario 7 with tax | g | 0.8 | 3.8 | 5.4 | 5.8 | g | 3.9 | u | −1.2 |
| reform | ca | 0.3 | −0.5 | −0.3 | −0.2 | g* | 4.3 | xnt | 0.7 |
| | def | 0.7 | 1.4 | 1.5 | 1.7 | ig | 5.8 | m | 1.4 |
| | | | | | | ip | 7.7 | | |

Scenarios 3 to 6 summarize the effects of the four major components of the macroeconomic policy announced in late 1990 and early 1991:[10] (1) the elimination of direct import controls (QRs), and (2) a reduction of import tariffs and export subsidies.[11] Given the strong dependence of the central government on import taxes (some 30% of total revenue over the past few years), this is equivalent to a gradual tax cut of some 0.7% of potential GDP. Lower tariffs also affect the relative price of tradables; although the current policy also includes a series of free trade agreements with Latin American countries (a free trade area in the Andean Group in 1992 and free trade with Mexico by July 1994, in particular), their effects on relative import prices and government revenue are not incorporated into the simulations. Other components are (3) a small (3%) real devaluation,[12] and (4) the elimination of the remaining consolidated public sector deficit in 1991.

The impacts of these policy decisions are simulated in a cumulative fashion. Except for devaluation, all tend to lift the domestic financing constraint, facilitating private capital inflows from the rest of the world or domestic credit creation for the private sector.

Their net effect on economic activity is contractionary; this means that expansionary devaluation is overwhelmed by the negative effects on capacity utilization of other elements of the macroeconomic package.[13] Private investment is boosted by all components (only very marginally so in the case of devaluation). On the contrary, whereas devaluation and the elimination of QRs increase government income and, thus, public-sector investment, the tariff reform and the more stringent fiscal target have the opposite effect. Overall, public sector investment is reduced by more than the increase in private investment. Potential GDP growth is thus adversely affected.[14]

The package reduces public sector investment significantly below the historical average (3.5% of potential GDP vs. 6.0% in the 1971–90 period. Such a low level may not be sustainable, as it risks deteriorating infrastructure and a reduction in mining exports. In fact, it reaches a range in which "crowding-in" rather than "crowding-out" (as assumed in the model) is certainly the rule. Contrary to this result, current macroeconomic programming assumes that public-sector investment must *increase* with respect to the fairly depressed 1990 level (DNP, 1991).

The last three scenarios in table 4.8 show the effects of increasing public investment to its 1987–88 level (5.8% of potential GDP). By itself, this decision would boost actual and potential GDP growth, bringing the former to average post-war levels (5 % of GDP), without hitting the external financing constraint (Scenario 7). However, the budget deficit increases to 2 % of GDP in 1991 and 3 % in 1992–94 and the domestic financing constraint is violated throughout the projection. To overcome this problem, two additional policy decisions are tried: a 10 % real appreciation of the peso (with respect to the 1990 level) and a tax reform equivalent to 1.7 % of potential GDP (some 2 % of current GDP). The latter can be understood also as a mix of tax hikes and cuts in current expenditures. Both policies are roughly of the magnitude required to relax the domestic financing constraint.

Revaluation will bring the economy under a foreign exchange gap and stun export diversification, the major objective of the structural reform program. It is unsustainable. In the face of growing external surpluses, largely augmented by massive capital inflows induced by contractionary monetary policy, this was the route followed by the authorities after June 1991. The decision to accelerate tariff reform by adopting in September 1991 the rates announced for 1994 reinforced the effects of exchange appreciation.

Given the medium term problems generated by revaluation, tax reform would be a better alternative. It is more contractionary in the short run, but economic growth would pick up rapidly after the initial recession. For the period as a whole, economic growth is higher than under the alternative scenario where public sector investment is adjusted to reach a zero deficit target (3.9 % vs. 3.8 % a year).

The tax increase required is, nonetheless, unusually large, as it must compensate for the reduction in government income generated by the tariff reform. It is similar to the big tax packages adopted in 1974 and 1982–85; given the low effective taxes typical of Colombia, it would require a 30 % increase in the rates on domestic economic activities (mainly sales, income and gasoline taxes).[15] The 20 % sales tax rate increase decreed by Congress in 1990 would do only a minor part of the job. The decision, adopted in early 1992, to present a new and more ambitious tax reform to Congress may be seen as a late recognition that the 1990 reform had not been enough.[16]

Despite obvious uncertainties—particularly those associated with the evolution of coffee and mining exports—these exercises show that there are no major constraints to growth of some 4 % per year in 1991–94. Given current population growth (1.8 % a year), it is not very different from the historical average in terms of per capita GDP.[17] Neither factor accumulation nor foreign exchange availability would be a binding constraint (the latter because of the aggressive exchange rate policy adopted in recent years).

The domestic financing constraint is likely to play a crucial role in the near future. The (correct) decision to devalue the exchange rate before the effects of trade liberalization were fully effective—to facilitate structural adjustment of the economy—has made short-run macroeconomic management difficult. Indeed, the exchange rate is undervalued from the point of view of the short-run macroeconomic balances. The resulting current account surpluses have an expansionary effect on monetary aggregates, which forces a fiscal adjustment that would otherwise not be required.

The contradiction between the long-term goals of exchange rate management and its short-run effect has thus made a domestic recession inevitable (at least if rising inflation is to be avoided). This is peculiar and perhaps unexpected contractionary effect of recent exchange rate management. A major tax reform emerges as the only mechanism to reconcile the exchange rate management required for a successful structural transformation with the levels of public sector investment required to guarantee adequate economic growth in the near future.

## 4.4   Trade Liberalization and Structural Change

The simulations suggest that a healthy balance of payments is likely for the next few years, accompanied by macroeconomic imbalances of a type that Colombia has only faced in the past when international coffee prices boomed. But what about structural change? The instability of the sectoral growth pattern experienced in recent years indicates that the economy has not overcome its paralysis dating from the mid-1970s. Particularly, the manufacturing sector has been incapable of leading and, in fact, has lagged behind during the recent recovery.

As in most Third World countries, the conventional interpretation of this crisis has been strongly influenced by orthodox academic analysis (World Bank, 1989; Roberts, 1988), emphasizing distortions in resource allocation generated by the "anti-export bias" of the trade regime, and the depressive effect on technical change induced by the lack of import competition and excessive industrial concentration. This story has been somewhat toned down by concern for the lack of an adequate infrastructure for foreign trade.

The orthodox-World Bank diagnosis is partly correct but certainly incomplete. It does not stand an adequate historical test. Colombian manufacturing has been strongly protected since at least the late nineteenth century, but this was no obstacle to technological advance during the period in which the sector experienced rapid structural change. Total factor productivity growth was dynamic up to the mid-1970s; the favorable performance was reflected in a long-run decline in the price of domestic manufactured goods relative to international prices and other domestic goods and prices. The productivity stagnation over the past 15 years could thus be interpreted as an effect rather than a cause of the structural paralysis experienced by the Colombian economy. Indeed, a brief period during the 1980s aside, poor productivity performance coincided with a long-term liberalization of tariff and nontariff barriers, that is, with a reduction of the "anti-export bias" as traditionally defined (Berry, 1983; Echavarría, 1989 and 1990b; Ocampo, 1990a and 1991a).

When exchange rate policy generated adequate incentives, export diversification has not been incompatible with the preservation of a protectionist structure, for example, Colombia's "mixed" development strategy generated an extraordinary growth of non-traditional exports beginning in the late 1950s. Active exchange rate management further deepened the process after 1967. When there was real appreciation induced by the Dutch disease effects of the foreign exchange boom, trade liberalization from the mid-1970s to the early 1980s coincided with stagnation of non-traditional exports. Since 1985, despite quantitative restrictions (QRs) and high tariffs, aggressive exchange rate policy has been reflected in a renewed boom of nontraditional exports.

High industrial concentration has been a feature of Colombian manufacturing since the early stages of industrial development. By itself, this is not necessarily a matter of great concern, as the relation between productivity and concentration is certainly more complex than the X-inefficiency aspects emphasized by the World Bank. According to the Schumpeterian and some European traditions of industrial policy, productivity may be positively linked to concentration, since it allows domestic firms to accumulate the scale economies necessary to reach international technological standards (see, for example, Hjalmarsson, 1991). European governments have actually encouraged concentration as a way to increase efficiency.

The lack of adequate infrastructure for foreign trade is worrisome but is not a novel feature either. In a country with the geographical complexity of Colombia, the strong tendency to regional market segmentation operates as a *pro*-export bias, as a cursory look at economic history reveals (Ocampo, 1991b). It is unclear what, if any, were the net effects of an inadequate foreign trade infrastructure combined with an equally insufficient integration of the domestic market.

The structural paralysis that the Colombian economy has experienced since the mid-1970s can hardly be attributed to features that have been permanent characteristics of modern manufacturing development in the country. The analysis should focus on the particular obstacles that the industrial sector has faced over the past 15 years and the absence of a consistent policy to overcome them.[18] In this regard, the easy and intermediate stages of import substitution were exhausted by the late 1960s. Moreover, during the past two decades, the aggregate income-elasticity of consumer demand for manufacturing goods experienced a strong decline and ceased to be an engine of growth.[19]

Industrial strategy in the late 1960s emphasized export promotion and the need for a larger market to deepen import substitution. When exchange rate policy provided adequate incentives, the export promotion element worked out satisfactorily. The import substitution component fared less well. The Andean Group as designed in the late 1960s was supposed to be an integrated and planned market where advanced import substitution would take place. However, the instruments for industrial programming at a regional level were extremely complex, never effective, and soon given up. In the early 1980s, regional integration virtually collapsed. Although it was revitalized in recent years, its initial concepts were abandoned.

Industrial policy failed in other regards to support manufacturing growth. The Industrial Development Institute (IFI) began in the 1940s to advance venture capital to new manufacturing firms but after the early 1970s, it ceased to play that role. The development banks (*Corporaciones Financieras*) had been designed in the 1960s to channel private risk capital and long-term lending to the industrial sector. This role was also significantly downplayed in the 1970s when the banks shifted toward short- rather than long-term financial intermediation.

Finally, the Colombian government never designed instruments essential for import substitution. It never sought to encourage technical change nor introduced an adequate state procurement policy. Public sector investment practices, heavily dependent on external financing, were characterized by an inherent import-bias (Londoño and Perry, 1985).

The lack of a consistent long-term policy amplified the adverse short-term shocks experienced by the industrial sector after the mid-1970s. Although the sector suffered Dutch disease and the effects of financial liberalization, short-term resources were increasingly used by productive firms for financial transactions. This portfolio structure generated a major financial crisis in the recession of the early 1980s. Profit margins remained depressed by historical standards throughout the decade. The cumulative effects of these events were relatively low investment rates and the accumulation of a significant technology gap.

Industrial paralysis thus reflects the cumulative effects of short-term shocks magnified by absence of a consistent industrial strategy. Given domestic market limitations and the lack of import substitution at the regional level, a package to overcome this structural crisis must certainly be outward-oriented. In light of the recent evolution of manufacturing, it is unlikely that trade liberalization would, by itself, be enough. Exports have been responding rapidly to exchange rate incentives and are unlikely to receive additional stimulus from the elimination of QRs and tariff cuts.[20] The econometric results suggest that the favorable effects of liberalization on factor productivity are uncertain, and in any case insufficient to generate a dynamic growth process.[21] Indeed, trade liberalization could well become just one more adverse shock.

From the perspective of recent structural trends, the current modernization program is thus a threat as well as a challenge. Its success would depend on its ability to inaugurate a new phase of structural change. Such an outcome relies on a wave of "innovations" in the broad Schumpeterian sense—including not only technological change but the development of new products, new organizations, the opening up of new markets, and so on—and *not* on the static and dynamic effects suggested by traditional neoclassical analysis.

To permit a cumulative process, trade liberalization must be complemented by a global industrial strategy. As our historical account indicates, the latter should (at least) include: (1) a special restructuring program for those sectors that have accumulated a significant technological gap over the past 15 years, (2) an aggressive policy to encourage technological catching up and innovations, (3) the restructuring of the IFI and the development banks, and the creation of new institutions to guarantee and adequate supply of risk capital and long-term finance, (4) a reform of government procurement policy, and (5) a redesign of sectoral planning.

## 4.5   The Effects of Violence

The role that violence plays in the current sociopolitical crisis of Colombia is apparent to all observers. It is essential to discern whether it is also adversely affecting economic activity.

The roots and characteristics of Colombian violence have varied over time (see, for example, Sanchez and Peñaranda, 1986). Its historical origins can be found in three distinct processes: regional conflicts associated with the painful construction of nationhood after independence from Spain in 1819; the lack of rules to settle democratically the struggle for power between the two major political parties; and land disputes in the open agrarian frontier and in those regions of the country where important Indian communities survived. Only the latter process has clear economic roots (LeGrand, 1988).

Conflicts for regional hegemonies became secondary or even disappeared after the longest and bloodiest civil war of the Republican period, the War of the Thousand Days (1899–1902) and its major sequel, the secession of Panama. With the birth of guerrilla warfare during the War of the Thousand Days, political violence took new forms (Bergquist, 1978). The old conservative-liberal political dispute finally erupted into a major undeclared civil war, known simply as *La Violencia*—after the assassination of Jorge Eliecer Gaitan, head of the Liberal party and popular urban leader in April 1948. With the alliance between the two major political parties to form a National Front in 1957, this form of violence also disappeared in the following decades. Former conservative and liberal guerrillas continued to operate at a microregional level increasingly detached from the national authorities. They were condemned by the establishment as *bandoleros* (bandit gangs) and openly repressed in the 1960s.

Thus, of the three "classical" forms of violence, only the last plagues the contemporary life of the country. It has actually become more virulent, as the agrarian frontier has been brought rapidly into commercial agriculture or cattle raising and narcotraffickers have become the landlord side of the dispute. Over the past three decades, two additional processes were superimposed on this complex historical background. The first was the rise of leftist guerrilla organizations since the 1960s. The second was the rise of narcotraffic in the late 1970s.

The oldest guerrilla group, FARC, is deeply rooted in the history of agrarian conflicts and has been loosely associated with the Communist party. The origins of the other groups were diverse: Some were associated with international ideological divisions of the communist movement (ELN and EPL, of Castroist and Maoist affections, respectively), with domestic populist experience (M-19), with the struggle of Indians for their land (Quintin Lame), and so on. Most participated in the peace negotiations supported by the last three Administrations and all but FARC and ELN are now disarmed.

The growth of violence became explosive when the methods typical of the cocaine mafia began to the used against guerrilla organizations, but also against disaffected peasants and workers, leftist urban and rural leaders and, finally, politicians from the traditional parties. Some army officials became involved, at a regional level, in alliances and even outright promotion of para-military groups financed by the cocaine lords. As a major study on the subject indicates (Comisión de Estudios sobre la Violencia, 1987), the characteristics and map of violence became extremely complex and intrinsically mixed with other social and political phenomena (the inadequate presence of the State in many parts of the country, the crisis of the judicial system, and so on). Deas (1990) argues, on the other hand, that the process was rooted in a more general trend towards the fragmentation of power.

The trend of the homicide rate indicates that violence was at a post-war low in the mid-1970s. Thereafter, it increased rapidly, particularly in the second half of the 1980s. In recent years, it has been higher than in the heyday of *La Violencia*. Its map certainly reflects the strong effect of narco-traffic, but also the activities of guerrilla organizations and the persistence of the old agrarian and Indian questions (Losada and Velez, 1989).

By itself, economic analysis cannot cope with the complex roots of the problem. Two economic processes have played a crucial role: the wealth generated by the cocaine trade and old and new social inequalities, particularly in rural areas. Much (mainly journalistic) speculation has been made on the size of the cocaine trade.[22] Careful quantification indicates that the Colombian drug business peaked in the early 1980s at 4% to 6% of GDP and declined later to 2%, equivalent to less than U.S. $1 billion (Gomez, 1988 and 1990). This estimate (correctly) excludes the share of the Colombian cocaine lords in the U.S. wholesale and retail business.

The persistence of unsatisfied basic needs and considerable income and wealth inequality are important characteristics of the Colombian socioeconomic structure. The usual social indicators (infant mortality, illiteracy, malnutrition, etc.) improved over the past decades, but remain in a median to lower Latin American range. In the mid-1960s, when the first complete estimates were made, Colombia had an extremely skewed distribution of income.

Recent studies indicate that distribution has improved considerably since the mid-1970s (Londoño, 1989b, 1990; Reyes, 1987; Urrutia, 1984), accompanied by improvements in poverty and nutrition levels (Carrizosa, 1987; Uribe, 1987). Moreover, land distribution also improved (Lorente et al., 1985). For rural areas subject to severe violence, the effects of the National Rehabilitation Plan implemented since the mid-1980s have been remarkable. There has been a significant improvement in economic conditions, as reflected in the rapid increase of Agricultural Trading Institute purchases in rehabilitation zones (IDEMA, 1990, p. 5).

The economic effects of violence are difficult to assess. The most severely affected areas accounted for no more than 10 % of agricultural production (Bejarano, 1988) and as we have seen, output has boomed in
rehabilitation zones. Certain forms of rural violence, particularly the kid-
napping of landlords, exercise a significant effect on the more entrepreneurial types of agricultural activities and cattle raising. The economic
effects of ELN terrorist attacks on oil pipelines are, however, much more
important. They have significantly affected production and foreign exchange earnings, particularly in 1988–89 and early 1991. Ecological destruction should also be included in the economic costs of oil terrorism.

The new wave of guerrilla violence in 1991 severely damaged transport
infrastructure, destroyed a sizable number of trucks and buses, and generated widespread uncertainty regarding transport security. Indeed, the combination of guerrilla attacks on oil pipelines, the transportation system,
and other economic targets reached unprecedented levels in the first few
months of 1991 and led the government to adopt a "war tax" to finance
the defense expenditures necessary to face the crisis[23] (DNP, 1991; Ministerio de Desarrollo Económico, 1991). As in previous episodes of sharp
escalation of guerrilla activities, this one was soon over.

The effects of violence on the manufacturing activities may be analyzed
with information provided by FEDESARROLLO's Entrepreneurial survey.
Table 4.9 shows the evolution of the sociopolitical investment climate. The
trend has generally been adverse over the past four years, but the fluctuations are striking. Detailed study in light of political events suggests that
investment decisions in the Colombian manufacturing sector have followed
the evolution of current economic rather than sociopolitical conditions.

In light of the sharp deterioration of social and political conditions that
the country has experienced in recent years, economic effects have been
rather mild. In particular, the general economic situation has not been
affected. This resiliance of the Colombian economy to violence is remarkable, paradoxical, and awaits a convincing explanation. A contributing factor may be the fact that the country's complex geography allows virtual
civil wars to take place in isolated regions, while the major economic
centers continue their normal lives. But this explanation is certainly incomplete, since the narco-traffic (and to a much lesser extent, guerrilla activity)
has affected the centers and projected a sense of sociopolitical crisis over
the whole of society. On the basis of recent trends, it seems likely that
violence will play a secondary economic role in the near future. Nonetheless, one can only speculate as to whether this paradoxical equilibrium will

**Table 4.9**
Business and investment climates in the manufacturing sector (% of firms)

| | Evaluation of current economic conditions | | Investment | | | |
| | | | Economic | | Sociopolitical | |
| | Favorable | Adverse | Favorable | Adverse | Favorable | Adverse |
|---|---|---|---|---|---|---|
| 1988-Feb | 46% | 6% | 78% | 9% | 24% | 49% |
| May | 38 | 7 | | | | |
| Aug | 34 | 8 | | | | |
| Nov | 29 | 11 | 24 | 35 | 8 | 58 |
| 1989-Feb | 29 | 9 | 27 | 23 | 10 | 49 |
| May | 27 | 12 | 19 | 30 | 13 | 40 |
| Aug | 24 | 11 | 8 | 52 | 2 | 77 |
| Nov | 32 | 10 | 11 | 47 | 3 | 67 |
| 1990-Feb | 33 | 7 | 22 | 25 | 11 | 45 |
| May | 34 | 8 | 20 | 34 | 8 | 55 |
| Aug | 30 | 9 | 27 | 27 | 30 | 25 |
| Nov | 39 | 8 | 20 | 30 | 18 | 40 |
| 1991-Feb | 24 | 15 | 14 | 51 | 7 | 63 |
| May | 24 | 11 | 18 | 39 | 13 | 47 |
| Aug | 20 | 18 | 18 | 46 | 13 | 41 |
| Nov | 28 | 12 | 25 | 33 | 19 | 37 |

Note: Other firms responded that economic conditions were "acceptable" or the investment climate "neutral."
Source: FEDESARROLLO, Entrepreneurial survey (unpublished data made available to the author).

break down, and to what extent the costs of the economic program now underway may contribute to an unfortunate outcome.

## Notes

1. This estimate assumes a capital-output ratio of 1.75 in 1925 (the first year for which National Accounts investment data are available) and depreciation rates of 2 % for public and private construction and 5 % for machinery and equipment. As Ocampo and Crane (1988) show, the trend and cycle of the capital-output ratio in the post-war period and the estimated growth of the capital stock are relatively independent of the assumptions on the initial stock and the depreciation rates. The estimate used is consistent with the stocks calculated by Harberger (1969) in a seminal article on the subject.

2. This is not true when this effect is not considered. See Ocampo and Crane (1988), Garcia (1988) and Clavijo (1990).

3. See Ocampo and Crane (1988), chapter 5. This result can also be obtained using alternative estimates of total factor productivity growth (see, for example, McCarthy et al., 1985; García 1988; Clavijo, 1990).

4. This is even so according to Roberts' (1988) work for the World Bank. Indeed, according to the statistical estimates of this study, an additional 1 % growth of industrial production is reflected in 0.4 % growth in total factor productivity. This effect explains, by itself, a difference in factor productivity growth of some 4 % between 1977−80 and 1980−83. On the contrary, the change in the ratio of imports to the domestic supply, which the author uses as the indicator of external competition, only explains a 0.2 % change in productivity during these years.

5. See the reference to Echavarría (1989) above and Sarmiento (1987).

6. Programa de Modernizacion de la Economía Colombiana, in Comercio Exterior, May, 1990.

7. This ratio is that necessary to define 1974 and 1979 as years of full capacity utilization, an assumption that is used in the model. According to the data provided in table 4.1, it took values of 4.2 in 1945−46, 3.9 in 1956−67, 2.6 in 1967−74, 3.3 in 1974−80 and 5.4 in 1980−87.

8. The "crowding-out" effect was obtained in simple econometric estimates of the parameters of the three-gap model. It largely reflects countercyclical management of public projects and structural changes in the roles of private and public investment in the 1970s. The latter were associated with increasing disregard for manufacturing and growing emphasis on the mining sector where public firms play a leading entrepreneurial role. More sophisticated econometric estimates have found a weak "crowding-in" effect of public on private capital formation.

9. Although the central government is a net debtor to the private sector, the decentralized public agencies are net creditors by an amount that makes the net internal debt of the consolidated public sector (excluding that with the central bank) negligible; 0.45 % of GDP in 1989 (see Restrepo, 1987, and FEDESARROLLO, Coyuntura Economica Andina, June 1988, pp. 80−87).

10. This macroeconomic package is part of a more general liberalization program, the elements of which are specified in Presidencia de la República and Departamento Nacional de Planeación, La Revolution Pacifica: Modernizacion y Apertura de la Economia Colombiana, vol. I, Bogotá, 1991.

11. The effects of these policies are simulated by revaluing the real exchange rate applicable to imports and nontraditional exports according to the tariff and subsidy schedules approved in late 1990. At the same time, the intercept of the government savings function is shifted downwards by the amount of the net reduction in fiscal revenue generated by these reforms.

12. This is actually a lagged effect on average annual levels of real devaluation implemented through 1990.

13. The expansionary effect of devaluation depends crucially on initial conditions, particularly the large current account surplus with the rest of the world. In fact, the relation between the real exchange rate and capacity utilization has a U shape, with

the minimum at a level of the real exchange rate somewhat below the historical average of the past two decades.

14. Preliminary estimates of economic growth and the consolidated public sector deficit in 1991 are not far from those projected in Scenario 6 (some 2 % and virtual fiscal equilibrium). The current account surplus was, on the contrary, significantly larger than the projection because a massive anti-inflation stabilization effort that was underway was reflected in a sharp cut in private investment. This weakened import demand despite real appreciation and the acceleration of tariff reform.

15. According to the information provided by the *Contraloria General de la Republica*, the ratio of central government taxes on domestic economic activities to GDP was only 6.9 % in 1990.

16. The acceleration of import tariff reforms in September 1991 as well as new government obligations created by the Constitutional Assembly in the same year generated additional fiscal complications, which the government attempted to deal with in its 1992 tax reform proposal.

17. Output expansion would be insufficient to absorb factor growth, including human capital (see table 4.1), and total factor productivity would continue to fall.

18. The account that follows is based on Echavarría et al. (1983), Chica (1988, 1990) and Ocampo (1991a).

19. See Ramirez (1990). This process seems to be associated basically with a movement along Engel's curve, reflecting the fall of processed foodstuffs, tobacco products, and clothing in consumer expenditure, accompanied by increasing service expenses.

20. Exporters were already allowed in 1985 to import, free of tariffs and licensing requirements, any intermediate and capital goods used in their productive processes, even if they were domestically produced. Thus, the elimination of QRs and tariffs will favorably affect exports only through general equilibrium channels. Given the aggressive exchange rate policy of recent years, however, both policy instruments held significant amounts of water and, thus, their liberalization would have weaker effects than usually claimed.

21. See note 4.

22. See a summary of some estimates in Caballero (1988).

## References

Bejarano, Jesús Antonio (1988). "Efectos de la Violencia en la Producción Agropecuaria." *Coyuntura Económica*, September.

Bergquist, Charles W. (1978). *Coffee and Conflict in Colombia, 1886–1910*. Durham: Duke University Press.

Berry, Albert 0. (1983). "A Descriptive History of Colombian Industrial Development in the Twentieth Century," in Albert Berry (ed.), *Essays on Industrialization in Colombia*. Tempe: Center for Latin American Studies, Arizona State University.

Caballero, Carlos (1988). "La Economía de la Cocaína, Algunos Estimativos para 1988," *Covuntura Económica*, September.

Carrizoza, Mauricio (1987). "Evolución y Determinantes de la Pobreza en Colombia," in José Antonio Ocampo and Manuel Ramírez, (eds.), *El Problema Laboral Colombiano: Informes Especiales de la Misión de Empleo*. Bogotá: Contraloría-DNP-SENA, chap. 7.

Chenery, Hollis, Sherman Robinson, and Moshe Syrquin (1986). *Industrialization and Growth: A Comparative Study*. New York: Oxford University Press.

Chica, Ricardo (1988). "Un Diagnóstico de la Crisis de la Acumulación de la Industrial Colombiana." *Desarrollo y Sociedad*, September.

Chica, Ricardo (1990). "El Estancamiento de la Industria Colombiana." *Coyuntura Económica*, June.

Clavijo, Sergio (1990). "Productividad Laboral, Multifactorial y Tasa de Cambio Real en Colombia." *Ensayos sobre Política Económica*, No. 17, June.

Comisión de Estudios Sobre la Violencia (1987). *Colombia: Violencia y Democracia*. Bogotá: Universidad Nacional de Colombia.

Correa, Patricia, and Jaime H. Escobar (1990). "Radiografia de la Inflación Actual." *Coyuntura Económica*, October.

de Gregorio, José (1991). "Economic Growth in Latin America." Paper presented at the Fourth Annual Interamerican Seminar on Economics. (Mimeo), Santiago.

Deas, Malcom (1990). "Una Tierra de Leones," *Lecturas Dominicales-El Tiempo*, Bogotá, March.

Departamento Nacional de Planeación (DNP, 1991a). "El Impacto de la Acción Terrorista sobre la Evolución de la Economía Colombiana en 1991." (Mimeo), February.

Departamento Nacional de Planeación (DNP, 1991b). "Programación Macroeconómica." (Mimeo), January.

Echavarría, Juan José (1989). "External Shocks and Industrialization in Colombia, 1920–1950." Oxford: Oxford University.

Echavarría, Juan José (1990a). "Cambio Técnico, Inversión y Reestructuración Industrial en Colombia." *Coyuntura Económica*, June.

Echavarría, Juan José (1990b). "Reestructuración, Apertura y Política Económica." *Debates de Covuntura Económica*, Bogotá, March.

Echavarría, Juan José, Carlos Caballero, and Juan Luis Londoño (1983). "El Proceso Colombiano de Industrialización: Algunas Ideas sobre un Viejo Debate." *Coyuntura Económica*, September.

Edwards, Sebastian (1984). "Coffee, Money and Inflation in Colombia." *World Development*, November–December.

FEDESARROLLO (1988). "La Inversión Privada en la Coyuntura Actual." *Coyuntura Económica*, March.

FEDESARROLLO (1990). "Editorial." *Coyuntura Económica*, March.

Garay, Luis Jorge and Alberto Carrasquilla (1987). "Dinámica del Desajuste y Proceso de Saneamiento Económico en Colombia en la Década de los Ochenta." *Ensayos sobre Política Economica*, June.

García, Jorge (1988). "Macroeconomic Crises, Macroeconomic Policies and Long-Run Growth (Part III): The Colombia Experience, 1950–1986," World Bank, July.

Gómez, Hernando José (1988). "La Economía Ilegal en Colombia: Tamaño, Evolución, Características e Impacto Económico," *Coyuntura Económica*, September.

Gómez, Hernando José (1990). "El Tamaño del Narcotráfico y su Impacto Económico," *Económia Colombiana*, February–March.

Harberger, Arnold (1969). "La Tasa de Rendimiento del Capital en Colombia," *Revista de Planeación y Desarrollo*, October.

Hjalmarsson, Lennart (1991). "The Scandinavian Model of Industrial Policy," in Magnus Blomström and Patricio Meller, eds., *Diverging Paths: A Century of Scandinavian and Latin American Economic Development*. Baltimore: John Hopkins University Press.

IDEMA (1990). "Propuesta para la Fijación de los Precios de Sustentación-Cosecha 1990," (Mimeo), February.

Junguito, Roberto (1986). *Memoria del Ministro de Hacienda*, Bogotá: Banco de la República.

Kalmanovitz, Salomón (1978). *El Desarrollo de la Agricultura en Colombia*, Bogotá: La Carreta.

Landau, Luis (1971). "Saving Functions for Latin America," in Hollis H. Chenery, ed., *Studies in Development Planning*, Cambridge: Harvard University Press.

LeGrand, Catherine (1988). *Colonización y Protesta Campesina en Colombia (1850–1950)*, Bogotá: Universidad Nacional de Colombia.

Londoño, Juan Luis (1987). "La Dinámica Laboral y el Ritmo de Actividad Económica: Un Repaso Empírico de la Última Década," in José Antonio Ocampo and Manuel Ramírez, eds., *El Problema Laboral Colombiano. Informes Especiales de la Misión de Empleo* (Vol. II). Bogotá: Contraloría General de la República-DNP-SENA.

Londoño, Juan Luis (1989a). "Agricultura y Transformación Estructural: Una Comparación Internacional," *Revista de Planeación y Desarrollo*, July–December.

Londoño, Juan Luis (1989b). "Distribución Nacional del Ingreso en 1988: Una Mirada en Perspectiva." *Coyuntura Social*, No. 1, December.

Londoño, Juan Luis (1990). *Income Distribution During the Structural Transformation: Colombia. 1938–1988*. Ph.D. Dissertation, Harvard University.

Londoño, Juan Luis, and Guillermo Perry (1985). "El Banco Muncial, el Fondo Monetario Internacional y Colombia: Análisis Crítico de sus Relaciones." *Coyuntura Económica*, October.

López, Hugo, Oliva Sierra, and Martha Luz Henao (1987). "Sector Informal: Entronque Económico y Desconexión Jurídico-Política con la Sociedad Moderna," in José Antonio Ocampo and Manuel Ramírez (eds.), *El Problema Laboral Colombiano. Informes Especiales de la Misión de Empleo*, Vol. 2. Bogotá: Contraloría General de la República-DNP-SENA.

Lora, Eduardo, and José Antonio Ocampo (1987). "Colombia," in *Stabilization* and Adjustment Policies and Programs. Country Study No. 6. Helsinki: WIDER.

Lora, Eduardo, and Catalina Crane (1991). "La Apertura y la Recuperación del Crecimiento Económico," in Eduardo Lora (ed.), *Apertura y Crecimiento: E Reto de los Noventa*. Bogotá: Tercer Mundo-FEDESARROLLO, Ch. 3.

Lorente, Juis, Armando Salazar, and Angela Gallo (1985). *Distribución de la Propiedad Rural en Colombia: 1960–1984*. Bogotá: Ministerio de Agricultura and CEGA.

Losada, Rodrigo, and Eduardo Vélez (1989). "Tendencias de Muertes Violentas en Colombia." *Coyuntura Social*, No. 1, December.

McCarthy, Desmond, James Hanson, and Soonwan Kwon (1985). "Fuentes de Crecimeinto en Colombia." *Revista de Planeación y Desarrollo*, June.

Ministerio de Desarrollo (1990). "La Coyuntura Inflacionaria y el Sector Externo." (Mimeo), October.

Ministerio de Desarrollo Económico (1991). "Propuesta de Medidas de Apoyo a los Afectados porel Terrorismo." (Mimeo), March.

Misión de Empleo (1986). "El Problema Laboral Colombiano: Disgnóstico, Perspectivas y Políticas." *Economía Colombiana*, Separata No. 10, August–September.

Ócampo, José Antonio (1988). "Una Nota sobre la Relación entre Financiamiento Externo, Ahorro e Inversión." *Ensayos sobre Política Económica*, No. 13, June.

Ócampo, José Antonio (1989a). "Ciclo Cafetero y Comportamiento Macroeconómico en Colombia, 1940–1987." *Coyuntura Económica*, October and December.

Ócampo, José Antonio (1989b). "Colombia and the Latin American Debt Crisis," in Sebastian Edwards and Felipe Larraín (eds.), *Debt, Adjustment and Recovery: Latin America's Prospects for Growth and Development*. Oxford: Basil Blackwell.

Ócampo, José Antonio (1989c). "El Desarrollo Económico," in Eduardo Lora and José Antonio Ocampo (eds.), *Introduccíon a la Macroeconomía Colombiana*. Bogotá: FEDESARROLLO-Tercer Mundo.

Ócampo, José Antonio (1989d). "El Proceso Ahorro-Inversión y sus Determinantes en Colombia," in Carlos Caballero Argáez (ed.), *Macroeconomía. Mercado de Capitales y Negocio Financiero*. Bogotá: Asociación Bancaria de Colombia.

Ócampo, José Antonio (1990a). "La Apertura Externa en Perspectiva," in Florángela Gómez (ed.), *Apertura Económica y Sistema Financiero*. Bogotá: Asociación Bancaria de Colombia.

Ócampo, José Antonio (1990b). "Import Controls, Prices and Economic Activity in Colombia." *Journal of Development Economics*, Vol. 32, No. 2, April.

Ócampo, José Antonio (1991). "The Transition from Primary Exports to Industrial Development in Colombia," in Magnus Blomström and Patricio Meller (eds.), *Diverging Paths: A Century of Scandinavian and Latin American Economic Development.* Baltimore: Johns Hopkins University Press.

Ócampo, José Antonio (1992). "Trade and Industrialization in Colombia (1967–1991)" in G. K. Helleiner (ed.), *Trade and Industrialization Reconsidered.* Forthcoming.

Ócampo, José Antonio (1993). "El Proceso Colombiano de Industrialización." Forthcoming in a volume on the History of Industrialization in Latin America, edited by Enrique Cárdenas. Mexico: Fondo de Cultura Económica.

Ócampo, José Antonio, and Catalina Crane (1988). *Ahorro, Inversión y Crecimiento Económico en Colombia.* Research Report presented to the Inter-American Development ment Bank, FEDESARROLLO. (A summary of this report was published in IDB, *Social and Economic Development of Latin America,* 1989, chapter 8, Part B).

Ramírez, Clara (1990). "Sector Productivo y Desarrollo Tecnológico: Incorporación de Innovaciones Tecnológicas a los Procesos Productivos," in Misión de Ciencia y Tecnología. *Estructura Científica, Desarrollo Tecnológico y Entorno Social,* Vol. II-2. Bogotá: DNP.

Restrepo, Jorge E. (1987). "Financiamiento del Déficit fiscal del Sector Público no Financiero." (Mimeo), Paper presented at the Meeting of Central Banks in Brasilia.

Reyes, Alvaro (1987). "Tendencias del Empleo y la Distribución del Ingreso," in José Antonio Ocampo and Manuel Ramírez (eds.), *El Problema Laboral Colomiano, Informes Especiales de la Misión de Empleo.* Bogotá: Contraloría General de la República-DNP-SENA.

Roberts, Mark J. (1988). "The Structure of Production in Colombian Manufacturing Industries, 1977–1985." (Mimeo), October.

Sánchez, Fabio (1992). "Tiene la Inversión Pública un Efecto "Crowding Out" sobre la Inversión Privada en Colombia?" (Mimeo), FEDESARROLLO, April.

Sánchez, Gonzalo, and Ricardo Peñaranda (eds.) (1986). *Pasado y Presente de la Violencia en Colombia.* Bogotá: CEREC.

Sandoval, Diego (1982). "Fuentes de Crecimiento en la Productividad de la Industria Manufacturera Colombiana, 1966–1975." *Desarrollo y Sociedad,* No. 7, January.

Sarmiento, Eduardo (1987). *Hacia un Modelo de Crecimiento Equitativo.* Bogotá: Universidad de los Andes.

Syrquin, Moshe (1987). "Crecimiento Económico y Cambio Estructural en Colombia: Una Comparación Internacional." *Coyuntura Económica,* December.

Uribe, Tomás (1987). "Evolución de la Inseguridad Alimentaria en Colombia." *Coyuntura Económica,* April.

Urrutia, Miguel (1984). *Los de Arriba y los de Abajo*. Bogotá: FEDESARROLLO-CEREC.

Villar, Leonardo (1991). "Las Restricciones al Crecimiento Económico: Un Modelo Sencillo de Tres Brechas," in Eduardo Lora (ed.), *Apertura y Crecimiento: El Reto de los Noventa*. Bogotá: Tercer Mundo-FEDESARROLLO, Ch. 4.

World Bank (1989). "Colombia: Commercial Policy Survey." (Mimeo), February.

# 5    Chile

## Andres Solimano

At the outset of the 1990, Chile's government switched from a 17-year-old authoritarian regime to an open democratic system. In light of this change, it is high time to look at the recent performance and the new challenges the economy is expected to face.

By 1991, Chile had been running a six-year expansion under conditions of moderate though stubborn inflation, without serious fundamental macro imbalances, and with significant progress in reducing external debt. However, poverty alleviation appeared in the agenda of all political groups in the last election and was taken as a major policy goal by the Aylwin administration, which took power in early 1990. Besides progressive redistribution, the economic issues of the day are how to preserve and enhance the output growth and export expansion and diversification of the last six years, while avoiding overheating (as in 1989) and preserving macroeconomic stability.

Three policy problems will be of critical importance in the near future. The first is how to conduct macroeconomics in the new institutional setting of an independent and indebted Central Bank. The bank's indebtedness sets a kind of "inflationary floor" under the economy, because the part of its debt service not covered by transfers from the treasury is financed by monetary emission.

A second area of concern is the macroeconomic effect of a fiscal package comprising a rise in corporate income taxes used to finance increased transfers to low income groups. An assessment of the likely effects on private investment is carried out. We also report simulation results of the effects of an expansion of social expenditure on GDP growth, the real exchange rate, and real wages. Third, a simple model is used to evaluate the quantitative effects of an increase in minimum wages on the price level, average real wages, and the real exchange rate. The paper closes with a discussion of the possibilities for growth and the political economy of the transition in Chile.

## 5.1  The Chilean Economy in the 1990s

The economy experienced sharp fluctuations in activity during the 1980s. They started with the exchange rate-based stabilization of the period 1979–82, when a debt-led boom developed, followed by a severe recession and the financial crises in 1982–83, until a period of recovery and growth began after 1984.

### 5.1.1  Exchange Rate Based Stabilization: 1979–82

A failed attempt at stabilization began in June 1979 when, after a moderate stepwise devaluation, the exchange rate was fixed for an undetermined period of time in an attempt to bring inflation to international levels. The absence of fiscal imbalances and a low, uniform tariff structure were thought to complement the exchange rate policy, but in fact the inflation rate remained stubbornly positive. The experiment had to be abandoned in June 1982, when the exchange rate was finally devalued in the midst of a severe recession and worsened external conditions.

The stabilization attempt took place during a period of booming economic activity, rising real wages, and overexpanding financial intermediation in a context of heavy foreign borrowing. Severe misalignments in key relative prices and foreign and domestic overindebtedness rendered the economy particularly vulnerable to adverse shocks. With ongoing inflation, the real exchange rate appreciated and unsustainable current accounts deficits developed—14.5 % of GDP in 1981—as exports started to be squeezed and imports boomed. High domestic real interest rates, mainly in 1981, sowed the seeds of financial crisis as debt accumulation by domestic firms and households with the financial system (the counterpart of heavy foreign borrowing) reached unsustainable levels.

### 5.1.2  The Crisis of 1982–83

During 1982–83, there was a severe recession as a consequence of external shocks and previous domestic policy mistakes.[1] In 1981, tight money and high real interest rates (without devaluing the exchange rate) were used in an attempt to correct the external imbalance, but by mid-1982, the government began to attack overvaluation by a series of discrete devaluations followed by a crawling peg. Fiscal and monetary policies were clearly restrictive to support the exchange rate policy and reduce domestic absorption. Real GDP fell by around 15 % in 1982–83, imports were cut by half in real terms, investment collapsed, and open unemployment rates climbed to almost 20 %. Many firms started to face large debts and depressed demand. The financial sector became very fragile, with an important part of the loans of the major financial institutions becoming nonperforming. The banking crisis further curtailed the supply of domestic credit, ultimately forcing the Central Bank to intervene in several financial institutions and undertake massive rescue operations and, in some cases, liquidation.

### 5.1.3   Recovery and Growth after 1984

Recovery began in 1984. During the period 1984–89, real GDP grew at an impressive 6.3 % per year, while annual inflation averaged 20.4 %, a low level by Latin American standards. Growth took place with reduced reliance on external savings (see the fall in the current account deficit in table 5.1) and consolidation of internal financial stability. Looking at this performance, important questions arise: What are the sources of growth in this period? Is the current record sustainable? What explains the fact that the recovery has been noninflationary while the real exchange rate depreciated by over 45 % in the last six years and a financial crisis led monetary authorities to reshuffle major intermediaries? To what extent have the benefits from higher growth been shared by labor and other low income groups?

Table 5.2 shows that growth since 1984 has been driven mostly by exports and investment rather than consumption. Total exports increased by 8.9 % per year whereas aggregate consumption averaged only 4.2 %. Investment has been growing from an initial low level at an average rate of 25 %, with large fluctuations that may reflect the building up of inventories. As a share of GDP, investment recovered from 13.6 % in 1984 to 22 % in 1989.

What explains the rapid increases in exports, investment, and growth in the last six years? The exchange rate policy played a preeminent role in the expansion of exports and import competing activities in that period. A higher and relatively stable real exchange rate enhanced profitability of producing for external markets—a stimulus mainly to noncopper exports. The increase in the basic tariff rate from 10 % to 20 % and indirect tax reimbursement for exports contributed to tradable goods expansion in general. Idle capacity (until 1987) and a large unemployed labor reserve also helped.

In addition to supportive macroeconomic policies and a competitive real exchange rate, the rapid expansion of nontraditional exports in Chile (fresh fruit, fish, paper, timber) was based upon institutional factors and structural

**Table 5.1**
Macroeconomic indicators for Chile, 1980–89

| | GDP growth (%) (1) | Inflation rate (%) (2) | Fiscal deficit[a] % of GDP (3) | Current account deficit (%) (4) | Real exchange rate (1980 = 100) (5) | Real interest rate (%) (90–365 days) (6) | Terms of trade (1980 = 100) (7) | Average real wages (8) | Real minimum wages (9) |
|---|---|---|---|---|---|---|---|---|---|
| 1980 | 7.8 | 31.2 | −3.1 | 7.1 | 100.0 | 8.4 | 100.0 | 100.0 | 100.0 |
| 1981 | 5.5 | 9.5 | −1.7 | 14.5 | 90.9 | 13.2 | 84.3 | 108.9 | 115.7 |
| 1982 | −14.1 | 20.7 | 2.3 | 9.5 | 108.8 | 12.1 | 80.4 | 108.6 | 117.2 |
| 1983 | −0.7 | 23.1 | 3.8 | 5.7 | 135.6 | 7.7 | 87.5 | 97.1 | 94.2 |
| 1984 | 6.3 | 23.0 | 4.0 | 10.7 | 144.1 | 8.4 | 83.2 | 97.2 | 80.7 |
| 1985 | 2.4 | 26.4 | 6.3 | 8.3 | 179.4 | 8.2 | 78.5 | 93.5 | 76.4 |
| 1986 | 5.7 | 17.4 | 2.8 | 6.5 | 175.5 | 4.1 | 79.0 | 95.1 | 73.6 |
| 1987 | 5.7 | 21.5 | 0.1 | 4.3 | 170.8 | 4.2 | 83.0 | 94.7 | 69.1 |
| 1988 | 7.4 | 12.7 | 1.7 | 0.8 | 181.9 | 4.6 | 100.0 | 101.0 | 73.4 |
| 1989 | 10.0 | 21.1 | −3.0 | 3.0 | 177.5 | 6.77 | 105.0 | 102.9 | 79.7 |
| 1990 | 2.1 | 27.3 | −1.3 | 3.5 | 161.8 | | 91.4 | 104.7 | 86.9 |

a. Minus indicates surplus.
Source: *Boletín Mensual* (Various issues). Banco Central de Chile, CEPAL (1990). Informe Preliminar de la Economía de America Latina, el Caribe, United Nations.

**Table 5.2**
Sources of growth in Chile, 1984–89

| | Consumption | | Investment | | Exports | | Imports | | GDP |
|---|---|---|---|---|---|---|---|---|---|
| | rate of growth (%) | share of GDP (%) | rate of growth (%) | share of GDP (%) | rate of growth (%) | share of GDP (%) | rate of growth (%) | share of GDP (%) | rate of growth (%) |
| 1984 | 1.3 | 87.4 | 75.4 | 13.6 | 6.8 | 24.3 | 16.5 | 25.3 | 6.3 |
| 1985 | − 1.0 | 83.5 | −6.7 | 13.7 | 6.9 | 29.1 | − 11.1 | 26.3 | 2.4 |
| 1986 | 3.8 | 81.6 | 14.3 | 14.6 | 9.8 | 30.6 | 9.6 | 26.8 | 5.7 |
| 1987 | 3.8 | 79.0 | 25.8 | 16.9 | 8.8 | 33.5 | 17.1 | 29.4 | 7.7 |
| 1988 | 9.0 | 75.8 | 8.5 | 17.0 | 6.1 | 37.4 | 12.1 | 30.2 | 7.4 |
| 1989[a] | 8.1 | 77.0 | 32.6 | 22.0 | 14.8 | 29.0 | 26.3 | 28.0 | 10.0 |

a. Estimate
Source: The World Bank

changes carried out in the 1960s and 1970s. CORFO's (Corporación de Fomento de la Producción) plan of fruit growing (1968) and the afforestation activities of 1966–73 boosted agricultural development and the ability to export in these areas. Despite transitional problems, the agrarian reform of 1965–73 modernized the sector from its *latifundio* (quasi-feudal) structure. After 1974 a new process of land redistribution, sale by tender and auctioning—starting from the structure left after the agrarian reform—took place, giving rise to an active land market needed to support a more competitive environment in agriculture.[2]

Investment has been stimulated by various factors.[3] In addition to the rebound of public investment, the reduction in real interest rates undoubtedly contributed to higher private investment. Monetary policy targeted real rates in a financial market characterized by the extensive use of indexed financial instruments.[4] Tax incentives also played an important role in the investment increase, as the rate on corporate incomes was reduced from 46 % to 10 %; the proportion of profits that are reinvested received a preferential tax treatment over the dividends (distributed profits).

As table 5.1 shows, growth accelerated at the end of the decade. One contributing factor was a period of unexpectedly high copper prices beginning in 1987. Another was related to the political business cycle. Highly expansionary monetary policy was pursued in the second half of 1988— $M_1$ grew nearly 50 %—as a plebiscite over the permanence of the military regime took place in October. Given the traditional lags, the stimulative effects of the late 1988 monetary expansion were largely felt in 1989.

The presidential and parliamentary election of December 1989 was also preceded by a rather lax monetary stance, reflected in an acceleration of inflation in the last quarter. During 1990, the Central Bank sharply tightened monetary policy in order to slow output growth, from 10% in 1989 to about 2% for 1990. At the same time, inflation accelerated slightly and the real minimum wage rose slightly (table 5.1).

### 5.1.4   Inflation Control

Two factors help explain Chile's success in controlling inflation.[5] First, the devaluations starting in 1982 were accompanied by deindexation of wages; thus a real depreciation did not require the erosion of real wages through a permanent acceleration in inflation. Unemployment, reaching levels over 20% in 1982–83 and remaining fairly high until 1987, deterred workers from attempting to recover the real wages lost after the crisis of 1982. Clearly absent in Chile was the "classic" price-wage-exchange rate spiral resulting from an attempt to modify the real exchange rate while maintaining wage indexation and monetary accommodation. However the "Chilean way" was not costless in terms of economic activity and regressive redistribution, although the costs were tilted toward the first phase of the adjustment process.

The second factor was fiscal. The strain on the public sector accounts (broadly defined) resulting from the crises of 1982–83 centered mainly on the quasi-fiscal deficit as realized in budget of the Central Bank. The deterioration stemmed from higher domestic currency costs of servicing the external debt and the rescue program for troubled financial institutions set up by the Central Bank. These adverse shocks were not strongly inflationary for two main reasons. First, the nonfinancial public sector in Chile ran a surplus before interest payments, transferring part to the Central Bank to cover its new losses. Second, the rescue operations for troubled financial institutions were carried out through issuing interest bearing liabilities of the Central Bank rather than high-powered money on a massive scale.

These novel Central Bank obligations were used to finance debt-relief schemes for borrowers from the banking system, to purchase risky loans by the Central Bank with a (generous) repurchase obligation on the part of a bank's shareholders, and to recapitalization and subsequent sale (financed with government credit and subsidies) of intervened banks to small investors (the "capitalismo popular" scheme).[6]

This whole scheme of reshuffling the banking system involved placement of large amounts of Central Bank bonds in local financial markets.

That required a corresponding increase in demand. The rapid recovery of the Chilean economy since 1984 certainly was instrumental in that regard. However, the new Central Bank interest-bearing liabilities are partly financed by money creation, making it difficult to reduce inflation below about 20 % per year in spite of the absence of fiscal imbalances.[7]

### 5.1.5    Benefits and Costs of Adjustment

A key and difficult question is the distributional incidence of macro policies in Chile. Table 5.1 shows that average real wages recovered their 1980 level just in 1988 and that minimum wages in real terms were still 20 percentage points below their 1980 level and 35 points below their 1982 level. Labor, and particularly low wage groups, paid a significant share of the costs of adjustment in Chile. The benefits for labor of the recovery after 1984 have taken more the form of higher employment rather than real wage growth.

The step from the functional to personal income distribution is hard to make, particularly in the case of Chile because of the absence of recent comprehensive information on distribution. However, actions such as cuts in some items of social spending, for example, pension payments, and the squeeze on public sector wages suggest that low and middle income groups suffered in the adjustment process. The incidence of the costs on high income groups is less clear since their income tax rates were reduced. Asset transfer in the privatizations that took place after 1985 and the granting of subsidies to the financial sector provide clues that high income groups were well shielded from the costs of adjustment.

## 5.2    Policy Issues for the 1990s

Three development issues appear to be central for the early and mid-1990s: (1) the new legislation of an independent Central Bank, its current indebtedness, and the interactions between fiscal and monetary policy under the new institutional setting, (2) the macroeconomic effects of financing fiscal transfers to poor income groups, and (3) the impact of wage policy and changes in labor legislation.

### 5.2.1    An Independent Central Bank

The new law for the Chilean Central Bank (CHCB) was released in 1989. It makes the CHCB autonomous and assigns as its basic role "the preservation of the stability of the currency and the normal operations of domestic and external payments." The Bank's board of directors is to be nominated by the President and ratified by Congress. Under this scheme the fiscal authorities play no explicit, formal, role in the appointment or removal of the CHCB's directors. In addition, the Bank is forbidden to provide directly or indirectly any credit to the Treasury, other fiscal entity, or public enterprise.

The notion of an independent central bank has a long history in the literature on monetary institutions (Yeager, 1962). Commodity standards, fixed exchange rates, constitutional monetary rules, and a currency tied to a stable partner are the staples of the no-government approach to monetary policy. Prominent monetary economists from David Ricardo through Henry Simons to Milton Friedman have preferred monetary rules over any other options to assure a sound currency.[8] More or less independent central banks operate in the United States, West Germany, and Switzerland, but the degree of fiscal involvement in the shaping of monetary policy in these countries seems to be greater than the one granted in the new CHCB charter in Chile (see Marshall, 1989).

Let us turn to the balance sheet of the CHCB in order to detect its current level of indebtedness and the direction and magnitude of the transfers between the Treasury and the Central Bank that are envisaged for the near future in Chile.

The debt of the Chilean Central bank is determined, to a large extent, by the role it played in the resolution of the financial crises of 1982–83. In 1983–85, the bank issued interest-bearing domestic liabilities (on behalf of the Treasury) valued at $7.8 billion (U.S.) to buy nonperforming assets of troubled financial institutions, to sell foreign exchange at a preferential rate for external debt servicing, and to finance debt rescheduling programs.[9] In exchange, the Central Bank received assets at a value of $6.8 billion although some $3.0 billion were non-performing:[10] a heavy burden on the net position of the Central Bank.

The counterpart of the increase in CHCB liabilities is a liability from the treasury to the Central Bank. In 1989 the treasury formalized the arrangement by placing a "big" bond of $7.3 billion with the Central Bank. The proceeds will let the CHCB to honor the interest payments associated with its liabilities. Following Rodriguez (1989), table 5.3 summarizes the balance sheet of the Central Bank for 1988.

The bank's new interest-bearing liabilities amount to 35 % of GDP, undoubtedly a large number. In terms of cash flows, total annual revenues of

**Table 5.3**
Balance sheet of the Central Bank of Chile (millions of dollars, December 1988)

| Assets | Liabilities |
|---|---|
| International reserves = 2600.0 | 7800.0 = Domestic interest bearing liabilities |
| Treasury bond    = 7300.0 | 4500.0 = Net external debt |
| Private sector assets held by the Central Bank    = 6800.0 | 1000.0 = Monetary base |
|  | 3400.0 = Capital and provisions |
| Total = 16700.0 | 16700.0 = Total |

Note: GDP in millions of dollars = 22068.0.

the Central Bank are estimated at around $711 million and its service on internal and external debt is $974 million. The resulting cash flow deficit of the Central Bank is about 1% of GDP. The interest burden of the treasury on the "big bond" is LIBOR plus 0.50%; however, the cash flow servicing has been stipulated at 2% on the present dollar value of the bond, the rest being capitalized. Current cash payments amount to $146 million. Ultimately this represents a transfer from taxpayers to domestic and foreign holders of debt issued by the CHCB. The outcome is that the newly independent Central Bank receives a net transfer from the treasury (the debt service of the government bond) but does not share the revenues from money creation (inflation tax receipts plus seignorage) with the fiscal authorities.

One important implication of the CHCB's independent status is that its flows of funds can no longer be consolidated with those of the "fisc" for purposes of financial programming, because provision of credit from the Central Bank to the government is forbidden. Solimano (1992) works through the details of the two institutions' budget constraints. For policy coordination several issues are important, with the potential budgetary impacts of exchange rate adjustment for both the Central Bank and the Treasury being particularly relevant. A real currency devaluation will worsen the budget of the Central Bank so long as its international reserves fall short of its outstanding external debt, a condition that is clearly fulfilled nowadays as table 5.3 indicates.

The impact on the fiscal budget of a currency depreciation depends on its effects on the revenue of trade taxes in domestic currency, the net profits of public enterprises (e.g., copper), and the real value in local currency of servicing the Treasury's external debt. Larrañaga and Marshall (1989) provide empirical evidence that in Chile the nonfinancial public sector budget improves with a higher real exchange rate.

Another question is raised by the fact that the liquidity and net worth of the Central Bank are dependent on the ability of the Treasury to continue servicing its $7.3 billion bond, that is, the Central Bank's main asset is the government's liability.

A third source of interdependence between both institutions lies in the fact that the seignorage accruing to the Central Bank (but not shared with any fiscal entity) depends on the rate of growth of GDP, a magnitude that can be influenced by fiscal policy variables such as the level of public investment, corporate taxes affecting private investment, and fiscal deficits affecting real interest rates.

A final set of questions hinges around debt. The new legislation assumes that both the government and the Central Bank can issue external as well as internal debt separately. On the one hand, external debt is sovereign, for example, it is assumed by the state of Chile and therefore subject to fiscal and parliamentary approval. On the other hand, the new CHCB charter requires the Central Bank to ensure "the maintenance of normal domestic and foreign payments operations." An obvious role for the bank to play is to advise the treasury to abstain from excessive external borrowing (in times of voluntary lending), that increases default risk and threatens compliance with the "normal external payments" proviso of the charter.

In regard to internal debt, the Central bank and the Treasury have to compete in domestic capital markets. Their placements will affect the interest rate, with obvious budgetary implications for both institutions. Here as in other areas, policy coordination will make the Bank and Treasury less independent than the framers of Chile's recent legislation may have desired.

### 5.2.2   Corporate Taxes and Social Spending

The new government in Chile is committed to reducing poverty and improving the personal income distribution. According to Pollack and Uthoff (1989) and Torche (1988), the population under the poverty line in Chile is sizable, in spite of the good macroeconomic performance of the economy over the last few years.

In 1990, an agreement was reached between government and congress to combine an increase in corporate and income taxes with a rise in the value-added tax rate, in order to increase revenues for financing a program of social expenditure. The targets include increased spending in education and health as well as augmented direct transfers to low income groups.[11]

To assess the likely impacts of this package, we can begin by asking how higher corporate taxes may affect economic growth. The issue is complex, and here we can only discuss the main channels and provide illustrative orders of magnitude of the effects of the tax on private investment.

One obvious channel is via profitability. Short-term demand consider-ations and the role of uncertainty are also examined in order to get a more complete picture of some likely effects of an increase in corporate income tax on private investment.

*The Profitability Effect*
What happens to the cost of capital as the corporate profit tax is increased? Considerations regarding how a firm finances investment (typically just by retained earnings and bank borrowing in Chile) and its anticipations of future tax changes are likely to arise.[12] The new tax code will eliminate the distinction between dividends and retained profits for the purpose of computing corporate profit taxes. The main effect is to increase the rela-tive cost of financing investment by retained earnings. The overall cost of capital would rise insofar as retained earnings and bank credit are imperfect substitutes.

What about the impact of the profitability effect on investment? An econometric estimation of a private investment function that incorporates profitability draws from Solimano (1989):[13]

$$\ln(IP/Y) = 3.68 + 0.22 \ln(Q) + 0.77 \ln(y) - 0.002 \ln(\sigma_Q) - 0.12 \ln(\sigma_y)$$
$$(3.17) \quad (2.09) \qquad (3.29) \qquad (-0.11) \qquad (-3.83)$$

$$+ 0.126 \ln(C/P) + 0.32 \ln(IP_{-1}/y) + 0.41 \text{ DUM} \qquad (5.1)$$
$$(2.78) \qquad (2.55) \qquad (2.93)$$

$R^2 = 0.83$

$DW = 2.19$

This log-linear equation shows that the (log) ratio of private investment to detrended GDP in Chile, $\ln(IP/y)$, is explained by profitability, $\ln(Q)$, measured as the ratio of the average stock price index over the replacement value of capital, by the level of (detrended) output, $\ln(y)$, the real stock of credit, $\ln(C/P)$, and the variances of profitability, $\ln(\sigma_Q)$, and output, $\ln(\sigma_y)$. The equation says that a 1% increase in profitability will raise private investment by 0.22%. If a corporate profits tax rate increase of 10 percentage points gives rise to a decline in investment profitability of, say, 2 percentage points,[14] then private investment will be reduced by 0.44 of a percentage point on account of the profitability effect.

*Demand Effects*
The econometrics suggests that private investment is sensitive to variations in spending and GDP. If the propensity to spend of profit earners (who will be paying higher taxes) is lower than the propensity to spend of low income groups (who will receive a higher real income from increased fiscal transfers financed by the rise in taxation), aggregate demand will increase. The size of this effect will depend on both the differences in the propensities to spend between income groups and the elasticity of private investment with respect to output.

*Uncertainty Macro Stability and Distortions*
Private investment is sensitive to the degree of macroeconomic instability in the economy. How is perceived (in)stability affected by an increase in corporate profit taxes? On the one hand, tax-financed social spending certainly tends to moderate macro imbalances—in terms of fiscal and current account deficits or inflation—as compared to a money-financed fiscal expansion. On the other hand, the choice between alternative taxes for financing the fiscal expansion in social sectors, for example, value-added taxes vis-à-vis corporate taxes—involves issues of efficiency in tax collection, the degree of tax-induced distortions, and effects on income distribution. How to balance these three criteria is basically a normative issue. Finally, the rules of the taxation game are as important as tax levels in terms of reducing uncertainty, a factor to which private investment is particularly sensitive.

We now turn to a quantitative assessment of some macro effects of raising public expenditure in social sectors. The size of the fiscal transfer is assumed to be 3 % of GDP: For a GDP of $22 billion that amounts to $660 million, close to the figure being considered by the authorities in Chile (Solimano, 1992).

A main result of table 5.4 is that an increase in public spending of 3 % of GDP without an accompanying tax increase slows the rate of growth of output by nearly 1 percentage point, due to the reduction in public savings and thereby aggregate investment in a savings-driven model closure.[15] This solution also requires a real appreciation of the exchange rate of 5.4 % to preserve goods market equilibrium at full capacity. The current account

**Table 5.4**
Effects of an increase in public spending of 3 % of potential GDP (capacity-constrained growth regime)

|  | Base year solution (1) | Solution with a 3 % increase in gov't. spending share (2) | Difference (2)−(1) percentage (3) |
|---|---|---|---|
| Rate of growth of GDP, % | 6.43 | 5.36 | −1.07 |
| Real exchange rate (index) | 110.27 | 104.88 | −5.39 |
| Real wages index | 100.00 | 104.36 | 4.36 |
| Rate of growth of GDP (%) under a balanced increase in public spending (matched extra fiscal revenue of 3 % of GDP | 6.43 | 6.43 | 0.0 |

Source: Solimano (1992).

deficit widens and will require additional external financing. On the other hand, the real appreciation brings about an increase in real wages by 4.4 %, potentially creating a trade-off between wages and employment growth.

A main lesson of this exercise is that in order to avoid a trade-off between enhanced social public expenditure (pursued through an unbalanced fiscal expansion) and growth in a capacity-constrained economy, it is necessary to avert a reduction in government savings. Because the terms of the trade-off are not trivial, social sector spending has to be met by increased taxation, lower tax evasion, or reduced government spending in other sectors.

### 5.2.3   Wage Policy and Changes in Labor Legislation

The new administration announced changes in wage policy and labor legislation with macroeconomic implications that are worth exploring. In addition, we can expect a change in the process of wage determination as a result of the ongoing process of redemocratization and changes in labor legislation.

For analytical purposes, it is appropriate to explore the effects of an increase in the minimum wage—a key policy instrument—on inflation, average real wages, and the real exchange rate. A simple three-equation model can be set up and evaluated empirically with plausible values of the parameters for the Chilean case.[16] The equations respectively describe

1. A cost-based inflation process wherein the growth rate of the national price level $P$ responds to growth in the nominal wage $W$ and the real cost of imports $EP^*$ (where $E$ is the nominal exchange rate and $P^*$ the foreign price level) with weights of $a$ and $1 - a$ respectively.

2. The nominal wage in turn responds to price increases (with $b$ as an indexation elasticity), the minimum wage (elasticity $c$), and the ratio of real to potential GDP (elasticity $d$).

3. The nominal exchange rate is indexed to the differential between the growth rates of national and foreign prices, with an elasticity $h$.

Under the assumption that the economy is at full capacity, an empirical evaluation of the macroeconomic effects of an increase in minimum wages of 20 % is provided in table 5.5. These estimates are carried out under various degrees of wage and exchange rate indexation. The results show that the inflationary effect of a rise in minimum wages is closely related to the degree of indexation in the economy. With no indexation, a 20 % increase in minimum wages will be associated with an increase in the price level of only 2.4 %. In the intermediate case, the rise in the price level reaches 7.1 %. In the high indexation case the rise in prices is about 85 % of the increase in minimum wages, say, 17.2 %.

The main result is the extreme sensitivity of the price level to the degree of wage and exchange rate indexation. An important policy conclusion is that for avoiding large inflationary effects of the wage policy it does not seem advisable to raise the degree of wage indexation in the economy.

**Table 5.5**
Effects of an increase of minimum wages by 20 % (percentages; $a = 0.4$, $c = 0.3$)[a]

| Degree of indexation | No indexation ($b = h = 0$) | Intermediate indexation ($b = 0.6$; $h = 0.7$) | High indexation ($b = 0.8$; $h = 0.9$) |
|---|---|---|---|
| Effect on: the price level, P | 2.4 | 7.1 | 17.2 |
| Average real wages W/P | 3.6 | 3.2 | 2.6 |
| Real exchange rate EP*/P | −2.4 | −2.2 | −1.7 |

a. The coefficient, $a$, draws from Jadresic (1985) and the coefficient, $c$, from Solimano (1988).

A further interesting result is that the effect of a rise in minimum wages on average real wages is inversely related to the degree of overall wage and exchange rate indexation. The rationale lies in the fact that a higher degree of wage and exchange rate indexation exacerbates the impact on the price level of an autonomous wage (or supply) shock, therefore eroding its effect on real wage. Finally, the size of the real appreciation that is expected to come along with an increase in minimum wages is rather small for moderate increases in minimum wages.

We can wind up our discussion of the labor market by sketching some effects a change in the labor legislation inherited from the military regime—the "Plan Laboral"—may have on employment and wages. The old legal framework, dating from 1979, was a permanent source of dispute because of its alleged role in allowing ample room for worker's dismissals, limiting the effectiveness of strikes, and imposing binding constraints to centralized wage bargaining. On the other hand, employers and business organizations supported this legislation, claiming that it had been instrumental in the rapid recovery of employment after the crises of 1982–83.

The modifications to the existing labor law are expected to affect (1) the costs of hiring and firing labor, (2) the relative bargaining power of labor unions, and (3) the target real wage.

An increase in the costs of hiring and firing labor may take place, although the idea is not to introduce complete job-security laws such as those in the pre-1973 labor code. If the costs of hiring and firing labor increase, the level and variability of employment over the cycle may be affected for the following reasons: First, a higher cost of changing the pool of labor employed at firm level will tend to make employment more stable along the business cycle. This could be termed a variance effect. Second, however, the increase in the costs of hiring and firing may lead to a reduction of the average level of employment as the present discounted value of unit labor costs increases. This level effect, in turn, may give rise to a bias toward a lower employment content per unit of output. Furthermore, those employed (insiders) will enjoy a more stable path of labor income, for a given wage, across cycles in potential detriment to the unemployed (outsiders).

From the perspective of efficiency wage theory, a reduction in labor turnover might be productivity-increasing. Two reasons stand behind this result: On the one hand, the losses of the human capital component that is firm-specific associated with the firing decision are reduced; on the other hand, the costs of job hiring and training also decline with a more stable employment pool.

A change in the labor legislation may affect the relative bargaining power of labor unions through a tendency toward a greater degree of centralization of the wage bargaining process. The international experience with a centralized versus decentralized wage bargaining schemes is far from conclusive.[17] In semi-industrialized economies with a centralized system of wage formation we find cases of cooperative centralized union behavior, for example Israel after the 1985-stabilization plan, but also uncooperative union stances in countries like Argentina. In addition to Chile under Plan Laboral, examples of decentralized labor market institutions concerning wage formation are provided by the United States or Japan.

The issue of the target real wage is less clear cut. The target wage is what workers desire and may well not coincide with the real wage actually paid. A discrepancy between desired and actual real wages may have adverse macroeconomic implications in terms of inflation or obstacles in allowing shifts in relative prices required from the point of view of attaining macroeconomic equilibrium. The income effects of such relative price shifts can be a source of distributive conflict in the economy. The determinants of the target real wage refer to the state of tightness or slack in the labor market, the level of labor productivity, and the relative bargaining power of labor. It is through these channels that a new labor legislation may affect the target wage.

## 5.3   Growth Possibilities and Political Economy

The Chilean economy needs to sustain growth in order to address social demands without serious distributive conflicts. Those conflicts would be destabilizing for a country in a political transition to democracy, a delicate process, as the experience of Chile's neighbors has shown.

What is going to drive the growth process? The private sector responded well to the incentives created in the second half of the 1980s and that dynamism must be preserved. Sustainable growth requires a significant effort for capital accumulation, suggesting that private profitability needs to be maintained. The high real interest rates of 1990 have to recede to more "normal" levels once the stabilization of inflation is consolidated. Further increases in taxation, if necessary in the future, must avoid a high reliance on taxes on corporate income that may adversely affect profitability and investment. Another reform that might affect the supply side is a change in labor legislation, although as discussed in the previous section, its effects on employment and labor productivity are not clear-cut.

Public investment in infrastructure is essential for complementarities with private investment and exports. A lack of capacity in ports in Chile seems to be evident and public investment in human capital, education, and health is another top priority. Finance for both public and private investment will have to rely on domestic savings. In the last five years the increase in public savings has contributed significantly to this effort and should be preserved.

The other important engine to growth lies in exports. Their expansion and diversification requires preserving a competitive and stable real exchange rate as well as the provision of adequate infrastructure and the encouragement of the adoption of technological innovation. The deepening of exports toward activities less based in natural resources and more intensive in value-added is still pending in Chile.

The satisfaction of social demands and particularly the reduction of poverty is envisaged to be a long process that will require that the economy grow at a satisfactory rate and that there is an efficient use of the instruments and resources of the state for doing the required internal transfer. A mismatch between the pace at which the social sectors want to see their demands satisfied and the potential of the economy and the ability of the state to actually fulfill them could be a source of social conflict that cannot be disregarded.

The overall performance of the economy in the years to come will depend on various factors, some in control of the new economic authorities and some not. A first factor, truly exogenous, is the terms of trade and in particular the price of copper; a drastic turnaround in copper or oil prices would adversely affect both the fiscal budget and the balance of payments. A second important factor is the continuation in the flow of external financing—ideally reversing the negative resource transfer—and certainly foreign borrowing is a variable that can be affected by domestic policy actions. A third element is domestic policies, an issue extensively dealt with in the paper. Good economic management is certainly the most important element for future success. Finally, a fourth element is the social setting; the government will be between demands for wages and social spending by workers and low income groups and the claims for setting stable "rules of the game" for the private sector in terms of property rights and business conditions. An adequate management of social demands combined with a stable institutional environment is, therefore, a crucial ingredient for a successful economic performance of the Chilean economy in the coming years.

## Notes

1. There is a vast literature about this period, e.g., Arellano (1988), Corbo (1985), Edwards and Edwards (1987), Foxley (1983).

2. See ECLA (1990) for a further discussion of these issues for the case of Chile.

3. An econometric analysis of the behavior of private investment in Chile during the 1980s is carried out in Solimano (1989).

4. According to Fontaine (1989), the level of the real interest rates was determined on the basis of two criteria: first, to provide a real return to domestic financial assets competitive with the return on financial instruments abroad so as to avoid capital flight and, second, the real interest rate should be consistent with a real cost of credit that does not hamper the recovery of investment.

5. See Corbo and Solimano (1990) for an econometric analysis of inflation and stabilization in Chile during the last two decades.

6. See Larraín (1989) for a detailed account of the management of the Chilean financial crises.

7. This point is analyzed in greater detail in the next section.

8. See for example Chapter 8 by M. Friedman in Yeager (1962).

9. Analysis of the Chilean financial crises and its fiscal implications appear in Arellano (1988), Arellano and Marfán (1987), Larrañaga and Marshall (1989) and Larraín (1989).

10. These estimates are drawn from Rodriguez (1989).

11. Those transfers may be in cash or kind. The transfers in cash may include an increase in some social security payments, for example, pensions and subsidies (asignacion familiar) to low income families. Subsidies in kind encompass the provision of free lunch, and food products (e.g., milk) to the children of poor families.

12. The specifics of a corporate tax code in terms of the treatment it gives to interest deductibility, depreciation, and allowances for inflation are another important element in determining the effect of a change in corporate income taxes on private investment.

13. The model was estimated using quarterly data from 1977 (5.1) to 1987 (5.4) for Chile. Estimation by instrumental variables corrects the endogeneity bias of the right-hand side variables of equation (5.1).

14. The share of retained earnings in total financing of investment has been around 20 % in Chile in periods of relative stability, see Hachette (1987).

15. The model used in Solimano (1992) presumes that relative prices are endogenous, output operates at full capacity, and growth is endogenously determined. The model is simulated using econometric estimates and plausible values of the key parameters. This analysis focuses in the short- and medium-run. Provided some social expenditure constitutes investment in human capital, it should have a positive effect on the rate of GDP growth in the long run.

16. See Solimano (1988) for a macroeconomic analysis of the impact of raising minimum wages in Chile.

17. See Bruno and Sachs (1985) for an anaLysis of this issue for the OECD countries.

## References

Arellano, J. P. (1988). "Crisis y Recuperación Económica en Chile en los años 80." *Collección Estudios Cieplan*, No. 24, Junio.

Arellano, J. P., and M. Marfán (1987). "Ahorro-Inversión y Relaciones Financieras en la actual Crisis Económica Chilena." *Colección Estudios Cieplan*, No. 20, Diciembre.

Bruno, M., and J. Sachs (1985). *Economics of Worldwide Stagflation.* Cambridge: Harvard University Press.

CEPALC (1990). "Balance Preliminar de la Economia de America Latina y el Caribe." Santiago: United Nations.

Corbo, V. (1985). "Reforms and Macroeconomic Adjustment in Chile During 1974–84." *World Development, 13:* 893–916.

Corbo, V., and A. Solimano (1990). "Stabilization Policies in Chile Revisited," in M. Bruno et al. (eds.), *Lessons of Economic Stabilization and Its Aftermath.* Cambridge, MA: MIT Press.

Edwards, S., and A. Edwards (1987). *Monetarism and Liberalization: The Chilean Experiment.* Lexington, MA: Ballinger Press.

Economic Commission for Latin America (1990). *Changing Production Patterns with Social Equity,* Santiago: United Nations.

Fontaine, J. A. (1989). "The Chilean Economy in the Eighties: Adjustment and Recovery"; also, "Comments" by E. Aninat, in S. Edwards and F. Larraín (eds.), *Debt. Adjustment and Recovery: Latin American Prospects for Growth and Recovery.* Oxford: Basil Blackwell.

Foxley, A. (1983). *Latin American Experiments in Neo-Conservative Economics.* Berkeley: University of California Press.

Friedman, M. (1962). "Should there be an Independent Monetary Authority?," in L. Yeager (ed.), *In Search of a Monetary Constitution.* Cambridge, MA: Harvard University Press.

Jadresic, E. (1985). "Formación de Precios Agregados en Chile: 1974-85," *Colección de Estudios Cieplan,* No. 16, Junio.

Larrañaga, O., and J. Marshall (1989). "Política Fiscal y Ajuste en Chile: 1982–88." (Mimeo), United Nations, Santiago.

Larraín, M. (1989). "How the 1981–83 Chilean Banking Crisis was Handled in Chile." *PRE Working Paper* No. 300. World Bank.

Marshall R. (1989). "Independencial o Autonomia del Banco Central?," in *Autonomia del Banco Central de Chile. Análisis de una Iniciativa*. Cuadernos de Economia, Universidad Católica de Chile, Abril.

Pollack, M., and A. Uthoff (1989). "Poverty and Labor Market: Greater Santiago, 1965–85," in G. Rodgers (ed.), *Urban Poverty and the Labor Market*. Geneva: International Labour Organization.

Rodriguez, C. A. (1989). "Revenues from Money Creation in Chile." (Mimeo), World Bank, Washington, DC.

Solimano, A. (1986). "Contractionary Devaluation in the Southern Cone: The Case of Chile." *Journal of Development Economics*, 23.

Solimano, A. (1988). "El Impacto Macroeconómico de los Salarios Mínimos en Chile." *Revista de Análisis Económico*, Vol. 3, No. 1, Junio.

Solimano, A. (1988). "Política de Remuneraciones en Chile: Experiencia Pasada, Instrumentos y Opciones a Futuro." *Colección de Estudios Cieplan*, No. 25, Diciembre.

Solimano, A. (1989). "How Private Investment Reacts to Changing Macroeconomic Conditions? The Case of Chile in the 1980's." *PPR Working Paper* No. 212, Washington, DC: World Bank.

Solimano, A. (1992). "Macroeconomic Constraints for Medium Term Growth and Distribution. A Model for Chile," in A. Chhibber et al. (eds.), *Reviving Private Investment in Developing Countries: Empirical Studies and Policy Lessons*. Amsterdam: North-Holland.

Torche, A. (1988). "Distribuir el Ingreso para Satisfacer las Necesidades Básicas," in F. Larraín (ed.), *Desarrollo Económico en Democracia*. Santiago: Universidad Católica de Chile.

# 6       Thailand

## Somchai Jitsuchon and Chalangphob Sussangkarn

In the last few years, the Thai economy went through a major transformation. The driving force for growth changed from traditional agriculture to manufacturing and services (particularly tourism). Manufactured exports boomed, along with the pace of growth. In 1988, real GDP increased by about 11 %, with another double-digit rise in 1989.

This paper describes these developments and their future implications. As the Thai Planning Agency, NESDB, was preparing the seventh five-year plan (1992—96), the key issues were (1) maintaining the high pace of growth with external stability and (2) making sure that the benefits of development are spread out more evenly than in the past. Human resource development more generally was an area of concern.

## 6.1   Background

Thailand is a country of 54 million people occupying an area of 514,000 square kilometers, about the size of Spain. Average real GDP growth was 6.8 % per annum between 1970 and 1988. During the same period, there was a rapid decrease in population growth, facilitated by quick acceptance of family planning. The rate declined from a peak of over 3 % per annum in the early 1960s to around 1.8 % in 1985 and is expected to approach the replacement level by the end of the century. Currently, Thailand's per capita GNP is about U.S.$1,100. (See table 6.1.) Although the agricultural sector long accounted for the largest share of GDP, 32.7 % in 1970, its share has steadily declined, and was only 16.9 % in 1988. Manufacturing is now the largest sector, accounting for 24.8 % of GDP in 1988, rising from 15.5 % in 1970.

As in most developing countries, Thailand's current account balance is in deficit because of the need to import capital goods and other primary and intermediate inputs. The gap was 5.2 billion baht in 1970, 12.4 billion in

**Table 6.1**
Past performance of the Thai economy

| Item | 1970 | 1975 | 1980 | 1985 | 1988 |
|---|---|---|---|---|---|
| Population (million) | 36.4 | 41.4 | 46.7 | 51.7 | 54.5 |
| GNP (million U.S.$, current prices) | 6,916 | 15,084 | 31,859 | 36,782 | 56,933 |
| GNP (per capita dollar, current prices) | 190 | 360 | 682 | 712 | 1,044 |
| | | 1970–75 | 1975–80 | 1980–85 | 1985–88 |
| Real growth of GDP (%) | | 6.09 | 7.21 | 5.70 | 9.20 |
| —Agriculture | | 5.09 | 3.17 | 4.70 | 3.10 |
| —Industry | | 6.80 | 10.86 | 5.00 | 11.80 |
| —Services | | 6.44 | 7.62 | 6.40 | 9.90 |
| Foreign trade (billion dollars) | 1970 | 1975 | 1980 | 1985 | 1988 |
| —Exchange rate (baht/dollar) | 20.8 | 20.38 | 20.50 | 27.10 | 25.30 |
| Balance of payments | | | | | |
| —Trade account (% of GNP) | −4.5 | −4.8 | −8.9 | −6.2 | −7.1 |
| —Current account (% of GNP) | −3.8 | −4.2 | −6.5 | −4.2 | −2.9 |

Sources: National income accounts of Thailand; Bank of Thailand, *Monthly Bulletin* (various issues).

1975, 42.4 billion in 1980, and 41.9 billion in 1985. This trend reversed in 1986, when Thailand's current account balance registered a surplus of around 6.5 billion baht. Since 1986, however, the current account has been negative again, although the level so far seems to be manageable.

In counterpoint to the deficit in current account, Thailand's capital account has usually been in surplus. In other words, Thailand has been accumulating external debt to finance its economic development. Estimates by the Thailand Development Research Institute (TDRI) of ratios of foreign debt outstanding to GDP are 2.3% in 1975, 16.1% in 1980, and 39.0% in 1985. Until recently, most external debt was incurred by the public sector (government and state enterprises), although the situation is rapidly changing due to a boom in private investment. In 1986, the estimated debt outstanding was about US $17 billion. Since then, because of rapid growth of exports, the debt/GDP ratio has declined substantially. (See figure 6.1)

In the early to mid-1980s, the persistent current account deficits and rapidly increasing foreign debt were of major concern to the government. Policy reforms were carried out, covering public sector resource mobilization and control of public expenditures; tax reform to give more incentives

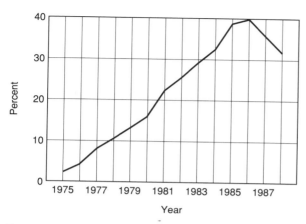

**Figure 6.1**
Ratio of stock of debt to GDP, 1975–1988

for exporting industries relative to importing competing industries (reduction of agricultural export taxes, and attempts to reduce the general level of tariffs); restructuring energy prices; and institutional changes to improve the management capacity of the public sector. Some reforms were taken through the government's own initiatives, and others were part of the World Bank's two structural adjustment loans (SALs) in 1982 and 1983.

In a TDRI study, Sahasakul et al. (1989) reviewed the impact of the SALs. They found that in general the programs benefited the economy, but that their quantitative effects were small. Simulations suggested that exports in 1987 would only have been 1 % lower without the SALs. Imports increased slightly due to an initial lowering of tariffs during the early SAL period, so that the current account worsened. Thereafter, due to the need to raise revenues, tariff rates gradually went up. Imports fell in comparison to a counterfactual with tariffs at the 1975–81 average, implying that the current account improved during the latter part of and after the SAL program.

The government also took measures outside the SAL framework that were regarded by the World Bank as the down payment for its loans. The most important were two devaluations in 1981 and 1984. These increased the baht/dollar rate from 20.5 in 1980 to about 27 at the end of 1984. Real depreciation helped keep external imbalances from getting out of hand, leaving Thailand in a position to benefit from major changes that occurred in the world economic environment starting in 1986.

The decline in oil prices and the exchange rate realignment between the Japanese yen and the dollar and major European currencies in 1986 helped substantially. The oil price decline cut the import bill, while the baht depreciated against the average currency of Thailand's trading partners, as it was closely tied to the dollar. There was a shift in comparative advantage between Japan and the Asian NIC's (South Korea, Taiwan, Hong Kong, and Singapore), which also tied their currencies to the dollar, allowing the latter to push into the export market for technologically and skill-intensive products such as cars and electronic consumer products. By 1986, the Asian NICs were probably already close to losing their comparative advantage in labor-intensive semi-skilled manufactured products (such as textiles) to other economies with plentiful supplies of low wage workers. Thereafter, their transition away from labor intensive manufacturing accelerated.

Without a serious structural adjustment overhang, the Thai economy was in an ideal position to take advantage of these developments. There was a plentiful supply of low wage workers with good basic education and skills. Particularly important was the quality of the female workers, who have historically been very active in the labor market, and who are needed for many of the key labor-intensive manufactured products such as textiles and electronics (Sussangkarn and Chalamwong, 1989).

A prominent feature has been the rapid growth of manufactured exports. In 1985 they surpassed agricultural exports in value for the first time, and continued rising thereafter. From 1984 to 1986, the ratio of manufactured to agricultural exports increased from 0.96 to 1.42. By 1988, it was 2.19.

Manufactured export increases have more than compensated for declines in Thailand's five major crop exports: rice, rubber, maize, sugar cane, and tapioca. Table 6.2 shows exports in millions of U.S. dollars by major groupings; also given are the shares in total exports, the yearly growth rates, and the average growth between 1980 and 1985, and 1985 and 1988. The rapid decline in the share of the five major crops in total exports stands out, despite high growth in 1988. Crop exports have been fluctuating almost yearly, depending on commodity prices and production.

Although exports of "canned fish" (mostly tuna) started rising fast in 1980, the other manufactured groups began sustained increases about 1986. The recent pace of growth of manufactured, as well as livestock and fisheries exports, has averaged 30% to 40% per annum. An important group is "clothing," including textiles and garments. Its share in total exports was 7.8% in 1980. This increased to 17.1% in 1988, and it is likely that the export value of "clothing" will surpass that of the major crops in the near future.

Small export items are currently expanding rapidly, and following recent trends, their importance will become more visible in a few years. One group that is now very prominent is "gems and jewelry." Starting from a base of 2.8 %, the share increased to 5.9 % in 1988. In 1989, its total export value is likely to pass the one billion dollar mark. The extent of export diversification can be seen in the "other" group, which started from a share of about 15 % to 16 % before 1984. Since that time it has gone up to over 30 %.

The export boom has been accompanied by accelerating economic activity since the bottom of the recession in 1985–86 when average growth was about 4 %. In 1987, real GDP growth was 8.4 %, rising to 11 % in 1988 and over 10 % in 1989. In 1990, the growth rate was close to double-digit again.

Given the current boom, Thailand is being mentioned as the leader of the next wave of NICs. The situation is, however, complex. Although it is true that manufactured exports are currently growing at rates similar to those achieved by the current NICs in their past transitions to newly industrialized status, Thailand's population and employment structures are still primarily rural and agriculturally based. In 1986, 66.8 % of the labor force had their main occupation in agriculture, and the current urbanization rate is just over 25 %.

It is this predominant influence of agriculture on the employment prospects of the current Thai labor force that makes any talk of the nation's reaching NIC status in the near future seem simplistic. At the very same time that manufactured exports were starting to boom in 1986 and 1987, agriculture was going through a second bad drought year in a row. Even ignoring the droughts, the period between the early 1980s until about 1987 was dismal for traditional agriculture.

The decline of agriculture is reflected in the rapid decrease in the share of crops in GDP; see table 6.3. The major source was the trend in commodity prices. Table 6.4 shows the average export price per ton of rice, rubber, maize, tapioca, and sugar for 1980–88. All five showed a declining trend until 1986. Since then, prices have recovered somewhat, with the exception of tapioca. However, apart from rubber, all prices in 1988 were lower than what they were in 1980.

The relative decline of agriculture in the early to mid-1980s also raises issues regarding the income distribution. Given that a very large proportion of the population is still dependent on that sector, the income distribution became steadily more unequal throughout the 1980s.

**Table 6.2**
Export performance

| Value (millions of dollars) | 1980 | 1981 | 1982 | 1983 | 1984 | 1985 | 1985 | 1985 | 1987 | 1988 |
|---|---|---|---|---|---|---|---|---|---|---|
| Five major crops | 2,778 | 3,272 | 3,167 | 2,696 | 2,993 | 2,389 | 2,696 | 2,696 | 2,961 | 3,835 |
| Other crops | 247 | 286 | 348 | 275 | 275 | 286 | 274 | 274 | 219 | 230 |
| Mining | 599 | 448 | 359 | 246 | 247 | 226 | 128 | 128 | 102 | 93 |
| Livestock and fisheries | 281 | 331 | 359 | 356 | 372 | 383 | 595 | 595 | 733 | 965 |
| Canned food exc. | 117 | 139 | 150 | 153 | 211 | 199 | 213 | 213 | 315 | 436 |
| Canned fish | 29 | 50 | 72 | 91 | 156 | 191 | 322 | 322 | 369 | 593 |
| Clothing | 507 | 629 | 676 | 707 | 910 | 966 | 1,323 | 1,323 | 2,129 | 2,716 |
| Gems and jewelery | 183 | 229 | 227 | 314 | 311 | 313 | 499 | 499 | 768 | 934 |
| Other industries | 579 | 537 | 500 | 504 | 666 | 644 | 839 | 839 | 1,169 | 1,229 |
| Others | 1,164 | 1,070 | 1,067 | 1,007 | 1,253 | 1,506 | 1,881 | 1,881 | 2,857 | 4,892 |
| Total | 6,489 | 6,995 | 6,929 | 6,354 | 7,397 | 7,106 | 8,775 | 8,775 | 11,622 | 15,924 |

| Share (percentage) | 1980 | 1981 | 1982 | 1983 | 1984 | 1985 | 1985 | 1985 | 1987 | 1988 |
|---|---|---|---|---|---|---|---|---|---|---|
| Five major crops | 42.8 | 46.8 | 45.7 | 42.4 | 40.5 | 33.6 | 30.7 | 30.7 | 25.5 | 24.1 |
| Other crops | 3.8 | 4.1 | 5.0 | 4.3 | 3.7 | 4.0 | 3.1 | 3.1 | 1.9 | 1.4 |
| Mining | 9.2 | 6.4 | 5.2 | 3.9 | 3.3 | 3.2 | 1.5 | 1.5 | 0.9 | 0.6 |
| Livestock and fisheries | 4.3 | 4.7 | 5.2 | 5.6 | 5.0 | 5.4 | 6.8 | 6.8 | 6.3 | 6.1 |
| Canned food exc. | 1.8 | 2.0 | 2.2 | 2.4 | 2.9 | 2.8 | 2.4 | 2.4 | 2.7 | 2.7 |
| Canned fish | 0.5 | 0.7 | 1.0 | 1.4 | 2.1 | 2.7 | 3.7 | 3.7 | 3.2 | 3.7 |
| Clothing | 7.8 | 9.0 | 9.8 | 11.1 | 12.3 | 13.6 | 15.1 | 15.1 | 18.3 | 17.1 |
| Gems and jewelery | 2.8 | 3.3 | 3.3 | 4.9 | 4.2 | 4.4 | 5.7 | 5.7 | 6.6 | 5.9 |
| Other industries | 8.9 | 7.7 | 7.2 | 7.9 | 9.0 | 9.1 | 9.6 | 9.6 | 10.1 | 7.7 |
| Others | 17.9 | 15.3 | 15.4 | 15.9 | 16.9 | 21.2 | 21.4 | 21.4 | 24.6 | 30.7 |
| Total | 100.0 | 100.0 | 100.0 | 100.0 | 100.0 | 100.0 | 100.0 | 100.0 | 100.0 | 100.0 |

**Table 6.2** (continued)

| Growth (percentage) | 1980 | 1981 | 1982 | 1983 | 1984 | 1985 | 1986 | 1987 | 1988 | Av. Gr. 1980–85 | Av. Gr. 1985–88 |
|---|---|---|---|---|---|---|---|---|---|---|---|
| Five major crops | 17.7 | 17.8 | −3.2 | −14.9 | 11.0 | −20.2 | 12.9 | 9.8 | 29.5 | −2.5 | 17.1 |
| Other crops | 18.1 | 15.8 | 21.4 | −20.9 | −1.0 | 4.1 | −4.1 | −20.1 | 5.2 | 2.5 | −7.0 |
| Mining | 21.2 | −25.3 | −19.7 | −31.4 | 0.4 | −5.6 | −43.2 | −20.1 | −9.2 | −15.5 | −25.7 |
| Livestock and fisheries | −5.7 | 17.7 | 8.5 | −0.9 | 4.6 | 2.9 | 55.2 | 23.2 | 31.7 | 5.3 | 36.1 |
| Canned food exc. | 15.5 | 18.3 | 8.1 | 1.8 | 37.8 | −5.5 | 6.7 | 47.7 | 38.4 | 9.3 | 29.8 |
| Canned fish | 60.7 | 72.6 | 42.5 | 27.1 | 70.0 | 22.6 | 68.6 | 14.5 | 60.9 | 36.9 | 45.9 |
| Clothing | 8.9 | 24.1 | 7.5 | 4.6 | 28.6 | 6.2 | 37.0 | 60.9 | 27.6 | 11.3 | 41.1 |
| Gems and jewelery | 36.7 | 24.7 | −0.6 | 38.0 | −0.8 | 0.4 | 59.6 | 53.9 | 21.7 | 9.4 | 44.0 |
| Other industries | 57.6 | −7.1 | −7.0 | 0.9 | 32.0 | −3.3 | 30.2 | 39.3 | 5.1 | 1.8 | 24.0 |
| Others | 39.3 | −8.1 | −0.3 | −5.6 | 24.4 | 20.2 | 25.0 | 51.9 | 71.2 | 4.4 | 48.1 |
| Total | 22.7 | 7.8 | −0.9 | −8.3 | 16.4 | −3.9 | 23.5 | 32.4 | 37.0 | 1.5 | 30.9 |

Source: Calculated from Bank of Thailand, *Monthly Bulletin* (various issues).

**Table 6.3**
Share of value-added by sector

| Industrial origin (%) | 1980 | 1981 | 1982 | 1983 | 1984 | 1985 | 1986 | 1987 | 1988 |
|---|---|---|---|---|---|---|---|---|---|
| Agriculture | 23.21 | 21.44 | 19.13 | 20.40 | 18.00 | 16.75 | 16.52 | 16.07 | 16.90 |
| Crops | 15.40 | 13.91 | 12.20 | 13.30 | 11.62 | 10.37 | 9.89 | 9.81 | 11.16 |
| Livestock | 2.35 | 2.08 | 1.71 | 2.09 | 1.73 | 1.48 | 1.82 | 1.83 | 1.70 |
| Fisheries | 1.23 | 1.40 | 1.34 | 1.36 | 1.16 | 1.26 | 1.38 | 1.16 | 1.03 |
| Forestry | 1.31 | 1.26 | 1.06 | 0.99 | 0.95 | 0.88 | 0.83 | 0.73 | 0.64 |
| Agricultural services | 0.83 | 0.88 | 0.85 | 0.68 | 0.70 | 0.73 | 0.65 | 0.58 | 0.53 |
| Simple agricultural processing products | 2.09 | 1.91 | 1.97 | 1.98 | 1.84 | 2.02 | 1.96 | 1.95 | 1.85 |
| Mining and quarrying | 3.36 | 2.84 | 3.06 | 2.90 | 3.39 | 3.96 | 3.14 | 3.10 | 3.02 |
| Manufacturing | 21.25 | 22.29 | 21.51 | 21.36 | 22.40 | 22.13 | 22.30 | 23.95 | 24.41 |
| Construction | 5.28 | 5.02 | 5.06 | 5.27 | 5.76 | 5.60 | 5.17 | 5.10 | 5.08 |
| Electricity and water supply | 0.96 | 1.43 | 1.91 | 1.88 | 1.91 | 2.33 | 2.62 | 2.58 | 2.56 |
| Transportation and communication | 5.75 | 6.03 | 6.79 | 6.68 | 7.14 | 7.70 | 7.80 | 7.53 | 7.29 |
| Wholesale and retail trade | 16.73 | 18.09 | 17.55 | 16.20 | 15.91 | 15.10 | 15.51 | 15.59 | 15.84 |
| Banking, insurance and real estate | 3.03 | 2.98 | 3.19 | 3.42 | 3.54 | 3.55 | 3.41 | 3.94 | 4.10 |
| Ownership of dwellings | 3.46 | 3.42 | 3.63 | 3.72 | 3.83 | | | | |
| Public administration and defense | 4.66 | 4.38 | 4.84 | 4.90 | 4.62 | | | | |
| Services | 12.31 | 12.08 | 13.34 | 13.27 | 13.50 | | | | |
| Gross domestic product (GDP) | 100.00 | 100.00 | 100.00 | 100.00 | 100.00 | | | | |

Source: NESDB, National Income of Thailand, New Series.

**Table 6.4**
Export price per ton for major crops (baht)

|  | Rice | Rubber | Maize | Tapioca | Sugar |
|---|---|---|---|---|---|
| 1980 | 6,968 | 27,145 | 3,314 | 2,853 | 6,586 |
| 1981 | 8,697 | 22,962 | 3,243 | 2,625 | 8,557 |
| 1982 | 5,949 | 17,429 | 2,943 | 2,527 | 5,862 |
| 1983 | 5,798 | 21,236 | 3,192 | 2,961 | 4,124 |
| 1984 | 5,618 | 21,969 | 3,227 | 2,527 | 4,205 |
| 1985 | 5,545 | 19,663 | 2,768 | 2,112 | 3,623 |
| 1986 | 4,491 | 19,867 | 2,308 | 3,021 | 3,708 |
| 1987 | 5,085 | 23,176 | 2,382 | 3,329 | 4,232 |
| 1988 | 6,576 | 27,733 | 3,181 | 2,688 | 5,207 |
| Growth 1980–88 | −4.08% | 0.50% | −2.86% | 0.82% | −6.83% |

Note: Average growth 1980–87 calculated by log regressions.
Source: Bank of Thailand.

## 6.2  The Medium Term

The goals of the seventh five-year development plan (1992–96) are to promote sustainable growth and improvements in the income distribution. It is fair to ask about the prospects for their attainment.

### 6.2.1  Growth with External Stability

In the early 1990s, most observers of Thailand view future development prospects with optimism. If the past growth pattern of the NICs can be a guide, then most of the impetus for the current export growth is coming through an increase in Thailand's market share of world trade in manufactured goods; greater sales depend more on market penetration than on world trade volumes. Given that the current share of Thai manufactured exports in world trade is very small, its prospects for growth are still good. The opening up of Eastern Europe may, of course, lead to further competition in the production of medium to low end manufactured products, but the extent to which these economies and their labor forces can adjust to new and unexplored economic environments remains to be seen.

One issue that needs careful monitoring is the widening trade and current account deficit as a result of the boom in economic activity. Table 6.5 shows the external balance figures between 1984 and 1988. Since the current account surplus year in 1986, the trade deficit has been widening substantially, reaching over four billion dollars in 1988. A major boost that

**Table 6.5**
External balance, 1984–88 (millions of US $)

|                      | 1984      | 1985      | 1986    | 1987      | 1988      |
|----------------------|-----------|-----------|---------|-----------|-----------|
| Trade balance        | − 2,904.1 | − 2,266.6 | − 545.3 | − 1,701.3 | − 4,031.4 |
| Net service accounts | 641.6     | 560.6     | 568.1   | 1,113.5   | 2,131.6   |
| Net transfers        | 174.3     | 165.2     | 224.4   | 224.8     | 233.2     |
| Current account      | − 2,088.2 | − 1,540.8 | 247.2   | − 363.1   | − 1,666.6 |
| Direct investment    | 406.3     | 160.9     | 261.1   | 182.7     | 1,090.1   |

Source: Bank of Thailand, *Monthly Report.*

has kept the current account to a manageable level has been the net surplus on the service accounts. The two main sources are remittances from Thai workers abroad and tourism. The former has been fairly stable at just over one billion U.S. dollars per year. Tourism has increased very fast. In 1984, earnings amounted to about $1.1 billion; by 1990, the figure was nearly $4 billion.

Another important development late in the 1980s was the large influx of foreign direct investment. Before 1988, direct investment into Thailand was only several hundred million dollars per year. Since then, the amount jumped significantly, increasing from $182.7 million in 1987 to over $1 billion in 1988. This influx has helped slow the increase in long-term external debt. Repatriation of profits has been minor because of a high reinvestment rate. If, however, the pace of direct investment continues for some time, then profit outflows may become an issue of some importance.

### 6.2.2   Income Distribution

The boom in manufactured exports and tourism together with the decline of traditional agriculture highlight a problem that is now regarded as a key policy issue for the medium term, that of income distribution.

As illustrated in table 6.6, the trend toward increasing inequality is unmistakable. The richest 20 % of the population increased its share of income from 49.3 % in 1975–76 to 55.6 % in 1986. All other quintiles showed decreasing shares. In fact, the real gainers are in the top 10 % of the population, since its share rose from 33.4 % in 1975–76 to 39.1 % in 1985–86. The largest share decline occurred for the poorest 20 %, from 6 % to 4.5 %. Over the period 1975–76 to 1985–86 the Gini coefficient increased from 0.43 to 0.5. The increase has been more rapid since 1981.

The worsening of the income distribution over the last 10 years reflects related imbalances along two fronts: between the production and employ-

**Table 6.6**
Income shares by quintile groups (percent of total)

| Quintile | 1975/6 | 1981 | 1985/6 |
|---|---|---|---|
| 1st | 49.3 | 51.5 | 55.6 |
| —top 10 % | 33.4 | 35.4 | 39.1 |
| —second 10 % | 15.9 | 16.1 | 16.5 |
| 2nd | 21.0 | 20.6 | 19.9 |
| 3rd | 14.0 | 13.4 | 12.1 |
| 4th | 9.7 | 9.1 | 7.9 |
| 5th | 6.0 | 5.4 | 4.5 |
| —second bottom 10 % | 3.6 | 3.3 | 2.7 |
| —bottom 10 % | 2.4 | 2.1 | 1.8 |

Source: NSO, Socio-economic Surveys 1975–56, 1981 and 1985–86.

ment structure, and between the locational distribution of industries and the population distribution (Sussangkarn, 1988).

Although the share of agriculture in GDP has been declining rapidly over the last decade, the share of employment mainly dependent on agriculture has not been falling as fast. Table 6.7 shows that in 1975, 73 % of the labor force were employed mostly in agriculture. In 1986, the share only declined to 66.8 %. The result is that value-added per head in agriculture had been increasing very slowly between 1975 and 1986, and in fact showed an absolute decline between 1980 and 1986. As the last line in the table indicates, the gap between agriculture and nonagriculture has been widening.

The second imbalance arises from the concentration of industries in and around Bangkok. Table 6.8 shows that per capita GDP in the capital and the surrounding five provinces was 7.3 times higher than that for the northeast, the poorest region. Although only 15.6 % of the population lives in the greater Bangkok area, it accounted for 45.5 % of GDP. Also, between 1975 and 1985, the growth rate of real per capita GDP was highest for greater Bangkok. The current boom in manufactured exports has a tendency to widen the disparities even more, as 75 % of manufacturing and 90 % of manufactured exports originate from the capital region.

## 6.3   Three-Gap Growth Projections

The background and recent developments of the Thai economy outlined previously provide a basis for projecting into the future. A standard three-

**Table 6.7**
GDP and employment by sector

| Year | 1975 | 1980 | 1986 |
|---|---|---|---|
| GDP (millions of baht) | 298,816 | 684,930 | 1,098,362 |
| Agriculture | 94,063 | 173,806 | 183,037 |
| Nonagriculture | 204,753 | 511,124 | 915,325 |
| Share | | | |
| Agriculture | 31.48% | 25.38% | 16.66% |
| Nonagriculture | 68.52% | 74.62% | 83.34% |
| Employment (millions) | 18.182 | 22.681 | 26.672 |
| Agriculture | 13.270 | 16.092 | 17.803 |
| Nonagriculture | 4.912 | 6.589 | 8.870 |
| Share | | | |
| Agriculture | 72.99% | 70.95% | 66.75% |
| Nonagriculture | 27.01% | 29.05% | 33.25% |
| Per captia GDP (baht/month) | 1,369.6 | 2,516.6 | 3,431.7 |
| Agriculture | 590.7 | 900.1 | 856.8 |
| Nonagriculture | 3,474.0 | 6,464.7 | 8,599.9 |
| Ratio Nonagriculture/agriculture | 5.88 | 7.18 | 10.04 |

Source: NESDB, National Income of Thailand; NSO, Labour Force Surveys (various issues).

**Table 6.8**
Gross domestic product at current market prices by region (1985, million baht)

| | Kingdom | N. East | North | South | Central | Bangkok[a] |
|---|---|---|---|---|---|---|
| Agriculture | 178,533 | 41,721 | 42,302 | 33,462 | 50,221 | 10,827 |
| Industry | 316,697 | 20,611 | 24,295 | 15,367 | 54,694 | 201,730 |
| Services | 564,124 | 83,365 | 68,799 | 49,126 | 83,209 | 261,625 |
| Total GDP | 1,041,354 | 145,697 | 135,395 | 97,955 | 188,123 | 474,182 |
| Per capita GDP (baht) | 20,148 | 8,083 | 13,304 | 14,737 | 21,395 | 58,963 |
| Population (million) | 51.684 | 18.025 | 10.177 | 6.647 | 8,793 | 8.042 |
| Row Shares | Kingdom | N. East | North | South | Central | Bangkok |
| Agriculture | 100.00% | 23.37% | 23.69% | 18.74% | 28.13% | 6.06% |
| Industry | 100.00% | 6.51% | 7.67% | 4.85% | 17.27% | 63.70% |
| Services | 100.00% | 15.26% | 12.60% | 9.00% | 15.24% | 47.91% |
| Total GDP | 100.00% | 13.99% | 13.00% | 9.41% | 18.07% | 45.54% |
| Population | 100.00% | 34.88% | 19.69% | 12.86% | 17.01% | 15.56% |
| Column shares | Kingdom | N. East | North | South | Central | Bangkok |
| Agriculture | 17.14% | 28.64% | 31.24% | 34.16% | 26.70% | 2.28% |
| Industry | 30.41% | 14.15% | 17.94% | 15.69% | 29.07% | 45.54% |
| Services | 52.44% | 57.22% | 50.81% | 50.15% | 44.23% | 55.17% |
| Total GDP | 100.00% | 100.00% | 100.00% | 100.00% | 100.00% | 100.00% |

a. Bangkok here includes the Bangkok metropolitan area and the five surrounding provinces.
Source: NESDB, GDP by province, 1985.

gap model is used to describe scenarios emphasizing two issues: the financing of each resource gap and the impacts on Thailand's external debt condition. In the next section, the model is combined with a Kuznets-type equation linking income distribution to growth, as well as other socioeconomic variables.

The detailed specification of the model resembles the one used for the other WIDER country studies, except that:

1. Private saving responds negatively to capital inflows (with a coefficient of −0.63) as well as positively to capacity use (coefficient = 0.53).

2. The share of exports in potential output has a positive time trend and also responds positively to capacity utilization. The interpretation is that increased sales abroad create domestic demand via a foreign trade multiplier.

### 6.3.1   A Short-Term Growth Exercise

Figure 6.2 shows the gap restrictions for 1987, the model's base year. We first explore adjustment between 1987 and 1990, fitting the equations to historical data as follows:

1. Capacity utilization in 1988 is assumed to be 1.0 (full utilization), because in that year Thailand experienced the highest real GDP growth rate since the second oil crisis, around 11 %.

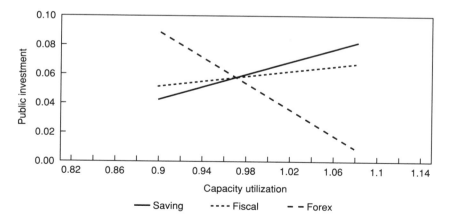

**Figure 6.2**
Three-gap diagram (base year = 1987)

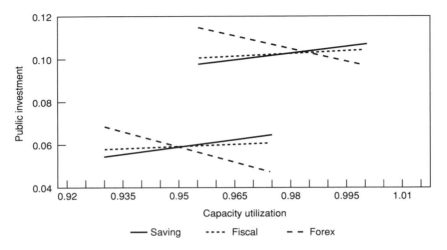

**Figure 6.3**
Short-term adjustment

2. During 1989 and 1990, potential and actual output are assumed to grow by 10 % and 9 % per year respectively.

3. There was an increase in the incremental output-capital ratio from 0.32 to 0.35, reflecting industrial modernization, while crowding-in of private by public investment may have become stronger (a coefficient of 0.8 instead of 0.55).

4. The increase in the export share of potential output from 28.5 % in 1987 to 37.7 % in 1990 is captured by the time trend.

5. There are changes in import and saving coefficients.

Figure 6.3 shows how the gap restrictions shift between the two years. Besides the export boom, a main adjusting variable behind the increases in public investment and capacity use is higher foreign saving, which rises from 0.65 % to 2.48 % of potential output in 1990. At the same time, the domestic saving share rose from 19.8 % to 28.6 % of potential output, due to a better tax effort (a 2.6 % increase in public saving) and strong growth in saving by enterprises. Since public investment rose by 4.6 % of potential output during the period, public sector borrowing had to go up, with the share in actual output increasing from 1.46 % to 3.2 %.

These changes raise several concerns, not least the question of how the soaring external deficit was financed. In 1987, Thailand's current account deficit amounted to 9,319 million baht (around $363 million), which was financed by $183 million inflow of foreign direct investment, $1,471 million of change in external debt (from $16,028 in 1986 to $17,499 in 1987), and $584 million net other outflows, making the overall balance of payments in surplus by $707 million. The following account shows all these figures in millions of baht, millions of dollars, and as a proportion of potential output ($Q$):

| Year 1987 | M. Baht | M. US $ | /Q |
|---|---|---|---|
| Current account deficit | 9,319 | 363 | 0.0065 |
| Debt change | 28,618 | 1,471 | 0.0201 |
| Dir. inv. + other inflows | −1,116 | −402 | −0.0008 |
| —Direct investment | 4,712 | 183 | 0.0033 |
| —Other inflows | −5,828 | −584 | −0.0041 |
| Balance of payments | 18,183 | 707 | 0.0127 |

The table suggests an identity,

$$\phi = dd + r - BOP,$$

$\phi$ is current account deficit or net foreign saving as a share of $Q$,
$dd$ is change in external debt/$Q$,
$r$ is net other capital inflow (including direct investment)/$Q$,
$BOP$ is surplus in balance of payment/$Q$,
and the data in 1987 are

$$0.0065 = 0.0201 - 0.0008 - 0.0127.$$

The stock of external debt in 1987 was $17,499 million, around 31.5% of $Q$ in the same year. Foreign direct investment, which was 4,712 million baht or about $184 million in 1987, has jumped sharply. We assume that the sum of direct investment and other net capital inflows will be no less than $1,600 million in 1990 (comprising $1,900 million of direct investment and -$300 million of net other inflow), which is equivalent to 2.19% of $Q$. We further assume that in 1990 Thailand maintained a surplus in the balance of payments at a similar level as that in 1987, that is, 1.3% of $Q$ or about $950 million at an exchange rate of 25.5 baht per U.S. dollar. With $\phi$ equal to 0.0248 as determined in the gap exercise, the debt growth identity for 1990 becomes

$$0.0248 = dd + 0.0219 - 0.0130.$$

To fill in the gap, an equivalent to 1.59% of $Q$ of external debt has to be created ($dd = 0.0159$). This corresponds to a $1,162 million increment of external debt in 1987 prices. To calculate debt stocks, we put in the actual figures of debt creation and debt stock during 1988–89 while the figures for 1990 were obtained from the model. Debt outstanding in 1990 will thus be \$20,466 million or 28 % of $Q$, declining gradually from 31.5 % in 1987. The following shows changes in Thailand's external debt:

(million US \$)

| Year | Debt creation | Debt stock | % Stock/Q |
|------|---------------|------------|-----------|
| 1987 |               | 17,499     | 31.54     |
| 1988 | 370           | 17,869     | 29.57     |
| 1989 | 1,434         | 19,303     | 29.04     |
| 1990 | 1,162         | 20,466     | 27.99     |

### 6.3.2 Medium-Term Growth

Economic prospects in the medium term are expected to vary in some aspects from the present. The major differences should be in foreign trade. Imports nowadays comprise mainly intermediate products and capital goods, and the latter may rise as Thailand enters more high technology industries and joint venture production grows. On the other hand, exports are expected to grow less rapidly than today. The emerging tendency toward regional trading zones may retard export growth of developing countries including Thailand. However, Thai exports are still capable of growing at a fairly high rate through increasing market share as explained earlier.

We assume that actual and potential output both grow at 8 % yearly between 1991 and 1995, holding capacity utilization at the level of 0.9819. With a stable growth equation, total investment of 25.3 % of potential output is required in 1995 to attain 8 % growth. The relationship between total and public investment is also assumed to be unchanged, making public investment equal to 7.2 % and private investment 18.1 % of $Q$.

Other key assumptions include the following:

1. The export share of potential output does not continue to grow, taking the value of 37.88 % in 1995. Imports stay fairly stable, except that the import content of investment is expected to increase from 38 % to 50 %. If interest payments are constant at 2 % of $Q$, the current account deficit in 1995 should be 5.41 % of potential output, up from 2.48 % in 1990.

2. The domestic saving rate is also likely to decline, as income differentials cease to widen (due to slower export growth and a possible ac-

celeration in trickle-down). Infrastructure investment must be put in place, but the overall public saving effort will probably slack off. We project private and public saving shares in potential output of 14.15 % and 5.78 %, respectively.

In terms of the debt accumulation equation given earlier, the requirement for additional debt creation $(dd)$ depends on other net capital inflows $(r)$ and the expected balance of payments (BOP). We assume that, as a proportion of $Q$, Thailand's balance of payments will keep on being in surplus at the same level as in 1990, that is, around 1.3 %. Other net capital inflows (direct investment included) will decline slightly as the requirement for capital accumulation will be less. We assume that in 1995 the real (1987) value of other net capital inflows except debt creation will be around 23 billion baht, which equals 1.95 % of $Q$ compared to 2.19 % in 1990. The debt creation requirement $(dd)$ is therefore 0.0575 $(= 0.541 - 0.0195 + 0.0130)$, equivalent to $5,106 million at 1987 prices.

If we assume that during 1991−94 Thailand's external debt increases smoothly, then the external debt profile between 1990 and 1995 may be displayed as:

| | (million US $, 1987 prices) | | |
| Year | Debt creation | Debt stock | % Stock/Q |
|------|---------------|------------|-----------|
| 1990 | 1,162 | 20,466 | 27.99 |
| 1991 | 1,635 | 22,101 | 27.99 |
| 1992 | 2,306 | 24,407 | 28.62 |
| 1993 | 3,173 | 27,580 | 29.95 |
| 1994 | 4,120 | 31,700 | 31.87 |
| 1995 | 5,106 | 36,806 | 34.25 |

This table suggests that Thailand's external debt situation in the medium term, after registering an improving trend during 1987−90, may be a source of concern in the 1990s.

## 6.4 Distributional Impacts of Expected Growth

The association between development (economic growth in particular) and the distribution of income has been long discussed. We start with the influential hypothesis put forward by Simon Kuznets (1955). He conjectured that income inequality is related to per capita national income in an inverted U-shape, that is, inequality initially rises during the first stages of development and then falls after the country has reached a certain income level. Many studies have attempted to test this "Kuznets Hypothesis". The conclusions are mixed.

Recently, Sussangkarn et al. (1988) carried out a study on the international long-term determination of income distribution. The model extends the standard Kuznets hypothesis by adding other economic and social factors as explanatory variables in order to capture the social transition process, not merely economic growth, in explaining distribution. The factors included are education, labor share in agriculture, and fertility growth. The regressions used a pooled cross section time-series country data set with 63 observations over 45 countries covering all ranges of income. The dependent variables are the Gini coefficient in one equation, and the income share of the poorest 40 % of the population. The independent variables are as follows:

1. Per capita income and per capita income squared are the standard Kuznets hypothesis regressors.

2. The share of agricultural labor in employment and its square (as ratios of agricultural workers to the total labor force). These variables are included to capture possible imbalances between income and production and the employment structure.

3. Regional dummies for Latin American and sub-Saharan Africa are included because most countries in those regions have more unequal distributions of income than countries elsewhere; institutional factors may be involved.

4. Education is measured by the ratio of secondary to primary enrollment rates. The variable is to measure the effect of transitions to higher-than-compulsory education on the distribution of income.

5. The fertility rate is to represent demographic development through success or failure in fertility control.

The main regression results are reproduced in tables 6.9 and 6.10. The findings seem to support the Kuznets hypothesis of an inverted U-shaped relationship between per capita income and inequality. The other socio-economic variables also prove to be highly related to distribution. Other things the same, countries with larger shares of agricultural labor tend to have more unequal distributions, while those with better education and more success in fertility control have greater income equality.

We use these regression estimates to simulate the distributional implications of the growth targets obtained from the previous section's growth

**Table 6.9**
Regression estimate of income inequality (Gini coefficient)

| Variable | Estimated value | T-statistic |
|---|---|---|
| Constant term | 0.010 | 0.062 |
| Economic factors | | |
| Income per capita | 0.084 | 2.150 |
| —Income per capita squared | −0.005 | −1.830 |
| —Share of agricultural labor | 0.301 | 2.940 |
| —Share of agricultural labor squared | −0.335 | −2.740 |
| Social variables | | |
| Regional dummies | | |
| —Latin America | 0.040 | 1.840 |
| —Africa (South Sahara) | 0.740 | 3.180 |
| Education | −0.122 | −3.870 |
| Fertility | 0.016 | 2.680 |
| No. observations | 63 | |
| $R^2$ | 0.7996 | |
| Adjusted $R^2$ | 0.7699 | |
| F-statistic | 26.93 | |

**Table 6.10**
Regression estimate of income inequality (share of poorest 40 %)

| Variable | Estimated value | T-statistic |
|---|---|---|
| Constant term | 42.730 | 4.640 |
| Economic factors | | |
| Income per capita | −5.840 | −2.600 |
| —Income per capita squared | 0.339 | 2.250 |
| —Share of agricultural labor | −3.350 | −1.220 |
| —Share of agricultural labor squared | — | — |
| Social variables | | |
| Regional dummies | | |
| —Latin America | −3.180 | −2.830 |
| —Africa (South Sahara) | −3.160 | −2.260 |
| Education | 3.725 | 2.060 |
| Fertility | −0.992 | −2.670 |
| No. observations | 63 | |
| $R^2$ | 0.7104 | |
| Adjusted $R^2$ | 0.6735 | |
| F-statistic | 19.27 | |

exercises. The future values of all other independent variables except national income have to be estimated. The following assumptions are used.

1. The fertility rate falls from 3.1 in 1987 to 2.9 and 2.5 in 1990 and 1995. This means that the population growth rate will decline to 1.1 % in the year 2000 from its current level (1987) of 1.5 %. Assuming that the rate of decline takes linear form, Thailand's population increases from 53.6 million in 1987 to 56.0 million in 1990, and 59.7 million in 1995.

2. The agricultural labor share in the total labor force decreases from 66 % in 1987 to 61 % and 53 % in 1990 and 1995 respectively.

3. The ratio of secondary enrollment to primary enrollment will increase from 0.31 in 1987 to 0.34 and 0.38 in 1990 and 1995 respectively.

Using these values for the explanatory variables, we get the estimated Gini coefficient and income share of the poorest 40 %. The summary results are presented in table 6.11.

The key finding is that one can expect a turning point in inequality around 1992. This happens to be the first year of the seventh five-year plan. Thus, it appears that the goal of achieving better income distribution is not too unrealistic. Of course, the underlying conditions as given by the various assumptions have to be fulfilled. Also, the estimated relationships between income distribution and the various socioeconomic variables are assumed to be valid for Thailand. On this point, it should be noted that, according to the estimated equation, the implied income inequality for Thailand in 1987 is lower than the actual figures (Hutaserani and Jitsuchon, 1988). We adjusted the equation by changing the intercept term in order to arrive at the base Gini coefficient of 0.5 for 1987, which is close to the actual figure, before carrying out the simulation.

## 6.5 Conclusions

In this paper we have described the past and recent developments of the Thai economy. Two key issues for the medium term were highlighted. These were (1) maintaining the high pace of economic growth with external stability, and (2) achieving a better income distribution than in the past. Simulation exercises were carried out to look at medium term prospects by using a three-gap model linked to Kuznets type equations.

The exercises reveal that the prospects for the Thai economy appear to be good. Maintaining a fairly rapid rate of growth without getting into serious external balance problems seems to be feasible, although growth in

**Table 6.11**
Simulation results from income distribution exercise

| | 1987 | 1988 | 1989 | 1990 | 1991 | 1992 | 1993 | 1994 | 1995 |
|---|---|---|---|---|---|---|---|---|---|
| GNP (1980 price, m. baht) | 787,431 | 863,467 | 946,846 | 1,038,275 | 1,117,489 | 1,202,745 | 1,294,507 | 1,393,269 | 1,499,565 |
| Population growth (%) | 1.50 | 1.47 | 1.44 | 1.41 | 1.38 | 1.35 | 1.32 | 1.28 | 1.25 |
| Population (million) | 53.61 | 54.40 | 55.18 | 55.96 | 56.73 | 57.49 | 58.25 | 59.00 | 59.74 |
| GDP per capita (US $) | 588 | 635 | 686 | 742 | 788 | 837 | 889 | 945 | 1,004 |
| Agricultural labor share (%) | 66 | 64 | 63 | 61 | 60 | 58 | 56 | 55 | 53 |
| Education (%) | 31 | 31.9 | 32.8 | 33.8 | 34.7 | 35.6 | 36.5 | 37.5 | 38.4 |
| Fertility (%) | 3.100 | 3.023 | 2.946 | 2.869 | 2.792 | 2.715 | 2.638 | 2.562 | 2.485 |
| Gini | 0.5000 | 0.5107 | 0.5196 | 0.5261 | 0.5289 | 0.5293 | 0.5271 | 0.5216 | 0.512 |
| Poorest 40 % share | 12.42 | 11.78 | 11.24 | 10.85 | 10.72 | 10.72 | 10.89 | 11.27 | 11.89 |

Note: The constant terms of all three regressions are adjusted to fit the actual value of Thailand in 1987.

foreign debt may prove to be an increasingly worrying issue. Further, using the Kuznets type relationships between socioeconomic development and income distribution shows that Thailand may be reaching a distributional turning point in the near future.

A particularly important policy in this regard concerns education. This is an area where Thailand lags far behind other countries. The gross secondary enrollment ratio in Thailand is only around 30 % at the present time. This compares with 94 % in South Korea, 91 % in Taiwan, 71 % in Singapore, 53 % in Malaysia, and 68 % in the Philippines. In order to raise the ratio to the levels assumed in the growth exercises, strong efforts will be needed. This will help with both achieving better income distribution and also promote growth, especially at a time when international competition is likely to be fierce, and Thailand has to upgrade the knowledge and skills of the labor force to keep up with technological developments.

## References

Hutaserani, Suganya, and Somchai Jitsuchon (1988). "Thailand's Income Distribution and Poverty Profile and their Current Situation." Bangkok: Thailand Development Research Institute.

Kuznets, Simon S. (1955). "Economic Growth and Income Inequality," *American Economic Review*, 65: 1–28.

Sahasakul, C., N. Thongpakde, and N. Kraisoraphong (1989). "Lessons from the World Bank's Experience of Structural Adjustment Loans (SALs): A Case Study of Thailand." Bangkok: Thailand Development Research Institute.

Sussangkarn, Chalongphob (1988). "Production Structures, Labor Markets, and Human Capital Investments: Issues of Balance for Thailand." Bangkok: Thailand Development Research Institute.

Sussangkarn, Chalongphob, and Yongyuth Chalamwong (1989). "Thailand's Economic Dynamism: Human Resource Contributions and Constraints." Bangkok: Thailand Development Research Institute.

Sussangkarn, Chalongphob, Direk Patamasiriwat, Teera Askakul, and Kobchai Chimkul (1988). "The Long-term View on Growth and Distribution." Bangkok: Thailand Development Research Institute.

# 7        Malaysia

## Jomo K. S.

Projecting structural change in Malaysia is fraught with difficulties owing to the highly open nature of the economy. In the late 1980s, exports were about two-thirds of GDP, compared with 45 % in 1957, the time of independence. From the twin pillars of rubber and tin in the colonial economy, Malaysia's major exports in 1990 included manufactured goods, petroleum, timber, palm oil, rubber, liquefied natural gas (LNG), tin, and cocoa, in that order of importance. Even this ranking has changed in recent years, with petroleum leading and timber a close second as recently as 1987.

Although the average real GDP growth rate was 6.75 % per year between 1971 and 1989 (table 7.1), there have been fluctuations. The 1985–86 recession seriously undermined the popular assumption among policy-makers that Malaysian economic performance closely follows the fortunes of the developed OECD economies. Despite the OECD's upturn in the mid-1980s, commodity prices did not recover for quite some time. Conversely, the vigorous 1987–89 Malaysian recovery outpaced more tentative upturns elsewhere.

There have also been major policy changes in the last couple of decades, for example, growth of the public sector and state intervention under the New Economic Policy (NEP) from the early 1970s and more gradual and less obvious structural adjustments since the mid-1980s. Malaysia's unhappy experience with external debt—interest rates reached new highs in the early 1980s—is likely to discourage massive new foreign borrowing in the near future. Recent tax reforms have reduced the base, especially for direct taxation, and seriously constrain the room for fiscal intervention.

With political turbulence in the country since the mid-1980s, it also seems foolhardy to make long-term assumptions. The recent unprecedented coalescing of opposition parties around a breakaway group from the long-dominant United Malay National Organization (UMNO) suggests that the future of electoral politics in Malaysia has reached a cross-

**Table 7.1**
Output and productivity, 1970–1989

| | 1970 | 1971 | 1972 | 1973 | 1974 | 1975 | 1976 | 1977 | 1978 | 1979 |
|---|---|---|---|---|---|---|---|---|---|---|
| GNP ($ million) | 11,644 | 12,592 | 13,842 | 18,064 | 21,861 | 21,606 | 26,988 | 31,064 | 36,186 | 44,354 |
| National income ($ million) | 9,732 | 10,582 | 11,556 | 14,990 | 17,769 | 17,936 | 22,229 | 25,284 | 29,568 | 36,309 |
| Population ('000) | 10,877 | 10,710 | 10,998 | 11,274 | 11,567 | 11,868 | 12,177 | 12,494 | 12,819 | 13,439 |
| Real GDP ($ million) | — | 22,149 | 24,228 | 27,063 | 29,315 | 29,550 | 32,966 | 35,522 | 37,886 | 41,428 |
| Potential GDP ($ million) | 21,722 | 23,202 | 24,784 | 26,473 | 28,277 | 30,204 | 32,262 | 34,461 | 36,810 | 39,319 |
| Capacity utility index (%) | — | 95 | 98 | 102 | 104 | 98 | 102 | 103 | 103 | 105 |
| GNP per capita ($) | 1,071 | 1,176 | 1,260 | 1,602 | 1,890 | 1,821 | 2,216 | 2,486 | 2,823 | 3,300 |
| National income per capita ($) | 895 | 988 | 1,052 | 1,330 | 1,536 | 1,511 | 1,825 | 2,024 | 2,307 | 2,702 |

| | 1980 | 1981 | 1982 | 1983 | 1984 | 1985 | 1986 | 1987 | 1988 | 1989 |
|---|---|---|---|---|---|---|---|---|---|---|
| GNP ($ million) | 51,390 | 55,602 | 59,690 | 65,530 | 74,182 | 72,039 | 66,364 | 75,339 | 85,800 | 96,600 |
| National income ($ million) | 41,486 | 45,505 | 49,618 | 53,719 | 61,321 | 59,916 | 56,021 | 64,436 | 72,247 | — |
| Population ('000) | 13,764 | 14,128 | 14,507 | 14,888 | 15,270 | 15,681 | 16,109 | 16,528 | 16,900 | 17,400 |
| Real GDP ($ million) | 44,512 | 47,602 | 50,430 | 53,582 | 57,741 | 57,150 | 57,859 | 60,929 | 66,258 | 71,871 |
| Potential GDP ($ million) | 41,998 | 44,861 | 47,918 | 51,184 | 54,672 | 58,399 | 62,379 | 66,630 | 71,171 | — |
| Capacity utility index (%) | 106 | 106 | 105 | 105 | 106 | 98 | 93 | 91 | 92 | — |
| GNP per capita ($) | 3,734 | 3,936 | 4,115 | 4,402 | 4,858 | 4,594 | 4,120 | 4,558 | 5,047 | 5,552 |
| National income per capita ($) | 3,014 | 3,221 | 3,420 | 3,608 | 4,016 | 3,821 | 3,478 | 3,899 | 4,275 | — |

Sources: Bank Negara Malaysia, *Quarterly Bulletin* (various issues); Malaysia, Ministry of Finance, *Economic Report* (various issues); Malaysian Institute of Economic Research.

roads. On the other hand, long-simmering ethnic tensions may have begun to abate. The growing wage-earning population, now comprising three-fifths of the labor force, resents increasingly anti-labor laws and policies despite the low level of unionization, ethnic schisms, and the absence of militant leadership.

Official data point to a worsening income distribution in the 1970s despite significant reductions in poverty during that period (Jomo and Ishak, 1986). Comparable data for the 1980s have not been publicly released, but highly aggregated government estimates suggest that the real incomes of the top twenty percent of the population declined slightly between 1984–87, while the average incomes of the rest increased (Malaysia, 1989). Scanty information suggests continuing concentration of corporate wealth (Mehmet, 1986), while the generally regressive tax reforms since the mid-1980s probably made the post-tax income profile more unequal.

## 7.1 Inflation, Sectoral Balance, and Debt

Against this background, following Jomo (1990) we need to explore three issues in more detail before we can consider alternative development strategies. They are inflation and its interactions with policy changes, the export mix and sectoral balance, and fiscal constraints and debt.

### 7.1.1 Inflation

After years of very low inflation, the rate began to pick up after 1987 with the economic recovery. The official consumer price index (CPI, 1980 = 100) for Malaysia increased by 2.5% in 1988, 2.8% in 1989, and 3.0% in 1990, to the disbelief of many observers. Meanwhile, the producer price index (PPI) rose by 3.7% in 1987, 7.4% in 1988, 4.0% in 1989, and 0.9% in 1990, after actually falling by −6.2% in 1986.

The recent resurgence of inflation has been popularly associated with the declining value of the ringgit, especially against the yen, sterling, and Singapore dollar, and even the U.S. dollar. The ringgit weakened (with fluctuations) from M$2.42 = U.S.$1 at the end of December 1984 to 2.71 at the end of December 1988, and declined further to 2.78 by mid-1991. However, there was little increase in the CPI in 1986 or even in 1987, partly due to the decline of rentals (due to the depressed real property and construction sectors) and imported food prices. The implication may be that inflation in 1988–91 is linked to increases in public expenditure, rentals, housing, and food prices. With the economic recovery raising incomes, including wages as unemployment declined, fears of a wage-price spiral reemerged. The threat of greater inflation probably constrains fiscal more than exchange rate policy, at least in the view of the government.

### 7.1.2    Sectoral Balance

Sectoral contributions to the economy have changed with economic growth. The primary sector's share declined from 44 % of Malayan (now Peninsular Malaysian, excluding Sabah and Sarawak, which joined Malaysia in 1963) GDP in 1960 to 29 % of Malaysian GDP in 1990. Conversely, the secondary sector's share rose from 12 % of Malaysian GDP in 1970 to 30 % in 1990.

Changes within sectors have also been important. For instance, the old primary sector comprised mainly tin mining, rubber, and food crops, especially rice. By the 1980s, petroleum, timber, and palm oil had overtaken rubber in significance, while cocoa continued to make important inroads through the decade. In 1988, Malaysia finally gave up its leading position in tin production internationally to Brazil, China and Indonesia. Petroleum production rose from the mid-1970s to the mid-1980s, transforming Malaysia into a net exporter, with petroleum revenue topping Malaysia's export earnings through the mid-1980s. Commercial natural gas production, mainly for export, began in 1983, and reserves are expected to last at least a century, although the export market is currently confined to Japan only.

Table 7.2 presents data on exports, with relevant post-1988 developments discussed in the following capsule sketches of the main items. The commodity history is complex, and we can only outline its main points along with future prospects.

First, Malaysian rubber supply appears to be quite elastic, with the volume of exports fluctuating with price. The world price declined in the early 1980s, largely because of increased production and supply, partly encouraged by international agencies such as the World Bank, which was providing rosy price forecasts. With the recent rubber recovery helped by AIDS, price and production picked up again from 1986, raising exports to $3.2 billion in 1986, $3.9 billion in 1987 and $5.3 billion in 1988, before falling to $3.9 billion in 1989 and $3.0 billion in 1990.

Second, palm oil fueled Malaysia's major post-independence commodity boom when exports rose from $264 million in 1970 to $1.3 billion in 1975 and $2.6 billion in 1980. The volume of palm oil exports has continued to grow steadily since then, but value peaked at $4.5 billion in 1984. As with rubber, world prices have recently been fluctuating widely, and future prospects are uncertain.

Third, timber extraction has grown tremendously, especially since the 1970s. Both sawlogs and sawn timber had double-digit growth rates of export value between 1960 and 1980, and again late in the 1980s. Peninsular Malaysia is considered nearly logged out, while the situation in Sabah is rapidly approaching similar status. Sarawak remains the last major frontier. Forests there may be exhausted by the late 1990s at current rates of extraction. Malaysia may thus stop exporting timber just as the World Bank expects prices to go up sharply.

Timber concessions, and hence logging, are essentially a state government prerogative, with the federal government disclaiming control. At least on paper, the federal government has had a decent forestry policy for the last decade, but to little effect in Sabah and Sarawak, or even on the ground in Peninsular Malaysia, according to environmentalist critics. In the face of growing environmentalist pressures, sustained yield forestry projects have expanded, especially in Sabah, to feed its new paper and pulp mill. Meanwhile, much of the timber exported from Sabah and Sarawak is still in the form of sawlogs with minimum value added, while the domestic wood-based industries, mainly located in the peninsula, have been crying out for supplies. Neither the national wood industry nor environmentalists have been able to undermine the nexus of Japanese financiers, local Chinese logging operators, and indigenous politicians with timber concessions who benefit most from logging in Malaysia. An increase in petroleum royalties for state governments, especially in Sabah and Sarawak, may well be the only effective way to reduce currently high logging rates.

Fourth, although the volume of tin exports did not change much, value rose from $1.2 billion in 1975 to $2.5 billion in 1980 as the price more than doubled. The value declined in the 1980s, especially after the price collapse of October 1985, before picking up in 1987 and 1988. After October 1985, gravel pump and other traditional mining methods were virtually suspended until the price recovered sufficiently. The subsequent recovery brought higher production cost methods into operation once again, but they are again at risk with the price decline since 1989.

Fifth, petroleum exports swelled from $0.7 billion in 1975 to $6.9 billion in 1981 and $8.7 billion in 1984 and 1985, before dropping to $5.4 billion in 1986 and $6.3 billion in 1987. Petroleum has been the leading primary commodity export earner since the late 1970s. Petroleum reserves in Sarawak and off the peninsula's east coast are not definitively established,

**Table 7.2**
Commodity exports, 1960–1988

| Commodity | 1960 | 1965 | 1970 | 1975 | 1980 | 1981 | 1982 | 1983 | 1984 | 1985 | 1986 | 1987[b] | 1988[b] | Average annual growth rate (%) | | |
|---|---|---|---|---|---|---|---|---|---|---|---|---|---|---|---|---|
| | | | | | | | | | | | | | | 1961–70 | 1971–80 | 1981–86 |
| Crude petroleum | | | | | | | | | | | | | | | | |
| Volume ('000 tons) | 2,515.1 | 1,747.4 | 4,696.2 | 3,794.5 | 11,226.9 | 10,143.2 | 11,973.9 | 14,224.0 | 16,497.4 | 16,701.3 | 18,792.0 | 17,999.0 | 19,879.0 | 6.4 | 9.1 | 9.0 |
| Unit value ($/ton) | 58.3 | 49.6 | 43.1 | 226.9 | 597.6 | 682.4 | 642.6 | 553.4 | 529.6 | 520.8 | 287.4 | 348.7 | 305.9 | -3.0 | 30.1 | -11.5 |
| Value ($ million) | 146.7 | 86.7 | 202.6 | 861.0 | 6,709.1 | 6,921.4 | 7,694.2 | 7,871.0 | 8,737.4 | 8,697.9 | 5,400.9 | 6,289.9 | 6,127.9 | 3.3 | 41.9 | -3.5 |
| Palm oil[a] | | | | | | | | | | | | | | | | |
| Volume ('000 tons) | 97.6 | 143.2 | 401.9 | 1,160.6 | 2,258.2 | 2,506.8 | 2,817.2 | 2,948.8 | 2,979.0 | 3,232.0 | 4,334.6 | 4,100.5 | 4,166.2 | 15.2 | 18.8 | 11.5 |
| Unit value ($/ton) | 620.9 | 728.8 | 657.5 | 1,136.9 | 1,152.7 | 1,131.1 | 973.4 | 1,015.6 | 1,524.7 | 1,226.2 | 696.6 | 802.7 | 1,039.8 | 0.6 | 5.8 | -8.0 |
| Value ($ million) | 60.6 | 107.2 | 264.3 | 1,319.5 | 2,603.1 | 2,835.5 | 2,742.3 | 2,994.9 | 4,542.1 | 3,963.1 | 3,019.5 | 3,291.9 | 4,540.2 | 15.9 | 25.7 | 2.5 |
| Rubber | | | | | | | | | | | | | | | | |
| Volume ('000 tons) | 853.2 | 966.0 | 1,345.4 | 1,456.9 | 1,525.7 | 1,485.3 | 1,378.1 | 1,563.0 | 1,590.6 | 1,497.4 | 1,516.1 | 1,620.3 | 1,610.6 | 4.7 | 1.3 | -0.1 |
| Unit value (cts./kg) | 234.5 | 151.3 | 128.1 | 138.8 | 302.7 | 250.0 | 192.7 | 234.4 | 230.8 | 191.8 | 209.9 | 241.6 | 326.3 | -5.9 | 9.0 | -5.9 |
| Value ($ million) | 2,001.0 | 1,461.8 | 1,723.7 | 2,025.6 | 4,618.0 | 3,713.1 | 2,655.1 | 3,663.6 | 3,671.5 | 2,872.2 | 3,182.7 | 3,915.1 | 5,255.9 | -1.5 | 10.4 | -6.0 |
| Sawlogs | | | | | | | | | | | | | | | | |
| Volume ('000 cu. m.) | 2,088.0 | 4,780.7 | 8,906.5 | 8,477.0 | 15,156.2 | 15,923.3 | 19,297.8 | 18,276.0 | 16,939.4 | 19,630.5 | 19,054.2 | 23,000.5 | 20,552.0 | 15.6 | 5.5 | 3.9 |
| Unit value ($/cu. m.) | 56.8 | 55.1 | 72.3 | 79.1 | 172.7 | 155.5 | 175.3 | 149.9 | 165.7 | 141.2 | 150.8 | 186.3 | 195.0 | 2.4 | 9.1 | -2.3 |
| Value ($ million) | 118.6 | 263.3 | 643.6 | 670.4 | 2,618.2 | 2,476.2 | 3,382.1 | 2,806.9 | 2,806.1 | 2,771.2 | 2,872.7 | 4,285.5 | 4,010.0 | 18.4 | 15.1 | 1.6 |
| LNG | | | | | | | | | | | | | | | | |
| Volume ('000 million tons) | — | — | — | — | — | — | — | 1,830.0 | 3,700.0 | 4,391.4 | 5,206.0 | 6,010.0 | 6,100.0 | — | — | — |
| Unit value ($/tons) | — | — | — | — | — | — | — | 454.3 | 479.6 | 523.7 | 364.0 | 290.0 | — | — | — | — |
| Value ($ million) | — | — | — | — | — | — | — | 831.3 | 1,774.7 | 2,299.8 | 1,895.0 | 1,742.0 | 1,800.0 | — | — | — |

**Table 7.2** (continued)

| | | | | | | | | | | | | | | Average annual growth rate (%) | | |
|---|---|---|---|---|---|---|---|---|---|---|---|---|---|---|---|---|
| **Tin** | | | | | | | | | | | | | | | | |
| Volume ('000 tons) | 77.9 | 75.3 | 91.9 | 77.9 | 69.5 | 66.4 | 48.6 | 57.1 | 39.6 | 57.4 | 40.4 | 49.6 | 45.1 | 1.7 | −2.8 | −8.6 |
| Unit value ($ tons) | 6,513.2 | 11,582.7 | 10,938.7 | 15,473.9 | 36,049.0 | 32,182.2 | 30,543.1 | 30,070.5 | 29,351.5 | 28,711.4 | 16,086.5 | 16,907.2 | 13,625.3 | 5.3 | 12.7 | −12.6 |
| Value ($ million) | 507.7 | 871.8 | 1,005.6 | 1,206.1 | 2,505.3 | 2,138.1 | 1,483.9 | 1,718.2 | 1,162.3 | 1,648.0 | 650.0 | 838.8 | 911.2 | 7.1 | 9.6 | −20.1 |
| **Sawn timber** | | | | | | | | | | | | | | | | |
| Volume ('000 cu. m.) | 573.2 | 753.0 | 1,392.9 | 1,883.5 | 3,245.2 | 2,907.8 | 3,116.4 | 3,437.6 | 2,872.8 | 2,780.1 | 2,999.3 | 3,921.7 | 4,000.0 | 9.3 | 8.8 | −1.9 |
| Unit value ($/cu. m.) | 131.0 | 128.7 | 147.7 | 223.9 | 414.2 | 384.5 | 373.7 | 392.6 | 409.3 | 408.9 | 435.1 | 444.2 | 461.1 | 1.2 | 10.9 | 0.8 |
| Value ($ million) | 75.1 | 96.9 | 205.8 | 440.6 | 1,344.1 | 1,118.9 | 1,164.6 | 1,349.7 | 1,175.7 | 1,136.8 | 1,305.0 | 1,769.8 | 1,344.4 | 10.6 | 20.6 | −0.6 |
| **Manufactures** | | | | | | | | | | | | | | | | |
| Value ($ million) | — | — | 615.0 | 1,786.0 | 6,269.8 | 6,328.3 | 7,398.5 | 9,501.8 | 12,148.5 | 12,470.8 | 15,351.9 | 20,343.8 | 26,865.2 | — | 26.1 | 15.8 |
| **Total gross commodity exports** | | | | | | | | | | | | | | | | |
| Value ($ million) | 3632.6 | 3782.5 | 5,163.1 | 9,230.9 | 28,171.6 | 27,109.4 | 28,108.2 | 32,771.2 | 38,646.9 | 38,016.7 | 35,720.9 | 45,138.4 | 55,433.0 | 3.6 | 18.5 | 4.1 |

Note: a. Includes processed palm oil. b. Estimate.
Sources: Bank Negara Malaysia, *Annual Report 1986, 1987*; Bank Negara Malaysia, *Quarterly Bulletin*, December 1989, Vol. 4, No. 3.

but at current rates of extraction, known or rather publicly acknowledged deposits are not supposed to last much beyond the beginning of the next decade.

Sixth, LNG exports, which only came onstream in 1983, have grown in value, from $0.8 billion in 1983 to $2.3 billion in 1985, before dropping to $1.9 billion in 1986 and $1.7 billion in 1987, mainly due to softening prices, before rising to $2.2 billion in 1990.

For the medium-term, the bottom line seems to be that Malaysia's two major export earners in the 1980s—petroleum and timber—cannot be counted upon to sustain growth beyond the next decade. Of course, in the interest of short-term expedience, the government can increase extraction, perhaps with dire consequences for the future. The handling of these irreplaceable natural resources will probably still be crucial to growth performance in the 1990s. It also seems likely, in the light of past experience, that the crucial decisions involved are likely to be made with short-term political considerations foremost, rather than with the long term economic interest of the nation in mind.

### 7.1.3   Foreign Debt and Internal Finance

Malaysia's debt problem is largely a phenomenon of the 1980s. Before then, borrowings were relatively modest, with a high proportion of project loans from multilateral as well as bilateral sources. Only with the collapse of primary commodity prices in the late 1970s did the Malaysian government begin to borrow heavily from private commercial sources, initially for countercyclical expansionary spending. After the April 1982 general election, the government abruptly embarked on an austerity campaign in June.

By this time, however, the new prime minister (since mid-1981), Mahathir Mohamad, was committed to financing several major heavy industrial projects including cement, steel, paper, and car industries with foreign commercial credit. New borrowings from abroad continued to grow until the mid-1980s. With Mahathir's "Look East" policy, yen-denominated loans financed heavy industrial projects at attractive interest rates.

Despite a reduction in new borrowing since 1984, the total size of the public foreign debt continued to rise in local currency terms until 1988 because of the ringgit depreciation in the interim. Partly due to the prepayment policy since 1987, outstanding foreign debt has declined from 1988, reducing Malaysia's vulnerability to external credit constraints or interest rate jumps. However, domestic public debt, particularly to finance government development expenditure, has grown faster since the mid-1980s to compensate for the decline in new foreign loans.

Central bank regulations have enabled commercial banks to enjoy handsome profits from margins between deposit and lending rates. The regulations have required banks to diversify ownership and lending from what they might have preferred. To maximize profits, many financial institutions in Malaysia became involved in financing quick profit and speculative activities. With collapses of the property market after 1983 and the stock market in late 1985 and October 1987, high-risk loans were adversely affected. The Central Bank has estimated commercial bank non-performing loans in the region of $25 billion as of 1988 (Bank Negara Malaysia 1989).

Before the 1980s, Malaysia's investment finance requirements could largely be met by domestic savings. However, the dramatic decline in foreign investments, particularly in manufacturing, mining, and agriculture, in the early and mid-1980s and the recession that followed may have marked a significant change. The recent recovery, primarily associated with renewed foreign investments, especially from Japan, Taiwan, and Singapore, suggests that for growth to be sustained, ever-rising net inflows of direct foreign investment may be required.

The recent foreign investment boom can be at least partly attributed to changes in relative factor costs in the wake of the Plaza II international currency realignments. While the Malaysian ringgit depreciated against even the U.S. dollar, other East Asian currencies all appreciated considerably. Labor shortages in these economies have also pushed up labor costs. Malaysia's new investment incentives—mainly directed at foreigners, and part of the mid-1980s "structural adjustments"—as well as its good infrastructure and other facilities and advantages have all helped to attract direct investment. The crucial question is how long this boom will last, as it is dependent on external factors well beyond Malaysian control.

There is also limited understanding of the sources of foreign investment. For example, Japanese investments rose from $25.2 million in 1978 to $152.7 million in 1979, before dropping to $32.6 million in 1980 and then rising to $136.7 million in 1982 before declining again until the late 1980s. Such fluctuations suggest that reliable forecasting about the sustainability of the current boom will not be an easy task.

Since the mid-1980s, the official line has been to discourage public investment—even in infrastructure if potentially lucrative—in favor of the private sector. Public foreign debt expansion has been curbed since 1986, with the subsequent increase in the public debt derived from domestic sources. There is little reason to believe that the foreign debt problem of the early 1980s will reemerge if current fiscal policies continue, which is likely to be the case.

## 7.2 Alternative Development Strategies

Consideration of the state in Malaysia is complicated by the popular perception of its role as a vehicle for particular ethnic interests. The New Economic Policy (NEP), announced in 1970, is ostensibly committed to creating the socioeconomic conditions for national unity by reducing poverty and the identification of race with economic function. In practice, the growth of the public sector and state intervention has been widely seen to be associated with advancing the economic interest of the indigenous (Bumiputera) community, especially the dominant Malay business class. Through the 1970s and the early 1980s, this ethnic identification with state expansionism colored most views about the desirability of state involvement in the economy.

In recent years, however, these perceptions have been changing in response to reforms popularly associated with Mahathir's appointee Daim Zainuddin (at the treasury since 1984). The new policies include efforts at improving relations between the state and the business community, privatization, reductions in public spending, new incentives to attract investors, and reduced taxes in the interest of business. Other measures seek to cut real wages as well as other costs and to promote export-oriented production. Despite this dramatic policy reorientation, the government has managed to retain its pro-Bumiputera image by publicizing its continued, albeit reduced, rural development efforts, and granting privatization opportunities, contracts, licenses and other lucrative rent-seeking opportunities to Malays, especially the politically well-connected.

In the recent debate, state actions generally have been associated with rent-seeking and the decline of public accountability among politicians and the bureaucracy. These perceptions obscure other important roles of the state in post-colonial Malaysia, for example, in terms of infrastructure development and social service provision. A fundamental problem is that public intervention to serve apparently ethnic, but actually class-factional, ends has contributed to widespread resentment or apathy toward the state, especially among the non-Malay population. There is a major constituency favoring deregulation and most other structural adjustments, though not necessarily privatization, as it has been implemented in Malaysia, because of ethnic bias. Any alternative economic strategy must take into account ethnic considerations as well as the current reputation of the Malaysian state.

## 7.3    Sectoral and Micro Issues

Because of its extreme openness, the Malaysian economy poses unique sectoral planning problems. In this section, we take up questions regarding industry, agriculture, planning and finance, and income distribution.

### 7.3.1    Industry

For its level of GDP per capita, Malaysia has been widely perceived as being "underindustrialized," in terms of the share of the manufacturing sector in GDP as well as in total employment. Malaysian exports consisted primarily of primary commodities, which accounted for 94 % of gross merchandise exports in 1965 but only 74 % in 1985 and 40 % in 1990. Malaysia's manufacturing base is still poorly developed with considerable potential for further import substitution and export diversification.

Industrial activities—especially in the free trade zones (FTZs) and licensed manufacturing warehouses (LMWs), for example, electronics and textiles—are only weakly linked to the rest of the economy. Although most successful earlier industrializers relied heavily on textiles for initial manufacturing growth, two factors blocked this role in Malaysia, namely, the sector is small and much of it is foreign controlled or located in the FTZs.

In 1986, the government announced its Industrial Master Plan (IMP) for 1986–95, prepared by a UNIDO team with the Malaysian Industrial Development Authority (MIDA). The IMP documents present a sober analysis of the nation's industrial heritage. They point out that Malaysia's success with primary commodities probably blunted the imperative to industrialize with the availability of other more profitable investment opportunities outside manufacturing, for example in real property, securities, finance, other services, mining, and agriculture.

Malaysia's initial moves toward import-substituting industrialization efforts began in the late 1950s and by the time of Singapore's secession in 1965, the limits had become clear. Nevertheless, the switch to export-oriented industrialization was slow, only really taking off in the 1970s. In the early 1980s, ill-considered efforts to develop certain heavy industries soon aborted a possible second round of import substitution.

The IMP also recognized that Malaysia's industrial structure is un-balanced. Dynamic subsectors are narrowly based on labor-intensive and resource-based activities. Manufactured exports accounted for less than 20 % of total manufactured goods in the early 1980s, while the share of resource-based manufactured products had actually declined to 19.7 % of all manufactured exports in 1983. Malaysia's nonresource-based manufac-tured exports mainly involve fairly simple, low-scale, labor-intensive as-sembly work, though there was some upgrading in the 1980s. In 1990, electronics and electrical products plus textiles and garments together accounted for 64 % of manufactured exports and 48 % of manufacturing sector workers.

Besides criticizing high levels of protection for ISI, the IMP emphasized the absence of domestic interindustry linkages. In 1982, only 6.5 % of the raw materials used in FTZs and LMWs were from local sources, whereas 64 % of total manufactured exports came from the zones. Although ac-knowledging that manufacturing is dominated by large, usually foreign-controlled firms, the document pays little attention to the massive outflows associated with foreign ownership and control.

The IMP's recommendations have only been selectively adopted. Pol-icies in the second half of the 1980s focused on manufacturing growth, almost at any cost, particularly stressing production for export. The empha-sis has been on enhanced industrial incentives, improved infrastructure, and reduced regulatory controls. These changes as well as the depreciation of the ringgit brought a tremendous resurgence, with manufacturing exports increasing by 33 % in 1987, 32 % in 1988, 36 % in 1989, and 29 % in 1990, with total industrial production rising by 92 % between 1985 and 1990.

Compared to the past, recent export processing involves greater capital-intensity, labor productivity, new skilling, and higher wages. The spread of "just in time" (JIT) processes requiring reduced inventories and supply flexibility has resulted in increasing local sourcing as well as relocation in Malaysia of component suppliers from abroad, strengthening domestic manufacturing linkages and the share of Malaysian value-added. Wide-spread transfer pricing, however, distorts the measures of manufacturing value-added in Malaysia, especially in the electronic and electrical compo-nents industry, which accounts for about half of Malaysia's gross manufac-tured exports.

Despite hearsay, there is little well-substantiated evidence of abrupt footloose investment behavior. Instead, investment relocation, when it oc-curs, generally appears to be more gradual, with new plants being set up abroad while existing plants are phased out with product or technological innovation, although usually for underlying cost and other related profit considerations.

## 7.3.2   Agriculture

The National Agriculture Policy (NAP) announced in January 1984 has been even less significant than the IMP. Nevertheless, its basic thrust of emphasizing commercial agriculture has increasingly become the order of the day, as subsidies for peasants have not increased since 1980, after their last mass demonstrations. Malaysia is now far less committed than in the past to self-sufficiency in rice, with domestic production accounting for much less than even the 80 % to 85 % envisaged by the NAP.

The most dynamic and profitable part of the agricultural sector remains the plantations, which are generally no longer able to grow in size, at least in peninsular Malaysia, because of land and political constraints. Productivity differences between plantation and peasant sectors appear to be widening despite the government's efforts to raise efficiency in the latter.

The agricultural sector's contribution to export earnings has remained in the region of about one-third in the 1980s. It also continues to account for about 32 % of the labor force, a growing proportion of whom are wage earners, rather than self-employed. During the recession of 1985–86, there was an apparent retreat to agriculture, as urban employment opportunities declined. There is persistent and concentrated poverty in peasant agriculture in peninsular Malaysia, leading the government to concentrate poverty eradication efforts in this sector, especially by trying to raise peasant productivity.

However, fundamental and sensitive problems of inequitable ownership and access to land and credit have barely been addressed. Land productivity is generally highest on the smallest farms, which nevertheless remain pockets of hard-core poverty. There is as yet no interest in, let alone commitment to, comprehensive agrarian or even land reform. The recent NAP emphasis on consolidating uneconomically sized farms into mini-estates is the official solution, although there is little evidence of progress on this front.

## 7.3.3   Planning and Public Finance

The idea of economic planning in Malaysia took shape in the late colonial period in the 1950s. For all intents and purposes, the first five-year plan (1956–60) continued to reflect colonial interests and priorities, especially those of British plantation and mining interests. The provision of social services was considered extravagant, except insofar as it was necessary to defeat the communist-led insurgency of the 1950s.

By contrast, in the second five-year plan (1961–65) and the First Malaysia Plan (1966–70), provision of social services was emphasized, with the corresponding resources rising from 8 % during 1950–55 to 27 % during 1966–70. This trend reversed with the promulgation of the NEP in 1971, as the social services budget share began to fall, reaching only 18 % under the Fifth Malaysia Plan (1986–90) allocations.

The revised allocations for the Fifth Plan totalled $49.3 billion for the period 1986–90, compared with $80.2 billion in the previous plan period. The reduction represents a considerable departure from the earlier increases in public expenditure. Of the new total, 76 % is expected to be allocated to the economic sector, 17 % to the social sector, and 7 % to administration and security. Of the social expenditures, education takes 13 %, followed by housing with 2 % and health with 2 %.

It is unlikely that public expenditure can be greatly reduced further without serious political and social strains, if only because political hegemony has been assured by a patronage system built around government regulations and public spending. Indeed, by the late 1980s, public (including development) expenditure was beginning to increase again. More surprisingly, the government began to announce economically unviable projects and commitments reminiscent of the early 1980s. These included a $1.5 billion Highland Highway, a multi-billion ringgit land reclamation project all the way down the west coast of Peninsular Malaysia, a $200 million communications tower, touted as the highest in the world, and $1.5 billion in arms purchases from Great Britain at inflated prices.

The limits of privatization are increasingly being recognized. Private capital is mainly interested in taking over profitable and potentially profitable activities currently in the public sector, leaving the government stuck with the most economically burdensome chores. The spending reductions that have occurred have reduced the number and scale of public projects as well as services, while increasing costs. Further slashes are unlikely to occur for political and bureaucratic reasons, in addition to the economic considerations involved.

On the revenue side, the regressive tax reforms since the mid-1980s have reduced the take, especially from direct taxes. Privatization of public enterprises has generated some revenue on a one-shot basis, but such sales will also imply long-term revenue declines. However, the buoyant economy since the late 1980s has raised overall receipts. The government is also expected to introduce a value-added tax in place of existing selective sales taxes. As discussed above, public revenue prospects from primary commodity exports are difficult to foretell.

### 7.3.4   Income Distribution

Owing to its rapid growth, Malaysia is now among the better-off middle-income countries. Income concentration probably increased after independence until the late 1970s (Jomo and Ishak, 1986). According to the treasury's *Economic Report 1974–75* (p. 85), "the top 10% of the households increased their average incomes by 46% from $766 in 1957–58 to $1130 in 1970. On the other hand, the income of the bottom 10% of the households seems to have declined from $48 to $33 during the corresponding period (−31%)."

More recent overall data have not been released, but official numbers suggest that poverty declined from 56.7% in 1970 to 39.6% in 1976, 18.4% in 1984, and 17.3% in 1987 (Jomo, 1989) while income inequality continued to grow until 1970, when the Gini ratio was 0.57. However, interethnic as well as urban rural disparities have declined since 1970, with the Malay mean income rising to 81% of the national average and the urban-rural disparity ratio declining to 1.7 by 1987. The limited data available for the 1980s suggest that the incomes of the lower deciles continued to rise while the upper income groups seem to have suffered some small reductions in average incomes due to the severe recessions of the early 1980s and 1985–86.

## 7.4   Prospects for Growth

The World Bank appears quite optimistic about the prices of Malaysia's main export commodities. If such forecasts influence policy, it is quite likely that the economy will be heavily reliant on primary exports while continuing to promote manufactures. However, the declining availability of non-renewable resources, such as timber, petroleum and even tin, means that these commodities can no longer be relied upon to sustain high growth. Prospects for future foreign investments are also uncertain, while domestic capital flight abroad is likely to continue to reflect the state of ethnic relations, political confidence in the government of the day, and other political developments.

Some major sources of inefficiency in the economy have been reduced with the structural adjustment policies since the mid-1980s. But the policies

**Table 7.3**
Malaysia: Gross domestic and national savings (% of GNP)

|          | GDS   | GNS   | NFPA   |
|----------|-------|-------|--------|
| 1961–65  | n.a.  | 15.3  | n.a.   |
| 1966–70  | n.a.  | 18.0  | n.a.   |
| 1971–75  | 25.9  | 22.0  | − 3.6  |
| 1976–80  | 35.0  | 30.6  | − 4.2  |
| 1981–85  | 33.5  | 27.2  | − 6.2  |
| 1986     | 33.8  | 27.3  | − 7.2  |
| 1987     | 40.4  | 34.4  | − 7.0  |
| 1988     | 37.5  | 32.1  | − 5.4  |

Source: Lin See-Yan (1989), "The Savings and Investment Gap—The Case of Malaysia."

have not created a coherent and balanced national economic structure. The government has recently begun to develop manpower serving the needs of transnational corporations, rather than those identified with a balanced, integrated, and less dependent national development strategy.

In the 1960s and 1970s, rapid growth could be sustained with little foreign borrowing. Private sector surpluses were enough to finance both private and public domestic investment. With the sharp increase in public spending in the early 1980s, domestic resources were no longer sufficient. By 1982, gross domestic investment (GDI) came to 39 % of GNP, while gross national savings (GNS) were only 25 %. Reductions in government spending from 1982 and in heavy industry investment by 1984 helped turn the situation around. Public investment's share of GNP fell from 19.6 % in 1982 to 13.8 % in 1985 and 10.1 % in 1987, before rising again slowly thereafter. At the same time, the external current account deficit compared to GNP was reduced from 14.1 % in 1982 to 2.1 % in 1985 and recorded a surplus of 8.1 % in 1987 (tables 7.3 and 7.4).

Although the growing savings gap in the early 1980s was closed by the middle of the decade with even a surplus in 1987, recent developments suggest that savings limitations may persist (Lin, 1989):

1. Growing net factor payments abroad (NFPA, currently equivalent to 7 % of GDP) have ensured the growing difference between gross national savings (GNS) and gross domestic savings (GDS).

2. GNS has been on a downward trend since 1979; since both total and private savings have been highly sensitive to income level and growth, rather than, say, interest rates, it may continue to be difficult to raise savings.

**Table 7.4**
Malaysia, savings-investment gap, 1961–1988 (% of GNP)

|          | GNS  | GDI  | Current account[a] |
|----------|------|------|--------------------|
| 1961–65  | 15.3 | 16.4 | − 1.1              |
| 1966–70  | 18.0 | 16.3 | 1.7                |
| 1971–75  | 22.0 | 25.7 | − 3.7              |
| 1976–80  | 30.6 | 28.4 | 2.2                |
| 1981–85  | 27.2 | 35.7 | − 8.5              |
| 1986     | 27.3 | 27.1 | 0.2                |
| 1987     | 33.5 | 25.7 | 8.9                |
| 1988     | 33.0 | 26.3 | 5.5                |

a. Surplus ( + ); Deficit ( − )
Source: Lin See-Yan (1989), "The Savings and Investment Gap—The Case of Malaysia,"
revised with data from Annual Reports of the Bank Negara Malaysia.

3. There appears to be a sharp fall in the elasticity of savings, both in terms of income level and growth.

Despite a high GDS of over 30 % of GNP, and the large and persistent current payments deficits in the early 1980s, real growth rates remained modest by local standards. This has been attributed to the rising factor payments abroad, which significantly reduced GNS. The negative ICOR trend in the early 1980s was mainly due to large investments in heavy industries and real property as well as countercyclical government spending, while investments in manufacturing, agriculture and mining declined to unprecedented low levels.

## 7.5  Toward Coherent Development?

Although the global economic environment has generally been kind to the open Malaysian economy in recent decades, the frequency and adversity of downturns in the 1980s raised crucial questions about the feasibility of continued export-led growth. International trade restrictions are expected by many to increase in the 1990s, with the increasing economic integration of Europe on the one hand and North America on the other. The failure of ASEAN to make significant headway as a framework for regional economic cooperation, and the recent Malaysian experience with U.S. protectionism against palm oil have only strengthened such fears. Although yen appreciation provided unexpected opportunities for Malaysia, there is little confidence in how much these may continue to offer through the 1990s.

There are also doubts about further industrialization, to which the current Malaysian government is strongly committed. Taiwan, South Korea, Hong Kong, and Singapore achieved NIC status 20 years ago in another world economic environment. The Malaysian manufacturing sector is very different from the Asian NICs besides Singapore, especially in terms of its extensive foreign ownership and control as well as technological dependence. Malaysia's current industrial dynamism is externally generated, rather than internally propelled and controlled, raising important questions about its coherence.

An important prerequisite for coherent development would be leadership by a regime recognizing the need for national integration and balance. Malaysia's political system—originally structured by British colonialism, and subsequently amended to mobilize ethnic groups in support of their economic and political interests—does not provide a framework conducive to such ends. At best, a few enlightened and visionary politicians and technocrats consider and advance the "national interest" in development as they see it.

Some economic policies associated with the early years of the Mahathir regime may have been intended as efforts for more coherent development. The heavy industrial projects of the early 1980s sought to balance the earlier emphasis on light manufacturing as well as to advance import substituting industrialization after the stress on export-oriented manufacturing in the 1970s. These industries turned out to be massive albatrosses, consuming finances and sinking the Malaysian economy and government into unprecedented levels of foreign debt. The heavy industries are poorly linked to the rest of the economy and require high levels of protection to ensure their survival, increasing production costs downstream.

Most other reforms associated with the Mahathir era have given priority to expanding export-led industrialization. The National Agriculture Policy has sought to promote cash crops for the market and to encourage more "economic" farm management, for example, by increasing farm size through managerial consolidation of small land parcels owned by peasants. The "Look East" policy, ostensibly meant to emulate Japan and South Korea's industrial successes, ended up offering privileges to construction firms and other suppliers from these two countries. It was then redefined to encourage new work ethics, which has turned out to be a rather hollow call to increase productivity, accept managerial and government prerogatives without complaint, and otherwise enhance industrial harmony without demanding or securing more tangible material benefits. The "Malaysia Incorporated" campaign turned out to be an aborted attempt to improve relations between the Malay-dominated government and the Chinese private sector, though it may well be revived if deemed necessary.

Meanwhile, the general political-economic environment has encouraged greater rent-seeking behavior by the politically influential and bureaucratically powerful. It has distorted investment priorities from production toward speculative and quickly remunerative activities, particularly in the property and stock markets. The fiscal and debt crises from the early 1980s made the government more amenable to the structural adjustment policies introduced since the early 1980s. With the 1985–86 collapse in commodity prices, these deflationary policies produced an unprecedented recession, with considerable fallouts in the economy, especially the corporate sector, and even in politics.

## 7.6   Political Stability

Political stability is a prerequistie for continued investment growth; in Malaysia, the uncertainties cluster around ethnic relations. Tension rose in the 1970s and 1980s, with the implementation of ethnically biased policies —often associated with the NEP—in most spheres of social life. More recent structural adjustment policies have helped to assuage non-Malay and especially foreign business interests. Yet, the non-Malays generally— especially, the highly influential, but discontented middle class, which dominates the managerial and professional positions in the private sector— remain frustrated, contributing to a continuous brain drain and capital flight. Ironically, influential members of the Malay elite seem pleased with this hemorrhage, believing that it will advance their economic power, besides consolidating their political hegemony. Although some Malay political leaders recognize the self-defeating consequences of such policies, the Malaysian political system of ethnic mobilization and patronage has generally forced them to maintain a discreet silence.

Another source of instability is regional. The federal fiscal system established at the time of Independence rendered state governments dependent on federal largess. Their main sources of revenue are related to land, over which they maintain jurisdiction. Despite additional prerogatives for the new states of Sabah and Sarawak with their integration into Malaysia in 1963, some argue that federal-state tensions in East Malaysia have worsened over the years. There have been dramatic changes in government in both Sabah and Sarawak, partly reflecting popular frustrations with the Kuala Lumpur government. Although secession is generally considered treasonous—despite the clearly artificial origins of the Malaysian federation to protect British interests in the twilight of its empire in Southeast Asia—these tensions continue to combine with ethnic and other political factors to sustain instability.

Other contradictions continue to grow in significance. Despite increased rural development efforts under the NEP, the two largest Malay peasant demonstrations ever occurred in late 1974 and early 1980, involving rubber smallholders and rice farmers respectively. There has been tremendous investment in rural and agricultural infrastructure and social services, and improved credit and even marketing facilities, although land schemes have been unable to keep up with the increasing numbers of the rural landless. Fortunately, increased wage and other employment opportunities have considerably reduced the pressures that otherwise would have mounted in the countryside. Since 1980, an effective system of political patronage and crisis management has minimized large-scale peasant unrest, although localized problems are quite widespread and continuously emerge.

Although three-fifths of the labor force were wage earners in the late 1980s, less than 10 % of the labor force is unionized, that is, less than a sixth of all wage earners. More than half the unionized employees are in the public sector, where workers' rights are further limited by law. Outside the public sector, labor laws and industrial relations policies have been revised from time to time to subjugate workers. Rapid economic growth since independence helped to defuse political instability. When growth was adversely affected, for example, in 1974–75 and 1985–86, unrest increased.

Other factors have contributed to the political ferment since the mid-1980s, for example, the electoral defeat of the then Sabah government in 1985, the increased votes for the opposition in the 1986 elections, the split of the UMNO leadership in 1987, and the near defeat of the state government in Sarawak in the same year. But it seems likely that if recession had not occurred, then some of this dissent might have been better contained. The economic recovery of the late 1980s strengthened the hegemony of the ruling coalition. More equitable growth in the medium term would strengthen it further, despite the fact that instability in Malaysia is related to ethnic, regional, and class inequalities.

However, one can never be too sure about the prospects of the Malaysian economy. The experience of the 1980s confounded both optimists and pessimists. Although external conditions have clearly been crucial in influencing Malaysia's performance, there have also been important changes in national economic management. If growth in the 1990s is more modest, it is very likely that the fiscal and political system will be under considerable stress. The improvement of its international credit rating in the late 1980s means that Malaysia recovered the maneuvering room it seemed to have lost in the mid-1980s. There are economic taps (e.g., petroleum and gas) that can be turned on at will in the interest of short-term political expediency. It is likely that all these and more will be called upon to preserve the regime, especially if growth rates decline. Although it is unlikely that the development process will become more equitable, except in enhancing the Malay economic position, and thus reducing interethnic disparities, continued tensions and preservation of the political status quo will probably mean that fundamentally different development strategies and policies are unlikely to emerge. And if allowed to fester, ethnic and regional tensions could have dire consequences for the future of the nation.

## References

Bank Negara Malaysia (various years). *Annual Reports*. Kuala Lumpur.

Edwards, C. B. (1975). *Protection, Profits and Policy: An Analysis of Industrialization in Malaysia* Ph.D. Thesis, University of East Anglia.

Jomo K. S. (1989). "Beyond 1990: Considerations for a New National Development Strategy." Kuala Lumpur: Institute of Advanced Studies, University of Malaya.

Jomo K. S. (1990). *Growth and Structural Changes in the Malaysian Economy*. London: Macmillan.

Jomo K. S., and Ishak Shari (1986). "Development Policies and Income Inequality in Peninsular Malaysia." Kuala Lumpur: Institute of Advanced Studies, University of Malaya.

Lin, See-Yan (1989). "The Savings and Investment Gap—The Case of Malaysia." Tokyo Symposium on "The Present and Future of the Pacific Basin Economy: A Comparison of Asia and Latin America," Institute of Developing Economies," Tokyo, July.

Malaysia (1989). *Mid-Term Review of the Fifth Malaysia Plan: 1986–1990*. Kuala Lumpur: Government Printers.

Malaysia (1991). *Sixth Malaysia Plan, 1991–95*. Kuala Lumpur.

Mehmet, Ozay (1986). *Development in Malaysia*. London: Croom Helm.

# 8        Sri Lanka

S. A. Karunaratne and
Carlo Fonseka

The present paper examines critical aspects of Sri Lanka's development problem in the decade of the 1990s. We begin with a historical introduction, followed in section 8.2 with a description of the main economic variables as they stood at the end of the 1980s. Section 8.3 takes up the main issues for the future, and in particular, the growth objective. It also describes the existing strategies in some detail.

## 8.1    Historical Introduction

When Sri Lanka became a politically independent country after four centuries of foreign domination, almost all characteristics of a typical dualistic economy had taken root. The enclave was plantation agriculture, consisting of growing and primary processing of tea and rubber, and to a lesser extent, coconuts. Physical infrastructure—roads, railways, and communication—were all geared to the needs of the enclave. The other segment of the economy that involved the large mass of rural population was basically subsistence agriculture, fisheries, mining, simple manufactures, handicrafts, and services.

In the pre-war period and up to the mid-1950s, surpluses generated in the plantation sector paid handsome dividends to foreign investors in addition to being a rich source of revenue for the government. The state was able to open new land for domestic agriculture, and initiate social services: health, education, and subsidized food, which mainly benefited the rural population outside the enclave economy but had generally favorable effects overall (see the international comparisons in table 8.1).

The system worked rather well in the given historical context and at the time of independence (1948), Sri Lanka had one of the highest incomes per capita in Southeast Asia. Nonetheless, there was substantial inequality.

**Table 8.1**
Sri Lanka—Quality of life indicators relative to low- and middle-income countries

| | Life expectancy at birth years (1987) | Crude death rates (1987) | Infant mortality rates (1987) | Population per physician (1984) | Per capita calorie consumption (1987) | Secondary school enrollment (1986) | ICP per capita including index US = 100 (1985)[a] |
|---|---|---|---|---|---|---|---|
| 1. Low-income countries average | 61 | 10 | 76 | 5410 | 2100 | 35 | 1.6–11.2 |
| 2. Sri Lanka | 70 | 6 | 33 | 5520 | 2400 | 66 | 11.2 |
| 3. Middle-income countries average | 65 | 8 | 56 | 2390 | 2700 | 54 | 7.0–35.5 |

a. Ranges rather than averages for the two sets of countries shown here.
Sources: *World Development Reports* (World Bank), 1989, 1990; *The World Bank Atlas*.

Among the poor were peasants in the hill country who were deprived of their land when the colonial rulers set up the plantations. There were also farmers in the dry and intermediate zones, who had to cope with difficult and unpredictable weather conditions. Indentured workers brought in from South India to work in the plantations were the third poverty group.

Sri Lanka acquired the right to universal suffrage almost as soon as some democracies in Europe. In the same period (1931), Sri Lankans won the right to almost full internal self-government, leading politicians to be responsive to the needs and aspirations of ordinary people even before the country became formally independent. Economic and social policies thus reflect an activist role for the government, principally aimed at strengthening the peasant agricultural sector and the provision of welfare services. A cornerstone of this strategy was the opening of new agricultural land in the dry zone of the island, under which water reservoirs (known as tanks) and connected irrigation systems of an older civilization were restored to establish new farming settlements.

At the time of independence, industrialization had not progressed beyond processing export crops and production of a few simple consumer items. Soon after, a number of government-owned industrial enterprises were set up but they invariably found it difficult to compete with cheap imports.

## 8.1.1   Social and Political Relations

For many centuries, Sri Lanka has been a multiracial, multireligious, multi-lingual society. In the present composition, the majority are Sinhalese (74 %) by ethnicity and Buddhist (69 %) by religion. The non-Sinhalese (26 %) are Sri Lankan Tamils (12 %), Indian Tamils (6 %), Moors (7 %), Burghers and others. The non-Buddhists are Hindus, Christians, and Muslims. Generally, but not exclusively, these groups have been associated with distinct economic functions.

At independence, power passed from the British to an elite drawn from the English-educated, propertied members of the different ethnic groups—Sinhalese, Tamils, Muslims, and Burghers. Among them, despite communal differences, a semblance of political unity was apparent at the time. The ruling elite owed power and prestige to inherited landed property, wealth acquired from enterprises such as the liquor trade, and to entry into the administrative service and professions such as law and medicine, through an English education.

In the four decades following independence, two political parties or groups alternatively took control of the government through a democratic electoral process. The more conservative United National Party (UNP) comprised a fair representation of all major ethnic communities and had wide support of the rural Sinhalese. The party emphasized agricultural development in its economic policy, and was committed to protect free enterprise, land ownership, and the old colonial values. The other groups was usually led by the Sri Lanka Freedom Party (SLFP), with social democratic leanings. This party was able to dislodge the powerful UNP only with the support of smaller, more radical groups or others having narrow ethnic or religious leanings. SLFP's policy aimed at a mixed economy with a strong public enterprise sector and usually gave greater weight to industrial development. Its rule, particularly in the 1970s, was marked by a proliferation of administrative controls of prices, trade, and foreign exchange.

The political cycle was associated with changes in economic growth rates. UNP-led governments, which applied relatively market-oriented economic strategies, succeeded in accelerating growth, while SLFP-led governments, which followed more welfare-oriented strategies, were not so successful in this regard. However, no definite conclusion on the efficacy of each policy regime in achieving either growth or equity can be drawn because it is clear that a number of other factors were at work.

One was the inflow of concessionary foreign capital (foreign aid). An examination of these inflows in the period since 1970 reveals a definite bias toward the market-oriented strategy, which probably contributed to acceleration of growth during these periods.

By the end of the 1950s, new problems associated with the pressure of population growth, and inequalities of income and wealth in a situation of declining terms of trade raised serious questions about the viability of the plantation export economy. A change in government at almost every parliamentary election indicated a general sense of dissatisfaction.

In the meantime, differences between the majority community and the largest ethnic minority—the Tamils—were growing. Adjustments were made in regard to language, education, employment, and new land settlements. Apparently these were intended to restore national resources, and economic and social opportunities to the majority Sinhalese. The Tamils saw a threat to their ethnic and cultural identity, which they attempted to redress by constitutional means. They repeatedly failed to obtain a measure of regional autonomy for predominantly Tamil-speaking parts of the country.

By 1976, mainstream Tamil opinion had resolved that their survival as a distinct ethnic group required nothing less than setting up a separate state called Tamil Ealam in the northern and eastern provinces. Before long, militant Tamil groups launched an armed struggle against the Sri Lankan state. The government attempted with varying degrees of success, and at great economic cost, to contain the revolt. In 1987 India intervened to help resolve the conflict on the basis of regional autonomy for Tamils within a unitary Sri Lankan state. This formula has been resented by extreme nationalist Sinhalese as well as by fiercely militant Tamils. The deep-seated conflict remains unresolved.

In the early 1960s, widespread unemployment began to appear on the socioeconomic scene. It is clear that the origin of most social ills including the ethnic division just discussed can be traced to this problem.

## 8.1.2   Evolution of Economic Variables

From 1948 to 1988, considerable changes occurred in the economic and social structure. The population increased at an average annual rate of 2.1 % to reach 16.6 million in 1988. This was accompanied by a slowing birth rate and an increase in the age composition in favor of higher age groups. The average annual rate of increase slowed to about 1.6 % in the 1980s.

Gross domestic product (GDP) grew only at an average annual rate of about 4 % in the period after independence, so that there has been a modest improvement in the living standards over time.

Domestic production became more complex. The relative contribution of plantation agriculture to GDP declined rapidly, even though dualism continued. Meanwhile, the composition of production shifted in favor of secondary and tertiary activities. The share of agriculture including plantations) fell from 38 % in 1950 to 27 % in 1987. Industry increased from 14 % to 19 %; the change would have been sharper if processing of agricultural exports was excluded. The share of services remained high at about 47 % (see table 8.2).

One of the most basic achievements was the increase in paddy (rice) output. In the 1948−1988 period, production rose from 18.7 to 118.2 million bushels, achieving an average rate of increase of nearly 5 % per year. This was clearly the foundation for economic growth and balance of payments viability of the island's economy in the period reviewed.

Foreign trade relative to the GDP declined in the years after 1948. Nevertheless, the economy continues to be exceedingly open by international standards. Compared to the situation in the early 1950s, exports as well as imports now show considerable diversity. Agricultural exports exceeded 90 % of the total in 1948 but now amount to about 43 %; the share of manufacturing exports has increased from almost zero to 48 %.

The more significant new exports are precious and semi-precious stones, marine products, ready-made garments, and refined petroleum products. Many such industries set up after 1970 were basically processing activities where the import content in the final product was high. Nevertheless, they were able to provide employment and a welcome stimulation to a slow-moving economy. There was also rapid growth of tourism in the period 1965 to 1982. At their peak, earnings from tourism reached 3 % of GDP.

Changes in import composition reflected not only growing complexity of domestic demand but also the achievement of a degree of import substitution. In 1948, imports of food alone amounted to about 53 % of the total, whereas the largest share at present is that of intermediate goods (57 %) while all consumer goods take up 24 %.

The domestic savings rate in Sri Lanka has not shown any appreciable increase. There was an improvement in the national saving rate in the 1978 to 1983 period, due to increased inflow of remittances by Sri Lankan workers employed abroad. In contrast to savings, gross domestic capital formation (GDCF) has risen in the post-1977 period. This helps explain the

**Table 8.2**
GDP by industrial origin, 1978–1988

| | (at constant 1982 factor cost) | | | | |
| | Rupees million | | Contribution to change 1978/88 % | Average rate of growth[a] % | Share of sector 1988 % |
| --- | --- | --- | --- | --- | --- |
| | 1978 | 1988 | | | |
| 1. Agriculture | 21820 | 27984 | 14.3 | 3.0 | 23.5 |
| Tea | 2571 | 2926 | 0.8 | 1.1 | 2.5 |
| Rubber | 963 | 770 | −0.4 | −1.4 | 0.6 |
| Coconuts | 2858 | 2501 | −0.8 | 0.6 | 2.1 |
| Paddy (rice) | 4829 | 6312 | 3.4 | 2.5 | 5.3 |
| Other agriculture | 10599 | 15475 | 11.3 | 4.1 | 13.0 |
| 2. Mining and quarrying | 1867 | 3392 | 3.5 | 5.4 | 2.8 |
| 3. Manufacturing | 11509 | 19622 | 18.8 | 5.5 | 16.5 |
| Proceeding of agricultural exports | 2967 | 3273 | 0.7 | 1.3 | 2.7 |
| Other manufacturing | 8542 | 16349 | 18.1   F | 7.1 | 13.7 |
| | | | Other | 4.6 | |
| 4. Construction | 6237 | 8463 | 5.2 | 1.7 | 7.1 |
| 5. Utilities | 8882 | 15118 | 14.5 | 5.6 | 12.7 |
| 6. Trade | | 25164 | | | 21.1 |
| | 17514 | | 31.3 | 5.7 | |
| 7. Finance and real estate | | 5819 | | | 4.9 |
| 8. Public administration and defense | | 5462 | | | 4.6 |
| | 8180 | | 12.3 | 5.2 | |
| 9. Other services | | 8026 | | | 6.7 |
| GDP | 76009 | 119050 | 100.0 | 4.6 | 100.0 |

a. Least square trend rates.
F: "Factory type" industry; Other: Other industry, including cottage industries.

improved growth performance achieved in the period after 1977. A particularly disturbing feature, however, is the apparent decline in the output-capital ratio over the four decades, suggesting in turn a decline in efficiency of capital use. One explanation in the 1980s has been a marked shift to infrastructure type capital projects with long gestation periods.

### 8.1.3   The Public Sector

In the post-independence period, the public sector in Sir Lanka grew in size and importance. Starting in the 1950s under the SLFP-led government, key business enterprises, particularly in the transport and services sectors, came under state control in accordance with the then current policy of nationalization. Later additions were tea, rubber, and coconut plantations taken over under the land reform laws of 1972 and 1975. New state-owned enterprises were established for manufacturing, including a refinery, a steel mill, a hardware factory, and textile, sugar, and tire factories.

Pricing and production in these (largely) monopoly industries were subject to state supervision. Broader social objectives such as provision of employment, reduction of the cost of living, employee welfare, and balanced geographical dispersal of industry were regarded as important. By 1975 the public sector contributed an estimated 70 % to GDP. Since 1977, growth in the economy has been basically in private sector activites, with the public sector showing zero or negative expansion: A crude estimate of its relative contribution to GDP in 1988 would be 50 to 55 %. In 1987, the total employment of the public sector was about 753,000 of which the central government proper employed about 445,000. That is, about 21 % of the employed population in Sri Lanka worked for the public sector. That sector now accounts for nearly 54 % of capital formation each year.

The steady expansion of the public sector is also reflected in the central government's fiscal aggregates. Total budgetary expenditures increased from 21.1 % of GDP in 1950 to about 34.1 % in 1988, while revenue increased from 16.6 % to 21 % in the same period, with domestic borrowing, foreign concessionary borrowing, and grants being the principal sources of finance. The two most important factors that contributed to the long-term increase in the budgetary expenditures were the growing governmental commitment to the provision of social expenditures (direct relief and welfare) on the one hand and the increase in development (capital expenditures) on the other. The jump in defense expenditure after 1983 is a relatively new phenomenon.

### 8.1.4   Public Investment

Public investment in Sri Lanka has been channelled mainly to irrigation, power, transport, and communications. It is often criticized as being wasteful. Since 1977, the size and character of the Public Investment Programme (PIP) has been influenced by its dependence on foreign concessionary financing.

One component of the PIP that made a significant impact on social, economic, and political conditions of the country but also led to controversy was the Accelerated Mahaweli Development Programme (AMDP). This was a set of development projects associated with the largest river basin in the country (the Mahaweli Ganga), involving construction of reservoirs, power houses, diversion tunnels, irrigation canals, and establishment of new settlements in irrigated land. The AMDP helped to double installed hydropower capacity, to settle 60,000 farmer families, and to create 55,000 jobs. This program has been criticized for being too costly in relation to the estimated benefits.

However, Mahaweli investments still hold considerable potential for increasing production and employment further as soon as the ongoing downstream development work is completed.

### 8.1.5   Social Welfare

As noted earlier, social welfare objectives have been given a great deal of emphasis in Sri Lanka. The widely debated food subsidy payments were started as a war time relief measure. In the war effort and immediately afterwards, there were definite advantages in maintaining low food prices as a means of controlling wage increases, particularly in the plantation sector.

Three major welfare policy instruments were used almost without a break: (1) the food subsidy for a number of basic items, (2) the free education system covering primary, secondary, and higher education, and (3) free health care service on a universal basis.

A continued emphasis on providing cheap food, free education, and health service over a long period helped Sri Lanka to perform exceptionally well on social indicators. Despite a low per capita income level, the nation can be placed among the middle and upper middle income countries in terms of its physical quality of life indicators (table 8.1). Even in the late 1950s, Sri Lanka had attained a level of welfare including low death rates, and high literacy levels that other South-Asian countries attained only 30 years later.

In the post-1977 period, there was some curtailment of these expenditures, particularly the food subsidy which was replaced by a nonindexed income transfer (Food and Kerosene Stamp Scheme) targetted to the lower 50 % of the income scale. Its real value was rapidly eroded by inflation.

### 8.1.6    Income Distribution

Compared to most countries similarly placed, disparities in income and wealth were historically less pronounced in Sri Lanka. The income distribution probably became more even in the period of welfare-oriented strategy in the 1970s as the relative incomes of the wealthy classes were leveled by nationalization and taxation on the one hand, and improvements of direct and indirect transfers and subsidies on the other. Of particular importance was the land reform in the 1970s in which all privately owned land in excess of 50 acres (25 acres in the case of paddy) was taken over by the state.

There are indications that income disparities have again increased in the 1980s, marking the start of a new market-oriented policy regime. This period also had rates of inflation averaging 12 % per annum, which weakened the relative income position of fixed money income earners particularly those in the lower wage categories. The share of incomes accruing to the bottom 40 % declined continuously while those accruing to the highest decile increased.

## 8.2    Current Trends

The present social and economic situation in Sri Lanka has to be viewed against the background of two important events: the far-reaching economic reforms during the latter part of 1977 and 1978,[1] and deterioration of the security situation in the country associated with the Tamil separatist movement, other ethnic conflicts, and foreign intervention.

The reforms consisted of the adoption of a package of policies leading to a market-oriented and outward-looking strategy of development. The main elements were the abolition of the dual exchange rate system, a substantial initial devaluation, and the elimination of controls in foreign trade, foreign exchange, and domestic prices. Further, a policy environment conducive to private sector activity including liberal fiscal incentives was created. Simultaneously, relatively large and ambitious public investment programs supported by foreign concessionary financing were launched.

Following the reforms, economic activity revived. In the 1977–82 period the average rate of growth exceeded 6.2 % per year, the average for the preceding seven years being less than 3 %. However, a slowdown appears to have set in since 1983, the most obvious explanation being the political instability and deterioration of the security situation in the country referred to earlier. There were also less obvious causes such as the loss of price stability and increased imbalance in the external payments position related to the emergence of excess demand conditions. The deterioration of the country's terms of trade and unfavorable weather conditions also contributed to this negative trend.

Tables 8.2 and 8.3 show the recent trends in the more important macroeconomic variables and their respective values in 1988. They show that economic activities such as trade and finance, utilities, and manufacturing made the largest contribution to growth in the period. If the weather-related setbacks are ignored, the performance of the agriculture sector has generally been satisfactory. Unemployment, on the other hand, continued to be a major problem, and has worsened since 1983. The 1988 rate of unemployment has been estimated at 18 %.

Significant features of the macroeconomic scenario in the initial year, 1988, may be summarized as follows:

1. Gross domestic capital formation was about 23 % of GDP in 1988. This gives a rather low short-term output-capital ratio.

2. About 54 % of total capital formation in the country was in the public sector. This has been typical of the period since 1977, when the public sector played a leadership and catalyst role in investment.

3. Domestic savings were about 12.8 % in 1988, lower than the long-term average of 13.5 % as a consequence of two consecutive years of low growth. The major contribution to domestic savings came from the private sector including households. The contribution of the public sector was negative in 1988. However, in a long-term context, it makes a small (less than 10 %) contribution to total savings.

4. Foreign savings have played a very important role in maintaining a satisfactory rate of investment in the period since 1978. They are defined here to be equivalent to the difference between imports of goods and nonfactor services and exports of goods and nonfactor services. Therefore these inflows include net factor incomes and net private transfers from

**Table 8.3**
Key macroeconomic indicators, 1978–1988

| | As % of potential | | | | | | |
| | Rupees billion | | As % of GDP | | Output Q* | | Average 1978– |
| | 1978 | 1988 | 1978 | 1988 | 1978 | 1988 | 1988 |
|---|---|---|---|---|---|---|---|
| 1. GDP mp | 42.3 | 223.0 | 100.0 | 100.0 | 83.3 | 79.5 | 82.1 |
| 2. Intermediate imports | 5.6 | 31.7 | 13.2 | 14.2 | 11.0 | 11.3 | 13.2 |
| 3. Output (X) | 47.9 | 254.7 | 113.2 | 114.2 | 94.3 | 90.8 | 95.3 |
| 4. Potential output (Q) | 50.8 | 280.5 | 120.1 | 125.8 | 100.0 | 100.0 | 100.0 |
| 5. GDCF of | 8.6 | 51.5 | 20.3 | 23.1 | 16.9 | 18.4 | 20.9 |
| Public sector | 5.1 | 27.9 | 12.1 | 12.5 | 10.0 | 9.9 | 12.0 |
| Private sector | 3.4 | 23.6 | 8.0 | 10.6 | 6.7 | 8.4 | 8.9 |
| 6. Consumption of | 35.8 | 194.4 | 84.6 | 87.2 | 70.5 | 69.3 | 71.2 |
| Public sector | 4.0 | 23.0 | 9.5 | 10.3 | 7.9 | 8.2 | 7.6 |
| Private sector | 31.8 | 171.4 | 75.2 | 76.9 | 62.6 | 61.1 | 63.6 |
| 7. Domestic savings of | 6.5 | 28.6 | 15.4 | 12.8 | 12.8 | 10.2 | 11.0 |
| Public sector | 1.0 | − 4.2 | 2.4 | − 1.9 | 2.0 | − 1.5 | 1.1 |
| Private sector | 5.5 | 32.8 | 13.0 | 14.7 | 10.8 | 11.7 | 9.9 |
| 8. Foreign savings | 2.1 | 22.9 | 5.0 | 10.3 | 4.1 | 8.2 | 10.0 |
| Export of goods and NFS | 14.8 | 57.1 | 35.0 | 25.6 | 29.1 | 20.3 | 22.3 |
| Import of goods and NFS | 16.9 | 80.0 | 40.0 | 35.9 | 33.3 | 28.5 | 32.2 |
| 9. Public saving after grants | 1.6 | 2.4 | 3.8 | 1.1 | 3.1 | 0.9 | 3.2 |
| 10. Public sector borrowing requirements | 3.5 | 25.5 | 8.3 | 11.4 | 6.9 | 9.1 | 8.7 |
| 11. External debt | 17.3 | 155.0 | 40.9 | 69.5 | 34.1 | 35.3 | — |
| 12. Debt servicing ratio | 15.5 | 28.7 | — | — | — | — | — |

a. Q Stands for potential output as defined in the growth exercise paper for Sri Lanka.

abroad. This aggregate accounted for about 10.8 % of GDP in 1988. A significant share of foreign savings came in the form of private and official unrequitted transfers and direct foreign investment. The net borrowing component was only about 3.1 % of GDP, typical of the period since 1978 when there has been a steady flow of official development assistance. Debt outstanding and service payments in 1988 were Rs 150 billion (69.5 % of GDP) and Rs 17.0 billion (28.7 % of exports of goods and services) respectively.

### 8.2.1   The Experiment in Structural Adjustment

A structural adjustment facility amounting to a total of SDR 141.7 million was negotiated with the IMF on the understanding that the government would work within an agreed-on policy framework (PF), involving implementation of a three-year structural adjustment program, from 1988 to 1990. This PF focused on the following areas: (1) budgetary management and fiscal policy, (2) public administration reform, (3) industrial policy, tariff reform, and export development, (4) restructuring of public enterprises, and (5) implementation of a reconstruction program with donor assistance.

In 1988, the government had to yield to rising wage demands and other pressures that normally occur in an election year. There was a marked drift toward expansionary fiscal and monetary policies, which led to an acceleration of inflation and increased external imbalances. Inflation rose to 14 % and gross official external reserves fell to 1.4 months of imports. There was a marked lack of enthusiasm about implementing key areas of the PF such as public administration reform and restructuring of public enterprises. Soon after the elections, the new administration embarked upon a number of expensive and hastily prepared poverty alleviation and other social expenditure programs, ignoring the commitment to the PF made by the previous government. Instead of reducing the number on the government payrolls as agreed, ambitious plans for additional employment were announced. The budgetary targets became impossible to achieve.

With the agreed PF targets not attained, the IMF decided to withhold the second installment of the SAF. Faced with a balance-of-payments crisis in mid-1989, the government was forced to request a new arrangement with the IMF. What was eventually worked out was basically a revival of the earlier PF with revised targets for fiscal deficits and government borrowing. It also included a sharp adjustment of the exchange rate to compensate for a substantial appreciation that occurred in the previous year.

The main areas of policy action under the new PF were:

1. Public administration reform on the lines of recommendations made by the Administrative Reforms Committee (ARC) appointed earlier by the government. These had the objective of creating a compact, effective, and better-paid public service geared to the present development needs of the country. The changes agreed upon also include a devolution of a large share of administrative powers and functions to eight elected provincial councils set up in 1988.

2. Restructuring public expenditure with a view to reducing the overall levels and increasing the effectiveness of those that remain. This involves a reduction of transfers to households and of subsidies that cannot be justified on economic grounds.

3. Public enterprise reforms to improve efficiency through privatization, joint ventures with foreign participation, and management reorganization.

4. Industrial and trade reform with a view to generating growth, export earnings, and employment.

It is clear that implementation of this package would entail unpopular measures such as retrenchment of public sector employment and corrective price increases. It appears that the authorities have no option other than to go through the adjustment exercise in full in 1990–91. The most important challenge will be the reconciliation of economic adjustment with the declared policy of large-scale social programs. The latter include the *Janasaviya* (income redistribution and employment), the School Mid-Day Meal Programme (nutrition), and the Food Stamps Programme (poverty alleviation). It is likely that the size of these social programs will be reduced and their targeting improved so that they will become safety nets that protect the more vulnerable groups from rigors of adjustment.

## 8.3 Basic Goals and Medium-Term Prospects

The basic goals of long-term development on which broad agreement exists are:

1. Achieving growth rates that are high enough to meet the rising aspirations of the people with respect to standards of living and employment, and

2. Further improvement of the quality of life, that is, achieving higher levels of nutrition, health, quality of human environment, education, and

**Table 8.4**
Goals to be attained by the year 2000

The following targets relating to selected quality of life indicators for Sri Lanka have been collected from a number of sources (not all official, however). Their existence suggests that the relevant official agencies are conscious of the need to work towards them. In the case of some, active programs are being implemented for their realization.

| Item | Reference year/period | Unit | Level | Target for 2000 |
|---|---|---|---|---|
| 1. Expectation of life at birth | 1984 | years | 70 | 70 |
| 2. Rate of population growth | 1985 | % | 1.7 | 1 |
| 3. Maternal mortality rate | 1982 | per 1000 | 0.6 | 0.3 |
| 4. Infant mortality rate | 1982–87 | per 1000 | 25 | 15 |
| 5. Child mortality rate under 5 years | 1982–87 | % | 35 | 25 |
| 6. Primary school enrollment | 1985 | % | 100 | 100 |
| 7. Adult literacy rate | 1981–82 | % | 85 | 95 |
| 8. Percentage of married women using contraception | 1980s | % | 62 | 85 |
| 9. Incidence of low birth weight | 1986 | % | 25 | 10 |
| 10. Incidence of severe undernourishment in children under 5 years | 1987 | % | 5 | 0 |
| 11. Incidence of diarrhea in children under 5 years | 1987 | % | 6 | 1 |
| 12. Incidence of acute respiratory diseases in children under 5 years | 1981 | % of all | 25 | 15 |
| 13. Immunization against: | | | | |
| (a) TB | 1987 | % | 95 | 100 |
| (b) Polio | 1987 | % | 90 | 95 |
| (c) DPT | 1987 | % | 90 | 95 |
| (d) Measles | 1987 | % | 65 | 90 |
| 14. Incidence of malaria | 1986 | per 10,000 | 831 | 0 |
| 15. Incidence of iodine deficiency | 1980s | per 10,000 | * | 0 |
| 16. Incidence of Vitamin A deficiency | 1980s | per 10,000 | * | 0 |
| 17. Access to safe drinking water | 1981 | % | 70 | 85 |
| 18. Sanitary disposal of excreta | 1981 | % | 67 | 80 |
| 19. Safe, sanitary environment free of | | | | |
| (a) radioactive pollutants | 1989 | sq. km. | na | na |
| (b) chemical pollutants | 1989 | sq. km. | na | na |
| (c) microbiological pollutants | 1989 | sq. km. | na | 100 |

* = "clinically significant numbers" in rows 15 and 16
Sources: World Bank (1986), *World Development Report*; (1988), *World Development Report*; (1987), *Demographic and Health Survey*; UNICEF (1987), *Situation Analysis of Children and Women in Sri Lanka, UNICEF*; (1986), *Annual Health Bulletin, Sri Lanka*.

cultural development (see table 8.4 for details of specific targets for the year 2000).

### 8.3.1 Boundary Conditions

The movements of key economic variables including production and income distribution in the next decade (1990–2000) will depend largely on three important factors: (1) restoration of peace and normalcy in the country, (2) success of the structural adjustment program, and (3) external factors, particularly those affecting the terms of trade and inflow of foreign capital.

These are not entirely independent in the sense that any positive developments can be mutually reinforcing. If there is some abatement of the internal strife, there is likely to be improvement in the inflows of foreign capital. There could also be a diversion of budgetary resources from defense to poverty alleviation and capital formation. A revival of economic activity will inevitably relieve unemployment, addressing one of the basic causes of social tension.

The political cycle appears to have ended with the continuation of the UNP government for three consecutive terms; but interestingly, the recent changes involving increased emphasis on poverty alleviation suggest that the underlying cyclical shift from market orientation to welfare is still present. However, a return to the *dirigiste* welfare formula of the 1970s is extremely unlikely.

External conditions have become uncertain due to sweeping changes in the international scene. In the immediate short term, the prices of Sri Lanka's main imports such as wheat, sugar, and fertilizer are likely to move up while mobilization of official development assistance may become increasingly difficult. This may also be true of foreign private capital even though Sri Lanka's present share in the total supply is negligible.

### 8.3.2 Sectoral Contributions to Growth

It is useful to analyze growth in terms of the three broad sectors: agriculture, industry, and services. Their current contribution to GDP are approximately 27%, 26%, and 47% respectively. In terms of employment, the ratios are 46, 18, and 36.

Given the overriding importance of the employment objective, emphasis on accelerating industrial growth may be expected in the next 10 years. Under normal circumstances, only a modest growth in agricultural activities is likely. The services sector also has an important potential; how-ever, here, only certain subsectors such as tourism, trade, and finance may achieve high rates of growth. By the year 2000, industry will probably increase its shares in GDP and employment.

Official thinking places objectives of sectoral growth in the following order of importance: employment generation, export earnings, and im-provement of income levels. Services being a heterogeneous sector, the objectives differ among various subsectors. The most important in terms of medium term growth perhaps are those related to infrastructure.

The specific strategies advocated for developing agriculture and indus-try possess common elements, the most important among them being: (1) reliance on private enterprise, (2) the role of the government to be that of a facilitator, (3) greater participation of foreign capital, and (4) increased emphasis on promoting research and communication of the results of re-search and training. Sectoral strategies—typically emphasizing market lib-eralization, private sector initiative, and foreign support—have also been enunciated.

## 8.3.3    Growth Scenarios

Table 8.5 shows the macroeconomic balances associated with two alterna-tive growth scenarios for the 1990–2000 period. These represent simula-tion results from a three-gap model and are intended to highlight the implications of alternative assumptions concerning a number of exogenous factors including policy variables.[2] The two alternative growth rates are basically targets to be reached by combining selected capacity growth rates and changes in capacity utilization. The specific combinations are: (1) Mod-erate growth—6 % output growth per annum consisting of (a) 5.5 % in capacity and 0.5 % in capacity utilization or (b) 5.8 % in capacity and 0.2 % in capacity utilization; (2) high growth—7.2 % consisting of (a) 6.2 % in capacity and 1 % in capacity utilization or (b) 6.5 % in capacity and 0.7 % in capacity utilization.

Selected simulations examined the possibilities of achieving these growth paths, within constraints imposed by external and internal stability, respectively represented by the size of foreign savings relative to potential output and by the size of the public sector borrowing requirement relative to actual output.

Sri Lanka's inability to achieve high growth rates in the last decade despite a sharp increase in the investment/GDP ratios can be attributed mainly to the character of the public investment program. Statistically this

**Table 8.5**
Sri Lanka alternative growth scenarios for 1990–2000 (identities may not be satisfied exactly due to rounding off errors)

| | Base | Moderate growth (1) | | | Moderate growth (2) | | | High growth (1) | | | High growth (2) | | |
|---|---|---|---|---|---|---|---|---|---|---|---|---|---|
| | 1987 | 1990 | 1995 | 2000 | 1990 | 1995 | 2000 | 1990 | 1995 | 2000 | 1990 | 1995 | 2000 |
| 1. GDP mp: Rs. billion | 27.6 | 29.1 | 37.8 | 50.9 | 29.2 | 37.6 | 49.9 | 29.7 | 41.1 | 59.0 | 29.8 | 41.1 | 58.7 |
| 2. Potential output [a] | 31.2 | 36.5 | 47.7 | 62.3 | 36.6 | 48.5 | 63.4 | 36.7 | 49.6 | 67.0 | 36.8 | 50.4 | 69.1 |
| 3. Growth rate of GDP % [b] | — | 1.8 | 5.4 | 6.1 | 1.9 | 5.2 | 5.8 | 2.5 | 6.7 | 7.3 | 2.6 | 6.6 | 7.4 |
| *As percentage of GDP* | | | | | | | | | | | | | |
| 4. Exports [a] | 26.9 | 26.4 | 28.9 | 27.6 | 26.4 | 29.8 | 29.2 | 25.9 | 27.1 | 24.7 | 25.9 | 27.9 | 25.2 |
| 5. Imports [a] | 33.9 | 33.7 | 37.1 | 35.6 | 33.7 | 38.3 | 37.5 | 33.0 | 34.9 | 32.1 | 33.1 | 35.8 | 33.8 |
| 6. GDCF | 23.3 | 25.7 | 25.9 | 25.1 | 27.0 | 27.8 | 27.4 | 28.6 | 27.9 | 26.3 | 29.8 | 29.7 | 28.4 |
| Public | 15.1 | 14.3 | 14.4 | 14.0 | 15.2 | 15.6 | 15.4 | 16.3 | 15.9 | 15.0 | 17.2 | 17.1 | 16.3 |
| Private | 8.2 | 11.4 | 11.5 | 11.1 | 11.8 | 12.2 | 12.0 | 12.3 | 12.0 | 11.3 | 12.6 | 12.6 | 12.1 |
| 7. Domestic savings | 16.3 | 18.4 | 17.7 | 17.2 | 19.7 | 19.3 | 19.2 | 21.4 | 20.1 | 18.9 | 22.6 | 21.7 | 20.8 |
| Public | 2.0 | 4.0 | 6.3 | 6.0 | 4.9 | 7.4 | 7.3 | 6.1 | 8.0 | 7.3 | 7.0 | 9.1 | 8.6 |
| Private | 14.3 | 14.4 | 11.4 | 11.2 | 14.8 | 11.9 | 11.9 | 15.3 | 12.1 | 11.6 | 15.6 | 12.6 | 12.2 |
| 8. Foreign savings | 7.0 | 7.3 | 8.2 | 8.0 | 7.3 | 8.5 | 8.3 | 7.1 | 7.8 | 7.4 | 7.2 | 7.9 | 7.6 |
| 9. PSBR | 10.7 | 7.7 | 5.7 | 5.7 | 7.7 | 5.8 | 5.7 | 7.6 | 5.6 | 5.5 | 7.6 | 5.7 | 5.5 |
| 10. Foreign grants | 2.4 | 2.6 | 2.4 | 2.3 | 2.6 | 2.4 | 2.4 | 2.6 | 2.3 | 2.2 | 2.6 | 2.3 | 2.2 |
| *Memorandum items* | | | | | | | | | | | | | |
| Capacity util. ratio | 92.9 | 88.4 | 90.6 | 92.7 | 88.2 | 89.0 | 89.9 | 88.9 | 93.1 | 97.6 | 88.6 | 94.6 | 94.6 |
| Growth rate of potential output | 5.2 | 5.5 | | | 5.8 | | | 6.2 | | | 6.5 | | |
| Growth rate of actual output | 1.6 | 6.0 | | | 6.0 | | | 7.2 | | | 7.2 | | |

Notes: a. Definitions are the same as those used in the Growth Exercise Paper. Exports refer to exports of goods and services. Imports refer to imports of goods and services adjusted for private inward transfers and a few other items.
b. Average rate for the period immediately preceding bounded by the years shown in the table; e.g. 1.8 shown in the first 1990 column is the average compound growth rate for the 3-year period 1988–90.

was reflected in low incremental output-capital ratios (IOCR) for the economy as a whole. It is likely that the particular phase is at an end. Thus it is possible to assume a higher IOCR for the simulations. This represents a 14 % improvement over its historical value and is quite significant. Fortunately, some of the required policy decisions have been already taken as a part of the current adjustment program, according to which the share of the private sector in the gross domestic capital formation is likely to increase rapidly in the next few years.

Given the foreign savings constraint in the model, any increase in the growth rate requires an upward adjustment of domestic savings. This adjustment has to be on the order of 1.5 to 3.0 percentage points in the case of the moderate growth and 4.5 to 5.5 percentage points in the case of the high growth scenario. One particularly significant fact brought forth by the simulations is that in each case, an increased savings effort is required from the public rather than the private sector. This is indicative of the weakness of the existing fiscal base.

A substantial upward adjustment of savings ratios in the economy cannot be made in the short term. Therefore a suitable strategy for Sri Lanka would be to mobilize a larger quantum of foreign savings than at present so that the required increase in domestic savings can be set at more realistic levels. The composition of such foreign inflows will be important in the present context. Ideally, the loans should be on highly concessionary terms and the total inflow should consist of a relatively high proportion of direct foreign investment. These conditions are suggested in view of the existence of a relatively high debt/GDP ratio on the one hand and the need to shift to private investment on the other. Meanwhile appropriate policies to improve the savings of the public sector have to be taken.

It may also be useful at this point to go beyond model simulations. Take, for example, the privatization program. It is bound to change the existing shares of the private sector and the public sector in total investment. Some attempt has been made to represent this indirectly as an increase in the IOCR. However, the impact of the changing shares on "crowding in" is not yet known.

One other assumption of the model that requires reexamination in the specific context of Sri Lanka relates to the growth of exports. In the growth exercise it was tacitly assumed that high capacity utilization led to a diversion of exportable surpluses to domestic use. This construction may not be appropriate in the present Sri Lankan situation where the underutilized capacity exists in export-oriented activities such as tourism.

## 8.4 Conclusions

The main conclusions that emerge from the above discussion may be summarized as follows:

First, under normal peaceful conditions, and given moderately favorable external conditions, Sri Lanka has the potential to reach growth rates of 6 to 7.5 % per year in the next decade. Such an acceleration will mean a total elimination of the unemployment problem—the most pressing social and economic problem of the day—within the next five to seven years. Some favorable initial conditions already exist and one component of a successful development strategy will be to exploit them to the maximum possible extent.

Second, higher growth also depends crucially on the success of the structural adjustment program.

Third, the strategies that have been suggested will probably lead to no immediate improvement in income distribution. On the contrary, it may get more unequal even in the short run. However, the large-scale welfare programs initiated last year, a quick improvement in the employment situation, and greater price stability should help alleviate temporary hardships that may accompany the process of adjustment.

### Notes

1. This stabilization and reform episode is reviewed by Jayawardena et al. (1988).

2. Details of the three-gap exercise for Sri Lanka appear in Karunaratne and Senanyake (1990).

### References

Jayawardena, Lal, Anne Maasland, and P. N. Radhakrishnan (1988). *Sri Lanka.* Country Study No. 15, SAPP project. Helsinki: WIDER.

Karunaratne, S. A., and M. D. R. Senanayake (1990). "Growth Exercise: Sri Lanka." (Mimeo), WIDER, Helsinki.

# 9    Turkey

Korkut Boratav and
Oktar Türel

Despite rapid growth through the 1980s, politics and economics in Turkey remain unsettled. In March 1989 the ruling Motherland Party (MP) came in third in local elections behind the newly renamed traditional parties of Turkish politics—the Social Democratic Populist Party (SDPP) and the conservative True Path Party (TPP). The MP's experience during 1987–90 seems to have shown the incompatibility of orthodox economic policies with political viability under a Turkish-style parliamentary system. The party's electoral success in 1987 coincided with the peak of an economic boom that public investment had started. Orthodox austerity in 1988, on the other hand, led to electoral disaster. The first reactions of the MP were to move in the direction of a new variant of populist economics. During preceding decades, populism with uninterrupted growth could be carried on for periods of seven to eight years, but the MP's expansion came to a standstill within three years under the external and internal conditions of the late 1980s.

By the spring of 1989, all major political parties responded to these developments by shifting the focus of policy debate into medium-term growth issues. In this endeavor they joined camps with economists of nonorthodox persuasion for whom growth had always been paramount. The implication is that analytical studies of alternative medium-term strategies will be of more than academic interest and may even contribute to decision-making processes in one way or another. In this paper, we extend the gap analysis of Boratav and Türel (1989) to address medium-term growth and distribution issues for Turkey.[1]

## 9.1    Background and Current Problems

Economic policy during the 1980s in Turkey is conventionally characterized as "liberalization and opening-up." A more careful formulation would see the new orientation as the antithesis of the internally oriented, interventionist, and populist model prevailing during the 1960s and 1970s.[2] But in addition, the emergence of new forms of selective and ad hoc government interventions in the economic process and the "bastard populism" of 1989 must be explained. An alternative characterization of the 1980s, this time in terms of class-state relations, may be useful at this stage. The focus should be on the bourgeoisie as the dominant class within the ruling bloc of social forces. The late 1970s were years of crisis for the Turkish bourgeoisie; the reorientation of economic policies and the new political structure that emerged during the 1980s can be interpreted as a response of the ruling class.

Why were the late 1970s critical years for the bourgeoisie and in what manner did the 1980s produce solutions? We believe that there were three components of the crisis and that different responses were required for each.

First, there was a crisis of distribution. There was a sharp rise in labor militancy during the late 1970s. The inability to cope with workers' demands and to impose discipline at the workplace convinced the bourgeoisie of the necessity of reorganizing the labor market on authoritarian lines. Heavy repression of the unions was implemented by the military regime during the early 1980s and by MP governments from 1984 onwards. The quantitative outcome can be observed in table 9.1: A dramatic regression of the wage share in industrial value added and almost continuous real wage declines from 1977. By the late 1980s, wages and labor relations were no longer considered primary problems by businessmen.

Second, there was recognition by the business community that there was no support coming from international financial capital to save the social democratic Ecevit government from external strangulation in the late 1970s. The extremely generous support extended by the Bretton Woods institutions and international finance to the post-1980 governments and the First World popularity of the MP leadership warmed the bourgeoisie's attitude toward the new regime.

Finally, there was a political crisis for the bourgeoisie, as it felt itself being pushed out of economic decision making, first by the fundamentalist-Islamic National Salvation Party and, second, when "leftist" elements with definite anti-business biases "infiltrated" the government in 1978–79. An extremely aggressive and effective public offensive of almost all business organizations and groups against the Ecevit government, particularly in 1979, accelerated its collapse. It was through the 1980 coup that the

**Table 9.1**
Indicators of primary relations of distribution

| | 1977 | 1980 | 1983 | 1984 | 1985 | 1986 | 1987 | 1988 | 1989 | 1990 |
|---|---|---|---|---|---|---|---|---|---|---|
| I. Manufacturing industry | | | | | | | | | | |
| A. Real wage index | 100.0 | 84.7 | 84.0 | 72.6 | 71.6 | 73.8 | 83.2 | 80.9 | | |
| B. Wages/value added (%) | | | | | | | | | | |
| 1. Total/Turkey | 36.9 | 30.7 | 24.8 | 23.5 | 21.2 | 16.1 | 17.3 | 15.4 | | |
| 2. Largest private | — | — | 42.7 | 38.2 | 39.4 | 32.6 | 29.5 | 31.8 | | |
| 3. Private/Eskisehir | — | 60.6 | 50.5 | 45.0 | 47.0 | 43.9 | | | | |
| II. Agriculture/industry terms of trade (GDP) | 100.0 | 57.2 | 49.6 | 51.2 | 47.5 | 46.7 | 48.9 | 44.5 | 50.9 | 57.7 |
| III. Commercial margins for agriculture (index) | | | | | | | | | | |
| A. Bread/wheat | 100.0 | 115.5 | 123.0 | 115.3 | 113.7 | 110.2 | 129.5 | 155.9 | | |
| B. Sugar/sugar beet | 100.0 | 207.3 | 129.4 | 129.4 | 122.5 | 126.4 | 111.9 | 108.9 | | |
| C. Cloth/cotton | 100.0 | 76.8 | 108.6 | 105.4 | 130.0 | 116.0 | 90.8 | 127.5 | | |
| D. Margarine/sunflower | 100.0 | 134.9 | 129.5 | 214.7 | 161.1 | 142.6 | 144.1 | 194.4 | | |
| E. Tobacco (export/farm) | 100.0 | 230.3 | 307.6 | 316.3 | 283.0 | 284.5 | 283.0 | 347.0 | | |
| F. Cotton (export/farm) | 100.0 | 89.6 | 169.3 | 185.2 | 220.7 | 184.5 | 182.3 | 233.2 | | |

bourgeoisie's domination over the state and specifically over economic decision making was reestablished.

There is a line of thought among Turkish social scientists that the increased political power of the bourgeoisie reflects its evolution toward greater "maturity," that is, the emergence of a political regime in which general and long-term interests of the ruling class prevail over sectional and short-term considerations. Under "mature" capitalism, class consciousness in its generalized form would be much more prominent than it would be under developing capitalism where oligarchic interests dominate decision making. With respect to the norms of behavior of the state, a longer-term and generalized perspective distinguishes maturity from underdevelopment and even decadence.

By the end of the 1970s, there was consensus within the ranks of the business community that both the short- and long-term (as well as the generalized) interests of the bourgeoisie were threatened. Reinstitutionalization of the state after 1980 constituted an attempt to resolve this basic problem. But as the 1980s came to an end, there was widespread agreement that the new institutions of the period (including the 1982 Constitution) could not function properly. The authoritarian "solution" of the 1980s turned out to be misguided.

On the other hand, there is no doubt that the new policy model aimed at broader class issues. Its attempted move from sectional into generalized class interests in decision making may be interpreted as a sign of maturity. Examples of a new orientation include continued restrictions on labor, an overall reduction of the tax burden on nonlabor income, consecutive pardons of "economic offenses," and the extremely easy access and liberal treatment extended to businessmen in resolving their problems with the government.

By the second half of the 1980s, however, there was a regression with respect to the class nature of the state from this perspective as well, reflecting the limits of economic liberalism in an underdeveloped capitalist economy where a weak bourgeoisie is dependent on the state and vulnerable to marginal policy changes. This was a period when the so-called "rents" due to allocations of foreign exchange were replaced by "superprofits" due to export subsidies on the basis of overinvoicing. An "antibureaucratic" campaign gave politicians a free hand in assigning state tenders among rival firms. Through ministries, they also fixed the import surcharge rates that replaced the old quota system. Finally, local politicians got control over speculative gains on urban land as restrictions on town planning were eased.

Such economic realities under the double myths of liberalism and anti-bureaucratic reform created extremely favorable conditions for the emergence and enrichment of privileged business groups and for discriminatory treatment of others. The MP government used these powers widely after 1985, enough to cause deep unrest within the business community.[3] These changes point toward decadence and away from maturity in terms of class rule.

### 9.1.1 Recent Economic Performance and Base-Year Conditions

The Turkish economy in 1990 allocated—in relative terms—about 20 % less for capital accumulation than a decade ago (table 9.2). Growth rates of potential output for the national economy (4.0 %) and the manufacturing sector (4.9 %) during the 1977–87 period were about one-third and one-half less than the rates of the preceding decade, respectively.

Despite these adverse changes, the 1980s have not been years of stagnation throughout. Capacity utilization improved continuously from 1980 to 1987 (table 9.3). A large increase (21.5 % in constant prices) in public investment in 1985 started the boom of 1985–87 with private investment in 1986 and 1987 (with 17.9 % and 14.1 % growth rates, respectively) following suit. This boom ended by 1988, and the administration tried to stimulate the economy again in 1990 through encouraging housebuilding and consumer spending. Investment has shifted away from the two largest productive sectors compared with the 1970s—a change the long-term effects of which we shall discuss presently.

The deficits of the public sector were at unsustainable levels by the end of the 1970s. The share of the PSBR in actual and potential output improved up to 1984 and then tended to rise again with rapid growth of transfers, that is, interest, pensions, and extra-budgetary subsidy-type payments partly to the business community. Public investment added significantly to the PSBR only in 1985 and 1986. There was improvement in the tax effort especially during the first half of the 1980s as a whole, which was due to an increased share of indirect taxation (table 9.4).

There was a gradual, but sustained improvement in the current account of the balance of payments (tables 9.5 and 9.6), with surpluses being registered in 1988–89 for the first time since 1973. The improvement is mainly due to strong exports—with a sizeable contribution from "fictitious" exports as well[4]—and high invisible earnings. There is, however, a discrepancy between balance of payments data and other estimates of Turkish external debt from 1984 onward: When all items are considered

**Table 9.2**
Investment-related macro data and relevant ratios, Bn, TL in 1987 prices

| | 1977 | 1980 | 1983 | 1984 | 1985 | 1986 | 1987 | 1988 | 1989 | 1990* |
|---|---|---|---|---|---|---|---|---|---|---|
| K-goods imports (Mk) | 3287 | 1769 | 2090 | 2272 | 2153 | 2880 | 3271 | 3287 | 3172 | 4221 |
| Investments (I) | 12391 | 10240 | 11090 | 10995 | 12393 | 14037 | 14823 | 13940 | 13749 | 17398 |
| Potential outout (Q) | 44807 | 49566 | 55245 | 58068 | 60269 | 62570 | 66513 | 69041 | 71943 | 74883 |
| Actual output (X) | 44454 | 44726 | 50252 | 53281 | 56132 | 60458 | 66166 | 67774 | 68182 | 74810 |
| Actual GDP | 39233 | 39700 | 45121 | 47336 | 50076 | 54274 | 58299 | 59608 | 59305 | 65180 |
| I/X | .279 | .229 | .221 | .206 | .221 | .232 | .224 | .206 | .202 | .233 |
| I/Q | .277 | .207 | .201 | .189 | .206 | .224 | .223 | .202 | .191 | .232 |
| I/GDP | .316 | .258 | .246 | .232 | .247 | .259 | .254 | .234 | .232 | .267 |
| Ig/GDP | .179 | .153 | .136 | .125 | .143 | .145 | .134 | .104 | .100 | .127 |
| Ip/GDP | .137 | .105 | .110 | .107 | .104 | .114 | .120 | .130 | .132 | .140 |
| Mk/I | .265 | .173 | .188 | .207 | .174 | .205 | .221 | .236 | .231 | .243 |

* Provisional

**Table 9.3**
Actual and potential GDP and output

| | 1977 | 1980 | 1983 | 1984 | 1985 | 1986 | 1987 | 1988 | 1989 | 1990 |
|---|---|---|---|---|---|---|---|---|---|---|
| **1. Potential GDP** | | | | | | | | | | |
| Mn, TL in 68 prices | 203425 | 228882 | 257525 | 267848 | 278585 | 289752 | 301367 | 312819 | 324080 | 335319 |
| a) Index 1987 = 100 | 65.5 | 75.9 | 85.5 | 88.9 | 92.4 | 96.1 | 100.0 | 103.8 | 107.5 | 111.3 |
| **2. Potential GDP** | | | | | | | | | | |
| Bn, TL in 87 prices | 39586 | 44540 | 50114 | 52123 | 54213 | 56386 | 58646 | 60875 | 63066 | 65253 |
| **3. Actual GDP** | | | | | | | | | | |
| Mn, TL in 68 prices | 201577 | 203956 | 231742 | 245038 | 257546 | 278955 | 299587 | 306316 | 304758 | 334949 |
| a) Index 1987 = 100 | 67.3 | 68.1 | 77.4 | 81.8 | 85.9 | 93.1 | 100.0 | 102.2 | 101.7 | 111.8 |
| **4. Actual GDP** | | | | | | | | | | |
| Bn, TL in 87 prices | 39233 | 39700 | 45121 | 47336 | 50076 | 54274 | 58299 | 59608 | 59305 | 65180 |
| **5. Intermediate imports** | | | | | | | | | | |
| a) In current mn $ | 3363 | 6158 | 6676 | 7624 | 7836 | 6675 | 9180 | 9241 | 10558 | 13491 |
| b) In real/87 mn $ | 6092 | 5865 | 5987 | 6937 | 7066 | 7216 | 9180 | 9529 | 10358 | 11237 |
| c) In real/87 bn TL ($1 = 857 TL) | 5221 | 5026 | 5131 | 5945 | 6056 | 6184 | 7867 | 8166 | 8877 | 9630 |
| **6. Potential output** (Q = 2 + 5c)(Bn, TL) | 44807 | 49566 | 55245 | 58068 | 60269 | 62570 | 66513 | 60041 | 71943 | 74883 |
| **7. Actual output** (X = 4 + 5c)(Bn, TL) | 44454 | 44726 | 50252 | 53281 | 56132 | 60458 | 66166 | 67774 | 68182 | 74810 |
| 8. V = X/Q | .992 | .902 | .910 | .918 | .931 | .966 | .995 | .982 | .948 | .999 |

**Table 9.4**
Public balances, 1977–1990 (billion total at 1987 prices)

| | 1977 | 1980 | 1983 | 1984 | 1985 | 1986 | 1987 | 1988 | 1989 | 1990 |
|---|---|---|---|---|---|---|---|---|---|---|
| 1. Tax revenue (V) | 6315 | 6624 | 8859 | 8777 | 10186 | 12773 | 12582 | 11859 | 10714 | 11350 |
| 1a. Of which, direct taxes (%) | 49.6 | 48.2 | 51.2 | 45.7 | 37.6 | 35.6 | 34.3 | 35.0 | 39.9 | 38.1 |
| 2. Parastatal profits (H) | 145 | 635 | 1424 | 2712 | 3254 | 3870 | 4230 | 4948 | 4113 | 3235 |
| 3. Public consumption (G) | 3452 | 3935 | 3996 | 4236 | 4474 | 4963 | 5320 | 5326 | 5382 | 5903 |
| 4. Non-interest transfers (W) | 214 | 569 | 1245 | 1510 | 2137 | 3472 | 4142 | 3283 | 2700 | 2259 |
| 5. Domestic interest (J) | 156 | 187 | 344 | 551 | 541 | 955 | 1261 | 1876 | 1541 | 1630 |
| 6. Foreign interest | 148 | 109 | 474 | 582 | 652 | 927 | 1040 | 1190 | 1268 | 1171 |
| 7. $Sg = V + H - G - W - J - SJ^*$ | 2490 | 2459 | 4224 | 4610 | 5636 | 6326 | 5049 | 5132 | 3936 | 3622 |
| 8. Public investment (Ig) | 7012 | 6059 | 6152 | 5891 | 7160 | 7869 | 7787 | 6174 | 5913 | 8262 |
| 9. PSBR (Ig − Sg) | 4522 | 3600 | 1928 | 1281 | 1524 | 1543 | 2738 | 1042 | 1977 | 4640 |
| 10. PSBR/GDP | .1153 | .0907 | .0427 | .0271 | .0304 | .0284 | .0470 | .0175 | .0333 | .0712 |
| 11. PSBR/X | .1017 | .0805 | .0384 | .0240 | .0272 | .0255 | .0414 | .0154 | .0290 | .0620 |
| 12. PSBR/Q | .1009 | .0726 | .0349 | .0221 | .0253 | .0247 | .0412 | .0150 | .0275 | .0619 |
| 13. V/GDP | .1610 | .1669 | .1963 | .1854 | .2034 | .2353 | .2158 | .1989 | .1807 | .1741 |
| 14. Ig/Q | .1565 | .1222 | .1114 | .1015 | .1188 | .1258 | .1171 | .0894 | .0822 | .1103 |
| 15. Ig/GDP | .1787 | .1526 | .1363 | .1245 | .1430 | .1450 | .1336 | .1036 | .0997 | .1268 |
| 16. Direct taxes/GDP | .0840 | .0960 | .0950 | .0840 | .0720 | .0790 | .0741 | .0702 | .0873 | .0915 |

Note: Current prices for 1a, 16.

**Table 9.5**
Foreign savings (major items) ($ million)

| Years | Consumer goods imports | Other items in current account (Net) | M (= 1 + 2) | Intermediate imports | Capital goods imports | Interest on debt | Exports | Current account Deficit (3 + 4 + 5 + 6 + 7) |
|---|---|---|---|---|---|---|---|---|
| 1977 | 178 | −978 | −800 | 3363 | 2255 | 320 | −1753 | 3385 |
| 1980 | 170 | −2572 | −2402 | 6158 | 1581 | 668 | −2910 | 3095 |
| 1983 | 242 | −3120 | −2878 | 6676 | 2317 | 1441 | −5728 | 1828 |
| 1984 | 474 | −3802 | −3328 | 7624 | 2659 | 1586 | −7134 | 1407 |
| 1985 | 905 | −4125 | −3220 | 7836 | 2603 | 1753 | −7959 | 1013 |
| 1986 | 956 | −4317 | −3361 | 6675 | 3474 | 2134 | −7457 | 1465 |
| 1987 | 1161 | −5549 | −4388 | 9180 | 3817 | 2387 | −10190 | 806 |
| 1988 | 1110 | −7073 | −5963 | 9241 | 3989 | 2799 | −11662 | −1596 |
| 1989 | 1389 | −8035 | −6646 | 10558 | 3845 | 2907 | −11625 | −961 |
| 1990 | 3024 | −9995 | −6971 | 13491 | 5787 | 3264 | −12960 | 2611 |

**Table 9.6**
Balance of payments: Capital movements (million dollars)

| Years | Capital inflows to increase debt (Net) | Other capital inflows | Direct foreign investment | Net errors and omissions | Reserve movements | D* + R = CAD (= 1 + 2 + 3 + 4 + 5) | Real CAD in 1987 dollars (7) | Exchange rate (TL per $) |
|---|---|---|---|---|---|---|---|---|
| 1977 | 3282 | 103 | 67 | -663 | 566 | 3385 | 6234 | 18 |
| 1980 | 2544 | 95 | 33 | 1030 | -607 | 3095 | 3275 | 76 |
| 1983 | 1266 | 161 | 46 | 507 | -152 | 1828 | 1738 | 226 |
| 1984 | 1082 | -171 | 113 | 317 | 66 | 1407 | 1329 | 367 |
| 1985 | 1642 | 233 | 99 | -837 | -124 | 1013 | 941 | 522 |
| 1986 | 1999 | 249 | 125 | -118 | -790 | 1465 | 1541 | 675 |
| 1987 | 1810 | 365 | 106 | -506 | -969 | 806 | 806 | 857 |
| 1988 | -1306 | -269 | 354 | 515 | -890 | -1596 | -1606 | 1422 |
| 1989 | 159 | 8 | 663 | 971 | -2762 | -961 | -937 | 2122 |
| 1990 | 3298 | 319 | 713 | -411 | -1308 | 2611 | 2194 | 2609 |

and corrections are made for exchange rate movements of creditor currencies, there still remains about $8 billion of unexplained debt growth.[5] A burst of foreign exchange earnings during 1988–89 (due largely to invisibles) helped hold the external debt service ratio to 33 % in 1989. However, the external miracle seemed to turn sour in 1990, when the year ended with a current account deficit of $2.6 billion (about 2.5 % of potential output).

With respect to indicators of distribution, the regression in labor incomes can be observed in table 9.1. Relative price declines for peasant agriculture are particularly striking. Higher agricultural productivity did not compensate for the reduction in relative on-farm prices up to 1985—the last year for which this estimate is possible. After nine years of enforced labor discipline, 1989 emerged as a year of massive popular reactions; this pattern is likely to continue. Substantial intersectoral changes have taken place during the 1980s in terms of relative price and investment movements, but the two phenomena have not been parallel. This observation points to the usefulness of an analysis linking the distributional impact of relative price changes with the investment propensities of various subgroups of the bourgeoisie.

### 9.1.2 Current Problems and Likely Evolution of the Policy Framework

In the early 1990s, there is great ambiguity about the conduct of economic policy. During 1989, there was a gradual movement from monetarist toward structuralist approaches, but there seems to be indecision on whether inflation or stagnation should be tackled first. The MP compromise has been to keep aggregate demand buoyant subject to a "monetary program" launched in January 1990, apparently aimed at checking the growth of monetary aggregates; and to tolerate real appreciation and sizeable public sector deficits.

Incentives for exporters were undermined when tax rebates were phased out after 1988 due to commitments to the GATT and when the currency appreciated by about 25 % from 1988 to 1990. Further, debt service is expected to remain high for the coming years. There is apprehension that the lack of political confidence in the government within the country may spread abroad (in case of an export decline), and reduce capital inflows. The low level of manufacturing investment during the 1980s is now starting to bite, and a belated effort on the part of the government to boost industrial capital formation is considered too late by many businessmen. The relatively advanced infrastructure—particularly thanks to recent investments in communications, transportation, energy, and municipal services—is a positive factor in attracting foreign investors. On the other hand, wages in dollar terms increased sharply after 1988 due to real currency appreciation and internal wage adjustments.

Further suppression of labor incomes seems to be no longer possible. On the contrary, 1989 was the first year in a decade when workers obtained wage increases substantially above the inflation rate. On the agricultural front, 1989 was a year of drought and the government committed itself to significant rises in support prices and input subsidies. Although the situation was fully reversed in 1990 with a bumper crop, the political uncertainty and the prospect of an early election precluded a return to the agricultural price policies of the earlier years. As noted earlier, there is some official talk of the importance of expansion of the internal market in overcoming stagnation.

### 9.2  Alternative Strategies

Evidently, the scene is uncertain and its outcome will depend on the development of the political framework. In Boratav and Türel (1989) three scenarious were envisaged, differing in economic logic as well as the political and social forces that might be willing to pursue them. The political setting of each can be summarized as follows.

Economic policies could conceivably shift back into an ultra-orthodox mode, as represented by scenario 3 of our exercise. If the MP overcomes its present disarray and manages to survive until 1992 and if effective pressure from abroad prevents heretical relapses into populism, a recommitment to orthodoxy is not unlikely. Such a model could also be implemented by a new undemocratic regime if politics take such a turn. The rentier-financial bourgeoisie and big business with MP ties would support the orthodox option.

More likely for the near future is a "moderate social democratic option" (scenario 2). The powerful right wing of SDPP is already committed to such an option. More significantly, the conservative TPP and even the ruling MP have been moving toward adopting some elements of scenario 2 in their economic programs. In class terms, this option would probably be welcomed by large segments of the industrial bourgeoisie, provided that external support is extended toward such a policy reorientation. If foreign assistance were not forthcoming, there is a likelihood that scenario 2 would be pushed into either of the extreme options, that is, scenarios 1 and 3. The political instability of scenario 2 is interesting, because in the growth exercises its economic viability was also found not to be high.

The radical scenario 1 represents a left or nationalistic strategy. It would be supported by a strong lobby within the SDPP as well as the radical wing of the Islamic political movements. However, the likelihood of a political coalition among these forces is small. This scenario has a potential worker-peasant social basis and depending on which political group takes the lead, disoriented elements of the provincial bourgeoisie might also join in.

### 9.2.1 Projections under the Scenarios

Projections under the three scenarios for 1991–95 are worked out in Boratav and Türel (1989), along with transitions for 1987–90.[6] The two phases reflected the presumption that policy would focus on stabilization through 1990, whereas medium-term questions would become more important thereafter.

In retrospect, electoral politics and consequent "populist" deformations precluded orthodox stabilization for the interim period. On the other hand, external pressures to lift trade and exchange controls coincided with the views of influential Turkish economic authorities. The decree of August 1989 No. 89/14391 (commonly known as Decree No. 32), which foresaw an extensive liberalization of invisible transactions and capital movements, is a reflection of this position. The economy moved toward 1990 combining "business as usual" with a modicum of liberalization, while fiscal balances failed to improve. Our comparison of different strategic orientations for 1991–95 takes its base-year parameters and variables from the expected outturn for 1990.

Our calculations show that the first scenario's growth performance is superior to the other two (table 9.7). It also presupposes some redistribution in favor of labor incomes. With respect to self-reliance, it requires a unilateral (or negotiated) debt rearrangement resulting in zero real interest transfers abroad and a zero current account to withstand adverse reactions from the external world, especially if Turkey acts unilaterally. Although the international economic and political climate is not favorable for such a rearrangement, it is conceivable that forthcoming Turkish governments could skillfully use opportunities created by unfolding events. In terms of trade prospects, scenario 1 (as well as scenario 2) is more feasible than the predicted export performance of scenario 3. Hence, Scenario 1 emerges as the desirable alternative for 1991–95. We will limit our discussion of the detailed policy implications to this strategy.

**Table 9.7**
Summary of policies and projections

| Policy elements | Strategy 1 | Strategy 2 | Strategy 3 |
|---|---|---|---|
| Imports | Substitution | Substitution | Liberalization |
| Export effort | Unchanged | Moderate increase | Increase |
| Debt management | Enforced debt relief | Unchanged | Unchanged |
| Tax/revenue effort | Increase | Moderate increase | Unchanged |
| Investment effectiveness (via planning, etc.) | Substantial improvement | Moderate improvement | Moderate improvement |
| Saving rates (via redistribution) | Decline | Unchanged | Unchanged |
| "Animal spirits" (via taxes and redistribution) | Decline | Improvement | Unchanged |
| *The Outcome* | | | |
| *1995 Ratios* | | | |
| —Inv./potential output | 0.2634 | 0.2105 | 0.1835 |
| —Exports/potential output | 0.1263 | 0.1310 | 0.1679 |
| —Actual/potential output | 0.9966 | 0.9943 | 0.9435 |
| *Average (1991—95) Growth* | | | |
| —Potential output | 0.0521 | 0.0420 | 0.0387 |
| —Actual GDP | 0.0524 | 0.0419 | 0.0268 |
| —Exports | 0.0517 | 0.0493 | 0.0992 |

### 9.2.2 Policy Implications of the Medium-Term Strategy

The medium-term strategy aims at raising potential output growth ($g$) from 4.0 % to 5.2 %, requiring increases in the investment share of potential output and the incremental output/capital ratio ($x$). The former should reach 26.3 % and the latter 0.25 by 1995, from 1990 values of 20.7 % and 0.18, respectively. If the increase in the investment/potential output ratio is divided into its private ($i_p$) and public ($i_g$) components, it turns out that $i_p$ can decrease modestly, but $i_g$ must climb from 9.0 % to 15.0 %.

Some improvement in $x$ during the 1990s will probably take place anyway due to the lagged impact of substantial infrastructure investment in recent years. However, the improvement foreseen by Scenario 1 requires careful planning. The increased share of $i_g$ in total capital formation provides the necessary condition. The aim should be to correct the distortions that occurred in the sectoral distribution of investments during the last decade. Capital formation in manufacturing fell by 49 % in real terms from 1977 to 1989 and the real decline in the investment levels of three productive sectors (agriculture, mining, and manufacturing) was 43 %.

Will private investment respond as the scenario requires? The inducement to invest in productive assets of private agents can be considered to be directly related to the share of gross profits in value-added (factor A), to the share of net before-tax profits (excluding interest charges and purely mercantile margins) within surplus (factor B), and to the share of net after-tax profits (inclusive of subsidies) in net before-tax profits (factor C). Finally, the standard positive effects of public investment and higher capacity utilization enter in.

Via these linkages, during the 1980s there were both adverse and favorable distributional effects on investment demand, as observed in tables 9.1, 9.4, and 9.8. Real investment trends for private manufacturing show that from 1977 to 1982 negative influences dominated, with modest improvement thereafter.

Scenario 1, given the social and political forces supporting it, would lead to significant distributional changes in favor of labor incomes, dampening animal spirits (factor A). The obsession with positive interest rates to savers would come to an end and policy elements designed to favor exporters against industry and merchants against farmers would probably have to be phased out. These changes would help $i_p$ (factor B). Tax burdens would have to shift primarily to rentier-type activities and the banking system; but secondarily to corporate profits and non-labor incomes as well. Private investment propensities would be affected adversely by these changes (factor C). When crowding-in and accelerator effects are taken into account, our projected end result is a moderate decrease in the ratio of private investment to potential output from 11.62 % in 1990 to 11.35 % in 1995.

Our "radical" strategy for the 1990s foresees a slight decline in savings propensities, due to redistribution in favor of labor incomes. This cautious prediction disregards the positive impacts on aggregate savings ratios of the internal redistribution of the surplus in favor of net profits and against interest payments. Empirical findings give strong support to such an outcome.[7]

With respect to public savings, the strategy is heavily dependent on a stronger tax effort and a savings on current public spending. There is, undoubtedly, substantial potential for economizing on military outlays. Simple economic reasoning suggests that there is significant scope for attaining higher tax/GDP ratios during the coming years.

**Table 9.8**
Indicators of secondary relations of distribution

| | 1977 | 1980 | 1983 | 1984 | 1985 | 1986 | 1987 | 1988 | 1989 | 1990 |
|---|---|---|---|---|---|---|---|---|---|---|
| I. Share of interest within industrial surplus (%) | | | | | | | | | | |
| A. Large private firms | | | 52.6 | 54.1 | 60.4 | 67.6 | 50.1 | 56.3 | | |
| B. Eskisehir Industry | | 22.1 | 53.7 | 42.0 | 46.0 | 39.0 | | | | |
| II. Trade and finance in GDP | | | | | | | | | | |
| A. Finance/GDP (%) | 2.5 | 1.8 | 1.9 | 2.7 | 2.9 | 2.9 | 2.8 | 2.8 | 3.1 | |
| B. Trade/GDP (%) | 13.5 | 15.9 | 17.6 | 18.1 | 17.2 | 17.1 | 17.6 | 17.6 | 17.6 | |
| C. Index of implicit deflators' ratios | | | | | | | | | | |
| 1. Trade/GDP | 100.0 | 123.1 | 128.0 | 129.0 | 122.1 | 119.0 | 116.8 | 117.6 | 112.8 | 107.7 |
| 2. Finance/GDP | 100.0 | 64.8 | 75.1 | 109.0 | 118.2 | 121.7 | 118.3 | 120.6 | 129.6 | 166.2 |
| D. Real bank profits (index) | | 247.3 | 329.0 | 636.7 | 617.6 | 968.8 | 1310.4 | | | |
| III. Rentier incomes | | | | | | | | | | |
| A. Deposit interests within GDP (%) | .3 | 1.4 | 5.6 | 7.7 | 10.8 | 9.2 | 7.7 | 10.6 | | |
| B. Interest on internal Government debt/GDP (%) | .5 | .5 | .7 | 1.0 | 1.0 | 1.8 | 2.4 | 3.5 | | |
| C. Total interest revenue/GDP (%) (IIIA + IIIB) | .8 | 1.9 | 6.3 | 8.7 | 11.8 | 11.0 | 10.1 | 14.1 | | |
| D. Real interest incomes (index) | 100 | 246 | 938 | 1357 | 1919 | 1978 | 1939 | 2775 | | |
| C. Real deposit interest rate (%) | −16.9 | −80.8 | 14.4 | −7.0 | 15.0 | 21.3 | 8.0 | .4 | | |

Changes in the taxation system during the 1980s raised the share of indirect taxes significantly. Generous incentives for selected activities (exports, tourism etc.) during the late 1980s seem to have resulted in significant declines in corporate tax/net pre-tax profit ratios from around 65 % to 38 % (Akyüz, 1990). The personal income tax, with 25 % to 50 % marginal rates, has been transformed into a levy mainly on workers and civil servants. In 1988 roughly 56 % of income tax revenue was collected from payrolls of wage and salary earners. Taxes on distributed corporate profits and (except a 10 % deduction on deposit interests) and on interest income do not constitute a major part of the remaining 44 % of personal income taxes.[8] A universal system of normally progressive personal income taxes and a simplified system of corporate taxation could definitely raise total revenue.

Assuming unchanged shares of public consumption and parastatal factor incomes in GDP for 1991–95, scenario 1 would require raising tax revenue and GDP from 22.0 % in 1990 to 25.0 % in 1995. In order to earmark greater public funds for neglected areas such as education and health, economies must be sought in other items of public spending, especially defense.

Strategy 1 projects a period average export growth rate of 5.2 % for the 1990s. After the boom of the 1980s, a realistic estimate of the elasticity of Turkish exports to world trade would be around unity. Considering IBRD and UNCTAD projections during the 1990s, the export growth rate of strategy 1 appears to be just about attainable.

The experience of the 1980s is not particularly instructive with respect to the impact of competing imports on the structure of Turkish industry. Quotas and reduced tariff rates were replaced with higher and arbitrarily fluctuating surcharges, effectively eliminating import policy. "Radical" strategies of the 1990s are characterized more in terms of their rejection of import liberalization than a strong commitment to import substitution. Effective control on the composition of imports will have to be linked closely to industrial policy.

The gap model used in Boratav and Türel (1989) does not directly incorporate inflation. However, because Scenario 1 foresees capacity utilization rates approaching unity, and because the 1980s have been years of endemic inflation fluctuating between 30 and 70 %, it will be difficult to disregard the issue for the 1990s.

A decade's experience suggests that it is essential to (1) avoid hyperinflation and (2) stabilize inflation at an "acceptable" rate and allow very moderate fluctuations around it. Even Central Bank (CB) economists have become convinced of the role of structural, cost-based factors in inflation as evidenced by the gradual reduction of indexation of the policy variables under their control since late 1988. The exchange rate has gradually been overvalued and net deposit interest rates have been pulled downward into negative values resulting in lower, but still significantly positive, loan interest rates. The election shock of March 1989 persuaded the government to soft pedal on price adjustment of intermediate inputs produced by state economic enterprises. These cost-based approaches prevented acceleration of inflation during 1989–90. The business community is also subscribing to a more or less "structuralist" diagnosis of inflation in Turkey, a subjective factor that shapes pricing behavior and the inflationary process.

Broadly speaking, pricing behavior in the Turkish economy can be disaggregated into three patterns: mark-up pricing in industry, flexible pricing in agriculture, and services roughly following industrial price movements. Administrative pricing has, however, been important in all three sectors (Boratav, 1987b).

With respect to industrial price movements, the exchange rate, state enterprise prices, wages, and the mark-up coefficient are the main factors determining the price level. The impact of the loan rate of interest remains controversial in Turkey.[9] In nonagricultural sectors as a whole, the exchange rate emerges as being more important than wages in influencing price movements (Uygur, 1987) Following Taylor (1987), a formulation like $\hat{p} = f(\hat{e}, \hat{s}, \hat{w}, \hat{f})$ in which the terms in parentheses represent (changes in) the exchange rate, the average mark-up coefficient specific for state enterprises, wages, and the private sector mark-up coefficient would probably explain aggregate price movements in four-fifths of the Turkish economy, especially for nonagricultural activities.

With respect to agricultural price movements, Uygur's (1987) econometric work suggests that support prices are more important than monetary variables. The 1980s can be characterized as a period when indexation coefficients of $\hat{e}$ and $\hat{s}$ have systematically exceeded unity and when repressive wage policies coupled with a gradual decline in the scope of agricultural support policies have been carried on. Attempts at monetary restraint have been present as well. These policy elements resulted in a decline in wage share, deterioration of agriculture's terms of trade, and increases in mark-up coefficients. It is not surprising that inflation has persisted.

Under strategy 1, wage and agricultural price movements are initially expected to exceed the general price movement. The problem is to prevent a drift into hyperinflation: There are financial limits to lowering the indexation coefficient of $\hat{s}$, because scenario 1 depends crucially on a stronger public revenue performance and erosion of state enterprise surpluses (or increased deficits) would undermine the strategy. Some degree of gradual overvaluation is permissible (i.e., $\hat{e} < \hat{p}$), probably within a dual exchange rate system in the manner of Kaldor. Beyond a point, however, it would be impossible to arrest adverse trade effects and moreover, the sizeable real appreciation during 1989–90 left very little room for maneuver in this respect. There is loose evidence that $\hat{f}$ may be inversely related to $\hat{w}$ (Boratav, 1990), and active but extremely careful price policy by public agencies may be required to reinforce this factor so as to narrow mark-up rates.

In short, the radical leftist-nationalist strategy faces the risk of hyper-inflation and eventual collapse. An effective social consensus around distributional issues will be required to prevent this eventuality.

The external debt management of Strategy 1 is based upon unilateral or negotiated restriction of interest payments abroad, attaining zero real interest rates by 1995, and realizing a zero current account deficit (CAD) by the same year.

These objectives have implications for the growth of the external debt and debt service; but it is not possible to project the debt stock from the foregoing assumptions directly. First, our estimates and parameter values are in constant dollar terms; interest payments affect the magnitude of CAD in nominal terms.

The second complication is due to the discrepancy between the capital accounts of the Turkish balance of payments series and external debt series particularly from 1984 onward.[10] The latter series, closely scrutinized by creditors, ought to be considered more reliable. According to our calculations, of the $19.3 billion growth in the Turkish external debt during the five years covering 1984 to 1988, $6.7 billion are reflected in debt-creating items in the recorded accounts, $4.2 billion are due to incidence of exchange rate fluctuations on the size of the debt stock in dollar terms, and there remains a residual of $8.4 billion. It results from a combination of unreliable Turkish statistics of the 1980s and reverse capital flight involving, inter alia, the repatriation of "black money." Overinvoicing exports and other foreign exchange earnings as observed in the "fictitious exports" are the major means by which the CAD is reduced but the reduction has no counterpart in the external debt figures.

If we start from a stock of $40.2 billion in 1987 and project external debt figures for 1995 in constant (1987) dollar terms, it turns out that strategy 1 succeeds in stabilizing the level at around $41.7 billion for 1995. The debt/GDP ratio starts at 59.1 % in 1987, and in 1995 falls to 42.5 %. Under our assumptions there seems to be no imminent debt crisis during the

1990s. On the other hand, these projections do not incorporate massive capital flights leading to an uncontrolled explosion of the external debt. Both orthodox and radical strategies face such a risk—the former with liberalized exchange and financial regimes that are vulnerable to adverse rentier behavior in response to nonfavorable" interest and exchange rate movements, the latter to politically motivated capital flight. The external debt trap is likely to remain on the agenda during the 1990s.

With respect to internal public debt, there has been an upsurge during the recent years as an outcome of fiscal laxity and high borrowing rates. The domestic public debt/GNP ratio (excluding advances from the CB) has risen from near zero to roughly 10 % and the PSBR/GNP ratio (inclusive of the inflationary component of interest payments on government bonds) reached 4.7 % by 1987. The relative improvement in 1988 turned out to be temporary, as the relevant ratios deteriorated again to values comparable with 1987.

Public debt creates problems due to the undeveloped nature of the securities market, which has been unable to absorb new issues of government instruments. Public agencies and the central government have marketed their tax-free obligations mainly to commercial banks which have held them as liquidity requirements and used them in short-term money market operations. Corporations have seen this pattern of public borrowing as creating "financial crowding-out" resulting from higher interest rates and portfolio displacement (Anand, et al., 1990). The unprecedented levels of nominal public debt have been creating extremely rigid constraints on the budget due to high interest components therein. As of 1990, it may be early to label these conditions as an "internal debt trap"; but there are, evidently, elements of a vicious cycle from which policymakers have been unable to liberate themselves.

### 9.2.3 Other Complications

The new orientation contrasts sharply with official policy positions in the 1980s. The new strategy is built around reemphasis of the productive role of the public sector, effective planning, selective import substitution, and control over internal and external finance. In contrast with these positions the official economic ideology of the recent past was built around privatization of productive public sector, deregulation, import liberalization, and financial liberalization. However, the apparent contradiction on all four points is misleading because it is difficult to speak about the prevalence of any model from 1987 onwards.

With respect to privatization of the public sector, attempts to sell public enterprises to local private business groups have failed. Privatization has turned into controversial sales of public companies to foreign firms and the marketing of parastatal shares at the local stock exchange. It is being used mainly to overcome immediate foreign exchange and/or financial problems of the public sector. The government's efforts to sell cement and petrochemical plants, in full or in part, to foreign capital has found some of its strongest critics within the ranks of influential business groups.

In the introductory section of this paper we discussed the limits to economic liberalism in Turkey on the basis of the arbitrary use of the economic levers controlled by the government in favor of or against individual business interests. The phenomenon is now so widespread that it has become impossible to speak about coherent deregulation during the last few years. The same general conclusion applies to import liberalization.

Financial liberalization has been an area where definite change has taken place compared with the pre-1980 period. However, the CB has not entirely given up its levers to impose restrictions on banks to control capital movements in either way. Its recent interventions have been in the direction of arresting the movement toward financial liberalization vis-à-vis the external world. Nevertheless, the new institutional arrangements have taken root and seem irreversible. Any new strategy must accommodate itself to this fait accompli in one way or another.

## 9.3  Sectoral and Micro Issues

Comparison of the real and nominal output trends of the major sectors and their decomposition from 1977 to 1990 points to a number of particularities in growth patterns and relative price movements.

Changes in the share of major sectors within GDP under constant prices have been in expected directions. From 1977 to 1988, the industry share rose by 1.9 % (to 25.5 %), offset by a 1.4 % fall in agriculture (to 21.7 %). From 1975 to 1985 industry's share within the economically active population increased from 9.1 % to 11.4 % , whereas the corresponding change in agriculture was from 67.3 % to 59.0 %, and in services from 23.6 % to 29.6 %. These shifts suggest that Turkey still preserves surplus labor in agriculture. There also appears to be hypertrophy of employment within "nonproductive" activities (defined as "services minus construction, transportation and communication"). Their employment share expanded from 54.2 % to 56.0 % during 1975−85.

When we shift our attention to changes in sectoral shares in current prices, a striking divergence between real output and relative price movements becomes apparent: Between 1977 and 1988 industry's share in current prices expanded from 19.8% to 32.4% and there was a reverse movement in agriculture (from 27.6% to 17.5%) and a moderate decline in services (from 52.6% to 50.1%). The resulting sectoral terms of trade movements (defined with respect to GDP implicit deflators) appear in table 9.9. Compared with 1977 index values of 100, the deterioration of relative agricultural prices in 1990 to 75.1 can be contrasted with the rise of industry's terms of trade to 130.2. Stability of service sector prices prevailed, with a 1990 index of 97.3.

An initial question is whether these movements can be considered a "return to a normal structure of relative prices" following the gradual opening-up of a protected economy and the elimination of "rents." On this issue it is interesting to note that the terms of trade of the predominantly nontraded service sector improved strongly in regard to agriculture.

Analysis within the framework of an alternative division between the nonproductive and productive sectors of the economy in which "government" has been excluded altogether and construction and transport and communications are shifted into the productive" group can also be useful. The terms of trade of nonproductive activities defined in this way improved by about 10% from 1977 to 1990, a finding that reinforces the preceding observation on nontradables (table 9.9). The dramatic improvement of industrial relative prices, on the other hand, was not only due to increased costs of imported or local inputs, but also due to higher mark-ups: The average mark-up rate for private manufacturing increased from 26.5% for 1975–77 to 32.1% for 1980–85 (Boratav, 1990, table IV). The expected relative price impact of opening-up (or of the "elimination of rents") does not seem to have operated with respect to major sectors. Further analysis based on table 9.9 suggests that the relative price movement of the service sector as a whole was determined by the composite effect of distributional changes relevant for its subsectors.[11]

A parallel inquiry should be extended to agricultural prices. A conventional analysis structured around income elasticities of demand for agricultural goods, and changes in agricultural supply and aggregate demand is not very illuminating: From 1977 to 1989 real agricultural value added grew annually by 2.9%, whereas the average growth rate of aggregate demand was 4.0%. Under any reasonable elasticity estimates, these growth rates cannot account for the deterioration of agriculture's terms of trade

**Table 9.9**
Sectoral terms of trade (sector implicit deflator/GDP deflator × 100)

| | 1977 | 1980 | 1983 | 1984 | 1985 | 1986 | 1987 | 1988 | 1989 | 1990 |
|---|---|---|---|---|---|---|---|---|---|---|
| 1. Agriculture | 100.0 | 78.6 | 72.1 | 73.8 | 71.9 | 70.5 | 70.4 | 66.2 | 71.6 | 75.1 |
| 2. Industry | 100.0 | 137.4 | 145.4 | 144.1 | 151.4 | 150.9 | 143.9 | 148.7 | 140.7 | 130.2 |
| 3. Services | 100.0 | 97.9 | 97.7 | 96.7 | 94.3 | 95.4 | 94.1 | 94.6 | 94.5 | 97.3 |
| 4. Construction | 100.0 | 92.7 | 81.9 | 82.7 | 77.6 | 81.8 | 82.3 | 90.4 | 81.8 | 88.2 |
| 5. Trade | 100.0 | 123.1 | 128.0 | 129.0 | 122.1 | 119.0 | 116.8 | 117.6 | 112.8 | 107.7 |
| 6. Communications & transport | 100.0 | 120.0 | 129.9 | 125.2 | 128.3 | 127.5 | 122.7 | 125.8 | 125.4 | 130.3 |
| 7. Finance | 100.0 | 64.8 | 75.1 | 109.0 | 118.2 | 121.7 | 118.3 | 120.6 | 129.6 | 166.2 |
| 8. Housing | 100.0 | 100.2 | 92.4 | 95.7 | 96.1 | 102.1 | 101.3 | 108.5 | 113.7 | 121.7 |
| 9. Liberal professions etc. | 100.0 | 106.9 | 108.3 | 109.5 | 105.0 | 102.9 | 101.1 | 102.4 | 103.9 | 103.6 |
| 10. Government[a] | 100.0 | 63.7 | 54.2 | 42.9 | 40.1 | 42.8 | 44.6 | 42.3 | 62.1 | 80.7 |
| 11. Unproductive/productive sectors[b] | 100.0 | 105.4 | 107.6 | | 106.4 | | 106.9 | 109.0 | 107.7 | 110.2 |

a. 1988–1990 figures are from SIS' new GDP series.
b. Unproductive sectors = Rows 5 + 7 + 8 + 9; Productive sectors = Rows 1 + 2 + 4 + 6 Government excluded from both groups.

vis-à-vis the rest of the economy by nearly 28.4 % during the same period (table 9.9).

An alternative explanation can be made on the basis of the structural features of agricultural markets in Turkey: During the preceding decades extensive government intervention created significant gaps between movements of prices paid by consumers (the relevant concept for analysis based on income elasticities of demand) and movements of prices received by farmers (which were predominantly influenced by government's support prices).[12] The agricultural prices used in terms of trade analysis are the latter. The gradual withdrawal of public agencies from agricultural markets during the 1980s seems to have led to steady deterioration of farmgate receipts.

Distributional changes to be expected during the 1990s under strategy 1 would probably lead to reversals of the relative price movements observed during the preceding decade. Would such a change lead to difficulties in macro balances and in the accumulation process? On the accumulation issue, our model solutions and the private investment function of this paper do not produce pessimistic outcomes. Moreover, improved relative prices for farmers would lead to higher rates of investment in agriculture, a factor left out of the foregoing investment analysis.

With respect to macro equilibrium, the consistency of the PSBR targets of Strategy 1 and a re-expansion of agricultural support and subsidy systems would have to be tested, while reintroduction of consumer subsidies on wage goods on the scale of the late 1970s may be impossible under the constraints imposed by the model. Extremely careful management of social policy will be required in order to prevent the emergence of worker-peasant distributional trade-offs and conflicts during the 1990s.

Specific planning problems arise with regard to manufacturing and agriculture. For the former, table 9.10 shows the dramatic regression in labor productivity observed in large-scale industry during the crisis years of 1978–80 and the gradual improvement thereafter. By 1986, most branches had still not attained the productivity levels of 1977. If we exclude the oil products, etc. (ISIC 35) sector, in which productivity indicators are highly sensitive to the margin between import costs and administrative prices, manufacturing as a whole in 1986 was operating at a productivity level 16 % lower than that attained in 1977.

This poor performance can be attributed to a variety of factors. First, in the business climate of the 1980s, industrial firms were mainly interested in raising capacity utilization and refrained from process innovations and significant additions to existing capacities. Because labor layoffs were pro-

**Table 9.10**
Indices of real value-added per worker in manufacturing (1977 = 100)

| ISIC code and subsector | 1979 | 1980 | 1981 | 1983 | 1985 | 1986 | 1987 | 1988 |
|---|---|---|---|---|---|---|---|---|
| 31 Food beverages & tobacco | 53.3 | 58.6 | 72.4 | 76.0 | 91.4 | 95.2 | 97.7 | 103.8 |
| 32 Textile, apparels & leather | 78.1 | 65.8 | 63.2 | 66.7 | 70.4 | 76.0 | 91.0 | 84.6 |
| 33 Wood products & furniture | 55.6 | 42.2 | 38.4 | 41.6 | 48.0 | 47.1 | 62.1 | 58.7 |
| 34 Pulp, paper & printing | 50.7 | 46.6 | 50.5 | 60.2 | 70.1 | 62.8 | 73.8 | 90.9 |
| 35 Chemicals & petroleum products[a] | 102.6 | 103.4 | 140.2 | 128.8 | 108.9 | 198.0 | 166.8 | 198.7 |
| 36 Nonmetallic products | 60.2 | 73.6 | 85.7 | 76.1 | 82.8 | 107.8 | 126.9 | 117.4 |
| 37 Basic metal industries | 56.8 | 59.1 | 54.2 | 57.8 | 66.2 | 72.4 | 91.2 | 105.4 |
| 38 Metal products, vehicles, mach | 78.2 | 67.9 | 69.2 | 73.2 | 78.9 | 91.4 | 102.1 | 101.1 |
| 39 Other manufacturing | 73.3 | 74.0 | 61.9 | 81.4 | 109.0 | 84.2 | 75.9 | — |
| 3 Manufacturing industry | 71.9 | 69.8 | 80.1 | 80.0 | 82.2 | 106.5 | 109.5 | 115.8 |
| 3 Manufacturing minus 35 | 64.9 | 62.2 | 65.7 | 68.3 | 76.5 | 83.9 | 94.9 | 95.9 |

a. Errors of data and/or deflation are highly likely for sector 35 for 1986–1988.

hibited by the military government from 1980 to 1984, higher capacity use with available labor increased productivity indicators even when capital stock had started suffering from obsolescence. Second, the Turkish manufacturing industry has continued to specialize in low-skill, low-productivity branches in an accentuated manner (Türel, 1987). The "star" industries of the export drive of the 1980s (i.e. textiles, leather, and iron and steel) did not exhibit significant productivity developments during this period. Real wage erosion and the preservation of comfortable mark-ups may have contributed to this pattern.

The pattern of international specialization exhibited by manufacturing industry has not changed much from the late 1970s onwards. As Türel (1987) shows, net export ratios (i.e. (Exp-Imp)/Output) in food, textiles, leather, glass, and, to a lesser extent, iron and steel rose considerably during the 1980s, but the same ratios registered declines in nonelectrical and electrical machinery and in transport equipment. Table 9.11 looks into the same issue by comparing indices of revealed comparative advantage of a few countries with relatively elaborate industrial structures in the WIDER sample. From the early 1970s to the early 1980s, the pattern of specialization of Turkish industry into products with higher capital or skill intensity is definitely lower than in Brazil and South Korea; even India exhibits a more mature structure of specialization.

During 1984–88, 31 % of the increment in manufacturing output was channeled to exports.[13] When extra output can no longer be realized on the basis of higher capacity use, export drives based on the manufacturing sector will be confronting constraints on production—another justification for the moderate export forecasts envisaged in scenario 1.

Agricultural value added per active person rose at an annual rate of 2.8 % from 1977 to 1985 and a parallel, but more moderate progression was registered in productivity per hectare of major crops between 1976–77 and 1986–87: Annual rates of change in land productivity—in ascending order—for tobacco, wheat, sunflower, cotton, and potatoes were between 0.3 % and 2.7 % and the only major crop with declining productivity was sugarbeet ($-1.5$ % per annum).[14] These positive productivity and output responses can be explained as an attempt by peasants to preserve real income levels by increasing marketed quantities at lower real prices. Increased self-exploitation of household labor and sustaining the level of productive inputs by depressing consumption levels and by increased indebtedness have probably been the means utilized to realise this outcome.

The capacity of such mechanisms to offset declining support policies and underinvestment in the sector has probably been exhausted. Future agricul-

**Table 9.11**
Revealed comparative advantage indices in selected industries of some countries

| ITC product group | Brazil 1970–72 | Brazil 1981–83 | India 1970–72 | India 1981–83 | South Korea 1970–72 | South Korea 1981–83 | Mexico 1970–72 | Mexico 1981–83 | Turkey 1970–72 | Turkey 1981–83 |
|---|---|---|---|---|---|---|---|---|---|---|
| 73 iron & steel bars | −0.7 | 1.60 | −.37 | −1.95 | −.32 | .64 | −.08 | −.49 | −3.03 | 2.42 |
| 74 Universal plates | −1.53 | 1.44 | −4.45 | −3.94 | .34 | 1.44 | .12 | −2.10 | −.69 | −2.41 |
| 91 Metal structures | −1.41 | −1.09 | 1.11 | .53 | −3.75 | 4.11 | −.42 | −.90 | −6.70 | .52 |
| 95 Tools | −1.67 | −.47 | .52 | 1.18 | −.58 | −.13 | −2.14 | −1.51 | −1.90 | −1.14 |
| 11 Power generators | −1.48 | .19 | −.85 | −.09 | −1.39 | −1.02 | −1.70 | −2.02 | −3.44 | −2.52 |
| 15 Metalworking machinery | −3.52 | −1.33 | −1.65 | −1.16 | −2.04 | −1.05 |  | −3.50 | −4.12 | −2.42 |
| 24 Telecommunication apparatus | −1.19 | .20 | −.53 | −.19 | −.70 | 1.45 | −1.42 | −.96 | −1.05 | −.65 |
| 32 Motor vehicles | −.19 | .73 | .10 | .09 | −.41 | −.03 | −1.43 | −1.86 | −.95 | −.41 |

Index of RCA: $(X_{ij} - M_{ij})/T_{ij}(T_{iw}/T_{tw})$, where X = Exports, M = Imports, T = $(X + M)/2$, and i, j, t, w, refer to product, country, total manufactures and world.
Source: UNIDO (1986).

tural growth will be heavily dependent on infrastructural investment. If, during the coming years, sufficient funds are allocated to the ambitious Southeastern Anatolia Project, which combines major irrigation schemes with infrastructural facilities and power plants, the early 1990s may witness a significant change in the crop pattern and yields. Price support policies roughly at comparable levels with the 1970s are another condition for sustained agricultural growth.

## 9.4  Conclusions

The foregoing discussion did not cover external factors that may influence the Turkish economy during the 1990s and certain international, social, and political implications of the new development strategy. This concluding section will briefly discuss these themes.

### 9.4.1  International Dimensions

There is a widespread expectation within government for massive direct foreign investment (DFI), a factor that may contribute to raising the overall rate of accumulation and to alleviating external difficulties.

Despite a liberal regime, DFI was meager up to 1987 with annual inflows rarely exceeding the $100 million threshhold (table 9.6). It is too early to foresee whether the upsurge after 1988 will end up with a real break-though. An investigation—covering 15 years from 1970 to 1985—on changes in the "degree of attractiveness of Turkey for direct foreign investment in industry" came to the conclusion that the dramatic regression in Turkish wages in dollar terms has partly been neutralized by relative stagnation in labor productivity in manufacturing in comparison with a number of "similar" countries likely to be competing for foreign investors (Boratav, 1987a). It is to be expected that an "enlarged" Europe may be promising for new exports; but a similar prediction cannot be made for capital flows.

A final question should, perhaps, be raised with respect to the external feasibility of our new strategy for the 1990s: How far is it possible to carry on nonorthodox economics in a world where orthodoxy still reigns supreme in those places where it matters, that is, at the financial centers of world capitalism? Attaining external equilibrium is a necessary condition, but not a sufficient one for a single nonconformist developing country to withstand the economic, political, and ideological pressures from a hostile external world through the well-known transmission mechanisms. Non-orthodox models will be more likely to succeed if there are several "dissident" developing countries broadly moving toward some sort of collective action and if there is a reemergence of neo-Keynesianism as the dominant economic orientation in metropoles of the Western world.

### 9.4.2    Class Collaboration or Class Conflict?

The viability of our new strategy is crucially dependent on some sort of a modus vivendi on a major economic and social issues, between the popular classes and an important segment of the bourgeoisie. The policy components of the strategy suggest that the industrial and nonmonopolistic segments of the business community are likely candidates for such "class collaboration." These groups have been taking an increasingly critical attitude vis-à-vis the pro-rentier, pro-mercantile and anti-industry components of MP policies since 1987, in part because of the "discriminatory" orientation of the government vis-à-vis individual members of the business community.

However, Turkish dominant classes may refuse to collaborate with popular social forces within the framework of a "radical" economic strategy. If the instinctive ideological conservatism of the bourgeoisie as a class prevails over its internal divisions, a generalized "strike" in the form of massive capital flight by all segments of the bourgeoisie may be likely. It is impossible to prevent such a development by economic means alone when it takes on a political dimension and is disseminated among all business groups.

If this pessimistic prognosis proves to be correct, the strategy developed in this paper may lead to class conflict and civil unrest. The final outcomes would be impossible to foretell.

### Notes

1. We updated the findings in Boratav and Türel (1989) and obtained slightly different numerical results. Nevertheless, the determining characteristics of comparative growth scenarios remained unchanged. With regard to the data presented herein, tables 9.1 and 9.8 are updated from similar tables in Boratav (1990). Türel (1987) presents data on maunfacturing value-added. All other data are based on official statistics from the State Planning Organization, Central Bank, Ministry of Finance, and State Institute of Statistics (SIS). In 1991, SIS revised its national accounting methods and produced a new series for 1987–90 resulting in (roughly) a 15 % upward adjustment for GDP; the old (unadjusted) GDP series will no longer be produced. In tables 9.2 to 9.4, GDP is estimated by starting from the unadjusted 1987 figure and applying the 1988–90 growth rates of the new series. Tables 9.5

and 9.6 are based on the three-gap model of Boratav and Türel (1989), where our calculations of entries in the balance of payments and potential output growth are also described.

2. See Boratav (1987b) for such a formulation.

3. The prosecution against Mr. Boyner, the then president of Turkish Association of Industrialists and Businessmen (TÜSIAD), in June 1990 on the charges of "interfering with politics" after his moderately critical remarks on economic policy is a bizarre case in point. Prior to this event, a Minister of State openly harassed Mr. Boyner, himself an industrialist in the textile and garment business, by a threat to slash import duties on rival textile products.

4. There is a discrepancy of 26.5 % between IMF and Turkish statistics on Turkish exports to OECD countries for 1984–87, a figure that may provide some estimate for the relative size of fictitious exports (Çetin, 1988, p. 53).

5. See Section 9.2 for a more complete treatment of this discrepancy.

6. The methodology in Boratav and Türel (1989) was based on the assumption that for 1977 and 1987 actual GDP = potential GDP. If actual growth rates for these years exceeded our estimates, it follows that our assumptions for both years ought to have been modified by adjusting the actual GDP/potential GDP ratio downwards, for example, present 1.00 towards 0.95.

7. See the persuasive reasoning and empirical findings in Akyüz (1990), who compares very low savings propensities of rentiers with high savings propensities out of corporate net pre-tax profits and analyses the implications of redistribution from the former to the latter: A lower interest burden on corporate gross profits would lead to higher aggregate savings ratios.

8. See ANKA, 31.5.89 for the 1988 figures and Oyan (1987) for a survey and evaluation of the changes in the taxation system during the 1980s.

9. The theoretical analysis in Akyüz (1984) and the persistent claims of the Turkish businessmen about the inflationary impact of loan interest rate increases conflict with the econometric evidence in Uygur (1987).

10. From 1972 to 1984 external debt growth corresponded broadly to the net capital inflows of the balance of payments data (See Boratav, 1987b). The discrepancy becomes serious after 1984.

11. It should be noted that the statistical agency's treatment of the service sector in its national accounts calculations is full of methodological problems and therefore any analysis based on GDP figures of the service sector (and subsectors thereof) should be interpreted with caution.

12. See the causality links in Boratav (1990) and Uygur (1987).

13. Calculations made by the authors on the basis of SPO data.

14. See Boratav (1990) for productivity per man estimates. Productivity per hectare estimates are based on SIS data.

# References

Akyüz, Y. (1984). "On Interest Rates and Inflation" (in Turkish), *Yapit*, 6 (August-September): 17–43.

Akyüz, Y. (1990). "Financial System and Policies in Turkey in the 1980s," in Aricanli and Rodrik (eds.), *The Political Economy of Turkey*. London: Macmillan.

Anand, R., A. Chhibber, and S. van Wijnbergen (1990). "External Balance and Growth in Turkey: Can They Be Reconciled?," in Aricanli and Rodrik (eds.), *The Political Economy of Turkey*. London: Macmillan.

Boratav, K. (1987a). "International Comparisons of Wages and Labor Productivity," in *Papers and Proceedings of the 1987 Congress Industry*, (in Turkish). Ankara: Makina Mühendisleri Odasi.

Boratav, K. (1987b). "Stabilization and Adjustment Policies and Programmes." *Country Study No 5: Turkey*, Helsinki: WIDER/UNU.

Boratav, K. (1990). "Inter-Class and Intra-Class Relations of Distribution under 'Structural Adjustment': Turkey during the 1980s," in Aricanli and Rodrik (eds.), *The Political Economy of Turkey*. London: Macmillan.

Boratav, K., and Türel, O. (1989). "Growth Projections for the Turkish Economy Under Alternative Scenarios." (Mimeo), Ankara.

Çetin, B. (1988). *The Dimensions of Fictitious Exports* (in Turkish). Ankara: Bilgi Yayinevi.

Oyan, O. (1987). *Opening-up and Fiscal Policies after the 24th of January Program* (in Turkish). Ankara: V. Yayinlari.

Taylor, L. (1987). "Macro Policy in the Tropics: How Sensible People Stand," *World Development*, 15: 1407–1436.

Türel, O. (1987). "An Overview of the Development of Industry in Turkey." *Papers and Proceedings of the 1987 Congress of Industry* (in Turkish). Ankara: Makine Mühendisleri Odasi.

UNIDO (1986). *International Comparative Advantage in Manufacturing/Changing Profiles of Resources and Trade*, ID/334. Vienna.

Uygur, E. (1987). *SESRTCIC Econometric Model of the Turkish Economy*. Ankara: Statistical, Economic and Social Research and Training Center for Islamic Countries.

# 10        The Philippines

Joseph Y. Lim,
Manuel F. Montes, and
Agnes R. Quisumbing

A broad coalition of political forces made possible what is now described as the "civilian-backed military overthrow" of Ferdinand Marcos's government in February 1986. Unified as an anti-Marcos faction under Corazón C. Aquino, the coalition's middle and upper class leadership ranged from the military, the Catholic church, and conservative elites. These forces deemed Marcos' greed and increasing ineffectiveness as the best recruiter for the Communist movement to the center-left, which sought to dismantle his authoritarian machinery. The broad civilian support for the inexperienced leadership of the resistance had as much to do with its consciousness-raising and nationalist economic declarations[1] as with the deep economic crisis of 1984–85.

The years 1986–87 saw the new government seeking its equilibrium, sometimes teetering on the brink[2] of collapse, as it attempted to accommodate the demands of a broader Filipino constituency while depending for its political survival on landlords, large businessmen, and the military. It did manage to replace officials down to the local level, install a new constitution and Congress, dismantle the Marcos agricultural monopolies, and liberalize imports of products not affecting its immediate supporters.

The rapid removal of selected structures made the nonconservative members of the coalition expendable by the end of 1987, as they had also resisted policies by which the government sought to take control of or benefit from structures Marcos left behind. Assets of Marcos and his supporters had been sequestered and either sold to government supporters or taken under government control. The military and paramilitary agencies have been reinvigorated. The Marcos agrarian reform was effectively taken over with the passage of a law that seeks to meet its targets in rice and corn lands by 1992, the end of the term of the present government. The same law expresses the intention of implementing more comprehensive coverage after 1992, though even at present it provides legal channels for evading future reform, especially in the case of plantations (Hayami et al., 1990).

The conservative consolidation has sought to create a more stable government, with a broader constituency within the elite than that of Marcos, who had sought to create his own elite. The stance toward economic reform is not qualitatively different from that of the previous government, albeit understandably more cautious. In the face of a continuing reliance on foreign financing, the agenda for reform depends upon a judgment about what will gratify the multilateral financing agencies in the country's consultative group.

The other significant source of pressure for reform is domestic and originates from the organized mass groups, who face deep-seated[3] poverty and economic inequality.

## 10.1   Recent Economic Performance

The conservative consolidation was carried out during (and, conceivably, made possible by) a brief but strong economic recovery in 1987–89. The recovery was made possible by lower international interest rates, lower oil prices, higher prices of traditional exports, and increasing inflows of foreign investment from Japan and the newly industrializing economies (NIEs) in the region.

When it took over, the Aquino government enjoyed the additional advantage of underutilized industrial capacity, left over from the IMF stabilization program of 1984–85. The government induced a demand-led recovery by driving up its real consumption by 7 % in 1987, 10.5 % in 1988, and 7.7 % in 1989. The average annual growth rate of real gross investment exceeded 25 % in 1987 and 1988, after falling by 33 % per year in 1984–85 (table 10.1). In 1989, the real gross investment growth rate declined to 16 %. Real durable equipment investment increased by 32 % in 1988, and by a slightly lower 28 % in 1989.

The structural adjustments now occurring in Asia provided breathing space for the recovery by permitting exports to grow rapidly, even though imports exploded as would be expected in demand-led growth. The private sector responded mainly with construction investment for residential and commercial purposes. (See table 10.2 for sectoral rates of growth). The growth of manufacturing is an important aspect of table 10.2. Domestic demand has permitted higher capacity utilization, rising from levels as low as 45 % in key sectors such as household appliances.

**Table 10.1**
Demand-side macroeconomic growth (average annual growth rates, %)

|  | 1967–74 | 1974–79 | 1979–83 | 1983–85 | 1985–88 | 1988 | 1989 |
|---|---|---|---|---|---|---|---|
| Personal consumption | 4.83 | 4.17 | 3.60 | 0.48 | 4.07 | 5.11 | 5.55 |
| Government consumption | 11.44 | 2.88 | 2.39 | −3.37 | 5.71 | 10.47 | 7.71 |
| Gross investment | 7.72 | 9.44 | −0.37 | −33.45 | 13.27 | 25.88 | 15.56 |
| Fixed capital | 5.19 | 10.98 | 2.09 | −28.45 | 6.07 | 21.39 | 19.76 |
| Construction | 0.42 | 17.53 | 3.36 | −23.13 | −0.10 | 11.82 | 11.56 |
| Government | 12.52 | 22.16 | −2.85 | −27.58 | 1.51 | 7.22 | 6.66 |
| Private | −3.86 | 14.21 | 8.16 | −20.62 | −0.91 | 14.42 | 14.04 |
| Durable equipment | 8.59 | 6.43 | 0.78 | −34.74 | 14.21 | 32.88 | 27.74 |
| Exports | 3.99 | 7.62 | 5.33 | 0.23 | 10.63 | 12.72 | 11.73 |
| Imports | 4.43 | 7.00 | 3.75 | −19.78 | 24.22 | 34.20 | 22.49 |
| GDP | 6.66 | 5.36 | 3.24 | −5.2 | 4.25 | 6.63 | 5.98 |
| GNP | 6.91 | 5.34 | 2.84 | −5.66 | 4.83 | 6.69 | 5.55 |

Source of basic data: National Statistics Office.

**Table 10.2**
Sectoral rates of growth (average annual %)

|  | 1967–74 | 1974–79 | 1979–83 | 1983–85 | 1985–88 | 1988 | 1989 |
|---|---|---|---|---|---|---|---|
| Agriculture | 5.17 | 2.39 | 2.79 | 1.87 | 3.42 | 3.42 | 3.00 |
| Industry | 8.40 | 8.31 | 2.98 | −10.19 | 4.70 | 8.90 | 7.50 |
| Mining & quarrying | 8.75 | −2.03 | −5.17 | −3.07 | 5.85 | 5.85 | 0.90 |
| Manufacturing | 8.42 | 5.86 | 3.08 | −7.38 | 5.36 | 8.74 | 7.30 |
| Construction | 5.61 | 19.75 | 3.28 | −25.58 | 1.63 | 12.76 | 10.80 |
| Electricity, gas & water | 13.07 | 7.75 | 9.01 | 9.64 | 11.92 | 5.29 | 6.50 |
| Service | 6.50 | 5.71 | 4.14 | −6.06 | 5.53 | 7.06 | 5.84 |
| Transportation, communication | 9.11 | 7.20 | 3.37 | −3.02 | 4.02 | 6.15 |  |
| Trade | 5.98 | 6.33 | 4.85 | 0.49 | 4.17 | 5.08 |  |
| Finance & housing | 4.75 | 6.16 | 4.17 | −25.52 | 13.66 | 7.92 |  |
| Private services |  |  |  |  | 1.40 | 3.72 |  |
| Government services |  |  |  |  | 7.92 | 15.89 |  |
| GDP | 6.66 | 5.36 | 3.24 | −5.20 | 4.25 | 6.63 | 5.98 |
| GNP | 6.91 | 5.34 | 2.84 | −5.66 | 4.83 | 6.69 | 5.55 |

Source of basic data: National Statistics Office.

The agricultural sector exhibited a secular slowdown even before the crisis began in 1983, probably as a result of the cumulation of anti-rural policies of the 1970s. The sector's average growth rate in 1974—79 was 2.4 %, and during the crisis years of 1983—85, it maintained positive growth. The principal explanation behind relatively slow growth after 1985 is unfavorable weather conditions in 1987 to 1989. The economy could have grown more strongly had agriculture attained the growth rates achieved in the mid-1970s.

The vigorous performance in 1988—89 was conditioned on an inflow of foreign support. But the recovery rekindled the pressures that caused the 1983 balance of payments crisis. Table 10.3 provides the information for 1982 and the years 1985—89. The trade deficit reached $1 billion in 1987 (about 18 % of the value of merchandise exports), stayed at about the same level in 1988, and more than doubled in 1989. In 1986, after the change in government, there was a one-time jump in inflows of overseas funds under Filipino control, which permitted the services account to turn positive. The critical item in the net services outflow is interest payments on foreign debt.

**Table 10.3**
Balance of payments, 1982—89 (U.S. $ millions)

|  | 1982 | 1985 | 1986 | 1987 | 1988 | 1989 |
|---|---|---|---|---|---|---|
| Merchandise exports | 5021 | 4629 | 4842 | 5720 | 7074 | 7890 |
| Merchandise imports | 7667 | 5111 | 5044 | 6737 | 8159 | 10245 |
| trade balance | −2646 | −482 | −202 | −1017 | −1085 | −2355 |
| Services (net) | −1040 | 85 | 715 | 0 | −126 | −36 |
| of which: interest | −1990 | −2208 | −2088 | −2107 | −2192 | −2465 |
| Transfers (net) | 486 | 379 | 441 | 573 | 780 | 815 |
| Current account | −3200 | −18 | 954 | −444 | −431 | −1576 |
| Selected capital account items: |  |  |  |  |  |  |
| Direct investments (net) | 17 | 17 | 140 | 326 | 986 | 757 |
| Medium-long-term loans (net) | 1548 | 890 | 732 | 159 | −329 | −618 |
| Short-term capital (net) | −263 | −721 | −23 | 390 | −205 | 22 |
| Monetization of gold, valuation adj. |  | 133 | 207 | 287 | 397 | 395 |
| Errors & ommissions | 277 | 638 | −102 | 89 | 190 | 151 |
| Change in net international reserves (—increase) |  | −991 | −1242 | −264 | −650 | −647 |

Source of basic data: Central Bank of the Philippines.

There has been a significant increase in net transfers received by the Philippines, mainly grants from Japan and the EEC. For 1988, extra grants of $200 million prevented worsening of the current account. As elsewhere in the region, direct foreign investment boomed. There was an eight-fold increase in net inflows between 1985 and 1986, and a three-fold increase between 1987 and 1988 (table 10.3), but then the level by $200 million in 1989. The first jump was induced by the reversal of loss of confidence as the new Aquino government took over in 1986. Finally, the continuing saga of Philippine debt is evident in the (net) medium and long-term loan entry in table 10.3, which exhibits a steady trend in the negative direction from 1985 to 1989.

The Aquino government contained a three-year extended fund facility from the IMF beginning in June 1989. The country's consultative group, renamed the Multilateral Aid Initiative (MAI), was spruced up with a "pledging" session in Tokyo in July 1989. For the most part, donor country commitments to existing projects identified in the medium-term plan were reaffirmed. A few other countries, notably Japan, indicated their readiness to increase commitments to the Philippines significantly.

The means by which the Philippines will obtain actual access to these additional pledges have as yet not been designed. There is a limit to additional infrastructure projects; there is also a limit, if not a fundamental inappropriateness,[4] to the quick utilization of additional funds for so-called countryside, rural development projects.

Table 10.4 provides information on rates of inflation, domestic interest rates, and exchange rates for the 1982–89 period. Until the end of 1988, inflation stayed below the double-digit level. The existence of significant excess capacity by end-1985 and the sharp plunge in domestic demand before that explains the almost-zero inflation rate in 1986 and the moderate 1987 rate of 4 %. There were three price rollbacks on oil products in 1988, but even then inflation approached 9 %.

Nominal interest rates were at unprecedented highs during the 1980s. In the 1984–85 stabilization, they exceeded 40 % for 91-day instruments as the government struggled to meet liquidity targets by offering Central Bank interest-bearing bills. The Treasury Bill rate, which the Central Bank currently uses as a lead instrument for interest rate determination has remained above 11 % since 1986,[5] approached 20 % in 1989, and exceeded 20 % in 1990. Interest rate setting is, in turn, motivated by the Central Bank's objective of preventing the exchange rate from depreciating "too fast" as part of the apparatus of a "market-determined exchange rate system" instituted in October 1984.[6]

**Table 10.4**
Rates of exchange, inflation, interest (%)

|  | 1982 | 1983 | 1984 | 1985 | 1986 | 1987 | 1988 | 1989 |
|---|---|---|---|---|---|---|---|---|
| Rate of exchange (average/year, pesos/U.S.$) | | | | | | | | |
| Nominal rate | 8.54 | 11.11 | 16.70 | 18.61 | 20.39 | 20.57 | 21.30 | 21.74 |
| Real effective rate | 109.10 | 92.30 | 91.50 | 100.00 | 78.00 | 71.80 | 69.80 | 73.80 |
| (1985 = 100) | | | | | | | | |
| Rates of inflation (average/year, %) | | | | | | | | |
| Consumer prices | 10.1 | 10.0 | 50.4 | 23.2 | 0.8 | 3.8 | 8.7 | 10.6 |
| Wholesale prices | 10.7 | 16.1 | 67.2 | 18.2 | −1.6 | 9.1 | 13.4 | 10.7 |
| Rates of interest (nominal) | | | | | | | | |
| Treasury bill | 13.78 | 14.23 | 28.53 | 26.73 | 16.08 | 11.51 | 14.67 | 18.65 |
| Deposit | 13.74 | 13.58 | 21.17 | 18.91 | 11.25 | 8.20 | 11.32 | 14.13 |
| Lending | 18.12 | 19.24 | 28.20 | 28.61 | 17.53 | 13.34 | 15.92 | 19.22 |

Source of basic data: IMF, *International Financial Statistics.*

The formal banking system, which is highly cartelized, is the principal beneficiary of this policy. As implied in table 10.4, real treasury bill rates have remained fiercely positive, while real deposit rates turned negative by 1988, but became positive again in 1989.

## 10.2  Income Distribution and Poverty

The Philippines has, more or less, recovered to the situation before the debt crisis, but the prospects for reforms directed at reducing economic inequality have dimmed as the Aquino administration paid more attention to the restoration of pre-martial law political institutions (e.g. the legislature) and economic recovery. In this regard, even public support for population programs has diminished, particularly in comparison to the Marcos years. The population growth rate, after falling to 2.4% per year in the mid-70s, is now estimated at 2.8%.

According to a recent World Bank (1988) report, although the incidence of poverty remained roughly constant at 52% between 1971 to 1985, the absolute number of the poor has increased by about 10 million individuals as a result of population growth. The balance between the urban and the rural poor also changed slightly since incidence increased in urban areas (from 38% to 42%) and did not change in the rural areas (at 58%). Nevertheless, the majority of the poor are still living in rural areas.

Although no income and expenditure surveys could be used to analyze the trends within the 1971−85 period, the report claims that poverty incidence decreased during the seventies and increased thereafter. First, GNP growth was not matched by personal income growth throughout the period. During 1971–79, personal income did grow, showing that some output growth was translated into higher household incomes. Since income distribution improved slightly during this period, personal income growth must have been translated into a reduction in poverty incidence. After 1979, however, personal income started a downward trend in spite of the fact that GNP continued to grow until 1981. It is probable that the incidence of poverty started to increase at this time. Poverty became even worse after 1981 when there was a sharp decline in both personal income and GNP per capita. By 1985, GNP per capita had fallen back to its 1975 level, and personal income to its 1972 level.

Although there may have been slight improvements over the 1971–85 period, the Philippines continues to have a highly skewed income distribution.[7] The Gini ratio in 1985 was 0.5, and during the same year the top decile of the population had more than 15 times the income of the lowest decile. Significant income disparities also exist between urban and rural areas; these have essentially remained unchanged over the past 25 years: Rural incomes are now 47% of average urban incomes, as compared to 40% in 1961. According to the World Bank (1988), this differential reflects the concentration of skilled occupations in urban areas, as well as policy biases in favor of industrialization in the past two decades. The use of state power to favor economic and political elites might also be mentioned as a causal factor.

The poverty problem continues to perturb the present administration. Recent releases of income distribution data indicate that poverty incidence dropped from 58% in 1985 to 48% in 1988, using the "official" poverty line; however, income distribution did not improve. Although the reduction in absolute poverty was hailed by the Aquino administration as a significant achievement, the persistence of economic inequality spurred the government to launch programs targeted at the "bottom 30%." It is ironic that much official rhetoric has been devoted to poverty while at the same time the implementation of agrarian reform has been stymied by corruption within the bureaucracy and the repeated resignations of the relevant cabinet secretaries.

The poor have been, and will continue to be, vulnerable to unfavorable changes in the macroeconomic environment. To cite recent history, the 1983–85 stabilization had a negative impact on the poor through the sharp increase in underemployment and the real drop in GDP. Although all sectors were affected by the contraction in output and government expenditure, the adverse effect on the poor was greatest, due to under-employment and inflation. The higher income groups were mostly hit by increasing real interest rates and the drop in economic activity.

The vulnerability of the poor to macroeconomic shocks is a complication that must be considered together with the difficult macroeconomic issues to be discussed in the next section. These problems will induce strains in the policy-making framework, which must be addressed in order to achieve sustainable growth in the medium-term.

## 10.3   Macroeconomic Issues

The 1987–92 development plan sets a GNP growth target of 6.5 % per year. The goal is to recover the highest per capita income achieved by the economy (in 1981) by the year 1991. In this section, we evaluate this objective by recounting the gap calculations in Montes, Lim, and Quisumbing (1990).

Our interpretation of the demand-led 1988 performance is that during that year there was 4 % growth of potential output,[8] 87 % Capacity utilization, and 6.6 % growth of current activity. The model parameters and other equilibrium values appear in table 10.5.

Our view is that high inflation (by Philippine standards, double-digit inflation) and higher imports will result if there is an effort to push capacity utilization beyond 90 %, which is about the 1988 situation. In addition, higher inflation reduces purchasing power for consumption and, given the immature capability of the economy to orient its manufacturing production toward exports, cuts back on domestic demand and the growth rate. These considerations are already evident in 1989. Inflation reached 8 % in 1988 and exceeded 10 % in 1989 (table 10.4); GNP growth was 5.5 %, clearly below the target and the observed growth rate in 1988 of 6.7 %.

The 4 % growth of potential activity was obtained in 1988 without a buildup in international reserves commensurate with the growth in imports. In order to achieve a sustainable 4.0 %, not 6.5 % growth rate of potential output, the model's results suggest that additional foreign financing in the amount of at least 2.0 % of potential economic activity is required. In comparison to foreign interest payments of 4.4 % of potential output, financing growth at 4 % will require a halving of these payments. This would represent an additional commitment, applicable to the current account, on the part of foreign creditors of $1 billion in 1988 prices.

**Table 10.5**
Equilibrium values of 1988 (values as a ratio to potential output, growth rates in percent)

| Variable | Value |
|---|---|
| Capacity utilization | 0.87 |
| Growth rate of actual economic activity | 6.6 |
| Growth of potential economic activity | 4.0 |
| Total investment, also equal to total savings rate | 0.1424 |
| Government investment | 0.0233 |
| Private investment | 0.1191 |
| Government savings | −0.000065 |
| Private savings | 0.1204 |
| Foreign savings | 0.0220 |
| PSBR as a proportion of potential output | 0.0234 |
| Foreign interest payments | 0.044 |
| Government share in foreign interest payments | 0.298 |
| Imports of raw materials and intermediate goods | 0.0889 |
| Imports of capital goods | 0.0337 |
| Other imports | 0.0823 |
| Merchandise exports | 0.1401 |
| Nonmerchandise export earnings | 0.0729 |
| Net foreign aid | 0.0159 |

Using the calibrated model, we can discuss the requirements of two possible scenarios, one pegged at a 6.5 % growth rate and the other at 5 %. As summarized in table 10.6, sustainable growth of 6.5 % requires an investment ratio of 23 %, while a 5 % rate of growth requires a 17.8 % investment ratio. Furthermore, a sustainable growth rate of 6.5 % requires a public investment rate of 7.7 % of potential (almost 9 % of actual) output, three times the 1988 level.

A target of 5 % would require a near-doubling of the public investment rate, still a significant effort. The required increase would be lower if the responsiveness of private-sector investment to public investment was stronger—the parameter is now set at 0.5. This would require reforms in public investment, and the drawing in of new types of investors (possibly foreign, but certainly domestic) whose response parameters are qualitatively different from those embodied in the 1988 data set.

In any case, the government must be judicious about the effects of its investment on the private sector. Even if one might quarrel about the parameterization in this exercise, there is still an argument that a more conservative growth target, by representing more feasible planning, will

**Table 10.6**
Foreign financing requirements (as percent of potential output and $ billion per year)

|  | 1988 | Growth rate | Targets |
|---|---|---|---|
| Growth rate | 6.7 | 6.5 | 5.0 |
| Total investment | 4.2 | 23.0 | 17.8 |
| Public investment | 2.3 | 7.7 | 4.3 |
| Capacity utilization | 0.87 | 1.0 | 0.987 |
| Extra foreign savings (in billions of $) | ($1.09) | ($3.79) | ($2.37) |
| Additional increase in fiscal effort ($z_0$) | — | 0.0223 | — |

attract investors with longer time horizons. However, a more conservative macroeconomic approach must be accompanied by close attention to social expenditures, rural development, and human resource development.

With no change in the ratio of interest payments to potential output,[9] $3.8 billion of foreign savings per year is required for the official target of 6.5 % growth and $2.4 billion for 5 %. A similar result would occur if foreign interest payments were reduced by the same amount (which is tantamount to a complete halt of required payments). Furthermore, for a 6.5 % growth rate, an additional increase in fiscal effort amounting to 0.022 of potential output is needed.

Given a starting debt level of $27 billion, it will be impossible to raise all external financing as debt, since this would imply a growth rate for foreign debt of close to 15 % per year for an economy growing at 6.5 % or, alternatively, debt growing at 9 % per year for an economy growing at 5 % per year. For the 6.5 % scenario, the required ratio of foreign savings to potential output exceeds even that of 1978 when foreign credit was still very much available.

There is a need to look seriously at net foreign investment of between $800 million to $1 billion per year, a not-insignificant target for the Philippines. In 1987, $326 million (of which $166 million were debt-equity conversions), and in 1988, $986 million (of which $437 million were debt-equity conversions) of net direct investment are recorded in the balance of payments (table 10.3). The figure declined to $757 million in 1989, and is expected to fall further in 1990 due to political instability, reduced economic potential, inadequate power supply and infrastructure, and a string of natural disasters that further harmed the economy and infrastructure.

These considerations point to a preferred scenario in addressing the foreign-debt issue. A combination of reduction in interest payments and new money are needed to provide the basis for external financing consistent with sustainable medium-term growth. Without such a condition, nonspeculative new foreign investment will not be within reach. Simply growing out from under the debt is not indicated.

Under the present program, $659 million per year in new loan commitments have been identified for 1989 to 1992 on average; an additional $881 million per year are under negotiation. This would only total $1.5 billion per year, $0.9 billion less than even the inflow needed for 5% growth. A $0.9 billion gap could reasonably be filled by increased direct investments and a more aggressive debt negotiation strategy as long as positive developments in the region continue and political instability is controlled.

The issue of direct foreign investment as gap financing is complicated. Even before the question of profit remittances in the medium term, foreign operations are likely to be more dependent on imported capital and inputs than the economy as a whole. Thus, additional net financing from new foreign investment per se is likely to be limited. Where it can be potentially helpful is labor absorption and in diversifying the structure of Philippine exports.[10]

The dollar value of merchandise exports increased 18% in 1987, 21% in 1988, and 12% in 1989. If exports are to improve sufficiently to cope with increased requirements for international reserves equivalent to around three months' worth of imports (additional foreign exchange to finance the growth is assumed to be obtained by increased foreign savings), the exercise points to the need for the value of merchandise exports to grow at least 20% per year.

The net financing advantages of both foreign investment and exports can be captured in the medium-term if embedded within an industrial policy that permits a progressive increase in domestic value-added of these operations. Otherwise, the pattern of the 1970s where a large shift in the make-up of exports occurred without creating a more robust foreign trade structure will be repeated in the 1990s.

Against this external backdrop, the next question is whether the government's policy goals are mutually consistent. Before delving into this in depth, it is good to clarify three points. First, the consensus in executive agencies and the legislative branches is that budget deficits can no longer be financed by money creation. Even the massive government pump priming in 1986 (with a budget deficit of 5% of GNP) was undertaken mostly with debt financing, especially via issuing treasury bills (T bills). This device has become more prominent as net foreign borrowing takes up a progressively smaller proportion of the government deficit.

Second, not just the national government is saddled with large liabilities and deficits. One of the big contributors to the consolidated public sector deficit is the Central Bank, with shortfalls of P15.5 billion in 1985 and over P20 billion in 1989. These deficits were due to large net interest payments on the Central Bank's external and domestic liabilities as well as stock revaluation and swap and forward-over losses arising from the depreciating peso. The need for the Central Bank to service these liabilities is the main cause of monetary base expansion. A second cause of base expansion is the various debt-to-equity and debt-swap schemes which involve Central Bank debt papers and which increase net foreign assets. Limits on such conversions were instituted in 1989.

Third, the Central Bank has an implicit policy of intervening in the foreign exchange market to prop up the depreciating peso. This policy has necessitated a contractionary monetary and high interest rate policy in order to restrain capital outflows.

With the Aquino government's new economic measures in 1990 stating categorically that inflation is the number one enemy (a view chillingly reminiscent of the extreme recessionary policy that led to the economic collapse in the mid 1980s), the contradictions that face the government heightened considerably. On one hand, the government is committed to pay all its foreign and domestic liabilities. On the other, the strong anti-inflation stance of the government, plus its commitment to IMF monetary base targets as well as its exchange rate policy, require periodic "mopping up of excess liquidity."

This dilemma has led to erratic monetary policies that first allow the monetary base to expand in order to service the Central Bank liabilities, and then when IMF review periods loom or when the peso starts depreciating alarmingly, there is massive issuance of treasury bills (resulting in an increase in idle treasury balances of the national government with the Central Bank), and the jacking up of required reserves. In a frantic effort, the required reserve ratio was raised from an already high 20% to 21% in the last week of March 1990 in order to meet the IMF base money target for the test period slated for the same week. This policy has put the financial system and the economy on a roller coaster.

In the first quarter of 1990, the interest rate on treasury bills peaked at 26%, bringing up most rates with it. The government finally admitted that the sale of short-term treasury bills will have to be reduced to avoid a debt-service crisis and that the high interest rates had slowed the economy and were threatening to slow it even further.

The solution the government adopted was to transfer much of the monetary authorities' deficits to the national government. The question is whether an increased fiscal effort will be sufficient to handle the massive deficit this move entailed. At present, the budget deficit already is 3 % of GNP, while the target is to bring this down to less than 2 %. The addition of the Central Bank deficits will make this goal very difficult to attain without substantial revenue increases.

The 1990 measures emphasized a stronger fiscal effort. Almost anticipatory of the U.S. fashion, sin taxes on alcohol and tobacco products were legislated and signed into law. There are plans to increase taxes on non-alcoholic beverages. Increased user charges on public utilities and deregulation of oil and fuel prices are in the pipeline. The government's inability to exact taxes on property and direct wealth have forced it to turn its efforts toward easy revenue sources that it claims are "progressive" and "directed against the rich."

The prospect for the early 1990s, therefore, would be an increasingly tight fiscal constraint with large indirect taxes and higher public utilities charges that may cause short-run inflationary pressures. But the size of the national and Central Bank deficits are so large that it is unlikely that increased taxes and other revenue generating measures can adequately cope with them. It is, therefore, likely that continued dependence on treasury bills and high interest rates will continue, especially if the Central Bank maintains its aversion to devaluing the peso. However, whether there are successive devaluations, high interest rates, or both, the medium-term prospect is more likely slow growth, ranging from 2 % to 4 %, depending on military coups, natural calamities, the international market, and the foreign debt and debt reduction programs. Growth prospects are not brightened by recently apparent infrastructural bottlenecks in power and energy, transport, and communication. With the extreme fiscal constraint facing the country, the capability to address long-term growth is seriously threatened.

Finally, a significant "other" constraint in the Philippine case is capital flight, which has been estimated to have cumulated to $21 billion (against a debt of $26 billion) in 1986 (Boyce and Zarsky, 1988). The sophisticated banking system and the overseas Chinese network provided the infrastructure for these flows. They force the government to "lead" in domestic interest rate setting to provide private asset holders the international rate of return in order to prevent exchange rate devaluation. With restricted entry into the formal financial system, the existing banks find the high-interest policy a satisfactory arrangement.

### 10.3.1   Changing Structural Parameters

In the language of economic modeling, structural parameters will have to improve significantly in the medium term to provide the basis for sustainable development. This is particularly urgent because the era of easy credit and low interest rates will not reappear soon. How to achieve improvements in the structural parameters and overall productivity is a task that cannot wholly be discussed in this paper because it involves questions of national cohesion, political coalitions, and industrial organization, as well as sound policies and political will.

In the three-gap gap exercises, it was estimated that an increase in potential output of 1 % for the base year 1988 could have been achieved with an influx of additional foreign savings equivalent to 0.0259 of potential economic activity, or $1.38 billion, and an expansion of capacity utilization from 0.87 to 0.99.

We consider cases in which no additional foreign transfers are obtained, but structural parameters improve to effect the additional 1 % growth in potential output: The first variant combines combines improvements in the fiscal parameters on one hand, and exports or the import coefficient of raw materials and intermediate goods of domestically produced goods, on the other. Fiscal parameters deteriorated drastically from 1978 to the latter part of the 1980s.[11] This was first brought about by the tremendous rise in government net lending to public corporations as the latter teetered toward near-bankruptcy in the economic crisis of the 1980s. Another important cause is the high interest rates on both foreign and domestic debt that the government has had to bear. Finally, the recession of the mid-1980s affected tax collection capacity adversely and it was only in 1988 and 1989 that tax effort has improved, although it still lags behind the capacity of 1978.

If the fiscal parameters were to recover to the 1978 position, the savings and fiscal equations would allow a 1 % additional growth in potential output with a reduction in the public-sector borrowing requirement to the 1978 level (that is, from 0.027 of actual economic activity to 0.011). This 1 % growth will not require additional foreign financing.

The foreign exchange constraint would also allow the additional 1 % growth without any additional financing if exports increased from 0.21 to around 0.25 of potential output or if the import coefficient for raw materials and intermediate goods of domestically produced goods decreased from 0.153 to 0.127.[12] A second, simpler exercise was done wherein a general productivity increase was assumed. It was found that a 1 % additional growth in potential output would be achieved if the ICOR is reduced from 3.5 to 2.8.

The thrust of the above exercises is to show that for continued, sustainable high growth rates to be achieved, the Philippines, in the medium term, will have to improve the structure of its economy. Rising productivity, an improved fiscal effort, export expansion, and forward and backward linkages will have to combine with better international markets and a healthy financial environment to bring the economy toward self-sustaining growth.

## 10.3.2 Broad Possibilities for State Intervention

Officially, the development goals expressed in the 1987–92 Medium Term Philippine Development Plan are: alleviation of poverty, generation of more productive employment, promotion of equity and social justice, and attainment of sustainable economic growth.[13] An employment-oriented, rural-based development strategy is the mechanism by which government planners intend to achieve the above objectives. The rationale for the strategy is the predominantly rural nature of the population and high poverty incidences in the rural areas: 60 % of the population lives in rural areas, and of the bottom 30 % of the income distribution, 80 % is in agriculture.

The policies that are supposed to attain these objectives can be broadly described as: (1) price reform with increased reliance on market forces to determine exchange rates and interest rates, (2) privatization and deregulation of trade, including the abolition of monopoly incentives, tariff reform, and import liberalization, (3) a stable set of investment policies, and (4) minimal government intervention except in the provision of public goods such as infrastructure, marketing, and communications facilities.

It is implicitly assumed that adherence to such policies will improve equity; this is consistent with the Aquino administration's "redistribution with growth" strategy, whereby incremental income can be channeled to the poor through the provision of social services. The only redistributive program is a comprehensive agrarian reform whose equity impact is doubtful.

For both agriculture and industry, the medium-term development plan clearly identifies liberalization policies as the main instrument of development. Such a development design has already been perverted by the politically powerful. For example, the most highly protected industries as of 1980 were meat processing and food canning, paper, grain milling, soft drinks, soap, made-up textile goods, bakery products, dairy products, tobacco products, electrical machinery, and glass, among others. The penalized industries (those with negative EPRs) included leather products, fabricated structural metal products, wood-based manufactures, and footwear. Highly protected industries with a high degree of spatial concentration in Metro Manila include: paper manufacturing, soap, tobacco products, batteries, glass, pulp and paper, chemicals, plastics, and paints. It can be argued that the furor over import liberalization raised by Manila-based big business groups can be interpreted as an effort to maintain monopoly privileges.

Despite pressure by multilateral institutions to implement import liberalization, the program has been manipulated by local business elites for their own ends. Consumer items have been liberalized relatively quickly—thus the abundance of imported goods—but the liberalization of intermediate products has dragged on, being the ongoing subject of legislative debate.[14] In the meantime, import liberalization has, for example, severely reduced the income of small fishermen, producers of final consumer products.

By studiously avoiding an industrial development program while attempting to implement import liberalization anyway, the government effectively is maintaining protection for the least dynamic sectors and further disprotecting those sectors with the greatest possibilities for growth.[15] As we pointed out previously, it will be difficult for the present government to generate its own reform agenda. Because of its need for foreign financing, it must respond to the suggestions of international agencies organized under its consultative group. Invariably, the suggestions of these agencies find an umbrella under the rhetoric of liberalization.

## 10.4   Political Economy

As a set of policies that seek to reform the relationship between the private sector and the state, liberalization could have very positive effects on Philippine development. But at this historic juncture, liberalization would be a necessary but not a sufficient program. Economies of scale, learning by doing, and other infant-industry realities plus the more modern concepts of bounded rationality and asset specificity furnish the grounds for economic intervention by a reformed state interacting with a reformed private sector (Lim, 1989).

Properly defined, liberalization should comprise not just price reform, which is apparently the view of the international agencies, but structural and property reform. These reforms can only be carried out within existing historical conditions; in contrast, liberalization is often thought of as a set of disembodied propositions about the best way to organize the economic activities of a society. "Reforms" based on such theory tend to subvert the role of social organizations, such as workers' unions but also including parts of the state, in setting social directions and mediating private conflicts. To the extent that they succeed in their objectives, such liberalization episodes will leave political and economic retrogression in their wake.

In the Philippine experience, many of the elements of a liberalization strategy have been significant components of past development policies. For example, except for quotas on agricultural products, the Philippines had free trade with the United States from the late 1940s to the mid-1960s. During this period and with a large participation by U.S. companies, the Philippines implemented an import-substitution policy aimed at serving its domestic market. Thus, the advantage of free trade with what was then the most dynamic market[16] in the world did not provide a sufficient basis for outward orientation and the hoped-for deepening of the industrial structure.

One might ask the counterfactual question: What if, instead, the policy regime had been consistent with increased manufactured goods penetration in the U.S. market? The answer would be: there would still have been a need for infant industry support at that juncture, because the manufacturing enterprises did not then exist.

There are many more examples that we can formulate. Here we would like to move into a discussion of an outline of an alternative development strategy. In the three-gap exercises, we advocate a more conservative growth rate target within which reforms will be carried out. Beyond that, the reform of state-private sector relations and property must be directed at eliminating the situation in which the state guarantees continued control of economic assets to those considered politically suitable regardless of their ability to develop the asset. Agrarian reform is a key liberalization strategy, aimed not only at the economic but also at sociopolitical structures that have made both interventionist and neoclassical policies detrimental to the nation.

It is unfortunate that the liberalization-as-development strategy has tended to view export orientation as a substitute for agrarian reform in particular and asset redistribution more generally. Neoclassical liberalization proponents have tended to view asset reform as, at best, a necessary political evil and, at worst, devastating to private initiative. In contrast, export orientation is supposed to provide the means to absorb rural unemployment rapidly. It is also supposed to be a more politically neutral policy, being one that can be supported by all "growth-oriented" classes in the liberalizing society.

The question of export orientation can be subtle in the Philippine context. Since the early 1960s, Philippine policymakers have utilized export orientation as a reason to exempt land planted to export crops from agrarian reform. In the 1980s, in the wake of a very poor international market for sugar, vast tracts of plantation sugar land were converted to ponds producing prawns for export. This shift is causing permanent environmental damage, reducing the labor absorption capacity of the land, and bears a high degree of technological and price uncertainty. The government's strategy has been to provide fiscal incentives for such export-oriented adjustments in land use.

From our viewpoint, the compelling macroeconomic argument for a serious development of exports is related to the savings gap. Any success in the redistributive policies of government, notably agrarian reform, will likely reduce the domestic savings elasticity, which in the three-gap model was set at 0.5, in line with recent estimates that capture the effects of the highly unequal income distribution in the country. A reduction in the marginal propensity to save will exacerbate the foreign financing problem in which case exports are the adjusting variable where a degree of freedom still exists.

The next key item of a development program is an industrial development program in which the state, representing the national interest instead of the interests of entrenched businessmen and landowners, provides a direction-setting evaluation, and a reward-and-disciplining role in the sectors where it intervenes. At this point in time, such a national industrialization program would put immediate priority on increasing agricultural productivity and in improving rural incomes.

Reform of the industrial sector will require privatization. The issues surrounding privatization in the Philippines are quite different from such efforts elsewhere. Except possibly for the national oil company, government corporations intended for privatization did not arise from a socialist bent to set up enterprises in order to publicly produce a good or service a need. There are assets that have fallen into government control as a result of failed public credit programs. There is little ideological controversy over whether the government should control these companies.

Because of this background, however, the consideration that the government must accept losses on these assets, while continuing to service associated foreign liabilities, looms particularly large. Privatization, Philippine-style, appears to consist of the socialization (nationalization) of private, including foreign, losses. For many of these companies, it would actually be more advantageous to view the asset disposal not as a privatization, but as a salvage sale combined with an effort to compel foreign creditors to share in the cost of the write off.

Unlike in other countries, the country's capital markets are too thin to provide the financial infrastructure that other privatization efforts have relied on. This means that politics plus competition among the large domestic business groupings for control over these enterprises (many of which enjoy significant monopoly power) play a critical role in the privatization effort.[17]

One final requirement that is not so abstract is the creation of a stronger governmental bureaucracy, an aspect in which the Philippines compares unfavorably with respect to Thailand, Indonesia, and Malaysia. The country's weak bureaucracy has been an important reason why it was also unable to operate a protectionist regime that genuinely protected the industries they were designed to protect, instead of creating government-mandated monopolies for the favored groups that happened to operate in those industries.[18]

## 10.5   Issues of Political Stability

Is political stability (or improvement) consistent with equitable medium term growth? If growth is not attained, what will happen?

The Philippines has the region's only significant Communist-organized insurgency. A rate of growth of less than 4% accompanied by limited asset reform provides fertile objective conditions for insurgency's growth. Whether the existing rebel groups will be able to exploit these conditions depends on their own fitness and the extent of foreign resistance.

The insurgency is a trend influence; the ebb and flow of political stability will depend on the conflicts among the country's leading families. Up until late November 1989, optimism prevailed among most professional circles about the future prospects of the Philippines. The drastic change in outlook after the failed December 1989 coup is a recognition that the country's leading families are once again deeply divided and will have insufficient political cohesion to carry out the needed restructuring of the economy's parameters, which the brief recovery since 1986 had only validated. Thus, political conflict induces economic uncertainty.

The question is whether the Philippines' leading families will stumble upon an orderly mechanism for mediating conflict. The controversies over trade and financial liberalization and privatization provide additional fuel to these conflicts. The experience of the Marcos years and his overthrow added to the arsenal of elite competition the maneuver of "revolution," which allows the setting aside of judicial and legislative tradition and condones the invalidation of contracts. The existence of mass poverty and the organized insurgency provide a natural setting for elite "revolutions."

Elite factions will have to compete not only for control of the state but also over access to external financing. Some may succeed in capturing the state, but will be unable to obtain foreign support (as the Marcos government was unable to do in its final years). Such situations, whose occurrences can also be convenient for foreign countries with geopolitical interests in the Philippines, will make it difficult to distinguish economic uncertainty from political instability in the 1990s.

## Notes

1. There were promises to implement a "comprehensive" agrarian reform program and to address the foreign debt problem with the complicity of foreign creditors in the Marcos regime in mind.

2. Conservative military units provided the most direct challenge through coup attempts in August 1987 and December 1989. The leadership of this coup came from the same group that led the successful anti-Marcos mutiny in 1986. The August 1987 coup failed to deliver political power to its leaders, but achieved its programmatic goals: the removal of "leftist" Cabinet members and greater attention to the demands of the military (including higher pay for soldiers). The most recent and most violent coup attempt in December 1989, however, nearly succeeded in overthrowing the civilian government.

3. A recent World Bank (1988) report states that poverty worsened between 1971 and 1985. Using comparable definitions, in 1971 the incomes of about 3 million families were insufficient to meet basic needs; in 1985 the figure had risen to 5 million families. Although the proportion of the poor remained at about 52%, the absolute number is higher in 1985, simply due to population expansion. As discussed later, the Philippines also has one of the most unequal income distributions among middle-income countries. Poverty and inequality have persisted despite high GNP growth rates in the 1970s.

4. Here we refer to the experience that throwing money at the rural sector in the form of subsidized credits and grants has been destructive of actual development in these areas.

5. The Central Bank keeps the proceeds of sales of these instruments as blocked cash balances of the national government.

6. This regime was part of the prior action commitments under the 18th IMF standby loan program.

7. There is no definitive conclusion on trends in income distribution between 1971 and 1985, despite the claims of the World Bank (1988) report. The poverty mission in 1987 based its conclusion on a comparison of two "comparable" income and

expenditure surveys. Earlier missions using noncomparable data sets arrived at different conclusions on trends in inequality.

8. Measured as gross domestic product plus noncompetitive imports.

9. This will decline if interest rates stay constant and positive growth rates in potential output are achieved.

10. See Urata (1989) for a discussion of the possibilities of the growth of intra-firm trade in the region.

11. We have the equation $z = z_0 + z_1 u$, where $z$ is equal to the fiscal effort defined as government saving before payment of foreign interest, as a proportion of potential economic activity; $u$ is equal to capacity utilization, $z_0 = 0.0091$ and $z_1 = 0.0364$ in 1978; and $z_0 = 0.0026$ and $z_1 = 0.0120$ in 1988.

12. The equation for imported inputs is $m_r = a_0 + a_1 u + (1 - a_2)x$, where $m_r$ is equal to the total imported inputs as a proportion of potential economic activity; $u$ is equal to capacity utilization; $x$ is equal to total exports as a proportion of total economic activity; $a_0 = -0.0871$; $a_1 = 0.1532$; and $a_2 = 0.2003$ in 1988. The text refers to an improvement in the parameter $a_1$.

13. Much of the text in this section is lifted from Quisumbing (1989).

14. Business groups are effectively wielding their political power in the import liberalization debate. It is difficult to speak of state autonomy in this area when the top-ranking trade and industry officials have interests in highly protected industries. This makes actions by the Department of Trade and Industry (DTI) highly suspicious. For example, there is new involvement of the DTI in licensing, ostensibly to "improve the data base." This will probably lead to a substantial increase in process protection at the very time when the enhanced liberalization of items on the list can be officially proclaimed.

15. The March 1989 Memorandum of Economic Policy submitted to the IMF includes a schedule, based on the number of items to be liberalized. One can question a planning approach that counts items to be liberalized, instead of determining a proper sequence of product lines to be liberalized. Even this schedule provides for liberalization of a certain number of items after 1992, after the end of the present IMF program.

16. It could also be said, as it can be said now, that trade was never really free. Under the treaty, individual states in the United States reserved the right to protect their products. It is still true, however, that the Philippines, by having this access to the U.S. market hypothetically enjoyed enormous advantages over many other countries that have since done better economically.

17. These considerations loom large role in the privatization of two of the largest corporations in the country: San Miguel Corporation, a diversified food products multinational, and the Manila Electric Company, the private distributor of electric power to the Metro Manila area.

18. For example, quantitative restrictions will provide high returns to smuggling. The advantage to the domestic company might not be so much that it is protected

from foreign competition, but that prospective entrants and smugglers of the product are prevented from arising.

## References

Boyce, James, and Lyuba Zarsky (1988). "Capital Flight from the Philippines, 1962–1986." *Journal of Philippine Development*, 15: 191–222.

Hayami, Yuhiro, Ma. Agnes Quisumbing, and Lourdes S. Adriano (1990). Toward a *New Land Reform Paradigm: A Philippine Perspective*, Quezon City: Ateneo de Manila University Press.

Lim, Joseph (1989). "An Application of Bacha's Three-Gap Model: The Case of the Philippines." (Mimeo), May.

Montes, Manuel, Joseph Lim, and Ma. Agnes R. Quisumbing (1990). "The Possibilities of Sustainable Growth in the Philippines: A Three Gap Analysis." (Mimeo), January.

Quisumbing, Ma. Agnes R. (1989). "Structural and Sectoral Constraints on Sustainable Growth." (Mimeo), June.

Urata, Shujiro (1989). "Recent Economic Developments in the Pacific Region and Changing Role of Japan in the Regional Interdependence." Paper presented at the Second Pacific Cooperations Conference, Fukuoka City, August 28–29, 1989.

World Bank (1988). *The Philippines: The Challenge of Poverty*. Report No. 7144-PH. Washington, DC: World Bank.

# 11 Mexico

## Nora Lustig and Jaime Ros

Overall, the Mexican economy turned in an impressive performance since World War II (table 11.1). The trend growth rate for 1950–81 was 6.4 % per year, over 3 % per capita. A profound transformation of economic and social structures accompanied this rapid growth. After 1982, however, the economy went into crisis and a prolonged adjustment process from which it may only be recovering a decade later. After presenting the historical background, we will concentrate on the factors underlying the crisis and its aftermath.[1]

## 11.1 Historical Background

The three decades after 1950 can be divided into three broad periods. The period from 1950 until the first oil shock in 1973 was characterized by high growth and low inflation rates, except for a short-lived crisis following the end of the war. This was the golden age of Mexico's development, reflected in an optimistic consensus that attributed rapid transformation to two features of the country's history and geography: the actions of the state and the stable political system that emerged from the 1910 revolution, as well as the challenges and opportunities presented by an economic and political superpower along the northern border. Yet the first signs of a worsening macroeconomic performance were already present by the first half of the 1970s.

In contrast with the first period, high growth continued but with relatively high inflation between 1973 and 1981. This period actually covered two brief but distinct growth episodes. The years between 1973 and a 1976–77 crisis were characterized by public expenditure-led growth and the narrowing of opportunities for import substitution. The years 1978–81 were marked by an aborted attempt to recover and sustain high growth based on the exploitation of massive oil revenues.

**Table 11.1**
Principal macroeconomic variables, 1956–1981 (percentages)

|  | 1956–72 | 1973–78 | 1977–81 |
|---|---|---|---|
| GDP[a] | 6.7 | 6.1 | 7.4 |
| Inflation rate[b] | 3.1 | 16.7 | 23.8 |
| Public deficit/GDP[c] | 2.5 | 8.0 | 10.2 |
| Current account deficit/GDP | 2.5 | 4.1 | 3.4 |

a. Rate of increase.
b. Based on the national consumer price index starting from 1969.
c. Information starting from 1965.
Source: From Alberro and Cambiazo (1986), table 1, p. 41.

### 11.1.1  The "Stabilizing Development" Period

The first period, commonly called "stabilizing development," combined an output growth rate of over 6% per year with a domestic inflation rate between 3 and 4% per year. High growth rates prevailed with the exception of two brief slowdowns: one in 1959 and the other in 1962–63. To some analysts of the time, these pauses indicated that the "stagnationist" tendencies characteristic of peripheral development were finally surfacing. For others, they reflected the obstacles to continued growth exerted by what Vernon's (1963) influential book described as a dysfunctional system of public-private relationships, characterized by a too large degree of discretion and particularism in the application of governmental regulations. The almost immediate resumption of the historical growth rate, however, removed those forebodings.[2]

Mexico followed an inward-oriented development path after the Second World War. The comparison in table 11.2 of the contribution of import substitution and domestic demand vis-à-vis external demand to overall manufacturing growth from 1950 to 1960 reveals the contrast between Mexico and outward-oriented economies such as Korea or Taiwan in the 1960s.

A substantial change in the structure of output during the entire period reflects the magnitude of industrial development. The sector's output was equal to 21.5% of the total in 1950; 25.4% in 1960; and, 30.1% in 1970. Shares of agriculture and other primary commodities declined, while services remained more or less steady (table 11.3). The structure of manufacturing also underwent substantial changes. The share in output of mass consumption and specific intermediate goods fell from 72% in 1950 to 49% in the mid-1970s, while the share of consumer durables and automo-

**Table 11.2**
Sources of change in manufacturing production

| | Average annual growth rate (%) | Sources (%) | | | | |
|---|---|---|---|---|---|---|
| | | Domestic demand expansion | Export expansion | Import sub-stitution | Changes in IO coefficients | Total |
| Korea | | | | | | |
| 1955–63 | 10.4 | 57.3 | 11.5 | 42.2 | −11.0 | 100.0 |
| 1963–70 | 18.9 | 70.1 | 30.4 | −0.6 | 0.1 | 100.0 |
| 1970–73 | 23.8 | 39.0 | 61.6 | −2.5 | 1.8 | 100.0 |
| Taiwan | | | | | | |
| 1956–61 | 11.2 | 34.8 | 27.5 | 25.4 | 12.3 | 100.0 |
| 1961–66 | 16.6 | 49.2 | 44.5 | 1.7 | 4.6 | 100.0 |
| 1966–71 | 21.1 | 34.9 | 57.0 | 3.8 | 4.3 | 100.0 |
| Mexico | | | | | | |
| 1950–60 | 7.0 | 71.8 | 3.0 | 10.9 | 14.4 | 100.0 |
| 1960–70 | 8.6 | 86.1 | 4.0 | 11.0 | −1.0 | 100.0 |
| 1970–75 | 7.2 | 81.5 | 7.7 | 2.6 | 8.2 | 100.0 |

Notes: Column 1 shows the average annual growth rates of total manufacturing gross output. The sources of growth contributions in columns 2–5 are expressed as percentages of the change in total gross manufacturing output, and add up to 100 % except for rounding errors. Results for Mexico are preliminary.
Source: Dervis et al. 1982, Table 4.3, p. 106.

**Table 11.3**
Mexico, percentage distribution of GDP, by sector, 1950–1985, for selected years

| | Agriculture and other primary activities | Mining, including oil extraction | Manufacturing, construction, electricity | Other (services, government, etc.) | Total GDP |
|---|---|---|---|---|---|
| 1950 | 19.1 | 5.1 | 21.5 | 54.4 | 100.0 |
| 1960 | 17.1 | 3.1 | 25.4 | 54.4 | 100.0 |
| 1970 | 12.2 | 2.5 | 30.1 | 55.2 | 100.0 |
| 1980 | 8.2 | 3.2 | 29.5 | 59.1 | 100.0 |
| 1985 | 9.1 | 4.7 | 28.7 | 57.5 | 100.0 |

Note: There might be differences in the definition of data included in each sector between 1950 and 1960–85 figures. Thus they are not strictly comparable.
Sources: Figures for 1950 based on Cuentas Nacionales, Bank of Mexico (1977, 1979), published in Lustig (1981). Figures for 1960–1979 based on official data from National Statistical Institute (INEGI) and Bank for Mexico.

biles doubled from 10 % to 20 %, and basic intermediate goods increased from 18 % to 30 %.

Population growth was quite high, reaching a yearly rate of almost 3.5 %. Rapid urbanization accompanied industrial development; the urban population[3] increased from 43.2 % to 60.4 % between 1950 and 1970. For most of the period, the agricultural sector recorded growth rates well above those of the population, supporting the continuity of the industrialization effort. Social and political stability and a low share of military spending were other important contributory factors.

The absence of capital flight was another major characteristic of the "stabilizing development" period. Confidence marked the overall financial and business environment, as the public sector followed a relatively prudent fiscal policy. Although information for the period prior to 1965 is not readily available, the public deficit to GDP ratio averaged about 2.5 % between 1965 and 1972 (table 11.1).

The combination of a relatively sound fiscal stance, absence of major external shocks or profound internal structural imbalances, and almost nonexistent wage-price conflicts explains why inflation rates were so low, especially when compared with the other large Latin American countries. Low inflation plus the overall stable environment made a fixed exchange rate policy credible and feasible. The rate was set at 12.50 pesos to the dollar in April 1954 and (with some effort) sustained until the early 1970s.

For all the positive qualities projected by the macroeconomic and industrial performance of the period, income disparities and poverty persisted. Although the surveys are not strictly comparable, in 1956 and 1963 the bottom 10 % of the population received 2.0 % and 1.5 % of total income respectively, while the top 5 % received 26.5 % and 30.3 % for the same years. In 1968 the corresponding numbers were 1.9 and 30.1 % (Altimir, 1982). Moreover, the shortcomings of the chosen industrialization path would eventually surface. Despite linkages created by the import substitution model, the contribution of total factor productivity to output expansion was small. Growth had been "accounted" for more by the supply of factors of production (especially capital) than by a rise in their productivity.[4]

The productivity increases that did occur were associated with labor saving technologies in industry and agriculture. The prevailing technology in the industrial sector was capital intensive because it was imported from and originally designed for regions with a different factor mix. The diffusion of these technologies—under the competitive pressure of multinational subsidiaries or of large local firms in market structures with initially low concentration ratios and a slight technological dualism and backward-ness—led to a rapid modernization of traditional industries. Capital inputs were cheap as a result of commercial, credit, and exchange rate policies (Hernandez-Laos, 1973; Fajnzylber and Martinez Tarrago, 1976; Casar, et al., 1986).

One of the controversial aspects of the policy mix pursued during the stabilizing development period was its commitment to a fixed exchange rate. In the face of a positive, albeit low, inflation differential with the rest of the world, there was increasing overvaluation of the peso. Together with protective barriers unaccompanied by clear performance criteria for the industries that benefited from them, the strong currency restrained the development of an ample and diversified export base (Bueno, 1987). Mexico's dependence on foreign financing increased over time.[5]

## 11.1.2 High Growth and High Inflation: The 1970s

The growing consensus among analysts of the Mexican economy is that its heterogeneous performance during the 1970s reflected maladjustment to changing world conditions of increased uncertainty, instability, and competition. In the early years, growth was around 6% per year while the average inflation rate was a little over 16% (table 11.1). There was active expansion of government expenditures, not accompanied by a rise in revenue. As a result, the fiscal deficit increased steadily from 2.5% of GDP in 1971 to 9.4% in 1975.[6] The gap was increasingly financed with foreign borrowing and external public debt rose from U.S. $6.5 billion in 1971 to U.S. $15.7 billion in 1975 (Zedillo, 1986).

The combined effect of the external oil shock in 1973, the stagnation of agricultural output and productivity (which began in the second half of the sixties), and expansionary fiscal policy fueled inflationary pressures. The low inflation rates of the "stabilizing development" years climbed into double digits (table 11.1). At the time, the government viewed faster price increases as an inevitable price that had to be paid in order for growth to be sustained. It also considered increased state intervention to be imperative for relieving the social tensions that had erupted in the bloody 1968 riots, student unrest, and localized guerrilla activity in the countryside. The government stepped up its social welfare outlays and adopted policies directed toward redistributing wealth and income, triggering political resistance on the part of the propertied class. The 1973 law regulating and limiting foreign direct investment strengthened the inward orientation of policy while foreign borrowing on the part of the government was increasing.

Financial confidence began to erode and capital flight occurred on a relatively large scale. In August 1976, the peso was allowed to float in the exchange market for the first time in 22 years. A devaluation of around 100 % followed the announcement. For the first time Mexico faced a type of crisis familiar in other Latin American countries which had experienced unsustainable macroeconomic misalignments and internal structural imbalances. A recession in 1976–77 followed during which the average growth rate fell to around 4 % per year and inflation reached an average of 21 %.

The crisis was short-lived after the discovery of massive oil reserves[7] and the upward trend in international oil prices. A period of very high growth ensued (table 11.1). During the oil boom, the average growth rate was over 8 % and the inflation rate rose from 16.2 % in 1978 to 28.7 % in 1981. To many Mexicans, including the government, oil wealth seemed to open the opportunity to increase living standards once and for all.

Highly expansionary policies were seen as risk-free, given the prospects of the world oil market: The government deficit rose, the trade deficit expanded, and foreign debt ballooned. The operational deficit, for example, rose from 5.7 % of GDP in 1978 to 9.8 % in 1981 (Alberro and Cambiazo, 1986). The trade deficit rose from $0.5 billion in 1978 to $5.3 billion in 1981. External public debt increased from $26.4 billion in 1978, to $33.9 billion in 1980, and $52.2 billion in 1981.

Fiscal expansion exacerbated the consequences of a resource-based export boom. Increased absorption generated inflationary pressure in the nontradeable sector and further appreciation of the exchange rate. Non-oil exports fell and there was import desubstitution because production and investment were geared mainly toward the internal market. Instead of providing the foundation for stable growth, the oil boom and the policies that were followed increased Mexico's real and financial vulnerability. Oil accounted for about 70 % of total exports by 1981, while the non-oil trade balance deteriorated sharply, and foreign debt expanded at alarming speeds.[8]

Capital flight accelerated sharply when the price of oil began to decline in mid-1981. In turn, public sector debt grew by about $20 billion. These difficulties were magnified when the flow of international lending was suddenly interrupted in August 1982. Crisis followed, on a grand and durable scale. There was a decline of 0.5 % in total GDP in 1982, with a yearly inflation rate of 58.9 % and a December-December rate of 98.9 %. Although most analysts concur that the 1982 crisis resulted primarily from internal policies and misperceptions about the evolution of oil prices and interest rates in international markets,[9] counterfactual exercises show that the required fiscal adjustment would not have been without costs in terms of inflationary impact and growth even if it was undertaken at an earlier date (Cordoba, 1986).

## 11.2  Macroeconomic Adjustment and Reform during the 1980s

Despite the initial perception that the 1982 crisis would be short lived, the actual outcomes were zero average growth and nearly 90 % average inflation for 1982–88 (table 11.4). For the first time in almost five decades the per capita growth rate was negative for a sustained period of time.

After several months of "chaotic" adjustment, the incoming administration put forward an orthodox stabilization program in December 1982, intending to restore price and exchange rate stability and balance of payments equilibrium. It was believed that price and financial stability would be regained through a drastic and permanent cut in the government deficit, and that speculation would be curtailed with an undervalued exchange rate. Both policy measures, in turn, would help to generate the needed surplus in the trade account. The required devaluation would necessarily imply a reduction in the real wage.

Debt servicing would also require a shift in the external accounts from a large trade deficit (characteristic of, especially, the oil boom years) to a trade surplus to meet interest payments. Because new lending and direct foreign investment would probably be scarce, domestic savings would have to replace foreign savings, which had averaged 3.4 % of GDP between 1970 and 1982 but declined to − 1.4 % between 1983 and 1987 (Ize, 1988).

Many policymakers also viewed the crisis as the result of the past development strategy in which protectionism and heavy state intervention had played major roles. The new economic policy aimed to address structural problems with trade liberalization, privatization of state enterprises, and deregulation of the economy in general. A full discussion of these structural reforms will be presented in section 11.3. The combined stabilization and adjustment policies[10] were relatively successful in keeping the balance of payments in check but failed to contain inflation until the implementation of a wide-reaching "Economic Solidarity Pact" in 1988.

Table 11. 5 shows that the years between 1982 and 1988 were ones of economic stagnation and declining living standards. The average growth rate of GDP was zero. Fixed investment as a percentage of GDP declined

**Table 11.4**
Aggregate performance of the Mexican economy

| | 1980 | 1981 | 1982 | 1983 | 1984 | 1985 | 1986 | 1987[p] | 1988[p] |
|---|---|---|---|---|---|---|---|---|---|
| GDP (real growth in percent)[a] | 8.3 | 8.8 | −0.6 | −4.2 | 3.6 | 2.5 | −3.7 | 1.5 | 1.1 |
| GDP per capita (real growth in percent)[a] | 5.4 | 5.3 | −2.9 | −6.3 | 1.4 | 0.4 | −5.9 | −0.6 | −0.8 |
| Consumer price index[a] (growth rate in percent) | | | | | | | | | |
| December/December | 29.8 | 28.7 | 98.8 | 80.8 | 59.2 | 63.7 | 105.7 | 159.2 | 51.7 |
| Yearly average | 26.3 | 27.9 | 58.9 | 101.9 | 65.4 | 57.7 | 86.2 | 131.8 | 114.2 |
| Gross fixed investment (as percent of GDP)[a] | 24.8 | 26.4 | 23.0 | 17.5 | 17.9 | 19.1 | 19.4 | 18.9 | n.a. |
| Yearly growth rate[b] (in percent)[a] | 14.9 | 14.7 | −16.8 | −25.3 | 5.1 | 6.7 | −11.7 | −0.7 | n.a. |
| Yearly growth rate of private investment[a] (in percent) | 19.5[g] | 13.9 | −17.3 | −24.2 | 9.0 | 13.4 | −8.8 | 2.1 | 10.1 |
| Public financial deficit[a] (as percent of GDP) | 7.5 | 14.1 | 16.9 | 8.6 | 8.5 | 9.6 | 16.0 | 16.1 | 12.3 |
| Current account (as percent of GDP)[c] | −4.3 | −5.8 | −3.7 | 3.8 | 2.5 | 0.7 | −1.0 | 3.1 | −2.1 |
| Stock of total foreign debt (US billion) | 50.8 | 74.9 | 87.6 | 93.8 | 96.7 | 97.8 | 100.5 | 105.6 | 107.0[e] |
| Foreign debt (as percent of GDP)[c] | 27.7 | 33.5 | 54.4 | 66.6 | 55.4 | 53.8 | 74.3 | 75.6 | 77.0 |
| Net foreign resource transfer (as percent of GDP)[c] | −2.5 | −7.4 | 2.8 | 5.3 | 6.6 | 6.1 | 6.5 | 5.5 | 6.4 |
| Terms of trade[d] | 100.0 | 103.0 | 97.0 | 77.0 | 77.0 | 73.0 | 58.0 | 62.0 | 59.0 |
| Non-oil exports (yearly growth in percent)[f] | −4.9 | −6.9 | 11.3 | 34.0 | 20.6 | −7.9 | 40.0 | 23.5 | 14.9 |
| GDP agriculture (real growth in percent)[a] | 7.1 | 6.1 | −2.0 | 2.0 | 2.7 | 2.9 | −1.4 | 1.1[p] | −1.6[p] |

p = preliminary
Sources: a. Banco de México (1989), *Indicadores Económicos*, April
b. From Zedillo (1986), Table 8, p. 974, for 1980–83; and Banco de México *Indicadores Economicos* (various years) for the rest.
c. From Dornbusch (1988), table 18, p. 265; and Dornbusch (1989), table 3, p. 8.
d. Barnes (1989).
e. Estimated.
f. CEPAL (1988) for 1985–88 and Banco de México, (1982–84, 1988), *Indicadores Economicos*, Ros (1989) for 1980 and 1981.
g. Nonresidential investment only.

**Table 11.5**
Real wages, unemployment, wage share, and government expenditures

| | On social development (GESD), in percentages | | | | | | | | |
|---|---|---|---|---|---|---|---|---|---|
| | 1980 | 1981 | 1982 | 1983 | 1984 | 1985 | 1986 | 1987[p] | 1988[p] |
| Real minimum wages (yearly growth rates)[a] | -7.4 | 1.3 | 3.3 | -25.2 | -8.3 | -1.2 | -10.8 | -4.7 | -12.7 |
| Real average wages (yearly growth rates)[b] | -0.8 | 4.2 | -2.4 | -26.5 | -4.9 | 1.0 | -9.9 | 5.5[p] | n.a. |
| Open unemployment rate[c] | 4.6 | 4.2 | 4.2 | 6.6 | 5.7 | 4.4 | 4.3 | 3.9[p] | 3.5[p] |
| Wage share[c] | 38.9 | 42.7 | 38.2 | 31.7 | 30.8 | 31.2 | 30.6 | n.a. | n.a. |
| Real GESD per capita (yearly growth rates)[d] | | 16.2 | -0.7 | -27.8 | -0.3 | 0.7 | -6.2 | -6.4 | n.a. |

Key: p = preliminary; n.a. = not available.
Sources: a. CEPAL (1988); *Banco de México, Informe Annual* for 1988.
b. *Banco de México*, Economic Indicators.
c. Calculated from National Accounts Ratio over the sum of wage pus non-wage income.
d. De la Madrid, *Informe*, various years.

from an average of 21 % in 1970–81 to 18 % in 1982–85. There were drastic cuts in real wages and government social expenditures, accompanied by a large shift from wage to non-wage income; available information indicates that the crisis led to a substantial deterioration in living standards.[11]

### 11.2.1   The Economic Solidarity Pact

The Economic Solidarity Pact was jointly signed in December 1987 by the government and formal representatives from labor, agricultural producers, and the business sector. Its basic components were further fiscal deficit cuts, tighter monetary policy, trade liberalization, and for the first time since the crisis erupted in 1982, a comprehensive incomes policy.[12]

The results of the pact were striking. During the second semester of 1988 average inflation was 1.2 % per month, far lower than the 8 % registered during the same period in 1987. Real GDP grew at 1.4 %, non-oil exports at 15.2 % and private investment at 10.9 % (table 11.4). The pact clearly fared better than the more orthodox 1983 stabilization program. In 1988 the reduction in inflation was much larger, growth was positive, and the reduction in real wages was considerably less than in 1983 (tables 11.4 and 11.6).[13]

What made the difference, and why had a pact-like program not been tried earlier? The unprecedented drop in the inflation rate should be attributed to the use of incomes policy as a centerpiece of the program, complemented by fiscal and monetary discipline. According to one econometric exercise, the contribution made by incomes policy to the reduction of inflation was significant (Gressani, 1989). In the past Mexican authorities were reluctant to use any sort of generalized price and wage control mechanism. Some opposed it because they were not convinced of its theoretical soundness.[14] Other policymakers were leery of using price controls for more pragmatic reasons. Memories of the failed Plan Austral in Argentina and Plan Cruzado in Brazil, which used incomes policies as their centerpieces, were too fresh. The pact implied an investment of government credibility, which may have been too dear to risk at a time when confidence in the government's ability was running particularly low. For several years the Mexican government felt that it was too discredited vis-à-vis the private sector to implement a price freeze.

Everything else had been tried to stabilize prices, and there was the example of Israel, which had curbed inflation using a package combining fiscal austerity and incomes policy. Moreover, there were several conditions that made the decision less risky in 1988 than before. First, though Mexico could not count on additional external finance as Israel had, the Bank of Mexico held record levels of foreign reserves. This would make the fixing of the exchange rate a more credible policy, and reserves could be partially used to finance expected deteriorations in the balance of trade. Second, the operational budget was already in surplus, thanks in part to continuing petroleum-based receipts. Third, the peso was undervalued so that the inevitable exchange rate appreciation following a freeze could be less damaging. Fourth, although the popularity of de la Madrid's government was rather low, the Mexican state had the institutional clout and authority to make implementing an incomes policy easier than in other places. Its corporatist character provided the government with adequate interlocutors to implement such a policy. Also, the long experience of the Mexican state in price regulation could be applied to the new circumstances.

All four conditions had been present since late 1986, or since 1983 apart from ample foreign reserves. Even so, Mexican policymakers still believed that fiscal austerity with a reduction in the rate of depreciation of the peso would suffice to bring inflation down. It took the unexpected exchange rate debacle in November 1987 and the jump in inflation that followed to change their minds.[15] Nevertheless, the time was ripe since the last quarter of 1986 for a pact-like program. An overcautious approach to policymaking may have resulted in a waste of valuable time.

The success of the pact relied on the prevailing initial conditions listed earlier, as well as the characteristics of its implementation. Among the latter there are several features worth mentioning. First, the pact included a large dose of strict "orthodox" measures, such as fiscal deficit cuts and credit tightening. Second, the form in which the program was implemented differed greatly from its analogues in Argentina and Brazil. Decisions were made through "concertation," rather than by decree. Weary of the bad reputation of price and wage freezes, the government never used the words "freeze" or "heterodox" in its propaganda. In addition, the government did not make any open-ended commitments to keep (controlled) exchange rates or public prices fixed. In principle, the policy was subject to revision each time the parties met to discuss the pact. This was a precaution to preserve government credibility in the event the package proved unsustainable.[16] Finally, from the start the government devised a mechanism to monitor the evolution of the pact on a weekly basis; this alerted policymakers to supply shortfalls and noncompliant participants with expediency.[17]

**Table 11.6**
Wages, non-wage income and employment 1980–1989

| (annual rates of change in percent) | 1980 | 1981 | 1982 | 1983 | 1984 | 1985 | 1986 | 1987 | 1988 | 1989 | Average 1983–88 | Cumulative change 1983–88 | Average 1983–85 | Average 1986–87 |
|---|---|---|---|---|---|---|---|---|---|---|---|---|---|---|
| Total wage income[a] | — | 11.3 | −5.4 | −24.6 | −2.7 | 2.0 | −10.7 | −2.0 | −7.9 | 4.2 | −8.1 | −39.7 | −9.2 | −6.5 |
| Total wage income per workplace national accounts[a] | — | 5.8 | −5.3 | −23.1 | −5.0 | −0.2 | −9.4 | −3.1 | −8.4 | 2.7 | −8.5 | −41.4 | −10.0 | −6.3 |
| Real wages quoted by industrial survey[b] | — | 5.0 | 0.1 | −24.1 | −6.8 | 1.1 | −6.9 | −1.4 | −6.3 | 8.8 | −7.8 | −38.5 | −10.6 | −4.2 |
| Minimum wage[c] | — | 1.0 | −0.1 | −21.9 | −9.0 | −1.2 | −10.5 | −6.3 | −13.4 | −6.6 | −10.6 | −49.0 | −11.1 | −8.4 |
| Private consumption per capita[d] | — | 4.6 | −4.9 | −7.8 | 1.1 | 1.7 | −4.8 | −2.2 | 0.3 | 3.7 | −2.0 | −11.5 | −1.8 | −3.5 |
| Non-wage income[e] | — | 4.8 | 2.0 | −7.2 | 9.9 | −0.2 | −9.2 | 5.4 | −3.4 | 9.8 | −1.0 | −5.9 | 0.6 | −2.2 |
| Share of non-wage income in total income[e] | 61.4 | 60.0 | 61.8 | 66.6 | 69.2 | 68.8 | 69.1 | 70.6 | 71.6 | 72.7 | 69.3 | — | 68.2 | 69.9 |
| Employment[f] | — | 6.3 | −0.3 | −2.3 | 2.3 | 2.2 | −1.4 | 1.1 | 0.6 | 1.4 | 0.4 | 6.3 | 0.7 | −0.2 |
| Urban open unemployment (percent)[g] | — | 4.2 | 4.2 | 6.6 | 5.7 | 4.4 | 4.3 | 3.9 | 3.5 | 3.0 | 4.7 | 27.5 | 5.6 | 4.1 |

a. Source: The figures for 1980 to 1985 are from the Comision Nacional de los Salarios Minimos, "Compendio de Indicadores de Empleo y Salarios," (Mexico, December 1989), p. 135–136. The figures for 1986 to 1989 are from the Instituto Nacional de Estadistica Geografia e Informatica (INEGI), "Sistema de Cuentas Nacionales de Mexico 1986–1989: Tomo I, Resumen General," [on diskette-filename "CTAPROD.WK1" in Lotus 2.0] (Mexico, 1991). Real figures were calculated using the CPI from the Banco de Mexico, "Indicadores Economicos," Resumen, p. f (Mexico, June 1990).

**Table 11.6** (continued)

b. Source: The Comision Nacional de los Salarios Minimos, "Compendio de Indicadores de Empleo y Salarios," pp. 157–160 (Mexico, December 1989). Real figures were calculated using the CPI from the Banco de Mexico, "Indicadores Economicos," Resumen, p. f (Mexico, June 1990).

c. Source: The figures for 1980 to 1986 are from the Comision Nacional de los Salarios Minimos, "Informe de la Direccion Tecnica," pp. 45–47 (Mexico, June 1987). The 1987 figure is from the Banco de Mexico, "Informe Anual: 1987," p. 119 (Mexico, 1988). The 1988 figure is calculated from the nominal figure in the Comision Nacional de los Salarios Minimos, "Compendio de Indicadores de Empleo y Salarios," p. 189 (Mexico, December 1989); and the 1988 monthly Consumer Price Index in the Centro de Analisis e Investigacion Economica (CAIE), "The Mexican Economy: A Monthly Report," p. 30 (Mexico, May 1990). The method used to calculate the real minimum wage is the same method used by the Comision de Salario Minimos. The nominal figures are converted into real monthly figures using the monthly CPI. The real minimum wage is the 12-month average of the monthly real minimum wage. At times of sharp changes in the inflation rate this yields very different results from alternative methods. For example, dividing the average unweighted nominal minimum wage by the average CPI for the year would not take into account the fact that the different nominal wages may have applied to different time periods within the year. Moreover, the average of ratio (the method used by the Comision) is not equal to the ratio of the averages.

d. Source: For the 1980 to 1984 figures the Instituto Nacional de Estadistica Geografia e Informatica (INEGI), "Sistema de Cuentas Nacionales de Mexico 1980–1986: Tomo I, Resumen General," pp. 118, 120, 123, 126 and 129 (Mexico, 1988). The 1985 figure is from INEGI, "Sistema de Cuentas Nacionales de Mexico 1985–1988: Tomo I, Resumen General," pp. 80 (Mexico 1990). The 1986 to 1989 figures are from INEGI, "Sistema de Cuentas Nacionales de Mexico 1986–1989: Tomo I—Resumen General," Tables 60–63 [on diskette-filename "OYUCONS.WKI" in Lotus 2.0] (Mexico, 1991). The preliminary 1990 figure is from the Banco de Mexico, "The Mexican Economy: 1991," Table 4, p. 178 (Mexico, 1991). Source for Population figures. Yearly levels are calculated using growth rates from Manuel Ordorica, "Las cifras preliminares del censo," which appeared in "Demos: Carta Demografica Sobre Mexico," pp. 4–6 (1990), and the 1980 population level of 66.9 million from INEGI, "10th Population Census" (Mexico). The INEGI "11th Population Census" indicates a 1990 population of 81.1 million.

e. Source: The figures for 1980–1984 are from the Instituto Nacional de Estadistica Geografia e Informatica (INEGI), "Sistema de Cuentas Nacionales de Mexico 1980–1986: Tomo I, Resumen General," tables 30–38, pp. 77–84 (Mexico, 1988). The figures for 1985 from INEGI "Sistema de Cuentas Nacionales de Mexico 1985–1988: Tomo I, Resumen General," Tables 24–32, pp. 57–61. (Mexico, 1990). The figures for 1986 to 1989 are from INEGI, "Sistema de Cuentas Nacionales de Mexico 1986–1989: Tomo I—Resumen General," [on diskette-filename "CTAPROD.WKI" in Lotus 2.0] (Mexico, 1991). Real figures were derived using the Consumer Price Index where 1980 = 100, from the Banco de Mexico, "The Mexican Economy: 1991," p. 204 (Mexico, 1991).

f. Source: The figures for the years 1980 to 1985 are from the Comision Nacional de los Salarios Minimos, "Compendio de Indicadores de Empleo y Salarios, No. 2," table 2.6, p. 67 (Mexico, 1989). The figures for the years 1986 to 1989 are from the Instituto Nacional de Estadistica Geografia e Informatica (INEGI), "Sistema de Cuentas Nacionales de Mexico: 1986–1989, Tomo I, Resumen General," [on diskette-filename "CTAPROD.WKI" in Lotus 2.0] (Mexico, 1991).

g. Source: Inter-American Development Bank "Economic and Social Progress in Latin American—1990 Report," table 10, p. 28 (1990).

Yet some features of the pact may have been counterproductive. An acceleration of trade liberalization[18] became the most controversial measure of the package. Combined with an appreciating exchange rate, it resulted in considerable worsening of the trade balance. This deterioration made the policy of keeping the value of the peso fixed less credible, made reserve losses larger than otherwise, and further stalled capital repatriation. To prevent capital from leaving the country, domestic real interest rates had to be high enough to compensate for the perceived exchange rate risk.

The high cost of credit persisted for two years. It significantly increased the burden of servicing the government's domestic debt, which in 1988 was about 18.5 % of GDP. With average real interest rates running close to 40 % per year, domestic debt servicing took about 8 % of GDP. This put pressure on the fiscal accounts, thereby endangering stabilization efforts (in particular, the need emerged to be tougher on non-interest expenditures and government revenues). It also entailed large transfers of resources to the private sector, especially to the upper income echelons.

An obvious question, then, is whether it was a good idea to engage in trade liberalization when it was known that an exchange rate appreciation would be inevitable; the nominal value of the peso was kept fixed while inflation, though lower, continued. The argument given by policymakers in favor of trade liberalization was the potential contribution to lowering inflation by making external prices work as a "ceiling." There is no strong evidence, however, that in the short run liberalization had a significant impact on curbing inflation (Ize, 1990).

Leaving aside immediate costs and benefits, if the long term goal was to move toward free trade, then the climate provided by the pact was politically conducive to accelerate liberalization. Record high reserves and an initially undervalued exchange rate were solid preconditions. Nonetheless, it may have been wiser not to accelerate liberalization until inflation was under control.

## 11.2.2 Economic Reform and Structural Change

The interactions of Mexico's traditional development strategy with negative international shocks in creating the crisis have not been fully clarified. But one could argue that the inward-oriented nature of the economy and its dependence on key capital and intermediate imports made handling the crisis more difficult. The strategy now being proposed by the government aims at redefining Mexico's position in the international division of labor. The country is to become an outward-oriented economy with a more limited role of the state in the economic sphere. We first take up the public sector's newly proposed role, and then changes in the foreign trade regime.

Since 1982, the consensus within the de la Madrid and Salinas de Gortari regimes has been that first, "public-expenditure-led-growth" as in the 1970s could not be continued. Second, the state had tolerated inefficiency beyond a viable level within its own structure as well as had protected inefficiency within some parts of the private sector. And, third, regulatory mechanisms had become an obstacle for increasing-efficiency rather than an instrument of adequate state intervention.[19]

On the other hand, the private sector's confidence had to be regained, especially after the nationalization of the banking system in 1982. In economic terms, this could be achieved by following the "right" mix of policies. Politically, the new government needed to convince the private sector that it did not consider the redistribution of assets through expropriatory means to be a "fair game." Government actions would be geared to enticing the private sector to agree to save and invest in Mexico.

Between 1982 and 1988, the most visible change in the government's economic role was the adjustment in public sector finances. The primary fiscal surplus (excluding interest payments on internal and external debt) as a proportion of GDP recovered from $-7.3\%$ in 1982 to a string of positive levels in the 5 % range after 1983. Yet, the structural allocation of the programmable expenditures (i.e., excluding total interest payments) has remained more or less the same. Unfortunately, the most prominent allocational change within each sector was the sharp decline in public investment vis-à-vis current expenditures.[20]

During this period the government also improved tax collection and broadened the tax base. In addition, privatization and restructuring of public enterprises was begun. In 1982 the government owned or controlled 1,155 entities. By 1990, 619 entities had been sold, liquidated, merged, transferred (to state governments), or eliminated. The government reiterated its commitment to retain ownership and control of PEMEX, radioactive minerals and nuclear energy, satellite communication, primary petrochemicals, the railroads, mail service, electricity production, and CONASUPO (food distribution). Among major divestments undertaken, or in process, Fundidora Monterrey (steel), Mexicana de Aviación (airlines), and Telmex (telephone company) stand out. In May 1990 the government announced its decision to reprivatize the banking system, which had been nationalized in September 1982. This move, together with the possibility of signing a free trade agreement with the United States, were bold-*cum*-desperate attempts to restore private sector confidence and attract potential investors, Mexican and foreigners alike, in sufficient amounts to finance a return to historical per capita growth rates.

The other fundamental component of the new development strategy is its "outward-oriented" character. This has materialized in the government's effort to maintain an "attractive" exchange rate, a process of trade liberalization, the decision to join GATT in 1986, and the pursuit of a free trade agreement with the United States and Canada beginning in 1990. At the same time, measures have been implemented to simplify bureaucratic processes regarding imports and exports. Export promotion policies include monitoring net export performance in exchange for domestic protection in the automobile and microcomputer sectors.

Trade liberalization began in mid-1985 and was accelerated at the end of 1987 with the Economic Solidarity Pact. In June 1985, the items covered by import licenses relative to tradeable output totaled 92.2 %. This share fell to 35.8 % in June 1987 and 23.2 % in May 1988. Items covered by reference prices relative to tradeable output went down from 18.7 % in June 1985, to 13.4 % in June 1987, and to zero in May 1988. The maximum tariff was lowered from 100 % in June 1985 to 20 % in December 1988. The trade-weighted average tariff went down from 23.5 % in June 1985 to little over 9.0 % in early 1990.

Nonoil exports grew at almost 20 % per year and manufactured exports even faster between 1983 and 1988. Although it is tempting to link this performance with the policies just mentioned, at the outset it resulted more from the contraction in internal demand than a shift in the underlying economic structure. Both the time and sectoral patterns of export growth suggest that trade policy changes since 1985 have not been its main driving force.

For example, manufactured exports grew rapidly both before and after 1985. The increases have been largely concentrated in some intermediate goods, that is, part of the boom is related to contraction of the domestic market.[21] Other sectors with expanding foreign sales include the (still protected) automobile industry, which benefitted from big investment programs of the late 1970s that came to maturity a few years later, and the *maquiladora* assembly plants in the northern border region. The latter sector has had a free trade regime for processing of imported raw materials for re-export since the mid-1960s; during the 1980s it profited from very low wages (in dollar terms) as well as the large and expanding U.S. market.

The implication is that even though the policies and reforms undertaken may be fundamental to supporting an outward-oriented strategy, their impact will only be seen in a longer time span. A Mexican "virtuous spiral" among exports, investment, productivity, and growth has yet to be established. Although capital inflows rose during 1990–91, the balance of payments still may not sustain the initial required expansion of capital formation. Short-run needs imposed by stabilization may run counter to the overall strategy as the case with the exchange rate shows.[22]

More fundamentally, a virtuous spiral would require heavy investments in human resources and physical infrastructure together with a full array of policies to take advantage of the positive externalities of industrial expansion. Without these, stagnation will loom in the form of a low wage/slow growth path with limited feedbacks between output and productivity gains and weak interindustry linkages. Mexico's *maquiladora* exports are a clear illustration of this danger.

### 11.2.3  Equity and Social Welfare

Despite three decades of growth and governmental efforts to improve living conditions in the post-World War II era, by the end of the 1970s poverty in Mexico was pervasive and levels of education and public health were low by international standards (Lustig, 1989). These conditions worsened after 1982.

More than any other indicator, Mexican wage income captures the extent of the consequences of the crisis and adjustment process. Total wage income declined an average of 8.1% per year between 1983 and 1988, as shown in table 11.6. As expected, the sharpest declines—24.6% in 1983 and 10.7% in 1986—occurred during the two years of deepest economic crisis.

This behavior is the combined result of the evolution of the real wage and employment, with contracting real labor payments playing the more important role. According to available estimates presented in table 11.6, employment[23] rose an average of 0.4% per year between 1983 and 1988. On the other hand, the contraction of wages was drastic.

In contrast to wage income, which declined on average 8.1% a year from 1983 to 1988, nonwage income fell at a rate of only 1.0% (table 11.6). The nonwage share of total income correspondingly rose from 61.9% in 1981 to 71.6% in 1988. This pattern reflects the fact that prices of goods and services (excluding those produced by the public sector and those subject to price control regimes) and especially the services performed by the self-employed are more "freely" set than wages.

It would be a mistake to believe, however, that nonwage income comprises only profits, rents, or interest income, which mostly accrue to the well-to-do. It includes earnings of poor peasants or small shop owners, as well as those of the rich modern businessmen. Given that per capita consumption declined considerably less than real wages, it is clear that part of the nonwage income went to income groups besides the wealthy.

Because most of the very poor in Mexico are engaged in agricultural activities, it is important to analyze the evolution of income flows in agriculture, as well as of the output and price of corn—the basic peasant crop—during the adjustment period.

Between 1983 and 1985 agricultural output and employment fared better than the overall economy. Real farm wages fell less than aggregate real wages and nonwage income rose while it contracted for the nonagricultural sector. Better prices for agricultural goods and unusually favorable weather conditions help explain this atypical performance. Real devaluations and attempts to align agricultural prices with world prices contributed to an improvement within Mexico. The on-farm price of corn was no exception. Because most poor peasants are corn-growers and most of the corn is grown by poor peasants, poor rural households may have suffered less during this crunch than their urban counterparts.

This favorable pattern reversed itself in 1986. By most indicators agriculture's performance was worse than the aggregate. Bad weather conditions and a deterioration in prices partly explain this downturn (Lustig, 1992), as do a reduction in agricultural subsidies and credit and an absence of new investment (Appendini, 1991). More recently, during 1988–89, the Economic Solidarity Pact was more effective in clamping down agricultural prices than those of other sectors. The conclusion is that economic hardship in agriculture must have been very severe in the 1988–89 period. More recently, data have shown a positive change in agricultural output and prices in 1990.

Besides direct earnings of households, government expenditures in the social sectors also have dropped. Outlays on education and health fell by a cumulative 30.2 % and 23.9 % respectively, between 1983 and 1988 (Lustig, 1992). Physical resources per capita in the provision of services were not reduced at all or reduced by less. The reduction in expenditures thus reflects lower wages and public investment in the social sectors.

The countrywide infant mortality rate continued to decline between 1982 and 1989.[24] Some indicators, however, reveal a deterioration in health standards. For instance, infant and preschool mortality caused by avitaminosis and other nutritional deficiencies increased from 1982 onward after years of steady decline. The infant mortality rate could have improved more rapidly had it not been for deteriorating nutritional conditions.

With regard to education, two phenomena may have resulted from the crisis. First, according to official statistics, the fall in the number of children registered for the first year of grammar school between 1981 and 1984 was lower than the population decline of the relevant age range.[25] Second, the proportion of each level of graduates entering the subsequent level decreased. These factors may explain why the average number of schooling years of the population during the 1980s improved by one year, while the improvement between 1970 and 1980 was two years. It may also imply a delay in the development of higher skills marked by a decline in the proportion of students advancing from one educational level to the next beyond primary school.

The question of who bore the brunt of the social costs of the crisis is of particular relevance in a country such as Mexico where the concentration of income is high and poverty is widespread. In table 11.7 we can observe that income concentration at the top 10 % of the population has been high for all years studied. The data show a slight improvement in the distribution of income between 1963 and 1977. It appears that some redistribution from the top to the middle sectors occurred. Table 11.7 shows a further improvement between 1977 and 1984. This result should, however, be taken with caution as the surveys are not strictly comparable.

The characteristics of the population by income level provide some hints about how the social costs of the crisis may have been distributed. First, because the bulk of the extremely poor are in agriculture and derive about two-thirds of their income from nonwage sources, the absolute and relative impact on poverty will depend on the performance of agricultural output

**Table 11.7**
The probable evolution of the income distribution in Mexico (percentages of total family income)

| | Percentile groups of households | | | |
| --- | --- | --- | --- | --- |
| | 40 lowest | 50 intermediate | 10 highest | Total |
| Family income and domestic expenditures, 1963 | 10.2 | 47.6 | 42.2 | 100.0 |
| Study of family incomes and expenditures, 1968 | 11.2 | 48.8 | 40.0 | 100.0 |
| Household incomes and expenditues, 1977 | 10.4 | 52.8 | 36.8 | 100.0 |

Source: Excerpted from Altimir (1981), p. 90, table 8.

and prices, and—to a lesser extent—on agricultural wages. Second, people in the middle ranges depend on wages as their principal source of income.

Because wage income contracted far more than nonwage income during the 1980s, it would appear that middle income groups suffered to a greater degree than those at either the bottom or the top.[26] Such households are far from being "middle class" by First World standards. Those at the bottom of the middle range are the poor living in urban areas. Because agricultural wage and nonwage incomes deteriorated sharply from 1986 onward, results may have been different during the second half of the the decade. Rather than the middle ranges, it was the rural poor who must have endured the sharpest decline in living standards.

Perhaps the most important source of inequity in the distribution of adjustment costs arose from portfolio shifts. The rich, that is, those who own a significant amount of assets, could always protect, and even improve, their wealth far more than the rest of society by simply transferring their capital abroad (recall that capital flight was estimated at about U.S. $36 billion between 1977 and 1987). Those without savings—the majority of Mexicans—did not have a similar option.

The crisis and its aftermath left Mexico with a relatively impoverished middle class, an increasing number of poor households, and probably with the poorest worse off than before. It is interesting to note that economic growth alone may be ineffective in reducing hard-core poverty. If the per capita income of the bottom 10 % in 1984 grew by 3 % per year, the historical average growth rate of GDP in the post-war period, it would still take this group about 16 years to reach an income level equal to the extreme poverty line (less than U.S. $50 per capita per quarter). If the income of the lowest decile grew at the 1988–89 per capita GDP growth rate of about 1 % per year, the waiting period would be almost 47 years. This still would only be enough income to buy essential foods.[27] It is clear that equity-oriented reforms are the major task ahead.

## 11.3  Macroeconomic Prospects and Problems

Macroeconomic policies during the 1980s succeeded in reducing inflation (from almost 160 % in 1987 to around 50 % in 1988 and 20 % in 1989), at the expense of a growing imbalance in the external current account—brought about by an appreciating real exchange rate in the midst of a radical import-liberalization program—and a temporary but sharp increase in domestic interest rates that remained at real levels of the order of 30 % in 1988 and 20 % in 1989.

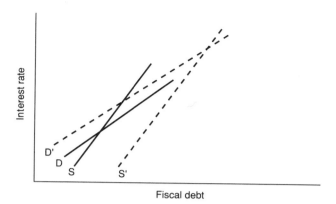

**Figure 11.1**
Note: A lower inflation tax shifts the supply schedule of interest-bearing government debt from S to S' as a consequence of an increased real fiscal deficit, and the demand schedule from D to D' by switching the public's desired portfolio away from nonmonetary assets

As illustrated in figure 11.1, this increase was the result of a shift in both the supply and demand schedules in the market for government debt, brought about by the reduction in the inflation tax. In the wake of the Economic Solidarity Pact, after additional adjustments in the primary fiscal surplus, real interest outlays on the government's domestic debt became the major source of fiscal imbalance, since at "normal" rates the current real deficit would have become a surplus.

The fundamental cause of the high rates was exchange rate uncertainty that had been introduced by the conflict between external and internal balance objectives, characteristic of the adjustment strategy adopted. With no further policy adjustments, the success or failure of the policy depended heavily on the level of capital repatriation and foreign direct investment being sufficient to moderate the trade-off between the internal and external macroeconomic balances, thereby removing exchange rate doubts.

The point is illustrated in figure 11.2 by means of a "critical mass" model where actual and expected capital inflows interact. Suppose that the perceived rate of return on public debt by an individual investor depends on the aggregate level of capital repatriation and foreign investment, because the larger these capital inflows, the lower is the exchange rate risk. Assuming a bell-shaped distribution of investors—ranging from a bullish group to a bearish one, with a majority in the intermediate category of "sheep"—yields an S-shaped relation between actual and expected capital repatriation.[28]

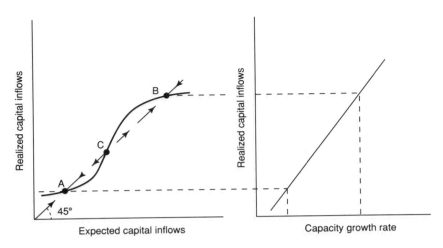

**Figure 11.2**
A critical mass model of capital inflows

With expectations being revised according to the actual outcome, stable self-fulfilling expectations equilibria will exist at A and B. Both are associated with the same non-interest balance in the current fiscal accounts, but one with no-or-low capital repatriation and the other with high capital inflows.

The implications for growth of these two scenarios can be briefly summarized as follows (Ros, 1989): If capital repatriation occurs, the economy can settle into a virtuous path of lower interest rates, higher public investment, and faster growth from 1991 or 1992 onwards. The decline in the government's domestic debt burden increases public savings by over 2 % of potential output, making possible both an increase in public investment and a reduction of the fiscal deficit to levels consistent with the reduced availability of foreign loans to the public sector after 1992.

Higher public investment crowds in private investment and raises capacity utilization, while private capital inflows rise further to match the larger gap between private investment and savings. In effect, the transition to lower interest rates removes the fiscal constraints on medium term growth that have been binding over the past eight years.[29] Sustained expansion could proceed at around 4 % per year, limited by a foreign exchange constraint. Minor trade and savings adjustments would push the GDP growth rate up to 5 % per year and, given the slowing down of population dynamics, permit a return to historical growth rates of per capita incomes in the range of 3 % to 3.5 %.

In contrast to this virtuous circle, the economy in the alternative scenario of no capital repatriation remains stuck in a vicious path of high interest rates, stagnant levels of public and private investment, and low growth. Fiscal constraints continue to bind as a result of the burden that real interest outlays represent in the government budget. The fall in foreign loans to the government after 1992 forces a cut in public investment, which in turn sets back accumulation and growth to 1988 levels or below. The high interest rate-low growth equilibrium is not sustainable over time. The implied accumulation of public debt and the low rate of GDP growth can easily degenerate into an internal debt crisis.

Before the pact was implemented, stabilization could not be achieved; thereafter, inflation was under control but economic recovery remained elusive. A comprehensive incomes policy and fiscal discipline sufficed to restore and maintain price and financial stability, but a "cooled down" economy could not stimulate private investment. The authorities were unwilling to attempt expansionary policies for fear of inflation and the loss of hard-won private sector confidence. Likewise, the private sector was unwilling to lead a recovery because it feared a failure or reversal of the policy package. Breaking this impasse was the challenge faced by the Salinas administration when it assumed office in December 1988.

After taking office, the new government introduced a Pact for Stability and Economic Growth, committing itself to economic expansion with price stability. The mechanism would be a reversal of the trend in resource transfers so that Mexico would not be forced into running large trade surpluses to finance debt service and capital flight, nor would it have to rely on high real domestic interest rates to hold down capital outflows. These goals would require efforts on three fronts: reducing the burden of debt service, encouraging capital repatriation, and attracting new foreign investment.

The authorities believed that a debt-reduction agreement with commercial banks was essential to enhance business confidence. The Mexican government's decisiveness was an important factor in persuading the United States to launch the Brady Plan (named for the incumbent Secretary of the Treasury) in March 1989. Mexico was the first country to sign a Brady-type debt agreement with commercial banks in February 1990.

The savings in cash flow from the agreement were not impressive, amounting to about U.S. $1 billion per year for the first five years, or 10% of total interest payments (Lustig, 1992). The government as well as many economists and other observers at the time were confident that the agreement would boost the private sector's animal spirits, encourage capital repatriation, and induce lower interest rates and economic growth.[30]

When these outcomes did not immediately occur, other alternatives were pursued. Since early 1990, the government has undertaken unprecedented and far-reaching initiatives to send the message that it is fully committed to an open economy and market-oriented reforms. Some initiatives such as deregulation and privatization of public enterprises conform to policy prescriptions stressed by the Bretton Woods institutions. Others, however, are sui generis. For example, the pursuit of a free trade agreement with the United States, announced in mid-1990, is meant to support economic reforms with a strong institutional boost.

The crucial question is whether the recent debt agreements and the acceleration of economic reform have been able to generate a level of capital inflows beyond the critical mass corresponding to the unstable equilibrium at point C in figure 11.2, sufficient to shift aggregate animal spirits from self-fulfilling pessimism at point A to optimism at point B. In the early 1990s, the results were decidedly positive. Capital repatriation, foreign investment, and Mexico's acceptance in the international capital market were on the rise and produced a radical turnaround in the capital account after 1989.[31] Domestic interest rates dropped throughout 1990 and 1991. First private and later public investment began to flow. Inflation, which had increased slightly in 1990, again began to decline. Output growth reached 4.4 % in 1990 but dropped off by about one percentage point the following year. The most significant unexpected feature of the recovery was a large current account deficit in the balance of payments. The gap in 1991 was of the same order of magnitude as the one 10 years previously, but financed an investment rate several points lower as a percentage of GDP. The massive task that remains is to transform this fragile, externally dependent economic recovery into sustained growth and a swift reduction of extreme poverty and blatant inequality of income and wealth.

## Notes

1. For a more detailed presentation, see Lustig (1992).

2. Growth pessimism was quite popular among the structuralist and dependency schools at the time. An analogous interpretation was also mistakenly given to the slowdown of the Brazilian economy in the early 1960s.

3. Defined as those people living in towns with populations larger than 2,500 inhabitants.

4. Hernandez-Laos (1973, p. 93). This result is also consistent with Bruton's (1967, p. 1115) findings for the period 1945–55.

5. Hirschman (1968) gives an insightful account of the inherent difficulties of import substitution industrialization.

6. The fiscal deficit here is equal to the operational deficit. the estimates were obtained from Alberro and Cambiazo (1986, Table 8, p. 48).

7. Proven reserves rose from 6 billion barrels in 1975 to 40 billion in 1978. By 1982 proven reserves equaled 70 billion barrels.

8. The stock of total foreign debt rose from U.S. $33.6 billion in 1978 to U.S. $74.1 billion in 1981 (Zedillo, 1986, Table 6, p. 972).

9. See for example, Alberro and Cambiazo (1986), Barker and Brailovsky (1983), Bazdresch (1983), Cordoba (1986), Dornbusch (1988), Garcia and Serra (1984), Ize and Ortiz (1985), Ize (1988), Ros (1986), Taylor (1985), and Zedillo (1986).

10. There are various studies that analyze this period. For example, see Alberro and Cambiazo (1988), Cordoba (1986), Dornbusch (1988), Ize (1988), Lustig (1992), Lustig and Ros (1987), and Ros (1986).

11. For discussion see Lustig (1989), Samaniego (1986), and Section 11.2.3.

12. The primary surplus of the public sector was to increase from 5.4 % of GDP in 1987 to 8.2 % in 1988. Private credit would be restricted by setting lending ceilings equal to 90 %, and later 85 % of the commercial banks' outstanding average balance in December 1987. See Aspe (1992) and Ortiz (1991) for details.

13. There is, however, one fundamental difference. The pact was launched when foreign reserves were high (estimated at about U.S. $13 billion), even increasing to U.S. $16 billion shortly afterwards. The reserves provided an objective basis for maintaining a fixed nominal exchange rate while import tariffs were reduced, and demand and output could experience a slight expansion. A year later in March 1989, foreign reserves were estimated at around U.S. $6 billion, meaning that the "cost" of the policy package, measured in terms of loss in reserves was about U.S. $10 billion. In a way, foreign reserves in Mexico played the role that U.S. financial support had played in the Israeli stabilization program. Since Mexico had no access to further sources of finance, short of a moratorium, it had to use its own "savings."

14. Mainstream economics, particularly at the IMF, regarded incomes policy with immense distrust and even contempt. It only gained respectability when its efficacy was argued analytically by some mainstream economists. Mexican policymakers concerned with risking a bad reputation with the official lending institutions chose more conventional policies. In fact, had Mexico been under an agreement with the IMF when it undertook the pact, it would have been practically impossible to apply price controls because the IMF would not have supported such measures.

15. Although some analysts argue that the November 1987 devaluation may have been unwarranted, it became one of the factors that set the stage for implementation of the pact. The acceleration in inflation to unprecedented levels encouraged the authorities to explore unchartered waters in stabilization policy in Mexico.

16. These periodic revisions also introduced uncertainty reflected in very high domestic interest rates.

17. The mechanism was a commission formed by very high ranking officials of the economic cabinet and the representatives of labor, agriculture, and business. Cordoba (1991) argues that the pact conveyed a sense of "justice." However, given the evolution of real wages and real interest rates this is questionable.

18. The maximum tariff was lowered from 45 % to 20 %, official import prices were eliminated, and import permits were removed from all items except parts of agriculture, automobiles, computers, and pharmaceuticals.

19. Although traditionally the "anti-statist" position has been identified with the ultra-liberal "right wing" position of Hayek or Nozick there has been a new current emerging from the social democratic "left," which also proposes reduction of state participation and regulation as part of a necessary development strategy. Among Mexican decision makers "ideological" positions coexist and effectively agree on policy decisions given the current consensus of both camps with respect to the role of the state.

20. The relatively high financial deficit to GDP ratio recorded in table 11.1 results from adding interest payments to the primary deficit including their inflationary component. In fact, the overall inflation-corrected operational deficit was equal to .88 % in 1988 (*Banco de Mexico, Informe Anual*, 1989, p. 268). The financial deficit for the same year was equal to 12.8 %.

21. These industries (petrochemicals, steel, cement) suffer from a structural trade deficit under normal demand conditions, but have recorded a trade surplus or a substantially reduced deficit as a result of the great underutilization of their productive capacities during the 1980s.

22. Export promotion requires a relatively undervalued and stable exchange rate whereas stabilization requires a certain degree of real appreciation. The latter is the unavoidable outcome of fixing the exchange rate in nominal terms while inflation is still positive even if slowing down. The pact demonstrated that stabilization can be helped to work if the exchange rate is temporarily fixed in nominal terms.

23. The definition of "employment" used by the National Accounts is of work-posts, that is, the number of laborers needed to produce a certain level of output given some labor/output coefficients. It is at best an indirect estimate of the number of people actually employed.

24. See UNICEF, *The State of the World's Children* (1984, 1985, 1986). It has been observed that the impact of an economic crisis is usually not reflected in average indicators and that its impact on health only becomes obvious over the long run. Perrot and Collins (1934) present a classic study for the United States during the Great Depression. Moreover, investigations completed in developed countries during the last 20 years have found that there is a statistically significant correlation between unemployment and a deterioration in physical and psychological health indicators. In Mexico, the available information usually refers to national aggregates, making it difficult to determine the differential impact of the crisis on various socioeconomic groups.

25. The number of children aged five to eight declined by 3.7% according to estimates provided by the National Council of Population (CONAPO), while the number of children enrolled in first grade for the same period fell by 7.9% (de la Madrid, *Tercer Informe del Govierno*, 1985, p. 576).

26. Care should be taken, however, as even a minimal decline in the income of the poor can have devastating effects on a household's present and future welfare.

27. By definition the extreme poverty line is defined as the total cost of a minimum food basket required to cover normal caloric and public needs.

28. In this context, the bulls are those investors who will repatriate capital even if nobody else does, the bears those who will not do so even if everybody else does, and the sheep those who follow the majority. The model follows Schelling's (1978) depiction of a "dying seminar."

29. When the three-gap model used by Ros (1989) is solved under a fiscal constraint, its 22.6% rate of accumulation—resulting from the expansion of public investment and its crowding-in effects on private investment—is associated with a current account deficit of 4.7%, which appears to be unsustainable. Total investment is simply too high, given domestic savings and plausible values for the net external indebtedness of the private sector.

30. For example, see van Wijnbergen (1990).

31. Capital repatriation in 1990 was U.S. $4.3 billion, according to information from the Secretaría de Hacienda y Credito Publico.

## References

Alberro, J., and J. Cambiazo (1986). "Characteristics of the Adjustment of the Mexican Economy." *Macro-economic Policies and the External Gap: Latin America in the 1980's*, LC/G. 1532-P. Santiago: UNDP/ECLAC.

Altimir, O. (1982). "La distribucion del ingreso en México: 1950–1977." *Distribucion del ingreso en México. Ensayos, Analisis Estructural*, Cuaderno 2, Tomo 1. Mexico City: Banco de México.

Appendini, K. (1991). "Los Campesinos Maizeros frente a la Politica de Abasto." Paper presented at Latin American Studies Association conference, Washington D.C.

Aspe, P. (1992). "Estabilizacion Macroeconomica y Cambio Estructural: La Experiencia de Mexico (1982–88)," in C. Bazdresch, N. Bucay, and N. Lustig (eds.), *Mexico: Auge, Crisis, y Ajuste*. Mexico, DF: Fondo de Cultura Economica.

Baillet, A. (1988). "La evolucion do las ingresos del sector publico: 1983–1988." (Mimeo) Mexico.

Banco de México (1987). *Indicadores de la Actividad Industrial*. Cuadro II-H-22–II-H-26, August.

Banco de México (1989). *Indicadores Economicos*. Mexico, April.

Banco de México (1988). *Indicadores Economicos, Acervos Historicos*, several years.

Banco de México (1988). *Informe Anual*, Mexico City.

Banco de México (1989). *Informe Anual*, Mexico City.

Barker, T., and V. Brailovsky (1983). *"La politica economica entre 1976 y 1982 y el Plan Nacional de Desarrollo Industrial."* *Investigacion Economica*, No. 166. Mexico City: Universidad Nacional Autonoma de México.

Bazdresch, C. (1983). *"Las causes de la crisis."* Paper presented at the seminar on the Mexican Economy, El Colegio de México, Mexico City, August.

Bruton, H. (1967). *"Productivity Growth in Latin America,"* *American Economic Review*, Vol. 57, No. 4.

Bueno, Gerardo (1987). *Policies on Exchange Rate, Foreign Trade and Capital.* (mimeo), El Colegio de México, Mexico City.

Casar, J., S. Zarayn, and C. Marquez (1986). *"Los determinantes del creacimiento do la productividad y la capacidad de absorcion de empleo en el sector manufactures."* *Economia Méxicana*, No. 6.

Casar, M. A., and W. Peres (1988). *El Estado empresario en México: Agotamiento o renovacion?.* Mexico City: Siglo XXI.

CEPAL (1988). *"Notas para el estudio economico de America Latina y el Caribe, 1987, México."* LC/MEX/L.82, July.

Cordoba, J. (1986). *"El programa mexicano de reordenacion economica, 1983–1984,"* in SELA (*Sistema Economico para America Latina*) *El FMI, el Banco Mundial y la Crisis Latinoamericana.* Mexico City: Siglo XXI.

Cordoba, J. (1991). *"Diez Lecciones de la Reforma Economica en Mexico."* *Nexos*, No. 158: 31–48.

De la Madrid, M. (1989). *Informe*, various years.

Dervis, K., J. De Melo, and S. Robinson (1982). *General Equilibrium Models for Development Policy.* A World Bank Research publication. Cambridge: Cambridge University Press.

Dornbusch, R. (1988). *"Mexico: Stabilization, Debt and Growth."* *Economic Policy*, 5 Great Britain, October.

Fajnzylber, F., and T. Martinez Tarrago (1976). *Las Empresas Transnacionales: Expansion a nivel mundial y proveccion en las Industria Mexicana.* Mexico: FCE.

Garcia, A., and P. Serra-Puche (1984). *"Causas y efectos de la crisis economica de México."* *Jornadas* No. 104. Mexico City: El Colegio de México.

Gressani, Daniela (1989). *"The Effects of the Mexican Stabilization Program on Inflation: Simulation Results from a Model with Wage and Price Determination."* Washington, D.C.: World Bank.

Hernandez-Laos, Enrique (1973). *Evolucion de la Productividad de los factores en México.* Mexico City: Centro Nacional de Productividad.

Hirschman, A. O. (1968). "The Political Economy of Import-Substituting Industrialization in Latin America." *The Quarterly Journal of Economics.*

Ize, A. (1988). "Savings, Investment and Growth in Mexico: Five Years after the Crisis," *International Monetary Fund* WP/88. Washington, DC, December.

Ize, A., and G. Ortiz (1985). "Default through Overshooting. The Case of Mexico." Paper presented at the seminar on the Mexican economy, El Colegio de México, Mexico City, August.

Lustig, Nora (1981). *Distribucion del ingreso y crecimiento en México: Un analisis de ideas estructuralistas.* Mexico: El Colegio de México.

Lustig, Nora (1989). "The Impact of the Crisis on Living Standards in Mexico: 1982–1985," (mimeo) Brookings Institution, Washington, D.C., June.

Lustig, Nora (1992). *Mexico: The Remaking of an Economy.* Brookings Institution: Washington, D.C.

Lustig, Nora, and Jaime Ros (1987). *Stabilization and Adjustment Policies and Programs, Country Study No. 7: Mexico.* Helsinki: WIDER.

Ortiz, G. (1991). "Mexico Beyond the Debt Crisis: Toward Sustainable Growth with Price Stability," in M. Bruno et. al. (eds.), *Lessons from Economic Stabilization and its Aftermath,* Cambridge, MA: MIT Press.

Perrot, G., and S. Collins (1934). "Sickness among the 'Depression Poor'," *American Journal of Public Health,* 24: 101–107.

Ros, Jaime (1986). "Mexico from the Oil Boom to the Debt Crisis. An Analysis of Policy Responses to External Shocks 1978–1985," in R. Thorp and L. Whitehead (eds.), *The Latin American Debt Crisis.* London: Macmillan.

Ros, Jaime (1989). "Medium-term Perspectives for the Mexican Economy." Prepared draft for WIDER, United Nations, Helsinki.

Samaniego, N. (1986). *"Los efectos de la crisis de 1982–1986 en las condiciones de vida de la poblacion en México."* Comision Economica para America Latina y el Caribe, LC/R.539. Santiago, Chile, November.

Schelling, T. (1978). *Micromotives and Macrobehavior,* New York: Norton.

Taylor, Lance (1985). "The Crisis and Thereafter: Macroeconomic Policy Problems in Mexico," in P. Musgrave (ed.), *Mexico and the United States: Studies in Economic Interaction.* Boulder, CO: Westview Press.

van Wijnbergen, Sweder (1990). "Mexico's External Debt Restructuring in 1989/1990." Washington, DC: World Bank.

Vernon, Ray (1963) *The Dilemma of Mexico's Development: The Roles of the Private and Public Sectors,* Cambridge MA: Harvard University Press.

Zedillo, E. (1986). "Mexico's Recent Balance of Payments Experience and Prospects for Growth." *World Development,* Vol. 14 No. 8.

# 12

## Nigeria

## T. Ademola Oyejide and Mufutau I. Raheem

Nigeria has had six successful military coups and only four years of civilian rule since 1966. In addition to these changes in government, the civil war that raged between 1967 and 1970 not only caused immediate disruption but also had political effects of a lasting nature. The present military government is working on a scheme to hand over power to a civilian regime by October 1992. If this program is successfully implemented, it would lead to the third attempt at civil rule in Nigeria. In contrast to the multi-party arrangement of the two previous republics, the government has fashioned a two-party structure on which the third republic will be based.

Whether a new civilian government can effectively manage the economy remains to be seen. Widespread pessimism is based on past experiences of gross mismanagement, endemic corruption, and short-sightedness. Political instability resulting from frequent changes of government may encourage initiatives with high short-term returns rather than an effective strategy that promotes meaningful long-term development. Each new government feels compelled to undertake new initiatives and projects rather than building on those of the past.

### 12.1 Economic Background

Nigeria's GDP increased by 4 % per annum in real terms between 1950 and 1960. But this first decade of independence set the stage for the economy's subsequent fluctuating performance. From an annual average of about 5.5 % during the first half of the 1960–1970 decade, the growth rate plummeted between 1966 and 1969 as a result of the civil war. However, it picked up again in 1970 with the restoration of peace. The most striking feature of the Nigerian economy between 1970 and 1973 was its remarkably rapid recovery, explained partly by the development of the oil sector—there were sharp increases in both quantity and price of crude oil exports—and partly by an element of catching up in response to the emerging post-war demand (Oyejide, 1987).

The 1970s witnessed perhaps the most significant structural changes. The fairly broad-based agricultural economy became considerably less diversified, as oil dominated the production and trade structures. Unlike the 1950s and 1960s when agriculture and manufacturing expanded, growth in the early 1970s was founded on the oil and government sectors. The oil boom (1974 to 1978) enabled the country to embark on a massive development program, which placed strong emphasis on infrastructure, social services, and heavy industry. GDP increased by 6% per annum in real terms between 1974 and 1978.

The collapse of oil prices, especially since the early 1980s, pushed the economy into deep recession. As table 12.1 illustrates, its performance during the past decade has been very weak. When a structural adjustment program was instituted in the fourth quarter of 1986, the reduction in domestic crude oil production and the even more dramatic fall in world prices led to a sharp deterioration in government finances and export revenues.

In the early 1990s, the economy confronts short-, medium-, and long-term development problems. In the immediate future, the authorities have to grapple with mounting debt service obligations. In the medium term, Nigeria has to deal with restoring and sustaining economic growth; bringing about an increase in per capita income in spite of rapid population growth; expanding employment opportunities; increasing capacity utilization in the industrial sector and promoting price stability; and creating incentives for increased production of food and agricultural raw materials

**Table 12.1**
GDP growth rates and sectoral composition of GDP (1950–1988)

|                        | 1950–60 | 1960–70 | 1970–80 | 1980–85 | 1985–88 |
|------------------------|---------|---------|---------|---------|---------|
| GDP growth rate (%)    | 4.2     | 6.2     | 4.9     | −3.1    | 1.0     |
| *Sectoral composition %* |       |         |         |         |         |
| Agriculture            | 62.8    | 52.3    | 26.1    | 24.5    | 33.5    |
| Oil and mining         | 1.4     | 7.0     | 25.0    | 20.4    | 16.4    |
| Manufacturing          | 3.2     | 6.9     | 4.9     | 6.3     | 9.5     |
| Infrastructures        | 9.5     | 10.3    | 16.2    | 17.1    | 7.2     |
| Services               | 23.1    | 23.5    | 28.0    | 31.7    | 33.4    |

Sources: Federal Office of Statistics' *Economic and Social Statistics Bulletin* (Various years), *Central Bank of Nigeria: Annual Report and Statements of Accounts* (Various years).

and non-oil export tradeables. In the long run, there is need to change the monocultural nature of the economy and diversify away from the heavy reliance on oil.

## 12.2  The Economic Crisis in the Medium Term

At the surface level, the immediate cause of the current economic depression may be traced to the collapse of the international oil market toward the end of 1981 and the consequent fall in revenues. But the deep causes can be anchored to structural defects in the economy and policies pursued since the early 1970s. Growth has been characterized by significant sectoral shifts, which in turn have left a legacy of distortions and imbalances.

In the 1960s, agriculture was the dominating sector. In the first half of the decade, it contributed as much as 60 % to the country's GDP. The average share fell to 52.3 % during 1960–70 and the drop continued unabated (see table 12.1). The share was at an all-time low of 19.4 % in 1981 before it started picking up and reached 28.1 % in 1986. During 1985–88, the sector recorded an improved contribution of almost 34 % to GDP as it began to recover from the worst effects of Nigeria's oil-induced Dutch disease.

This lackluster performance is a source of growing concern. Once a net agricultural exporter, Nigeria now spends more on agricultural imports than it earns from exports. Studies such as those by Oyejide (1987) and the World Bank (1987) have analyzed the causal factors that underlie this decline. The current importance of petroleum notwithstanding, agriculture continues to be the real base of the economy.

Growth in the 1970s and thereafter was founded on the oil sector. Its leading role is evident in tables 12.1, 12.2, and 12.3. Starting in 1974, oil has been contributing more than 90 % of total exports on average. From 1970 through 1988, the petroleum profit tax, royalties, rents, and premiums have been the major sources of federal government revenue: The sector's contribution has not been less than 60 % of the total since 1974.

The sharp increases in oil revenues as well as output in 1973–74 and again in 1979–80 had pervasive effects on the economy (Tallroth 1987). The objective of the Nigerian government was to convert oil returns into investment in infrastructure and to develop other sectors. Progress was recorded in some areas, but many investment projects were undertaken that were later found to be unviable, constituting a dead-weight loss in terms of net benefits to the economy.

**Table 12.2**
Crude oil exports (quantity and value), 1960—1988

| Year (1) | Quantity (barrels million) (2) | Oil exports (N million) (3) | Total exports (N million) (4) | (3) as % of (4) (5) |
|---|---|---|---|---|
| 1960 | 6.24 | 8.4 | 339.0 | 2.5 |
| 1965 | 96.99 | 136.2 | 537.0 | 25.4 |
| 1970 | 383.46 | 509.6 | 886.0 | 57.5 |
| 1971 | 542.55 | 1053.0 | 1293.0 | 81.4 |
| 1972 | 650.98 | 1176.2 | 1434.0 | 82.0 |
| 1973 | 723.3 | 1893.5 | 2277.0 | 83.2 |
| 1974 | 795.71 | 5365.7 | 5795.7 | 92.6 |
| 1975 | 627.84 | 4565.1 | 4925.0 | 92.7 |
| 1976 | 736.82 | 6321.7 | 6751.0 | 93.6 |
| 1977 | 744.41 | 7072.8 | 7631.0 | 92.7 |
| 1978 | 667.39 | 5401.6 | 6328.0 | 85.4 |
| 1979 | 812.73 | 10166.8 | 10398.0 | 97.8 |
| 1980 | 701.26 | 13523.0 | 14187.0 | 95.3 |
| 1981 | 458.16 | 10280.3 | 11024.0 | 93.5 |
| 1982 | na | 8003.0 | 8206.0 | 97.5 |
| 1983 | 341.4 | 7201.2 | 7502.5 | 95.9 |
| 1984 | 401.0 | 8840.6 | 9008.0 | 98.1 |
| 1985 | 453.8 | 11223.7 | 11720.8 | 95.8 |
| 1986 | 445.7 | 8368.5 | 8920.5 | 93.8 |
| 1987 | 389.5 | 28208.6 | 30360.6 | 92.9 |
| 1988 | 408.8 | 29292.7 | 33138.1 | 88.4 |

Source: Compiled from Central Bank of Nigeria and Nigeria National Petroleum Company files.

Consequent upon the expansionary effect of income from the oil enclave, Nigeria's savings and investment ratios rose rapidly, at least during the 1973—78 period. As indicated in table 12.4, the savings ratio increased from 11.3 % in 1960—65 to reach 23.3 % in 1970—73 and 30.1 % in 1973—78. It went down thereafter to 19 % in 1981—84 before rising to almost 26 % in 1984—88. Following a similar pattern, the investment ratio rose from almost 15 % in 1960—65 to 21.0 % and 26.5 % in 1970—73 and 1973—78, respectively. During the first seven or eight years of the 1970s, domestic savings was higher than investment as the oil boom produced positive net exports.

Table 12.4 also shows that reliance on external resources to finance domestic investments became prominent as the oil slump replaced the oil

**Table 12.3**
Federal government revenue from crude petroleum, 1970–88 (N million)

| Year | Oil revenue | Total current revenue | Oil revenue as % of total |
|------|-------------|-----------------------|---------------------------|
| 1970 | 166.4 | 633.2 | 26.3 |
| 1971 | 510.2 | 1169.0 | 43.6 |
| 1972 | 764.3 | 1404.8 | 54.4 |
| 1973 | 1016.0 | 1695.3 | 59.9 |
| 1974 | 3726.7 | 4537.0 | 82.1 |
| 1975 | 4271.5 | 5514.7 | 77.5 |
| 1976 | 5365.2 | 6765.9 | 79.3 |
| 1977 | 6080.6 | 8080.6 | 75.2 |
| 1978 | 4654.1 | 7371.1 | 63.1 |
| 1979 | 8880.9 | 10913.1 | 81.4 |
| 1980 | 10990.2 | 15813.1 | 69.5 |
| 1981 | 9193.6 | 14745.7 | 62.4 |
| 1982 | 6867.8 | 10143.9 | 67.9 |
| 1983 | 7253.0 | 10811.4 | 67.1 |
| 1984 | 8029.7 | 11738.5 | 70.0 |
| 1985 | 10915.1 | 14606.1 | 74.7 |
| 1986 | 8107.3 | 12302.0 | 65.9 |
| 1987 | 19027.0 | 25099.8 | 75.8 |
| 1988 | 20933.8 | 27310.8 | 76.8 |

Sources: Federal Government Gazette, Central Bank of Nigeria and Federal Inland Revenue Department publications (various years).

**Table 12.4**
Nigeria's savings ratio, investment ratios, fiscal deficits and current account balance, 1960–88.

| | 1960–65 | 1965–70 | 1970–73 | 1973–78 | 1978–81 | 1981–84 | 1984–88 |
|---|---------|---------|---------|---------|---------|---------|---------|
| Domestic savings (as % of GDP) | 11.3 | 15.0 | 23.3 | 30.1 | 26.9 | 19.0 | 25.6 |
| Gross domestic investment (as % of GDP) | 15.2 | 16.8 | 21.0 | 26.5 | 26.3 | 22.9 | 27.5 |
| Net exports (as % of GDP) | −3.9 | −1.8 | 2.3 | 3.6 | 0.6 | −3.9 | 8.0 |
| Current account balance (as % of GDP) | −5.1 | −5.4 | −3.4 | 1.4 | −1.5 | −6.0 | −0.48 |
| Fiscal deficits (as % of GDP) | na | na | −0.1 | −2.5 | −3.6 | −8.3 | −7.3 |

Source: World Bank (1985) and Central Bank of Nigeria publications.

boom. External deficits were entrenched by 1981, after the second oil price shock. A surplus recorded in 1984 and 1985 was a result of large reduction in imports brought about by the stabilization measures. The current account once again turned negative in 1987–88.

The external terms of trade are dictated by the price of oil, given that it accounts for about 95 % of export earnings. Changes in the terms of trade explain about 90 % of the movements of Nigeria's current account. Prior to 1986, there was a more or less fixed nominal exchange rate for a nonconvertible currency with extensive capital controls. Significant real exchange appreciation rate was inevitable, about 68 % between 1973 and 1984.

The exchange rate was allowed to strengthen in line with increasing oil earnings in the early 1970s as a matter of deliberate policy, but the authorities did not allow the naira to depreciate in periods of declining earnings in the early 1980s. The effect has been to exacerbate the deficit in the balance of payments.

Besides reduced oil export earnings, external indebtedness has constituted another significant source of pressure on the balance of payments since the early 1980s. The magnitude of Nigeria's external debt remains controversial because statistical information is deficient and unreliable. From the available information, however, public and publicly guaranteed external debt rose from less than U.S. $0.5 billion in 1970 to U.S. $1.067 billion by the end of 1972. It subsequently increased sharply to $11.75 billion in 1981. Since then, Nigeria's external indebtedness (total drawings) has grown almost geometrically to $28.7 billion in 1987 (see table 12.5 for the breakdown). At the end of 1988, the total external debt of Nigeria was estimated to be slightly over $30 billion. Within about a decade, the country moved boldly from a negligible level of external borrowing to a situation characterized by heavy indebtedness.

The problem of debt overhang remains heavy (Raheem, 1988, 1989). As much as about 44 % of total foreign exchange went into debt servicing in 1985. However, the debt rescheduling agreements reached with some creditors enabled the debt service ratio to fall to slightly less than 30 % between 1986 and 1988.

From the foregoing, it is clear that Nigeria passed through most of the 1980s with an overvalued exchange rate, a distorted production structure, an import-intensive economy, and excessive dependence on the volatile international oil market for its export earnings and most of federal government revenue as well as unrealistic expectations about the future. Instead of instituting reforms to arrest the economic decline in the early 1980s, the authorities perceived the problem to be short-lived; consequently, they

**Table 12.5**
Nigeria's external debt profile, 1986 to 1988 (U.S. million $)

|  | December 1986 | October 1987 | September 1988[a] |
|---|---|---|---|
| 1. Total commitments | 21,973.1 | 33,102.1 | 34,768.2 |
| 2. Total drawings | 18,830.0 | 28,733.4 | 30,893.5 |
| (a) Conventional | (13,976.3) | (17,662.4) | (23,121.8) |
| (b) Trade debt | (4,853.7) | (11,071.0) | (11,771.7) |
| 3. Less total repayments | 2,970.8 | 5,288.5 | 6,493.1 |
| 4. Total outstanding | 15,859.2 | 23,445.0 | 28,400.4 |
| (a) Fed. Government debt obligations | (11,927.4) | (19,172.0) | (22,880.3) |
| (i) I.C.M.[b] loans | 5,267.4 | 5,874.5 | 6,652.8 |
| (ii) World Bank | 1,484.3 | 1,384.5 | 1,423.2 |
| (iii) Bilateral loans | 322.1 | 342.0 | 589.5 |
| (iv) Capitalized interest | — | 500.0 | 240.9 |
| (v) Promisory notes | 1,600.0 | 4,800.0 | 5,457.7 |
| (vi) Accrued interest on L/C | — | 500.0 | 433.9 |
| (vii) Letters of credit (L/C) | 3,253.7 | 5,771.0 | 5,880.2 |
| (viii) Uninsured suppliers Credit | — | — | 1,202.2 |
| (b) Federal parastatals (I.C.M.) | — | (610.3) | (690.9) |
| (c) State governments | (3,931.7) | (3,438.4) | (4,267.7) |
| (i) I.C.M. loans | 3,103.3 | 2,446.9 | 2,771.6 |
| (ii) World Bank | 314.8 | 658.2 | 695.2 |
| (iii) Bilateral loans | 12.4 | 116.0 | 112.0 |
| (iv) Unguaranteed loans | 500.9 | 217.2 | 688.9 |
| (d) Private sector (Unguaranteed loans) | na | (224.4) | (561.6) |

a. International capital market; b. Provisional.
Sources: Central Bank of Nigeria, Federal Ministry of Finance and Economic Development.

resorted to stabilization measures and massive deficit financing. The size of the deficits, as shown in table 12.6, moved from N 0.2 billion in 1980 to N 4.6 billion in 1982 and finally reached N 12.6 billion in 1988.

## 12.3 Public-Private Sector Balance and Income Distribution

The roles played by and the relative sizes assigned to the public and private sectors in any economy are rather normative, depending on social, economic, political, and even philosophical considerations. They will differ from one country to another and over time. Nigeria exhibits the features of

**Table 12.6**
Federal government revenue and expenditure, 1980 to 1988 (N billion, current prices)

| Values | 1980 | 1981 | 1982 | 1983 | 1984 | 1985 | 1986 | 1987 | 1988 |
|---|---|---|---|---|---|---|---|---|---|
| Federal collected revenue | 15.1 | 13.0 | 13.1 | 11.7 | 11.1 | 14.6 | 12.3 | 25.09 | 27.31 |
| Federal retained revenue | 12.0 | 8.0 | 8.2 | 7.5 | 6.9 | 9.6 | 7.9 | 16.13 | 15.59 |
| Total federal expenditure of which: | 12.2 | 12.8 | 12.8 | 14.1 | 9.5 | 13.2 | 16.2 | 22.02 | 27.75 |
| Recurrent | 5.2 | 4.9 | 4.9 | 8.4 | 6.3 | 7.2 | 7.7 | 15.65 | 19.41 |
| Capital | 7.0 | 7.9 | 7.9 | 5.7 | 3.2 | 6.0 | 8.5 | 6.37 | 8.34 |
| Federal budget deficit | −0.2 | −4.8 | −4.6 | −6.6 | −2.6 | −3.6 | −8.3 | −5.89 | −12.16 |

Source: CBN Annual Report and Statement of Account (various years).

**Table 12.7**
The relative size of private sector in Nigeria's national development plans: 1962–85

| Plans and period | Contribution of the private sector to total outlay (N billion) | Total plan outlay (N billion) | Percentage contribution of the private sector |
|---|---|---|---|
| 1st Plan: 1962–68 | 0.78 | 2.37 | 32.9 |
| 2nd Plan: 1970–74 | 1.63 | 3.19 | 51.1 |
| 3rd Plan: 1975–80 | 9.0 | 43.3 | 20.8 |
| 4th Plan: 1981–85 | 11.5 | 82.0 | 14.0 |

Source: Nigeria's National Development Plans (Various years).

a mixed economy with the ownership of the means of production and exchange shared between the public and private sectors. Prior to 1986, the public sector assumed an increasing proportion of productive activities.

An expanding public sector was inevitable following the influx of oil revenues in the early 1970s; it was also essential for economic reconstruction and rehabilitation as well as nation building after the civil war. The relative share of the private sector in the outlay for the total national development plans dropped from 51.1 % under the second plan to 20.8 % in the third plan (table 12.7). The fourth plan assigned about 14 % to the private sector.

By the beginning of the 1980s, the public sector accounted for about one-half of the GDP and two-thirds of modern sector employment (table 12.8). The increase in public sector employment since the early 1970s has averaged about 11.5 % per annum. Even during the 1980s, public sector employment continued to grow, although at a lower rate. Parastatals have spread over agricultural, mining, manufacturing, transport, commercial, and other business activities. By 1985, there were about 120 noncommercial and commercial federal parastatals; there was an equally large number of these units at the state government level. As of 1986, public investment in the parastatal sector was estimated to be over 30 billion. Nigerian governments have gone beyond the provision of public goods and services to carry a relatively high investment profile in most economic activities.

The public enterprise sector, by and large, has in the past been viewed as an extension of the government and a convenient vehicle for pursuing social objectives such as providing employment. The performance of public enterprises has often run short of expectations because of their inefficiency relative to their private counterparts. Rather than generating revenue, a large percentage of these businesses have constituted financial drains. Their

**Table 12.8**
Sectoral wage employment in Nigeria: 1973–83

| Sector | 1973 | | 1975 | | 1980 | | 1983[a] | |
|---|---|---|---|---|---|---|---|---|
| | Number | % | Number | % | Number | % | Number | % |
| Public | 901,828 | 64.87 | 1,009,600 | 67.3 | 1,350,000 | 60.0 | na | 75.3 |
| Private | 488,172 | 35.13 | 490,400 | 32.7 | 900,000 | 40.0 | na | 24.7 |
| Total | 1,390,000 | 100.0 | 1,500,000 | 100.0 | 2,250,000 | 100.0 | — | 100.0 |

a. Estimated values.
Source: National Manpower Board, Report of the Shuttle Employment Enquiries, 1983.

**Table 12.9**
Gross capital formation and banking system credit to the economy (N million, current prices)

|                             | 1960  | 1965  | 1970   | 1975  | 1980   | 1985    |
|-----------------------------|-------|-------|--------|-------|--------|---------|
| Gross capital formation     |       |       |        |       |        |         |
| Total (N million)           | 315.8 | 463.0 | 397.2  | 963.8 | 8564.3 | 4551.0  |
| Public sector (%)           | 39.7  | 37.5  | 33.6   | 40.0  | 37.0   | 37.0    |
| Private sector (%)          | 60.3  | 62.5  | 66.4   | 60.0  | 63.0   | 63.0    |
| *Bank credit to the economy*|       |       |        |       |        |         |
| Total (M million)           | 114.0 | 339.4 | 1140.4 | 275.4 | 9066.4 | 31335.3 |
| Public sector (%)           | 89.7  | 17.4  | 58.1   | 51.5  | 31.4   | 58.3    |
| Private sector (%)          | 10.3  | 82.6  | 41.9   | 48.5  | 68.6   | 41.7    |

Source: Central Bank of Nigeria, *Annual Reports and Statements of Accounts,* Various years.

operations are subject to excessive interference, misuse of funds, gross waste, over-staffing, mismanagement and corruption, as well as overinvestment in poorly conceived projects. These problems, combined with its diminished resource position, have forced the government to start divesting from many parastatals. The goal of the reform is that the public sector should withdraw from those activities that could be better managed by the private sector.

An important dimension of the public-private sector split in the economy emerges from an analysis of their contributions to gross capital formation in relation to their access to credit. As table 12.9 shows, the private sector consistently accounted for not less than 60 % of the nation's gross fixed capital formation over the 1960–88 period. But the public sector had a much larger reliance on the banking system for financing its activities. In other words, private savings played a significant role in financing public sector capital formation and other activities.

Turning to distributional issues, a first observation is that lack of adequate and up-to-date information precludes a comprehensive and in-depth study, but that some broad conclusions can still be drawn. On the average, urban dwellers earn more income than rural dwellers who constitute the largest segment of Nigerian society. Although this categorization is dual-natured, it is possible to break each category into further subcomponents.

As regards trends in wages and household income the general picture is a declining pattern, especially in the 1980s. Based on the information presented in table 12.10, particular segments of the Nigerian population seem to have suffered greater real wage and income declines than others. In 1980 (the base year), the rural self-employed earned almost half of the income of

**Table 12.10**
Trends of wages and income, 1980–85

|  | 1980 | 1981 | 1982 | 1983 | 1984 | 1985 |
|---|---|---|---|---|---|---|
| *Index of real wages (1980 = 100)* | | | | | | |
| Urban wage earner | 100 | 87 | 81 | 69 | 50 | 55 |
| Public sector wages | 100 | 103 | 99 | 83 | 60 | 55 |
| *Real household income (index: Rural self-employed in 1980 = 100)* | | | | | | |
| Rural self-employed | 100 | 103 | 91 | 86 | 73 | 79 |
| Rural wage earners | 178 | 159 | 147 | 135 | 92 | 101 |
| All rural households | 105 | 107 | 99 | 89 | 74 | 82 |
| Urban self-employed | 150 | 124 | 106 | 94 | 69 | 76 |
| Urban wage earners | 203 | 177 | 164 | 140 | 101 | 111 |
| All urban households | 166 | 142 | 129 | 109 | 80 | na |

Source: Adapted from Oyejide (1988).

urban wage earners. Urban self-employed workers earned 50 % more than their counterparts in the rural sector. The income differential between wage earners in the rural and urban sectors was not as high, amounting to about 25 %. In the aggregate, urban households earned more (about 61 %) than rural households.

The index of real urban wages fell by 50 % between 1980 and 1984 before picking up slightly in 1985. The index of public sector wages declined more gently, although it fell to the same level as that of the index of urban wage earners by 1985. Over the years, changes in real household incomes were more revealing. Between 1980 and 1985, while the rural self-employed suffered a 21 % decline in real income, wage earners lost about 56 %. In the aggregate, all rural households suffered a real income decline of over 20 %. Comparatively, the real income of urban households fell much more sharply (about 48 % between 1980 and 1984); the urban self-employed posted a 50 % loss in real income, while the decline for urban wage-earners was 45 %.

## 12.4 The Structural Adjustment Program

Faced with the problems previously described, in the early 1980s the government began stabilization measures, including drastic import controls. The coverage and intensity of the regime increased substantially between 1983 and 1985. In spite of the tighter controls, sizeable fiscal and external deficits emerged; the policy response was a switch toward demand management. An austerity program was in effect over the 1983–85 period, with objectives to reduce fiscal deficits and to cut imports as a means of eliminating the accumulation of further external payments arrears. At the same time, the exchange rate policy continued to be geared toward strength. Real effective appreciation was as high as 88 % between 1980 and 1984.

The austerity program did achieve some of its objectives. Both fiscal and external deficits fell sharply: The overall public sector deficit was brought down from 12 % of GDP in 1983 to 3 % in 1985. The use of very tight monetary policy also produced some results. The growth of net domestic credit declined from an annual rate of 47 % in 1980 and an average of 13 % over 1981–83 to 10 % during 1984–85. The banking system's credit to the government increased at a rate of 15 % in 1984–84 compared to 28.6 % in 1983. Finally, the import level was reduced from $18 billion in 1981 to $8.3 billion in 1985.

This "success" was achieved at a high real cost to the economy. The annual growth rate of the GDP was negative in each year between 1981 and 1984. Compared with 1980, per capita GNP was down by 26 % in 1984 while the real wage declined by 50 % over the same period. The emergence of a new political regime in August 1985 and another sharp fall in oil prices during the first quarter of 1986 prepared the ground for more comprehensive reform.

## 12.4.1 Reform Program Objectives and Strategy

In December 1985, Nigeria launched its comprehensive structural adjustment program in the recognition "that more austerity without structural adjustment constitutes an inadequate response to the fundamental economic and financial problems confronting the country" (FGN 1986). The basic focus was alteration and realignment of the economic structure to make absorption less import-intensive and production more export-oriented.

In terms of development strategy, the program heralds a sharp break from the past in several respects. In Nigeria, an attempt to diversify the economy's productive base and reduce reliance on oil translates into the adoption of an agriculture-led growth model; it is the only sector that has the potential for boosting output and exports of nonoil tradeables. This orientation contrasts sharply with the focus of the 1960s and 1970s on protected import-substituting industrialization. Greater importance is now assigned to the private sector and its growth potential than before. Combined with the objective of increased efficiency in the public sector, greater reliance on the private sector means that economic decisions will be guided more by markets and market forces than by administrative and government discretionary controls.

## 12.4.2   Structural Adjustment Policies

The structural adjustment program calls for a shift from reliance on demand management to a combination of these with supply-side measures aimed at the promotion of economic efficiency and long-term growth. The entire package represents a mix of expenditure-reducing, expenditure-switching, market liberalization, and structural measures. The main policies are described as follows (FGN 1986, p. 9):

(i) strengthening of the hitherto strong demand management policies;

(ii) adoption of measures to stimulate domestic production and broaden the supply base of the economy;

(iii) adoption of a realistic exchange rate policy;

(iv) further rationalization and restructuring of the tariffs in order to aid the promotion of industrial diversification;

(v) move towards improved trade and payments liberalization;

(vi) reduction of complex administrative controls simultaneously with a greater reliance on market forces;

(vii) adoption of appropriate pricing policies, especially for petroleum products and public enterprises; and

(viii) encouragement to rationalization and privatization of public sector enterprises."

## 12.4.3   A Tentative Assessment

This program's success will depend quite crucially on the degree and speed at which non-oil tradable sectors, particularly agriculture, respond to increased production incentives. It is too early to discern how strong these responses will be, but a few observations can be made.

First, the reforms have, to some extent, arrested the deterioration of the economy and produced a modest increase in domestic output. A sizeable proportion of the overvaluation of the exchange rate has been eliminated. The introduction of SAP and the generous export promotion incentives associated with it may have induced increases in nonoil exports. Besides improving export price competitiveness, the change in relative prices due to naira depreciation has enhanced the attractiveness of exports, particularly primary products. The government's local currency revenue has risen substantially through monetization of petrodollars at the new exchange rate. This has provided a good revenue base for settling public domestic debt and funding vital programs.

Implementation of the structural reform has, however, left in its wake some problems and difficulties. It has severely aggravated the operational problems and constraints of the manufacturing sector. Unusually high interest rates coupled with restrictive monetary and fiscal policies have reduced aggregate credit and this has constrained the expansion of investment. The level of unemployment has remained high while inflationary pressures have become more devastating and chronic. The living standard of the people has been eroded markedly and the most frightening aspect is the adverse effect on the living conditions of the vulnerable groups.

The external sector continues to operate under severe pressure, and there is some evidence that the reform has triggered capital flight. Although external debt rescheduling is one of the program's goals, not much has been achieved along this line. The government introduced debt-conversion in 1988 but the amount redeemed so far amounts to a paltry $70 million as of April 1989.

The overall picture is that the Nigerian economy may not experience substantial growth in the early to mid-1990s. Beyond the mid-1990s, a more comfortable growth rate may be achievable, driven by the agricultural and manufacturing sectors. Over the next 10 years, therefore, economic development in Nigeria will depend significantly on the policies that the authorities choose to pursue in the near-term.

As regards structural adjustment, an urgent issue is the sociopolitical viability of the economic reform. The outcome will depend on factors such as the relationship between the state and the society, the relationship between labor unions and other mass organizations on one hand and between labor unions and the state, on the other hand, as well as the values of the leadership or the ruling class as perceived by the ruled. A reform program has a high chance of being acceptable to the generality of the people if it is perceived by them that first, the adjustment cost or burden is being equitably distributed across social strata and second, the state is willing and ready to give adequate relief measures to the segments of the society that are adversely affected.

This issue becomes more relevant because policy reforms inevitably set in motion changes with direct and significant implications for redistribution of income and wealth across sectors and among owners of resources. Too much of reforms within relatively short periods of time may not be endurable given the nature of sociopolitical set-up of the country. The issue of an optimal time profile of policy reform boils down, therefore, to the question of trade-offs between reducing the adjustment costs and sustaining efficiency gains.

Meanwhile, the potential that Nigeria has for lightening its current external debt burden within a reasonable period of time by creating an export base should not be understated. Even though openings exist for Nigerian goods in the West African market, the government is interested in a more varied and diversified international market in the long-term.

One of the basic tenets underlying the ongoing reform is the withdrawal of government participation in activities that are better handled by the private sector. This partly explains why the government is divesting itself of parastatals. The new role being cut for the government is to limit itself to only the provision of an adequate infrastructural base and policy incentives-that would encourage the private sector to respond positively to emerging opportunities. The incentive package in this regard should include getting the prices right, administering an efficient tax structure, and removing all bottlenecks in the administrative and production systems.

The involvement of the public sector in the funding and managing of the "commanding heights" industrial plants in the economy calls for serious assessment. Several reasons have been adduced to justify direct participation of the government in these projects. First, they are very costly and highly capital intensive to the extent that the private sector may not be capable of mobilizing adequate resources to fund them. Second, some of the projects such as the iron and steel complex are supposed to provide a solid base for technological and industrial development, given the prospects of their considerable backward and forward linkages with the rest of the economy. Third, they (for instance, the petrochemical complex) can serve as a springboard for the production of manufactured exports.

Regarding project funding, two options can be identified. In the first case, the public sector will solely finance a project with the assistance of foreign technical partners. A good example is the iron and steel complex and the steel rolling mills in the country. The second approach involves joint ventureship between the public sector and the foreign and domestic private sector. This is what is being planned for the LNG project. There are clear indications that a scheme under the second approach will be more efficiently run and managed than the iron and steel complex whose operation since inception has been bedevilled with gross inefficiency and wanton resource mismanagement.

## 12.5   Macroeconomic Constraints in the Medium Term

This section presents the medium-term outlook of the Nigerian economy based on the results and conclusion of a three-gap growth exercise (Oyejide and Raheem, 1990). This approach emphasizes the importance of investment in promoting economic growth. A worrisome problem is that a large share of the required investment has to be undertaken by the public sector.

The medium-term evolution of key macro-economic variables based on simulation of the growth model is presented in table 12.11. The basic scenario is that the economy will continue to grow at the rate of about 4.5 % on the average between 1990 and 1995, to prevent per capita income and consumption from falling in the medium term. It is assumed that the three gaps jointly determine this minimum permissible growth rate.

The foreign exchange constraint seems to be heavily binding in the period 1990 through 1993 with the peak being reached in 1992 when the current account deficit constitutes about 6.5 % of the GNP. This outlook is informed by the assumption that the economy will continue to rely, in the next couple of years, on oil exports whose market is envisaged not to be strong enough to ensure a sustainable and enhanced level of foreign exchange receipts. The intensity of the constraint may be reduced from 1994 when the impact of the non-oil export promotion measures will start bearing fruit.

The continued deterioration of the world oil market coupled with an increasing debt service payments implies that Nigeria will continue to grapple with a severe balance of payments problem. The outstanding total external debt is projected to rise from U.S. $30.61 billion in 1990 to $37.5 billion in 1995 under a moderate growth scenario. Given the debt repayment structure, the debt service ratio is expected to be more than 35 % throughout the period if there is no relief from the international creditor community. Nigeria is debt distressed, and will urgently need both an alleviation of her debt burden and additional concessional assistance if the economy is to achieve sustained growth.

For a consistent 4.5 % growth rate in the medium term, the required gross domestic investment ranges between N 18.09 billion in 1990 to almost N 25 billion by the end of 1992 and further to N 35.5 billion in 1995. At this level, investment will constitute about 26 % of GDP on the average. Much of it will have to come from the public sector, especially in the early 1990s.

**Table 12.11**
Projected trend values of selected macroeconomic indicators

| Macro-indicators | 1990 | 1991 | 1992 | 1993 | 1994 | 1995 |
|---|---|---|---|---|---|---|
| 1. GDP (at 1984 Mkt. Prices (N billion) | 89.68 | 93.72 | 97.94 | 102.35 | 107.06 | 112.87 |
| 2. Potential output (N bil.) | 119.56 | 121.15 | 123.69 | 126.82 | 129.11 | 113.82 |
| 3. Gross domestic investment (N billion) | 18.09 | 20.60 | 24.40 | 28.56 | 31.67 | 35.50 |
| of which: | | | | | | |
| *Public sector | 10.89 | 11.69 | 13.43 | 15.69 | 16.38 | 17.29 |
| *Private sector | 7.20 | 8.91 | 10.97 | 12.87 | 15.29 | 18.01 |
| 4. Gross domestic investment as % of GDP | 20.17 | 21.98 | 24.91 | 27.90 | 29.58 | 31.45 |
| 5. Gross domestic savings (N billion) | 14.07 | 16.29 | 18.24 | 22.91 | 24.67 | 27.35 |
| 6. Gross domestic savings as % of GDP | 15.7 | 17.4 | 18.6 | 22.38 | 23.0 | 24.23 |
| 7. Current account balance (N billion) | −5.389 | −5.749 | −6.341 | −6.528 | −5.842 | −5.449 |
| 8. Current account balance as % of GDP | −6.0 | −6.1 | −6.5 | −6.4 | −5.5 | −4.8 |
| 9. Fiscal deficits (N bil.) | −14.52 | −15.69 | −12.02 | −11.39 | −10.21 | −8.69 |
| 10. Fiscal deficits as % of GDP | −16.19 | −16.74 | −12.27 | −11.13 | −9.54 | −7.70 |
| 11. Total external debt (U.S.$ billion) | 30.61 | 31.54 | 32.73 | 34.36 | 35.93 | 37.45 |

A comparison of this picture with the savings trend reveals how serious the savings gap can be. Total domestic savings of N 20.17 billion level at the end of 1990 are expected to jump to almost N 28 billion in 1993 and N 31.5 billion in 1995. Two problems are identifiable from this scenario. First, the required investment level is higher than the saving capacity of the economy. Second, the savings rate has to improve considerably. The ongoing economic reform with an attendant resumption of growth in the medium term may provide an environment conducive for this achievement.

The fiscal constraint puts its own pressure on the evolution of the economy. Resources for public expenditures for the next six years are not projected to increase markedly. Partly because of the inability of the government to mobilize enough revenue for investment, it may have to continue to rely on deficit financing. The fiscal deficit as a percentage of GDP is projected to be well above 10 % between 1990 and 1994. Given the economic structure as it is now, it will be difficult to get this proportion reduced to a 4 % target level as envisaged in the IMF/World Bank-supervised structural adjustment documents.

On a comparative basis, the size of the fiscal deficit was relatively high in the 1980s, reaching 14.9 % in 1984. The major causal factor remains excessive and unsustainable government expenditure programs in the face of dwindling revenue. The options that have been used to finance the deficit include running down public sector accumulated cash balances, net borrowing from the banking system, issuing of new currency or money creation by the Central Bank, net borrowing from abroad, and drawing down of foreign assets. The effect of running such a high deficit, especially in terms of compounding the inflationary spiral, should not be underestimated. There is an urgent need for the public sector to introduce measures that will significantly improve revenue mobilization. More efficient investment project selection and appraisal is expected to follow from the policy reforms.

Informing the projections above is a set of assumptions that the agricultural sector will grow much more rapidly than the rest of the economy, that the diversification of the Nigerian export structure is not achievable in the medium run, that the structural adjustment program will continue to be implemented tenaciously, and that the external environment will be conducive enough to promote growth. As the emphasis of the Nigerian government is now on agriculture, the sector is expected to contribute in no small way to transforming the economy. There is likelihood that the contribution of agriculture to GDP would rise gradually from 30 % in 1989 to about 34 % in 1995.

Without a boost from oil, the agricultural sector which will once again determine the overall growth rate. Based on the priority now being given to the development of the sector, in particular the production of food and export crops as well as raw materials for agro-industries, it may be expected that the country will eventually reverse its deficit in food products and restructure the industrial set-up to be based on domestic raw materials and intermediate goods. The success of the reform program will depend to a large extent on the speed at which the agricultural and manufacturing sectors are rehabilitated.

The medium term outlook indicates that the share of manufacturing could increase from almost 10 % in 1988 to 13.5 % by the end of 1995. This growth may be justified on the grounds that first, a greater use of local resource inputs by the sector will emerge; second, the commanding heights of the sector such as the liquified natural gas project, iron and steel as well as petrochemical complexes would have come on stream; and given appropriate incentives and policy backing, the sector has potential to produce for the West African export market.

The projections reported in table 12.11 can be usefully compared with the result of a similar exercise undertaken by the World Bank (1987). The World Bank used an extended version of its standard macroeconomic projection (RMSM) model that was adjusted for the specific characteristics of the Nigerian economy in analyzing development through 1995. These projections are presented in table 12.12.

The difference in the estimated GDP values of the two projections is marginal, predicated on different perceptions about the likely growth rate. While the World Bank presumed a 3.9 % average growth rate in the medium term, the Growth Exercise (hereafter GE) model worked on a 4.5 % growth benchmark. Starting almost around the same GDP level in 1990 (N 89.68 and N 89.15 billion for the GE study and the Bank respectively), the growth trajectory assumes corresponding values of N 112.87 and N 107.94 billion respectively in 1995. The divergence between the two projections with respect to gross domestic investment and savings is, however, quite large.

First on gross domestic investment: The World Bank's projection takes off from N 7.67 billion in 1990 to N 9.28 billion at the end of 1995. It is questionable whether this level of investment, in the medium term, is sufficient to generate enough growth to achieve the target rate of almost 4 % 'hat is envisaged. The inadequacy of this trend becomes more glaring when it is compared to the past level.

**Table 12.12**
World bank's projected values of selected macroeconomic indicators for Nigeria

| Macro-indicators | 1990 | 1991 | 1992 | 1993 | 1994 | 1995 |
|---|---|---|---|---|---|---|
| 1. GDP (at 1984 market prices, N billion) | 89.15 | 92.63 | 96.24 | 99.99 | 103.89 | 107.94 |
| 2. Gross domestic investment (N billion) | 7.67 | 7.97 | 8.28 | 8.60 | 8.93 | 9.28 |
| 3. Gross national savings (N billion) | 12.66 | 13.15 | 13.67 | 14.20 | 14.75 | 15.33 |
| 4. Current account balance (N billion) | −17.39 | −12.01 | −8.58 | −4.21 | −1.17 | −5.30 |
| 5. Current account balance as % of GDP | −19.51 | −12.97 | −8.92 | −4.21 | −1.13 | −4.91 |
| 6. Total external debt outstanding (U.S.$billion) | 28.4 | — | 29.0 | — | — | 29.2 |

Source: Computed from World Bank (1987).

The GE model places premium on the investment-growth linkage and therefore takes cognizance of the investment quantum that can promote sustainable growth. For a 4.5 % growth target to be achievable, it projects an investment volume that ranges between N 18 billion in 1990 to almost N 36 billion by the end of 1995. Comparatively, this represents about 26 % on the average when investment is taken as a proportion of GDP over the period as opposed to a corresponding value of 8.6% derived from the World Bank's projections.

A comparison of the two different savings trends tends to show another underestimation of the World Bank's projections. Whereas the GE assumes a savings ratio of about 20 %, the World Bank's ratio is on the low side— just 6.2 %. Thus, when these savings trends are compared to the investment streams, it can be deduced that, given the World Bank's position, available savings will be more than sufficient to finance the required investment level and consequently external savings may not be necessary after all.

At the external front, although both projections agree that the current account balance will remain in deficit in the medium term, however, the magnitude of the deficit differs. The World Bank's projection started on a high N 17.4 billion deficit in 1990 and this thereafter declines dramatically on a consistent basis until it hits N 1.2 billion level in 1994. It shoots up again to N 5.3 billion in 1995. Viewed from the GE position, the current account deficits hovers around N 5 to N 6 billion throughout the period.

The generated external debt values by the two projections also exhibits wide divergences. The GE estimates that the debt level will increase from U.S. $30.61 billion in 1990 to U.S. $34.4 billion in 1993 and further up to almost U.S. $37.5 billion by the end of 1995. The corresponding trend projected by the World Bank presents a debt level of $28.4 billion in 1990, which then increases marginally to $29 billion in both 1992 and 1995. This debt level and trend are unrealistic; the actual total debt level by mid-1989 was estimated at about $30 billion. Given the structure and prospects of the Nigerian economy as discussed in this paper, the expectation is that the debt level would continue to growth at a rate that is higher than that envisaged by the Bank.

Taken together, while the World Bank's projections are based on a lower target rate than that of our growth exercise, the explicit three-gap analytical framework of the latter permits more realistic estimates of investment, saving, and financing needs of the Nigerian economy over the medium term.

### References

Bangura, Yusuf (1987). "IMF/World Bank Conditionality and Nigeria's Structural Adjustment Program." (Mimeo).

Betrand, T., and Robertson, J. (1981). "The Structure of Industrial Incentives in Nigeria." World Bank Report on Nigeria.

Central Bank of Nigeria (CBN, 1988). *Annual Report and Statements of Account.* Lagos: CBN.

Federal Government of Nigeria (FGN 1967). *First National Development Plan.* Lagos: Government Printer.

Federal Government of Nigeria (FGN 1970). *Second National Development Plan.* Lagos: Government Printer.

Federal Government of Nigeria (FGN 1975). *Third National Development Plan.* Lagos: Government Printer.

Federal Government of Nigeria (FGN 1980). *Fourth National Development Plan.* Lagos: Government Printer.

Federal Government of Nigeria (FGN 1986). *Structural Adjustment Programme.* Lagos: Government Printer.

Helleiner, G. K. (1966). *Peasant Agriculture. Government and Economic Growth in Nigeria.* Homewood, Illinois: Richard D. Irwin.

Oyejide, T. A. (1975). *Tariff Policy and Industrialization in Nigeria.* Ibadan: University Press.

Oyejide, T. A. (1986). "Sector Proportion and Growth in the Development of the Nigerian Economy." Paper prepared for Session 2 of the International Economic Association's Annual Conference, New Delhi, India.

Oyejide, T. A. (1987). "Resource Exports, Adjustment Problems and Liberalization Prospects in Nigeria." Paper prepared for the Ford Foundation Project on Trade Policy and the Developing World. University of Ibadan.

Oyejide, T. A. (1988). "Food Insecurity in Nigeria: Issues and Policy Options." Report to the World Bank.

Oyejide, T. A. and M. I. Raheem (1990). "Macro-Economic Constraints and Growth Programming: Empirical Evidence from Nigeria." Revised draft of the paper prepared for a Research Project on Medium Term Adjustment Strategy sponsored by WIDER, Helsinki.

Pickett, T. (1989). "Reflections on the Market and the State in Sub-Saharan Africa." *African Development Review*, Vol. 1., No. 3, (May): 419–445.

Raheem, M. I. (1988). "External Debt in the Development Process: A Macro-econometric Case Study of Nigeria," unpublished Ph.D. thesis, Department of Economics, University of Ibadan, Ibadan, Nigeria.

Tallroth, N. B. (1987). "Structural Adjustment in Nigeria." *Finance and Development*, 24: 327–330.

World Bank (1985). "Nigeria: Country Economic Memorandum." Washington, DC: World Bank.

World Bank (1987). "Nigeria: Country Economic Memorandum." Washington, DC: World Bank.

# 13    Zimbabwe

## Rob Davies and Jørn Rattsø

Zimbabwe's development problems and economic policies it has adopted
are like those in the rest of the sub-Saharan African region, where all
countries are vulnerable to shifting weather and world market conditions.
Debt service burdens and foreign exchange constraints are common concerns. The usual response has been to choose regimes involving regulation
of foreign trade and domestic prices. Compared to Tanzania and Zambia,
which have pursued broadly similar policies, the government in Harare has
not allowed the foreign exchange situation to get out of hand while
maintaining a comparable growth performance. In effect, Zimbabwe's disadvantage of lower capital inflows has been offset by greater macroeconomic stability. Presumably, this stable past can help provide a starting
point for future growth.

Zimbabwe achieved independence in 1980 after a long period of colonial
and settler rule. After 1965, the country was subject to international sanctions and a war economy. These 15 years are called the UDI period,
referring to the illegal Unilateral Declaration of Independence (UDI) by the
white government. The international community did not recognize the
settler regime and the United Nations introduced sanctions in 1968. The
guerrilla war intensified during the 1970s, partly related to the independence of Mozambique in 1975.

By African standards, Rhodesia in 1965 was rich. The settler state had
developed large-scale farming oriented toward exports, in particular tobacco. Industry, mining, and infrastructure had expanded based on copper
revenues from Zambia (through the Central African Federation, which also
included Malawi), foreign capital, and cheap black labor. Sanctions induced
a period of import substituting industrialization, leading to economic diversification Real GDP grew at an annual average of over 7 % between 1965
and 1974.

This growth was not sustained in the second half of the seventies. Real income per capita decreased by more than 20 % from 1974 to independence in 1980, with most of the burden falling on the black population. International conditions were unfavorable following the oil crisis. External problems motivated contractionary macroeconomic policies, which restored current account balance but also reduced capacity utilization and investment. The escalating war for independence disrupted internal and external transportation and the farming sector and placed strains on skilled labor supplies. From the point of view of this paper, the most significant fact was that the potential for import substitution was exhausted and no new engine for growth was found.

## 13.1 Macroeconomics after Independence

At independence, the new government faced challenges familiar in many developing countries: The distribution of income and wealth was highly skewed, unemployment and underemployment were growing, and basic social services did not reach the majority of the population. There were also specific problems of rehabilitating capacity and infrastructure after the war, and of a threatened shortage of skilled manpower due to a white exodus.

The government responded with a policy package aimed at both rapid growth and redistribution (Government of Zimbabwe 1981, 1983, 1986), but the deterioration of real income per capita observed from 1975 continued except for short episodes. Understanding the sources of this stagnation can give some insights when considering future growth prospects and policy options.

Economic developments in the 1980s generally have been periodized into a post-independence growth period (1980–81), followed by prolonged stagnation with short growth spurts in 1985 and 1988–89 (Green and Kadhani, 1986; Davies and Sanders, 1988). A longer view suggests a different interpretation: The economy has essentially been stagnant since 1975, arguably due to a crisis of the underlying import substituting model of development, adopted during UDI and not substantially altered by independence. The 1980–81 and 1985 growth spurts were just deviations from structural stagnation, caused by contingent factors (sanctions removal and/or exceptional rains) that relieved the growth constraints temporarily, but did not alter any underlying factors on a permanent basis. Reorientation towards export promotion in 1986–87 relaxed the foreign exchange

**Table 13.1**
ZIMBABWE performance indicators, 1975–87

|        | GDP   | GDP per head | Employment % of population | Investment % of GDP[a] | Inflation | Trade balance |
|--------|-------|--------------|----------------------------|------------------------|-----------|---------------|
| 1966–74 | 7.6  | 4.3          | na                         | 22.3                   | 4.6[b]    | na            |
| 1975   | 0.9   | −2.0         | 16.7                       | 27.3                   | 6.4       | −1.2          |
| 1976   | −0.9  | −3.7         | 15.9                       | 22.3                   | 9.3       | 3.9           |
| 1977   | −5.6  | −8.3         | 15.1                       | 18.1                   | 7.5       | 2.4           |
| 1978   | −2.5  | −5.3         | 14.3                       | 14.7                   | 10.1      | 3.5           |
| 1979   | 2.8   | −0.1         | 13.8                       | 14.3                   | 16.3      | −0.2          |
| 1980   | 11.4  | 8.2          | 13.7                       | 15.3                   | 9.5       | −3.0          |
| 1981   | 12.6  | 9.3          | 13.7                       | 18.6                   | 14.5      | −7.3          |
| 1982   | 3.2   | 0.3          | 13.7                       | 19.7                   | 13.6      | −5.9          |
| 1983   | 1.6   | −1.2         | 13.4                       | 18.8                   | 19.5      | −3.1          |
| 1984   | −1.8  | −4.5         | 13.0                       | 15.5                   | 3.4       | −4.1          |
| 1985   | 6.0   | 3.1          | 12.9                       | 11.9                   | 3.4       | 1.2           |
| 1986   | 2.6   | 0.2          | 12.8                       | 12.0                   | 15.2      | 4.3           |
| 1987   | −1.5  | −4.1         | 12.3                       | 11.6                   | 9.2       | 4.1           |
| 1988   | 7.0[c] | 4.2[c]      | 12.9[d]                    | 11.6                   | 12.0      | na            |
| 1989   | 5.4[c] | 2.6[c]      | 13.1[d]                    | na                     | 12.6      | na            |

Notes a. Gross fixed capital formation
b. Average for 1970–74
c. Preliminary figures based on World Bank data
d. Based on employment as of June
Sources: Central Statistical Office (1990), *National Income and Expenditure Report 1989*, Harare.
Central Statistical Office (1989), *Quarterly Digest of Statistics*, June, Harare.

constraint, but it is at present too early to draw definite conclusions about future prospects.

The existence of a structural crisis is suggested by, among other things, stagnant formal employment and no growth in real income per capita. The performance indicators shown in table 13.1 suggest that the decade of high growth prior to 1975 was achieved on the basis of existing excess capacity and stimulated by relative autarchy. Sustaining these rates would have required investment (to increase capacity, to refurbish existing plant, and for technical progress). But investment was limited, before independence, by the capacity to import capital goods and lack of public projects, as well as pessimistic expectations. After independence, better terms of trade (caused by sanctions removal) and potential foreign assistance raised import limits. Structural import-dependence of production and investment remained. Table 13.1 documents the decline in investment measured in 1980 prices.

### 13.1.1   Growth Patterns

The economy has not shown balanced growth between productive sectors, reflecting different responses to shocks and policies: Agriculture has been fluctuating around a slow growth path, construction and services have contracted, and mining and manufacturing have shown stagnation. Only public administration, education, and health services have been steadily increasing at a real rate of about 7 % annually.

The performance of agriculture is closely linked to rainfall. Drought from 1982 to 1984 help explain slow overall growth. Drought cycles have economy-wide effects, even though the share of agriculture in GDP is below 15 %. The sector's income generation of the masses, industrial processing of agricultural raw materials, and agro-exports are key linkages to the rest of the economy.

There has been a shift in the balance between commercial and peasant agriculture, with the share of the latter in marketed output rising from 6 % in 1980 to 21 % by 1985. Although higher sales probably reflect more output, there is evidence that this increase has been concentrated in a small number of households and that rural differentiation is increasing.

The contracting and stagnating sectors point to other factors as well. Declining investment after the first boom strongly affected the construction industry. Reduced activity of services has its counterpart in the decline of private consumption. The stagnation of mining and manufacturing is related both to import compression and the fall in investment.

### 13.1.2   The Policy Regime

The government has chosen direct regulation of prices, wages, and foreign trade to ensure macroeconomic stability. The focus on controls may have drawn attention away from structural adjustments needed to stimulate growth. Import rationing has held down the trade deficit, but at a low level of economic activity. Wage and price controls have constrained relative price movements and have hidden underlying inflationary pressure from the fiscal imbalance.

Fiscal performance has reflected the government's ambitions to build up social services. Total current disbursements of general government rose from 18.2 % of GDP in 1975 to 30.6 % by 1978, because of the war.

Substitution within expenditures allowed rapid social service expansion after independence without increasing overall disbursements dramatically: By 1983 they stood at 29.3 % of GDP, but 1984 saw a sharp jump to 36.6 % as the government was unable to restrict defense expenditure further in the face of South African destabilization. The commitment to social services is reflected in the fact that the share of education and health rose from 20.6 % of total disbursements in 1979 to 41.6 % in 1982; since then it has fluctuated around 40 %.

Revenues have been mobilized, but with increasing reliance on inflation. Total revenue of local and central government rose from 30.5 % of GDP in 1979 to 43.5 % in 1985. This growth relied increasingly on indirect taxes (from 30.2 % of revenue in 1979 to 39.1 % in 1985), and particularly customs duties. Income tax on individuals also has increased, particularly relative to company taxes, mainly because of inflation.

The resulting public deficit of about 10 % of GDP has affected the economy in two ways. First, the financial system has been forced to accept long-term government debt and there has been upward pressure on the interest rate. It is a puzzle that the deficit has not produced more inflation. Price controls and the failure of official price indices to include transactions on the parallel market may be part of the answer. In addition, the private savings rate has risen dramatically.

Second, the fiscal situation has motivated the government to reduce public investment. Fixed capital formation in the public sector nearly tripled in real terms between 1980 and 1983 (including social investment, infrastructure, and productive investment by parastatals). The deterioration of public finances during 1983 forced retrenchment in these programs.

The fiscal situation led gross public debt of central government to rise from $1.5 billion in 1979 to $8.6 billion in 1989. Because of financial sanctions, Zimbabwe was underborrowed at independence, with a total external debt of 16.4 % of GDP. Initially the government was willing to borrow heavily abroad: The external share of total central government borrowing rose from 17 % in 1980 to 85.5 % in 1982. Thereafter, concern about debt service implications induced a switch to the domestic market. Since 1982, the foreign share has never been higher than 50.5 %, and was 30.3 % in 1988. Government operations largely determine Zimbabwe's overall debt profile. Total outstanding external debt, which had risen to 54 % of GDP by 1984, stood at 49.6 % in 1988. The debt service ratio peaked at 33.3 % in 1987; in 1988 it was 27.5 %.

In dealing with the current account deficit, the government has preferred to compress imports rather than run arrears on debt service. The system of direct management of trade was inherited from the UDI period under sanctions. Foreign exchange allocation committees follow rules that tend to favor established users. For new customers and investment projects the guidelines give priority to the generation or saving of foreign exchange. The main post-independence modifications have been the introduction of commodity import programs (funded by bilateral donors) and incentives for exporters, both providing alternative channels of access to foreign exchange (Davies, 1989). Import quotas have been used as a macroeconomic instrument to control the current account, with their protective effects being an incidental by-product.

The government also inherited extensive price controls, initially introduced as a means to restrain inflation in an oligopolistic market under trade restrictions. In essence they allow mark-ups on material costs to be maintained; however, the bureaucratic delays in granting permission for increases have led to periodic profit squeezes. In 1987 there was an official price freeze. It was effective mainly with regard to large producers' wholesale prices, which were easily monitored; Retailers were less affected. Some undesirable changes in relative prices were thus probably induced. The history of inflation and relative prices is discussed by Chhibber et al. (1989).

Shortly after independence, the government introduced a system of national minimum wages, used until 1982 to raise wages for low-paid workers. Since then the legislation has been applied, overtly in some periods, to control wage increases. The price freeze in 1987 was coupled with a wage and salary freeze, eroding the gains in real wages made before 1983.

### 13.1.3 Foreign Trade

Compared to other countries in the region, Zimbabwe's exports are diversified among agricultural, mining, and manufacturing goods. Important items are tobacco, cotton lint, asbestos, gold and processed minerals such as ferro-chrome and nickel metal. Because about 80 % of the exports are raw materials, the economy is subject to fluctuations in its terms of trade.

South Africa is the largest trading partner, representing 15 % of exports. Sub-Saharan Africa (SSA) takes about the same share. The greatest part thus goes to industrialized countries, mainly in Europe but also the United States and Japan. There has been a shift from South Africa since independence. Stagnation in the OECD area has influenced demand and price conditions.

**Table 13.2**
Foreign trade indices

|      | Import volume | Export volume | Import unit value | Export unit value | Net barter terms of trade | Real exchange rate |
|------|---------------|---------------|-------------------|-------------------|---------------------------|--------------------|
| 1974 | 125 | 115 | 44  | 53  | 122 |     |
| 1975 | 120 | 107 | 48  | 57  | 118 |     |
| 1976 | 87  | 108 | 54  | 59  | 109 |     |
| 1977 | 81  | 102 | 60  | 62  | 103 |     |
| 1978 | 74  | 107 | 68  | 66  | 96  |     |
| 1979 | 73  | 105 | 93  | 76  | 81  |     |
| 1980 | 100 | 100 | 100 | 100 | 100 | 100 |
| 1981 | 124 | 95  | 100 | 111 | 111 | 104 |
| 1982 | 133 | 98  | 99  | 107 | 108 | 103 |
| 1983 | 112 | 102 | 116 | 121 | 104 | 94  |
| 1984 | 111 | 100 | 131 | 158 | 121 | 95  |
| 1985 | 97  | 96  | 153 | 189 | 123 | 83  |
| 1986 | 118 | 119 | 160 | 192 | 120 | 79  |
| 1987 | 122 | 128 | 183 | 194 | 106 | 78  |

Sources: Central Statistical Office (1989), *Quarterly Digest of Statistics,* Harare: Davies.

Export volumes have been constant between 1980 and 1985 as shown in table 13.2 (the upswing in 1986 was related to gold). The overall performance masks varied results at the commodity level. Exports of tobacco and cotton had a steady rise in value terms, while most industrial exports were stagnant. Volumes of asbestos and ferro-chrome have fallen over time. Supply constraints due to lack of imported intermediates seem to be the main explanation.

Exports are not determined by external factors alone. Profitability of export production as determined by the exchange rate and domestic costs plays a role. Exports from commercial farming, notably tobacco and cotton, respond to supply conditions in agriculture. Production in mining and other raw materials is affected by the availability of imported inputs, rehabilitation, and investment. Domestic demand conditions affect foreign sales of maize, as well as some manufactured goods.

The exchange rate is determined through a managed float, with reference to a trade-weighted basket of currencies. The authorities change the weights periodically and since 1982 have followed a policy of not allowing the dollar to appreciate in real terms. Movements in the foreign terms of trade have not been unfavorable for Zimbabwe in the 1980s.

Imported intermediate and capital goods account for most of the import bill. South Africa, the major source of imported manufactured goods, supplies more than 20 % of the imports while SSA provides less than 10 %. The United Kingdom, West Germany, and the United States are the main suppliers from outside Africa. Imports of consumer goods (electronics, cars, clothing, etc.) have been as low as 2 to 3% of imports. Needless to say, the underlying demand is high.

The dependence on imported machinery, equipment, spare parts, fuels, and other intermediate imports explains the contractionary effect of import compression. Capacity utilization of existing industries is necessarily hurt by reductions in the availability of foreign inputs. Over years of relative autarchy, spells of import compression have reduced the scope for further cuts which will not affect production or investment levels.

### 13.1.4  Macroeconomic Performance

Between 1975 and 1979 public sector savings declined from 6.9 % to −3.3 % of GDP, due entirely to central government spending related to the war. Table 13.3 describes the development of the savings-investment

**Table 13.3**
Investment-savings balances (percent of GDP)

|      | Investment | | | | Savings | | | Savings surplus | |
|------|-----------------|----------------|---------------|-------|----------------|--------|----------------------|----------------|--------|
|      | Private GFCF | Public GFCF | Stock Inc. | Total | Private | Public | Foreign[a] | Private | Public |
| 1975 | 13.7 | 9.7 | 3.6 | 27.0 | 15.8 | 6.9 | 4.4 | 2.1 | −2.8 |
| 1976 | 11.2 | 8.5 | −0.9 | 18.8 | 14.5 | 4.7 | −0.3 | 3.3 | −3.8 |
| 1977 | 10.1 | 7.1 | 1.9 | 19.1 | 16.6 | 2.1 | 0.4 | 6.5 | −5.0 |
| 1978 | 8.4 | 6.1 | −2.5 | 12.0 | 16.2 | −3.3 | 2.6 | 4.1 | −8.1 |
| 1979 | 9.2 | 4.8 | −1.3 | 12.7 | 13.3 | −3.3 | 2.6 | 4.1 | −8.1 |
| 1980 | 10.6 | 4.7 | 3.5 | 18.8 | 19.7 | −5.4 | 4.6 | 9.1 | −10.1 |
| 1981 | 13.4 | 5.3 | 4.4 | 23.1 | 12.7 | 0.5 | 9.9 | −0.7 | −4.8 |
| 1982 | 10.1 | 9.9 | 1.2 | 21.2 | 12.0 | −1.1 | 10.3 | 1.9 | −8.8 |
| 1983 | 8.0 | 11.6 | −3.7 | 15.9 | 5.1 | 3.6 | 7.2 | −2.9 | −8.0 |
| 1984 | 8.7 | 9.8 | 0.4 | 18.9 | 17.7 | −0.4 | 1.6 | 9.0 | −10.2 |
| 1985 | 6.7 | 9.5 | 4.9 | 21.3 | 23.3 | −4.3 | 2.3 | 15.6 | −13.8 |
| 1986 | 15.8 | 15.8 | 3.6 | 19.4 | 22.0 | −2.6 | −2.0 | na | na |
| 1987 | na | na | na | 19.1 | na | na | na | na | na |

a. Defined as deficit on current transactions with the rest of the world.
Source: CSO, *National Income and Expenditure Report* update, various years.

balance in current prices. Strict import controls meant that the current account balance did not deteriorate significantly; public sector investment was reduced and private sector investment fell, allowing a private sector savings surplus to release resources to accommodate the public sector shortfall. Private investment fell due to a combination of weak expectations and capital goods import controls.

The post-independence boom saw private sector investment rise as removal of sanctions and relaxation of controls reduced foreign exchange constraints. Although private sector savings rose, the public sector savings deficit widened, with foreign savings filling the gap. A large current account deficit (4.6 % of GDP) materialized and worsened over the next two years. The fiscal deficit was due to expanded social expenditures.

After 1983, the growing fiscal and declining trade deficits had serious macroeconomic consequences. Because foreign savings fell to zero (or even an outflow), high public dissavings required a large private savings surplus. This was achieved by increased savings and reduced private investment. The private savings share rose above 20 % of GDP in 1985, as consumption fell by 20 % in real terms in response to import compression. Reduced access to consumer durable and other imports led the upper income classes to store money in the financial system. The balance achieved is fragile: Improvement in the foreign exchange situation or a more liberal trade regime could start up a consumption boom.

The share of gross fixed capital formation in the GDP has been strongly reduced in constant prices, as shown in table 13.1. The fall in the investment share in current prices is much less, because of the increased relative price of capital goods due to devaluation. Most of the reduction is seen in the public civil works sector. The development of private investment in the past few years is not yet well documented.

## 13.2   Growth Constraints

The 1980s policy package held the capacity utilization rate in the region of 80 to 90%. The fall in the investment share of GDP since the 1980–81 boom reduced the growth of potential output. As just described, investment has been constrained by, first, the foreign exchange bottleneck and, second, the fiscal balance.

In the short run, investment is affected by capacity utilization, which is positively linked to imports of intermediate goods. There are three key channels: First, given import capacity, higher imports of intermediates crowd out imports of investment goods and negatively affect growth.

Second, the increase in capacity utilization associated with increased intermediate imports stimulates investment demand. Finally, higher capacity use improves the fiscal balance, allowing greater public investment, which crowds in private capital formation.

The three-gap model developed by Bacha (1989) and Taylor (1991) serves as an analytical framework to understand the growth constraints. We have modified the gap model to take into account the importance of intermediate imports for capacity utilization (Davies and Rattsø, 1989, 1990). Theoretical macroeconomic models of import compression have been developed to support the analysis, for example, Rattsø (1989a) and (1989b), but have not been empirically tested. The discussion here concentrates on adjustment mechanisms to understand medium-run policy alternatives.

The first and third channels just described summarize the foreign exchange and fiscal gaps, respectively. (The overall saving-investment balance is the third gap.) The former is related to stagnant export earnings in the first years after independence, when policies were oriented towards domestic challenges. Zimbabwe's traditional exports are largely produced for stagnating markets, and there have not been sufficient incentives to move into new areas. At the same time, the government's independent economic policy has not drawn support and participation of multilateral agencies, thereby limiting net transfers from the rest of the world.

Most developing countries experience limited foreign exchange inflows compared to import demands for production inputs, investment projects, and consumption. Many try to avoid the disadvantages of the standard remedies, expenditure reduction, and expenditure switching, by imposing quantitative restrictions. In Zimbabwe's case, import compression has kept foreign debt at manageable levels, but has set up a hard choice between imports of intermediates and investment goods. The foreign exchange balance thus defines a negative relation between capacity utilization and growth.

There is another relationship between capacity utilization and growth defined through the fiscal balance, which affects economic growth via the level of public investment. Reduced public investment implies lower capital formation overall, both because of its direct impact and the effect of observed complementarity between public and private projects.

Current government savings respond endogenously to economic events. Tax revenues and public enterprise profits vary with the level of national economic activity. Expenditure items are also affected by fluctuations; in particular subsidies tend to increase during downswings. It follows that government savings are positively related to capacity utilization.

The fiscal balance defines a constraint to growth because the ratio of public debt to GDP cannot grow indefinitely. Given an implied limit to the current public deficit as a share of GDP, public investment can only increase with capacity utilization that improves the fiscal position. In Zimbabwe, public investment has been squeezed between expanding current expenditure and stagnating tax revenues, as the government sought to avoid unmanageable deficits.

Our calculation of the growth constraints in Zimbabwe assumes a trend growth rate of potential output of 3.5 %, the result of an investment share (of potential output) of about 18 % and a capital-output ratio of 5. A constant share of imports in investment of about 1/3 is assumed. Public investment accounts for more than half total investment. The capacity utilization rate is 88 % in the base year 1986.

Import compression tightly limits growth. If imports of intermediates are increased by 1 % of potential output, the growth rate is reduced by almost 0.5 percentage point along the foreign exchange restriction. However, such an increase in imported intermediates will relax the fiscal constraint via higher capacity utilization. The rise in fiscal savings allows for higher public investment, increasing the growth rate by more than 0.5 percentage point. If the growth rate is to be raised above 3.5 % per year, policy intervention must bring all the constraints into consistency.

The First National Development Plan 1986—90 (Government of Zimbabwe, 1986) aimed for a growth rate of 5 % per year. Even with capital productivity growth of 3 % per year, the investment share of potential GDP must increase by close to 6 % to reach that target. The growth projections of Green and Kadhani (1986) also aim at 5 % output growth, but assume that half of it can be achieved through increased capacity utilization. It is optimistic to hope for a capacity utilization rate well above 90 % without macroeconomic surprises. Except for that, their results are similar to ours.

Higher public investment is needed to increase the overall level. The required increase can be calculated from the fiscal gap, and the result comes out at about 3.5 % of potential output. The remaining 2.5 % of extra private investment is crowded in by public investment and higher activity.

The constraints show that other adjustments are also needed to support the higher growth rate. Public savings have to increase to finance the higher public investment when the ratio of public sector borrowing to potential output is assumed to stay constant. About 3 % of potential GDP must be mobilized by fiscal policies. Simultaneously, the foreign exchange balance must adjust to permit higher imports of capital goods. The current account deficit has to increase by about 2 % of potential output.

Although it is optimistic to expect exports to grow faster than potential output under the present international conditions, export-oriented policies may help improve performance. But even if the export share of potential output rises by 1 % during the period, some imports still must be saved to accommodate investment. Policies to reduce import coefficients seem necessary to support 5 % economic growth.

## 13.3 Structural Adjustment

The foregoing analysis identifies the public sector deficit and the foreign exchange constraint as key restrictions on growth. Higher public investment financed by government savings is necessary to get growth going; the required imports of capital goods must be paid for by higher exports or a reduction in intermediate imports. The final macroeconomic complication is that if the overall savings-investment balance and a fixed public deficit share of GDP are to be respected, then forced private and public savings seem to be required. The latter can be understood as active government involvement to implement the public deficit target.

Empirical and theoretical understanding of the macroeconomic mechanisms that force private saving to equilibrium in Zimbabwe are weak. A common explanation involves the import compression policy—it has reduced private investment and stimulated saving through rationing of imported consumption goods. The first factor implies that it may be hard to achieve an investment share above 20 % even if public investments go up significantly. The other factor says that private savings are sensitive to the foreign trade regime.

We think that forced savings through inflation also plays a role. High profits in protected, domestically oriented industries are the main source of the savings buildup. There is also an inflation tax factor affecting the public finances. This savings mechanism is likely to be more important with a growth-oriented program increasing investments. Reforms of the trade regime that has held down consumption will increase the burden of inflationary adjustment even more.

The growth aspects of structural adjustment concern the coefficients of the gap model. The analysis of the preceding section made several assumptions about underlying parameters. Two are especially important for the discussion of policy alternatives. First, import coefficients—particularly of investment—were assumed to be fixed. Reducing these was seen to be necessary to support a growth rate above 5 %, by relaxing the foreign exchange constraint. Second, the capital-output ratio was assumed constant. If capital productivity is improved, the investment requirements of a given growth rate are reduced. Structural adjustment must contribute to reduced import dependence and improved productivity.

The import dependency issue is complex in an economy that long has regulated imports. On the one hand, industry oriented toward the domestic market has been built up under a protected shelter. The regulations have increased the relative price of importables and stimulated a transfer of resources into this sector. On the other hand, the same industries are strongly dependent on imported inputs and spare parts. If structural adjustment is to reduce import dependency, the protected sector must restructure. Resources must be transferred to the traded sector, that is, industries that can compete at world market standards at home and abroad.

Import dependency is related to productivity growth, which has almost certainly been reduced by the protected domestic atmosphere. The foreign exchange allocation system that has given intermediate inputs priority has at the same time restricted structural change that could have increased their productivity. Structural adjustment is first and for all about allowing such structural changes to happen.

### 13.4  Policy Alternatives

Current debate in Zimbabwe focuses on two areas in which policy choices must be made: the direct allocation of foreign exchange (and more generally the direct control of price and wage formation) and public sector finances. The first issue is at the center of international debate over structural adjustment programs. The public deficit is seen as being a crucial determinant of the pace of liberalization. The growth analysis above suggests it is important in revitalizing growth.

Three alternative strategies are discussed below. Direct controls can be used to defend the status quo (section 13.4.1) or to promote structural change (section 13.4.2). Alternatively, direct controls can be scrapped in a program of liberalizing domestic markets and foreign trade (section 13.4.3). Our evaluation concentrates on possible trade-offs between growth and stabilization.

Exogenous factors set the scene for growth in Zimbabwe, in particular weather conditions and international markets. In addition, political and economic relations within southern Africa, certainly in regard to South Africa, are of importance.

To begin with weather: Average annual rainfall is about 700 mm. The historical record shows variations between 400 mm and 1000 mm. Shifts may be dramatic from season to season and show sharp geographical variations within seasons. Because a robust rainfall forecasting model does not exist, the government cannot plan for a stable growth path. Strategies for handling future supply shocks must be developed.

The international environment determines the conditions for foreign trade and financing. The growth of export revenues is strongly influenced by economic growth in industrialized countries and by international commodity prices, but Zimbabwe did not maintain its share of the world market through the 1980s. The export response to recent incentive programs suggests that the loss may be gained back during the present decade. Global forecasts from the World Bank suggest that Zimbabwe will face roughly stable terms of trade.

### 13.4.1 Regulated Status Quo Regime

Although the need for reforms of some kind is widely recognized, it is possible that a combination of political stalemate, special interests, and bureaucratic inertia will prevent any substantial change from the current regime. This section discusses likely trends in these circumstances.

Continuation of import compression will not allow much improvement in the foreign exchange situation. Exports will not grow faster than the economy if more forceful incentives are not put in. Foreign borrowing opportunities will be restricted because of the failure to undertake policy reforms. The compression will hold back on the growth of imported investment goods, while the local construction and capital goods sectors will be constrained by lack of intermediate inputs. Growth of the supply of both foreign and domestically produced investment goods will be slow.

Public investment is not likely to increase as a share of GDP without reform of public finances. The fiscal deficit will continue to capture private savings that could otherwise flow into investment. Private investment will remain low—growing at about the overall growth rate—because of the lack of imported inputs, the low level of complementary public investment, and uncertainty regarding the politically determined conditions for business activity. Continuation of high private savings will depend upon continued low consumption and sustained profitability of protected firms, closing the circle back to import compression.

On the financial side, intermediaries will have to continue accommodating public borrowing. Up to now, government has avoided financing by money creation, and most of the borrowing has taken place in non-bank financial institutions. However, public debt as share of GDP is increasing, which will, in a no-growth context, make it increasingly difficult to borrow further.

Lack of substantial reforms will require continued reliance on direct controls of foreign exchange allocation, prices, and wages. Such interventions have been effective in promoting macroeconomic stability up to now. Even if the trade-off of growth for stability is accepted, however, it is not clear how long these measures will continue to function.

This precarious balance can be seriously disturbed by three factors. First, an expansion of investment together with higher public sector borrowing will put pressure on savings generation. Second, a fall in the private savings rate back to the pre-1984 level will give a strong demand injection to the economy. Third, a worsening of public finances with increased reliance on borrowing or inflation tax financing represents a problematic scenario.

If foreign exchange controls are held in place, and the scope for increased capacity utilization remains limited, demand injection from either increased investment or falling private savings will give an inflationary push. High inflation has several unfavorable effects: International competitiveness is hurt and income distributions shift against the poor. An inflationary spiral could be sparked, with claims for wage compensation and nominal depreciation of the currency fueling further price increases. Use of wage controls to prevent this has severe political implications. The pressures on the public finances will mean that the social wage currently provided by government will continue to erode, providing more pressure for wage increases.

The recent signals are that this scenario is unlikely in its starkest form. Some policy reforms have already occurred, and further, more far reaching ones are on the way. It is not, however, certain that the changes will happen soon enough to prevent at least some of the scenario from materializing. Moreover, it seems clear that government intends to continue substantial regulation of the economy; true-believing liberalizers might question whether even a reformed regulatory system is capable of delivering growth and macroeconomic stability.

### 13.4.2   Growth-Oriented Regulation Regime

It is possible that the current regulatory apparatus could be used in a more growth-oriented way. A possible package to do so would include the following ingredients:

1. Public investment could be increased by several percentage points of GDP, while reducing public consumption and transfers to hold the public deficit constant. The new public investments would be in infrastructure, stimulating exporting sectors in general, and more specifically agricultural production and the transport sector.

2. The volume of imports would have to increase and the allocation of foreign exchange would be reoriented towards export promotion. Higher imports of industrial intermediates and investment goods can be financed partly from higher export earnings and partly by import-related credits, so that foreign savings would rise. It is assumed that Zimbabwe would not face international credit rationing when such a policy package is presented.

3. Exports would be stimulated by reallocation of subsidies, by moderate nominal devaluation, by the reallocation of foreign exchange, and through new public investment reducing infrastructural bottlenecks.

4. Producer prices in agriculture would be increased to stimulate profitability. Consumer prices would have to be raised to defend the margins of the marketing authorities. Higher agricultural production should follow from the combination of increased prices and higher public investment in rural infrastructure and transportation.

In the short run this policy package should allow expansion due to agricultural response, increased capacity utilization of import-dependent industries, and increased exports. The growth bottlenecks associated with production capacities, foreign exchange revenues, and agricultural output are widened. The package's effect on private investment and productivity growth would be limited because of the uncertain conditions for business activity set by government and the foreign exchange allocation system.

Why does this program allow a more optimistic outlook than the previous one? In the "business as usual" case, expanded investment was constrained by lack of imports. In this case, it is assumed that increased import demand is accommodated by export expansion and foreign borrowing. In the previous case, the injection of demand by raising investment was problematic because it reduced the private savings surplus necessary to finance the public deficit. Here, the reduction in the private surplus is offset by a rise in foreign savings, permitted by external borrowing. To the extent that this is not possible, the public deficit has to be cut, especially current expenditures and *not* public investment, which would have a negative effect on private investment and growth.

The crucial element is the rise in foreign savings, which depends on the assumption that Zimbabwe would not face rationing in international credit markets. At present the country's credit rating is high; the constraint on foreign borrowing appears to have been self-imposed, rather than externally caused. If this assumption is wrong, the result of growth stimulation is likely to be inflation, with all the negative consequences described at the end of the previous section.

It is thus possible that growth can be stimulated through appropriate use of the current regulatory system. The parallels between such a program and the episode in 1980–81 are obvious. The higher excess capacity existing then allowed growth to take place at low levels of investment.

This parallel raises the question of the sustainability of growth induced by the current package. The difference would be the role that investment plays. The foreign savings generated in the earlier episode were channelled into current consumption to feed social programs. Under the proposed package, the government would have to channel its own expenditure into investment designed to relieve the bottlenecks on export expansion and allow private investment to grow as much as possible. Whether it has the political strength or desire to exercise this restraint is debatable.

There are many aspects of current policies that are similar to the package just sketched, and it reflects broadly what the authorities want to do: grow and keep control of the economy. The reforms to the foreign exchange system in the latter half of the 1980s provided greater incentives to exporters, which generated some response. The 1989–90 budget for the first time showed a small surplus of current revenue over current expenditure, so that there was a use of borrowing for investment proposed (although it is likely that supplementary estimates will change this). The government has made some efforts to encourage foreign investment, which is an alternative way of easing the external constraint. The reduction in debt servicing has provided space for this as well. Price controls have been relaxed, although in practice very ineffectually, and the government has made strong noises about allowing free collective bargaining over wages.

### 13.4.3  Growth-Oriented Liberalization Regime

Although Zimbabwe has had no formal structural adjustment agreement with the World Bank or the IMF, the question of liberalization had been at the forefront of policy debates over the past five years. A study to look at possible liberalization measures and their consequences, commissioned by the government under the stimulus of the World Bank, was completed at the end of 1988. It seems likely that some reforms that fall under the rubric of liberalization will definitely be introduced, but there is a great deal of speculation and uncertainty about what the precise contents and speed will be.

The liberalization alternative represents a regime shift since policy controls in important areas must be given up. It is put forward as a way of improving incentives for private investment and productivity growth. The regulation of foreign trade and domestic prices are the central targets of policy reforms.

It is likely that any liberalization package will include some or all of the following ingredients:

1. A shift in trade policy from quantitative restrictions to tariffs for the majority of imports. The tariff-based system is expected to generate short-run efficiency improvements and faster structural change. Alternative tariff policies can be chosen regarding the level and composition of tariffs and their development over time. Macroeconomic considerations and efficiency aspects may conflict.

2. The lifting of price controls for most consumer goods and services. This reform is intended to allow relative prices to adjust to market conditions and to stimulate resource reallocation to areas of shortage.

3. Allowing the wage structure to respond to labor market conditions. Minimum wages and labor regulations—especially restrictions on firing labor—are hot issues in this debate. Minimum wages in real terms are below what they were 10 years ago so that in themselves they are unlikely to be a problem for labor demand. Rather it is the inability to reduce the labor force in times of trouble that has induced employers not to expand it on the upswing.

4. Rearranging public finances similar to the growth-oriented regulation alternative. A shift from current government expenditures to public investment is a necessary component of the package.

Liberalization enthusiasts would include market-determined exchange rates and free movements of capital across national boarders. It seems unlikely, however, that (at least in the early stages of liberalization) the capital account will be included. There is a fear of capital flight, arising not simply from the usual reasons in a controlled economy but also because of Zimbabwe's potential regional instability arising from South Africa, and the historical concentration of local capital in the hands of whites, many of whom would still like to get it out.

The growth effect of the liberalization package is expected to flow from more competition and the opening up of new profit opportunities. Additional measures to stimulate investment would probably be necessary. A free transition to liberalization may discourage investment, through an impact on expectations (which is ambiguous) and a potential profit squeeze.

Domestically oriented industries are worried that they cannot live with international competition, and the scrapping of old facilities represents a short run contraction. Against this, firms recognize the need to refurbish existing facilities to make them technologically competitive. If liberalization is allowed to feed consumer import demand there may be a crowding out of investment goods. Finally, increased international competition can potentially squeeze profits of domestic market oriented firms in the short run, reducing a major source of investment finance. No sensible model can quantify the effects of the regime shift.

Liberalization is likely to bring the underlying stabilization problems of the economy to the surface. The inflation rate would be more responsive to macroeconomic imbalances under a less regulated regime. If controls are lifted and prices adjust, higher inflation would be hard to avoid without substantial fiscal contraction. Without an improbably fast output response, there would be demand-induced price jumps, which might feed into a spiral.

Faster nominal devaluation of the Zimbabwe dollar (or, if the tariff system replicates exactly the effects of the current quantitative trade controls, the cost implications of the tariff increase) would also induce cost inflation. In these circumstances, nominal wage formation is of increased importance to economic stability. Organized labor is weak; government has used labor legislation to set minimum wages with little reference to labor leaders. Nominal wages are therefore unlikely to keep pace with inflation, that is, real wages would fall.

The inflationary effect of increased investments with a continued high public deficit is a result of the necessary adjustment of savings. The inflation implies a shift in income distribution that generates more savings. The management of the public deficit has important consequences for the income distribution in this situation. If the government runs a high deficit, the inflationary effect would cut real wages and increase profits. A reduced deficit would favor wage earners by holding inflation in check. Liberalizing reforms to promote structural change and efficiency must be supported by active stabilization.

### 13.4.4   Consequences of Shocks

Alternative policy regimes are usually compared under the assumption of a stable environment. In the case of Zimbabwe, normal rainfall and trend development of world market conditions are assumed in the scenarios presented by the government and the World Bank. Experience shows that economic growth responds strongly to disturbances affecting agricultural production and the foreign exchange situation.

The contractionary effects of agricultural drought work though three main channels: price and income effects, import compression, and intermediate deliveries to other sectors. The composition of price and income reactions depends on the price regulations. When prices are controlled, the income effects may be quite strong. Reduced agricultural income leads to a contraction of consumption demand. Loss of earnings from agricultural exports tightens the foreign exchange constraint. Finally, the decline of production of raw materials reduces activity in manufacturing industries. The immediate contraction following a drought may be as much as 3 % to 5 % of GDP.

At present, the government balances the agricultural market by intervention in stocks, foreign trade, and possibly rationing. Running down stocks helps reduce the shortage of food in a drought year and improves the financial situation of the marketing boards. Foreign trade is used as an instrument of market regulation, adding to the foreign exchange burden. Imports of food in a drought year take up part of the import capacity. The government has run a destabilizing price policy in the past, reducing prices in drought years. The consequent demand reduction due to lower farm incomes has probably been the most important factor in the overall contraction besides the drought itself.

With liberalization, the terms of trade between agriculture and the rest of the economy would be allowed to go up with drought. Price changes would stabilize agricultural incomes, that is, contraction is offset at the cost of food inflation. The income distribution effects for the rest of the economy may induce a further fall in demand. If the immediate real wage loss is compensated by nominal wage adjustments, more inflation is fueled. This type of inflation is likely even if the public finances are well controlled.

Shifts in the foreign terms of trade affect the income of exporters and the current account. The income effect of a fall in key export prices induces reduced consumption demand and contraction in domestically oriented sectors. Different responses between regimes concern the current account. When foreign exchange allocation is administered, imports are adjusted to the fall in export earnings through rationing. Reduced intermediate imports decrease capacity utilization of import-dependent industries. When foreign trade is liberalized, lower export prices automatically generate a current account deficit, which must be financed or eliminated by government intervention.

When external shocks are permanent, the two regimes offer different conditions for restructuring. Under the regulated system, policymakers must make hard decisions on the reallocation of imports. In practice, they are seldom taken. Consequently import regulations tend to restrict structural change.

The liberalized regime hopes for market pressures to promote restructuring. Exchange rate adjustments are central to the story: Radical liberalizers recommend floating the exchange rate to guarantee efficient relative prices. Currency depreciation to give correct incentives has the possible disadvantage of increasing the inflation rate. Once more there is a tradeoff between efficiency and stabilization. Floating the exchange rate in an economy vulnerable to external shocks may confuse producers and start up inflationary pressures.

## References

Bacha, E. (1989). "A Three-Gap Model of Foreign Transfers and the GDP Growth Rate in Developing Countries." *Journal of Development Economics*, 32: 279–296.

Central Statistical Office (1990). *National Accounts*, (early release). February, Harare.

Chhibber, A. et al. (1989). "Inflation, Price Control and Fiscal Adjustment: the Case of Zimbabwe." (Mimeo), Public Economics Division, World Bank.

Davies, R. (1989). "Trade, Trade Management and Development in Zimbabwe." (Mimeo), Department of Economics, University of Zimbabwe.

Davies, R., and J. Rattsø (1990). "Restrictions to Economic Growth: Growth Programming for Zimbabwe." (Mimeo), University of Zimbabwe and University of Trondheim.

Davies, R., and D. Sanders (1988). "Adjustment Policies and the Welfare of Children in Zimbabwe, 1980–85," in A. Cornia, R. Jolly, and F. Stewart (eds.), *Adjustment with a Human Face*, Vol. 2. Oxford: Oxford University Press.

Government of Zimbabwe (1981). *Growth with Equity: A Policy Statement*. Harare.

Government of Zimbabwe (1983). *Transitional National Development Plan 1982/83–1984/85*, Vols. 1 and 2. Harare.

Government of Zimbabwe (1986). *First National Development Plan 1986–90*, Vol. 1. Harare.

Green, R., and X. Kadhani (1986). "Zimbabwe: Transition to Economic Crisis 1981–83: Retrospect and Prospect." *World Development*, 14: 1059–1083.

Rattsø, J. (1989a). "Comparison of Adjustment Mechanisms under Regulation and Liberalization Regimes: A Macroeconomic Model for Zimbabwe." (Mimeo), Institute of Economics, University of Trondheim.

Rattsø, J. (1989b). "Import Compression Macro Dynamics: Macroeconomic Analysis for Sub-Saharan Africa." (Mimeo), Institute of Economics, University of Trondheim.

Taylor, L. (1991). "Gap Disequilibria: Inflation, Investment, Saving and Foreign Exchange," in *Income Distribution, Inflation and Growth*. Cambridge, MA: MIT Press.

# 14

## Tanzania

### Benno J. Ndulu

Like many developing economies, Tanzania faces structural constraints that limit its potential growth in the long run and the efficacy of policy in the short and medium term. Key among the constraints are the low level of technology for its dominant rain-fed agriculture, weak and dependent openness, a fragile and immature institutional structure, and distorted markets. The lack of response of producing and consuming sectors to policy instruments in the short to medium term is partly explained by these structural rigidities.

It is important to distinguish between weakness of an economy, which can only be tackled via structural transformation, and maladaptation, which results from economic management undertaken. Although structural rigidities place the ultimate limits, maladaptation prevents an economy from realizing what is achievable in the medium term. Tanzania's development during the last three decades has been subject to both rigidities and maladaptation, especially after the mid-1970s.

Although structural constraints are considered, this paper focuses on maladaptation and its impacts. We first review Tanzania's development strategy during the first two decades and draws implications for sustainable growth. We then discuss responses adopted to close resource gaps in the post-1978 period. Finally, emerging issues for the future are analyzed, drawing heavily from the previous discussions.

## 14.1 Development during the First Two Decades

During the first two decades of independence (1961–81), Tanzania's development strategy concentrated on structural transformation in two main areas: infrastructure and human resources to raise productivity and absorptive capacity of the economy; and the industrial sector to support dynamic growth. In the first 15 years, investment was concentrated on infrastructure, geared towards providing transportation links for integrating the economy, increased commercialization of agriculture, and facilitation of industrial production. The share of fixed capital formation going to economic infrastructure (transport, water and power) averaged 48.9 % during 1966–75 (Ndulu, 1985). Most of this investment was implemented through capital intensive turn-key projects to circumvent the paucity of skills.

After the mid-1970s, concentration switched to industrialization. Two changes were notable in this effort. First, the expansion of industrial capacity received a tremendous boost, increasing its share of total investment from an average of 14 % during 1964–74 to 33.5 % between 1975 and 1982. Second, emphasis shifted from simple import substitution to what was termed Basic Industrialization. The objectives were to link production to the domestic resource base and to domestic demand—predominantly for mass-consumed goods. Industrial expansion concentrated in the subsectors producing basic needs, processing of agricultural and livestock products, and intermediate and capital goods (Wangwe, 1983). The strategy implied deepening import substitution and raising the level of interdependence within the economy.

Expansion of capacity to provide social services during 1964–75 did not involve much fixed capital formation, its share of the total averaging 3.1 %. The structure of expenditure within the sector was shifted in favor of basic services. Spending on primary education and literacy programs rose from 9 % to 29 % of the education budget, the rural health share increased from 30 % to 49 % of the health budget, and the rural water share increased from 19 % to 45 %. The investment share of social services increased during 1976–80 to 5.9 %, dominated by an increase in educational capital expenditure needed to implement universal primary education (Ndulu, 1985).

Throughout the first two decades, direct investment in agriculture was deemphasized. During 1964–75 the share of investment into agriculture declined by 42 %. In real terms fixed capital formation in this sector fell by 38 % between 1976 and 1980. The bulk of government investment went into expansion of state farms, sugar cane plantations, and marketing authorities. Supportive services to small holders received little attention.

Incentives at both the macroeconomic and sectoral levels were geared toward the chosen strategy. The tariff structure, quantitative restrictions, and exchange rate policy enforced protection for the industrial sector. Agricultural taxation, both direct and indirect (via protection of the industrial sector), led to massive resource outflows, leaving little available for growth of the very sector that was key to resource generation. Low inter-

**Table 14.1**
Growth of production, investment and external trade (percent)

|                              | 1965–73 | 1973–80 | 1980–87 | 1980–84 | 1984–88 |
|------------------------------|---------|---------|---------|---------|---------|
| GDP (real)                   | 4.8     | 2.3     | 1.7     | 0.7     | 3.3     |
| GDP per capita               | 1.6     | −1.0    | −1.8    | −2.8    | −0.2    |
| Agriculture                  | 3.1     | 0.2     | 3.8     | 2.6     | 5.2     |
| Manufacturing                | 8.7     | 2.6     | −3.5    | −5.1    | 0.9     |
| Services                     | 6.9     | 5.5     | 0.8     |         |         |
| Gross domestic investments[a]| 9.6     | 3.8     | −5.6    |         |         |
| Exports (real)               | 4.2     | −5.6    | −7.4    |         |         |
| Imports (real)               | 4.6     | −0.2    | −0.5    |         |         |
| Implicit GDP deflator        | 3.4     | 15.4    | 24.9    |         |         |
| CPI[b]                       | 6.6     | 14.2    | 30.5    | 29.6    | 31.7    |

Notes: a. Gross domestic investment outlays on additions to fixed assets plus net changes in the level of inventories. It is important to note that depreciation is excluded and hence the definition used by the Bank is "non-conventional gross."
b. Consumer price index, national from 1969.
Source: World Bank (1989), *Sub-Saharan Africa: From Crisis to Sustainable Growth*, Appendices; URT, *Economic Survey*, various issues.

est rates and allocation of investible resources favored development of industry and within agriculture, the state sector.

Four problems were implicit in the strategy. First, neglect of agriculture (especially small holders), led the economy into a financial-foreign exchange bottleneck. The import dependence of the industrial sector required hard currency both for its continued expansion and operation of installed capacity. Coupled with institutional obstacles to exporting, industry itself remained a large net importer. Agricultural growth declined from 3.1% during 1965–73 to 0.2% during 1973–80. Exports over the same periods declined from an annual average growth rate of 4.2% to −5.6% (table 14.1).

Second, capacity expansion was largely driven by external finance while operations were limited to nationally generated resources. Although optimistic projections were made regarding availability of recurrent resources to support utilization and maintenance of increased capacity, they were far off the mark. Export growth, for example, was projected at an annual rate of 5% for 1976–81 compared to the actual of −5.6%.

Inflexibility in shifting external resources from projects to operational and maintenance finance exacerbated the gap. At the margin new projects were doomed to negative returns, signalling a serious debt problem in the future. The rapid decline in capacity utilization of the manufacturing sector and precipitous drop in the sector's real growth rate to an average −3.5 % during 1980−87 (table 14.1) is a result of this inconsistency. The manufacturing sector now faces a solvency problem in view of the fact that its debt service rate was positive while growth rate was negative.

Third, fiscal capacity to support redistributive policies as well as maintain and use capacity of social services became unsustainable. The recurrent expenditure requirements implied by the rapid expansion of demand could not be matched by revenue growth in view of decline in the tax base as retrenchment of economic activity set in. Rapid growth of parallel markets and the informal sector to evade both controls and tax collection worsened the problem. Redistributive policy via consumption and input subsidies through fiscal absorption of losses of marketing parastatals added to this pressure. Unit costs increased with a decline in the share of volumes handled officially as parallel markets grew, raising unit subsidy requirements (Amani et al., 1988).

Fourth, with retrenchment in the growth of real income, domestic saving declined, led by government dissaving during the late 1970s and early 1980s. This resulted in pressure for cutting down investment (especially in the public sector) and hence potential growth. Reduced accumulation was partly reflective of measures to protect levels of current consumption (both private and public), and partly a decline in the inflow of new external resources during the early eighties as Tanzania quickly built up arrears in debt servicing and lost credit worthiness (Ndulu, 1986).

On the positive side the initial strategy did have several achievements. Investment in human capacity through education and health programs set up a potential for raising productivity in the long run. This is vindicated by the relative high literacy rate and improvement in health indicators achieved (table 14.2). Capacity-wise, the structure of production created a basis for enhanced interlinkages within the economy although capacity underutilization restricted its realization. A major gap in the strategy was

**Table 14.2**
Indices of human well-being

|                                            | 1960 | 1970 | 1980 | 1987 |
| ------------------------------------------ | ---- | ---- | ---- | ---- |
| Life expectancy at birth (total yrs.)      | 41   | 45   | 52   | 53   |
| Infant mortality (per 1,000 live births)   | 146  |      | 120  | 107  |
| Literacy rate (%)                          |      | 33   |      | 90   |

Source: UNICEF, *Annual Reports for Tanzania and Seychelles* (various years), J. H. Wagao (1981).

the absence of an articulated short to medium term set of policies consistent with sustenance of longer term development.

## 14.2  Gap Constraints on Medium-Term Growth

Three gaps are discussed here: saving, foreign exchange, and fiscal (Taylor 1993). The following section describes the policy measures adopted in response to the widening gaps.

The evolution of the domestic saving and investment is presented in table 14.3. During 1966–73, domestic saving financed 72 % of domestic gross capital formation. The balance came from foreign saving, mostly in the form of project finance for economic infrastructure. During the period of accelerated investment, 1973–82, the savings-investment gap widened considerably, with domestic finance for only 65 % of gross domestic capital formation. The widening was more the result of a higher investment rate than a decline in savings. After 1982, although the investment rate declined, the gap increased. During the 1982–86 period, domestic saving on average financed only 43 % of investment.

For the period for which complete data are available (1966–87), the widening of the savings-investment gap after 1973 was largely driven by government. The fiscal deficit as a proportion of GDP widened from an average of 6.3 % during 1966–73 to 11.6 % during 1973–78, and to 14.5 % during 1978–82. Between 1966 and 1978, the deficit was driven by a public investment increase rather than dissaving. The recurrent budget

**Table 14.3**
Basic indicators of resource gaps (%)

|                                            | 1966–73 | 1973–78 | 1978–82 | 1982–87 |
|--------------------------------------------|---------|---------|---------|---------|
| (1) Estimated current account deficit/GDP  | −1.4    | −8.0    | −10.0   | −8.0    |
| (2) Gross domestic saving GDP[a]           | 18.1    | 18.4    | 16.5    | 11.6    |
| (3) Gross capital formation GDP[b]         | 25.2    | 27.5    | 27.5    | 26.9    |
| (4) Fiscal deficit/GDP                     | −6.3    | −11.6   | −14.5   | −11.0   |
| (5) Recurrent budget balance/GDP           | 0.8     | 0.9     | −3.9    | −3.5    |
| (6) Imports/official exports               | 1.14    | 1.72    | 2.26    | 2.60    |

Notes: a. Last column is for 1982–86.
b. Unlike the World Bank's estimates depreciation is not netted out. The ratio is that of real magnitudes. Ratios of current values significantly understate the share of investment due to differentials in deflators. Thus the rates are significantly higher than those appearing in *World Development Reports*. Since savings are estimated gross of depreciation, we felt that this was more accurate presentation.
Source: URT, *National Accounts* and *Economic Survey* (various years).

surplus as a proportion of GDP increased from 0.8 % during 1966—73 to 0.9 % between 1973—78 while the fiscal deficit deteriorated steeply over the same period. The situation changed during 1978—82. While public investment rate remained more or less constant, recurrent budget balance deteriorated rapidly to − 3.9 % of GDP (table 14.3).

The foreign exchange gap is measured here as the ratio of the current account deficit to GDP. This deteriorated from − 1.4 % during 1966—73 to − 8 % during 1973—78 to − 10 % during 1978—82. The worsening between 1966 and 1978 was led by relative expansion of imports of capital goods for the investment program, and intermediates for utilization of expanded industrial capacity. The observed increase of average domestic savings from 1966—73 to 1973—78, when foreign saving (the negative of current account balance) was increasing indicates that during this period foreign resource inflows did support capital formation. During 1978—82, however, a lower rate of domestic saving was imperfectly matched by foreign inflows. The deterioration of the current account deficit during this period was more a result of a drop in exports due to a combination of external shocks and anti-export bias in policy.

It is clear from table 14.3 that the import/export ratio jumped after 1973. From an average of 1.14 during 1966—73, it rose to 1.722 during 1973—78 (dominated by expansion of imports for investment), and to 2.35 during 1978—86. Although imports in real terms were compressed after 1978, the ratio rose due to a relatively steeper decline in exports.

## 14.3 Medium-Term Responses to the Resource Gaps

The resource gaps arising from Tanzania's long term development strategy were exacerbated by external shocks during the late 1970s and early 1980s. Apart from the aftermath of expenditures on the Kagera War, two other shocks are noteworthy. Barter terms of trade deteriorated at an annual average rate of − 5.15 % between 1977 and 1985 (table 14.4) as a result of a combination of increased import prices, especially for oil and products, and the collapse of world commodity prices. The world recession of the early 1980s led to a reduction in net resource transfers and a rise in the interest rate on debt.

### 14.3.1 The 1978—82 Adjustment

This period was characterized by a combination of import compression via quantitative restrictions and measures to protect against declines in the investment rate and public current consumption.

**Table 14.4**
Real export growth and its explanation

| Period | Growth rate of real exports (%) | Quantity growth rate | Barter TOT variation | Variation of real exports explained by quantum variation | Variation of real exports explained by TOT |
|--------|--------|--------|--------|--------|--------|
| 1960–72 | 3.03 | 2.97 | 0.05[a] | 98.0 | 1.9 |
| 1972–85 | −8.88 | −6.20 | −2.70 | 69.8 | 30.4 |
| 1977–85 | −11.92 | −6.76 | −5.15 | 56.8 | 43.2 |

a. Trend co-efficient not statistically significant.
Source: Trend growth rates estimated using data from UNCTAD (1980, 1986), *Handbook of International Trade and Development*. Table from Lipumba and Ndulu (1989), "Long-Term Trends in Exports," ERB *Tanzanian Economic Trends: A Quarterly Review of the Economy*, Vol. 2, No. 1, April.

Real imports fell at an annual rate of −13.5 % over the period, with the steepest cuts in consumer goods and intermediates at annual rates of −33.1 % and −21.9 % respectively. Capital goods imports declined at an annual average rate of −11.7 %, thereby increasing their share in total. This pro-investment shift in structure of imports was largely a result of continued implementation of projects under the basic industrialization program financed externally.

The use of import quotas for balance of payments management was intensified, implemented through an administrative foreign exchange allocation system. This system by and large tried to keep all production sectors alive (sometimes barely), resulting in across-the-board involuntary import compression and lower capacity utilization. The latter rate fell steadily from 83.9 % in 1978 to 76.7 % in 1982. Real GDP growth rate declined from an annual average of 3.6 % during 1967–78 to 2.2 % between 1978 and 1982, despite sustained high investment.

To ameliorate the impacts of import compression on growth, several offsetting mechanisms were put into motion. Some substitution away from imports in production at the aggregate level was achieved, as evidenced by the decline in the real intermediate import content of GDP from 13.7 % in 1978 to 4.7 % in 1982 (table 14.5). This occurred as a result of a relative decline of the more import-dependent sectors in their contribution to real GDP.

Maintenance of high investment rates was achieved through continued inflows of external finance. Foreign saving defined as the negative of the current account balance plus unrequited net transfers increased from 5.7 %

**Table 14.5**
Shifts in the structure of real imports (1978–86)

|      | Consumer imports/GDP (%) | Intermediate Imports/GDP (%) | Capital goods Imports/GDP (%) |
|------|------|------|------|
| 1978 | 8.1  | 13.7 | 8.2 |
| 1979 | 3.8  | 11.0 | 6.9 |
| 1980 | 2.8  | 11.6 | 5.5 |
| 1981 | 1.8  | 10.6 | 5.3 |
| 1982 | 1.5  | 4.7  | 4.5 |
| 1983 | 1.2  | 6.8  | 4.7 |
| 1984 | 1.3  | 9.5  | 8.1 |
| 1985 | 1.3  | 8.0  | 8.7 |
| 1986 | 1.0  | 5.9  | 9.3 |

Source: URT (1986, 1987), *Foreign Trade Statistics, Economic Survey* (various issues).

of GDP in 1977 to 14.2 % in 1980 before tapering down to 11.6 % in 1981 (table 14.6), closing the widened gap between a continued high rate of investment and a reduced savings rate.

On the fiscal front, the overall deficit grew sharply at an annual rate of 21.1 % in nominal terms, with the steepest increase occurring between 1977–78 and 1980–81. The deficit as a proportion of GDP rose from 10.8 % in 1977 to 16.1 % in 1981. Although the initial high rate of increase (1977–79) was related to war finance, its continuation reflected fiscal populism.

Net foreign resource transfers to the government financed on average 20.6 % of the fiscal deficit during this period, with higher rates between 1977 and 1980. The inflation tax and forced saving closed a much larger proportion of the gap. From 9.7 % in 1977, the proportion of the deficit that was monetized rose sharply to 62.3 % in 1979 and tapered down to an average of 41 % during 1980–82. The rise in the inflation rate from an average of 13 % per annum before 1978 to 30 % is predominantly linked to this type of financing, although the slowdown in real growth had its explanatory share. A rise in commercial margins, as supplies dwindled, redistributed income in favor of private traders to generate forced saving.

14.3.2  The 1982–89 Adjustment

Two sub-periods can be distinguished, 1982–86 when the first structural adjustment program (SAP 1982–83 to 85–86) was implemented, and 1986–89 with the Economic Recovery Programme (ERP) supported by the

**Table 14.6**
Indicators for closure of resource gaps (percent)

| Year | GDP growth rate | Foreign savings[a]/GDP | Adjusted foreign savings[b]/GDP | Adjusted foreign savings[b]/imports | Net foreign transfer to government/fiscal deficit | Government bank borrowing/fiscal deficit | Inflation rate | Real imports/GDP |
|---|---|---|---|---|---|---|---|---|
| 1977 | 0.4 | 5.7 | 5.7 | 23.7 | 28.9 | 9.7 | 11.63 | |
| 1978 | 2.1 | 17.2 | 17.2 | 55.7 | 29.5 | 48.4 | 12.18 | 31.0 |
| 1979 | 2.9 | 13.3 | 13.3 | 47.2 | 25.0 | 62.3 | 12.93 | 21.0 |
| 1980 | 2.5 | 14.2 | 14.2 | 56.9 | 15.7 | 44.7 | 30.22 | 18.3 |
| 1981 | −0.5 | 10.1 | 10.1 | 46.3 | 12.6 | 34.8 | 25.65 | 16.3 |
| 1982 | 0.6 | 11.6 | 11.6 | 59.2 | 12.1 | 42.1 | 28.93 | 13.2 |
| 1983 | −2.4 | 7.3 | 7.3 | 50.5 | 14.1 | 65.2 | 27.07 | 11.8 |
| 1984 | 3.4 | 10.3 | 8.7 | 51.0 | 17.6 | 46.4 | 36.13 | 16.2 |
| 1985 | 2.6 | 12.6 | 7.8 | 48.2 | 23.9 | 42.1 | 33.28 | 16.9 |
| 1986 | 3.0 | 18.3 | 11.0 | 43.2 | 51.1 | 23.3 | 32.43 | 15.6 |
| 1987 | 3.6 | 32.4 | 13.2 | 43.7 | 75.4 | 5.5 | 29.95 | |
| 1988 | 4.1* | 38.3 | 16.0 | 42.0 | | 11.2 | 31.19 | |

Notes: a. Foreign savings defined as negative of current account balance plus net transfers.
b. Foreign savings as in note 1, less own funded imports less net service payments.
Sources: Bank of Tanzania, *Economic and Operations Reports* (Various issues), URT, *Economic Survey* (Various issues).

Fund, the World Bank, and bilateral donors. The ERP was essentially an intensification of SAP with two major differences. A much more active use of policy instruments for alignment of incentives was adopted and agreement with the IMF in late 1986 opened doors for new inflows of foreign resources and debt rescheduling.

For purposes of subsequent analysis we need to redefine foreign savings to take into account two factors. First, starting in July 1984, the government allowed importers to use their own foreign exchange to bring in a range of items and dispose of them at scarcity prices. This implicit exchange rate depreciation on the side of imports induced holders of unofficial reserves abroad and those engaged in unofficial exports to redirect their earnings to imports for home use. The reduced risk of penalty on the side of importation enhanced the profitability of unofficial trade. Official records of own exchange financing, although a gross underestimate (Ndulu and Hyuha, 1990), show an increase from 4.5 % of total imports in 1984 to 23.2 % in 1985, 23.6 % in 1986, 26.1 % in 1987 and 26.6 % in 1988 (Bank of Tanzania, 1986, 1989). Most analysts now conclude that a flow (through unofficial exports) rather than a stock of foreign assets is the major source of financing such imports.

Second, since 1983 the balance on services has turned negative, indicating a net payment driven predominantly by foreign debt servicing.

These developments lead us to adjust foreign savings as previously defined by subtracting the value of own exchange imports and net payments on services to arrive at "authentic" flow available for financing investment and current consumption. With this adjustment, the picture on the relative shares of financing of adjustment between own resources and foreign resources change drastically from the conventional measures (table 14.6). As a proportion of imports, own resources (official and unofficial exports) played a much more significant role in the adjustment process since 1984 than generally acknowledged.

### 14.3.3   The SAP, 1982–86

Starting July 1982 Tanzania implemented its own structural adjustment program with ran through June 1986. The focus was on reducing both external and internal imbalances in the economy. Import compression was further intensified between 1982 and 1984 as export earnings continued to fall and foreign savings sharply declined from 11.6 % of GDP in 1982 to 7.3 % in 1983. The government slashed its investment and initiated measures to boost revenues. The result was a reduction in the fiscal deficit from 16.1% of GDP in 1981 to 9% in 1985. Between 1982 and 1985 the gross investment rate declined with the savings rate, though relatively less.

Continued monetary expansion during this period had two key sources. The first was widening of the recurrent budget deficit, 1982–85, which could not be financed through external resources that were declining and in any case still were directed predominantly to project finance. Indirectly, crop authorities' losses increased and were absorbed as a build up of unserviced overdrafts within the banking system.

To cushion continued import compression, debt servicing arrears were rapidly accumulated between 1982 and 1985, reaching 132% of the value of official export earnings by 1985. Any easing of compression between 1984 and 1986 was largely due to the own exchange import scheme. Negotiations with the IMF were in progress and doors to new foreign resource still closed. The contribution of own exchange imports (financed by the importer, with no questions asked) to the revival of growth went through four channels. First, increased availability of consumer goods improved incentives for agricultural production by reducing "frustrated" demand. Second, official sources of foreign exchange could now be used relatively more for importation of intermediates and capital goods. Third, since the second half of 1985 the structure of own funded imports shifted heavily in favor of capital goods (Ndulu and Hyuha, 1989), supporting the observed revival of investment during 1984–86. Fourth, they contributed towards increased revenues from import duties and sales tax on imports, easing the fiscal constraint.

### 14.3.4   The ERP, 1986–89

Three major new areas for adjustment were identified during this period: (1) There was an intensified use of policy instruments for realignment of incentives geared toward improvement of allocative efficiency; (2) an agreement with the IMF opened doors to new foreign resources; and (3) institutional reforms to support adjustment were pursued. Key price revisions included real devaluation, raising nominal interest rates toward achieving real positive levels, and a pricing policy that ensures pass-through of incentives to producers, distributors, and consumers in the domestic market.

Between 1986 and 1989, the Tanzanian shilling was depreciated by 73% in nominal dollar terms and (using annual average exchange rates) by 52% in real terms. This helped align the implicit exchange rate on the import side and the official exchange rate on the export side. Externally, real purchasing power parity was largely restored. In spite of depreciation, the inflation rate actually declined from 33.3 % in 1985 to 28 % in 1988 and further, to 25.8 %, in 1989 (United Republic of Tanzania, 1989). Real GDP growth rose from 2.9 % in 1985 to reach 4.5 % in 1989.

Several factors offset potential inflationary and contractionary effects of the maxi-devaluations. First, as far as final imports are concerned, the relevant effective implicit exchange rate had been far above the official rate since the trade liberalization of 1984. Domestic supplies were being priced at retail to match foreign counterparts, resulting in large rent to retailers. The import cost increase was absorbed via lower margins. Significant increases in food supplies and imports of consumer goods under the own exchange scheme ameliorated cost-based inflationary pressure. Reduction in import compression via net foreign resource inflows and repatriation of earnings from unofficial exports counteracted the contractionary effects of devaluation.

Depreciation eased the fiscal constraint, by reducing the budgetary burden of financing high export producer prices through losses of marketing authorities. Import tax receipts also rose, due to the higher value in shillings of their base. A large part of this increase was a transfer of margins from importers to government as the gap between the implicit and official exchange rate (used for tax valuation) narrowed. On the expenditure side, depreciation raised unit costs of public imports and the burden of foreign debt servicing. If one includes new foreign resources made possible by agreement on exchange rate adjustment, the net impact for the period 1985–86 to 1987–88 came out positive (Rutayisire and Mgonja, 1989).

The impact on production for exports was more dramatic than on earnings. Output of cotton more than doubled, while the perennial crops (coffee, tea, and sisal) registered marginal increases on aggregate. Due partly to processing and transportation bottlenecks, exported quantities rose significantly less than output. With declining world market prices, earnings in dollar terms remained stagnant.

The share of nontraditional exports (manufactures, horticultural, and minerals) steadily increased from 27.15 % of total official earnings in 1985 to 40 % in 1988. The fastest growth in nontraditional exports was in manufactures and new items not in the basket earlier, for example, horticultural products, tourism, livestock, marine products, and small crops. Streamlining of export procedures to lessen administrative bottlenecks and various incentive schemes played a role in this improvement.

Nominal interest rates on deposits and government securities were raised from a range of 5 % to 14 % to 16 % to 29 %. On the lending side, interest on commercial debt rose from a range of 11 %−16 % to 20 %−31 % while those for housing mortgages rose from 7 %−16 % to 9 %−29 % (Bank of Tanzania, 1988). Due to the high inflation rate, positive real interest rates were not achieved until 1989. The preliminary inflation estimate for 1990 is 19 %, making real interest rates significantly positive.

The objectives of the interest rate increases were savings mobilization and to induce more efficient utilization of credit. Although some evidence on positive effects of real interest rates on savings exists (Lipumba et at., 1989), there are two main negative implications that have come to the fore. The first is related to the precarious solvency of the official banks. Over the last decade, the system built up a huge stock of nonperforming assets, predominantly from an accumulation of overdrafts by the crop authorities. The banks, although honoring increased interest payments on the liabilities side, are not de facto receiving interest on much of their loan portfolio. Increased reliance on the central bank for liquidity has been the result. The second problem is the recessionary impact of a crunch in the availability of working capital, especially at a time when devaluation and producer price increases have considerably raised credit requirements in domestic currency terms and ceilings are tight.

There has been considerable movement toward freeing the pricing structure, with official mechanisms tracing market signals as much as possible. Support pricing is still in force for food producer prices, and the exchange rate has been used to cushion recent steep world market prices for major export commodities such as cotton and coffee.

With the signing of the agreement with the IMF, direct and indirect resource inflows from both multilateral and bilateral sources increased via higher loans and transfers as well as debt rescheduling and forgiveness. From $487 million in 1985, net official development assistance increased to $681 million in 1986 and $882 million in 1987 (World Bank, 1988). At the same time $1,143.7 million and $188.0 million of Tanzania's debt were rescheduled during 1986 and 1987 respectively (31.3 % and 4.6 % of the totals during the two years). As a proportion of GDP, adjusted foreign savings increased steadily from 7.8 % in 1985 to 16 % in 1988. As a proportion of current imports, however, having netted out debt servicing, an own exchange import decline was recorded (table 14.6).

Foreign resource inflows as a share of total government expenditure increased from 9.4 % in 1985−86 to 28.0 % in 1986−87 and 29.4 % in

1987–88. Although foreign debt servicing also increased as a proportion of expenditure, a net inflow was recorded. Its structure changed in favor of import support, which rose from 42 % of the total 56.6 %.

Ample foreign inflows allowed the government to reduce its reliance on inflationary finance. The proportion of the central government's fiscal deficit monetized declined from 42.1 % during 1985 to 5.5 % in 1987 (table 14.6). The continued high growth rate of money supply is currently dominated by finance requirements of the cooperatives and crop boards along with reserve increases in the very recent period.

Import compression has been attacked on several fronts. The tariff structure has been reviewed with the aim of achieving neutrality in protection across industrial sectors and enhanced revenue collection. An open general license system has been introduced for intermediate imports. Its coverage will be extended as remaining overvaluation is eliminated.

With reduced import compression, major improvements in food supplies, and reduced monetization of the fiscal deficit, real GDP growth recovered from 2.6 % in 1985 to 4.1 % in 1988. The inflation rate fell from 36.1 % in 1984 to approximately 26 % in 1989. The external current account deficit as a proportion of GDP declined steadily from 12.5 % in 1985, reaching 9.8 % in 1988. The large increases in net foreign transfers explain the bulk of this improvement: otherwise with appropriate adjustments there is actually a widening of the deficit from 7.8 % in 1985 to 16 % of GDP in 1988 (table 14.6). This, in turn, is reflected in a higher ratio of the fiscal deficit to GDP: from 9 % in 1985 to 12.0 % in 1987 and more in 1988. The share of net foreign transfers to the government in financing the deficit rose sharply from 23.9 % in 1985 to 75.4 % in 1987.

## 14.4 Emerging Issues for the Future

Several questions about future prospects arise. One is whether import compression can be eased on a sustainable basis. Partly linked to this (via growth) is controlling inflation. Here a sustainable fiscal deficit and modalities for its closure are central. A need for intersectoral resource balance between capacity utilization and investment came out clearly from our review of the development strategy during the first two decades. Redefining the role of state in supporting growth in the light of changing economic environment is important. Finally, redistributive policy is closely linked to growth and fiscal performance. We briefly take up each of these issues.

## 14.4.1    Import Compression

The critical role of imports in expanding and sustaining production cannot be overemphasized. Investment requires capital goods that are not domestically produced while at the same time availability of intermediate imports has been shown to be a critical constraint to capacity utilization (Wangwe, 1983; Helleiner, 1986; Ndulu, 1986; Rattsø, 1988).

The main sources of foreign exchange for imports are the nation's exports and net foreign resource inflows. Although foreign inflows can be considered exogenous, exports are supply-constrained (Lipumba et al., 1988) and dependent on imports (Khan and Knight, 1988). These considerations raise two issues. Dependence on foreign resource inflows for import capacity ties growth to economic conditions in the donor countries. Rattsø (1989) argues that the pattern of flows had tended to be procyclical. World economic recessions reduce resource transfers, as observed in the late 1970s and early 1980s.

The second issue refers to allocation of import capacity between expansion and utilization of installed capacity. The latter affects growth through productivity of new and previous investment and helps explain the debt problems of many Tanzanian firms even as growth recovered.

Sustainable export growth emerges as being central to achieving and maintaining output growth. Looking at export performance in Tanzania, one can distinguish between two sets of factors, exogenous and policy-related. Table 14.4 presents the contributions of quantum changes and the barter terms of trade to explaining growth in the real value of exports. If volume is supply-constrained (the small country assumption), quantities exported are predominantly policy determined through both capacity expansion (investment) and its utilization. Barter terms of trade can be considered exogenous.

Table 14.4 shows that prior to 1973 the growth rate of quantities exported explained more than 90 % of the variation in real export earnings, barter terms of trade being more or less neutral considering the period as a whole. After 1977, however, both a quantum decline and the terms of trade contributed significantly to the steep drop in the growth of real exports.

These observations suggest that the problem of export performance has to be dealt with from two angles. One is the need to continue bolstering incentives and investment in favor of exporting sectors. Here, not only the level of remuneration to export efforts (pricing) but also infrastructural support are important. The second is higher productivity in traditional lines. Appropriate real exchange rate policy is, of course, important for correct alignment of internal terms of trade that do not penalize exporters and for reducing hindrances to international competitiveness in the medium term. Increased productivity, removal of institutional constraints to exporters, and provision of necessary economic infrastructure are, however, essential for sustained performance, especially in light of continued downward trends in world prices of primary commodities.

For the next years, at least, it makes sense to use imports to raise capacity utilization. Scarce foreign exchange can more effectively raise growth by supporting movement toward the capacity frontier rather than shifting it. Nevertheless some investment is critical in view of the deterioration in infrastructure during the past decade. Growth in savings associated with higher utilization can finance further investment.

Fungibility of use of foreign resources between investment and capacity utilization has improved significantly over the last four years. However, a new problem is appearing insofar as donors tie import support to projects they helped finance regardless of relative returns economy-wide. To enhance efficiency in the use of scarce foreign exchange, selectivity will have to be exercised based on strict economic criteria. The current trend of shifting resources from import support to the Open General License System will enhance fungibility. Some deindustrialization may have to be accepted as part of the process of selection.

## 14.4.2   Controlling Inflation

The need to control inflation arises out of several concerns. With revenue collection lags, a sustainable fiscal deficit requires price stability (Tanzi 1977, 1978; Olivera, 1967; Kilindo, 1982). To protect against tendencies for exchange rate overvaluation and avoid reliance on continuing nominal depreciation to sustain real prices of exports, inflation has to be brought down closer to the levels in countries Tanzania trades with. Further, protection of nonindexed real wages and achievement of a positive real interest rate need slower inflation. Otherwise, there is a risk of contractionary impacts of interest rate increases.

The inflationary process in Tanzania can be understood by segmenting the pricing system into flex-price and fix-price components. The basic cost of production or procurement is assumed to be the floor price level in both segments. Cost mark-ups are determined administratively in the case of controlled prices and by excess demand pressures where such controls are not applicable or ineffective due to violation. The aggregate price level will thus be a weighted average of the two segments. The weights are determined institutionally where controls are effective; otherwise ability to enforce control is the key determinant. Because Tanzania has moved away from controls, the flex-price segment can now be regarded as dominant.

Two key channels of inflationary pressure are thus identified. Factors that influence cost of production are one and those that influence excess demand the other. Given the level of technology, policy instruments that increase cost of production include exchange rate depreciation, wage costs, and interest rates. Import compression has contributed through higher unit overhead costs as capacity utilization declined. Within the policy sphere, a trade-off exists between the impact of exchange rate depreciation in raising direct costs of production in domestic currency and reduction in import compression via stimulation of exports.

On the side of excess demand, two sources are identified: the fiscal-monetary process and growth of real output. The former operates via monetization of the fiscal deficit. To the extent that ensuing money supply growth exceeds real output-income growth, inflationary pressure will be generated, raising mark-up margins on cost. Real output growth counters inflationary pressure from monetization. With public sector savings falling far short of required investment, public spending to support overall growth of the economy was recently financed through net foreign transfers (table 14.6). Although such inflows may be critical for provision of breathing space in the medium term, they are not sustainable. Raising national savings is critical; rationalization of expenditure growth to be consistent with growth in revenue is ultimately inescapable.

The fiscal deficit as defined here is narrow in the sense that it does not include the losses of parastatals, especially crop boards that still continue building up unserviced overdrafts with the banking system (although the parastatal sector as a whole is in surplus). Crop boards and cooperatives are the institutions accounting for most of the continued high growth rate of monetization of the economy. As explained earlier, a large part of the increase in parastatal indebtedness comes from higher interest charged to accumulated debt, which was not absorbed by the government budget. This problem may have to be dealt with from a stock point of view with several parties (government, banks, and the debtors) sharing its absorption.

## 14.4.3 Intersectoral Resource Allocation and the Role of the State

In the review of the development strategy for the first two decades, we saw that concern with structural transformation had led to neglect of the agricultural sector. Subsequent faltering of agricultural and industrial performance arose out of the inconsistency between the resource base and expanded requirements of this strategy.

The last decade saw some rectification of this problem as agriculture received renewed emphasis, and recovery of the industrial sector proceeded slowly after 1985. The key channel of resource allocation has been increased prices to producers. The role of government in agriculture shifted toward supporting infrastructure including marketing, extension service, and research. Modernizing production and marketing within the framework of small-holder farmers is the appropriate development strategy to ensure growth with equitable income distribution.

Transportation, storage, processing capacity, and marketing arrangements are still the major bottlenecks to increased agricultural production. The wedge between production and exports of cotton is a typical example. Abundant national food supplies co-existing with price increases in deficit areas are another. Although resources beyond those generated internally are necessary for supporting rehabilitation of physical infrastructure, sustained upkeep of improvements in the future will need additional measures. The contribution by infrastructure users to its maintenance needs to be raised.

Provision of social services is key to raising human capacity and productivity in the long term. In this sense, expenditures in education, health, and water should not purely be regarded as consumption. In view of prevalence of externalities in this sector and social returns that exceed private benefits (Jimenez, 1989). the public sector's role is central. A sustainable social service delivery system hinges on a solid fiscal resource base.

The crisis period demonstrated that some segments of the society were willing and able to finance a large portion of their own education and health expenditures, once public services deteriorated below a certain standard, as exemplified by the proliferation of private schools and health services. This experience should help to establish a basis for careful assessment of private contributions while providing for the poorer segments of the society.

Although the role of the state in providing both economic and social infrastructure to support growth has been emphasized thus far, there is a need to redefine its role in other spheres in the light of changing conditions. The state in Tanzania has actively participated in directly productive activities through statal and parastatal enterprises. It has regulated resource use in the rest of the economy through administrative allocations, its financial institutions, and price controls. Over time, strains on the state's managerial capacity for effective control and efficient utilization of resources came to the fore, primarily because of overextension of its efforts.

The role of state as a modernizing agent is still important in view of the continued lack of resource concentration in private hands for large-scale investment as well as undeveloped indigenous entrepreneurial skills. Development of the nonagricultural sector and improvements in agricultural productivity will in the foreseeable future depend on public support. The state has to create room for private initiative to grow, and then not stifle it. This will require and efficient interventionist stance that does not grossly distort incentives and enhances accountability to the community to ensure effectiveness of resource use in relation to policy targets.

Major reforms are currently underway in redefining the role of state. Where public enterprises show no promise of contributing to resource mobilization, the state has decided against indefinitely keeping them afloat. Realignment of state participation in productive activities will take time and careful consideration in order to minimize transitional costs.

### 14.4.4 Sustainable Redistribution

Primary income distribution in Tanzania is determined by human endowments (skills, education) and assets. Land, the basic asset for the majority of Tanzanians, is public property: Proprietorship is granted upon improvement from its natural state. Less than 10 % of arable land is currently put to use. Other assets contributing to differentiation in income earning capacities include livestock and real estate. Income earning potentials from the land, however, depend on its fertility and climate, which are naturally determined, as well as accessibility to major domestic markets and export points. The historical development of transportation infrastructure has significantly affected geographical distribution of potential earnings from land. Opening up of remote areas has been one of the main concerns of government. Equalization of access to education, actively promoted since 1972, was geared toward increasing equality of human endowments.

The state has also been active in the redistributive sphere. Guided by the principles of Ujamaa, the government actively redistributed income at the secondary level though progressive taxation and transfers. At the tertiary level, price control was the key instrument for redistribution. Green (1974), Wagao (1981), Semboja (1983), ILO (1978, 1983), Valentine (1983), and Bukuku (1990) have all concluded that reduction of inequality after tax among wage and salary earners was achieved. They obtained different results when account is taken of the rural sector and the impact of pricing policy. The available evidence seems to point toward worsening of the relative position of the rural population vis-à-vis the urban population up to the late 1970s and its reverse in the 1980s. Both groups seem to have lost to the private commercial sector as price controls became ineffective during the 1980s, much more so on the side of the urban population.

Trade-offs between growth and equity are central to the issue of sustainable redistribution. Policy instruments for achieving equitable income distribution and poverty alleviation involve intervention in both product and factor markets, with effects on investment and fiscal deficits. The issue at hand is not whether to intervene but how to shape socially efficient intervention. Efficiency here is defined in terms of reaching targeted segments of the population and sustainability of intervention, which entails maintaining its base—real growth.

Effectiveness of market-wide subsidy programs faltered with reduced budgetary capacity after the late 1970s. Low real prices for agricultural producers reduced domestic supplies of consumer goods through stagnant food production and exports. This scarcity led to growth of parallel markets and ineffectiveness of control, with the brunt of the ensuing rationing falling on the less influential poor. Deterioration of the fiscal capacity to finance expansion and maintain delivery of social services had similar effects.

Sustainable growth with equity remains a fundamental objective of a welfare-oriented development strategy. Providing the poor with income-generating assets and supportive infrastructure to raise their productivity is central to redistribution with growth. In view of the deterioration of both economic and social infrastructure, external resources for returning the situation to normalcy are needed for bridging purposes. In the longer run, however, development must rely on national efforts.

### References

Amani, H. K. R., S. M. Kapunda, N. H. Lipumba, and B. J. Ndulu (1988). "Effects of Market Liberalization on Food Security in Tanzania," in Rukuni, M. and R. H. Bernstein (eds.), *Southern Africa: Food Security Policy Options*. University of Zimbabwe and Michigan State University.

Bank of Tanzania (1986, 1987, 1988). *Economic and Operations Report*. Dar-Es-Salaam.

Bukuku, E. (1990). *Income Distribution and Economic Growth in Tanzania*. Unpublished Ph.D. Thesis, University of Dar-es-Salaam.

Green, R. H. (1974). "Towards Ujamaa no Kujitegemea: Income Distribution Aspects of the Tanzania Transition to Socialism." IDS Discussion Paper, No. 66. Sussex.

Helleiner, G. (1986). "Outward Orientation Import Stability and African Economic Growth: An Empirical Investigation," in Sanjayahall and Stewart, F., *Theory and Reality in Development*. New York: Macmillan.

International Labour Organization (1978). *Towards Self-Reliance: Development, Employment and Equity Issues in Tanzania*. Addis Ababa.

International Labour Organization (1983). *Distributional Aspects of Stabilization Programs in the United Republic of Tanzania, 1979–84*. Geneva.

Jimenez, E. (1989). "Social Sector Pricing Policy Revisited: A Survey of Some Recent Controversies in Developing Countries." Paper presented at the *First Annual World Bank Conference in Development Economics*. Washington, DC.: World Bank.

Khan, M. S. and M. D. Knight (1988). "Import Compression and Export Performance in Developing Countries." *Review of Economics and Statistics*, May: 359–364.

Kilindo, A. L. (1982). "Government Deficits and the Process of Inflation in Tanzania." Unpublished M.A. Thesis, University of Dar-es-Salaam.

Lipumba, N., B. Ndulu, S. Horton, and A. Plourde (1988). "A Supply-Constrained Macroeconometric Model of Tanzania." *Economic Modelling*, Vol. 5, No. 4.

Lipumba, N., and B. Ndulu (1989). "Long Term Trends in Exports: Tanzania." *Tanzanian Economic Trends: A Quarterly Review of the Economy*, Vol. 2, No. 1.

Lipumba, N., Osoro, N., and B. Nyagetera (1989). "The Determinants of Financial Savings in Tanzania." Paper presented at African Economic Research Consortium Workshop, Harare.

Ndulu, B. J. (1985). "Investment and Resource Gaps in Tanzania, 1964–1982." African-American Issues Center, Discussion Paper No. 4. Boston University.

Ndulu, B. J. (1986). "Investment Output Growth and Capacity Utilization in an African Economy: The Case of Manufacturing Sector in Tanzania." *East African Economic Review*, Vol. 2.

Ndulu, B. J., and M. Hyuha (1990). "Inflation and Economic Recovery in Tanzania." *UCHUMI Journal of Economic Society of Tanzania*, Vol. 2, No. 1.

Olivera, H. (1967). "Money, Prices and Fiscal Lags: A Note on the Dynamics of Inflation." *Banca Nazionale del Lavoro Quarterly Review*.

Rattsø, J. (1988). "Import Compression Macro-dynamics: Macroeconomic Analysis for Sub-Saharan Africa." (Mimeo), University of Trondheim.

Rattso, J. (1989). "The Asymmetric Relation Between Sub-Saharan Africa and the Rest of the World: A Theoretical Analysis of the Role of Import Compression." (Mimeo), University of Trondheim.

Rutayisire, L., and G. Mgonja (1989). "The Effect of Devaluation on Government Budget Deficit: A Case Study of Tanzania." paper presented at AERC Workshop, Harare.

Semboja, J. (1983). "Income Distribution in Tanzania: An Analysis of Trends." Unpublished Ph.D. Thesis, University of Illinois, Urbana-Champagne.

Tanzi, V. (1977). "Inflation, Lags in Collection and the Real Value of Tax Revenues." *IMF Staff Papers*, Vol. 24, pp. 154–167.

Tanzi, V. (1978). "Inflation, Real Tax Revenue and the Case for Inflationary Finance: Theory and Application to Argentina." *IMF Staff Papers*, Vol. 25, No. 3.

Taylor, L. (1993). "Foreign Resource Flows and Developing Country Growth: A Three-Gap Analysis." this volume.

United Republic of Tanzania (1986, 1987, 1988, 1989). *Economic Survey*, Dar-es-Salaam.

United Republic of Tanzania (1986b). *Foreign Trade Statistics*, Dar-es-Salaam.

United Republic of Tanzania (1986c). *National Accounts*, Dar-es-Salaam.

Valentine, T. (1983). "Wage Adjustments, Progressive Tax Rates, and Accelerated Inflation: Issues of Equity in the Wage Sector of Tanzania." *African Studies Review*, Vol. 26, No. 1.

Wagao, J. H. (1981). "Income Distribution in a Developing Country: The Case of Tanzania." Unpublished Ph.D. Thesis, University of Sussex.

Wangwe, S. M. (1983). "Industrialization and Resource Allocation in a Developing Country." *World Development*, Vol. 2, No. 6.

World Bank (1988). *World Development Report 1988*. Oxford: Oxford University Press.

World Bank (1989). *Sub-Saharan Africa: From Crisis to Sustainable Growth*. Washington, DC: IBRD.

# 15  Uganda

## Ardeshir Sepehri

After a decade and a half of economic and political crisis the National Resistance Movement (NRM) government has gone to great lengths to restore economic and political stability in Uganda, once one of the most prosperous nations in Sub-Saharan Africa. The government initiated a three-year rehabilitation and development plan, which is expected to ease the transition to an "independent, self-sustaining, and integrated economy." The program, well received by the foreign donors, aims at achieving a moderate growth rate of 5 % per annum over the plan period.

Against this political background, this chapter is devoted to an examination of the current macroeconomic problems faced by Uganda, policy measures taken by the government to address them, and the likely effects of the measures on key macroeconomic variables as well as the evolution of the reform framework. A three-gap model provides the quantitative framework, and the role of the state and its agricultural and industrial strategies are also discussed.

### 15.1  The Economy: Past, Present, and Future

During its first post-independence decade, Uganda experienced a relatively high rate of economic growth with a more or less stable political environment. Uganda's abundant fertile land, together with sufficient rain, made it possible for the country to feed its population and generate a surplus to support the development of manufacturing and infrastructure, and the fiscal and balance of payments situation showed little sign of imbalance. During this period (1963–70), real GDP grew at an average rate of 4.8 % and per capita GDP at about 3 % per annum (see table 15.1). The high national saving rate (13.4 % of GDP) was sufficient to finance the moderate rate of capital accumulation which amounted to less than 13 % of GDP.

**Table 15.1**
Macroeconomic indicators, 1963–1988 (percentages)

| | 1963–1970 | 1971–1978 | 1979–1980 | 1981–1983 | 1984 | 1985 | 1986 | 1987 | 1988 |
|---|---|---|---|---|---|---|---|---|---|
| Growth rates: GDP[a] | 4.8 | −0.2 | −9.7 | 5.5 | −5.4 | −1.1 | −2.7 | 7.7 | 6.8 |
| Monetary GDP | 4.6 | −1.6 | −6.8 | 4.9 | −1.1 | 2.6 | −1.3 | 4.0 | 8.2 |
| Manufacturing | 6.5 | −5.9 | −17.0 | 7.4 | 4.9 | −12.0 | −8.4 | 24.3 | 25.0 |
| Nonmonetary GDP | 3.9 | 3.4 | −14.3 | 8.1 | −11.6 | −7.0 | −5.4 | 5.6 | 5.2 |
| Inflation rate[b] | 8.2[c] | 40.4 | 16.7 | 35.0 | 41.3 | 167.7 | 152.7 | 198.2 | 136.2 |
| Gross investment[d] (% of GDP) | 12.7 | 8.6 | 6.0 | 8.5 | 16.3 | 8.6 | 8.1 | 14.4 | 15.1 |
| National savings (% of GDP) | 13.4 | 7.7 | 2.6 | 9.6 | 17.3 | 6.5 | 8.1 | 9.2 | 7.4 |
| Recurrent revenue[e] (% of GDP) | 14.6 | 9.7 | 2.2 | 10.5 | 12.7 | 8.7 | 7.1 | 9.4 | 7.4 |
| Total government expenditure[f] (% of GDP) | 17.5 | 15.5 | 5.9 | 15.5 | 17.7 | 13.9 | 12.6 | 17.5 | 13.4 |
| Imports[g] (% of GDP) | 22.9 | 11.9 | 2.1 | 12.3 | 16.1 | 12.7 | 12.0 | 16.9 | 16.9 |
| Exports[h] (% of GDP) | 25.0 | 12.0 | 1.8 | 8.8 | 15.8 | 9.4 | 9.4 | 9.6 | 6.1 |
| Current account (% of GDP) | −0.4 | −1.3 | −0.4 | −2.0 | 1.7 | 0.6 | 0.0 | −3.7 | −4.7 |

a. Real GDP at factor cost (1966 = 100).
b. Based on Kampala cost of living index for low income groups.
c. For the period 1967–1970.
d. Gross domestic investment as a percentage of GDP at market prices. Since GDP deflators for the more recent years are both large and unreliable, only limited reliance can be placed on these ratios.
e. Current revenues for calendar years are estimated using moving average of fiscal year estimates.
f. Includes unallocated expenditures.
g. Goods and nonfactor services.
h. Goods and nonfactor services.
Sources: Government of Tanzania, Background to the Budget, various issues; World Bank (1982, 1988).

Underlying economic growth was a conventional development strategy focusing on the promotion of a few export crops, as well as domestic production of basic consumer and intermediate goods. Exports of goods and nonfactor services amounted to 25 % of GDP, more or less sufficient to pay for imports. Although state intervention in the economy was strengthened by expanding the role of the Uganda Development Corporation in the ownership and management of the industrial sector, the overall control exercised by the government and African entrepreneurs over key sectors of the economy remained insignificant until the end of the 1960s. Of the major export crops, coffee and cotton production came entirely from small peasant holdings while tobacco and tea production were undertaken by both small holders and large foreign owned plantations. Mining, finance and the management of foreign trade were mainly in the hands of foreign companies, leaving the manufacturing sector and domestic trade to the Asian business class.

In 1970, the Obote government, frustrated with the slow growth of African control over the economy, resorted to the "Nakivubo Pronouncements," which sought 60 % state participation in a number of private industrial, commercial, and financial enterprises. The government's shift to the "left" was, however, soon interrupted by a coup d'etat let by Idi Amin in 1971.

Following the change in government in 1971, the situation deteriorated abruptly and the subsequent eight years of brutal state repression marked a turning point in the political economy of Uganda. During this period, economic policy was aimed primarily at enhancing "state intervention, often in arbitrary and contradictory ways, by the extensive use of direct controls, the undermining of market incentives, the erosion of official market transactions, and the unhinging of foreign exchange, monetary, and fiscal balances" (Loxley, 1989, p. 69). In 1972, the state launched the "Economic War," which led to the expulsion of 50,000 Asians and foreigners, and the expropriation of their assets. The larger and more complex enterprises were transferred to parastatals and the rest were redistributed, often randomly and with violence, among the regime's military and tribal affiliates. State control over the economy was further extended by the Land Decree of 1975, which abolished customary communal land tenure and replaced it with public ownership. Regulation was tightened as well as the extent and intensity of "road blocks" and "border controls," which provided the military and other officials with extra instruments to supplement their income.

These measures led to disastrous consequences. The expulsion of Asians and foreigners entailed an abrupt loss of the country's entrepreneurial class and skilled professionals who could not be easily replaced as many of the best Ugandan administrators, managers, and other trained personnel also left the country. The frequent and arbitrary redistribution of Asian assets, together with the gross mismanagement of parastatals, led to rapid decay of existing capital assets and dominance of speculative and rent-seeking activities over long-term productive real investment. The effect of these changes, combined with a series of external shocks (the oil shocks of the mid 1970s and the break down of the East African Community) was severe. Real GDP declined at an average rate of 0.2 % per annum during 1971–78 and despite official price controls inflation skyrocketed to over 40.4 % per annum, as compared with an average rate of 8.2 % per annum during 1967–70.[1]

Only the subsistence sector remained resilient and continued to grow at an average rate of 3.4 % per annum. In the public sector, huge deficits developed as government revenue sources dried up with the stagnation of the economy, imports and exports declined, and economic activities shifted into the *magendo* (parallel) economy. Recurrent revenues declined from 14.6 % of GDP in the 1960s to 9.7 % while total expenditures declined only marginally from 17.5 % of GDP to 15.5 % (see table 15.1). Spending went primarily toward unproductive activities relating to internal security, defense, and prisons, which absorbed over 40 % of the recurrent and development budget (World Bank, 1982).

Faced with infrequent price adjustments, export crop producers reverted to subsistence farming and food production to supply the thriving *magendo* markets. Exports of goods and nonfactor services fell from 25 % of GDP in the 1960s to 12 %. Lower export earnings, together with reductions in tourism and external capital inflow reduced imports drastically from 22.9 % of GDP in the 1960s to 11.9 % (table 15.1).

The war of liberation of 1979 and the overthrow of the Amin government imposed a severe hardship on an already fragile and shattered economy. The war and subsequent lootings heavily damaged many houses, factories, and the country's social and physical infrastructure. By 1980, the monetary sector and its manufacturing subsector were producing 27 % and 60 % below their 1971 peak levels, respectively (Government of Uganda, 1988).

Nine years of economic and political instability came temporarily to an end in 1981 when Obote regained power. For most of his leadership

(1981–85) the country was in a recovery program under IMF/IBRD auspices. The program aimed at a speedy rehabilitation of the export sector, manufacturing sector, and the physical infrastructure as well as bringing fiscal deficits and credit under tight control. After an initial devaluation of the shilling, the fixed exchange rate was replaced by a two-window exchange rate system in which most key transactions (traditional export crops, imports of petroleum and foreign aid-financed products, official grants, and servicing of debt) took place at an official rate and the balance of transactions were handled under an auction system through Window II.

The new exchange rate regime led to a substantial fall of the currency as the official dollar rate depreciated from 7.5 shillings in 1981 to 271.3 shillings in 1984, and the effective exchange rate index declined from 100 in 1979 to as low as 17.2 in 1984 (World Bank, 1985). The drastic devaluation of the shilling, along with major increases in producers' prices shifted income distribution in favor of the rural export crop growers. The internal terms of trade index, as measured by the price index of coffee over the consumer price index (excluding food items), rose steadily from 1 in the third quarter of 1981 to as high as 6.36 in the third quarter of 1984 (Belshaw, 1988, p. 122). This left the main burden of the adjustment on urban wage and salary earners whose real incomes were steadily eroded by increases in the cost of living. By the end of 1984 the real minimum wage-index stood at 15 % of its level of 1971 (Loxley, 1989, table 3.3). By 1984, however, the program collapsed as Uganda entered into another civil war. The atrocities committed by Obote and his army surpassed those of Amin and undermined the morality and integrity of the state and its administration. The result was even more devastating for the country than before.[2]

Uganda's history over the past generation reveals the country's rich potential and some of the obstacles to its realization. The lessons that have been learned are summarized as follows:

1. Given political stability and law and order, the economy can achieve a relatively high rate of growth (higher than many countries in sub-Saharan Africa) even under a very conventional development strategy.

2. The normal functioning of the economy can seriously be disrupted once regional, political, and economic conflicts are settled though the use of force.

3. Uganda's unsuccessful experience with the economic recovery program of 1981–84 does reaffirm the observation made by the Commonwealth

Team of Experts (1979) in reviewing conditions in Uganda: "the task of rehabilitation is not, or even fundamentally, a financial one. The really important need is to reform the institutions and politics the Government inherited. More fundamentally still, successful rehabilitation depends on political leadership to bridge the rifts in Ugandan society—some long standing, some of more recent origin—and to create law, order and political stability."

### 15.1.1   Macroeconomic Issues, 1986–89

In January 1986, the National Resistance Army (NRA) marched triumphantly into Kampala and the National Resistance Movement (NRM, the political wing of the NRA) formed a government of national reconciliation. The NRM inherited a country in which law and order hardly existed, thousands of innocent people were displaced, social infrastructure was all but destroyed, the transport system was in disarray, inflation was running at over 168 % per annum, the budget was completely out of control, and many economic activities were transferred to a flourishing *magendo* economy providing a demoralized civil service and many others with an alternative source of income. Following its victory the NRM formed a government whose platform, as set out in the Ten Point Program included democratization, provision of security, consolidation of national unity, building of an independent, integrated and self-sustaining national economy, restoration and improvement of social services, elimination of corruption and misuse of power, and following a strategy of a mixed economy.

During its first two years in power the NRM went to great lengths to restore law and order, to resolve regional problems by creating a broad-based government encompassing different regional, ethnic, and ideological strands, and to provide relief to war-damaged areas. The government was, however, slow in undertaking comprehensive medium-term reform. After a short experience with an ill-defined interim macroeconomic policy program the authorities formulated a more comprehensive short- and medium-term policy package in early 1987, which was used subsequently for its negotiations with the IMF/IBRD.[3]

The Economic Policy Package for Reconstruction and Development included demand-management and supply-stimulation measures to restore internal and external balances. The package's main feature was a currency reform, according to which the currency was re-scaled by a factor of 100 and a conversion tax of 30 % across the board was imposed on cash holdings, time and saving deposits, and on the treasury bills and government stocks held by the public. The program also provided for price increases of between three to five times for traditional export crops, a devaluation of the currency by 329% (77% in foreign currency), and an upward adjustment in prices of essential consumer items. These measures, supported by IMF/IBRD, were incorporated into a three-year rehabilitation and development plan (RDP).

Although this reform package resembled the National Recovery Program of 1981–84, the NRM considered it to be superior in several ways. Instead of short-term and high-cost external financing, the RDP drew mainly on grants and concessional loans. It also provided for a direct allocation of foreign exchange to priority sectors and projects, allowing for a balanced recovery in line with government priorities and goals. No such detailed allocation was attempted in the National Recovery Program of 1981–84, and consequently more scarce foreign exchange was spend on imports of consumer items, many of which could be produced locally.

Adjustment in the exchange rate and changes in producers' prices of export crops were both more moderate and less frequent than before. These ensured that price incentives were synchronized with the removal of supply bottlenecks and that shifts in income distribution in favor of the rural sector of the economy were not so large and abrupt as to be politically destabilizing. Finally, the recent policy reform provided not only for control over total government spending but also for a restructuring of the recurrent budget by controlling the administration of government spending, broadening the tax base, and improving the administration of the tax collection system.

Growth performance during the first two years of the program was impressive, but the pace of reconstruction remained slow. Foreign exchange requirements were much higher than anticipated by the World Bank and IMF. Slow output growth of export crops and the slump in world coffee prices further worsened the trade account. Faced with shrinking export earnings and the slow disbursement of foreign aid, the government gradually compromised its policy stance under IMF and World Bank urging.

This change became evident in late 1988 and early 1989, as the pace of trade and price liberalization quickened and unpopular budget cuts were imposed. Following the introduction of an export retention scheme allowing exporters of nontraditional agricultural products to use their foreign exchange earnings to make payments on imports, the government introduced a special import program (SIP) in December 1988. It permitted allocation of foreign exchange for a very broad list of imports on a first-come, first-served basis.

In early 1989, the ERP was extended for an additional three years and the annual structural adjustment program was replaced by a three-year extended adjustment facility (ESAF). The goals were (among others) the maintenance of an annual GDP growth rate of 5 %, a reduction in inflation to 7.5 %, the attainment of a sustainable external position by the end of the program, more frequent adjustment of the exchange rate, an improvement in the fiscal budgetary position via better tax collection, expenditure control, and civil service restructuring, and the suspension of foreign exchange surrender requirements for non-coffee exports.

Subsequent devaluations steadily reduced the real effective exchange rate index from 131.6 in 1987 to 86.1 in the fourth quarter of 1989, and to as low as 53.4 in the first quarter of 1991. On the fiscal front, the government's deficit as a share of GDP (cash basis) was project to decline from 5 % in fiscal year 1987—88 to 2.4 % in 1988—89 and 1.6 % in 1989—90.

### 15.1.2   Potential Problems in the Medium Run

There has been concern that the government's long-term development objectives will be submerged by short- and medium-term attempts to cope with immediate crises and rehabilitating the economy. This perceived danger is reinforced by two factors. First, Mamdani (1988), among others, argues that the broad-based government created by the NRM has not been organized around a minimum program, but around a distribution of offices. The NRM's failure to define a comprehensive long-term economic and social policy strategy has led to a policy-making environment in which "state policy is simply responding to pressures, moving in the directions where they are strongest" (Mamdani, 1988, p. 1164). In its reconciliation with political reality, the NRM aligned itself mainly with the southern propertied class and other organized forces of the old order. Their well-established political parties within the government serve "to hold back any attempt to usher in fundamental social change" (Mamdani, 1988, p. 1168).

Second, the NRM's failure to define a comprehensive long-term development strategy has led, among other things, to a recovery program that is influenced more by a desire (mainly held by some senior government officials and foreign aid donors) to reconstruct the prevailing economic structure of the 1960s instead of aiming for "an integrated self-sustaining independent economy." Rehabilitation of the capital-intensive, import-intensive, and mostly urban-based manufacturing units, promotion of the traditional export crops, and rebuilding an expensive urban-based health care delivery system are in direct contradiction with this stated NRM goal.

The program also raises the issue of reliance on foreign financing and the growing debt burden. The government was initially hesitant in its approach to the IMF and IBRD. The experience of the first year in power demonstrated that a rapid economic recovery and reconstruction require foreign financing. In its negotiation with the IMF/IBRD and other aid donors the government has been quite successful in attracting grants and concessional money, which relax the foreign exchange constraint and reduce the debt servicing burden.

A resort to foreign financing is not, however, without its shortcomings. The government has taken several steps to ensure the effective utilization of external resources according to national priorities, but its investment program depends heavily on foreign aid donors who influence the pace and allocation of resources. Furthermore, the deterioration in the machinery of public administration during the past 15 years, low morale among the civil service, lack of technical and managerial skills, and widespread corruption all mitigate against effective utilization of the external resources.

Finally, in its rehabilitation efforts the government has relied increasingly on a few ministries with little input from the community at large. This bureaucratic approach to recovery has alienated many Ugandans.

## 15.2 Macroeconomic Issues: External, Saving, and Fiscal Constraints

To assess the extent of medium- and long-term macroeconomic constraints to the economic growth we formulated and estimated a three-gap model, the results of which are summarized in table 15.2 (see Sepehri and Loxley 1989).

According to the most likely scenario, output and capacity are expected to grow at an average rate of 5 % and 3 % per annum over the medium-term (1988–90), respectively. This scenario represents a slow recovery process, providing Uganda with a per capita income by the end of the reform program, which is 60 % of its 1971 peak level. Underlying this growth path lie several structural-parameter changes, which are all expected to ease fiscal, saving, and foreign exchange constraints.

A projected increase in public investment from 2.8 % of potential output to 3.7 % removes infrastructural bottlenecks, rehabilitates agricultural-industrial productive capacity, and relaxes the foreign exchange gap by increasing exports and reducing imports through import substitution. It

**Table 15.2**
Projected growth paths (millions of U.S.$)

|  | Base year (1987) | Scenarios | | Long term (1991–95) |
| --- | --- | --- | --- | --- |
|  |  | Medium term (1988–90) | | |
|  |  | Most likely | Socially desirable | Most likely |
| Potential output (Q) | 4,685 | 5,119 | 5,270 | 5,935 |
| Output (X)[a] | 3,514 | 4,068 | 4,245 | 5,192 |
| Capacity utilization (X/Q*100) | 75.0 | 79.5 | 80.0 | 87.5 |
| Gross capital inflows |  | 510 | 680 | — |
| Net capital inflows |  | 390 | 561 | 330 |
|  |  | As % of Q | | |
| Investment | 12.1 | 14.2 | 18.8 | 15.1 |
| Government investment | 2.8 | 3.7 | 5.7 | 2.8 |
| Government saving[b] | −3.9 | −1.9 | −0.6 | −1.1 |
| Government financing req. | 6.7 | 5.6 | 7.0 | 3.9 |

Notes: a. Output (X) is defined as real GDP + intermediate imports.
 b. Government saving is adjusted for the inflationary component of interest payments.

also has a crowding-in effect on private investment by raising it from 9.3 % of potential output to 10.5 %.

To fill the saving gap, after allowing for the effect of higher output on private and public savings, the government has to improve its marginal propensity to save. It has taken measures to broaden the tax base, improve the efficiency of tax collection, and control recurrent expenditures. Higher output and an additional public revenue effort reduced the government borrowing requirement from 6.7 % of potential output to 5.6 %. This fiscal gap is much larger than the projection given in the Policy Framework Paper (PFP) prepared jointly by the Government of Uganda, the IMF, and the IBRD. It assumes that government expenditures and borrowing requirements rise initially and then by 1990 decline slightly below their 1987 levels.

These budgetary operations raise two interesting points. First, the last thing Uganda needs is a cut in total government spending. The level per capita is among the lowest in the world and further real cuts would undermine what remains of social expenditures and civil service morale. The government has been understandably cautious about taking quick action despite increasing pressure from IMF/IBRD to cut drastically public sector employment (Government of Uganda, et al., 1987; World Bank, 1988). With the economic recovery and with a gradual decline in inflation, the government will be in a better position to restructure the civil service and wages.

Second, the fiscal position is likely to stay vulnerable to the performance of foreign trade in general and of export earnings from coffee in particular. In the fiscal year 1976–77, taxes on foreign trade accounted for 51 % of recurrent revenue and the export duty on coffee for 40 % (Government of Uganda, *Background to the Budget*, 1988). This dangerous dependence on coffee, which accounted for over 90 % of foreign exchange earnings during the past 15 years, is not expected to change substantially in the medium-term.

With regard to the foreign sector, the growth of output and new investments are projected to increase imports of intermediate and capital goods by as much as 20 % and 5.6 % per annum during 1988–90, respectively. Assuming that the government's measures toward export expansion succeed in increasing earnings by 7 % per annum, total gross capital inflows required to close the foreign exchange gap are estimated to amount to $510 million per annum. This is about 30 % higher than the initial PFP projection, but almost identical to the latest revision. Financing this foreign exchange gap will be less problematic if foreign aid donors meet commitments they made in 1987 and 1988.[4]

A second projection—for a socially desirable growth path, including a 6.5 % output growth rate per annum and a 4 % capacity growth rate per annum—includes a more aggressive role for public investment as well as higher needs for capital inflows than assumed under the first scenario. Public investment rises from 2.8 % of potential output to 5.7 % and the government borrowing requirement drops from 6.7 % of potential output to 6.3 %. The foreign exchange requirement is $680 million per annum.

A long-term projection to 1995 based on the most likely scenario indicates that the availability of foreign exchange continues to be the most severe constraint and the fiscal gap will be far less binding. Public investment can decline to its 1987 level as the rehabilitation of the key sectors of the economy is completed. This reduction and higher capacity utilization imply that the government borrowing requirement per unit of potential output will decline to 40 % below its 1987 level. The foreign exchange requirements per annum under this long-term scenario are expected to decline only moderately (based on an optimistic export growth rate of 4 % per annum and rapid import substitution, which reduces the output elasticity for intermediate imports from 4 to as low as 1.6).

### 15.2.1   Other Macroeconomic Constraints

The Land Reform Decree of 1975 and the recent increases in transfers of land ownership have created an urgent need for an institutional reform to give security of tenure to tenants.

The limited accessibility of the public to the banking system is another major obstacle to a speedy economic recovery. Uganda has one of the lowest banking densities in the world (179,000 people per bank office), and few commercial banks have offices outside Kampala, Jinja, and other urban centers. Commercial banks should be encouraged to mobilize domestic savings by expanding their branches and agency networks into the rural areas. The Cooperative Bank should be encouraged to renew its services to those for whom it was originally established, and alternative grass roots credit and saving societies should also be encouraged.

### 15.2.2   The Role of the State

In Uganda, as in most developing countries, the state has historically played a significant role in the process of economic change. In the 1960s, it was instrumental in widening and strengthening industry and social infrastructure. During Amin's military regime, public control and regulation was drastically enhanced, often in arbitrary and contradictory ways. The expulsion of the Asians and foreigners and appropriation of their assets by the state brought about a substantial shift in the nation's wealth.

Every government in the post-Amin era tried to redistribute the former Asian assets among its own military-tribal affiliates, as well as carry out its own "economic war" against opponents. Besides frequent appropriation and redistribution of property, every government used its control over public enterprises, whose number mushroomed after Amin's initial "war," to transform them into little kingdoms for political supporters of the ruling party. These measures undermined profoundly the integrity and legitimacy of the state.

Among the questions confronting the NRM government today are how to resolve the uncertainty surrounding former Asian assets; to restore the morale and integrity of the state and its administration; and to restructure public enterprises. There are pressures, both inside and outside of the country, to privatize some of the existing parastatals, to limit government intervention in marketing of food crops and basic consumer goods, and to liberalize trade.

Up to now, the government has been very cautious in its approach to the privatization and liberalization. Control over parastatal operations has been nonexistent since 1971 and subsidies and subventions to these enterprises in 1986 amounted to over 14 billion shillings (Uganda Study Team, 1987, p. 25). Whatever the ideological undertone of the current debate over the role of the private versus the public sector, there are structural and institutional factors that should influence any evaluation.

First, the private sector has yet to recover from the expulsion of Asian entrepreneurs and the departure of many qualified Ugandan managers and technical personnel. Second, in the absence of a sufficiently well developed, regionally broad-based bourgeoisie, the privatization of parastatals, even if effectively carried out, will generally benefit a few propertied groups (mainly former supporters of Obote and Okello) who got their wealth from redistribution under past corrupt governments, as well as aspiring, mainly southern-based, entrepreneurs. This likely outcome is clearly not consistent with the government's commitment to regional and income equality.

Third, the economic and political crises of the last 15 years have affected adversely the performance of both private and public enterprises. The poor financial state of many parastatals is, to some degree, a reflection of the past economic environment, as characterized by (1) the haphazard manner in which parastatals were created, (2) excessive government intervention in day-to-day operations, (3) a hiring policy based on party or tribal affiliation rather than qualification, and (4) frequent disruptions in economic activity. Finally, in the absence of an equitable tax system and well-developed financial markets, the budgetary benefits of privatization are minimal.

As regards trade, there has been concern that unplanned and indiscriminate import liberalization threatens rehabilitation and reconstruction of most industries. Uganda's experience with liberalization and the auction system of exchange rate determination and allocation under the recovery program of 1981–84 provides the reason. Not only did the recovery program permit a large proportion (40–60 %) of scarce foreign exchange to be used for the importation of consumer goods, but it also facilitated capital flight (Uganda Study Team, 1987). There was little foreign exchange left to import spare parts and raw materials. The implication is that rehabilitation and reconstruction of industry must be planned under a protective environment: This needs a change in the nature of state regulation of foreign trade rather than a reduction in its degree.

## 15.3 Microeconomic Issues

Against this macroeconomic background, Uganda also faces pressing sectoral problems in agriculture, industry, mining, and with the income distribution.

### 15.3.1    Agriculture

The agricultural sector is usually seen as central to the rehabilitation of the economy, both in the short and medium term. In 1987, it accounted for 50% of real GDP, over 95% of total export earnings, and 40% of government revenue, and provided employment to 80% of the working population.

Agriculture suffered dramatically over the past 15 years. In 1987, the monetary part of the sector, which was more adversely affected than its subsistence counterpart, produced an output that was about 28% below its 1973 peak level; officially marketed coffee was 43% below its 1969 peak level, and the production of the other export cash crops such as cotton, tea, and tobacco had declined to as low as less than 10% of their former peak levels.

High output levels for many export cash crops in the early 1970s and self-sufficiency in food, even during the turbulent past 15 years, demonstrate the potential of agricultural capacity. However, its realization requires appropriate and effective institutional, technical, and microeconomic measures designed to address constraints faced by each major individual cash crop, in both production and marketing.[5]

Regarding food self-sufficiency, there are two major obstacles. As the Agricultural Secretariat (1986) concludes, Uganda "is now existing at a very delicate level of food self-sufficiency." In the past, the country could feed itself and during an abnormally good harvest have a surplus for export. However, food production has increasingly come under stress by past export expansion and promotion measures, shortages of land, and the low level of technology used to meet growing domestic needs. During 1971–81, the overall annual growth rate in food production (1.1%) did not keep up with population growth (2.8%) and the result was a rapid decline in per capital availability of food for consumption, mainly cereal, pulses, and oil seeds (Agricultural Secretariat, 1987). Demand for food is estimated to grow at an average annual rate of 5 to 6% over the period 1988–91 with projected population growth rate of 2.8% and a significant improvement in per capita income (Agricultural Secretariat, 1987). To achieve food sufficiency, an innovative strategic policy must be articulated that aims at the following:

1. to rehabilitate and redirect research, extension services, marketing, and credit in a more balanced way toward food production as well as export cash crops;

2. to build up national food reserves to guard against unexpected disruptions in food supply from the producing areas;

3. to open up new arable land for cultivation of food crops;

4. to investigate the possibility for both food export and import-substitution; and

5. to improve the efficiency of institutions as regards the sale of agriculture inputs, processing and the purchase of food crops by promoting the participation of parastatals, cooperatives, and private institutions.

For cash crops, the main challenge is to reverse declining trends in the production of traditional exports. The major problems in recent years include severe inadequacy in the provision of agricultural inputs and extension services, inadequate transport equipment and poor roads, crop financing and payments difficulties, and unreliable power supplies. Low producers' prices, high inflation rates, and shortages of basic consumer items have seriously undermined producers' incentives. Ugandan farmers have been paid poorly, even in comparison to neighboring countries. Farmers' share in the world price of clean robusta coffee, Uganda's main export crop, amounted to less than 40 % in 1987–88, and the real producer price in July 1988 (after the official upward price adjustment) was 44 % below its average level for the period 1967–70.

For the purpose of making the structural adjustment to the foreign exchange constraint and to diversify exports, it is vital to promote the production and export of nontraditional export crops. Measures already taken include promotion of barter trade, which allows exporters to retain some of their earnings to import goods. A more effective and comprehensive effort must yet be taken toward (1) establishing an efficient marketing system which provides producers with a guaranteed market and a competitive price, (2) providing financial and technical support to both producers and exporters, (3) clarifying the role of the private sector in the marketing and exporting of food crops, and (4) analyzing the cost efficiency of various crops and their comparative advantages.

## 15.3.2 Manufacturing

During its first post-independence decade, Uganda built up its manufacturing base by active import substitution. The manufacturing sector, although relatively small, did satisfy domestic demand for a range of basic consumer and intermediate goods (sugar, textiles, edible oils, fertilizers, cement) and exported some of its products, which accounted for almost 20 % of total foreign exchange earnings at its peak. Many medium- and large-scale enterprises are today publicly owned and managed by the Uganda Development Corporation. These companies account for about 50 % of the turnover in manufacturing. Agro-industries (cotton ginning, coffee curing, and sugar) provide 17 % of the value added by the sector, food processing 6 % and miscellaneous manufacturing (steel, textile, tobacco, paper, soap, leather) 77 % (World Bank, 1988, p.2).

No other sector was as adversely affected by the economic and political crises as manufacturing. In 1987, output was less than 43 % of the 1971 peak level. Many enterprises are now operating at less than one-fourth of their capacity and face enormous problems: obsolete and poorly maintained equipment and machinery, frequent power supply failures, inadequate working capital, shortages of managerial and technical expertise, ownership problems, shortages of spare parts and intermediate imports, a bad debt record, and negative effective rates of protection.

The basic objectives of government industrial policy are to help the sector recover in the short run, and to create a base for long-term growth. Several potential problems arise. The first is incompatibility between the short and medium term objective of achieving self-sufficiency in basic consumer goods through the rehabilitation of existing industries and the need to restructure the sector in the long run. Many existing firms are urban-based, and are capital- and foreign-exchange intensive. They were created and developed mainly under a very protective environment. Nonetheless, renewed activity of some existing light industries is essential for relaxing the foreign exchange and fiscal constraints. Beyond that, however, cost efficiency, foreign exchange savings efficiency, and capital-intensity of the industrial strategy should be given serious consideration, especially if the overall economic objective is to achieve an independent, integrated, and self-sustaining national economy.

The second question concerns the economic viability of rehabilitating the existing industries. Many were created and managed by Asian entrepreneurs and other professionals under an overvalued fixed exchange rate regime. The expulsion of Asian entrepreneurs and the departure of many of Uganda's best managers and skilled personnel created a vacuum that is yet to be filled by emerging African entrepreneurs. Moreover, it is now difficult for Uganda to provide the protective environment that industry had in the past.

The third question relates to the role of large formal versus small informal industrial units. It might be more appropriate in terms of job creation, both in rural and urban areas, and in the use of raw materials and in-digenous technology, to utilize the potential offered by the informal manu-facturing sector rather than concentrating on the rehabilitation of formal sector firms. During the past 15 years, the small informal manufacturing sector has grown rapidly. It is estimated to account for more than 78 % of total industrial establishments employing two or more people, producing more than 50 % of the value-added, and accounting for 80 % of the total employment in industry (Uganda Economic Study Team, 1987, p. 14).

Finally, there is the question of foreign exchange requirements for recon-struction and utilization of industrial capacity. According to past estimates, an increase in average capacity utilization from 20 % to 60 % over two years (1982–83) for 125 selective industries would cost more than U.S. $340 million in direct foreign exchange (World Bank, 1982, table 5.3). Part of this expenditure would be recovered through a reduction in imports, but it is still high considering the import bill of U.S. $600 million for 1987. Given the poor state of machinery and equipment of many industrial units, the high foreign exchange cost implies not only the need for a careful selection of industries but also a very slow improvement in capacity use.

15.3.3   Income Redistribution and Basic Needs

The income distribution and provision of basic needs have been pro-foundly affected by the last 15 years of economic stagnation and decline, war and physical insecurity, and the destruction of social infrastructure. In the absence of data it is not possible to document the extent of misery and hardship. The available evidence, including some anecdotal information, indicates the basic trends:

1. a steady reduction in rural/urban cash income differentials throughout the 1970s and more sharply in the 1980s;

2. a decline in urban real wages;

3. a general increase in income concentration; and

4. a breakdown in the distinction between formal and informal sectors and emergence of a grand trader-cum wage earner-cum *shamba* (small private garden) growing class.

The urban-rural cash income differential that widened in the 1960s was reversed with the stagnation and decline of output of the formal urban economy and an extremely buoyant rural sector. The average wage bill for the public and private formal sectors rose by 6.2 % per annum between 1970 and 1977 (the latest year for which data are available) while coffee prices and coffee producers' earnings rose by 24.3 % and 18 %, respectively, during 1972–78. The estimated rural-urban cash income differential continued to decline from an average of about 1:4 in 1980 to 1:2 in 1985 (Uganda Economic Study Team, 1987, p. 7).

Nominal income growth of formal urban wage earners was completely offset by a growing inflation throughout the 1970s and 1980s. The real wage index, according to one estimate, declined from 100 in 1972, to 35 in 1976, and to as low as 9 in November 1984 (Jamal and Weeks, 1988, p. 288). According to the most recent Census of Civil Servants, the official monetary salaries for the top and the lowest grade scale accounted for 3 % and 0.7 % of monthly monetary income needed to sustain a family of five in Kampala, respectively (Government of Uganda, 1988). To compensate for these substantial declines in real income, urban wage earners relied increasingly on other sources. The result has been an emergence of the "trader-cum-wage-earner-cum-*shamba*" class that blurs the distinction between the formal and informal sectors.

Cash crop growers also experienced a substantial decline in their purchasing power. The coffee producers' real price index declined steadily from 100 in 1972 to 21 in 1979 and after a rapid recovery during the period 1981–84 continued to drop to as low as 44 in 1986 (Loxley, 1989, table 3.3).

The general worsening income distribution has hit women and children as they have to supplement family income by engaging in petty trading, growing and marketing food crops, and brewing and handicrafts, in addition to their normal activities and household chores. The result of general deterioration in the quality of life has been low morale among wage earners, low productivity, corruption, and theft.

Years of war, destruction, and negligence also have affected adversely the provision of basic needs services. Primary health care facilities have virtually collapsed and availability and quality of education have deteriorated drastically.[6] Although exact figures are not known, it is commonly believed in Uganda that the infant mortality rate, the under-five mortality rate, and the maternal mortality rate are all very high.[7] The infant mortality rate in 1985 was estimated at 120 per 1,000 live births, the same level achieved in 1969 (Dodge, 1987).

Real growth at 5 % per annum, an upward adjustment in wages and producers' prices, a decline in inflation, and an improvement in the long-term sense of stability may reverse the decline in incomes experienced during the past 15 years. But these expected benefits are yet to materialize, especially for the urban wage and salary earners and for some sections of the rural sector, for whom inflation continues to erode purchasing power.

Experiences of other countries under IMF structural adjustment, in general, and Ghana (one supposedly successful model of IMF structural adjustment), in particular, indicate clearly that the trickle-down effects of the structural adjustment have seldom been realized.[8] In recognition of this fact, the IBRD and other donors recently initiated several projects targeted at alleviating the adverse effect of the structural adjustment on the disadvantaged groups. Although these attempts constitute a step in the direction of design of structural adjustment programs with a human face, they still fall short of incorporating distributional considerations directly into the design of structural adjustment programs. Any policy attempt towards restoring output growth must also strive to achieve an equitable distribution of income, which guarantees that people's basic needs are met.

The government has committed itself to rehabilitation and reorganization of social services, as well as to a more equitable distribution of income. However, its approach is often viewed as a "top-down bureaucratic one with little input from the community at large." It is further argued by Dodge (1987), among others, that the government "must decide if the simple but expensive rehabilitation of a 1960s-style system is desirable and possible, or if the more difficult but potentially more appropriate redefinition of health services is needed for the remainder of the 1980s and beyond" (pp. 110–111).

## Notes

1. Macroeconomic indicators for this period and parts of the 1980s should be interpreted with care. As the economy steadily deteriorated, the quality of its statistics fell.

2. For an evaluation of the 1981–84 program, see Loxley (1989) and Belshaw (1988).

3. The Interim Macroeconomic Measures are summarized by the Uganda Study Team (1987).

4. In a recent donor meeting, the Consultative Group for Uganda raised their commitments by 26 % to 2.1 billion dollars over the period 1988–91 (World Bank, 1988).

5. Belshaw (1988) examines factors contributing to the failure of the 1981–85 agricultural recovery program and draws policy lessons.

6. UNICEF (1989) reviews the state of primary health care.

7. Based on hospital surveys and statistics, it is estimated that over half of all deaths in Uganda are among children younger than five years.

8. The United Nations (1989) report on the world social situation argues that structural adjustment policies of the World Bank and International Monetary Fund have not addressed the problems of alleviating rural poverty, unemployment, food scarcity, malnutrition, and inadequate health and education services.

## References

Agricultural Secretariat (1986). *The Food Crops in Uganda: A Review of the Situation Between 1971 and 1985, Factors Contributing to Stagnation in Production and Strategies for Improved Future Production*. Kampala: Bank of Uganda.

Agricultural Secretariat (1987). *Food Production in Uganda—Past Trends, Projection and Policy Issues*. Kampala: Bank of Uganda.

Belshaw, Deryke (1988). "Agriculture-led Recovery in Post-Amin Uganda: Causes of Failure and the Bases for Success," in Bernt Hensen and Michael Twaddle (eds.), *Uganda Now: Between Decay and Development*. London: Lames Currey.

Commonwealth Team of Experts (1979). *The Rehabilitation of the Economy of Uganda*. A report prepared for the Commonwealth Secretariat, London.

Dodge, Cole (1987). "Rehabilitation or Redefinition of Health Services," in Paul Wiebe and Cole Dodge (eds.), *Beyond Crisis: Development Issues in Uganda*. Kampala: Makerere Institute of Social Research.

Government of Uganda, (various issues). *Background to the Budget*, Ministry of Planning and Economic Development, Kampala.

Government of Uganda (1987a). *The Rehabilitation and Development Plan: 1987/88– 1990/91*. Kampala: Ministry of Planning and Economic Development.

Government of Uganda (1987b). *Uganda's Economic Policy Package for Reconstruction and Development*. An address to the nation by H. E. President Yoweri K. Museveni. Entebbe: Government printer (May).

Government of Uganda (1988). *Census of Civil Servants*. Kampala: Ministry of Information.

Government of Uganda, the IMF, and the World Bank (1987). "Uganda: Policy Framework Paper." Washington, DC: IBRD and IDA.

Jamal, Vali, and John Weeks (1988). "The Vanishing Rural-Urban Gap in Sub-Saharan Africa." *International Labour Review*, 27: 271–292.

Loxley, John (1989). "The IMF, the World Bank and Reconstruction in Uganda," in Bonnie Campbell and John Loxley (eds.), *Structural Adjustment in Africa*. London: Macmillan.

Mamdani, Mahmood (1988). "Uganda in Transition: Two Years of the NRA/ NRM." *Third World Quarterly*, 10: 1155–1181.

Sepehri, A., and J. Loxley (1989). "Uganda: Constraints to Economic Growth." (Mimeo), University of Manitoba, Winnipeg.

Uganda Economic Study Team (1987). *Economic Adjustment and Long-term Development in Uganda*. A report prepared for the Government of Uganda and the International Development Research Center. Ottawa: IDRC.

UNICEF (1989). *State of the World's Children*, New York: United Nations.

World Bank (1982). *Uganda: Country Economic Memorandum*. Washington, DC: World Bank.

World Bank (1985). *Uganda: Progress Towards Recovery and Prospects for Development*. Washington, DC: World Bank.

World Bank (1988). *Uganda: Toward Stabilization and Economic Recovery*. Washington, DC: World Bank.

# 16        Argentina

José María Fanelli and
Robert Frenkel

This study provides a global approach to Argentina's medium term development issues. The first section reviews the development strategy followed by the country in the post-war period. Emphasis is placed on the role of the state as a locomotive of growth, the characteristics of the investment-saving financing process, and the consequences of the policies pursued for the income distribution and the behavior of the entrepreneurial class. Likewise, the roles of the late 1970s liberalization attempt and the 1975 crisis in generating the present economic situation are examined. The second section analyzes growth prospects in terms of saving, external and fiscal gaps. The third section evaluates medium-term development issues in the public, industrial, and agricultural sectors, and there is a brief reference to employment and income distribution.

## 16.1    The Postwar Development Strategy

Just after World War II, Argentina was relatively prosperous, but was beginning to show the signs of the distributional and policy conflicts that would constrict the growth process three decades later. The first important feature of the 1946–74 period is that Argentina was able to sustain economic growth relatively well in spite of its inflationary and balance-of-payments problems. The performance of the economy was much better than that observed after 1975, even though its growth rate was lower than those in the most successful countries in the region such as Mexico and Brazil.

### 16.1.1    From Unstable Growth to Stagnation: 1946–74

The growth rate averaged 3.5 % per year over the period.[1] Given the relatively slow growth of population (around 1.6 %), there was a steady

**Table 16.1**
Inflation and GDP (annual growth rates in percentage)

| Year | Inflation | GDP | Agriculture | Industry |
|------|-----------|-----|-------------|----------|
| 1971 | 34.7 | 3.76 | 1.57 | 6.14 |
| 1972 | 58.4 | 2.08 | 1.92 | 4.02 |
| 1973 | 60.3 | 3.74 | 10.71 | 3.97 |
| 1974 | 24.2 | 5.41 | 2.73 | 5.87 |
| 1975 | 182.8 | −0.59 | −2.75 | −2.55 |
| 1976 | 444.1 | −0.01 | 4.53 | −3.03 |
| 1977 | 176.0 | 6.38 | 2.46 | 7.81 |
| 1978 | 175.5 | −3.22 | 2.82 | −10.52 |
| 1979 | 159.5 | 7.02 | 2.82 | 10.19 |
| 1980 | 100.8 | 1.53 | −5.51 | −3.79 |
| 1981 | 104.5 | −6.71 | 1.93 | −15.98 |
| 1982 | 164.8 | −4.98 | 6.92 | −4.73 |
| 1983 | 343.8 | 2.93 | 1.89 | 10.81 |
| 1984 | 626.7 | 2.46 | 3.57 | 4.03 |
| 1985 | 672.2 | −4.38 | −2.57 | −10.51 |
| 1986 | 90.1 | 5.38 | −2.79 | 12.88 |
| 1987 | 131.3 | 2.00 | 3.40 | −0.57 |
| 1988 | 342.9 | −2.80 | 0.20 | −6.80 |

Source: BCRA and INDEC.

improvement in per capita GDP of about 2% per year. However, the growth rate showed a wide variance. The higher levels were registered in the late 1940s and mid-1960s. The most stable period, on the other hand, was between 1964 and 1974. During those 10 years there was not one year in which the growth rate was negative and it averaged 4.5% per year, similar to the first three decades of the present century, when the economy had its greatest success.

Typically, there was marked instability in the short run, taking the form of recurrent crises in the external sector followed by IMF-inspired stabilization policies designed to restore an equilibrium between domestic absorption and domestic income. The prominent role that the balance of payments played in explaining the short-run behavior of the economy was inherent to the development strategy that was chosen.

The basic source of growth was import substitution, which led to rapid development of the industrial sector, but exports did not expand fast enough to cover a secularly increasing demand for foreign exchange. Especially just after the war, disequilibrium arose because policy stressed

**Table 16.2**
Balance of payments (current million dollars)

| Year | Trade surplus | Financial services surplus | Current account surplus |
|------|---------------|----------------------------|-------------------------|
| 1970 | 79.1 | −222.5 | −158.9 |
| 1971 | −127.7 | −255.9 | −388.7 |
| 1972 | 36.4 | −333.6 | −222.9 |
| 1973 | 1036.5 | −394.4 | 720.7 |
| 1974 | 295.8 | −333.3 | 127.2 |
| 1975 | −985.2 | −429.6 | −1284.6 |
| 1976 | 883.1 | −492.5 | 649.6 |
| 1977 | 1409.3 | −578.5 | 1289.9 |
| 1978 | 2565.8 | −680.8 | 1833.6 |
| 1979 | 1109.9 | −920.0 | −536.4 |
| 1980 | −2519.2 | −1531.4 | −4767.8 |
| 1981 | −287.0 | −3699.7 | −4714.0 |
| 1982 | 2286.8 | −4718.5 | −2657.7 |
| 1983 | 3320.0 | −5407.9 | −2437.5 |
| 1984 | 3523.0 | −5712.0 | −2390.9 |
| 1985 | 4351.0 | −5305.0 | −952.8 |
| 1986 | 1555.0 | −4416.0 | −2859.0 |
| 1987 | 257.0 | −4485.0 | −4236.0 |
| 1988 | 3550.0 | −5181.0 | −1631.0 |

Source: BCRA.

import substitution rather than export diversification. Another factor that amplified the short-run effects of the cyclical shortage of foreign exchange was the difficulty that Argentina faced in obtaining credit from abroad. Across the cycles, however, foreign saving was not important in financing domestic investment and Argentina utilized comparatively much less external financing than Brazil or Mexico in the same period.

Due to these structural features, in the short run the economy followed a "stop-and-go" model:[2] As the activity level rose, imports would rise faster given that their income-elasticity was higher in the short than long run. Because of the short-run rigidity of exports and the scarcity of credit from abroad, the increment in the activity level was brought to a halt by the shortage of foreign exchange. At that stage of the cycle, a stabilization program was usually implemented in order to equilibrate the current account. Even though the economy was able to generate the amount of saving and the foreign exchange necessary for self-sustaining growth,

**Table 16.3**
Foreign debt (billion dollars)

| Period | External debt | | |
|--------|-------|--------|---------|
|        | Total | Public | Private |
| 1975 | 7.875  | 4.021  | 3.854  |
| 1976 | 8.279  | 5.189  | 3.090  |
| 1977 | 9.678  | 6.044  | 3.634  |
| 1978 | 12.496 | 8.357  | 4.139  |
| 1979 | 19.034 | 9.960  | 9.074  |
| 1980 | 27.162 | 14.459 | 12.703 |
| 1981 | 35.671 | 20.024 | 15.647 |
| 1982 | 43.634 | 28.616 | 15.018 |
| 1983 | 45.069 | 31.709 | 13.360 |
| 1984 | 46.903 | 36.139 | 10.764 |
| 1985 | 49.326 | 39.868 | 8.444  |
| 1986 | 51.422 | 44.000 | 7.400  |
| 1987 | 54.700 | 44.000 | 7.400  |
| 1988 | 57.000 | nd     | nd     |
| 1989 | 57.000 | nd     | nd     |

Source: BCRA.

it was achieved at the cost of generating an unstable macroeconomic environment.

Although development policies were never fully able to prevent the countercyclical behavior of the supply of foreign exchange, it is true that this constraint weakened over the years. The trade gap was "much more" binding in the 1950s than in the 1970s due to the fact that, although imports were effectively substituted throughout the period, other explicit policies designed to correct anti-trade biases and diversify exports were adopted. New goods became tradable and long-run forces that helped to equilibrate the current account emerged. The economy moved from the marked stop and go of the 1950s to the more stable growth process of 1964–74.

Two additional characteristics of the foreign-exchange constraint are worth emphasizing. As already mentioned, the disequilibrium in the current account stemmed from an excess of absorption (i.e., consumption plus investment expenditures) over income: The counterpart was a greater over-all supply of goods and services on the domestic side of the economy.

This kind of disequilibrium is notably different from the one that Argentina would suffer throughout the most recent decade. Today, the current

**Table 16.4**
Fiscal deficit (as a proportion of GDP)

| Year | Deficit |
| --- | --- |
| 1971–75 | 8.2 |
| 1976–80 | 7.5 |
| 1981–85 | 12.5 |
| 1986 | 4.1 |
| 1987 | 7.4 |
| 1988 | 4.2 |

Source: Secretaria de Hacienda.

account deficit cannot be attributed to the fact that real imports of goods and services are greater than exports. Since the debt crisis, the country has systematically shown a surplus on these accounts. Rather, imbalance persists because the increment in the country's indebtedness forced a structural disequilibrium in the financial services account and, as a consequence, policies intended to maximize the trade surplus were put into practice so as to equilibrate the current account.

A second characteristic of the external gap prior to 1975 was that when balance-of-payments problems arose, the stabilization episodes were not long lasting because absorption usually adjusted quickly to a level consistent with the country's income. There was even a propensity to generate an overkill in the adjustment. This characteristic of the stabilization process is completely at variance with what has happened throughout the 1980s. The external disequilibrium now being experienced cannot be eliminated in a short period of time because it does not stem from a disadjustment between income and domestic expenditure flows, but from disequilibrium between the flow of income and the stock of debt accumulated. Restoring any imbalance between stocks and flows takes time and tends to be difficult. In fact, during the 1980s, not only was the Argentine economy unable to reverse disequilibrium, but it could not prevent a widening of it.

Another general point that should be highlighted with regard to the 1946–74 period is that repeated strong variations in effective demand and relative prices in a context of policy shocks created a behavior pattern characterized by marked risk-aversion in the entrepreneurial class. The private sector diversified away from higher risk-long maturity investment projects. Despite a saving/output ratio of 20 %, the observed growth rate was not high precisely because of the risk-averse pattern followed in allocating resources for investment.

This conservative conduct on the part of the private sector, in turn, obliged the government to assume responsibility for investment projects with a low risk-adjusted rate of return that the private sector did not undertake. Most direct public-sector economic activity ended up in the energy, transport, steel, petrochemical, and urban infrastructure sectors. Likewise, the unstable macroeconomic environment induced firms to insulate themselves from shocks by seeking institutional agreements with the public sector which that would ensure profitability. The outcome was the buildup of a whole structure of market regulations and state interventions that often did not take into account either efficiency or income distribution.

So far we have referred to the roles played by the external constraint and macroeconomic instability in generating disequilibria. The last feature that should be stressed is the "heterodox" nature of the investment-saving process. It deserves attention because the way in which investment was financed induced long-standing effects that contributed to the deeper problems now seen in both the financial and the public sectors.

Throughout the post-war period there was no firm consensus on how much effort each sector of society was to make to provide the savings required for financing the import-substitution strategy of development. Even though *ex post* investment averaged 20 % of GDP, ex ante there would have been a gap between investment and saving. This would have been the case not so much because of an extreme preference for present consumption, but rather because of uncertainty as to which sector would receive the benefits of austerity. In great measure, this uncertainty stemmed from the abrupt changes in the distribution of income induced by the policy shocks.

Support for the hypothesis of an ex ante gap between investment and saving can be seen in the way in which the financing of investment was actually carried out: A good part of required saving was obtained by means of both forced saving (via manipulation of relative prices) and redistributions of the stocks of financial wealth (regulating prices and/or quantities on the monetary side of the economy).

Many devices were used to generate forced saving through variations in relative prices. However, the principal role was played by public policies via manipulations of absolute prices that were directly or indirectly under the control of the economic authorities: wages, exchange rates, and public enterprise prices. The changes induced in the structure of relative prices produced redistributions of income favoring the accumulation of capital in both the industrial and public sectors. Different sectors were adversely affected by these policies in distinct periods but, in general, the rural sector and low-wage workers carried the heaviest burdens.

Of the variety of mechanisms employed to generate forced saving, three can be said to be typical. First, the relationship between internal and external prices was biased to shelter the industrial sector. This was done by building up protectionist barriers via tariff or import prohibitions and taxing agricultural exports. Because of adverse terms of trade, there was a transfer of incomes from the rural to the urban sector. Urban workers and the public sector were not necessarily favored since both were obliged to pay for costly industrial goods. A second mechanism was control of wages (either their level or rate of growth). Finally, numerous tax exemptions and subsidies were created to promote industry through a complex system of investment incentives. There were several reimbursement regimes for non-traditional exports. Certain imports were exempt from paying tariffs, and a "buy national" regime was put into practice.[3]

Diverse policy instruments also were utilized to redistribute financial wealth to favor the sectors that the government sought to promote. Within the financial system these took the form of interest-rate ceilings. With excess demand for credit, rationing mechanisms were implemented that resulted in an allocation of loanable funds that favored firms over households and industry over other economic activities. The ceilings usually induced negative real interest rates, resulting in a redistribution of financial wealth from creditors to debtors. Likewise, as the inflation rate was systematically high during this period, the so-called inflation tax played a significant role in financing public expenditures. Low interest rates and high inflation rates both led to the demonetization of the economy, as savers holding financial assets issued by either the banks or the government suffered a loss of financial wealth.

A second, policy-induced redistribution of financial wealth went through the retirement and pension system that was set up in the post-war period. At first there was a high surplus, between 1950 and 1960 accumulating to 28% of GDP.[4] The government tapped these funds for partial cover of its borrowing requirements. But from the mid-1970s on, when the number of retired workers began to grow, the system developed a structural deficit that was partly offset by adjusting the transfers to retired workers downward.

The outcome of all these features of the development strategy adopted between the end of the war and the mid-1970s was to produce an economic structure with increasingly unmanageable tensions.

The public sector was at center stage because it played a crucial role in both generating and allocating resources for investment. This "locomotive of growth" role turned the state into the place where distributive conflicts were resolved and, likewise, obliged it to assume productive activities well beyond its managerial capacity.

In the second place, abrupt and repeated policy shocks that induced significant redistributions of income and financial wealth exacerbated the conflict. All sectors tried to establish institutional agreements directed to protecting their real incomes. Strong oligopolies developed within the sheltered industrial sector, which used infant industry arguments to favor established incumbents over potential entrants. So long as rents generated in industry were shared with workers, each trade union strove to raise its proportion. A segmented labor market developed as select unions appeared with strong enough political power to resist policies designed to reduce incomes originating in the oligopolistic sector.

Third, the financial and monetary policies that induced segmentation of the financial markets and demonetization of the economy exacerbated macroeconomic instability; it became increasingly difficult to obtain funds for financing the fiscal deficit and firms' borrowing needs. Negative real interest rates reduced the cost of investment in physical assets in the long run. It is possible that this was why the growth rate was low in spite of the high investment/output ratio. Investment promotion policies also acted similarly in that they favored capital-intensive industries to the detriment of more labor-intensive ones.

Finally, given downward inflexibility of nominal prices, which implied that changes in relative prices had to be realized through a rising overall price level, the distributional conflict, the external crises, and the industry promotion policies interacted with each other to foster inflation.

To summarize, while the import substitution strategy succeeded in promoting industrial growth and, to a certain extent, in weakening the foreign exchange constraint, the policies implemented induced severe disequilibria in the financial system, the government budget, resource allocation, and the distribution of income. While the growth rate was acceptable, it was obtained at the cost of a highly unstable environment in the short run. The deepening of all these disequilibria provoked the economic crises of the mid-1970s.

## 16.1.2   From Stagnation to Financial Squeeze: 1975—88

In 1975, there was a fiscal deficit that reached 15 % of GDP, a spurt of inflation that led the economy to the brink of hyperinflation, and an unprecedented billion dollar current account deficit accompanied by massive capital flight. During the period following this crisis (between 1976 and 1981)[5] a market-oriented package of policy measures was put into place, in an attempt to overcome short-term disequilibria as well as the distortions induced by import substitution. The pillars of the new strategy were financial and trade reforms and liberalization of the foreign-exchange market, set firmly in place after an orthodox policy closely following IMF recommendations succeeded in stabilizing the economy during 1976–78. The ultimate outcomes were the worst economic disruptions that Argentina faced in the post-war period. Because the nation is still suffering the consequences, the salient features of the 1975–81 period are worth pointing out.

First, a long-lasting consequence of the 1975 spurt of inflation was the consolidation of a *high inflation regime* (Frenkel, 1989). Although Argentina had previously suffered from chronic inflation, there was an upward break after 1975. The annual rate would fall below 100 % only twice after the crisis, in 1980 owing to a huge overvaluation of the domestic currency and in 1986 during the Austral plan.

The persistence of high inflation rates over such an extended period accentuated the macroeconomic instability of the post-war period. There were widening oscillations of relative prices, resulting in a concomitant shortening of the time length of contracts. Specifically, wage negotiations became more frequent, and, on the financial side, the already scarce supply of medium and long-run loans disappeared. Greater uncertainty reflected itself into worsened short-run instability and stagnation in the long run.

The second characteristic of the 1976–81 period that must be highlighted has to do with the puzzling performance of the external sector. For the first time after World War II, a rapid succession of disequilibria of opposite signs was observed in the balance of payments. The final result was a huge increment of the foreign debt.

Following expansionary policies in 1973–74, there was a severe deficit in the current account in 1975. Exports grew steadily from 1976 on, mainly because of a rightward shift in the supply of tradable goods produced by the agricultural sector. The trade gap was not binding between 1976 and 1978, when the accumulated current account surplus amounted to U.S. $3.6 billion. In great measure this outcome was due to the fact that the stabilization policy implemented between 1976 and 1978 induced an overkill in the adjustment of the economy.[6]

This outstanding current account performance rapidly reversed after 1979. Trade reform and liberalization of the foreign-exchange market together with a new stabilization program, which in turn led to a huge overvaluation of the domestic currency, were the main causes. The reduction in protection via lower tariffs resulted in a spurt of imports (especially finished goods because the level of protection for intermediates had not been changed significantly), while overvaluation of the peso in the context of a higher degree of international capital mobility led to a sharp increase in the outflow of capital.

During 1979–81 the current account showed a deficit of about U.S. $10 billion. Capital flight amounted to U.S. $16.2 billion (around 23 % of Argentina's GDP). Given that the accumulated current account surplus of 1976–78 was insufficient to finance such financial outflows, the country's indebtedness rose. External debt went from U.S. $9.7 billion in 1977 to U.S. $35.7 billion in 1981. The government's external liabilities greatly increased, that is, private financial outflows were in great measure subsidized by the public sector.[7]

Finally, the liberalization attempt of the late 1970s disarticulated the financial system. Narrowed credit markets would later play a prominent role in constraining the degrees of freedom of the stabilization policies that would be attempted after the 1981 external crisis.

The liberalization of the domestic financial market 1977 did partially reverse the demonetization process that the economy went through after 1975.

But during 1977–81, the M2/GDP ratio averaged 19.7 %, while during the sixties it had averaged 20.5 %. In other words, the repressed financial markets of the sixties generated more credit than the freed ones of the 1977–81 period. Likewise, there was no lengthening of contract durations because the financial reform did not reduce uncertainty.

Even worse, lax market regulation helped lead to a crash in 1980, which contributed to the widening of the external crisis of 1981. Given that the higher level of financial fragility perceived during 1980 motivated private agents to substitute foreign financial assets for holdings denominated in domestic currency, the financial turmoil accelerated the fall in the Central Bank's reserves.

There were two long-lasting consequences for the monetary side of the economy. First, there was dollarization of private portfolios because of capital flight, which expanded in part because the absence of exchange controls helped people learn how to operate in international financial markets. Second, as the Central Bank acted as a lender of last resort during and after the 1980 financial crisis, it grew to be the most important financial intermediary. The monetary authorities turned into "partners" of the private sector in financing the cost of the financial crash of 1980.

Both the huge external debt that resulted from the failure of the liberalization attempt and the long-lasting effects of the exhaustion of import substitution are now visible in structural disequilibrium of the external and the public sectors. Throughout the 1980s the Argentine economy would show its worst performance in the whole post-war period. Between 1981 and 1988, inflation averaged 166.2 % per year; the average growth rate was slightly negative; the fiscal deficit/GDP ratio was more than 10 %; and the foreign debt rose from U.S. $35.6 billion to U.S. $58.5 billion.

In the following section, we will analyze the present situation and the prospects of the economy in terms of the external, fiscal, and saving gaps. Before that, however, it is worthwhile stressing that during the 1980s, key macroeconomic variables have shown divergent trends, which, in turn, exacerbated short-run instability. In the first place, even though the accumulated trade surplus between 1981 and 1988 was U.S. $20.1 billion, the current account deficit was U.S. $22.8 billion. That is, over eight years, the transfer of resources abroad was about a third of Argentina's GDP. Despite this effort, the foreign debt grew by about U.S. $20 billion. With output stagnant, the debt-output ratio is rising at an ominous pace.

Second, while the public deficit increased as a consequence of servicing foreign debt, the dollarization of the economy deepened. This fall in the demand for domestic assets has given rise to destabilizing forces such as increasing financial fragility and attempts to cut the fiscal deficit in ways that disrupt growth, for example, reducing public investment below the minimum required to preserve the stock of capital.

Finally, as policy shocks took the form of maxidevaluations and disproportionate increases in public prices, the high inflation regime tended to become hyperinflationary.

## 16.2 Macroeconomic Constraints and Growth Projections

The purpose of this section is two-fold. First it intends to analyze the main factors determining the behavior of the economy in terms of the fiscal, domestic, and external gaps. Second, following Fanelli, et al. (1989), it describes growth exercises for the Argentine economy under alternative scenarios.

As we have observed, the huge increment in Argentina's foreign debt was the counterpart of capital flight rather than excessive domestic absorption. In other words, the increased liabilities did not add to production capacity but rather to the stock of external assets held by the private sector. Because the capital flight was largely financed, directly or indirectly, by the public sector, today, the government holds almost 90 % of the external debt.

There have been four important consequences. First, there has been a permanent change in the relationship between GDP and GNP. The GNP/GDP ratio fell from 98.7 % in the 1970s to 91.9 % in the 1980s, almost entirely due to higher debt service. In the second place, as a result of the increase in interest payments abroad the current account has shown a permanent deficit since the early 1980s. Third, as the debt is mainly public, the external crisis has taken the form of a fiscal one. Finally, the increase in the fiscal deficit has had disturbing effects on the financial side of the economy. These facts have significantly changed the features of the external, fiscal, and saving gaps.

Let us begin with the saving gap. It may be interpreted as a measure of the disequilibrium between aggregate investment and saving. With regard to saving, the main aggregated agents (the government, the rest of the world, and the private sector) greatly changed their behavior during the 1980s as compared to the 1970s: While both private and government savings dropped sharply, external savings rose. In the earlier decade, government savings averaged 1.9 % of GDP; those of the private sector averaged 19.2 %; and the external sector provided funds for about 0.6 % of GDP. After the debt crisis during the 1980s, the saving/GDP ratios for the government, the private sector, and the external sector were − 3.4 %, 13.2 %, and 4.3 %, respectively.

The investment/GDP ratio also dropped during the 1980s. Historically, it was around 20 %; after the crisis it averaged 14 %. There are several explanations for the downward trend. One of the most important is that as debt service rose the government attempted to reduce other expenditures. Of these, investment was the hardest hit. In turn, as there is a complementarity between public and private investment, the latter declined. Fluctuations in relative prices, high interest rates (both in the domestic economy and abroad), and reverse accelerator effects were also causes of the downward trend in the investment/GDP ratio.

The *ex post* evolution of investment and savings suggests that the saving constraint might become binding when Argentina attempts to resume growth. There are at least two reasons for this. First, while the saving/GDP ratio fell by 53.3 % after the crisis, the fall in the investment/GDP ratio was lower: 34.5 %. Second, the increment in foreign saving that closes the gap between internal saving and investment was not voluntarily provided by the rest of the world. In fact, Argentina was able to utilize external saving mainly because of its arrears in foreign payments.

When the saving gap is binding: (1) there is a positive relationship between the availability of financing from abroad and growth, (2) the larger both the marginal propensity to save and the tax burden are, the faster is the rate of growth, and (3) if there is an increase in current public expenditures, there will be a fall in the rate of growth. Available data suggest that the private sector did not dramatically change its propensity to save. Therefore, the fall in the saving/output ratio was in all likelihood due to two factors: the increment in foreign payments (i.e., the downward trend in national income) and the denationalization of domestic saving that took the form of capital flight. Overinvoicing of imports and the underinvoicing of exports were the main mechanisms used to send capital abroad.

The increment in the interest payments influenced government saving. In the 1975−80 period, the government's total internal and external interest payments were 2.56 % of the potential output while in 1988 they amounted to 5.3 %. The *ex post* value of external saving, on the other hand, rose during the 1980s by about 4 % of the potential output.

According to the calculations made by Fanelli et al. (1989), taking into account 1988 values of the variables, the growth rate of potential output permitted by the saving gap would be 0.46 % per year. Given available external financing, however, if interest payments had been similar to their average value in the 1976−80 period, potential output could have grown at 3.3 % without opening the saving gap. The implication is that Argentina must lower consumption at each level of the potential output before it can begin to resume growth. Also, transfers abroad should be reduced. In order to have a complete picture of the constraints that the economy faces, however, we must take into account the other gaps.

As noted in the previous section, the character of the trade gap changed after the debt crisis. Today's deficit in the current account originates in financial services. Consequently, in the absence of "fresh" money, the country has to maintain a continuous trade surplus to offset the financial deficit. Accordingly, domestic absorption has to be continuously lower than domestic product. Although Argentina received some fresh money between 1981 and 1987, the country has maintained a permanent surplus in the trade account of about 3 % of GDP. This not only served to depress investment, but also reduced consumption and employment as well.

There is a sharp trade-off between growth and capacity utilization when the trade gap binds. Given the availability of foreign exchange, higher capacity utilization and therefore higher intermediate imports mean lower imports of capital goods, that is, both investment and the growth rate must fall. For the same reasons, faster growth would result from extra net capital inflows; a rise in the share of exports in the potential output, or a decline in foreign payments.

The increment in foreign payments after 1980–81 was a principal cause of slower potential output growth. Its effects can be seen by comparing the growth rates predicted by the model when the capital inflows/output and foreign interest payments/output ratios take average values for the period 1975–80 (0.59% and 0.56% respectively) and when they take the values of 1988 (3.6% and 5.4% respectively). In the first case, we would obtain a growth rate of 4.4% while in the second it would be 0.46%.

Two additional points must be highlighted. First, between 1980 and 1988 the volume of exports increased by 46% but their value rose only slightly due to a 35% deterioration in the terms of trade. Second, deindustrialization induced by the liberalization of the late 1970s partially reversed the import substitution process underway since World War II.

Finally, the debt crisis adversely shifted the fiscal and financial gap by creating a domestic transfer problem. The core of this issue is that although the government has to pay the interest on the foreign debt, the private sector "owns" the surplus of the trade account, which provides the necessary foreign exchange. The public sector must buy the external surplus from the private sector, obtaining the funds to do so by reducing expenditures or raising taxes. Both measures depress the activity level and restrain growth, and there are also financial complications:

If neither expenditures nor taxes are modified, ceteris paribus, the fiscal deficit is higher and must be financed by issuing money or placing more public debt with the private sector. With the former, the government loses control over the stock of money; with the latter, the interest rate tends to rise and investment is further depressed. Moreover, these alternatives cannot be maintained indefinitely, because they imply higher growth rates of financial assets than GDP (i.e., for financial market equilibrium in the long run, the growth rates of GDP and financial assets must be roughly the same, and this is not the present case). In fact, the dollarization that the economy has been undergoing since 1980 tends to accelerate when there is an increase in the issue of domestic financial assets. That is, domestically generated savings goes abroad instead of financing investment within the country.

In sum, when the government budget constraint is integrated into the analysis, it becomes clear that if Argentina resumes self-sustained growth it will be on a kind of "knife edge" from the fiscal point of view. While a fiscal reform to increase government saving is a necessary condition for growth, the subsequent increase in the tax burden (or the decrease in expenditures) should be designed to prevent possibly depressing effects on the "animal spirits" of the private sector (Frenkel and Rozenwurcel, 1988).

The need for a structural reform in the public sector can be illustrated quantitatively with the following example. If the policy parameters that define public sector saving are unchanged, the only "endogenous" variables allowing an increment in public investment would be the output level (rising national income adds to net government revenue) and the fiscal deficit. For the growth rate to go up ceteris paribus by 1%, either the activity level would have to increase by 10.9% of potential output or the fiscal deficit by 2.5%. Given that capacity utilization is restricted to being under 100%, the first option would be feasible only if the economy were in a deep recession. As we shall discuss later, the second alternative might not be feasible because of the disturbing effects of placing more fiscal debt in asset markets in order to finance public capital formation.

The three gaps underline the factors that have determined the long-term deterioration of the Argentine economy. Our simulations of its performance in the future show that if the destabilizing forces at work in the external and the public sectors are not deactivated, its problems will persist. To illustrate possible outcomes, we can briefly describe the main features of alternative status quo and 3% annual growth rate scenarios.

Let us begin with the analysis of the status quo. It is assumed that (1) there is no change in the structural parameters that define the three gaps, (2) capacity utilization is maintained at the 1988 level, and (3) exports grow at 3% per year (which is similar to the 1980s observed rate).

Table 16.5 shows the evolution of the endogenous variables from 1988 to 2000. This scenario reproduces the principal patterns of behavior that the economy has shown since the debt crisis: a continuous fall in the investment/potential output ratio, a low or negative rate of growth, and upward trends in both internal and external debt. Due to the rising debt ratios, the proportion of interest payments in public spending steadily goes up. The share of public saving in potential output falls, and public investment has to be reduced accordingly.

On the side of trade, slow growth and a stable capacity utilization rate imply that neither intermediate nor capital good imports increase as shares

**Table 16.5**
A "status quo" scenario (variables in %)

| | $e$ | $u$ | $g$ | $ig$ | $\pi$ | $\phi$ | $sg$ | $sp$ | $dig$ | $deg$ | $det$ | $dgt$ | $i$ |
|---|---|---|---|---|---|---|---|---|---|---|---|---|---|
| 1987 | 7.60 | 97.00 | 0.16 | 6.30 | 8.00 | 5.20 | −1.70 | 8.60 | 13.30 | 59.40 | 67.47 | 72.70 | 12.10 |
| 1988 | 11.50 | 97.80 | 0.45 | 7.05 | 6.30 | 3.60 | 0.75 | 8.89 | 15.94 | 62.72 | 70.52 | 78.66 | 13.23 |
| 1989 | 11.85 | 97.80 | 0.32 | 6.71 | 6.64 | 3.77 | 0.07 | 8.89 | 18.76 | 66.28 | 73.68 | 85.04 | 12.71 |
| 1990 | 12.20 | 97.80 | 0.16 | 6.31 | 6.60 | 3.53 | −0.28 | 8.89 | 21.80 | 69.70 | 76.70 | 91.49 | 12.12 |
| 1991 | 12.57 | 97.80 | 0.01 | 5.91 | 6.53 | 3.27 | −0.62 | 8.89 | 25.05 | 72.96 | 79.59 | 98.02 | 11.51 |
| 1992 | 12.94 | 97.80 | −0.16 | 5.48 | 6.36 | 2.90 | −0.88 | 8.89 | 28.56 | 75.98 | 82.28 | 104.54 | 10.08 |
| 1993 | 13.33 | 97.80 | −0.33 | 5.05 | 6.08 | 2.40 | −1.03 | 8.89 | 32.31 | 78.64 | 84.66 | 110.98 | 10.22 |
| 1994 | 13.73 | 97.80 | −0.51 | 4.59 | 5.59 | 1.67 | −1.00 | 8.89 | 36.42 | 80.73 | 86.50 | 117.15 | 9.53 |
| 1995 | 14.14 | 97.80 | −0.67 | 4.12 | 5.11 | 0.96 | −0.99 | 8.89 | 40.82 | 82.28 | 87.83 | 123.10 | 8.82 |
| 1996 | 14.57 | 97.80 | −0.88 | 3.64 | 4.92 | 0.54 | −1.28 | 8.89 | 45.56 | 82.58 | 88.93 | 129.14 | 8.12 |
| 1997 | 15.00 | 97.80 | −1.07 | 3.15 | 4.62 | −0.01 | −1.47 | 8.89 | 50.68 | 84.52 | 89.68 | 135.20 | 7.37 |
| 1998 | 15.46 | 97.80 | −1.27 | 2.64 | 4.38 | −0.51 | −1.74 | 8.89 | 56.21 | 85.16 | 90.13 | 141.37 | 6.60 |
| 1999 | 15.72 | 97.80 | −1.48 | 2.10 | 4.11 | −1.04 | −2.00 | 8.89 | 62.20 | 85.46 | 90.27 | 147.66 | 5.80 |
| 2000 | 16.40 | 97.80 | −1.69 | 1.54 | 3.81 | −1.62 | −2.26 | 8.89 | 68.69 | 85.39 | 90.06 | 154.08 | 4.97 |

Key: $e$, exports; $u$, activity level; $g$, growth rate; $ig$, public investment; $\pi$, fiscal deficit; $\phi$, foreign saving; $sg$, government saving; $sp$, private saving; $dig$, government domestic debt; $deg$, government foreign debt; $det$, total foreign debt; $dgt$, total government debt; $i$, investment. All variables are expressed as proportions of potential output.
Source: Fanelli et al. (1989).

of potential output. With 3 % export growth, foreign saving decreases; indeed there is a current account surplus after 1997. In other words, there is a negative trade-off between growth and capacity utilization on the one hand, and the requirements of external financing on the other.

Finally, note the exponential increase of the ratio of domestic government debt to potential output (the variable "dig"), which illustrates the long-run consequences of the domestic transfer problem. The upward trend in the public sector's interest payments results in an ever-increasing deficit even though government investment is cut back.

Table 16.6 shows the evolution of key macroeconomic variables required to maintain 3 % potential output growth. There is a significant jump in the investment/potential output ratio, that is, both overall saving and the investment ratio of the public sector have to increase. Moreover, because we have assumed full capacity utilization and a higher growth rate, imports would be rising. Therefore, an increase in the share of the rest of the world's saving in potential output is needed in order to maintain external balance. The required inflows decline *pari passu* with the increment in Argentine exports.

On the financial side, the projection shows that if the economy were growing at 3 % per year, the evolution of the stock of public debt would not be explosive. This growth target requires a strong adjustment in the public sector's policy parameters to raise government saving. Otherwise, there would be a gap of about 7 % of potential output between current public sector savings and the level required at the beginning of the program.

The required fiscal improvement would be smaller if (1) there were a reversal in the process of denationalization of saving, which in the model's accounting would signify an increase in the private sector saving share; or (2) there were an autonomous increase either in private investment demand or in the efficiency of the economy (i.e., a lower capital/output ratio) because the same growth rate could be then achieved with lower public investment.

## 16.3   Sector Adjustment and Growth

In the previous section we emphasized the constraints that macroeconomic consistency puts on growth. We now analyze at a more disaggregated level other factors that are constraining the economy in the present situation as well as the reforms that should be put into practice in key sectors.

**Table 16.6**
A 3% growth scenario (variables in %)

| | $e$ | $u$ | $g$ | $ig$ | $\pi$ | $\phi$ | $sg$ | $sp$ | $dig$ | $deg$ | $det$ | $dgt$ | $i$ |
|---|---|---|---|---|---|---|---|---|---|---|---|---|---|
| 1987 | 7.60 | 97.00 | 0.16 | 6.30 | 8.00 | 5.20 | −1.70 | 8.60 | 13.30 | 59.40 | 67.47 | 72.70 | 12.10 |
| 1988 | 11.50 | 97.80 | 0.46 | 7.07 | 6.33 | 3.62 | 0.74 | 8.89 | 15.95 | 62.74 | 70.54 | 78.69 | 13.25 |
| 1989 | 11.85 | 100.00 | 3.00 | 13.58 | 5.61 | 5.36 | 7.97 | 9.69 | 15.73 | 66.19 | 73.40 | 81.92 | 23.02 |
| 1990 | 12.20 | 100.00 | 3.00 | 13.58 | 5.43 | 5.18 | 8.16 | 9.69 | 15.52 | 69.34 | 75.97 | 81.86 | 23.02 |
| 1991 | 12.57 | 100.00 | 3.00 | 13.58 | 5.20 | 4.75 | 8.38 | 9.69 | 15.32 | 72.16 | 78.25 | 87.48 | 23.02 |
| 1992 | 12.94 | 100.00 | 3.00 | 13.58 | 4.86 | 4.61 | 8.73 | 9.69 | 15.12 | 74.56 | 80.17 | 89.68 | 23.02 |
| 1993 | 13.33 | 100.00 | 3.00 | 13.58 | 4.38 | 4.13 | 9.20 | 9.69 | 14.93 | 76.41 | 81.60 | 71.34 | 23.02 |
| 1994 | 13.73 | 100.00 | 3.00 | 13.58 | 3.69 | 3.44 | 9.87 | 9.69 | 14.74 | 77.52 | 82.33 | 92.26 | 23.02 |
| 1995 | 14.14 | 100.00 | 3.00 | 13.58 | 3.00 | 2.75 | 10.58 | 9.69 | 14.53 | 77.91 | 82.37 | 92.47 | 23.02 |
| 1996 | 14.57 | 100.00 | 3.00 | 13.58 | 2.58 | 2.33 | 11.00 | 9.69 | 14.39 | 77.87 | 82.00 | 92.75 | 23.02 |
| 1997 | 15.00 | 100.00 | 3.00 | 13.58 | 2.03 | 1.78 | 11.55 | 9.69 | 14.22 | 77.27 | 81.10 | 91.47 | 23.02 |
| 1998 | 15.46 | 100.00 | 3.00 | 13.58 | 1.52 | 1.27 | 12.06 | 9.69 | 14.05 | 76.19 | 79.73 | 90.24 | 23.02 |
| 1999 | 15.72 | 100.00 | 3.00 | 13.58 | 0.36 | 0.72 | 12.62 | 9.69 | 13.89 | 74.58 | 77.86 | 88.47 | 23.02 |
| 2000 | 16.40 | 100.00 | 3.00 | 13.58 | 0.36 | 0.11 | 13.22 | 9.69 | 13.74 | 72.42 | 75.45 | 86.45 | 23.02 |

Key: $e$, exports; $u$, activity level; $g$, growth rate; $ig$, public investment; $\pi$, fiscal deficit; $\phi$, foreign saving; $sg$, government saving; $sp$, private saving; $dig$, government domestic debt; $deg$, government foreign debt; $det$, total foreign debt; $dgt$, total government debt; $i$, investment. All variables are expressed as proportions of potential output.
Source: Fanelli et al. (1989).

## 16.3.1 The Public Sector[8]

The development strategy followed during the post-war period had created serious difficulties for the public sector well before the present decade. The government's inability to realign taxes and expenditures after the debt crisis was a direct consequence of the inertial behavior of the main fiscal variables. Their movements were determined by structural characteristics of the public sector and the existing legislation such as that concerning industrial promotion and the investment incentive regime.[9]

The public expenditure/output ratio was increasing before the debt crisis. As income stagnated in the late 1970s, public spending maintained its post-war rate of growth, and the expenditure/GDP ratio rose from 25% in the early seventies to 38% in the early 1980s. Thereafter, the ratio declined under successive stabilization plans; by 1987–88 it was 31%. The kind of expenditures that were reduced were not determined by efficiency or equity considerations.

The principal budgetary items are wage and social security payments, interest on public debt, the deficit of public enterprises, and overall government investment.[10] Wages and investment have carried the burden of the public sector adjustment for two significant reasons. First, the authorities cannot exert control over the amount of interest due; and second, public enterprises underwent a budgetary squeeze because of their foreign indebtedness. Wages were adjusted by depressing their real level (in order to minimize the consequences on employment) while the public investment/output ratio fell from 12% in the late 1970s to less than 7% in 1988.

This public expenditure cut, nonetheless, was insufficient to close the fiscal gap. Public revenues in the best years reached 28% of GDP (including social security revenues) and averaged 25% in the adjustment period. The distorted tax structure as well as severe shortcomings in administration prevented an increase of the tax burden *pari passu* with the increment in foreign payments.[11]

One of the most important ways in which the tax structure impeded a rise in receipts was the erosion of the tax base which affected both direct and indirect taxes. The amount of direct tax collected was less than 1% of GDP. This poor performance was due first, to denationalization of part of the private sector's wealth as a result of capital flight; second, to legislative weaknesses concerning taxes on profits;[12] and third, to authorized tax deferments and exemptions under the investment incentive regime. The only viable taxes were indirect, on value-added, and on fuel and international trade.[13]

Even for indirect taxes, erosion of the tax base was a serious impediment to obtaining a permanent increase in the amount collected, regardless of equity considerations. The value-added tax base narrowed because pre-existing legislation regarding industrial promotion (both sectoral and regional) was based on value-added and other tax exemptions.[14] At the same time, the international trade base fluctuated erratically—especially with regard to taxes on agricultural exports—due to movements in the terms of trade and instability of the activity level.

One consequence of all this was increasing reliance on the fuel tax as an instrument to raise the government's revenue. The policy of offsetting lower collections by raising this tax was an important cause of macroeconomic instability. It contributed to the acceleration of inflation and the worsening of distortions in relative prices.[15]

Finally, macroeconomic instability in itself was an autonomous factor in narrowing the tax base. The Olivera-Tanzi effect[16] and the increase in fiscal evasion were the principal factors. The former was important because of the acceleration of inflation after 1975; the latter widened after the debt crisis *pari passu* with the dollarization of the economy and administrative difficulties in the public sector.

The erosion of the-base, tax evasion, and the Olivera-Tanzi effect have induced a reduction in total receipts of more than 10 % of GDP (by conservative estimates).[17] This amount is similar to the average size of the fiscal deficit experienced during the 1980s.

In the previous section we saw that a fiscal reform is necessary because of the significant increment in public sector savings required for a 3 % growth rate: The factors impeding an increment in government revenues must be removed. Specifically, evasion must be reduced by means of improved tax administration and at the same time, legislation concerning industrial promotion and investment incentives must be restricted since the public sector cannot bear the implicit fiscal cost. Complete success cannot be obtained without stabilizing the economy as the widening of the underground economy and the high inflation regime are the basic causes of the fall in tax receipts.

With regard to expenditures, improvement of the performance of public investment is a necessary condition. It is a difficult task because there must be an efficient allocation of investment funds given the extreme resource constraint yet at the same time there are institutional obstacles to designing a rational public investment program. For example, existing legislation regarding public works reduces investment options by earmarking funds (especially in the energy and transport sectors). The "buy national" system makes it difficult for the public sector to optimize the allocation of funds.

Second, costly projects initiated in the past under optimistic assumptions on the future growth of the economy are now unprofitable, but are difficult to discontinue because of sunk cost and the high cost of cancellation. Finally, vested interests are active in impeding the reallocation of resources to priority areas. The state is the most important customer of 20 of the 100 leading firms of the economy, ranked by sales (Kosakoff, 1988).

Notwithstanding, the priorities of public investment should be: First, infrastructure maintenance to prevent further quality deterioration, especially in urban services, health, education, and transport. Second, private sector participation should be allowed in those activities that the public sector can no longer cover because of a lack of resources.[18] Third, there should be a concentration of net investment in cases of suboptimal resource use (such as oil and gas exploitation) and in order to overcome bottlenecks (pipelines, ports, power distribution). Fourth, given the regressive income distribution that resulted from the adjustment period, resources should be allocated to improve social services.

## 16.3.2    Industry and Rural Sectors

For most of the post-war period, the industrial share of GDP increased. The liberalization attempt of the late seventies brought this process to a halt. The industrial product/GDP ratio fell from 28 % in 1975 to 22 % in 1982 and thereafter fluctuated around this level. In 1988, it was 22.6 %.[19]

The deindustrialization that followed the debt crisis affected distinct sectors in varying ways. Metal products and electrical machinery were hardest hit, while the food, aluminum, and petrochemical industries maintained their previous levels of development. Traditional sectors such as oil and leather showed an acceptable evolution, especially regarding exports. The industries that suffered the greatest deterioration were those that were technologically more complex. A consequence was a reduction in the employment of skilled workers and an increment in the demand for unskilled ones as the overall industrial employment level remained unchanged.

Deindustrialization and the lack of a consistent pattern in designing industrial policy (especially regarding the trade and investment regimes and industrial promotion)[20] resulted in the many distortions that the industrial structure is now showing. A growth-oriented policy must necessarily address industrial reform.

In the first place, there is a bias toward activities characterized by high capital intensity and low value-added, a direct consequence of incentive regimes which favored investment to the detriment of employment. Tax deferments and exemptions from taxable profits and from imported capital goods are examples.

Second, heavy intermediates have received disproportionate benefits: the petrochemical and chemical sector, ferrous metal sectors, and cellulose sectors showed increase in the industrial product to the detriment of other sectors. This pattern of specialization resulted from a sectoral-incentive regime that concentrated the allocation of incentive funds within a reduced group of no more than 50 highly capital-intensive projects.

Third, there is a regional bias induced by the regional-promotion regime, which not only distorted the location of industries but also favored assembly operations to the detriment of others using highly skilled workers.

In the fourth place, there has been a process of concentration favored by the incentive regime, protection barriers, and the financial crisis (which allowed firms with a hedge financial position to purchase at "bargain prices" enterprises affected by the lack of credit and high interest rates experienced after 1980–81).[21]

Finally, the government buying system must be changed in order to improve its efficiency and reduce the effects on the fiscal deficit of the higher prices that the public sector must pay as a consequence of the buy national regime.

The severe restraint experienced by domestic effective demand was one of the prominent factors that contributed to industrial stagnation. The regressive income redistribution that resulted from adjustment following the 1975 crisis explains in great measure the fall in effective demand. The sharp drop in the investment/output ratio after the debt-crisis was a second important factor.

Given the present prospects for the probable evolution of the economy, a rapid recovery of the domestic components of effective demand cannot be expected. Therefore, exports should be privileged as a source of demand for industry. Changes in the incentive regimes should be made in order to correct the biases that impeded a rapid increment in Argentina's industrial exports.

Although rural sector production represents only 15 % of GDP, it plays a fundamental role with regard to both short-run stability and growth. In effect, (1) land and cattle production is the main source of foreign exchange (60 % of total exports originate in this sector); (2) goods produced by the sector represent 15 % of the consumer basket; and (3) it contributes significantly to government revenues (although its overall contribution tends to fluctuate widely in the short run).[22]

From 1975 on, industry stagnated while agricultural production showed a marked upward trend. This can be seen in the annual growth rates of the production of wheat and oilseeds: They were 0.5 % and 2.4 % respectively between 1960 and 1970, 3.1 % and 12.2 % in 1970–80, and 7.5 % and 12.2 % between 1980 and 1985. This outstanding evolution by agriculture was mainly a consequence of deep technological change in both oil cultivation and in the organization of work, especially in the Pampa Humeda region.[23] The positive evolution of productivity in crop agriculture displaced cattle production and, as a result, the latter lost importance in exports from the rural sector. Likewise, there was a displacement of cattle production to less productive land.

According to specialists (e.g., Barsky, 1989), future prospects, especially for the major crops, seem to be promising. In great measure, however, they will be conditioned by the overall evolution of the economy. Two factors should be stressed. First, the sharp drop in public investment in infrastructure (railways, roads, ports, and storage systems) has generated a series of difficulties that will worsen in the future if the upward trend in crop production is maintained. Second, the reduced supply of credit has created a severe liquidity constraint. So, stopping demonetization and increasing public sector investment would greatly benefit rural production.

16.3.3 The External Sector

During the import-substitution period, the growing industrial sector increased its participation in exports, from 3 % in 1960 to 24 % in 1975. Afterwards, however, growth stagnated. In 1988 the share of industry in total exports was 23.5 %. Likewise, the structural changes that took place in industry after the debt crisis changed the pattern of goods exported. As machinery lost influence, industrial goods originating in the primary sector and heavy intermediates with low value-added augmented their participation. The participation of the latter in industrial exports was countercyclical, as firms tended to offset the short term decrease in domestic demand by selling abroad.[24]

Rural exports have shown a steadily upward trend as a consequence of the aforementioned increment in agricultural productivity. Argentina's grain exports rose from 8.9 million tons in 1970 to 15.6 in 1980 and 20.5

in 1985. Following that, there was a decline because of bad weather conditions, but sales are improving again. Projections regarding both grain and cattle exports are optimistic (Barsky, 1989). The outcomes will depend heavily on agricultural policy in the OECD. Over the last few years, European and U.S. agricultural subsidies have depressed Argentina's terms of trade.

Even though the country must improve the growth rate of exports, it should not try to maximize the trade surplus. The result would be an accelerated amortization of foreign debt but no solution to the macroeconomic disequilibria we have discussed. Indeed, if the private sector leads export growth, the domestic transfer problem would worsen. The growth strategy should be to reach a reasonable long-run agreement with foreign creditors and induce an increment in imports as exports steadily rise.

A trade reform is necessary to attain these goals. It should aim at significantly reducing the level of domestic protection. Given the disappointing results of reforms in the late 1970s, however, the liberalization should be carefully implemented. Specifically, it should avoid the two distortionary features of the earlier reform: it should not be too fast, and it should prevent the reduction in the protection of final goods while maintaining a pre-trade reform shelter for intermediate producers.

### 16.3.4    Employment and Income Distribution[25]

During the adjustment period, macroeconomic instability generated fluctuations in the labor market. In spite of output stagnation, however, there was a slight upward trend in employment and the increment in unemployment was not dramatic. This fact is surprising, when compared with what happened in other Latin American countries that have undergone severe economic crises during the 1980s.

The growth in employment is explained by various factors. First, there was more underemployment, which rose from 4.5 % of the labor force in 1980 to 7.8 % in 1988. There was also a reduction in average productivity as a consequence of deindustrialization accompanied by an increasing trend in the participation of services in total output. Although 29.7 % of the total labor force was employed in industry in 1980, that proportion had fallen to 26.6 % in 1988. Finally, the labor supply tended to vary procyclically. This helped to offset the effects of activity changes on observed unemployment. After a significant jump at the beginning of the debt crisis (from 2.6 % in 1980 to 6 % in 1982), the unemployment rate oscillated between 4.5 % and 6.5 %.

Even though there are no available official data on income distribution, estimates that have been made suggest that there was a structural change after the development strategy crisis in 1975. Worker's participation fell from 43.4 % of GDP in 1975 to 27.9 % in 1976, and afterwards averaged 30 % in the liberalization period of 1976–80. The debt crisis, on the other hand, did not further worsen income distribution. In fact, the average participation of workers in total income improved slightly between 1981 and 1988 (33 %).

The prospects for the future evolution of income distribution and employment heavily depend on whether or not Argentina succeeds in resuming growth, since rising employment in response to productivity reductions is not viable in the long run. Given that the income elasticity of employment is about 0.5 % and the labor supply is growing at a rate of 2 % per year, *ceteris paribus*, the economy should grow at a rate of 4 % per year in order to maintain the labor market in equilibrium.

**Notes**

1. Basic references are Diaz Alejandro (1969 and 1970) and Mallon and Sourrouille (1975).

2. See Canitrot (1975), Porto (1975), and Diaz Alejandro (1963).

3. For a detailed analysis of these mechanisms see Santamaria, et al. (1967).

4. See Carciofi (1988) and Gerchunoff and Vicens (1989).

5. Basic references for this period are Canitrot (1981), Feldmann and Sommer (1989), and Frenkel (1984).

6. See Fanelli and Frenkel (1985) and Fanelli, Frenkel, and Winograd (1987) where this policy is analyzed together with the concept of overkill.

7. For a more detailed account of the process of increasing foreign indebtedness see Fanelli, Frenkel, and Sommer (1987).

8. For a detailed analysis of the public sector in Argentina see Gerchunoff and Vicens (1989); Carciofi (1988) and Programa de Asistencia Técnica para la Gestión del Sector Público Argentino (1989).

9. The most important laws are analyzed in Azpiazu (1988).

10. The participation in total public expenditures (as percentages of GDP) are wages: 9.4 %; social security: 9.5 %; interest: 2.4 % and investment: 6.9 %. The deficit of public enterprises fluctuates between 0 and 2 %, but is important on the margin.

11. For a detailed analysis of the tax structure see Programa de Asistencia Técnica para la Gestión del Sector Público Argentino (1989).

12. Specially with regard to the calculation of benefits after the inflation-adjustment of balances.

13. Value-added represents 24.5 % of total tax collecting while the participation of fuel, foreign trade and profit taxes are, respectively, 16.7 %, 18.2 %, and 8.9 %.

14. The fiscal cost of tax expenditures is about 3.4 % of GDP, see Artana (1989).

15. Attempts to close the fiscal gap by increasing the prices of public enterprises fostered inflation was well.

16. Domper and Streb (1987) calculate that this effect represented around 2.5 % of GDP.

17. See Programa de Asistencia Técnica para la Gestión del Sector Público Argentino (1989).

18. It should be taken into account, however, that privatization is not an easy task. With regard to this see Werneck (1989).

19. For a study of the interaction between the macroeconomic evolution of the economy and industry see Kosakoff (1988).

20. The consequences of the industrial promotion on the industrial structure are evaluated in Azpiazu (1988).

21. Damill and Fanelli (1988) analyzed the balance shuts of the 122 largest firms in the industrial sector and found that they invested heavily in buying small firms undergoing financial problems.

22. For an evaluation of the rural sector's present situation and prospects see Barsky (1989); see also Garramon et al. (1988).

23. For an overview of the factors that helped to increase productivity see Barsky (1989).

24. The evolution of industrial exports is analyzed in detail in Azpiazu et al. (1986).

25. Damill (1989) and Beccaria (1988) extensively analyze these topics.

## References

Artana, D. (1989). "La Promoción Económica en la Argentina." Buenos Aires: Instituto Torcuato Di Tella.

Azpiazu, D. (1988). "La Promoción a la Inversión Industrial en la Argentina. Efectos sobre la Estructura Industrial 1974–87." Buenos Aires: CEPAL.

Azpiazu, D., R. Bisang, and B. Kosacoff (1986). "Desarrollo Industrial y Exportación de Manufacturas." D. T. No. 22, Buenos Aires: CEPAL.

Barsky, O. (1989). "Perspectivas del Sector Agropecuario Pampeano en una Estrategia de Crecimiento con Equidad." (Mimeo), Instituto de Investigaciones Económicas de la CGE, buenos Aires.

Beccaria, L. (1988). "Políticas Sociales en una Estrategia de Crecimiento con Equidad." (Mimeo), Instituto de Económicas de la CGE, Buenos Aires.

Canitrot, A. (1975). "La Experiencia Populista de Redistribución de Ingresos." *Desarrollo Económico*, 59.

Canitrot, A. (1981). "Teoría y Práctica del Liberalismo: Política Antiinflacionaria y Apertura Económica en la Argentina." *Desarrollo Económico*, 82.

Carciofi, R. (1988). "Crecimiento con Equidad: Apuntes para una Reforma del Sector Público." (Mimeo), Instituto de Investigactiones Económicas de la CGE, Buenos Aires.

Damill, M., and J. M. Fanelli (1988). "Decisiones de Cartera y Transferencias de Riqueza en un Período de Inestabilidad Macroeconómica." *Documentos CEDES*, 12.

Damill, M. (1989). "Ocupación y Desempleo en la Argentina Durante el Período de Ajuste." (Mimeo), CEDES, Buenos Aires.

Diaz Alejandro, C. (1963). "A Note on the Impact of the Devaluation and Distributive Effect." *Journal of Political Economy*, 71.

Diaz Alejandro, C. (1969). "Devaluación de la Tasa de Cambio en un País Semi-Industrializado: La Experiencia de la Argentina 1955−1961." Buenos Aires: Instituto T. Di Tella.

Diaz Alejandro, C. (1970). *Ensayos sobre Historia Económica Argentina*. Buenos Aires: Amorrortu.

Domper, J., and J. Streb (1987). "Influencia de la Esabilización de Precios sobre la Recaudación Tributaria." *Ensayos Económicos*, 38.

Fanelli, J. M., and R. Frenkel (1987). "La Argentina y el Fondo en la Década Pasada." *El Trimestre Económico*, 44.

Fanelli, J. M., R. Frenkel, and J. Sommer (1987). "El Proceso de Endedudamiento Externo Argentino." Caracas: Sistema Económico Latinoamericano.

Fanelli, J. M., R. Frenkel, and C. Winograd (1987). "Stabilization and Adjustment Policies and Programs." *Country Study* No. 12. Helsinki: WIDER.

Fanelli, J. M., R. Frenkel, and C. Winograd (1989). "Growth Exercise for Argentina." Helsinki: WIDER.

Feldman, E., and J. Sommer (1989). *Crisis Financiera y Endeudamiento Externo*, Buenos Aires: CET/IPAL.

Frenkel, R. (1984). "Salarios Industriales e Inflación: El Período 1976−1982." *Desarrollo Económico*, 95.

Frenkel, R., and G. Rozenwurcel (1988). "Restricción Externa y Generación de Recursos para el Crecimiento en América Latina." *Documento CEDES* No. 15.

Frenkel, R. (1989). "El Régimen de Alta Inflación y el Nivel de Actividad." Buenos Aires: CEDES.

Garramon, C., et al. (1988). *Ajuste Macroeconómico y Sector Agropecuario en América Latina*. Buenos Aires: IICA.

Gerchunoff, P., and M. Vicens (1989). "Gasto Público, Recursos Públicos y Financiamiento en una Economía en Crisis: El Caso Argentino." Buenos Aires: Instituto T. Di Tella.

Kosakoff, B. (1988). "Desarrollo Industrial e Inestabilidad Macroeconómica. La Experiencia Argentina Reciente." Buenos Aires: CEPAL.

Mallon, R., and J. Sourrouille (1975). *La Política Económica en una Sociedad Conflictiva: El Caso Argentino*. Buenos Aires: Amorrortu.

Porto, A. (1975). "Un Modelo Simple Sobre el Comportamiento Macroeconómico Argentino en el Corto Plazo." *Desarrollo Económico*, 59.

Programa de Asistencia Técnica para la Gestión del Sector Público Argentino (1989). "Síntesis y Conclusiones de los Documentos de Investigación." Buenos Aires: Program de Estudios Sobre Política Tributaria.

Santamaria, M., O. Altimir, and J. Sourrouille (1967). "Los Instrumentos de Promoción Industrial en la Posguerra." *Desarrollo Económico*, 38.

Werneck, R. (1989). "Aspectos Macroeconómicos da Privatização no Brasil." Rio de Janeiro: PUC.

# 17      Brazil

Dionisio D. Carneiro and
Rogerio L. F. Werneck

In the early 1990s, the Brazilian economy is undergoing the longest crisis of its development process. Despite the political success of redemocratization, economic stagnation, high inflation, and a critical level of uncertainty have led to a very low rate of investment and self-fulfilling pessimism concerning economic prospects. The present disarray, as well as the deep imbalances that helped to brew the present crisis, leave no option but to launch a frontal attack on the economy's problems, if there is any hope for a successful recovery of growth.

From 1940 to 1980, Brazil's average annual GDP growth rate was above 7%. This performance was achieved in spite of the serious economic and political difficulties the country faced during those four decades. Expansion was not only fast, but remarkably steady. Only in 6 of the 40 years was the growth rate below 4%: 1942, 1947, 1956, and 1963–65. And in only one year (1942) was there a fall in aggregate output. Real per capita GDP increased by a factor of five, in 1989 prices, from $490 to $2,450.

These facts give perspective to the extent and consequences of the slowdown of growth in the 1980s.[1] During 1981–89, the average annual growth rate fell to approximately 2.3%. In five of the nine years it was below 4%, and in two of them (1981 and 1983) there were significant declines in GDP. As the average population growth rate was slightly above 2.2%, there was practically no growth in per capita terms. Moreover, the evolution of per capita output was highly unstable. Only in 1987 did it again reach the 1980 level, after an accumulated 13.1% fall in the 1981–83 recession.

Had the historical trend of the previous 40 years prevailed through the 1980s, the value of Brazilian GDP at the century's end would correspond to around U.S. $1 trillion, or about one-quarter the size of the U.S. economy today, with a per capita income equivalent to the poorest countries of the European Community.

One cannot argue that growth could have been maintained notwithstanding the difficulties—the external ones in particular—faced by Brazil in the early 1980s. But from a long-run perspective, this period may be seen as an interruption that will have cost an estimated 40% of the per capita income before it is over. For a poor country that has never been able to solve its inhabitants' most elementary needs such as food, health, education, and housing, the social dimensions of this lost decade are even more dramatic than the idea of riches foregone.

This paper addresses the nature of a feasible growth path for the next five to ten years and the main obstacles in the way of the necessary policies. It is divided into three main sections, following this introduction. The first covers general background issues. The second analyzes macro policy problems and some sectoral implications. The third section examines the political economy of adjustment to a new growth regime.

## 17.1  The Public Sector in the Brazilian Crisis

It is useful to begin with a broad perspective on what happened to the public sector from the early 1970s to the mid-1980s, a period notable for its external shocks.[2] During the growth-cum-debt period of the 1970s, public sector adjustment was characterized by two trends that proved to be inconsistent in the long run. A huge import-substituting and export-promoting program constituted the core of Brazil's adjustment strategy to the oil shocks, with the public sector undertaking a sizable and central part in the required investment effort. But despite its enhanced commitments, the sector's share in aggregate income shrank significantly during the decade. The latter trend stemmed from a falling gross tax burden, rising transfers and subsidies to the private sector, and decreasing real prices and tariffs charged for the goods and services produced by public enterprises.

Although untenable in the long run, the coexistence of the two trends was the crux of the adjustment strategy. It required maximizing growth, even at a rate inconsistent with equilibrium in the external current account. The public sector's increasing borrowing requirements constituted a secure way to assure the steady flow of foreign loans required to finance the external deficit. Had the high self-financing capacity that public enterprises displayed in the early 1970s been maintained, the growth policy would have had to rely extensively on the nervous and risk-averting private sector's investment to accomplish the increasingly difficult foreign capital inflow targets.

In other words, the implicit logic of the chosen policy was the following: As public enterprises had easy access to badly needed foreign loans to finance their investments, there seemed to be no problem in reducing their self-financing capacity. Actually, it would induce them to resort to debt in order to carry on their investment plans. There was, therefore, room to let their real prices and tariffs erode somewhat, which would be particularly convenient because it would avoid unnecessary pressures on the worrisome evolution of inflation.[3]

The reduction in the net tax burden and in public enterprises' real prices and tariffs allowed the burden of the adjustment to fall upon the public sector, delaying the required adjustment on the part of the private sector. But the public sector's shrinking share in national income forced it to abdicate the important role it had been playing as a net source of savings. As there was no offsetting enhancement of private savings, adjustment throughout the 1970s meant substituting foreign savings for domestic savings without any fall in consumption (Werneck, 1986).

As interest payments on foreign debt (predominantly the burden of the public sector) soared in the wake of higher international interest rates after 1979, there was still no effort to recover the public share in aggregate income in order to accommodate the mounting expenditures. Avoiding a rise in taxes and fearing the inflationary impact of a correction in public enterprises' real prices and tariffs, the government simply resorted to more and more foreign and domestic indebtedness.

With further acceleration of inflation following a bout of inconsistent macroeconomic policies of 1979–80, the government decided to adopt a stricter monetary policy in 1981, without support either from tighter fiscal policy or an IMF program.[4] The resulting rise in domestic public debt and the pressure on interest rates in financial markets contributed to increase the resource transfer from the public to the private sector over the 1980s. When the external debt crisis came in 1982 there was an effort to bail out private sector borrowers through arrangements that permitted the absorption of foreign exchange risks by the Central Bank, further aggravating the public sector's financial strains.

The concentration of the adjustment burden on the public sector, revealed in its shrinking share of aggregate income, and the consequent disappearance of its savings capacity poses important questions about the ability of the Brazilian economy to return again to the high average 1940–80 growth rate. There would have to be a significant enhancement of the present low domestic saving effort, which could hardly be obtained without re-establishing the importance of public savings.[5]

Before this healthy development can occur, however, the extremely difficult short-term situation must be sorted out. Stabilization schemes proliferated endlessly under both the Sarney and Collor governments, while confrontations with foreign lenders were called on and off. Ultimately, fiscal reform will have to be combined with inflation control to refurbish the public budget and increase government savings in order to open room for a sustained growth path. Details of different types of fiscal adjustment are discussed in section 17.2.

Regrettably, two likely scenarios may divert the economy from such a path. The first one could result either from premature populist reheating of demand or from the sheer impossibility of negotiating thorough reform with Congress. In this scenario, a return to generalized indexation with a high monthly inflation rate could mean a continuation of the stop-and-go policies that prevailed before the first Cruzado plan, with low economic growth. The second one, either in view of the difficulties of increasing public savings or from pure ideological persuasion would try to implement liberalizing reforms aimed at reducing the role of the state via lowering import tariffs. After a possibly long stabilization crisis, growth possibilities would depend fundamentally on the cooperation of bankers and multilateral institutions in the first moves, as well as on the willingness of foreign investors to finance a possibly long period of high current account deficits.

## 17.2 Macroeconomic Issues

Carneiro and Werneck (1990a) use a three-gap model to assess the importance of public capital formation under the assumption of complementarity of public and private investment, as well as of sensitivity of private investment to capacity utilization. The question of a sustainable level of capacity utilization is likely to be crucial in the next years after the failures of heterodox attempts at stopping inflation in Brazil. Short-run changes in output that may derive from the need to keep prices and mark-ups under control could have a lasting adverse effect on the level of investment. In other words, the long run effects of short-run macro policies are transmitted via the level of capacity utilization, which is judged to be sustainable in light of anti-inflation maneuvers.

In the basic scenario, the public sector borrowing requirement and the current account deficit in the balance of payments were both set to zero, in order to provide benchmarks. The former represents no increase in domestic public debt after years of uncertainty about the willingness of the private sector to hold any more. Setting the current account to zero represents independence from external sources of savings in the aftermath of the external debt crisis.

Under this basic scenario the saving and the foreign exchange constraints jointly determine a maximum feasible growth rate—approximately 3.1 %—well below the historical 7 % rate for 1940–80. By itself, a higher current deficit would have little effect the growth rate. A steady flow of foreign finance of $3.5 billion per year in the first year and 1 % of GDP thereafter would make the foreign exchange constraint nonbinding. The resulting shift in the saving constraint could allow a maximum growth rate of 3.5 %, but only at the cost of keeping the capacity utilization rate very close to 100 %. That could mean, in practice, a more overheated economy than might be advisable from the viewpoint of inflation control, illustrating the short-run limitations to long-run performance.

Growth rates higher than 3.5 % would only become feasible through policies to improve the fiscal and saving constraints. If a current account deficit of 1 % of GDP is feasible, growth would be limited by savings for levels of capacity utilization above 90 %. Higher fiscal deficits under these conditions would not increase growth possibilities. This means that policies are required to improve jointly the saving and fiscal constraints. A strong fiscal adjustment is essential for a significant upward shift in both restrictions.

The pattern of fiscal adjustment is also of great importance. A change is needed not only to open room in the fiscal budget for more public investment, but also to make the global saving constraint less severe. Two additional experiments were made to illustrate the issue. With no external finance, an increase in public savings by 3 % of GDP allows a growth rate similar to that of the basic scenario to be attained with lower capacity utilization. But there is little point in increasing public savings if overall investment cannot respond, for example, because private savings are not forthcoming. The adjustment turns out to be an overkill, since the fiscal constraint becomes nonbinding and practically no additional growth is possible, for lack of savings.

There is thus no point in increasing the investment financing capacity of the public sector if the overall saving capacity of the economy remains binding. The overkill can be eliminated if the fiscal adjustment is combined with an offsetting negative PSBR, achieved (say) by a higher net tax rate not matched by a simultaneous equivalent rise in current public expenditure. This package would permit the public sector to finance a significant portion of private investment, thereby increasing total investment capacity.

The adjustment acts basically upon the saving constraint, avoiding a fiscal impact that would be unavailing from the viewpoint of faster growth.

To summarize, high growth rates are possible without high, potentially unstable levels of capacity utilization, if a vigorous fiscal adjustment is combined with high net financial transfers from the public to the private sector, and a move to a more favorable external constraint. A scenario for 5 % growth would involve a fiscal adjustment of 6.8 % and a reduction of the PSBR by 6.5 % of GDP. Most of the fiscal adjustment (6 %) would stem from tax increases or current spending cuts. The remainder could be generated by a 40 % cutback in interest payments on the public sector's foreign debt, that would also make the external constraint significantly less adverse.

## 17.2.1    Other Constraints and Sectoral Implications

Even if macroeconomic policies can be correctly directed toward the removal of growth constraints, key sectoral issues have to be addressed. Without going into detail, two important ones may be mentioned. First is the role of agriculture and the search for "new dynamic sectors," which hinges in a special way on the role of the state in the next phase of growth. And second are the possibilities and consequences of further deepening of capital goods import substitution that started in the late 1970s.

Agriculture was never given a leading role in the post-war development experience. The average growth rate of the rural sector has been around 4 % over the past 40 years. Deviations from trend can be explained by the years of unfavorable climatic developments such as droughts or floods.

In the 1970s, substantial resources were committed to agricultural research and experimentation designed to develop and adapt new varieties to specific regional conditions. As a result of a continuous effort, in the 1980s a substantial increase in agricultural output has been achieved especially through expansion of the agricultural frontier in the direction of the *cerrado* area, which occupies about one-third of Brazilian territory, but until the 1960s was considered to be land of bad quality.

Combined with the progress made in adapting new varieties to the soil and climatic conditions of the new lands, a favorable weather cycle permitted the grain crop to grow above its trend rate late in the 1980s, with successive records of production both in exports and in crops for domestic markets. Specialists point to a new era of agricultural growth and underline the role played by domestic price policies as well as by favorable stimulus from the international market.

Two important implications follow in regard to growth constraints for the coming years. The first has to do with the pressure for improvement in transportation and storage facilities brought about by the simple fact that the new production areas may be located 3,000 to 4,000 kilometers from the nearest port. A necessary condition to maintain competitive prices at the port is a total refurbishing of the transportation network connecting production areas to the export outlets.

The second issue relates to the sectoral implications of the agricultural boom, for example, derived demand for manufactured goods such as transportation equipment, agricultural machinery, and storage and refrigeration equipment. Migration flows toward the new areas, as well as to middle-sized prosperous new towns with their demands for the comforts of modern life, will mark a clear contrast with the concentrating nature of the industrialization waves of the 1950s and 1970s. In fact, it is hard to see import substitution playing again the role it had in the past. Yet, the identification of new dynamic sectors is important for the assessment of the relevance of the external constraint.

The impact of additional investment on the demand for imported capital goods is an important linkage in this regard. In the model used by Carneiro and Werneck (1990a), this effect is captured by a parameter $(\gamma_1)$ that makes the share of imported capital goods in total investment depend on the investment ratio.

The magnitude of $\gamma_1$ will depend on the investment pattern that prevails in the 1990s, as well as the effects of import substitution policies in the capital goods industry. The success of the last round of import substitution in the second half of the 1970s is hard to evaluate at this point, due to the fall in investment following the stabilization crisis in 1982–83. In the first half of the 1970s, typical figures for the share of imports in total machinery and equipment outlays were above 20%, and this figure declined to 13.2% in 1980 and 9% in 1982. As a fraction of total fixed investment, imported capital goods declined from 10% in 1973 to 5.4% in 1980 and 3.4% in 1982. In the growth model, $\gamma_1$ was taken as 0.15, meaning that an increase of 1% of GDP in the rate of investment leads to an increase in the imports of capital goods of 0.15% of GDP. Between 1973 and 1975, the observed value for $\gamma_1$ was 0.125 and between 1980 and 1982 the figure was 0.14.

The sensitivity of the growth rate to $\gamma_1$ is acute. When this parameter is set to 0.15, an increase in the current account deficit equivalent to 1% of GDP would raise the maximum feasible growth rate by 1.9% from the viewpoint of the foreign exchange constraint. If, instead, $\gamma_1$ is equal to 0.1, the same increase in the current account deficit would raise the externally-constrained growth rate by 2.9%.

These results suggest that the level of the external limit to growth is responsive to policies aimed at capital-goods import substitution. But on the other hand, they could also lead to an increase in the incremental capital-output ratio, and that would be detrimental to growth. Although the latter effect was not considered in the simulations, data on investment in past years suggest that a substantial rise in the relative price of capital goods—as reflected in the difference between the rate of investment at constant and current prices—may be indicating declining productivity. These questions deserve prompt investigation.

## 17.2.2 The State and Economic Change

Under the new configuration of aggregate and sectoral constraints that we have discussed, a natural question is how the public sector should modify its historical role to support a new growth strategy.

The recent weakening of state initiative in Brazil has two identifiable and interdependent causes: the public sector financial crisis and a loss of political grip on strategic economic issues. During the 1980s, for lack of a sound financial basis, as well as convincing long-term projects, the Brazilian state lost good deal of the legitimacy of its power of intervention in economic matters. In the past, free market ideas have not been popular in the country even in the early times of the military government, despite the official liberal rhetoric. However, they have recently become widespread among politicians and were present even in the late 1980s program of self-styled leftist intellectuals, after the "New Republic" regime failed to produce a credible growth strategy.

The difficulties of the 1985–89 period project into the 1990s because the public sector financial crisis and the menace of hyperinflation undermine the credibility of any plan based on official sources of finance without a convincing fiscal reform. From the viewpoint of growth, fiscal reform is a way to dismantle the plethora of fiscal exemptions, tax expenditures, cheap inputs, and special credit facilities, which mushroomed after the first oil shock, as part of the effort to mobilize private investors toward the top priority sectors of the Second National Development Plan. An estimated 3–4% of GDP in government expenditures or forgone revenue were transferred each year to the private sector during the 1980s. If a reform of the tax system manages to give this share of income back to the federal government, a substantial increase in government savings will be available to support a new investment effort.

In the previous growth experience, government financial capability was used to cement solidarity between state enterprises, representing the modern face of the government, and a host of new entrepreneurs who accepted the challenge to invest in capital and intermediate goods producing sectors, as part of the effort at import substitution and export expansion. The system implied the choice of selected capitalists to receive substantial transfers from the treasury. In return, the level of direct bureaucratic controls over imports, prices, and exports permits was probably never so high and widespread in the Brazilian economy.

More recently, the obsolescence of incentives coupled with bankruptcy of the state have given rise to ever-increasing calls for less state intervention and more reliance on market forces, with scarcely any support for the view that there may be a need for the state in the next stage of economic growth.

A competing vision may be offered by arguing that: (1) after present high uncertainty, the role of the state in warranting the feasibility of the new growth path is bound to be crucial; and (2) as in other moments of Brazilian economic history, the infrastructure sectors (transport, energy, communications, water supply, etc.) are once again those which will have to be given special attention, because the past five years have witnessed a visible deterioration of public services. These verities contrast with the new mainstream view, which tends to see deregulation, privatization, and import liberalization as the key issues for development.

The pace and the limits of privatization in Brazil will be shaped by strict economic constraints, which are bound to impose difficulties quite different from those that stem from vested interests and political opposition. Privatization represents a structural change that has to be justified in terms of long-run policy objectives.[6] The central problem of the Brazilian economy today is the resumption of economic growth. The effective advancement of privatization in Brazil will be determined by the extent to which it will help or hinder the search for a solution.

It is certainly true that as part of a more general effort to reform and modernize the public sector and to enhance economic efficiency, privatization may have a significant contribution to make.[7] But Brazil will not be able to maintain again the high average annual growth rate of the past without a sizable increase in its present investment ratio. And this poses important questions about the economy's ability to pay for the required additional investment and about whether privatization may make that finance easier or more difficult.

The case for privatization in Brazil has been partly made in terms of the positive effects it could have on investment financing, particularly in those sectors that have been controlled by public enterprises. It has been argued that, given the serious financial difficulties that have been faced by the public sector, the transfer of capital-intensive public enterprises to the private sector would be the natural way to increase investment in those enterprises, and indeed overall. The problem with this kind of argument is that it lacks macroeconomic consistency. There is an aggregate savings constraint to be faced. Shifting the investment responsibility from the public to the private sector will not lead to a higher sustainable overall investment ratio, unless aggregate savings are increased accordingly.

Discussion of the financial absorptive capacity of the private sector in privatization programs has centered on stocks, as opposed to flows, that is, whether the private sector would be able to buy the transferred assets and pay what they are worth. There is no doubt about the relevance of such discussion, but it is at least as important to discuss also the privatized enterprises' financial ability to maintain the required investment effort in the sectors they operate. In capital-intensive operations such as electricity, telecommunications, and railroads, even the largest Brazilian groups would face serious difficulties.

Of course, the expansion could be extensively financed by the state, as has been done in the past in many sectors, but in this case the privatization argument would naturally become less forceful. Furthermore, the large-scale channeling of required public funds into private enterprises may also pose difficulties, already observed in the past, if giveaways are to be avoided and the private character of the enterprise preserved.[8] Indeed, the need to avoid giveaways of public funds and assets may prove a strong impediment to privatization in the first place. Significant public-to-private capital transfers were possible in the 1970s, under the military government. But obvious distributional considerations would make them difficult in the very different political circumstances of today. If giveaways are to be avoided, even top public officials directly involved in the Brazilian privatization program acknowledge that it would be difficult to sell control of most of the largest public enterprises.

The ability of the private sector to absorb the assets to be transferred, as well as to maintain the required investment effort in the privatized sectors, will in some measure depend on the role allowed to foreign investors.

Speculation about this raises difficult questions as to the relative power of the nationalist coalition within Congress.

## 17.3 Political Economy

The long transition of the 1980s led to growing pessimism about growth possibilities for Brazil. Its less radical aspect is a belief that the historical 7 % rate is no longer sustainable, and therefore one should settle for something less. This may be turned into a gloomier prospect if one believes that absorption of new additions to the work force (still expanding at approximately 3.5 % yearly, despite the sharp fall in population growth) will require economic growth close to the historical rate during the next decade.[9]

There seems to be no evidence that recovery of the historical rate of economic growth has become unfeasible. But there are several important obstacles to such recovery. The first is the political difficulty of gathering support for a serious stabilization program directed toward restoring the country's growth capability. With high inflation and its paralyzing effect on investment and any kind of long run planning, there is no way a successful recovery can be forthcoming. Lower inflation, together with a continuous effort to maintain a high level of exports to prevent import capacity from being strangled by recovery, are essential elements in the strategy. Another is certainly an increase in the aggregate rate of investment.

The rate of investment in the second half of the 1980s was well below the threshold required for historical growth rates, even if one disregards the probable decline in productivity of investment. One cannot help looking at the financing aspects to explain part of the fall. A mixture of factors must be considered, ranging from the high uncertainty generated by a long period of outrageously high rates of inflation, to the high level of transfers abroad after the debt crisis of 1982 and the virtual disappearance of public savings.

Recovery of investment will require an increase in the domestic savings rate even in overoptimistic scenarios concerning the prospects of foreign finance. Because in the near future foreign savings are not likely to be of any importance compared with the past, recovery of investment will require an inevitable decline in consumption as a proportion of GDP, side by side with a decline in transfers of real resources. An important part of the challenge ahead is how to obtain this result without aggravating distributional equity. These observations tend to reinforce our doubts concerning the possibility of a smaller role for the state in the new growth model.

Consensus on these issues is far from easy. At the peak of an inflationary outburst, distributive conflicts are as important as ever. For the time being, the only agreement seems to refer to the need to contain government current expenditures, which is far less than sufficient to promote higher investment.

### 17.3.1    Difficulties of Fiscal Adjustment

It has been argued that the financial crisis of the public sector has been behind most of the difficulties recently faced by the Brazilian economy. Both a feasible stabilization effort and the recovery of economic growth depend on its resolution. As suggested earlier, however, general recognition of this fact has not been sufficient to generate the substantial fiscal effort required. Repeated attempts in this direction have faced strong and unsurmountable political opposition.

In fact, the apparent consensus around the idea of a fiscal adjustment hides a strong coalition that has been able to create political obstacles to its implementation (Werneck, 1990). In order to increase public sector savings one has to combine cuts in current expenditures, subsidies, tax expenditures, and simple transfers to the private sector, on one hand, and an increase in gross tax-burden and public prices. Any such measure creates clear losers: public employees, contractors, clients of public firms, holders of public debt, and so on, whose interests are immediately affected. In sharp contrast, gains from a successful adjustment are at best a promise for the future, with a strong flavor of a public good. There are perverse incentives to postpone adjustment, and the political system has not been able to produce a majority coalition to support a time-consistent collective choice.

These somewhat commonplace difficulties have been amplified by special conditions in the Brazilian case. One such is the visible deterioration of sector-specific public services, creating opposition to increases in the net tax rate (Bacha and Werneck, 1988). Another aspect is a widespread corporatist vision in some segments of the public establishment, which helps to generate obstacles to any transfer of command over resources to the government.

Finally, years of half-hearted budget control measures have not managed to cut back the public deficit, but rather undermine funding of important functions of the public sector from education to health services, as well as to erode the credibility of budgeting techniques and expenditure control practices. Systematic underestimation of inflation has been turned into a device to increase centralized control over effective disbursements, as actual disbursements have to be negotiated every quarter when allocated expenditures become obsolete due to spiraling prices. Such practices contribute to further demoralize attempts at budget control and fiscal adjustment.

## 17.3.2 Difficulties of an Effective Anti-inflation Policy

Two types of challenges have to be faced by anti-inflation policy. The first relates to the costs involved in stabilization after mounting frustration associated with the failed attempts over the past six years. The second is due to the long tradition of inflation, which has contributed to establish a view (dominant among politicians as well as specialized analysts who contribute to public opinion) that inflation is "part of the culture," a "necessary lubricant" to structural changes, or even "beneficial to development." This view is so embedded in some minds that any program aiming to bring inflation down to (say) European levels is rapidly dismissed as being absurd. Politicians and practical men have very modest goals regarding inflation. Therefore, it is very difficult to form a political coalition to support anti-inflation policy.

On top of these perceptions, the fact is that heterodox promises of putting an end to inflation with small social cost in terms of recession have led to anguish in Brazil. Expectations following the announcement of any new policy shock are bound to be dim: the costs of stabilization are perceived now to be inevitably higher than five years ago (Carneiro, 1989a).

## 17.3.3 Political Stability and Medium-Term Growth

What will happen if growth and stability are not attained reasonably soon? It has been a long decade of very slow growth and macroeconomic disarray. There is room to believe that if the new president, elected in late 1989, fails during his term to put the country back on the road to sustainable and fairly rapid growth, escalation of political and social tension will become unavoidable. After all, the labor force is still growing very fast. That trend is expected to last until at least the end of the century, despite the recent surprisingly sharp fall in population growth.

Latent social unrest in the country's large metropolitan areas is evidenced by the rise in the importance of informal jobs and criminality during the decade, in the wake of a general decay in the quality of urban services. If demand for labor does not start to grow steadily in the early to mid-

1990s, and if the quality of urban life and the supply of basic services as elementary schools, health care, police protection and mass transport cannot be improved in a significant way, there may be social and political unrest.

If that is accepted, the relevant question is how this unrest will feed back into the political sphere. One possible, more optimistic scenario, would foresee growing concern about a social explosion making it less difficult to build up a majority coalition that could implement the needed adjustment measures, for example, by reducing the pervading fierce resistance to any loss that could stem from an effective fiscal adjustment. Another, more pessimistic scenario would mean that democratic rule has failed to generate political support for reasonable economic policies in Brazil.

## Notes

1. The following analysis is based on Werneck (1988).

2. See Werneck (1991) for a detailed analysis of the public sector behavior in the period.

3. In fact, in the mid-1970s public enterprises were forbidden to resort to new equity capital from minority private shareholders and were forced to limit their borrowing in the domestic financial markets, in order to induce them to resort to foreign loans. There is no room in the Brazilian case to ascribe the explosive behavior of the foreign debt to a liberalization of borrowing restrictions imposed on public enterprises and agencies, that would have led to unwanted indebtedness from the point of view of the central government. Strict control on foreign exchange and external credit operations was maintained throughout the period under analysis in this paper. Foreign borrowing targets were explicitly established by government and their accomplishment carefully surveyed month after month by the Central Bank.

4. See Carneiro (1987) for a description of stabilization and adjustment programs of the early 1980s.

5. The design of a policy that could effectively generate the required enhancement of the domestic savings effort in Brazil involves some important trade-offs that are analyzed in Werneck (1987), through simulations based on two simple consistency models. Those simulations outline what would be the required increase in the private sector's saving effort in different scenarios, that involve distinct sets of hypotheses on the evolution of income distribution and of variables that determine the public sector's savings capacity. The results stress the lack of realism of savings policies that do not restore the importance of public savings, which used to represent—in the mid-1970s—one-third of total domestic savings in Brazil. The need to restore the importance of public sector savings becomes particularly clear when one considers scenarios involving even a modest—and highly probable—redistri-

bution of income in favor of labor in the near future, and takes into account the consequent impact on the private savings ratio.

6. For a deeper analysis of the privatization issue in Brazil see Werneck (1989).

7. See Bacha and Werneck (1988) for a brief discussion on the urgent need for a drastic public sector reform in Brazil.

8. Such difficulties were faced during the 1970s in many sectors. Very often there was either resort to large giveaways of public funds or the firms fell under state control. See Werneck (1991) and Najberg (1989).

9. Of course such estimates reflect the past growth experience. Very little is known about the pattern of job creation of recent growth in services and the new agricultural regions and their supporting sectors.

**References**

Bacha, E. L. and R. L. F. Werneck (1988). "Reforma do Setor Público: O Primeiro Desafio," in "Estratégias de Desenvolvimento: Alternativas para o Brasil." *Relatório Interno* No. 108. INPES/IPEA.

Carneiro, D. (1987). "Brazil Stabilization and Adjustment," *Country Study* No. 11. Helsinki: WIDER.

Carneiro, D. (1989a). "Alternativas para a Política de Estabilização." (Mimeo), PUC-RJ.

Carneiro, D. (1989b). "The Limping Eighties and Beyond." (Mimeo).

Carneiro, D., and R. L. F. Werneck (1990a). "Brazil: Growth Exercises for the Nineties," revised version, Mimeo.

Carneiro, D., and R. L. F. Werneck (1990b). "Divida Externa, Crescimento Economico e Ajuste Fiscal." *Pesquisa e Planejamento Econômico*, Vol. 20, No. 1.

Carneiro, D., and R. L. F. Werneck (1990c). "Public Savings, Private Investment, and Growth Resumption in Brazil." *Texto para Discussão* No. 239, Departamento de Economia, PUC-Rio de Janeiro.

Najberg, S. (1989). *Privatização de Recursos Públicos: Os Empréstimos do BNDES ao Setor Privado Nacional com Correção Monetária Parcial*. Unpublished M.A. Thesis, Departamento de Economia, PUC-RJ.

Werneck, R. L. F. (1986). "Poupança Estatal, Divida Externa e Crise Financeira do Setor Público." *Pesquisa e Planejamento Econômico*, Vol. 16, No. 3.

Werneck, R. L. F. (1987). "Retomada do Crescimento e Esforço de Poupança: Limitações e Possibilidades." *Pesquisa e Planejamento Econômico*.

Werneck, R. L. F. (1988). "A Longa Transição do Anos 80." *Carta Econômica*, ANBID, year VIII.

Werneck, R. L. F. (1989). "Aspectos Macroeconômicos da Privatação no Brasil." *Pesquisa e Planejamento Econômico*, Vol. 19, No. 2.

Werneck, R. L. F. (1990). "A Questão de Financiamento de Setor Publico na Economia Brasileira: O Espaço para Ajuste nos Dispêndios Não-Financeiros." *Revista de Economia Política*, Vol. 20, No. 1.

Werneck, R. L. F. (1991). "Public Sector Adjustment to External Shocks and Domestic Pressures in Brazil, 1970–85," in M. Selowsky and F. Larrain (eds.), *The Public Sector and the Latin American Crisis, 1970–1985*. San Francisco: International Center for Economic Growth.

# 18

## Nicaragua

## Bill Gibson

This chapter assesses prospects for the Nicaraguan economy using the three-gap methodology up to end of the decade. The general conclusion is that growth will be slow, with little chance of any increase in per capita income, because Nicaragua will not be able to sustain the current account deficits of either the Sandinista or immediate post-Sandinista regimes. To increase exports will require (1) a restructuring of the economy in fundamental ways, (2) a further decline in real incomes of workers and peasants, (3) continued success in the fight against inflation, (4) recovery and integration into the regional economy, and (5) continued political support of the Sandinista party, the Frente Sandinista de Liberción Nacional (FSLN). Only once the restructuring has taken place can redistributive policies be placed on the political agenda.

This chapter is organized as follows: The next section provides the backdrop for the discussion of the gap projections by providing some details of the economic policies and performance of the Sandinista regime during the 1980s. Section 18.2 takes up the transition to the new government of Violeta Chamorro. Section 18.3 discusses the gap projections for the remainder of the decade. A fourth section concludes and the mathematics of the model appears in an appendix.

## 18.1 The Sandinista Model of the Mixed Economy

For the first few years after the FSLN took power from the deeply corrupt, U.S.-backed government of Anastasio Somoza Debayle, the economy grew relatively smoothly.[1] In 1983, the growth in Nicaraguan GDP was the highest in Latin America. Tax collections were up, the fiscal deficit was under control and inflation was moderate (see table 18.1). Capital flight prior to the revolution was intense, and it continued after the revolution, but there was some capital formation though public sector enterprises,

**Table 18.1**
Basic macro data

| Year | GDP growth rate | Per capita GDP[a] | Inflation[b] | Imports[c] | Deficits Fiscal[d] | Current account[e] |
|---|---|---|---|---|---|---|
| 1970–74 | 6.3 | 102.9 | 9.8 | | 3.0 | 85.7 |
| 1975–79 | −4.5 | 100.0 | 14.2 | | 5.7 | 122.3 |
| 1980 | 4.5 | 68.7 | 24.8 | 100.0 | 8.9 | 430.1 |
| 1981 | 5.4 | 70.1 | 23.2 | 110.1 | 8.8 | 590.6 |
| 1982 | −0.8 | 67.3 | 22.2 | 87.7 | 12.4 | 491.6 |
| 1983 | 4.6 | 68.1 | 35.5 | 99.4 | 21.8 | 507.7 |
| 1984 | −1.6 | 64.8 | 47.3 | 105.5 | 23.5 | 596.8 |
| 1985 | −4.1 | 60.1 | 334.3 | 111.9 | 22.5 | 725.7 |
| 1986 | −1.0 | 57.5 | 747.4 | 115.6 | 17.1 | 687.8 |
| 1987 | −0.7 | 55.8 | 1,347.4 | 89.9 | 16.4 | 679.1 |
| 1988 | −13.4 | 47.2 | 33,602.6 | 86.6 | 20.7 | 581.3 |
| 1989 | −5.1 | 43.6 | 1,690.0 | 65.4 | 2.5 | 361.6 |
| 1990 | 1.0 | 42.4 | 13,490.9 | 70.0 | 12.3 | 357.4 |
| 1991 | −0.7 | 41.1 | 1,183.2[p] | 81.0[p] | 2.3 | 357.5 |

Notes: a. 1975–79 = 100.
b. CPI.
c. Quantity index; 1980 = 100.
d. As a percent of GDP.
e. $U.S. × $10^{-6}$.
p. preliminary.
Sources: 1970–86 IMF (1989); 1987–1988; Taylor et al., (1989) CEPAL, (1988, 1990, 1991) and Ocampo (1992).

created through the expropriation of the properties of the Somoza family and its associates.

The intellectual model at the base of Sandinista policy was the mixed economy and not classical populism as described by Sachs (1989) and Dornbusch and Edwards (1990). In the populist regime, the government earns political support from the urban working class by raising real wages. This leads to an increase in capacity utilization that puts pressure on the balance of payments by increasing imports and, possibly, decreasing exports. Prices of nontraded goods are held in check initially either by surplus import capacity (funds that would have otherwise retired debt) and, often, price controls. In the second phase of populism, inflation breaks out. The nominal exchange rate is pegged and the real exchange rate appreciates. Capital flight increases as the domestic bourgeoisie anticipates the coming devaluation. The capital base of the economy shrinks, output falls, and inflation accelerates. To prevent the erosion of political support from their only constituency, the populist regime allows nominal wages to increase, but not on par. With falling real wages, high inflation, and possibly capital and exchange controls, the government is deserted. With no foreign exchange reserves and exports at an all time low, government is forced to seek help, typically with the IMF. But for a populist government, IMF conditionality implies, above all, that the populist measures be dismantled. Real wages plunge far below their initial level as nominal wage increases stop and a maxi-devaluation is undertaken. In the end, the populist regime has failed as a vehicle for improving the lot of the popular classes. They are worse off than if the stabilization and structural adjustment policies of the old regime had continued.

The conception of the nixed economy advanced by the Sandinistas departed from this pattern in important ways. Many of the Sandinista top leadership were intellectuals rather than workers and the policies of the revolution were shaped by their analysis of why the agroexport model had failed (Wheelock, 1980; Hodges, 1986). Departing from classical Marxism, the Sandinistas located the source of exploitation and inequality not in property ownership, per se, but in the control of key areas of the economy —finance, commerce and international trade. Their politics were nationalist, anti-imperialist flowing from real history of U.S. intervention, intervention that was usually more political than economic (Close, 1988).

Although the details of the mixed economy were never clearly spelled out, they are somewhat clearer in retrospect. The productive apparatus was to remain essentially in the hands of the private sector, with the state controlling distribution. Immediately after the revolution, the Sandinistas put into place capital and exchange controls, adopted a fairly repressive wage structure, and embarked on a series of "social wage" projects in the areas of health, education, housing, and literacy that were completely unheard of in prerevolutionary Nicaragua. State-controlled marketing boards were set up to eliminate speculative and exploitative middlemen and clearing houses for exports were instituted to stop underinvoicing. The foreign exchange constraint was institutionalized through elaborate procedures to allocate increasingly scarce hard currency.

In exchange for political control, the Sandinistas intended to deliver low wage labor to the private sector. Profits would be maintained and in no way would capitalists be oppressed by the state (Wheelock, 1983). Large growers would be unaffected by the agrarian reform and provided with low wage labor and if not an adequate real exchange rate, input subsidies in order to maintain profitability. Only land of the Somoza family and "unpatriotic" or unproductive capitalists would be expropriated.

Labor's part of the bargain would come in the form of the social wage. Presumably, labor would be content and sufficiently loyal to exchange a lower private wage for a higher social wage. In the countryside, displaced workers would benefit from the agrarian reform and although there might be pressure for radical land redistribution, it would be contained through an expansion of credit to poor- to medium-sized producers, who never in the past had access to the financial system.

Given the degree to which the Sandinistas' own clients have had to bear the costs of the revolution, the prima facie evidence seems to suggest that Nicaragua has indeed followed a populist trajectory. Under the Sandinistas, per capita output declined to levels of 1940s and, as shown by table 18.1, is now only 41.1 % of its prerevolutionary level. Real wages have declined by at least 65 % since 1978, the year before the revolution (Ocampo, 1992). (Using the CPI to deflate nominal increases gives a much more dramatic fall in the index than does the GDP deflator, due to the presence of scarce consumer goods in the CPI.) Most of this fall occurred during the period of hyperinflation, roughly 1987 to 1991, but in no year did the index rise above its prerevolutionary level. This seems to dispel the idea that the Sandinistas engaged in simple wage led expansion that led to difficulties with the current account as foretold by the populist story.

Nevertheless, inflation followed a populist path in that prices of at least basic consumer commodities were controlled, and there was sufficient foreign exchange to allow imports to dampen any potential increase. Nicaraguan inflation was less than half that of the rest of Latin America until 1984 (CEPAL, 1988, p. 19) but then accelerated rapidly as seen in table 18.1. In 1988, the CPI advanced by more than 33,600 % but then fell precipitously in 1989 as the result of a contractionary stabilization program introduced by the Sandinistas. At its worst, the inflation surpassed Bolivia's record rate of 11,750 %; for two months at the end of 1988 Nicaragua's monthly inflation rate was more than 100 % (Arana, 1990, Cuadro 6). Then after a period of relative calm leading up to the election, the inflation rate again surpassed 100 % per month in May and June 1990.[2]

There is a second sense in which the Nicaraguan model is similar to the populist framework identified by Sachs (1989) and, Dornbusch and Edwards (1990). In the standard model, the urban popular classes are enticed to support the new regime because of previous belt-tightening policies introduced to stabilize the economy. The latter comes about through a combination of wage repression and devaluation, which is designed to shift income from wage earners and importers to exporters. The populist party exploits the inequity of the standard adjustment package to form a political base. Debt that would under more normal circumstances be inflated away is now being repaid with real resources. There appears to be some slack in the balance of payments due to adjustment process.

Table 18.1 shows that Nicaragua nay have also suffered from the delusion of sufficient foreign exchange for whatever plans the Sandinistas may have had. With enough foreign exchange to purchase intermediate imports and capital goods, the economy began to recover from the revolution which had reduced GDP by 25 % in 1979. Current account deficits on average of four times the 1975–79 levels became commonplace during the first few years, and grew to a maximum of $725.7 million in 1985. For perspective, this last figure is just above 1978 exports but almost three times 1991 exports.

How much Nicaragua could import seemed to have little connection with the local economy, but rather how the revolution was received by donor countries. Initially the list was long and included the United States as well as significant contributions from other Latin American countries and Western Europe. Mexico and Venezuela entered into an agreement to supply oil at concessionary terms. Even when the United States withdrew, citing alleged arms shipments to the FMLN guerrillas in El Salvador, other donors were found to make up the difference. But when it became apparent that Nicaragua would not meet minimum payments for oil shipments, Mexico and Venezuela cut off supplies. Pressured by the United States to cut off funding, sources in Europe and Latin American began to dry up and Nicaragua turned increasingly to the Soviet Union and the Eastern bloc. After 1986, tied aid restricted real import capacity, as seen in table 18.1. All together, some 70 % of total imports took the form of commodities tied both to donor supply and to specific destinations (Taylor, et al., 1989, p. 14).

The progressive deterioration in export performance is shown in table 18.2. Over the period, exports have never done better than about 80 % of their prerevolutionary levels, and often much worse. Nontraditional exports virtually disappeared along with the Central American Common Market (CACM), which in 1980 supported $1.1 billion in trade compared to $0.4 billion in 1986. Much of the explanation lies in the U.S. embargo and the loss of Nicaragua's principal export market. There was also substantial deterioration in the terms of trade as seen in the fourth column of table 18.2. Some point to the lack of sufficient incentives for large, private sector exporters especially as expressed in the overvaluation of the ex-

**Table 18.2**
Foreign trade (millions of U.S. $)

| Year | Total exports $mn | Non-traditional % | Terms of trade | Exchange rates Official rate | Exchange rates Black market | Foreign exchange losses |
|---|---|---|---|---|---|---|
| 1975–79 | 552.7 | 28.7 | 112 | | | 0.0 |
| 1980 | 445.1 | 20.4 | 100 | 100.0 | 100.0 | 0.0 |
| 1981 | 513.8 | 18.5 | 90 | 86.3 | 141.5 | 0.0 |
| 1982 | 408.6 | 16.9 | 85 | 75.6 | 241.6 | 2.7 |
| 1983 | 451.9 | 14.8 | 82 | 65.2 | 454.4 | 4.0 |
| 1984 | 412.4 | 13.9 | 103 | 48.5 | 749.3 | 5.5 |
| 1985 | 305.1 | 12.0 | 94 | 50.1 | 814.2 | 2.8 |
| 1986 | 257.2 | 15.3 | 99 | 35.1 | 627.4 | 7.6 |
| 1987 | 295.0 | 13.6 | 101 | 9.4 | 535.3 | 5.3 |
| 1988 | 232.7 | 18.4 | 101 | 100.7 | 301.5 | 0.0 |
| 1989 | 310.7 | 25.4 | 92 | 199.0 | 181.6 | n.d. |
| 1990 | 330.3 | 20.7 | 82 | 126.0 | n.d. | n.d. |
| 1991 | 262.8 | 23.3 | 85 | 126.0 | n.d. | n.d. |

Sources: Ocampo (1990); Taylor et al., 1989

change rate. Taylor describes the 1986–87 exchange rate as one of the "most impressive cases of overvaluation in the economic history of Latin America, or indeed the world" (Taylor, et al., 1989, p. 39).

As the current account deficits piled up, public sector foreign debt reached $6 billion in 1986 almost double the 1981 figure. On a per capita basis, Nicaragua led the region as the most indebted. In the early 1980s, total liabilities were several times GDP while accrued interest was 78.3 % of total exports in 1985 (CEPAL, 1991). Total interest paid, however, was far less, some 8 % of exports in 1985, increasing the rate of resource transfer to Nicaragua to extremely high levels (Timossi, 1989). During their tenure, the Sandinistas managed to pay only about 30 % of the total interest bill (*Envio*, May, 1989, p. 21). There was an air of unreality about the way Nicaragua was able to manage its foreign accounts: while most countries of Latin America were transferring resources abroad, the inflow into Nicaragua kept increasing. In contrast to Peru under Garcia (one of the explicitly recognized populist experiments by Dornbusch and Edwards), Nicaragua was able to get away with an effective moratorium on its debt. Secondary debt sold for a little as 4 % of face value and 1 to 2 % in the late 1980s (CEPAL, 1988).

Most populist regimes do not have the luxury of increasing foreign resource flow from abroad, in fact, the problem is that credit dries up. Clearly, the inflow is what kept the Sandinista experiment going as long as it did. A principal factor at work was the Contra War, which began slowly in 1982 but was significant by 1985. The disproportionate hostility of the Reagan administration probably increased the flow of foreign resources, at least initially, from other donors. The idea that a small country of just more than 2 million could possibly pose a military threat to the United States was widely regarded as preposterous. Moreover, the utter disregard by the United States for judgments entered by the World Court against it for CIA activities undoubtedly provided Nicaragua with some political leverage that otherwise would have been unavailable.

The reaction of the United States to events in Nicaragua went far beyond the usual resistance offered by the international financial community to populist mismanagement. The damage to the country done by the Contras has been surveyed by numerous authors, all based on different methodologies (FitzGerald, 1987; Delgado, 1988). Roughly speaking, the fiscal deficit could have been reduced by almost half had the country been at peace. According to estimates at the end of 1988, some 29,400 Nicaraguans were killed, including 12,457 civilians. Official estimates place the total economic losses on the order of $12.2 billion, or approximately 6 years of GDP (*Envio* Feb. 1989, p. 16). In addition to the loss of life, there was an enormous waste of "human capital." The best and brightest minds in Nicaragua were often dedicated to solving logistical and strategic problems of the war, rather than directing the economy. At one point a fifth of the draft age population had been mobilized, creating a cultural atmosphere in which formal education was accorded low priority.

The counterpart to the war was the trade and aid blockade. Shortly after taking power in 1981, the Reagan administration ended bilateral aid of U.S. $15 million to Nicaragua and then cut off PL 480 funds in 1981. The administration pressured Western Europe not to participate in a $130 million credit line organized in London in 1982 and in 1983 cut Nicaragua's sugar quota by 90% (Conroy, 1984, p. 1028). It stopped support through the Export-Import Bank, Overseas Private Investment Corporation and downgraded Nicaragua's creditworthiness from "substandard" to "doubtful," even though at the time (1983), Nicaragua was on schedule with its debt payments (Leogrand, 1985, p. 434). The United States blocked credit from the World Bank and Inter-American Development Bank and in 1985, imposed a total economic embargo on Nicaragua. The embargo, combined

**Table 18.3**
Central government accounts (% of GDP)

| Year | Revenue | Total expenditure | Defense | Social spending | Infrastructure & production |
|------|---------|-------------------|---------|-----------------|------------------------------|
| 1981 | 24.4 | 34.5 | 7.6 | 10.2 | 7.6 |
| 1982 | 25.7 | 39.2 | 7.4 | 9.5 | 10.1 |
| 1983 | 31.2 | 61.0 | 11.0 | 11.4 | 24.7 |
| 1984 | 35.2 | 59.7 | 12.4 | 13.0 | 16.9 |
| 1985 | 32.3 | 55.6 | 17.6 | 12.1 | 9.5 |
| 1986 | 32.4 | 50.0 | 18.5 | 11.9 | 6.7 |
| 1987 | 27.8 | 44.3 | 18.1 | 10.9 | 4.8 |
| 1988 | 22.6 | 46.4 | 18.5 | 11.2 | 4.9 |
| 1989 | 21.4 | 19.6 | 8.0 | 4.8 | 2.1 |
| 1990 | 17.7 | 27.1 | 8.0 | 10.7 | 2.6 |
| 1991 | 25.3 | 26.7 | 6.6 | 10.4 | 4.5 |

Source: Ocampo, 1992.

with the effect of the lost sugar revenues and the CIA mining of the Nicaragua's principal harbor, cost the country an estimated U.S. $335 million in lost revenues from 1985 through 1988 (*Envio* Apr. 1989, p. 16).

Typically, populist regimes are cited for their failure to successfully manage public finances, but in Nicaragua, fiscal system was basically sound up until 1983. Then the fiscal deficit jumped from 12.4 % to 21.8 % of GDP (see table 18.1). Thereafter, the war forced the government to rely on deficit financing.

The fiscal crisis imposed by the war restricted the terms of agreement under which the mixed economy was to function (see table 18.3). Without some latitude to advance the social wage through infrastructural investment and social spending, there was no reason for workers and peasants to support the accord. In order to maintain social spending (which had increased three-fold over the Somoza years) the only available option was to reduce public accumulation. Defense expenditure began to crowd out public investment which had peaked at 24.7 % of GDP in 1983, the year of the highest growth in output. By 1988, public investment dropped to only 4.9 % of GDP. By 1985, the social compact began to unravel.

The money supply began to accelerate with the deepening of the war effort in 1982–83, as seen in table 18.4. Even though inflation remained low, liquidity began to build, preparing for a massive assault on the *córdoba*. By 1984, the central government and the Area de Propriedad Publica (APP) were absorbing more than two-thirds of total credit. Credit to the

**Table 18.4**
Monetary data

| Year | M1[a] | Quasi-money[a] | Official exchange rate[b] | Black market[c] | Black market premium[d] | Foreign exchange losses[a] |
|------|-------|----------------|---------------------------|-----------------|-------------------------|----------------------------|
| 1980 | 20.9 | 12.1 | 100.0 | 100.0 | 73.3 | 0.0 |
| 1981 | 20.0 | 12.5 | 85.0 | 139.3 | 184.7 | 0.0 |
| 1982 | 21.8 | 11.9 | 74.1 | 237.1 | 454.2 | 2.7 |
| 1983 | 27.2 | 12.7 | 64.7 | 451.0 | 1,129.2 | 4.0 |
| 1984 | 36.4 | 15.4 | 49.3 | 760.1 | 2,658.3 | 5.5 |
| 1985 | 36.8 | 10.4 | 54.6 | 863.3 | 2,643.2 | 2.8 |
| 1986 | 35.0 | 5.9 | 39.1 | 702.2 | 3,183.2 | 7.6 |
| 1987 | 28.2 | 3.6 | 11.1 | 630.6 | 17,614.3 | 5.0 |
| 1988 | 17.0 | 1.2 | 92.8 | 264.9 | 361.3 | 8.3 |
| 1989 | 8.1 | 1.1 | 137.7 | 107.3 | 28.3 | 13.9 |
| 1990 | 6.7 | 1.2 | 105.2 | 84.1 | 12.2 | 2.8 |
| 1991 | 6.2 | 1.3 | n.d. | n.d. | n.d | n.d. |

Notes: a. Percent of GDP.
b. Real exchange rate index using GDP deflator.
c. 1980 = 100.
d. percent
Sources: Banco Central; Taylor, et al., 1989; IMF, 1987 Ocampo, 1992.

private sector dried up more than proportionally, as much a result of the drop in private sector demand for credit as it was limited by supply. As inflation intensified, the real burden of loans disappeared, owing to the fixed nominal interest rates. Credit amounted to a direct subsidy, at least until early 1989 when a significant financial reform required monthly adjustments of nominal rates (Taylor, et al. 1989, p. 60).

The inflation tax was particularly successful in 1984 through 1986 (Taylor, et al., 1989). For no obvious reason, the private sector was willing to hold large quantities of money subject to accelerated erosion, as shown in table 18.4. Part of the explanation was undoubtedly price controls, at least in the beginning. A second reason lay perhaps in the lack of formal information about current inflation rates. There was also the inflow of CIA money to supply the Contra. CIA dollars injected through the black market allowed for average liquidity ratios to rise while the effect on prices would be temporarily slowed by increased imports. Capital flight began to offset the effect on supply, however, as early as 1982 and the real black-market exchange rate began to rise steeply. The premium over the official rate jumped from 184.7 % in 1981 to 454.2 % in 1982, as seen in table 18.4.

A substantial fraction of the fiscal deficit is tied to policies that attempted to garner the support of domestic bourgeoisie. By 1984, the multiple exchange had gotten out of hand, causing foreign exchange losses of 5.5 % of GDP, as seen in table 18.4 . Foreign exchange losses rose to 7.6 % of GDP in 1986, but declined thereafter, as the import and export exchange rates were brought together.

Public sector investment projects also contributed to the inflationary push because the bulk of state projects obtained 100 % financing at highly subsidized, mostly negative interest rates. They also benefited from the overvalued exchange rate. Medal, argues that "financial discipline" had virtually disappeared and that the Central Bank presided over a massive transfer of resources from domestic savers to questionable state projects. The only effective limit on credit creation was the associated need for foreign exchange for intermediate inputs. Concerns about the inflationary consequences of credit creation expressed through the normal mechanisms of credit regulation were simply not present (Medal, 1988, p. 88). On the other hand, these projects were to some extent self-financing through the inflation tax they induced.

Thus, it is unclear that Nicaragua fits closely the populist paradigm as set forth by Sachs (1989) and others. Nicaragua may be a case of blatant disregard for principles of sound financial management, but the problems were not the simple mistakes of a government solicitous of political support from the urban working class. As argued, the situation was complicated by the war, and in particular, the failure of the domestic bourgeoisie to cooperate with the regime. The latter undermined the Sandinista notion of a mixed economy and caused Nicaragua to seem to parrot other failed populist schemes. It was a failure of will, of domestic policy, and of U.S. foreign policy.

## Will

In the prerevolutionary period, the private sector served as the engine of accumulation, investing as much as 16.8 % of GDP in the 1970–74 period. Immediately following the revolution, a capital strike began and the Sandinistas denounced the domestic bourgeoisie for "decapitalizing" the economy (Gilbert, 1985, p. 172). Private sector investment throughout the revolutionary period never recovered, despite persistent policies of price guarantees, preferential access to foreign exchange at subsidized rates, relatively low taxes and direct subsidies. Regressions on investment data show that prior to the devastating earthquake in 1972, the stimulative effect of government investment on private investment, crowding in, was weak, with barely a significant coefficient of lagged public-sector investment on private investment. Thereafter, the coefficient becomes highly significant, indicating strong crowding in.[3] Thus, the idea that the private sector would play a predominant role in the recovery and future of the mixed economy simply never materialized.

Vilas (1984) and many others have pointed out that the domestic, *antisomocista* bourgeoisie only wanted to destroy the dictatorship and certainly not the class structure that supported it. For them the crisis of the dictatorship was strictly a political crisis and had nothing to do with an economic restructuring of society. Historically, Nicaragua has been politically stable with a superimposed lineage of statist control leading to a constituency inexperienced in constitutional government. There is no history of effective multiparty politics as an arena in which class conflict could play itself out. Prior to 1979, distributional conflicts were resolved by rule of the dictatorship with little need for persuasion. What the traditional private sector had in mind was a continuation of the old, anti-democratic power structure in which power came in proportion to economic position rather than numbers.

*Domestic Policy*

Throughout the revolutionary period, the overvalued exchange rate was substantially offset by implicit and explicit subsidies as well as negative real interest rates. In 1982, the government introduced a system of multiple exchange rates, although the implicit rate of devaluation was only 20 % the first year and 15 % for the next two years[4] (De Franco, 1985, p. 6). Gibson (1985) argued, using a computable general equilibrium model, that the Sandinistas should have undertaken a major currency devaluation much earlier on, at least in 1983. But implicit in the agreement with labor was that the real wage would not come under serious attack. Devaluation was widely regarded as reneging on the agreement. Moreover, given the hostile attitude of the domestic bourgeoisie, official devaluation would trigger a run-up in the black market rate, stimulating capital flight.[5] The Sandinistas were unwilling to face the political consequences of an open assault on real wages and in so doing crippled the export market. The various schemes to make up for the overvalued exchange rate were too little too late and not evenly applied. What the Sandinistas apparently failed to recognize was that a successful real devaluation, however achieved, would necessarily transfer income from workers and urban capital to agroexporters. They could not simultaneously protect their clients and stimulate exports.

*U.S. Foreign Policy*

The Contra war brought an enormous amount of physical devastation to Nicaragua, but the ideological effects of the dominant power in the hemisphere's supporting the counterrevolutionaries probably did even more long-term damage. Bolstered by the United States, the domestic bourgeoisie simply failed to take part in the revolutionary experiment. Certainly, the Sandinistas are themselves to blame for their fiery rhetoric on the issue of the transition to socialism. A socially progressive model of some fashion could have been born out of negotiations with the domestic bourgeoisie supported by the United States. Instead, local capital rejected virtually all aspects of the Sandinista model, especially state production of private goods, capital and exchange controls, and control of the financial system. It is not at all surprising that the Chamorro regime intends to dismantle, piece, by piece, these artifacts of the Sandinista economy.

## 18.2   The Macroeconomy in the Transition to the Chamorro Regime

In summarizing recent macropolicy, it useful to break down the last decade into four distinct phases. July 1979 through December 1981 was a period of revolutionary euphoria, consolidation, and reconstruction after the insurrection. Agroexports were recovering, and ample foreign assistance kept the foreign exchange constraint from binding and the economy grew without inflation. Stabilization amounted to containing the growth in domestic credit which was exploding to cover the new social programs ushered in after the fall of Somoza.

The second phase, from December 1981 to October 1983, was a period of transition to a war economy. The Contras obtained U.S. $19 million in CIA financing and the government deficit began to swell as the arms buildup began. External financing was no longer abundant and the increase in emissions began to show up in a substantial black-market premium as seen above.

After November 1983, the economy entered the third phase, a full war economy with attendant macroeconomic chaos. Several factors coalesced to undermine the Sandinista policy. As the pressure of war expenditure increased, the extra purchasing power injected by the monetary creation caused the black-market exchange rate to rise. The *córdoba* ceased to be an instrument for savings. As the capital flight accelerated, extra-legal imports (a factor that had been important in keeping inflation under control) dwindled, setting in motion a vicious cycle of stagflation. Capitalists and the petty bourgeoisie were awash with cash due to the forced savings brought about by rigid nominal wages and large nominal expenditure. The demand for any stable asset exploded and the premium over the official rate (shown in table 18.4) increased from 4.5 to 26.5 times between 1982 and 1984.

There were weak-willed attempts at stabilization in 1985 (e.g., the first devaluation since 1979) but the Sandinistas did not undertake serious reform until 1988. By the end of 1987, the black-market premium was wildly out of line with the official exchange, inflation was at more than 1,300 % per year and real growth had ended. The Sandinista economy entered its fourth and final phase, characterized as orthodox shock stabilization policy.

In February 1988, President Daniel Ortega announced monetary reform, implying a maximum devaluation of the *córdoba* from 70 to 10,000 to the dollar. The reform was highly contractionary, designed to restore profitability and eliminate the more egregious distortions in the system. Formal sector real wage increased by a factor five and government spending was slated to fall by 10 %. Public sector employment was to contract by 8,000 and the numerous nominal exchange rates collapsed into an official and parallel rate. Access to foreign exchange, for whatever use, was to be liberalized and price controls abandoned.

This was the first of two drastic stabilization plans introduced by the Sandinistas in 1988–89. In June 1988, the exchange rate was against devalued by 700 %, followed by smaller devaluations in a vain attempt to bring the official and black-market rates together. Little progress was made in 1988 in controlling monetary growth, other than an attempt to increase domestic deposit rates. There was a massive contraction of 13.4 % in activity as shown in table 18.1.

As third adjustment program announced in January 1989 was more effective. As the Contra War wound down, the Sandinistas were able to reduce government spending to 5.6 % of GDP (Ocampo, 1992). In 1989, 8,000 civilian and 13,000 military jobs were eliminated, causing the rate of unemployment to increase from 24.7 % to 32.7 % (*Envio*, Aug. 1990, p. 15). The 1989 overall fiscal deficit was reduced to 10 % of the government budget and to 2.5 % of GDP (see table 18.1). Expropriations were disavowed, interest rates actively managed and crawling peg was instituted. Initially, inflation fell rapidly, demonetization stopped and international reserves began to build.

Despite the intensity of the shocks, the reforms were insufficient to stop the hyperinflation. First, the nominal devaluation was followed by several more maxi-devaluations in 1988 and then a milder and more frequent crawl in 1989. Despite this, the exchange rate remained clearly overvalued. Government spending, and hence, Central Bank credit, was not contained as planned, due to hurricane Joan and Olivera-Tanzi real revenue losses. With the elections in 1990, came massive injections of liquidity, first to finance the reelection campaign and second to maintain the flow the private sector credit at a time when it was considered politically indispensable.

Beginning with the months just prior to the February 1990 election the Sandinista stabilization program began to completely unravel. The exchange rate was frozen, as were government prices, which had been kept high to absorb some of the excess liquidity. To encourage production, the government decided to pay exporters the parallel market exchange rate, effectively reviving the multiple exchange rate system. Central Bank losses on foreign exchange transactions (13.9% of GDP) along with a liberal program of debt forgiveness returned the rate of monetary emissions to crisis levels (see table 18.4). At the end of the year, the government deficit ballooned to 28% of GDP at an annual rate. The price level almost doubled every month toward the end of 1989 and there was severe demonetization of the economy as seen in table 18.4.

By the time the economy lapsed into hyperinflation in 1987–88, there was very little left of the Sandinista project. It became common for the left to criticize the government as "more monetarist that the monetarists" or worse, "monetarism without the money." Any progress to be made on land reform, real (private or social) wages or even production in the APP was clearly going to have to be put off until some unspecified future date. But with outcome of the elections, the date was postponed indefinitely.

With the inauguration of Chamorro in April 1990, all efforts turned toward ridding the economy of the hyperinflation. The polices effected by Chamorro's coalition, Union Nacional Opositora (UNO), in fact differed little from those of the ousted Sandinistas. Apart from specific programs, the principal areas in which the two policy regimes differed was in their ability to contract fresh funds from abroad and in their positions on privatization. Had the Sandinistas continued in office, they would have undoubtedly tried to maintain some remnants of the APP parastatals. Chamorro, on the other hand, immediately combined state enterprises in a holding company, Corporaciones Nacionales del Sector Publico (CORNAP) with the objective of privatizing some 90% of them by 1993. With few buyers available, the program got off to a slow start; as of September 1990, only 16 out of 350 state enterprises were privatized and six of these were immediately taken over by their workers (Envio Nov. 1990, p. 9). By August 1991, however, another 70 enterprises had been privatized.

Soon after the election, the new government introduced a five-point program to combat the generalized economic crisis: (1) stop inflation through a continuation of the orthodox shock, (2) introduce currency reform to achieve convertibility, (3) secure foreign financing unavailable to the Sandinistas, (4) promote exports by progressive real devaluation, and (5) privatize the parastatals to the extent possible, while leaving the majority of the agrarian reform intact.

The attention of the new government throughout the first year was to stabilize the economy, points 1 through 3. The most visible component of the stabilization effort was the *córdoba oro*, introduced by Central Bank President Francisco Mayorga at one-to-one parity with the U.S. dollar in May of 1990. Mayorga had promised in the presidential campaign to stop the hyperinflation by imposing fiscal and financial responsibility through monetary reform within 100 days. But the "Plan Mayorga" did not work and the central bank president was eventually forced to resign. As the currency reform began to fail, it enhanced capital flight which caused the foreign exchange constraint to bind even more tightly. A third of the new *córdobas* returned to the central bank, having been exchanged for dollars (Ocampo, 1992, p.43). Exchange parity with the dollar was ultimately lost and the credibility of the new government severely strained.

The effective dollarization of the Nicaraguan economy then accelerated inflation as has the attempt by the government to bring the official exchange rate in line with the black market rate. Indexation became more deeply rooted in the Nicaraguan economy than ever before, making real devaluation ever more elusive. Mayorga's *córdoba oro* simply convinced the private sector that the ordinary *córdoba* would inflate along with the rate of devaluation.

But perhaps the most damaging effect of the so-called "Plan Mayorga" was to sharpen the conflict between organized labor and new the government (Neira, 1990). The nominal exchange rate became a highly visible indicator of the rate of expected price increases allowing unions to anticipate inflation in their demands. Taxes and public utility payments were also indexed as were new deposits in the banking system. Together with the perceived weakness of the regime, dollarization promoted two devastating strikes in May and June of the first year, virtually eliminating any hope of immediate stabilization.

Fueling the 1990 hyperinflation was UNO's inability to get government spending fully under control. Table 18.1 shows the fiscal deficit returned to approximately 12 % of GDP in 1990 (still low by Sandinista standards). There were numerous reasons: First, the complete demobilization of the

Contras did not go through, delaying further savings on the military budget. Moreover, UNO's attempt to reduce the size of the state bureaucracy was frustrated by strikes. That year, the size of the government expanded, with new ministries and an "occupational conversion program" in which displaced workers were offered either four months severance pay and credit to start a small business or a tax credit to a prospective employer worth half a year's salary.

Initially, the principal barrier to fiscal compression was the size of the armed forces. As of May, 1990 the army was 80,000 men, but has been pared back to 28,000, now the smallest army in Central America (*Envio* Jan.-Feb. 1991, p. 16).[6] Reintegration costs were substantial, although mostly a one-time charge. There was also initial difficulty with foreign financing. As of April 1991, the United States has pledged $541 million, but only $207 had been disbursed (*New York Times*, 4/18/91, p. 3). UNO's limited ability to secure external financing for the fiscal deficit forced a return to the printing press and ultimately the devaluation of the *córdoba oro*. The evidence of the failure of the Plan Mayorga in controlling the hyperinflation is seen in table 18.5.

Another attempt to stabilize the economy, the fifth in three years, came in March 1991 when yet a new program, the Plan Lacayo, was announced. It combined the usual tactics of a 400% devaluation of the *córdoba oro* with monetary reform unifying it with the *córdoba* at a rate of 5 million to one. There were wage adjustments, backward indexation of term deposits and

**Table 18.5**
Monthly inflation data

|        | 1989 | 1990  | 1991 | 1992 |
|--------|------|-------|------|------|
| Jan.   | 91.8 | 25.9  | 52   | −1   |
| Feb.   | 45.8 | 14.7  | 42   | 1    |
| Mar.   | 20.1 | 15.0  | 261  | 0    |
| Apr.   | 12.6 | 36.2  | 20   |      |
| May    | 15.5 | 116.4 | −6   |      |
| June   | 62.2 | 100.6 | −7   |      |
| July   | 32.3 | 86.4  | 1    |      |
| Aug.   | 7.7  | 82.5  | −2   |      |
| Sept.  | 11.9 | 58.8  | 1    |      |
| Oct.   | 14.4 | 30.5  | 6    |      |
| Nov.   | 16.2 | 33.0  | 1    |      |
| Dec.   | 19.2 | 47.5  | 0    |      |

Source: *Envio* May, 1992; Ocampo, 1992.

unification of loan criteria across social sectors. But most important, there were serious credit controls: no new credit to public sector and credit ceilings imposed on commercial banks (Ocampo, 1992).

Table 18.5 shows the trajectory for the monthly inflation rate and how it precipitously dropped off after the announcement of the plan. In a sense, the plan was a "miracle" in that it was expansionary and at the same time decreased the fiscal deficit and increase the level of foreign reserves. One important aspect was fixing the exchange rate as a signal that prices would stop rising (Dornbusch, 1986).

But the truly important factors in the success of the Plan Lacayo were the foreign exchange bonanza that finally arrived in 1991 and the end of the war and the resettlement program. The armed forces had been reduced by some 70,000 in 1990 and approximately 30,000 had been released from the public sector and parastatals. Thus, the current fiscal account went into surplus, due largely to the effects of ending the war. The United States had spent U.S. $9 billion to oust the Sandinistas and it would take another U.S. $500 million to stop the hyperinflation the war had caused. Real wages fell by half from the time the *córdoba oro* was introduced to the initiation of the Plan Lacayo. With a 1985 base of 100, the index was at 15 at the end of 1991 (Ocampo, 1992).

In 1990 Chamorro's first request for an emergency aid package of U.S. $40 million was turned down on the grounds that Nicaragua would not be able to repay the loan. But then Nicaragua was able to negotiate a stunning writedown of approximately 75% of the debt owed those countries. But the Paris Club only represents 6.9% of a total debt of approximately U.S. $10 billion, however, with another U.S. $4 billion owed to the Soviet Union and Eastern Bloc, U.S. $2 billion to Latin American Countries and U.S. $1 billion to multilateral banks and U.S. $2 billion to commercial banks (*Envio*, Apr. 1992, p. 18). In order to qualify, Nicaragua had to be up to date on all outstanding payments, which required renegotiation with Mexico, Venezuela, and Colombia, in regard to their loans, all of which were written down by at least 95% of their value. By establishing bridge loans, Nicaragua was able to cancel arrears with the World Bank and the Interamerican Development Bank, and Nicaragua is now firmly locked into the world financial system. Official transfers for 1990 and 1991 amounted to U.S. $201.6 million and U.S. $528.1 million, the latter more than two and a half times the value of exports. For 1992, new loans and donations will be on the order of U.S. $740 million with interest payments of U.S. $179 million. This constitutes a significant flow of resources that cannot be expected to continue indefinitely. Although the international financial community has signalled its approval of Nicaragua's policies (especially Chamorro's decision to dropping its case against the United States in the World Court) there is little productive use being made of the inflow of new resources. Rather than spending on project development, the money is being used to import consumer goods, thereby undercutting local producers.

## 18.3  A Model of the Medium Term

With prices under control, there is some reason to be optimistic about an economic recovery from the devastation of the last decade. Nicaragua's natural trading base has been restored with the lifting of the embargo and the price of cotton is remain too low for profitable production, producers are being encouraged to switch to bananas. With incentives restored, the stage is now set for some export growth, if only the private sector cooperates. It will, nonetheless, be a difficult recovery because the domestic bourgeoisie has not invested in a decade and is no longer competitive even by Central American standards. It is also true that perceived risk is higher now because of the absence of state subsidies. (There were very few bankruptcies under the Sandinistas.)

The review of the current situation in the previous section shows that Nicaragua is still in a deep bind. The option of limping along, heavily subsidized by foreign capital, will not last, and in the coming decade the economy must be restructured in fundamental ways. Exports should be increased, but it is just as clear that increasing exports will come at additional social cost. Nicaragua now follows Haiti as the poorest country in the hemisphere, with 70% of its people living in poverty. The purpose of this section is to quantify the tradeoffs involved in the needed restructuring.

Growth projections are based on a two-sector, two-class, three-gap macro model summarized in the appendix and discussed in greater detail in Gibson (1990). The two sectors are traded and nontraded goods and the two classes are capitalists and workers. Given information on traded supply elasticity, investment, and government expenditure, the model calculates exports, nontraded output, the foreign deficit and the public sector borrowing requirement (PSBR) or the amount the government must raise to cover its deficit. The crucial assumption of the model is that the foreign exchange constraint does not bind. The model then calculates the amount of foreign exchange required to keep the foreign exchange constraint at bay; If this amount of resources is not available, either through exports or foreign loans, the behavior of model changes radically. Although the benchmark projections assume the required quantity of foreign exchange will be forthcoming, the assumption of no foreign exchange constraint will dropped below. The consequences of this change in regime are seen to be catastrophic.

Table 18.6 reports the findings of the model for projections on to the year 2000. External resource requirements are computed for a somewhat optimistic set of assumptions about government expenditure, investment, and traded good price elasticity. The key assumptions are that nominal government expenditure grows at only 2 % and government investment at 3 %, also in nominal terms. The nominal exchange rate grows at 5 % per year while the nominal wage grows at only 3 % per year. Debt repayment is assumed to grow at 2 %. Agricultural capitalists respond to the real exchange rate by increasing output by 1 % for every 1 % depreciation.[7]

Although the findings are based on very optimistic assumptions, they are not terribly encouraging. The results for real GDP growth are shown in the first column of table 18.6. Real GDP grows by less than 1 % until 1995 and only slightly above 1 % thereafter. With the population growth rate at 3.35 %, the result means continued contraction of per capita income throughout the 1990s. Inflation, however, remains under control, with prices increasing by only 60 % to the end of the decade. Real wages fall by only 1 % per year, but employment grows more slowly than output. What little optimism there is in these results hinges on private sector response in agroexports. All of the growth over the next decade is concentrated in the agricultural sector, which grows at an average of 2.9 % per year. Because the real exchange rate depreciates, domestic expenditure switches to non-tradables and exports grow by 13.6 % per year.[8] The non-tradable sector, on the other hand, limps along at less than 0.2 % per annum.

The simulations stress the essential role of exports. The message of the model is that the agricultural sector must grow much more rapidly than the rest of the economy. But even under the favorable conditions of the model, the fourth column of the table shows that there will be no surplus on the trade account until 1999. Faster demand-induced growth would put this point off even further into the future. A brisker rate of nominal exchange rate depreciation, on the other hand, would help advance the date, but at the cost of substantial deterioration in the distribution of income.

The origin of the surplus with which the economy will make its recovery is clear in the last two columns of the table. The share of workers' income in total GDP falls by 6.9 % over the period. The nominal devaluation is here real, transferring income from workers to agricultural capitalists as the needed incentive to raise production. But it is clear from the discussion

**Table 18.6**
Results of growth exercises

| Year | Real GDP growth | Inflation CPI[a] | Real exchange rate[a] | Savings[b] | | PSBR[b] | Workers' share[c] | Employment[a] |
|------|------|------|------|------|------|------|------|------|
| | | | | Foreign | Government | | | |
| 1990 | 0.83 | 1.04 | 1.02 | 9.0 | −15.2 | 25.0 | 58.8 | 100.5 |
| 1991 | 0.86 | 1.09 | 1.03 | 7.6 | −15.1 | 24.2 | 58.1 | 101.1 |
| 1992 | 0.90 | 1.14 | 1.05 | 6.1 | −14.9 | 23.5 | 57.5 | 101.8 |
| 1993 | 0.93 | 1.19 | 1.06 | 4.7 | −14.8 | 22.8 | 56.8 | 102.5 |
| 1994 | 0.96 | 1.24 | 1.08 | 3.3 | −14.6 | 22.1 | 56.1 | 103.2 |
| 1995 | 1.00 | 1.30 | 1.09 | 1.9 | −14.4 | 21.3 | 55.4 | 103.9 |
| 1996 | 1.03 | 1.36 | 1.11 | 0.6 | −14.2 | 20.6 | 54.7 | 104.8 |
| 1997 | 1.06 | 1.42 | 1.13 | 0.7 | −13.9 | 19.9 | 54.0 | 105.6 |
| 1998 | 1.09 | 1.48 | 1.14 | 1.9 | −13.6 | 19.2 | 53.3 | 106.5 |
| 1999 | 1.12 | 1.54 | 1.16 | −3.2 | −13.2 | 18.5 | 52.6 | 107.5 |
| 2000 | 1.15 | 1.61 | 1.18 | −4.4 | −12.8 | 17.8 | 51.9 | 108.5 |

Notes: a. 1989 = 100.
b. % of GDP.
c. % of total income.
Source: Model computations

above that to the extent the Sandinistas remain major players, the UNO coalition cannot permit the economy to recover exclusively on the backs of the working poor and the peasantry. Any real devaluation stronger than that along the path of table 18.6 will probably be judged politically infeasible, despite Chamorro's mandate.

Although an employed worker is slightly less well off during the recovery due to the falling real wage, unemployed or underemployed workers benefit from the rise in employment. These workers emerge from the bulging informal sector to present themselves for formal sector work, some for the first time since the revolution. But note that the gain in employment is only 8.5 % over the decade. Reducing the enormous informal sector was always an explicit goal of the Sandinistas, but these simulations make clear that the goal cannot be an immediate priority in the new regime.

As mentioned previously, UNO has identified private sector initiative as the driving force of their recovery program. So far the private sector has turned in a lackluster performance, but it is highly unlikely that the coalition will change its approach in the medium term. The simulations show that if the private sector were only more responsive to the real devaluation, the share of workers would have to fall less. This coincidence of interests was a bitter irony to the Sandinistas, but will become the essential feature of any workable program under UNO.

In the short run, the deficit will remain a problem. To avoid high rates of emission, much of the foreign capital will have to go to financing the government deficit. Firms should be encouraged to go abroad to arrange private financing to reduce the pressure on internal credit expansion. This should allow the government to maintain at least some existing social programs. The simulations show that the economy will not come out of the inflationary "danger range" of a current deficit of 10–12 % of GDP by 2000 (and this is assuming that foreign financing can be found for public investment projects). Although PSBR declines steadily, the table 18.6 shows that it is still high, in the vicinity of 17.8 % of GDP, even by the year 2000.

Above all the economy must avoid debilitating foreign exchange bottlenecks. In this regard, untied foreign resources will play a crucial role (Taylor, et al., 1989). The model can be used to illustrate just how essential the foreign capital inflow will be to the post-war recovery. Simulation results show that a 1 % drop in foreign savings corresponds to a 1.7 % appreciation of the real exchange rate. Given the assumptions made above about the price responsiveness of export agriculture, the appreciation causes agricultural output to fall by the same percentage. This leads to a vicious cycle: As agricultural output falls, exports fall as well and the foreign exchange constraint begins to bind even more tightly. The restriction on foreign exchange causes the supply of nontradables to diminish, thus producing an excess demand for nontradables. With a binding foreign exchange constraint, the real exchange rate must then appreciate.

The 1% drop in foreign savings causes the CPI to rise by 0.6% and real wages to fall in proportion. The price-cost ratio in the nontradable sector rises and labor's share in total income falls by 0.6%. Employment falls by 2%. Because taxes fall with output, there is a rise in the government deficit by 0.4% and the PSBR increases accordingly. Investment declines because it is tied to the level of output. Although this presumably reduces productive capacity in the future, the short-run effect is stabilizing. Because investment falls, the real exchange rate does not appreciate as much as it otherwise would.

## 18.4   Conclusions

It is clear that Sandinista Nicaragua was in no sense a classical Marxist-Leninist revolution. But neither was it classical populism in the sense discussed by Sachs (1989) and others. In essence, the populist outcome, in which the clients of the regime are the ones who end up suffering the most from it, was forced on the Sandinistas through a combination of events far beyond their control. The shift to a right-wing, confrontational government in the United States combined with the lack of a clearly articulated, coherent and stable conception of the mixed economy are the two main reasons identified here.

There was nothing ingenious about Chamorro's stabilization plan, which ended hyperinflation. It was the product of the same kind of shock therapy, with the same regressive implications, that had been applied three previous times by the Sandinistas. What did make an enormous difference, and caused the program to work, was the end of the war and the large foreign exchange bonanza that was orchestrated by the United States. The private sector had nothing to do with the success; had the Sandinistas been in power under the same circumstances, they would have achieved the same results, despite mistrust by the domestic bourgeoisie.

The question is how the economy will develop from here, given that it is firmly entrenched in neoliberal policies. Here the private sector will make an enormous difference. Even under reasonably optimistic assumptions, three-gap projections document a painfully slow path to recovery the economy will have to undertake. Progress cannot be measured in terms of the overall growth rate (seen to be low in the simulations above) given the contraction of the nontradable sector the restructuring will require. Success will require a delicate balance of incentives for private sector exports (through the maintenance of a realistic real exchange rate), demand restraint, and attention to social programs.

## Notes

1. There are numerous overviews of the revolutionary period, e.g., Gibson (1987) and Close (1988).

2. Finally, in March 1991, monthly inflation hit 261%, a rate which surpassed Bolivia's monthly maximum of 182% in February 1985.

3. The stability of the process is in question, however, the data show clear evidence of heteroskedasticity after 1972. To conserve space neither the regressions nor the data are presented; both are available from the author.

4. In 1982 the government also introduced the PIE, a program of export incentives, which provided for foreign exchange "certificates." These could theoretically be used to import both intermediate and luxury goods. Dollar denominated accounts were established but then later frozen by the government; producers never had effective access to dollars.

5. The black market for foreign exchange was tolerated as a social safety valve, imparting a degree of flexibility to the rigorous system of foreign exchange allocation. A direct confrontation with the domestic bourgeoisie could thereby be avoided (De Franco, 1989, p. 32). But from the point of view of the domestic bourgeoisie, the mixed economy was a transitory tactic in the struggle for a Marxist-Leninist state.

6. This does not count the Costa Rican National Guard.

7. This is roughly equivalent to recent econometric estimates; see Taylor, et al., 1989, p. 37, n. 7).

8. This is slower than the 20% suggested by Arana, but consistent with Taylor, et al., who note that a "highly successful strategy" would allow exports to grow to U.S. $1 billion by the year 2000 (Arana, 1990, p. 32; Taylor, et al., 1989, p. 44).

## Appendix 18.1

The purpose of this appendix is to sketch the model used for the projections. Full details appear in Gibson (1990). The two sectors of the model are agriculture and nonagriculture and the social classes are divided into capitalists and workers. Potential agricultural output, $Q$, corresponds to the maximum amount which could be produced assuming full utilization of the means of agricultural production. $x_1 \leq Q$ is the level of output corresponding to the current planting decision. The ratio:

$$\mu = x_1/Q \tag{18.1}$$

defines capacity utilization in the agricultural sector. Agricultural output is either consumed as food by workers or is exported:

$$ep_1\mu = m(1 - s_w)(1 - t_w)(wl_1\mu + wl_2u + w_g) + ep_1\varepsilon \tag{18.2}$$

where $e$ is the exchange rate, $p_1$ the price of agriculture, $m$ the fraction of workers' income spent on food, $s_w$ the fraction of workers' income saved and $t_w$ the tax rate on workers' income. $w$ is the wage rate and the $l_i$ are the direct labor coefficients. $u$ is defined as the normalized level of nonagricultural output. $w_g$ is government wages and $\varepsilon$ the level of net exports, both normalized by $Q$. Note two assumptions: 1. there is no capitalist consumption of agricultural goods; and 2. there is no investment demand for agriculture.

Rather than present a demand-supply balance for the nonagricultural sector as in equation 2, we write the savings-investment balance directly:

$$s_c(1 - t_c)(\pi_1\mu_1 + \pi_2u + j_c) + s_w(1 - t_w)(wl_1\mu_1 + wl_2u + w_g)$$
$$+ e\Phi + s_g = [p_2\theta + (1 - \theta)ep_0]i \tag{18.3}$$

where $s_c$ and $t_c$ are the savings and tax parameters for capitalists. The $\pi_i$ are unit profits defined as:

$$\pi_1 = (ep_1 - wl_1) \tag{18.4}$$

$$\pi_2 = (p_2 - ep_0a - wl_2) \tag{18.5}$$

where $p_0$ is the foreign price of imports and $a$ is the input-output coefficient for noncompetitive intermediate imports. $j_c$, in equation (3), is payments to capitalists by the government normalized by $Q$. $\Phi$ is normalized foreign savings, defined as:

$$\Phi = p_0[au + (1 - \theta)I + m_g] + j^* - p_1\varepsilon \tag{18.6}$$

and $\theta$ the fraction of investment, $I$, which is imported. $m_g$ are normalized government noncompetitive imports and $j^*$ is normalized government debt service.

$s_g$ is normalized government savings:

$$s_g = (t_c\pi_1 + t_wwl_1)\mu + (t_c\pi_2 + t_wwl_2)u - p_2g - w_g - j_c - ej^* - ep_0mg \tag{18.7}$$

where $g$ is the level of government consumption, normalized by $Q$.

Total investment is divided into public, $i_g$, and private, $i_p$, both normalized by $Q$:

$$i = i_0 + (1 + \alpha)i_g + \beta\mu \qquad (18.8)$$

where a represents a "crowding-in" effect of public on private investment. $\beta$ is the responsiveness of total investment demand to agricultural harvests. $p_2$ is defined as:

$$p_2 = (1 + \tau)(ep_0 a + wl_2) \qquad (18.9)$$

where $\tau$ is a fixed and given mark-up over costs. Finally the PSBR is defined as:

$$\sigma = \frac{p_2\theta i_g + (1 - \theta)ep_0 i_g - s_g}{[ep_1\mu + (p_2 - ep_0 a)u]} \qquad (18.10)$$

The model now consists of the 10 equations in the 10 unknowns: $\mu$, $\varepsilon$, $u$, $\pi_1$, $\pi_2$, $\Phi$, $s_g$, $i$, $p_2$ and $\sigma$. The rest of the variables are taken as given parameters. See Gibson (1990) for details on the data base employed and other results of the model.

## References

Arana, M. (1990). "Nicaragua: Estabilización, Ajuste y Estrategia Economíca," in M. Arana and, R. Stahler-Sholk and C. Vilas, (eds.), *Políticas de ajuste en Nicaragua: Reflexiones sobre sus implicaiones estratégicas.* Managua: CRIES.

Banco Central de Nicaragua. Various internal documents.

CEPAL (1988, 1990, 1991). "Balance Preliminar de la Economía Latinoamericana." Chile: Santiago.

Close, D. (1988). *Nicaragua: Politics, Economics and Society.* London: Pinter.

Conroy, M. (1984). "False Polarization: Economic Strategies of Post-Revolutionary Nicaragua." *Third World Quarterly* 6(4): 993–1032.

De Franco, M. (1985). "An Analysis of the Black Market in Dollars in a Computable General Equilibrium Model for Nicaragua." Ph.D. dissertation prospectus, Department of Economics, University of Massachusetts, Amherst.

De Franco, M. (1989). "An Analysis of the Black Market for Foreign Exchange in a Computable General Equilibrium Model: The Case of Nicaragua." Ph.D. dissertation, University of Massachusetts, Amherst.

Delgado, R. (1988). "Los Costos Económicos de la Agresión," in INIES, *Nicaragua: Cambios Estructurales y Políticas Económicas 1979–87.* Managua: INIES.

Dornbusch, R. (1986). "Inflation, Exchange Rates and Stabilization." *Princeton Essays in International Finance* No. 165.

Dornbusch, R. and S. Edwards (1990). "Macroeconomic Populism," *Journal of Development Economics* 32(2): 247–249.

*Envio* (various years). Managua, Instituto Historíco Centroamericano, and Washington, D.C., Central American Historical Institute.

FitzGerald, E. (1987). "An Evaluation of the Economic Costs to Nicaragua of U.S. Aggression," in R. Spalding (ed.), *The Political Economy of Revolutionary Nicaragua*. Winchester, MA: Allen and Unwin.

Gibson, B. (1985). "A Structuralist Macromodel for Post-Revolutionary Nicaragua." *Cambridge Journal of Economics* 9: 347–369.

Gibson, B. (1987). "A Structural Overview of the Nicaraguan Economy," in R. Spalding (ed.), *The Political Economy of Revolutionary Nicaragua*. Winchester, MA: Allen and Unwin.

Gibson, B. (1990). "Restructuring the Nicaraguan Economy." *International Journal of Political Economy* 20(3).

Gilbert, D. (1985). "The Bourgeoisie," in T. Walker (ed.), *Nicaragua: The First Five Years*. New York: Praeger.

Hodges, D. (1986). *The Intellectual Foundations of the Nicaraguan Revolution*. Austin: University of Texas Press.

IMF (1987). "Nicaragua: Mission Report."

IMF (various issues). *International Financial Statistics*.

Leogrand, W. (1985). "The United States and Nicaragua," in T. Walker (ed.), *Nicaragua: The First Five Years*. New York: Praeger.

Medal, J. (1988). *Nicaragua: Política Económica, Crisis y Cambio Social*. DILESA: Managua.

Neira, O. (1990). "La caída de zar." *Pensamiento Propio*, 9(76) (Nov.-Dec.): 8–10.

Ocampo, J. (1992). "Hyperinflation and Stabilization in Nicaragua." (Mimeo), FEDESARROLLO, Bogota.

Sachs, J. (1989). "Social Conflict and Populist Policies in Latin America," in Brunetta, Renato and Carlo Pell'Aringa (eds.), *Labour Relations and Economic Performance*. Basingstoke : Macmillan.

Taylor, L., R. Aguilar, S. Vylder, and J. Ocampo (1989). *Nicaragua: The Transition from Economic Chaos toward Sustainable Growth*. Mission Report of the Swedish International Development Authority.

Timossi, G. (1989). *Centroamerica: Deuda Externa y Ajuste Estructural*. Managua: CRIES.

Vilas, C. (1984). *Perfiles de la Revolucion Sandinista*. La Habana:Casa de las Americas.

Wheelock, J. (1980). *Imperialismo y Dictadura*, Mexico: Siglo XXI.

Wheelock, J. (1983). *El Gran Desafío*, Managua: Editorial Nueva Nicaragua.

# 19     Zambia

## Thandika Mkandawire

Few nations in Africa have witnessed as dramatic changes in their fortunes as Zambia's since independence in 1964. Once a country characterized by its president as having been born with the proverbial silver spoon in its mouth, enjoying one of the highest per capita incomes in Africa south of the Sahara, Zambia now clearly has a "low income" economy.

At independence, Zambia was a mineral enclave economy par excellence. At one end of the economy were the modern industrial and large-scale commercial farming sectors while, at the other end was a basically stagnant peasant agriculture, which, because it was treated by the colonial governments essentially as a source of cheap labor, never witnessed the kind of cash crop boom experienced in such countries as the Gold Coast (cocoa) and Senegal (groundnuts). Underpinning this duality was a racist structure that was reflected in income differentials and patterns of urbanization that effectively blocked the emergence of an "informal sector" (Mkandawire, 1986).

Two salient features of the mining industry were its high ownership concentration and the rather large-scale character of its production units. Socially, these facilitated the creation of a relatively stable working class that quickly learned to organize itself, forging one of the most highly organized unions in Africa south of the Sahara.

### 19.1   Past Performance of the Economy

Until the onset of the copper crisis in 1974, the overall annual growth rate was 6% (table 19.1). This was twice the rate of population growth and ensured a steady increase in per capita income from U.S. $203 in 1964 to U.S. $524 in 1974 (in 1980 U.S. $). Government expenditure grew by 9% while tax revenue grew at 5%. Investment expanded by 11%, increasing its share from 11% in 1964 to a peak of 41% in 1975. The high growth

**Table 19.1**
Growth rates of key variables (from regression equations)

|                        | 1964–74 | 1975–87 | 1964–87 |
|------------------------|---------|---------|---------|
| GDP                    | 0.06    | −0.01   | 0.02    |
| Government expenditure | 0.09    | −0.02   | 0.04    |
| Tax revenue            | 0.05    | −0.01   | 0.01    |
| Public consumption     | 0.15    | −0.08   | 0.08    |
| Investment             | 0.11    | −0.09   | 0.00    |
| Savings                | 0.04    | −0.03   | −0.07   |
| Exports                | 0.02    | −0.03   | −0.01   |
| Imports                | 0.05    | −0.05   | 0.02    |
| Copper exports         | 0.03    | −0.05   | −0.03   |

rate was dependent on copper, which accounted for 95 % of exports and more than half of state revenue.

With the collapse of copper prices in 1975 (from an average of $.93 per pound in 1964–74 to $.56), the Zambian economy was thrown into a crisis from which it has yet to recover. Public revenues and the balance of payments were shaken, with repercussions throughout the entire economy. With declines in copper receipts, total taxes shrank at the annual rate of 3 % from 1975 to 1980 and so did government expenditure. Investment collapsed to 13 % of GDP in 1984. For most years prior to 1974, Zambia enjoyed a current account surplus. This turned into a deficit that rose from 5 % of GDP in 1975 to 17 % in 1984, while exports declined at an annual rate of 10 % from 1975 to 1983. GDP declined by 1 % annually between 1975 and 1987 while the population growth rate was estimated at slightly over 3 %.

## 19.2   Policy Responses

If one were to identify phases over which major economic relations have remained stable and those moments of "rupture" when totally new relationships emerged, one would divide policymaking in Zambia into three periods: 1964–68, 1968–74, and from 1975 to the present.

### 19.2.1   The First Phase

In the immediate post-independence period, the government pursued a liberal policy in which "industrialization by invitation" was central. Economic growth was constrained not by foreign exchange as is the case today, but by manpower shortages and lack of "viable projects," at least in the eyes of the private sector, which the government assiduously sought to attract. Unable to absorb its export earnings, Zambia was a net exporter of capital. Gross domestic expenditure (consumption plus investment) was around two-thirds of gross national income. The relatively low level of expenditure was inherited from the days when Zambia belonged to the Federation of Rhodesia and Nyasaland, an arrangement which systematically transferred Zambian surpluses to the then white-dominated Southern Rhodesia.

### 19.2.2    The Second Phase

The second phase (1968–74) involved greater state participation in the economy, underpinned by a nationalist-populist ideology. This new line reflected frustration with the unsatisfactory response of the private sector to a battery of incentives. To encourage investment and make use of its trade surpluses and reserves, the state adopted a more activist role, crystallized in the Mulungushi Declaration of 1968, which mapped the ideological framework of the "shift to the left."

The shift involved an increased state share in mining industry, creation of parastatals to oversee industrialization, extensive provision of social services (especially education), and acceleration of the Africanization of the management of the economy. The government acquired 51% or more of the equity of some 25 previously private firms in building materials, manufacturing, transport, and fisheries. The IDECO (The Industrial Development Cooperation), which had hitherto limited itself to promotion and finance of industries, assumed the role of a holding company to operate these enterprises, as well as those established through public investment. The three main objectives were: to accelerate the pace of Zambianization, to insure reinvestment of surpluses in Zambia, and to minimize "profiteering." Additional goals were employment creation, diversification, and rural employment.[1]

The firms nationalized during this period scarcely constituted a dynamic private sector that state policy somehow foolhardily thwarted. Indeed, most of the public activities were in entirely new activities. Privatization today would therefore not be "returning" nationalized industries to the private sector whose vibrancy has yet to be demonstrated. The distinction is of great political significance in understanding the reluctance of the state to privatize and the unlikelihood that there will be a rush of buyers.

One should also add that the geographical location of Zambia—its proximity to Rhodesia, which declared unilateral independence only a year after Zambia's independence, the liberation struggles that raged in neighboring countries, and the sympathy that many whites in Zambia openly expressed towards Rhodesia—meant that Zambia would not be enthusiastic about reliance on a private sector that would be largely in non-Zambian (and most likely South African) hands. In a racially divided society where private ownership was coterminous with white ownership, there was bound to be enormous pressure for state activism and indigenization. Even had the private sector reacted positively to incentives, the state would have been under pressure to assume an active role.

Greater state participation dramatically increased investment in manufacturing—quadrupling it in real terms over 1965–72 and doubling its share of total investment to reach 13 % in 1972. By 1980, manufacturing contributed 18 % of Zambia's GDP, a figure that was threefold the figure at independence and was higher than any other sub-Saharan African country except Zimbabwe.

The first decade of Zambia's independence was, in retrospect, a veritable boom period, but high growth had some disturbing features (table 19.2). First was its reliance on an import-intensive industrial sector; second was the lethargic performance of the mining sector, which had underwritten the process of industrialization with its surpluses and foreign exchange earnings; third was the poor performance of agriculture; and fourth was the failure to diversify the country's export base.

Industrialization was soon to exhibit classical problems associated with import substitution. First, the distribution of imports changed rather sharply. The share of consumer goods fell from a third to a fifth of the total. Significant for our later discussions of the relationship between imports and capacity utilization was the increased reliance on imported intermediate inputs, despite some efforts at substitution.

A major socioeconomic characteristic of Zambia was that it was a relatively high wage and highly urbanized country. The mining industry was

**Table 19.2**
Sectoral GDP growth rates

|               | 1965–70 | 1970–74 | 1974–75 | 1975–79 | 1979–83 |
|---------------|---------|---------|---------|---------|---------|
| Manufacturing | 11.4    | 7.8     | −11.9   | −2.3    | 1.1     |
| Mining        | 0.4     | 0.8     | −9.8    | −2.2    | 4.7     |
| Agriculture   | −2.1    | 2.5     | 4.3     | 0.5     | 1.8     |

Source: World Bank, Industrial Policy Study.

patterned very much along South African lines, with a racially differentiated wage structure and a reservation system that excluded blacks from certain jobs. Average earnings of non-Africans were around nine times those of African workers (Daniel, 1979). With independence, this situation had to change.

The Brown Commission, which was set up to examine the pay scales, recommended raising the wages of the blacks to those of the whites although the process of "job fragmentation" and redefinition of posts meant that only a few black workers were to achieve equalized wages. Nonetheless, the index of real earnings by black workers rose by 33 % in 1967 and by a further 15 % in the period up to 1973. This reunification of pay placed Zambian wage scales at relatively high levels, further accentuating the dualism of the income structure, not along racial lines, but along spatial (rural-urban) and sectoral (formal-informal) lines. The attractiveness of urban employment rose, helping turn Zambia into the most urbanized country in sub-Saharan Africa.

In many ways, Zambia's policies conformed to the normal nationalist response in Africa. Whenever foreign exchange positions improved, African regimes have sought to increase their control of the economy either through indigenization or outright nationalization, only to retreat during hard times when they are vulnerable to external pressure. What was specific to Zambia's nationalist response was its populist or leftist content. An explanation can be found in the unusually strong position that Zambian labor unions have played in political life. They are among the best organized in Africa and have fiercely defended their autonomy against government encroachment or co-optation efforts.

The organization of the trade unions and the rapid increases in real wages in the organized sectors in the immediate post-independence period led some observers to argue that there was a "labor aristocracy" collaborating with other classes to constitute a coalition against agriculture.[2] Some even give the coalition credit for the country's farming disaster.[3] Looking at the broad program of the labor movement, the nature of conflicts of interests in the urban areas, and the fate that has befallen the incomes of the putative "labor aristocracy," it is difficult to subscribe to this version of the roots of the agrarian problem in Zambia. The government did invest considerable amounts of funds in agriculture and although it subsidized consumers, it also tended to subsidize farmers. The irony is that because it did not need it as a source of surpluses, state policies towards agriculture tended to be "welfarist" rather than extractive. Kydd (1988) notes:

in an important way Zambia does not fit the Berg stereotype ... taxation of farmers (large or small) by the device of monopsonistic marketing organizations has not been present to a great extent. Zambia has had state monopsonies which have effectively taxed some farmers (those in locationally favoured areas) in order to subsidize others. But the failure of Zambian agriculture cannot be explained in terms of excessive surplus extraction from farmers or even, on the aggregate, of a lack of government commitment to investment in rural areas.

In fact, Zambia—the most urbanized sub-Saharan African country—has traditionally allocated about 20 % of its state budget to agriculture, twice the level in places such as Malawi and Ivory Coast, which are usually considered to favor the sector. The failure of agricultural policy was not so much due to "urban bias" as it was due to a "bias" towards large scale. The government sought to reduce dependency on white settler farmers while remaining skeptical of small farmers' capacity. The tendency, therefore, was toward the establishment of state farms or large-scale indigenous capitalist farming through massive investments that failed to pay off.

### 19.2.3    Planning under Duress

Zambia, like most African economies, draws up periodic development plans to guide the economy. Currently, the country is going through its fourth national development plan. Implementation of the First Plan of Zambia was relatively smooth sailing, with the only constraints being lack of management and technical skills and, later, transport problems caused by the declaration of independence in Rhodesia. Foreign exchange resources were plentiful and the country's current account balances were positive. Foreign reserve holdings at any time usually exceeded annual imports. This picture was to change dramatically with the collapse of copper prices in 1974, which ushered in the third policy phase.

The collapse drastically reduced state revenue, with the share of total receipts provided by the industry falling from 60 % to near zero. In some recent years, copper was actually a drain on the state budget. All this led to fiscal and accumulation crises that were to force the government to seek the assistance of international financial institutions. Planning and plan im-plementation, never a well-mastered art even in the best of times, became a highly uncertain activity. Since then the move from one plan period to another has been interrupted by "interim plans" aimed at introducing cor-rective measures in the face of dramatically changed circumstances.

Thus, prior to embarking on its current fourth national development plan and following the most recent rupture with the IMF, the government adopted a New Economic Recovery Plan and an Interim National Development Plan. The main objectives centered around relaxing the foreign exchange constraint by better use of resources, reduction of import dependence of the economy, and rationalization of the use of foreign exchange as a strategic resource.

For a while the policy posture was that the fall in copper prices would be reversed. The state sought to maintain levels of consumption and investment by borrowing. This sharply reversed the historical positive resource balance (gross domestic saving minus gross domestic investment) in 1975 and led to the dramatic increase in the debt service ratio, forcing the state toward international organizations.

The turning point in fiscal policy came in 1983. To ease its serious foreign exchange constraints, the government entered into an agreement with the IMF. One immediate demand was reduction in government expenditure, which in 1983 dropped to 60 % of its level in 1975. The budget deficit fell from 9 % of potential output in 1982 to yield a temporary surplus of 2 % in 1983. Capital expenditure was also sharply reduced. The inability of the government to provide counterpart funds also meant that disbursement of grants was slowed down. Adverse shifts in the terms of trade following the two oil shocks increased the foreign exchange squeeze. Current account deficits continued to rise despite reductions in imports; their level in 1983 was 42 % lower than in 1975. Debt obligations including arrears would have been 115 % of export earnings. The result of all this was decline in real GDP for three years in a row.

Recourse to international financial institutions put to test the entire political economy of the post-independence period. It soured the already tenuous relationship between the state and labor, and undermined the nationalist-populist alliance that had given the state a decent degree of legitimacy. The government increasingly resorted to force in its relations with labor, helping set up the "IMF riots" that led to loss of lives in 1987 and more recently in June 1990.

## 19.3 Modeling the Economy

Given the convulsions that the economy has undergone, it may seem foolhardy to conduct growth exercises on rigid assumptions about crucial variables. Although we rely heavily on econometric results, we have modified some of these in light of our knowledge of the Zambian economy and used "guesstimates" instead.

The growth exercises are carried out along the lines made familiar by Bacha (1990) and Taylor (Chapter 2, this volume) and used by others in the WIDER network. To fit Zambia's particular situation, the standard model was modified in several ways.

First, the net fiscal surplus was assumed to depend on the level of copper exports. Econometric results suggest that about 30 % of export revenue is transferred to the state. The regressions also show that higher capacity utilization *reduces* the budget surplus. This result contradicts the stylized fact that the greater the level of economic activity, the greater the revenue base of the state. The negative relationship may reflect low profitability of parastatals that are generally highly subsidized. It may also be a reflection of the historical fact that with the existence of a fairly easy sector to tax— mining—there was no development of fiscal and administrative instruments to tax other sectors. This is a common feature of mineral *rentier* economies in Africa (as opposed to mercantile states that rely on taxes on peasants and consumers). The low responsiveness of net fiscal revenue to capacity utilization is countered by this variable's high responsiveness to the share of copper in potential output.

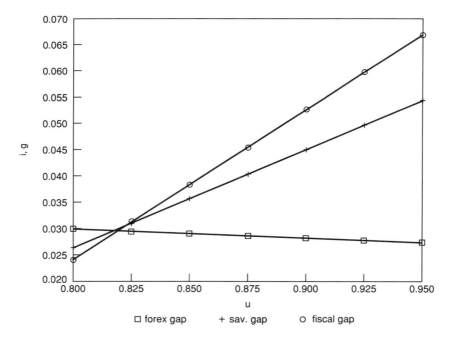

**Figure 19.1**
Gap constraints for Zambia

Second, private saving is crowded-out by capital inflows with a coefficient of −0.69, but rises strongly with capacity use (a coefficient of 0.78).

Third, as in other countries, imports seem insensitive to the real exchange rate. In Zambia, one reason has been tight state control over trade. In practice, experience with currency auctions and trade liberalization suggests that such moves may be associated with higher consumer imports and capital flight, reducing foreign exchange available for investment and intermediate imports in the short run.

Fourth, exports appear to be an increasing function of capacity utilization, in contrast to other WIDER studies. In Zambia, the picture is complicated by copper's dominance and import repression. The metal has virtually no domestic market and its production is extremely import-intensive. Any greater availability of imports immediately flows toward the mines, bringing higher noncopper capacity utilization in train.

On the basis of our estimates, gap equations for Zambia are plotted in Figure 19.1, while Figure 19.2 illustrates gap-constrained growth rates since 1973.

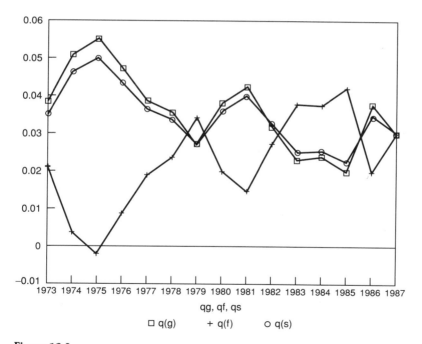

**Figure 19.2**
Binding growth constraints in Zambia

### 19.3.1    Growth Constraints

The results in Figure 19.2 suggest that between 1973 and 1979, the main constraint on growth was foreign exchange. As described by Fundanga (1989), Young and Loxley (1990), and SIDA (1989), the government entered into arrangements with the IMF in an attempt to relax this constraint.

The first standby arrangement in 1973 was a low-conditional, first*tranche* drawing with requirements to reduce domestic absorption. In 1976 another standby arrangement was made. It involved greater conditionality, calling for removal of domestic subsidies, reduction in demand through a wage freeze and diversification of exports. A continued decline in the terms of trade, intensification of the conflict in Rhodesia, and the disruption of Zambia's access to the sea undermined the program. It could neither arrest the decline in GDP nor restore the balance of payments.

Zambia entered into another standby with the IMF for the period 1978–80. This arrangement was for SDR 250 million, equivalent to 177 % of the nation's quota. It imposed rigorous quantitative targets to constrain expansion of domestic credit and raise agricultural prices. More significantly, Zambia was required to eliminate arrears on external credit. The share of amortization of foreign loans by the state jumped from 4 % to 7 % of potential output. The foreign exchange position of the country improved as a result of copper export prices and a reduction in imports, at the cost of a drastic decline in capacity utilization.

The new arrangement coupled with improvements in the price of copper led to a temporary relaxation of the foreign exchange constraint. In 1979, the fiscal constraint appeared to bind. But in the following year, foreign exchange limits asserted themselves again. There were declines in copper prices and output, largely due to poor agricultural performance and the need to import food as well as higher oil prices. Although exports fell as a share of potential output, imports rose sharply, leading to deterioration in the balance of payments. The sequel was a reduction of import capacity and declines in capacity utilization by as much as 11 % between 1980 and 1982.

Between 1983 and 1987, policymaking in Zambia was very much under IMF tutelage. In 1983, a one-year standby for SDR 211 million was agreed upon. The arrangement called for devaluation and reduction in the state deficit. Government expenditure was drastically reduced. Significantly, there were sharp cuts in welfare expenditure. The arrangement was suspended by the end of the year due to disagreement between the governments and the IMF. In 1984–86, a standby for SDR 225 million was reached with the objective of stabilization of external and internal balances. Measures included the introduction of foreign exchange auctions, further cuts in state expenditure, higher prices for agricultural produce, and generalized deregulation. Until the policy reversal in April 1987, the economy functioned under a highly liberalized regime.

One of the effects of the new policies was an increase in the "fiscal effort" as the net current surplus changed from −0.06 of GDP in 1982 to a +0.06 in 1985, but this could not overweigh the higher amortization payments for foreign loans, which jumped up sharply in 1985 and remained at a rate that was at least twice as high as the average of the preceding 10 years. An improvement in the balance of payments was achieved through further contraction in imports, leading to further declines in capacity utilization. One characteristic of the auctions was that the big manufacturers and the mining industry were the principal beneficiaries. This may explain the temporary increase in capacity utilization in 1986.

The hardship caused by the austerity package, the high burden of debt repayment, and the sudden appearance of luxury goods in the face of penury for many created such political tension that the package became politically unsustainable. In December 1986, there was extensive rioting following the government's decision to remove subsidies on maize meal, doubling the price. The riots caused extensive damage and 16 people died.

19.3.2 Homemade Adjustment

This regime was discontinued in May 1987 together with IMF-World Bank supported programs. President Kaunda gave as a reason the fact that the reform program was disintegrating the country's social fabric. A "home grown" New Economic Recovery Program was announced. The new policies included abandonment of the auction system, introduction of price and trade controls, and restriction of foreign debt service to 10 % of net exports.

The central preoccupation was to raise capacity utilization by a judicious relaxation of foreign exchange constraint. This was to be achieved by greater reliance on domestic products, reduction of the import dependence of production, and a more efficient use of foreign exchange. To combat inflation, interest rates were controlled at between 15 % and 20 % per year until November when the ceiling was raised to 25 %. Prices on a number of commodities also were controlled.

The plan called for an incomes policy that would contribute to the stimulation of effective demand and would make wages in the civil service competitive with those of the private and parastatals sector. Wages would be allowed to increase through collective bargaining and through income support programs for the unemployed.

The thrust of the plan was clearly "unorthodox," and the immediate effect was the decision by donors to restrict their aid sharply while awaiting an IMF-World Bank seal of approval. Meanwhile, the terms of trade improved as a result of a sharp increase in the price of copper and the fall of oil prices. Both these events helped to release investment funds. During a two-year period the economy enjoyed positive real growth rates. Manufacturing performed especially well (Young and Loxley, 1990).

## 19.4   Medium-Term Prospects

For a mid-term projection we use the New Recovery Program-Fourth National Development Plan as a benchmark, examining its internal consistency and drawing out implications for key economic policy variables and parameters. We also examine an orthodox alternative to the Zambian Plan.

We accept the government estimates of both the initial and terminal values for transfers to the government, foreign saving, public sector borrowing, public saving, and debt repayments. These values give 4.8 % as the underlying growth rate of potential output.

The government assumed 2.3 % GDP growth in the interim period 1987–89. Although this fell below the population growth of 3.4 % per year, it signaled an improvement on recent trends. It was hoped that improved capacity utilization would play an important role. We have, therefore, assumed that capacity utilization increases to 86 %. The government planned to raise investment from 6.7 % of potential output to 12.7 %. This was to be done largely by increasing public investment from 4.99 % to 9.43 %. Private investment was expected to also increase, from 1.95 % to 3.7 %.

The most important deviations from the 1987 benchmark were the doubling of grants and the halving of foreign amortization. These measures had the effect of allowing for increased imports, and would also favorably affect the deficit. Public borrowing would remain at its rather high level of over 20 % of potential output. The budget deficit would not change much, hovering around 10 % of potential output while creating some room for redistributive allocation of public expenditure. On the other hand, the private savings function was supposed to shift upwards.

In the terminal year of 1993, the plan yields figures suggesting substantially different assumptions about the economy than in the initial phase.

Potential growth rate would be 5.9 %. Investment would be 18 % of potential GDP, led by public investment, which would be 12.2 %. The current account deficit is sharply reduced to 1 % of potential output. The fiscal deficit is replaced by a surplus and public borrowing is reduced to 4.7 %. These are fairly substantial changes in the comportment of both the economy and the state.

There are three key assumptions that were inserted into the gap model to generate these expectations. The first is increased austerity by the state, suggested by a shift in the base level of the current public surplus of 10.5 % from the base year. The second is an improvement in the trade account. The export function shifts upwards. There is also either a reduction in the use of imported intermediate and competitive goods or greater domestic import substitution of these commodities.

The third key assumption is on foreign amortization, which plays a crucial role by both affecting the country's capacity to import and the government's saving and investment possibilities. The plan simply assumed that Zambia would carry heavy arrears through the entire period, amounting to 26 % of exports in 1989. They would still amount to 25 % in 1993.

## 19.4.1 How Realistic Are These Assumptions?

On the political level, the documents describing the Zambian plan were astute at least with respect to domestic factors, taking into account the presence of a whole number of significant interests.

Increasing the "fiscal effort" in Zambia by the magnitudes suggested by the plan would seem politically possible if stretched over the entire plan period. The plan expected to achieve a greater effort largely by increasing taxes while leaving subsidies and other transfers intact. "Shock treatment" measures in the context of the Zambian political economy would run into definite difficulty, as demonstrated by "IMF riots" and loss of lives.

The assumption of increased aid and a unilateral rescheduling of the debt is obviously unrealistic or at least merely indicative of the extent of international goodwill Zambia needs in order to ease the foreign exchange crunch. The reaction of the international community to Zambia's plight does not auger well. Following the break with the IMF most donors withheld their aid money and are unlikely to release it without the IMF's stamp of approval.

The upward shift in the export function is possible, given the improvements in the political climate of the region. Zambia's access to her traditional export routes via Benguela and Beira should cut costs, although not enough to offset the poor performance of copper in world markets. Although improvements in agricultural exports have been registered, they are too small to make much of an impact in an economy where copper still determines the overall performance.

It is unlikely that Zambia will get more aid than it does today. One of the moral arguments for supporting Zambia was its "frontline state" status during the liberation wars. With the dramatic political changes in the region, the Zambian case for financial support will be greatly diminished.

The plan also expected an upward shift in the private investment function, suggesting an exhilaration of the "animal spirits" of the private sector. The plan actually states that attraction of foreign direct investment will be pursued more vigorously than hitherto. The political economy of southern Africa is such that the investment prospects depend on events in South Africa. That country and perhaps Zimbabwe and Mozambique would benefit from any initial investment flows.

Zambia's historical attraction to private investment—mining—has lost most of its allure and both the country's geographical position and economic status do not make it particularly desirable to private capital. Zambia will therefore continue to depend on the parastatals and, perhaps, capital owned by an emergent "national bourgeoisie." The best midterm option is not privatization (for there are no takers) but more efficient management of the nation's already rather substantial industry.

### 19.4.2   The Orthodox Option

Already the "plan" has been shelved as Zambia had to go back to the Bretton Woods institutions, which sought to push the economy back to the course abandoned in 1987. Zambia has also returned to the Paris Club to renegotiate rescheduling of its debt.

But what do orthodox policies entail? We do not have access to the exact details of the package to be adopted. Let us assume a rather "orthodox" adjustment program. Both the current account deficit and the budget deficit are drastically reduced. As a sweetener to the dose, aid allocations are increased so that they are double the 1987 share in potential output. At the same time, debt repayment is twice the 1987 level, which was kept artificially low by Zambia's decision to restrict its debt servicing to 10 % of exports.

Apparently using what Bacha (1987) suspects is the IMF rule of thumb with respect to the budget deficit ratio to GDP ("measure its size and cut in half"), the orthodox version called for the reduction of the budget deficit, which was 11.6 % of GDP in 1988 to 5 % in 1990. Access to new loans and rescheduling will demand as a precondition, repaying of past outstanding debt at least to the World Bank, which amounted to $200 million. With dramatic depreciation in the Kwacha, servicing such a debt would impact on the budget.

The effect of such a policy would be a fall in public investment. This in turn would bring down private investment. The overall effect would be a contraction in total investment and growth rate of potential output of only 1.47 %. To maintain the same level of capacity utilization, Zambia would have to sharply increase its efficiency in the utilization of imported intermediates or engage in further import substitution.

Reduction of the fiscal deficit would lead to an upward shift in the fiscal surplus: for any given level of capacity utilization, the state would exhibit greater "fiscal effort" than is currently the case. This leaves little room for redistributive measures as subsidies would have to be removed, user charges for public services introduced, and so on. It should be noted that the increase in the fiscal effort would not be as high as is suggested in the "plan" but this is only so because it takes place in a regime of slow growth or decline in potential output per capita. Were the orthodox package to have as high growth as is in the plan, the "fiscal effort" would increase sharply to accommodate both the required public investments and external financial commitments.

## 19.5   Concluding Remarks

Zambia is not exactly a great democracy. Partly because of the high levels of urbanization and unionization, howeve:. Zambian politics generally have tended to be less repressive than is usually the case in African one-party states. State-trade union relationships have maintained a precarious act of collaboration and conflict. The adoption of orthodox measures has soured the relationship between the state and unions and the state has gradually drifted toward openly repressive practices. Low capacity and negative output growth rates will not reverse this trend.

Zambia's immediate prospects do not look good. An important message of the exercises is that changes in the external environment are of enormous importance to a socially acceptable recovery process. It has been often stated that the Zambian leadership has not been determined enough in the implementation of its policies and has lacked the "political will" of the Ghanaian and Nigerian leadership, to cite a few examples. What much of this comparison conveniently forgets is that Zambia is not a military regime and its political structure does not facilitate riding roughshod over popular demands as is often the case elsewhere.

The implementation of Zambia's Plan would either require unilaterally rescheduling of the debt (which was attempted for two years) and inviting the wrath of the international community and all that entails in terms of new funds, or would demand such shifts in the international environment as to allow for smooth rescheduling of its debts without pushing the economy into a deep recession. For the international system such rescheduling is virtually costless although the gains to Zambia would be substantial. Attempts to once again push through the package that was attempted in 1985 can only lead to unpopular policies implementable only through ruthless measures.

This raises the weighty problem of reconciliation of orthodox adjustment problems with the democratization process now taking place in Zambia. The last two years has witnessed the rise of a strong movement for multi-party democracy. The movement is broad-based and the trade unions have played a central role in its growth. It has not spelled out a clear economic policy but there are intimations that there will be strong pressures for "macroeconomic populism" that will run counter to prevailing orthodox stabilization and adjustment nostrums.

## Notes

1. Turok (1979) describes the extent of state participation in this period.

2. It may be interesting to note here that the case of Zambia was used by both the left and right in arguing the "labor aristocracy" and "urban bias" theses and is still widely cited for such evidence. See Arrighi and Saul (1973) and Bates (1981), respectively.

3. Ravi Gulhati (1989) of the World Bank is quite emphatic on this: "Rural development programmes came to naught because of the ascendancy of urban interest groups, namely, local business groups, civil servants, and formal sector workers. A new urban middle class has emerged since independence. It is not well organized politically, and it contains a number of subgroups with partly conflicting economic interests, but despite these differences, this new middle class has prevented a forceful policy of rural development."

## References

Arrighi, Giovanni, and John Saul (1973). "International Corporations, Labor Aristocracies, and Economic Development in Tropical Africa," in G. Arrighi and J. Saul (eds.), *Essays on the Political Economy of Africa*. New York: Monthly Review Press.

Bacha, Edmar L. (1987). "IMF Conditionality: Conceptual Problems and Policy Alternatives." *World Development*, 15 : 1457–1468.

Bacha, Edmar L. (1990). "A Three-Gap Model of Foreign Transfers and the GDP Growth Rate in Developing Countries." *Journal of Development Economics*, 32 : 279–296.

Bates, Robert H. (1981). *Markets and States in Tropical Africa*. Berkeley: University of California Press.

Daniel, Phillip (1979). *Africanization, Nationalization, and Inequality: Mining Labor and the Copperbelt in Zambian Development*. Cambridge: Cambridge University Press.

Fundanga, Caleb (1989). "The Role of the IMF and the World Bank in Zambia," in Bade Onimode (ed.), *The IMF, the World Bank, and the African Debt*. London: Zed Books.

Gulhati, Ravi (1989). "Impasse in Zambia: The Economics and Politics of Reform." Washington, DC: World Bank.

Kydd, Jonathan (1988). "Zambia," in Charles Harvey (ed.), *Agricultural Pricing Policy in Africa: Four Country Case Studies*. London: Macmillan.

Mkandawire, Thandika (1986). "The Informal Sector in the Labor Reserve Economies of Southern Africa: With Special Reference to Zimbabwe." *Africa Development*, 1.

Swedish International Development Authority (SIDA, 1989). *Zambia: Exchange Rate Policy*. Stockholm: SIDA.

Turok, Ben (1979). "The Penalties of Zambia's Mixed Economy," in B. Turok (ed.), *Development in Zambia*. London: Zed Press.

Young, Roger, and John Loxley (1990). *Zambia: An Assessment of Zambia's Structural Adjustment Experience*. Ottawa: North-South Institute.

# 20 Senegal

## François Boye

Senegal has always had an unbalanced economy, reliant upon external contributions to get its foreign and fiscal gaps financed. Unlike the case in most Third World countries, this dependency on the outside has, up to now, not been counterproductive. First, there has been no trade-off between debt service and imports; domestic production and demand have not been sacrificed to foreign interests. Indeed, real domestic consumption, by far the biggest component of domestic demand, has been so impervious to post-independence slumps in production that there was negative saving in 1980 and 1981.

Second, imports have always bridged the gap between domestic demand and production, keeping any inflationary shock in check. Third, policy-makers have not been forced to crush domestic demand through repeated devaluations or price hikes so as to bring the import bill into line with limited foreign exchange. Current account deficits in Senegal have never been transitory imbalances doomed to disappear as a result of their un-sustainability. On the contrary, they have attracted as much capital inflow as necessary to prevent a binding external constraint from dictating macro-economic outcomes.

Fourth, the state has been protected from black markets sprouting all across the country and thwarting control of the economy. Black markets have been transitory opportunities that last so long as (before the era of adjustment programs) the state enforced irrational taxes, that is, taxes keeping domestic prices out of step with the ones in Gambia, Mali, or Mauritania. Parallel transactions have not become a permanent plague stripping the state of both tax resources and authority for the reasons that (1) no speculation against the Franc CFA can occur, (2) assured convertibility between the Franc CFA and the French Franc allows free access to foreign goods, and (3) scarcity of goods has never been the order of the day.

Fifth, public investments have been propped up under all circumstances. When the state was awash in cash (in the aftermath of the first oil shock) as well as when it became cash strapped (after 1978), foreign funding agencies did not shrink from financing the public sector's projects. As a result, Senegal must be one of the few countries on earth where availability of domestic savings has not been a factor driving the state's intervention and regulatory capabilities.

Growth in Senegal is, therefore, independent of both the current account and public saving. Potential output growth, as calculated in Boye (1989), is how real GDP would have increased had the trend of the primary sector's value-added not been reversed at the end of the 1960s. It is unaffected by investment because capital formation from 1971 onwards failed to set the economy above its initial growth path. Two facts explain this poor performance: On the one hand, a series of droughts drove down yields and production in the primary sector while capacity was being built up through huge public investment programs in the 1970s; on the other hand, over-capacity industrial sectors were not goaded until 1986, the year of the launching of the New Industrial Policy, into shifting toward international markets.

## 20.1   Macroeconomic Linkages

Real GDP increases have been a godsend since the second half of the 1960s. Overall activity has been boosted whenever there have been plentiful rainfalls; recession has been the order of the day whenever drought has been rife in the countryside. Senegal is an agriculture-based economy. Describing its macroeconomics boils down to specifying how a change in agricultural activity feeds into the system.

The secondary sector fits into the primary sector through (1) the oil mills' dependency on groundnut production, (2) use of fertilizers and ploughs by peasants, and (3) peasants' demand for import substituting products. The tertiary sector is given a fillip by agricultural production as a result of the money made out of the marketing of raw as well as processed crops (groundnut, millet, rice).

The trade deficit fluctuates with the primary sector's value added because groundnut is the preponderant crop in Senegal, and the major credit entry of the current account is made up of groundnut products (oil, meal) exports. Climatic vagaries are disruptive of public finance in that marketing boards in Senegal are state controlled, less marketed value means that the public sector's financial resources are deflated, drought increases default in paying back advances in seeds and fertilizers to peasants from parastatals, and financially squeezed parastatals, if not liquidated, have to be granted subsidies, overdrafts, or tax exemptions by the treasury.

Inflation may be driven up by revision of state controlled prices (foodstuffs, public utilities) whenever the treasury feels the pinch following a recession in the primary sector concomitant with slump in international commodity markets. Operating costs of producing and marketing agricultural products are covered by bank credits entitled to refinancing from the Central Bank without limit, meaning that booming activity in the country is automatically financed by an increase in the money supply. Domestic demand, albeit proof against recession, goes through an upsurge in case of expansion in the agricultural sector.

The franc currency zone and the openhandedness of donor countries make up the two specific factors that account for fluctuations in Senegal being ascribed to the ups and downs of the agricultural sector, no matter the course of foreign and saving gaps.

### 20.1.1 The Contribution of the Franc Zone

From the perspective of open economy macroeconomics, the franc zone supports the unorthodox properties of the Senegalese economy, for several reasons. Foreign exchange reserves have no bearing on demand for foreign goods and services: Member countries of the Franc zone pool their reserves, 65 % of which have to be deposited in an account—the operations account—located in the French treasury. As a result, so long as the operations account balance is positive, at least one specific member country can have its imports financed regardless of its earnings in foreign exchange. Senegal has transformed this facility into a permanent source of support; its current account balance has been negative save in 1972.

The exchange rate and the balance of payments are uncorrelated; the rate is pegged at its 1948 level of 50 francs CFA to one French franc. This oddity reflects two major facts. On the one hand, the franc CFA is the currency of the whole currency zone, hence it cannot be only tied to Senegal's economic course. On the other hand, the 1948 exchange rate of the franc CFA is still the one at which France guarantees the convertibility without limit of the two currencies. It follows that external disequilibrium never feeds into the domestic economy through the exchange rate: dwindling foreign exchange reserves cannot lure Senegalese transactors into speculating against the Franc CFA if France sticks to her position as the guarantor of the convertibility of the franc zone's currency. Moreover, the exchange rate cannot contribute to any inflationary process being self-sustained since its determination has nothing to do with supply and demand.

The more money supply, the more foreign exchange: As a consequence of France unconditionally guaranteeing the convertibility of the franc CFA, the French franc and the franc CFA can freely and limitlessly be swapped for each other. So Senegal's possibilities for acquiring foreign exchange each year are bounded not by her net foreign assets registered in the operations account, but by the money issued by the Central Bank. Despite losses in foreign exchange piling up since 1973, neither net overdrafts to the treasury nor credits to private transactors have gone through a contraction before as well as after Senegal embarked on implementing adjustment programs.

There is no such thing as a shortage of foreign exchange: So long as the convertibility of the franc CFA is maintained unconditional, Senegalese transactors cannot be deprived of either French francs or transactions with French traders. As for doing business with non-French transactors, no obstacle is likely to lie before Senegalese businessmen. As a result of the convertibility of the French currency, they can either convert their French franc denominated monetary assets into any non-French currency to suit their counterparts' financial requests, or pay off their bills by using French francs. That is why the current account's being permanently in deficit has not implied any shrinkage of imports. On the contrary, there have never been so many Senegalese traders roving in the world and shipping goods to Senegal as in this moment in time. The only activity that has proved proof against recession since the 1970s is the import trading business.

### 20.1.2   The Contribution of Foreign Aid

Donor countries' openhandedness toward Senegal has contributed to scotching the effects of foreign and fiscal gaps in several ways. Unrequited transfers from foreign public agencies to the treasury have repeatedly headed off financial bankruptcy since 1979. In keeping public finance afloat, donors have saved the state the political and social trouble of trimming the civil service, retreating from spending, and contracting domestic demand. The Paris Club's conceding six reschedulings of the Senegalese debt in this decade has allowed the public sector to build up debt without interest payments shooting up and setting Senegal's GNP on a downward trend; and it has covered the current account deficit and curbed Senegal's needs for funds from the outside.

Bilateral donors' permanent readiness to finance investments in Senegal has made investment insensitive to domestic saving (insignificant), capacity use (low in industrial plants) and external disequilibrium (deep). In contributing to long-term growth problems being partially addressed, it has put off the emergence of a trade-off between consuming and investing, between capital formation and capacity use, and between capital goods imports and the restoration of external balance. Finally, many multinational organizations are headquartered in Dakar and, by African standards, there are many embassies. These result in the banking system enjoying business opportunities and capital inflows regardless of the course of the local economy, and the service industry thriving on exports independent of its competitiveness and sophistication.

## 20.2   Medium-Term Prospects

Medium-term prospects depend on the extent to which bilateral and multilateral financiers will remain intent on neutralizing contractionary effects of both fiscal and foreign gaps, and the extent to which the agricultural sector will keep dictating its course to the whole economy.

### 20.2.1   Capital Inflows

Senegal cannot bank on her capital suppliers' lavishness in the decade to come as the result of the economy not fulfilling expectations in the 1980s. After a ten year period of adjustment, no indicator bears witness of a turnaround, a rebound, or a structural change.

Booming domestic consumption is still the obstacle to domestic saving being markedly boosted and sustaining growth through internally financed investments. No industrial export has as yet plugged Senegal into the world economy and stemmed the depressing effects of climatic shocks on GDP. Losses in foreign exchange per annum, despite improvements in 1986 and 1987, more than trebled between 1980 and 1988.

Senegal has drawn from all extended facilities the IMF has launched since the beginning of the 1980s, but despite Fund pressure the state still puts off bringing domestic prices of petrol, rice and groundnut oil into line with international prices. Subsidies still have to be poured into the agricultural sector to compensate for terms of trade out of step with either export markets or the restoration of budgetary balance. Despite the implementation of the New Industrial Policy since 1986, the Dakar-based free zone remains unattractive, and the whole industrial sector cannot withstand international competition because of an overvalued exchange rate and overcharged industrial inputs (fuel, power, water, telecommunications, transportation).

How Senegal's financiers will react to this set of poor results is the riddle medium-term forecasting has to unravel. Juding by current interactions between the Senegalese government and its fund suppliers, we make these three key assumptions relative to the first half of the 1990s: (1) the 1980s adjustment agenda will carry on; (2) the Senegalese economy will have less access to financial resources; and (3) the franc zone will remain unchanged.

The following facts give credit to the first assumption: (1) the medium- and long-term adjustment plan (MLTP henceforth) endorsed by bilateral and multilateral donors in December 1984 is still the agreed-upon yard-stick with which to gauge the Senegalese economy's performance; (2) the MLTP's objectives are the ones that molded the three-year plan, in return for which the IMF allowed the Senegalese government to draw funds from its enhanced structural adjustment facility in December 1989; and (3) it is along the lines of the MLTP that the World Bank negotiated last year a fourth structural adjustment loan with Senegal.

The second assumption is substantiated by the following evidence: (1) development agencies in the West are revising their view that Senegal is the typical financially overassisted country struggling to find a way out of the vicious cycles of underdevelopment; (2) the structural adjustment loan being implemented in Senegal is the fourth in ten years; (3) there is no extra IMF facility Senegal can resort to; and (4) the World Bank's making available all the outlays of the fourth SAL is conditional upon the treasury contracting its financial needs through trimming the civil service and hand-ing over some public enterprises to private business. Few steps have been taken in this direction, and indeed the treasury is being pushed into increas-ingly financing crops and their export—the result of state-controlled banks having gone bankrupt and private banks setting harsher conditions to finance the agricultural sector.

Our assumption of a stable franc zone takes the opposite view to wide-spread cconcerns about the post-1992 monetary integration of Europe sapping the zone's fabric. It allows for the fact that France's position within the EEC does and will depend upon the country's economic, cultural, and political influence worldwide in which African countries are participants and for which the franc zone stands. It also rules out the Franc CFA being devalued for the following reasons: (1) French companies' and banks' sway in francophone African can deny any devaluation effectiveness, (2) French sensitivity to the African plight notwithstanding, France has no intention of providing African economies in stagnation with a competitive edge to flood the French market with cheap and labor-intensive goods, and (3) rendering francophone African competitive vis-à-vis the rest of the world cannot but weaken its hitherto close economic and political links with France.

Our second and third assumptions are not in contradiction with each other in that the franc zone can be run in a way consistent with a reduction in deficits and capital needs. France's current commitment to the franc zone reflects less a pledge of largesse than a mood to tighten her grip on the BCEAO whose laxity has left banking resolutions unenforced, public enterprises' demand for credit unchecked, capital outflows out of control, and public treasuries more and more in the red. As far as Senegal is concerned, these criticisms of the Central Bank boil down to reduced financial resources at the disposal of the Senegalese economy in the years to come.

### 20.2.2   The Agricultural Sector

In all likelihood, during the first half of the 1990s we will not witness the emergence of a new leading industry replacing the oilmills, smothering the effects of climatic shocks, and freeing the whole economy from the dictatorship of groundnut.

Several factors account for this pessimistic view. First, its commitment to the New Agricultural Policy (NAP) notwithstanding, the treasury cannot concede higher producer prices for food crops because low international prices of groundnut oil have kept SONACOS (the state-owned company that is the sole buyer and processor of groundnut) in the red and have drained public finances since 1986.

Second, it is a forlorn hope that more of the cereal crop could be marketed to generate macroeconomic effects as large as groundnut production if peasants face both cuts in their subsidies and a freeze on their prices. Moreover, two new dams on the Senegal River will not allow the substitution of irrigation for rainfall as the predominant factor of production in the countryside, because of financial and political limitations that are unlikely to disappear.

The impact of agricultural stagnation will be severe because the New Industrial Policy that has been in place since 1986 is unlikely to bear fruit in the 1990s no matter what Senegal's endeavors to emulate successful export-led developing countries may be. This is because (1) the world economy is turning into an interplay between three blocs—American, European and Japanese—that are undermining the free-market system in

**Table 20.1**
National accounts (billions of CFA francs at 1977 prices)

|      | GDP    | Imports | Exports | Public consumption | Private consumption | Investment |
|------|--------|---------|---------|--------------------|---------------------|------------|
| 1990 | 596.52 | 225.97  | 161.42  | 114.47             | 461.13              | 85.45      |
| 1991 | 602.78 | 233.12  | 170.88  | 116.26             | 463.80              | 84.94      |
| 1992 | 609.23 | 240.29  | 180.69  | 117.92             | 465.96              | 85.14      |
| 1993 | 616.23 | 248.84  | 190.61  | 117.51             | 467.51              | 85.43      |
| 1994 | 624.09 | 258.13  | 201.31  | 120.96             | 474.42              | 85.53      |
| 1995 | 631.81 | 267.92  | 211.72  | 122.37             | 479.89              | 85.75      |

force since 1945. (2) Ireland, Southern Europe, Eastern Europe, the Asian NICs, and Mexico are not to be rivaled as the foci of direct investments from OECD countries because of the specific industrial and commercial advantages they offer in this context of geographical upheaval. And (3) if unreversed in the medium term, the dollar's downward trend and the invariable exchange rate of the franc CFA will combine to rule out setting up more tradables producing plants in Senegal as well as banking on booming exports from the current manufacturing industries.

The sad conclusion is that given Senegal's nonexistent prospects of being economically turned about in the years ahead, the dictatorship of groundnut will bite harder as international prices of oil-bearing products go down in consequence of Europe getting more and more integrated and consequently more self-sufficient in fats.

20.2.3    Evolution of Key Economic Variables

Tables 20.1 through 20.4 summarize projections of key economic variables for the first half of the 1990s, from a simple model incorporating the macroeconomic linkages sketched in Section 20.1. The projections presuppose that the upward trend of rainfall during the 1980s will remain unchanged in the five years ahead, and are compatible with groundnut production topping one million tons each year as well as real value-added of the primary sector growing at 2.4 % per annum on average. For 1990–95, average real GDP growth is 1 %; the current account deficit is to revolve around 10 % nominal GDP; and the overall fiscal deficit remains high.

Falling per capita income in the forthcoming quinquennium will stem from the deflationary impacts of the measures incidental to pursuing the adjustment process. Layoffs in the civil service and restructuring the public

**Table 20.2**
Monetary survey (billions of CFA frances)

|      | Net foreign assets | Net credit to the government | Credit to the economy | M2 | Credit from the central bank to deposit banks |
|------|--------|--------|--------|--------|--------|
| 1990 | −248.25 | 256.99 | 466.11 | 474.85 | 144.92 |
| 1991 | −255.07 | 275.12 | 473.15 | 493.20 | 149.83 |
| 1992 | −261.07 | 275.12 | 480.20 | 511.14 | 155.12 |
| 1993 | −270.82 | 318.88 | 486.99 | 535.05 | 160.61 |
| 1994 | −282.60 | 350.38 | 495.20 | 562.98 | 166.42 |
| 1995 | −294.24 | 384.35 | 502.57 | 562.69 | 172.18 |

**Table 20.3**
Government financial operations (billions of CFA francs)

|      | Total revenues | Total expenditures | Wages and salaries | Interest payments | Margins on groundnut marketing | Public sector deficit |
|------|--------|--------|--------|--------|--------|--------|
| 1990 | 242.2 | 293.5 | 136.9 | 59.1 | −30.0 | 33.9 |
| 1991 | 257.3 | 307.3 | 143.0 | 62.1 | −31.0 | 33.0 |
| 1992 | 272.6 | 321.9 | 149.4 | 65.8 | −53.2 | 100.1 |
| 1993 | 288.8 | 336.03 | 155.9 | 68.7 | −56.3 | 125.5 |
| 1994 | 305.7 | 350.9 | 162.7 | 72.6 | −57.0 | 131.5 |
| 1995 | 323.0 | 364.8 | 169.6 | 75.2 | −70.2 | 143.7 |

**Table 20.4**
Current account (billions of CFA francs; one U.S. dollar = 265 CFA francs)

|      | Exports | Imports | Service balance | Net unrequited transfers | Current account deficit | Public debt |
|------|--------|--------|--------|--------|--------|--------|
| 1990 | 230.8 | 388.4 | −85 | +81.8 | 160.8 | 1865.59 |
| 1991 | 236.8 | 393.2 | −83 | +78.6 | 164.8 | 2061.51 |
| 1992 | 235.1 | 390.0 | −90 | +76.2 | 168.7 | 2252.93 |
| 1993 | 275.83 | 404.4 | −120 | +74.5 | 174.07 | 2466.37 |
| 1994 | 292.94 | 412.4 | −135 | +73.5 | 180.96 | 2677.51 |
| 1995 | 306.85 | 420.5 | −147 | +72.9 | 187.75 | 2896.23 |

service will result in a three-point cut in the growth (from 8 % in the 1980s to 5 % in the forecast period) of salaries from central government. The state's retreat from some productive activities in conjunction with deepening financial imbalances will keep growth of real public consumption sluggish (1.4 % each year) up to 1995. The shutdown of banks unsecure against insolvency and the overhaul of public enterprises will reduce demand for refinancing from commercial banks; the Central Bank's credits to the banking system up to 1993 will fall short of their 1986 amount (160.6 billions of CFA Francs). Losses in jobs and curbed credits will let the driving factor of domestic demand—real private consumption—grow no faster than 3 % from 1990 to 1995.

Exports are forecast to have 6 % growth per annum throughout the first half of the 1990s in consequence of bumper crops of groundnut predicated on the current trend of rainfalls holding in the medium term. The positive effects on demand will be more than offset by the ongoing adjustment policies. As the result of Senegal's permanent deficit in saving and her recurring demands for rescheduling, foreign financiers will hold capital formation in real terms down to its 1990 level. The growth of their capital inflows will just be commensurate with inflation.

The current account deficit ratio ( + 10 % in 1995) is forecast to worsen despite export growth because the disequilibrium in Senegal's balance of payments will neither level off nor trend downward while stagnation grips domestic activity and curbs import growth ( + 18 % in real terms from 1990 to 1995). The underlying causes of this paradoxical finding are as follows: (1) the export price ( − 18 %) is to tumble as the result of an oversupply of fats in the world economy; (2) the import price index ( + 24 %) is to keep its upward trend because the dollar's tendency to fall ( − 5 %) will foster inflationary pressures thereby worldwide; (3) unrequited transfers to Senegal ( − 10 %) are to be cut as financiers press to have her go further and faster down the road of structural adjustment; (4) through Senegal's indebtedness to the IMF, her debt outstanding will be boosted by the dollar's downward trend because a depreciating dollar amounts to an appreciation ( + 18 %) of the IMF's numéraire; and (5) interest payments ( + 24 %) will shoot up in the 1990s, matching the steep rise ( + 31 %) in debt.

A low inflation rate (4.5 % per annum) will come along with stagnation and deficits in both public finance and the balance of payments. This paradox reflects the fact that prices in Senegal are driven up by exogenous factors. The first is imported inflation that our model expects to be moderate (4.0 % per annum), that is, in line with its trend in the second half of the 1980s. The second is the key role of state controlled prices. Producer prices in agriculture are forecast to be sticky upwards because the treasury will remain cash strapped in the years ahead. Consumer prices are not expected to shoot up because any deviation from their current trend would be counterproductive in terms of government revenue as a depressing factor in an already stagnant economy. The above macroeconomic imbalances are ruled out as determinants of the inflation rate because as long as Senegal enjoys the favors of the franc zone, no stagnation in production will bring about a dearth of goods and services, nor will growth in money supply translate into frustrated excess demand.

### 20.2.4   Microeconomic Impacts

The medium term assumptions and forecasts will naturally dictate the abilities of the state to carry on the reforms whereby it has been trying to reshape the economic environment and to promote free enterprise since 1984. As far as the new agricultural policy (launched in 1984) is concerned, the 1990s will be the decade of its being rolled back. First, the state cannot improve the terms of trade between the primary and the secondary sector through agricultural price hikes because the treasury cannot cover the implied subsidies. Second, at the current exchange rate, the financial need to tie the domestic to the international price of groundnut will lead to peasants curtailing their demand for fertilizers and turning their backs on modern productive processes as the result of their costs not being covered and their purchasing power being eroded. Third, the austere monetary policy going hand in hand with the adjustment process will prove detrimental to private newcomers starting out as farmers and taking over production activities from disengaging agriculture-oriented parastatals because the credit squeeze will be inconsistent with specific credits attuned to the constraints in farming being launched. It follows that the current peasants will be denied the room for maneuver to set up businesses of their own responsive to the market and capable of moving beyond the quasi-command economy that has been shackling the countryside since 1960.

Nor is the New Industrial Policy set to have less gloomy a future. The termination of quantitative restrictions and the lowering of tariffs, concomitant with its launching in 1986 and designed to open the economy, will collide head on with the treasury's urgent needs for extra tax revenues to forestall a downfall in government intervention and to meet the IMF's conditionalities. The shutdown of state-controlled banks in conjunction with harsher access to credit will keep away from entrepreneurship the nationals who were supposed to shift from the civil service towards business as a result of structural adjustment policies. The cash-strapped treasury will frown upon conceding big tax cuts on petroleum imports to cut the costs of transportation, electricity, and water enough to make domestic firms competitive; as the result, not only will foreign producers thrive on our domestic market in consequence of the opening of the economy, but more shutdowns of industrial plants are lying down the road. Finally, overall stagnation will be a deterrent, crippling private investment and putting off the launching of new industrial projects.

All in all, the economic revolution—rolling back state controlled activities plus opening the economy plus promoting free enterprise—that policymakers set out to implement since the mid-1980s will dash during the five years to come. Short-term concerns such as correcting public finance, rebuilding the banking system and paying off the debt will override its being carried on. Stated differently, the Senegalese government will continue to experience incompatibility between growth and adjustment in the 1990s.

Whether such a strategy of abdication is feasible in social or political terms is the question we have to take up next.

## 20.3   Political Economy and History

In the early 1990s, when it came to making collective decisions in Senegal, the actors of consequence could be described as follows:

*The Ruling Party*
In Third World fashion, it controls both the government and the state apparatus. Through the size of the public sector, its influence extends to the whole economy.

It is made up of citizens of any background because being an integral part of its intricate machinery is unquestionably the best opportunity to get ahead in a stagnant economy. Thus, it brings together the different regions, ethnic groups, and religions of Senegal. There are two offsetting implications: the ruling party is a stabilizing factor as an all-encompassing body bridging the gap between heterogeneous groups; but it also is unstability-ridden—the stage where rivals pit themselves against one another to climb up a political ladder that is also an economic ladder.

The ruling party has claimed to stand for socialism since 1960. It has, however, attracted as much private capital as possible and has never alienated the support of France. It is rooted in the community-based traditions of Africa and the need for the state to redress the socioeconomic biases put upon Senegal by colonialism. Its originality is twofold: (1) barring private ownership of the land in order for collective exploitation of plots in the countryside to be the basic agricultural decision-making unit, and (2) promoting public intervention into the driving force of the economy.

According to the 1980s adjustment programs, socialism has not benefited the economy given its inability to tackle macroeconomic imbalances and rekindle growth. Still, it remains the commitment on behalf of which Senegal moderates her financiers' pressure for policy changes and the asset the ruling party cashes in among its peers of the Socialist Internationale.

### The Opposition

It is a coalition of a dozen political parties. However tiny by parliamentary standards (less than ten MPs), it has set the political agenda of the 1980s. First, it has ridden the tide of discontent swollen by the adjustment process, thus gaining more militants in the rank and file than the ruling party. Second, through its harshly critical papers it has provided a countervailing power outside parliament the catchword of which, sopi—change—has shattered the ruling party's credibility. Third, the controversy-stricken 1988 elections left the opposition as the champion of democracy calling for the separation of the state from the ruling party and the submission of new election regulations to the people.

### The Islamic Brotherhoods

Senegal is an overwhelmingly Islamic country where Muslims freely allocate themselves among several brotherhoods claiming each to be a way to salvation. The most prominent are the Murid and Tijaan brotherhoods. Both date back to the end of the nineteenth century and were founded by an ascetic versed in the Koran. Historically, they were not only the channels through which Islam became widespread in Senegal, but also the new political and social entities after the colonial power had crushed the nineteenth-century kingdoms. That is why their relationships with France were confrontational from the onset: Ahmadou Bamba, the founder the Muridism, was either under house arrest or in exile from 1895 until his death in 1927.

From the First World War onward, however, the Islamic brotherhoods and France had no option but to cooperate. The colonial power needed to lean on local notables and organizations to ensure its rule and to minimize the cost of administering the colony. Facing a new administrative and economic order beyond their control, the Islamic brotherhoods had to adapt and compromise. Being the intermediary between the French administration and the natives became their new role. From an economic standpoint, that consisted up to the end of the colonial era (1960) of carrying out the French project of concentrating groundnut production in Senegal and promoting France-based oil mills to process tropical oil products. From a sociopolitical standpoint, the alliance with the colonial power allowed Islam to dominate Senegal through an unassailable control over the cash crop, and the use of the colonial state to expand its faith in the cities and outside the groundnut basin.

The post-independence era has been the heyday of Islam. Instead of the almighty colonial state, it has been dealing with a state under endless pressure to widen its political bases, increase its tax revenues, expand its control over the national territory, and shape the nation. In return for ideological and political support of the ruling party, it has extended its influence throughout the state apparatus and secured many privileges undreamt of in colonial times. First, the Islamic brotherhoods have always had their own representatives within the government, the parliament, and among the managers of the public sector. Second, their own religious (pilgrimages, mosque buildings) and economic projects have been taken on by the state, no matter what their impact on public finance. Third, backed up by the state controlled banks and the state's largesse, they have diversified their activities away from the drought crippled agriculture to all sectors —formal or informal—of the economy.

*Funding Agencies*
They are now an integral part of the decision-making process. As the economy can neither run surpluses nor finance its own deficits, Senegalese decision makers always have to approach donors to be informed of available forms of financial support from OECD countries (United States, Canada, France, and Italy). As a consequence, key decisions are made so as to fit into the schemes of at least one benevolent funding agency. Playing funding agencies against one another is the state's only strategy to forestall bumping into financial rationing. IMF and World Bank conditions do not bite hard because nonmultilateral funding agencies vie with one another for alleviating the pain incidental to the adjustment process.

Stated differently, funding agencies make up a group of different objectives. They do not, therefore, speak with one voice; Senegal has always taken advantage of this to further her interest as a nation short of funds.

## Foreign Companies

They are concentrated in the import-substitution sector. Domestic demand is, therefore, the determinant of their plight. They suffer from a low capacity utilization as the result of domestic consumption (investment goods are imported) being adjusted not to industrial capacity but to the stagnating GNP. They are getting more and more short of cash as the treasury's illiquidity spills over into the whole economy through all the suppliers of the public sector.

As yet, nothing has been done to fix these problems, with the consequence that foreign companies either are pulling out of Senegal altogether or coalescing behind French funding agencies to have their interests enforced upon the whole nation.

## Senegalese Businessmen

They stand for economic nationalism. Their platform states that foreign companies' grip on key activities (banking, insurance, mines, oil mills) has to be loosened by state intervention; specific financial schemes have to be launched to increase the number of national companies in all sectors; foreign tenderers must be discriminated against so as to balance the lopsided playing field that keeps Senegalese nationals from making inroads into business at home; tariffs have to be lowered in order for Senegalese traders (most Senegalese businessmen are traders) to thrive on domestic market at the expense of the foreign companies unwilling to address the common people's needs; and finally France's privileges in Senegal have to be terminated.

To be sure, this platform is a piece of wishful thinking, given the need to maintain the flow of foreign funds into Senegal. It does not follow, however, that it has no chance of being translated into policy because it is being aired by members of the opposition, the Islamic brotherhoods, or the ruling party, many of whom happen to run businesses.

## Peasants

They are the backbone of the economy. No growth can set in and last unless it meets their demands. Still, their control over the economic environment is insignificant. They cannot set their output prices. State intervention does not allow them to bid down the price of fertilizers and seeds. They are restricted from selling their groundnut output to anybody but the marketing board. The banking system does not target peasants at all, putting them in a permanent state of financial rationing. This paradox has not yet been counterproductive from a macroeconomic standpoint because, as the constituency of the ruling party, peasants have always enjoyed a flow of financial resources and services (food, health, infrastructure) independent of their crops and compensating for their bondage to the state's control over their economic opportunities.

### The Urban Middle Class

This group was supposed to reap all the benefits of the post-independence era: protected jobs in the bloated civil service, highly paid jobs in public enterprises, subsidized foodstuffs and utilities, comfortable infrastructure, cheap access to imports, strong and feared unions, first-class education and health services, and a near-Western standard of living. The 1980s crisis has shattered this rosy picture. The only way the middle class is being adjusted is down, and in city areas it has become disgruntled at the ruling party and gets more responsive to the opposition.

As the result of the ruling party being a coalition of diverse interests, interaction among the groups just described has up to now resulted in a stable society. Foreign funding agencies have basically and in all circumstances tided over the state from all its financial worries. Shielded from bankruptcy, the state apparatus has developed into a huge provider of (1) business opportunities to foreign companies, Senegalese businessmen, and Islamic brotherhoods, (2) jobs to the urban middle class and urban youth, (3) privileges to the ruling party, and (4) gifts to peasants. In return, the ruling party has seen its power unshaken despite the sluggish economy in the 1980s and the opposition's relentless onslaught on the state's corrupting practices, and mismanagement on a large scale. Consequently, the IMF and the World Bank's conditions have been met without any social uprising deterring the government.

The afore-displayed forecasts might prove devastating to this stability. Beset with increasing cuts in capital inflows, the state will have to adjudicate among competing groups. If it targets the ruling party's prominent militants whose privileges do not accord with public finance, it will behead the patronage system whereby the rulers have enlarged their constituency in the rank and file. If it tries to force the Islamic brotherhoods to pay for their mammoth arrears of taxes and interest and lose their economic power, it will take the risk of Islam shifting loyalty and siding with the Opposition. If its toll on the productive sector gets higher, many ailing companies, Senegalese or not, will have no option but to close up shop, lay off workers, and set the stage for social unrest.

Fairness will be difficult as each group will suffer from the determinants of the forthcoming stagnation. The Islamic brotherhoods' businesses will face rationing in credit and foreign exchange due to the overhaul of state controlled banks and the absolute enforcement of banking regulations. The ruling party's militants will have to allocate among themselves fewer and fewer financial resources and jobs as the civil service and the public sector are downsized. Senegal-based and inward-looking companies will see domestic markets shrink as the result of the implementation of contractionary policies. Peasants will confront an overconstrained state unable either to increase agriculture's terms of trade or to provide food and infrastructure. Senegalese businessmen will deal not only with a contracting public sector issuing less and less tenders, but also with a convalescent banking system less and less prone to open-handedness. The urban middle classes' standard of living will be hard hit by rising unemployment and hikes in public utility prices in the midst of an environment of decaying infrastructure and poor public services. The urban youth will have no opportunity but to remain where it is now: on the sidelines of a decreasing per capita income economy.

Does it follow that Senegal is on the eve of a political upheaval, or that the countdown has begun for the takeover by the opposition, or that the ruling party is heading for a resounding defeat at the 1993 elections? The recent social unrest throughout French-speaking Africa renders the answer problematic. As the region becomes locked in stalemate, France is being pushed into staving off chaos through the launching of an initiative on a large scale designed to reshape African economies. Should such an expectation come true, this would mean that, in contrast with the beginning of the 1980s, France is intent on controlling the whole adjustment process in the 1990s at the expense of the IMF and the World Bank. Will she be more successful than the multilateral agencies? In complete ignorance of her new vision, nobody can respond. However, my guess is that France, as mindful of her big stakes in her former colonies as ever, will not rock the boat, that is, promote the political forces that are challenging her grip on French-speaking Africa by allowing the medium term forecasts presented above to be self-fulfilling.

## Reference

Boye, François (1989). "Gap Exercises for Senegal." Helsinki: WIDER.

# Index